T0189071

Lecture Notes of the Institute for Computer Sciences, Social Informatics and Telecommunications Engineering 358

More information about this series at http://www.springer.com/series/8197

Qihui Wu · Kanglian Zhao ·
Xiaojin Ding (Eds.)

Wireless and Satellite Systems

11th EAI International Conference, WiSATS 2020
Nanjing, China, September 17–18, 2020
Proceedings, Part II

Editors
Qihui Wu
Nanjing University of Aeronautics
and Astronautics
Nanjing, Jiangsu, China

Kanglian Zhao
Nanjing University
Nanjing, China

Xiaojin Ding
Nanjing University of Posts
and Telecommunications
Nanjing, China

ISSN 1867-8211 ISSN 1867-822X (electronic)
Lecture Notes of the Institute for Computer Sciences, Social Informatics
and Telecommunications Engineering
ISBN 978-3-030-69071-7 ISBN 978-3-030-69072-4 (eBook)
https://doi.org/10.1007/978-3-030-69072-4

This Springer imprint is published by the registered company Springer Nature Switzerland AG
The registered company address is: Gewerbestrasse 11, 6330 Cham, Switzerland

Preface

We are delighted to introduce the proceedings of the 11th edition of the European Alliance for Innovation (EAI) International Conference on Wireless and Satellite Systems (WiSATS 2020 formerly PSATS). This conference brought together researchers, developers and practitioners around the world who are leveraging and developing wireless and satellite technology for a smarter global communication architecture. The theme of WiSATS 2020 was "Intelligent Wireless and Satellite Communications for Beyond 5G".

The technical program of WiSATS 2020 consisted of 91 full papers. The conference main track was organized into 5 sessions. Aside from the high-quality technical paper presentations, the technical program also featured three keynote speeches and six technical workshops. The three keynote speakers were Dr. Sastri Kota (Associate Fellow of AIAA) from SoHum Consultants, USA, Professor Geoffrey Ye Li (Fellow of IEEE) from the School of Electrical and Computer Engineering, Georgia Tech, USA and Professor Tony Q.S. Quek (Fellow of IEEE) from Singapore University of Technology and Design, Singapore. The 6 workshops organized were (1) High Speed Space Communication and Space Information Networks (HSSCSIN), (2) Integrated Space and Onboard Networks (ISON), (3) Intelligent Satellite Operations, Managements and Applications (ISOMA), (4) Intelligent Satellites in Future Space Networked System (ISFSNS), (5) Satellite Communications, Networking and Applications (SCNA), (6) Satellite Internet of Things, Trusted Data Sharing, Secure Communication (SIOTTDSSC). The HSSCSIN workshop aimed to address the requirements challenges and promising new technology of broadband communications in future space information networks. The ISON workshop aimed to gain insights into research and development of future integration of onboard and space networks. The ISOMA workshop aimed to discuss the development, operation, management and application of future intelligent satellites. The ISFSNS workshop focused on the role of intelligence and networking in future space systems. The SCNA workshop aimed to achieve a deeper understanding of the future of satellite communications and networking and their applications in a connected world. The SIOTTDSSC workshop aimed to gain understanding of the architecture of satellite-based IoT and the guarantee of security in such networks.

Coordination with the steering chairs, Imrich Chlamtac, Kandeepan Sithamparanathan, Mario Marchese, Weixiao Meng and Min Jia, was essential for the success of the conference. We sincerely appreciate their constant support and guidance. It was also a great pleasure to work with such an excellent organizing committee team for their hard work in organizing and supporting the conference. In particular, the Technical Program Committee, led by our TPC Co-Chairs, Prof. Zhili Sun, Prof. Guangxia Li, Prof. Kanglian Zhao and Prof. Min Jia, completed the peer-review process of technical papers and made a high-quality technical program. We are also grateful to the Conference Managers, Barbora Cintava and Radka Pincakova, for their support and to all the authors who submitted their papers to the WiSATS 2020 conference and workshops.

We strongly believe that the WiSATS conference provides a good forum for all researchers, developers and practitioners to discuss all scientific and technological aspects that are relevant to wireless and satellite technology. We also expect that future WiSATS conferences will be as successful and stimulating, as indicated by the contributions presented in this volume.

Qihui Wu
Biaobin Jin
Qing Guo
Jian Guo
Jun Yang

Conference Organization

Steering Committee

Imrich Chlamtac University of Trento, Italy
Kandeepan Sithamparanathan RMIT, Australia
Mario Marchese University of Genoa, Italy
Weixiao Meng Harbin Institute of Technology, China
Min Jia Harbin Institute of Technology, China

Organizing Committee

Honorary Chairs

Zhicheng Zhou Chinese Academy of Engineering, China
De Ben Chinese Academy of Engineering, China

General Chairs

Qihui Wu Nanjing University of Aeronautics and Astronautics, China
Biaobin Jin Nanjing University, China

General Co-chairs

Qing Guo Harbin Institute of Technology, China
Jian Guo Beijing Institute of Spacecraft System Engineering, China
Jun Yang The Sixty-Third Research Institute, National University of Defense Technology, China

TPC Chair and Co-chairs

Zhili Sun University of Surrey, UK
Guangxia Li Jiangsu Collaborative Innovation Center for Satellite Communications and Navigation, China
Kanglian Zhao Nanjing University, China
Min Jia Harbin Institute of Technology, China

Sponsorship and Exhibit Chair

Wei Sheng Nanjing China-Spacenet Satellite Telecom Co., Ltd., China

Local Chair

Lu Lu	Jiangsu Collaborative Innovation Center for Satellite Communications and Navigation, China

Workshops Chair

Xiongwen He	Beijing Institute of Spacecraft System Engineering, China

Publicity and Social Media Chair

Guohua Kang	Nanjing University of Aeronautics and Astronautics, China

Publications Chair

Xiaojin Ding	Nanjing University of Posts and Telecommunications, China

Web Chair

Peng Li	Nanjing University of Information Science and Technology, China

Posters and PhD Track Chair

Shaochuan Wu	Harbin Institute of Technology, China

Panels Chair

Xuanli Wu	Harbin Institute of Technology, China

Demos Chair

Xin Liu	Dalian University of Technology, China

Tutorials Chairs

Gongliang Liu	Harbin Institute of Technology, China
Wei Wu	Harbin Institute of Technology, China

Technical Program Committee

Li Yang	Dalian University, China
Huaifeng Shi	Nanjing University of Information Science and Technology, China
Zhiguo Liu	Dalian University, China
Debin Wei	Dalian University, China.
Yuanming Ding	Dalian University, China
Xiaojin Ding	Nanjing University of Posts and Telecommunications, China

Contents – Part II

International Workshop on Intelligent Satellites in Future Space Networked System

International Workshop on Satellite Internet of Things, Trusted Data sharing, Secure Communication

Contents – Part I

Main Track

International Workshop on Intelligent Satellite Operations, Managements, and Applications

General Technology Research of GEO Space Debris Exploration System Based on Hosted Situation Awareness Payload

Donglei He[1](✉), Feng Shi[1], Guoxian Zheng[2], and Kunpeng Wang[3]

[1] Beijing Institute of Spacecraft System Engineering, Beijing 100094, China
hdl_hitsat@163.com
[2] Beijing Institute of Space Mechanics and Electricity, Beijing 100094, China
[3] Beijing Institute of Communication and Tracking Technology, Beijing 100094, China

Abstract. Hosted payload is a typical pattern which is capable of realizing flexibility and separate space system. In this paper, aiming at the shortage that the ground-based facility can not detect small and medium scale space debris, the general index of GEO hosted payload was analyzed, and the working pattern of GEO hosted payload system was designed. The general framework of GEO hosted payload system was studied, accordingly, the efficiency of the system was analyzed. It is hoped that the study will be helpful reference for technology development of hosted payload system general design and space-based debris cataloging.

Keywords: GEO space debris · Hosted payload · Space-based detection · Feasibility research

1 Introduction

Hosted payload is a typical pattern which can be capable of realizing flexibility and separate space system [1, 2]. Putting the payload made from the third party, which has the advantage of relatively small volume and little resource consumption, onto the platform made from another company, and accordingly the hosting platform needs some improvement to supply the setting space, carrying capacity, power supply, orientation control and data transfer to the hosted payload, then some value-added service can be brought to satisfy different need from the consumer, which doesn't affect the satellite's original function. There are many tasks which can be fulfilled by the hosted payload, such as information access, space debris exploration and new technology experiment, etc. [3].

As the human develop more and more space activity, the number of spacecraft and the debirs gets larger and larger. Currently, the debris density of the LEO, especially the polar has already approached critical point, the possibility of the Kessler effect will take place progressively. As to the GEO, there will be no orbit place resource to use in 20 years as long as the trend goes on [4]. As the number of space traffic gets larger and

Q. Wu et al. (Eds.): WiSATS 2020, LNICST 358, pp. 3–13, 2021.
https://doi.org/10.1007/978-3-030-69072-4_1

larger, the collision possibility between the spacecrafts and debris increase progressively, which will threaten the safety of our GEO space assets.

Developing the GEO hosted payload system of space debris exploration, namely, to host the space debris exploration payload onto the GEO satellite, then, we can take full advantage of GEO orbit and close-distance observation, high efficiency exploration and small debris detection capability for local important area will be developed relatively rapidly and economically. In this paper, aiming at the shortcomings that the current ground-based equipments can not detect small and medium scale debris, the feasibility of hosted payload detection for GEO debris was studied. General index of the hosted payload was analyzed, the working pattern for hosted payload detection was designed, the general frame design approach for GEO hosted payload was put forward and the system efficiency was studied. This paper will offer beneficial reference to the study of hosted payload system.

2 General Index Analysis for the GEO Hosted Payload

2.1 Analysis for Detection Pattern and the Spectrum

According the distribution characteristic of the space debris, there are quite a few GEO space debris more than 97%, whose orbit altitude distribution is at the range of GEO ± 100 km and the orbit inclination is no bigger than 15°.

During the period when the space debris move on the orbit, in quite a few percent of the duration, the debris is in the period of sunlight, then the debris can be detected by using the reflex spectrum characteristic. There are short umbrage at vernal equinox or at autumnal equinox, for different space debris of different inclination, the duration when the debris is in the umbrage is shown as the following table (Table 1).

Table 1. Duration in the umbrage for different debris of different inclination

Inclination	The time of day	umbral/h	penumbra/h	umbrage/h
0°	Vernal equinox	1.12	0.04	1.16
	Midsummer	0	0	0
	Autumnal equinox	1.12	0.04	1.16
	Midwinter	0	0	0
15°	Vernal equinox	0	0	0
	Midsummer	0	0.45	0.45
	Autumnal equinox	0	0	0
	Midwinter	0	0	0

In one year, for debris of different inclination, the duration when the debris is in the daylight and in the umbrage are shown as the following table (Table 2).

Table 2. The umbrage duration of different inclination space debris in one year

Debris inclination	Daylight	umbrage	umbrage percent
0°	363.33 day	3.67 day	1%
10°	363.27 day	3.73 day	1%
15°	363.43 day	3.57 day	1%

In summary, the duration when the debris moving in the umbrage is very small, which takes up almost 1% time percent. At the same time, to detect these debris, the long wave infrared approach will be used. So, thinking about the efficiency-expense ration, the visible light camera will be used as the detection payload. Synthetically thinking about the permeance ability of the optical material and the spectrum response of the detector, the spectrum is determined as 0.45–0.85 μm.

2.2 Analysis for the Detection Ability

In this paper, 30 cm debris will be used as the typical scale object to be detected. Thinking about the feasibility of the payload, the detection ability is chosen as 10 cm@3000 km. The illumination angle is chosen as 45°, then the detection ability of the optics should be 15.4 Mv.

2.3 Analysis for the Centroid Determination Precision

Angle precision and centroid determination precision have the influence on the measurement precision of chronometer angle [5]. According to the precision analysis of STARE, the measurement error caused by angle precision and centroid determination precision is relatively bigger, which is above 25% for STARE and above 40% for MOST, so the angle precision and centroid determination precision should be optimized. According the centroid determination ability of foreign payload, the angle precision is required to be 60 μrad and centroid determination precision should be 1/3pixel.

2.4 Relative Motion of Detection Payload

The bigger the inclination of the debris is,the relative motion magnitude of the hosted payload will get bigger. Take the debris of 15° inclination as classical object, relative motion between the debris and the hosted payload was analyzed. When the pointing longitude difference between the debris and hosted payload vary from 1° to 12.25°, the maximum azimuth, elevation and relative angular motion are shown as the following table (Fig. 1 and Table 3).

2.5 Analysis of the Caliber of the Hosted Payload

We chose the detector of 12 μm dimension pixel, and the field of view is 6° × 6°, the pixel number is not smaller than 2k × 2k. Then the focal length of the camera is 235 mm.

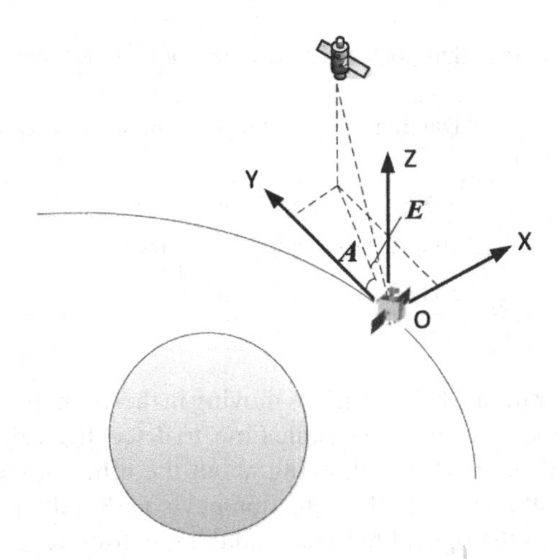

Fig. 1. Sketch of relative motion reference frame.

Table 3. Relative motion of 15° inclination debris

Pointing longitude difference between the debris and hosted payload	Maximum azimuth	Maximum elevation	Maximum relative angular motion
1°	89.97°	86.80°	0.0630°/s
5°	25.12°	72.07°	0.0126°/s
10°	16.30°	56.80°	0.0063°/s
12.25°	15.3057	50.9696	0.0051°/s

The integration time was considered as 0.5 s, then as to the debris of 15° inclination whose pointing longitude between itself and the payload is 12.25°, we can see that during the period of integration time the movement of debris onto the detector is no longer than one pixel. We chose the SNR as 5, then the caliber was almost 135 mm, and the F number was 1.74, the camera like this will have a relatively better engineering feasibility.

In summary, the general technology index demand of the hosted payload is:

- detection spectrum: 0.45–0.85 μm.
- detection ability: 30 cm@9000 km (15.4 Mv).
- field of view: 6° × 6°
- pixel number: 2k × 2k.
- caliber: 135 mm.
- focal length: 235 mm.
- SNR: 5

3 System of the GEO Hosted Payload

3.1 Detection Pattern of Hosted Payload

The hosted payload is fixed on the eastern and western side of the hosting satellite platform, taking the advantage of big field of view, high detection sensitivity and space-based observation distance, to detect and catalogue the GEO debris near to the hosting platform. As is known from the knowledge of GEO characteristic, as long as the sunlight condition is available, the hosted payload can detect the debris real time, which will make up the deficiency that the current ground-based equipment can not detect small and medium scale debris. At the same time, for the same debris, the observation angle from eastern and western payload will be different as almost 90°, which can make up the time-window that the ground-based equipment can not work at the daytime, and it will be benefical for long-term surveillance ability come into being (Fig. 2).

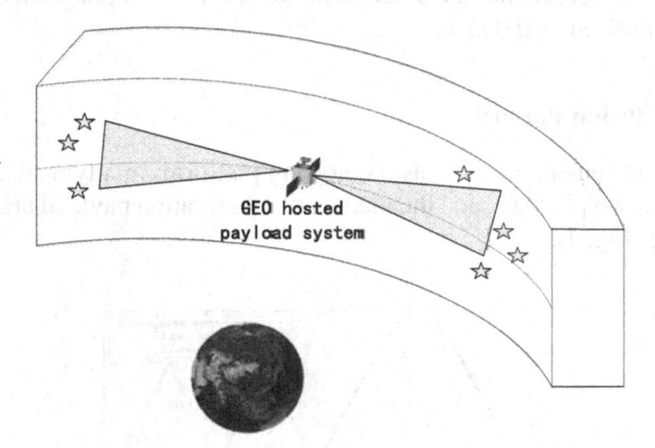

Fig. 2. Working pattern of hosted payload detection

Duration of the Hosted Payload Along Sunlight Observation
The table below shows that when the host-payload is at the along sunlight observation condition, the duration of observation at the vernal equinox, the autumnal equinox, the midsummer, and the midwinter will be as long as 5–8 h (Fig. 3 and Table 4).

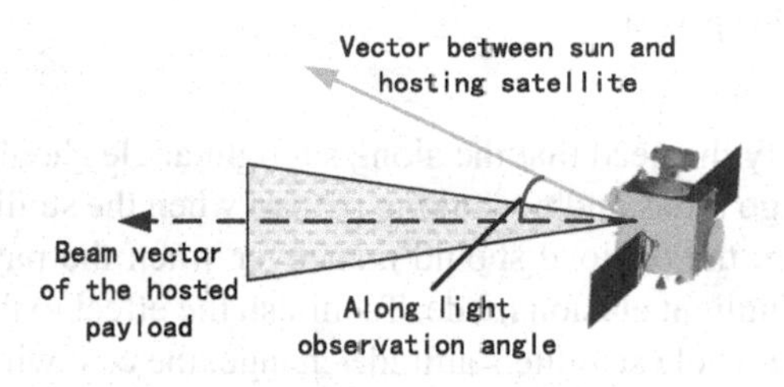

Fig. 3. Along sunlight observation angle.

Table 4. Total duration of the hosted payload along sunlight observation in one day

Observation time	Total duration of the hosted payload	
	Along sunlight observation angle 45°	Along sunlight observation angle 60°
The vernal equinox, the autumnal equinox	6 h	8 h
The midsummer, and the midwinter	5.27 h	7.62 h

The Platform Stability Demand from the Payload
The integration time was considered as 0.5 s, the platform should offer enough stability, to make the drift of debris onto the detector no longer than 1/3 pixel, then the platform stability can be derived as 0.002°/s.

3.2 Sunlight Elusion Pattern

Taking the remote sensing satellite as the hosting platform, in a typical day, the along sunlight angle of two payloads and the main earth observation payload are shown as the following figure (Fig. 4).

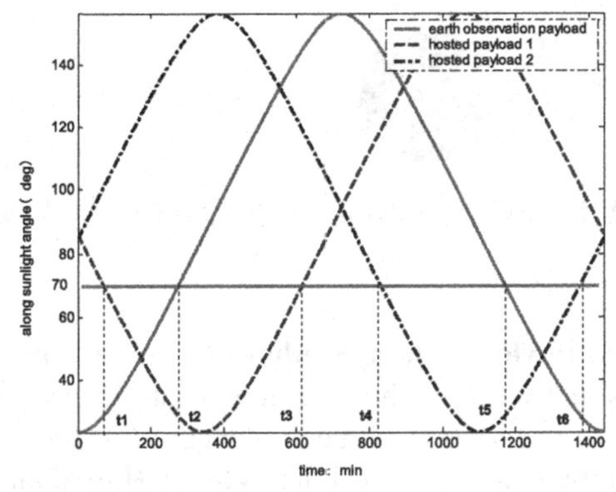

Fig. 4. The along sunlight observation duration alternate with time for the hosted payload and the main earth observation payload.

Therefore,to satisfy the need that the along sunlight angle should be no bigger than 70°, the payload will go into standby working pattern when the sunlight condition is not permitted. In addition, the payload should maneuver when the payload is against the sunlight and go into sunlight elusion mode. To minish the effect to the hosting platform, considering that if the whole satellite's attitude change, the cost will be too high for the platform to accept, so the payload should be designed with two-dimensional rotational machine collocated as shown as following figure (Fig. 5).

Fig. 5. Hosted payload with two-dimensional rotational machine collocated.

4 General Design and Efficiency Evaluation of GEO Hosted Payload System

Ideally, suppose hosted payload system constellation can be disposed according to demand, and the hosted payload can be placed onto the eastern and western side of the GEO satellites, then the debris between two neighbor hosting satellites can be detected one-fold coverage or two-fold coverage.

4.1 Design Approach

As is shown from the figure below, the hosted payloads are placed onto N evenly distributed GEO satellites. To realize one-fold coverage, the smallest detection range of the payload should be (Fig. 6)

$$L = R \cdot tan(\alpha)$$

$$\text{where}\, \alpha = \frac{360}{2\text{N}}$$

The smallest field of view should be

$$\theta = \frac{\pi}{2} - \left(\frac{\pi - \alpha}{2}\right) = \frac{\alpha}{2} = \frac{360}{4N}$$

To realize two-fold coverage, the smallest detection range of the payload should be (Fig. 7)

$$L = 2R \cdot \sin(\alpha)$$

The smallest field of view should be

$$\theta = \alpha = \frac{360}{2N}$$

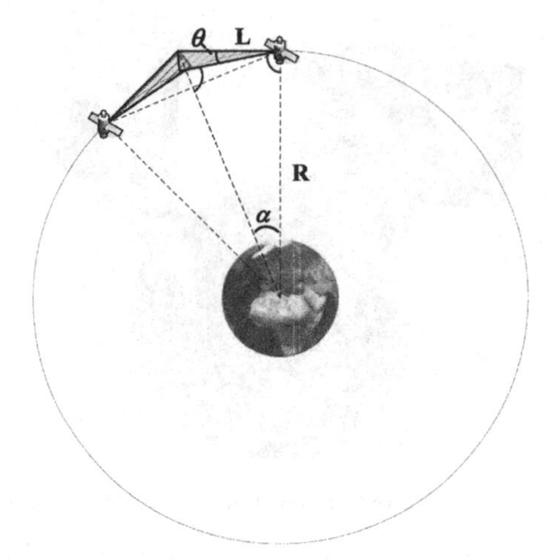

Fig. 6. Sketch of one-fold coverage.

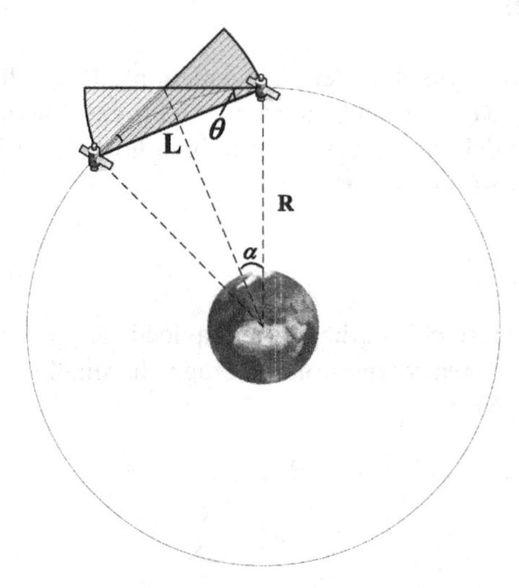

Fig. 7. Sketch of two-fold coverage.

4.2 Design Result

To realize one-fold or two-fold coverage real time to the whole GEO belt debris, when the number of constellation is from 12 to 30, the required detection range, detection ability and the minimum field of view are shown as the table below (Tables 5 and 6).

So, according to general index analysis of the hosted payload, one-fold coverage can be realized when the number of satellites of constellation is at least 15, and two-fold coverage can be realized when the number of satellites of constellation is at least 30.

Table 5. GEO hosted payload constellation design of one-fold coverage

The number of satellite	One-fold coverage design		
	Detection range (km)	detection ability (Mv)	Field of view (°)
12 sats	11297.9	15.8971	7.5
14 sats	9623.7	15.5488	6.43
15 sats	8962.3	15.3942	6
16 sats	8387	15.2502	5.625
28 sats	4750.8	14.0160	3.2143
29 sats	4585.6	13.9391	3.1034
30 sats	4431.6	13.8649	3

Table 6. GEO hosted payload constellation design of two-fold coverage

The number of satellite	Two-fold coverage design		
	Detection range (km)	Detection Ability (Mv)	Detection range (km)
12 sats	21825.8	17.3270	15
14 sats	18764.8	16.9988	12.86
15 sats	17533	16.8514	12
16 sats	16452	16.7132	11.25
28 sats	9441.8	15.5074	6.4286
29 sats	9117.5	15.4315	6.2069
30 sats	8814.7	15.3582	6

4.3 Efficiency Estimation

From the hosted payload constellation, 15 satellites and 30 satellites constellation are shown as the figure below (Figs. 8 and 9).

Hundreds of GEO debris were selected to do simulation, the simulation duration was one day. From the table below it can be seen that compared with one-fold coverage constellation, two-fold coverage constellation can make up working time window between the eastern and western neighbor payload caused by the sunlight condition, and mean detection duration will be increased from 485.93 min to 888.43 min, which will be benefical to constant detection for GEO debris (Table 7).

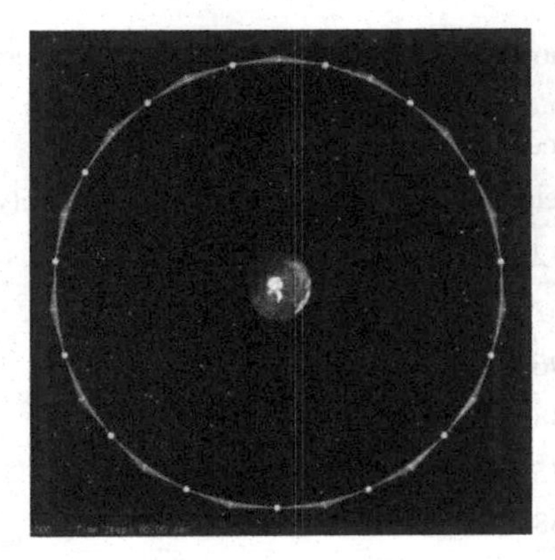

Fig. 8. One-fold coverage constellation made up of 15 satellites

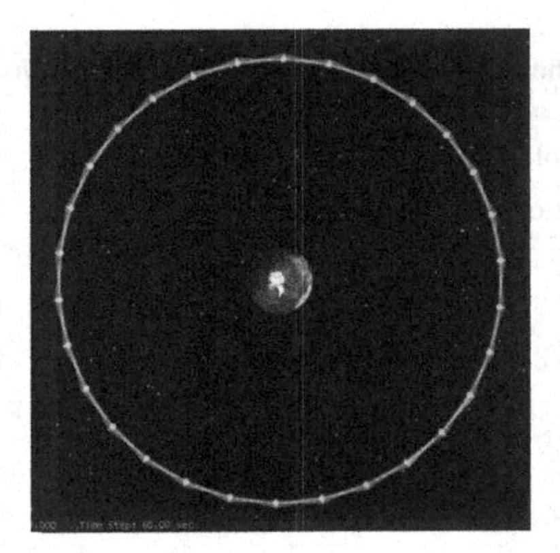

Fig. 9. Two-fold coverage constellation made up of 30 satellites

Table 7. One-fold and two-fold observation efficiency of GEO hosted payload constellation.

Number of constellation	Detection proportion of the GEO debris	Mean observation times	Mean single time detection duration	Mean total detection duration
One sat	8.17%	1.94 times	417.45 min	833.31 min
One-fold coverage 15sats	96.78%	1.92 times	485.93 min	880.49 min
Two-fold coverage 30sats	99.75%	1.54 times	888.43 min	1032.11 min

5 Conclusion

By analyzing the general index, designing the working pattern, developing general design and efficiency evaluation for the hosted payload of GEO debris detection, the feasibility of the hosted payload system was completed. In conclusion, the proposed GEO debris hosted payload can be capable of detecting small and medium scale debris, which will provide support to the development of integral space-based and ground-based debris detection system.

References

1. Hong, H., Ni, S., Chai, L.: Hosted payload can the development situation. China Space **2014**(8), 25–28 (2014)
2. Liu, H.: Research on hosted payload development of foreign commercial satellitesp. Foreign Space **2014**(1), 24–30 (2014)
3. Kalmanson, P.C., Schueler, C.: A standardized interface and accommodation methodology for commercially hosted payloads on the Star Bus. In: Proceedings of SPIE, vol. 7087, p. 70870R (2008)
4. Gong, Z., Xu, K., Mou, Y., Cao, Y.: Current space debris situation and active removing technology. Spacecraft Environ. Eng. **2014**(1), 24–30 (2014)
5. Yu, J., Su, Z., Tan, Q.: Space-based detection mode of space objects. Quant. Electron. J. **2006**(6), 772–776 (2006)

A New Problem of Resource Scheduling for Cooperative Awareness

Haixiao Zhuang[1(✉)], Zongbo He[1], Yuan Tian[2], Qiang Zhang[1], and Feilong Jiang[3]

[1] Beijing Institute of Spacecraft System Engineering, Beijing 100094, China
zhx03@126.com
[2] China Academy of Space Technology, Beijing 100094, China
[3] Harbin Institute of Technology, Harbin 150006, China

Abstract. In order to realize the situational awareness of the free space and strengthen the ability to perceive the random targets in free space, firstly the free space situational awareness could be realized on the foundation of cooperative surveillance. An important problem of the space surveillance system is presented and a relevant compete design project as well as a relevant object function were proposed. Besides, a new system schemes based on tabu genetic algorithm was put forward to improve the cooperative surveillance model. Through a series of theoretical derivation and some corresponding simulation experiments, it is proved that the system schemes is in possession of stronger ability for solving speed and precision, even detect and track the space object more than 1000.

Keywords: Space object · Cooperative surveillance · Resource scheduling

1 Introduction

Because of the high speed movement, large quantity and complex observation conditions of space objects, it is always a difficult problem to perceive them effectively. In order to improve the perception accuracy and timeliness, China has developed various means successively, including foundation, space-based and other resources. But there are limits to all of these [1, 2].

The ground-based system can be free from volume and power, and has high observation accuracy. However, due to the limited deployment position, there are dead corners in the observation area. In addition, it is limited by weather conditions, observation height and observation time, which leads to the restriction of the perception ability of spatial targets, especially high-orbit spatial targets. The space-based systems have the advantage of all-time, all-weather, all-day domain, can operate in the space orbit outside the earth's atmosphere, and can be effectively supplemented. Scheduling determines the efficiency of resource utilization. Space-oriented cooperative sensing resource scheduling technology is used to solve the problem of collision of detecting, tracking, imaging

This research was supported by the project: 2019001TJ20172A04097-4.

Q. Wu et al. (Eds.): WiSATS 2020, LNICST 358, pp. 14–21, 2021.
https://doi.org/10.1007/978-3-030-69072-4_2

and other satellite resources, ground-based optical array, passive monitoring system and so on.

In the future, all-day, all-weather, all-orbit, wide-scale, multi-means sensing ability would make the task increasingly refined and complicated [3, 4], This makes the traditional single-equipment implementation task mode difficult to cope with, so it is urgent to develop to the direction of autonomy and synergy, that is, resource collaborative scheduling, autonomous decision-making, autonomous multi-star collaboration [5, 6] become a new trend of spatial activity collaborative perception system task mode development.

This paper discusses the problem of spatial activity co-perceived resource scheduling, which is the key to ensure the coordinated and efficient operation of equipment and improve the comprehensive performance of the system [7], It is of great significance to give full play to the advantages of space and earth sensing resources, to allocate resources effectively, and to enhance the overall efficiency of spatial goal perception and even the ability of spatial dynamic perception.

2 Resource Scheduling Modeling for Spatial Activity Collaborative Awareness

The constraints of resource scheduling problem for spatial activity collaborative sensing are more complex, the task includes point target and area target, and the area target sensing task needs to decompose the task before resource scheduling, so it needs to preprocess the observation task before task modeling. The task pre-processing stage mainly analyzes the user task requirements and standardizes the task processing and task decomposition, processes the task constraints in the task decomposition process, and prepares the data for the modeling process.

2.1 Analysis on the Resource Scheduling Problem

Considering the characteristics of multi-star sensing resource scheduling problem and combining with engineering practice, the constraints of cooperative sensing resource scheduling problem are divided into the following four categories according to the constrained objects.

Resource constraints, time constraints, state constraints, relational constraints and so on. The cooperative sensing resource scheduling problem of space-ground equipment can be used to analyze various constraints and scheduling objectives in the joint perception, abstract the basic elements such as perceived demand, scheduling target, perceived resource and so on, and establish a multi-objective optimization model.

Overall Functional Analysis and Design
Analyze multi-device collaborative sensing modeling task requirements, clarify model functions, and determine appropriate application scenarios. Wide Area Surveillance Mode: general mission programmes. The basic requirement is to make as many observations of the target as possible with minimal energy consumption. Continuous tracking mode: After discovering the task plan of the key observation object, the requirement is

to realize the cumulative observation of the target as long as possible under the minimum energy consumption. Contingency mode: In the case of sudden-onset scenarios, the demand does not take into account the energy consumption to capture the target as soon as possible, and the target as much observation as possible.

Definition and Description of Input and Output Specification

Input information includes space-based sensing resources, ground-based sensing resources, measurement and control resources and digital transmission and reception resources. The output information includes the space-based system operation scenario, the Gantt chart of the observation task planning, the evolution curve of the observation task planning, and the definition description of the change map of the observation direction.

Analysis and Determination of Objective Function

As shown in Table 1, According to the requirements of wide area monitoring mode, continuous tracking mode and emergency mode, this paper establish the corresponding optimization target, then construct the concrete objective function.

Table 1. Objective function on Typical Scenarios.

Scene	Optimized goal 1	Optimized goal 2	Optimized goal 3	Optimized goal 4
Wide Area Surveillance Mode	Maximum number of observed targets	Maximum average single-objective observations	Minimum energy consumption	Star Mission Balance
Continuous tracking mode	Maximum cumulative duration of target observations	Maximum observed benefits	Minimum energy consumption	Star Mission Balance
Emergency mode	Target capture	Maximum average single-objective observations	Null	Null

In wide area monitoring mode, multiple observation devices cooperate to observe a large number of spatial targets. There are three kinds of planning targets which can be selected: the largest number of observation targets, the most number of average single target observations, and the balance of each star task. The corresponding objective functions are:

$$Max \sum x_i, i \in I \tag{1}$$

$$Max \sum (x_i \cdot times_i) / \sum x_i, i \in I \tag{2}$$

$$MinD(x_i \cdot times_i), i \in I \tag{3}$$

In the formula, if $x_i = 1$, the target is selected to be observed, if selected, otherwise, $x_i = 0$, $times_i$ is the times of the target to be observed, $D(\cdots)$ is the variance operator, and I is the set of observations for the target.

In the continuous tracking mode, multiple observation equipment carries on the relay continuous observation to the key target. There are three kinds of planning targets which can be selected: the longest cumulative observation time, the best observation conditions, and the balance of each star task. The corresponding objective functions are:

$$Max \sum\nolimits_r \left(\sum\nolimits_k dur_{rk} \right), r \in R, k \in O_r \tag{4}$$

$$Max \sum\nolimits_r \left(\sum\nolimits_k fit_{rk} \right), r \in R, k \in O_r \tag{5}$$

$$MinD(x_i \cdot times_i), i \in I \tag{6}$$

In the formula, dur_{rk} is the duration of k observation missions carried out by the r observation apparatus, fit_{rk} is the observation gains of k observation missions carried out by the r observation apparatus, $D(\cdots)$ is the variance operator, $times_i$ is the number of times the target is observed, x$_i$$x_i$ and I is the same as above.

In emergency mode, multiple observation devices need to respond quickly and cooperate to complete the fast capture of target groups. There are two types of planning targets that can be selected: the fastest capture of all targets and the maximum number of average single target observations. The corresponding objective functions are:

$$\min \sum\nolimits_i \left(\min_n (TAs_{in}) \right), i \in I, n \in TO_i \tag{7}$$

$$\max \sum (x_i * times_i) / \sum x_i, i \in I \tag{8}$$

In the formula, TAs_{in} is the initial time of observation missions TO_{in} for the observation target i, TO_i is the Observation sets of observation missions for the observation target i, $D(\cdots)$ is the variance operator, $times_i$ is the number of times the target is observed, x_i and I is the same as above.

Resource Scheduling Model of Spatial Activity Collaborative Awareness.

The objective function model includes four aspects: maximum number of observations, maximum number of average single-objective observations, minimum energy consumption and minimum variance of each star task.

Maximum number of observed targets:

$$Q_1 = \max\left(\sum V_i x_i \right), i \in I \tag{9}$$

Maximum average single-objective observations:

$$Q_2 = \max\left(\sum V_i x_i - \sum e_i x_i \right), i \in I \tag{10}$$

Minimum energy consumption:

$$Q_3 = \max\left(\sum V_i x_i y_i + \sum V_i x_i z_i\right), i \in I \tag{11}$$

Minimum variance of star:

$$Q_4 = \min\left[\left(\sum (V_i x_i - u)^2\right)/N\right], i \in I \tag{12}$$

In the formula, V_i is the times the observed target, if $x_i = 1$, the target is selected to be observed, otherwise, $x_i = 0$, $times_i$ is the times of the target to be observed, e_i is the cost of observation missions. if $y_i = 1$, the objective is observed in the same way as the original mission, otherwise, $y_i = \beta, \beta \in (0, 1)$. z_i indicates whether the target is a burst target, if $z_i = 1$,the target is non-expected one, otherwise, $z_i = 0$.

2.2 Analysis on Resource Scheduling Algorithm

In the collaborative sensing resource scheduling problem, scenario and perceptual requirements are the input of the problem. it is the purpose of resource scheduling to meet the perceptual requirements as much as possible under the consideration of various constraints, and the principle of giving priority to ensuring that high priority task requirements are served. Different solutions can be chosen according to the level and urgency of requirements, When the time requirement is high and the time requirement is not high, the requirement-oriented heuristic algorithm can be used to generate the available scheduling scheme quickly. Among the many evolutionary algorithms, genetic algorithm is one of the best tools to find satisfactory solutions to combinatorial optimization problems. Some scholars have applied genetic algorithm to solve the related problems of observation resource scheduling. Although genetic algorithm has the advantages of parallel search and high search efficiency, it also has the disadvantages of weak local search ability and easy precocity.

As a complex combinatorial optimization problem with time window constraints, the genetic algorithm is a stochastic search algorithm, which needs to be searched step by step in the whole solution space. The number of decision variables of the multi-star resource scheduling problem is large, and the corresponding solution space is also naturally huge, so the time cost of the algorithm will be large.

Based on the factors of satellite resource, ground resource and task requirement, this paper proposes an optimal solution method of collaborative sensing resource scheduling based on tabu genetic algorithm. The basic idea of tabu genetic algorithm is to use the evolutionary function of genetic algorithm to make the search quickly concentrate around the better solution, and then use the tabu search method to further search the optimal solution in a small range.

By combining the advantages of genetic algorithm ideas and tabu search methods, we can effectively use global information and the information obtained in the search process to search repeatedly in the neighborhood and move quickly and effectively in the direction of the optimal solution, so as to effectively overcome the local optimization and achieve the purpose of improving the solution effect and search efficiency. The concrete realization process is mainly divided into three stages: preliminary optimization, taboo processing and termination judgment.

Step 1: Initial optimization.
Input the original data and the required parameters, form the initial population, calculate the fitness value and make the preliminary optimization.
Step 2: Taboo handling.
Select based on elite selection, cross and mutate based on tabu search, and update tabu table.
Step 3: Termination judgement.
Determine whether the tabu algorithm termination condition is satisfied, If satisfied, jump out of taboo optimization, and genetic optimization operation. if not satisfied, continue to taboo operation, until the survival probability of the largest chromosome.

3 Analysis of Examples Based on Simulation Verification

3.1 System Testing and Validation

Based on the aforementioned cooperative sensing resource scheduling algorithm, Based on the idea of modularity, a software module of collaborative sensing resource scheduling based on Tabu Genetic Algorithm is developed, and related test applications are carried out, The typical interface of the software module is shown in Fig. 1. Figure 2 shows a preliminary optimization scheme for resource scheduling of a sensing task: The software plans space—ground resource allocation plans based on a programme of collaborative sensing tasks for space activities, Generating work task sequences and time windows for various available resources; The change curve of attitude angle is a guarantee requirement for the platform to support the smooth implementation of space-based detection, tracking, imaging load work plan and measurement and control data transmission plan, The software system can respond quickly to the task requirement.

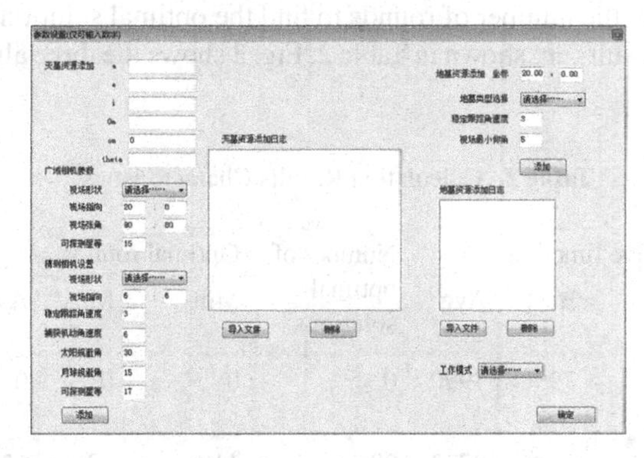

Fig. 1. Design of scheduling Software Interface Based on Cooperative surveillance

3.2 Comparative Analysis

In order to test the advantages of the system introduced in this paper, a comparative analysis is carried out based on the application background of the joint perception task of space and ground, and to obtain the maximum task income as the objective function.

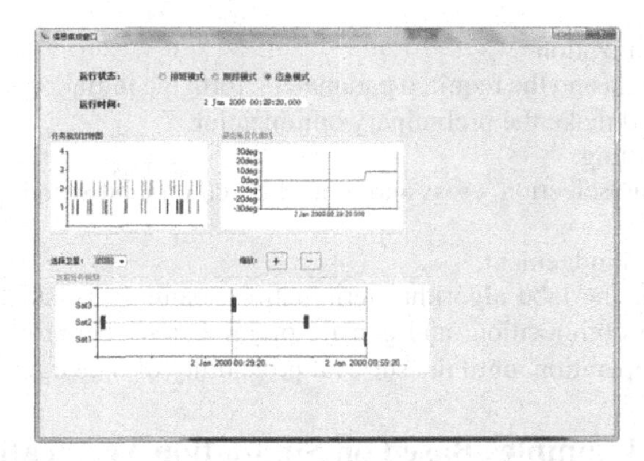

Fig. 2. Preliminary result of scheduling on Cooperative surveillance

objective function: Maximum cumulative gain

$$\max \sum\nolimits_r \left(\sum\nolimits_k fit_{rk} \right), r \in R, k \in o_r \tag{13}$$

In the formula: fit_{rk} is the benefits of k observation missions carried out by the observation subjects, R is the collection of observation subjects, o_r is the collection of observation missions from observation subject r. In the background of satellite and ground station joint sensing mission planning, the simulation calculation of observation task scheduling is now in progress, in which Three algorithms are applied to optimize the solution based on objective function.

In order to reduce the influence of contingency, each algorithm runs independently for 30 times when solving, recording the solution it finds, the number of times it finds the optimal solution, the number of rounds to find the optimal solution, and the average running time. The results are shown in Table 2, Fig. 3 shows the three algorithms running at one time.

Table 2. Calculation Results Characteristics

Algorithm	Objective function			Number of optimal solutions	Optimal rounds			Mean time (s)
	Worst	Best	Avg		Min	Max	Avg	
Priority heuristic	7990	7990	7990	0	0	0	0	1.1812
tabu genetic	8075	8984	8772	23	110	130	125.3	189.135
Ant colony hybrid	8053	8984	8922	28	81	98	88.7	173.413

As we can see, Under the compound optimization objective function, The cooperative sensing resource scheduling system proposed in this paper has faster convergence speed and stronger ability to find the optimal solution.

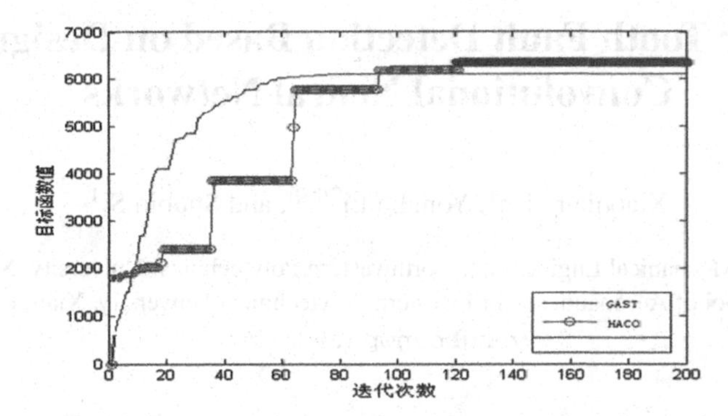

Fig. 3. Comparison of processes based on different algorithm

4 Conclusion

In this paper, the requirement, current problems and countermeasures of resource scheduling system for spatial activity cooperative sensing are expounded in detail. Taking the task income as the specific measurement value, it proves that the resource scheduling system has obvious advantages in the speed of scheduling optimization, the speed of algorithm convergence, the accuracy of solution, and so on.

References

1. Han, C., Liu, Y., Li, H.: Mission planning for small satellite constellations based on improved genetic algorithm. Chin. J. Space Sci. **39**(1), 129–134 (2019)
2. Zhang, H., Yang, J., Wang, H.: Development and inspiration of space surveillance equipment and technique. Modern Radar **33**(12), 11–14 (2011)
3. Huang, Z.: Space weaponization and space deterrence. Stud. Int. Technol. Econ. **17**(1), 24–28 (2006)
4. Wang, J., Yu, X.: The current development and characteristics analysis of foreign space-based space surveillance. J. Equip. Acad. **32**(6), 24–27 (2011)
5. Xu, Z., Huang, Y.: A scheduling method for cataloging observation tasks based on greedy algorithm. J. Spacecraft TT & C Technol. **31**(02), 89–94 (2012)
6. Guo, Y.: Research on Key Technologies of Joint Task plannIng for Multi-type Earth Observation Satellite. National University of Defense Technology, Changsha (2009)
7. Zhang, C., Jin, P., Chen, J., et al.: Virtual constellation task planning technology for emergency observation. Syst. Eng. Electron. **41**(4), 819–825 (2019)

Gear Tooth Fault Detection Based on Designed Convolutional Neural Networks

Xiaoqiang Du[1], Yongbo Li[2](✉), and Shubin Si[1]

[1] School of Mechanical Engineering, Northwestern Polytechnical University, Xian, China
[2] School of Aeronautics, Northwestern Polytechnical University, Xian, China
yongbo@nwpu.edu.cn

Abstract. Gearbox is one of the most important parts of the rotating machinery, so health monitoring of the gearbox is essential. The accurate positioning of tooth failure of gear is an important function of the fault diagnosis system. This paper proposes a detection strategy based on designed convolutional neural networks to detect and locate gear tooth failure. The detection strategy aims to compare the characteristic gap between the normal gear and the faulty gear in the same period extracted by the convolutional neural network, and assign weights to the faulty gear vibration signal to obtain the weight sequence of the faulty vibration signal, so as to obtain the faulty tooth weight. Finally, the health condition of the gear can be evaluated by comparing the weight between all teeth of the gear. The proposed detection strategy is tested through simulation vibration signal and experiment vibration signal. The result shows that the proposed method can successfully identify gear failure and effectively detect single tooth failure on gear.

Keywords: Gear tooth · Detection strategy · Designed convolutional neural networks

1 Introduction

Gearbox is a vital transmission element, which has widely applied in small, medium and large machines. Excessive load, overspeed and improper operating conditions may cause defects on its surface, which can cause abnormal vibration for the entire machine structure. This may eventually lead to accidental casualties and property damage. Therefore, the fault diagnosis of the gearbox is of great significance to the reliability and safety of the mechanical system [1–4].

The accurate positioning of tooth failure of gear is an important function of the fault diagnosis system. In the past researches on gearbox, many researchers have devoted themselves to the detection of gear tooth failure. Liang et al. [5] proposed a windowing and mapping strategy to interpret the vibration signal of a planetary gear at the tooth level and detect the gear tooth failure by comparing the differences among the signals of all teeth. Xue et al. [6] developed a 20 degree of freedom planetary gear lumped-parameter model to obtain the gear dynamic response and detect the gear failure further. Shahin et al. [7] presented a statistical analysis on a fault index computed based on the stator

Q. Wu et al. (Eds.): WiSATS 2020, LNICST 358, pp. 22–32, 2021.
https://doi.org/10.1007/978-3-030-69072-4_3

current space vector instantaneous frequency on a real-time platform, which can evaluate gear tooth surface damage fault detection using a threshold. Liu et al. [8] proposed a new time-domain fault detection method combining fast dynamic time warping (DTW) and correlated kurtosis techniques to detect and identify damaged planetary gear and its position. Yang et al. [9] proposed a method using an autoregressive model with exogenous variables (ARX) to detect and localize the gear failure for varying load conditions.

All of them use the artificial design features to evaluate the health condition of the gearbox. As we know, feature extraction is the core of the entire fault diagnosis work and determines the effectiveness of the entire diagnosis system. Traditional feature extraction methods use artificial design features that experts design features based on experience. However, due to limited expert experience, artificial design features will inevitably bring many errors.

Therefore, in order to overcome the shortcomings of artificial design features, it's a better choice to use deep learning methods for feature extraction. In recent years, deep learning has been used widely in fault diagnosis [10–12], performance evaluation [13, 14], remaining life prediction [15, 16] and many other aspects. Compared with traditional fault diagnosis methods, deep learning can directly process the original data to achieve adaptive feature learning, which reduces manual participation and helps to improve the adaptability and intelligence of prediction methods. Layer-by-layer feature learning is more likely to learn the basic features hidden in the monitoring data, which improves prediction accuracy. Convolutional neural networks (CNN), as an effective neural network of deep learning, has been widely used in the field of fault diagnosis [17, 18]. CNN can automatically extract the original features of the input signal, which greatly avoids the diagnostic errors caused by human factors. The design operation of convolution and pooling has a non-negligible effect on data feature extraction and dimensionality reduction.

In this paper, this designed CNN has 3 stages including data preprocessing stage, feature extraction stage, and classification stage [19]. The data preprocessing stage is a key part of the implementation of the detection strategy, which mainly includes the symbolization process [20] and the one-hot encoding process [21]. The symbolization process aims to denoise the vibration signal and recombine the sequence in an integer manner. The one-hot encoding process aims to convert the recombination sequence from a 1-dimensional signal to a 2-dimensional signal. The feature extraction stage is through convolutional layers and pooling layers. The final classification stage uses binary classification logistic regression to score the extracted features.

The detection strategy is mainly based on the idea of probability. For a binary classification problem, suppose that the normal signal label is 0 and the abnormal signal label is 1. The higher score of the test signal, the more fault information characteristics the signal has. And for high-score test signals, they must have some special properties that are different from normal signals in certain areas. Therefore, when there are enough high-score signals, by calculating the probability value of the symbol value of each point of the high-score signals, the weight sequence can be characterized by the maximum probability value.

Therefore, by combining the designed CNN and the detection strategy, we proposed a method of gearbox fault region location based on convolutional neural network (CNN).

The method mainly consists of three steps. First, train a designed CNN model with dataset. Then, use the detection strategy to obtain the weight sequence of the fault signal. Finally, detect the gear tooth failure by processing the weight sequence The main contributions of this paper can be summarized as follows.

(1) A designed CNN structure is proposed by introducing symbolization and one-hot encoding. The designed CNN model can automatically learn to discriminate features directly from the original vibration signal without much prior knowledge about vibration signal feature extraction. And the designed CNN can effectively identify gear fault.
(2) A detection strategy is proposed to locate the gear tooth failure. The effectiveness is validated by the simulation signal and the experiment signal. The detection result can give certain instructions for failure mechanism.

The focus of this article is gearbox fault area detection based on the designed CNN. The rest comment is as follows. Section 2 gives the designed CNN model and the explanation of fault area detection of gearbox. Section 3 is the validation using the simulation signal. Section 4 is the validation using experiment signal. Finally, conclusions are given in Section 5.

2 Methodology

Figure 1 gives the flowchart of the gear tooth failure detection. As we can see from that, firstly, it's essential to train a designed CNN model. Then, obtain the weight sequence of the fault signal using the detection strategy. Finally, detect the position of the gear tooth failure by calculating the weights of all teeth.

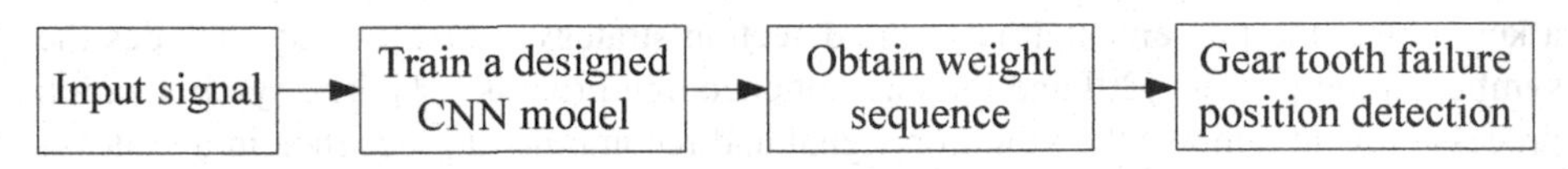

Fig. 1. Implementation process of proposed mythology

2.1 The Designed CNN Model

Figure 2 gives the schematic diagram of the designed CNN model. For training, the scoring CNN model uses a set of sequences. For each sequence, binary class label is adopted. As we can see from Fig. 2, the designed CNN model consists of three stages: data preprocessing stage, feature learning stage, and classification stage. The data preprocessing stage plays a vital role for the tooth failure detection.

For data preprocessing, it contains symbolization step and one-hot encoding step. In this paper, equal probability symbolization is used to symbolize the vibration data.

The idea of equal probability symbolization was first introduced by Lin et al. [22] in 2007. It is widely used in the field of data mining. The equal probability symbolization

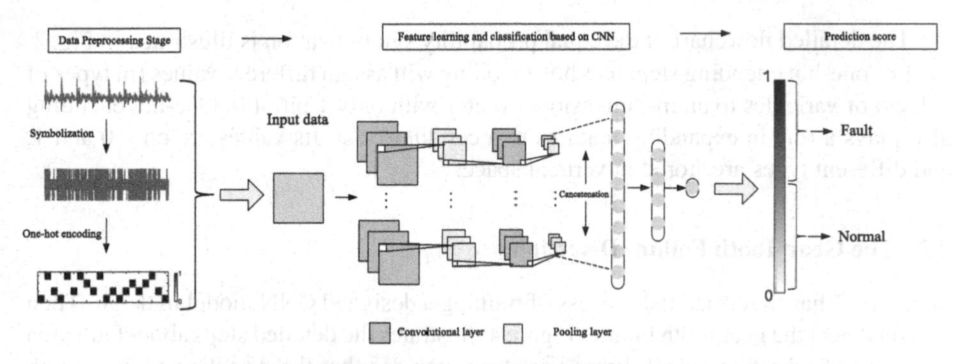

Fig. 2. The designed CNN model structure.

process is briefly described as follows: For time sequence $\{x_i : 1 \le i \le N\}$, the sequence is sorted by amplitude first. When the number n of symbols is given, n-1 bisectors (denoted as $t_1, t_2, ..., t_{n-1}$) can be found as the threshold of symbol division. After that, a new symbolic sequence is obtained according to the rule as follows:

$$s_i = \begin{cases} 0 & (x_i \le t_1), \\ 1 & (t_1 < x_i \le t_2), \\ \dots & \\ n-2 & (t_{n-2} < x_i \le t_{n-1}), \\ n-1 & (t_{n-1} < x_i), \end{cases}$$

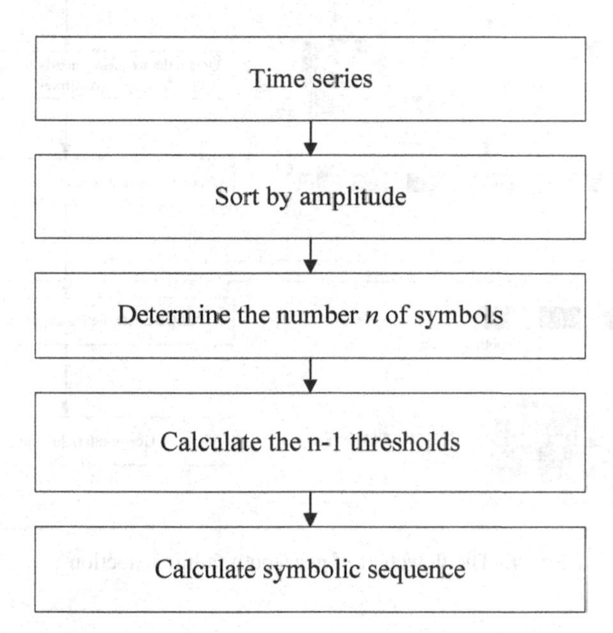

Fig. 3. The flowchart of the equal probability symbolization.

The detailed flowchart of the equal probability symbolization is illustrated in Fig. 3.

For one-hot encoding step, one-hot encoding will assign different values (m types of values) of variables to an m-dimensional vector with only 1 bit of 0. One-hot encoding also plays a role in expanding features to a certain extent. Its values are only 0 and 1, and different types are stored in vertical space.

2.2 The Gear Tooth Failure Detection

Section 2.1 has described the process of training a designed CNN model in detail. Then we can detect the gear tooth failure. Figure 4 illustrates the detailed steps about fault area detection of vibration signal. From Fig. 4, we can see that the detection of gear tooth failure can be divided into two parts: the detection strategy and tooth failure detection.

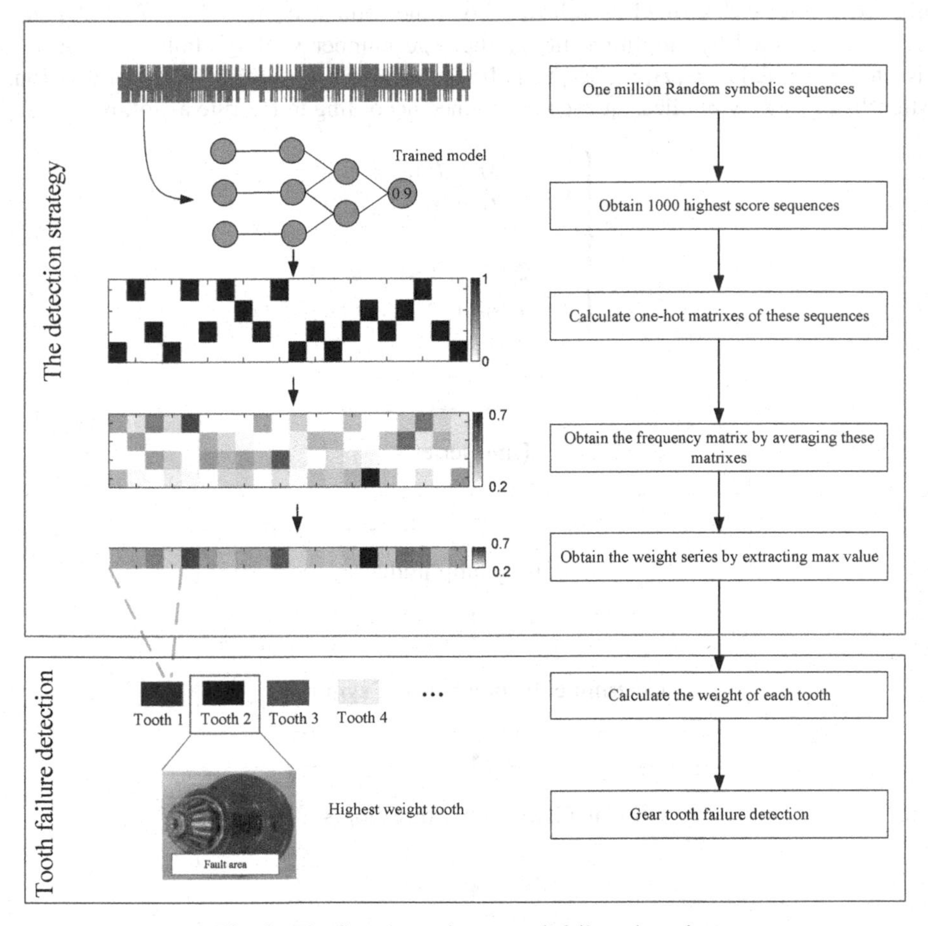

Fig. 4. The flowchart of gear tooth failure detection

2.2.1 The Detection Strategy

As we can see from Fig. 4, five steps are required for high score sequences acquisition as follows:

Step 1: Randomly generate 1,000,000 sets of symbol sequences.
Step 2: Using the trained CNN model to test these symbol sequences. Each symbol sequences would generate a score between 0 and 1. Then rank these sequences according to the output score from high to low. Finally, select the top 1000 highest scoring sequences. These high score sequences acquisition aims to provide the sequences which have more fault information.
Step 3: Obtain the one-hot matrixes of these highest scoring sequences by one-hot encoding.
Step 4: For these top 1000 highest-scoring sequences, they have the same fault features in certain areas. This means they must have some same values in certain areas. By adding the 1000 corresponding one-hot matrixes and averaging the final result, each position shows the frequency. When a position of a column have higher value compared with the other values of this column, this indicates this value is more effective and this position can be important. When the value is near to the other values of this column, this demonstrates this point of the vibration signal is not important. Therefore, the average matrix is the weight matrix.
Step 5: Due to the importance for each position of the vibration signal can be reflected by the max value of each position. Therefore, for the weight matrix, we can extract the max weight for each column to obtain the weight series. The weight series shows the importance of each position of the vibration signal for the classification result.

2.2.2 Tooth Failure Detection

When we have obtained the weight series for the signal of fault condition. It's easy to calculate the weight of each tooth. To get the weight of each tooth, it's essential to calculate how many points a tooth has according to the related parameters of the experiment data. Then we can get the weight of each tooth by adding these weights for each tooth and each period.

In the end, by normalizing the final result, we can get relative importance of each tooth. By observing the tooth of highest weight, the fault area of gearbox can be found.

3 Simulation Validation

In this section, we use the simulation signal to validate the effectiveness of the proposed method.

For dataset, we use a normal gearbox vibration signal and a fault vibration signal. Each fault type number is 2000, and the length of each sample is 512. The training rate is 0.8, which means each condition has 1600 samples to train and 400 samples to test. The simulation vibration signal is shown in Fig. 5.

By symbolizing and one-hot encoding, we can use the dataset to train the designed CNN model. The parameter setting of CNN model is given in Table 1. The learning

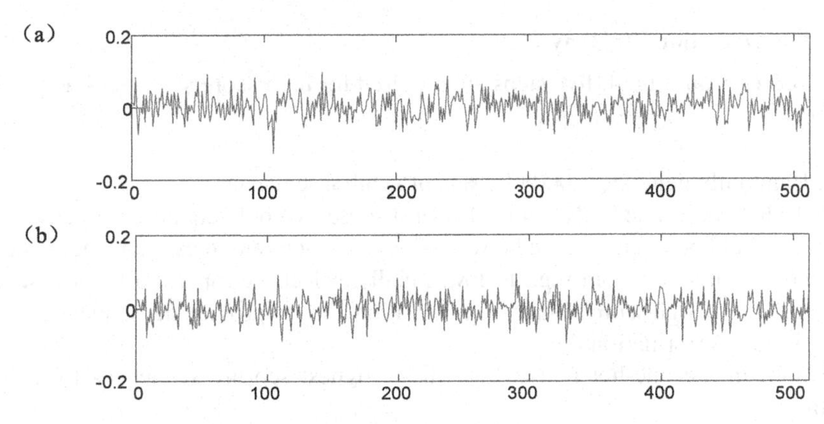

Fig. 5. Simulation signal: (a) normal (b) fault

rate is 0.0001, and the epoch is 100. The Adam optimization algorithm [23] is use to minimize the loss function.

Table 1. The adopted CNN structure

Layer Type	Number of Filter	Size of the feature map	Size of kernel	Number of Stride	Activation function
Input layer	–	4 × 512 × 1	–	–	–
C1	12	1 × 488 × 12	4 × 25	1 × 1	ReLu
P1	–	1 × 244 × 12	1 × 2	1 × 2	–
C2	24	1 × 244 × 12	1 × 2	1 × 1	ReLu
P2	–	1 × 244 × 12	1 × 2	1 × 2	–
F1	–	200	–	–	ReLu
F2	–	40	–	–	ReLu
Output layer	–	1	–	–	Sigmoid

For the testing result, the testing accuracy of 100% after 20 epochs almost, which means we get a very effective model to distinguish these two fault types. Then, we can randomly generate 1,000,000 symbolic sequences to test the trained model. Each sequence's length is the same as the sample of the dataset and each vibration point's value is between 1 and 4. Finally, we get the average one-hot matrix by averaging the top 1000 highest score samples' one-hot matrixes.

According to the average matrix, we can get the weight series by extracting the biggest value for each column. The weight series means the weight of each position in the diagnosis process, which is shown in Fig. 6. The high weight of the fault signal position shows which part of the fault signal is more important than others for the diagnosis result.

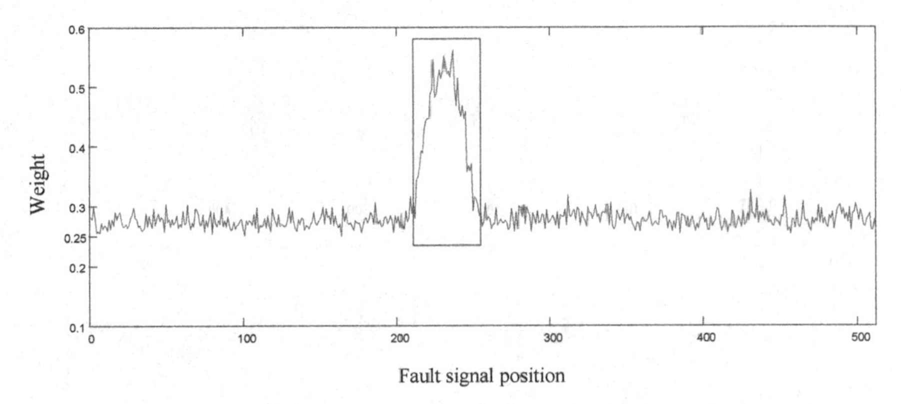

Fig. 6. The weight series for fault condition

4 Experiment Validation

In this section, the gear fault experiments were conducted on rotating machinery called SpectraQuest Machinery Fault Simulator (MFS). The test rig is shown in Fig. 7. An accelerometer was installed on the top of the gearbox to collect the vibration signals. The sampling frequency was 12800 Hz and the rotating speed was 3000 rpm.

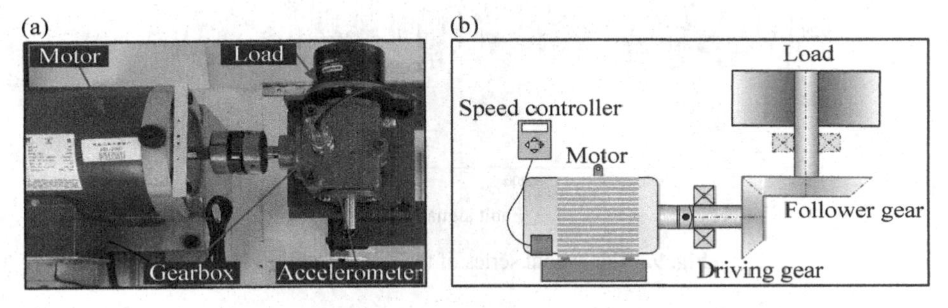

Fig. 7. (a) The machinery fault simulator system; (b) the layout of the test rig.

The proposed method is used for binary problem. In the experiment, 2 conditions are introduced including normal condition and missing tooth condition (fault condition). For the dataset, each condition has 480 samples and the length of each sample is 512. The length contains 2 period for the vibration signal. The training rate is 0.8. So, the total number of training samples is 768 and the testing number is 192. An example of dataset is given in Fig. 8.

By symbolizing and one-hot encoding, we can use the dataset to train a designed CNN model. The testing accuracy keeps 100% after almost epoch 20, which means the model is effective to distinguish the fault. Then, by testing 1,000,000 random sequence, we can get the wight matrix. After that, a weight series is obtained by extracting the biggest value for each column, which is shown in Fig. 9.

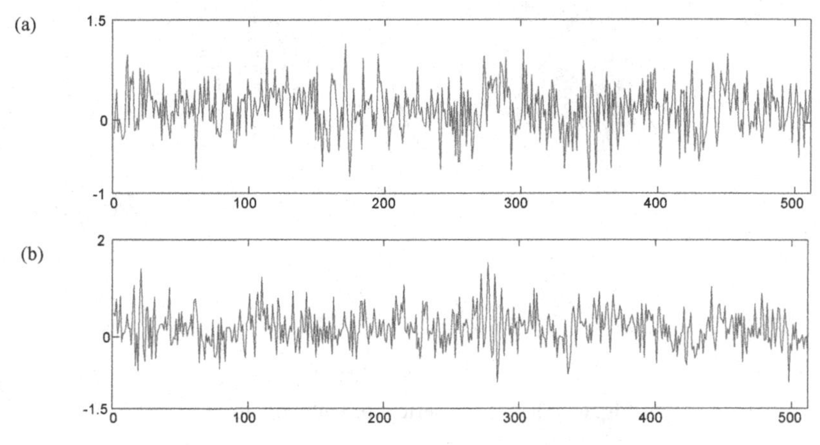

Fig. 8. The experiment vibration signal: (a) normal (b) fault

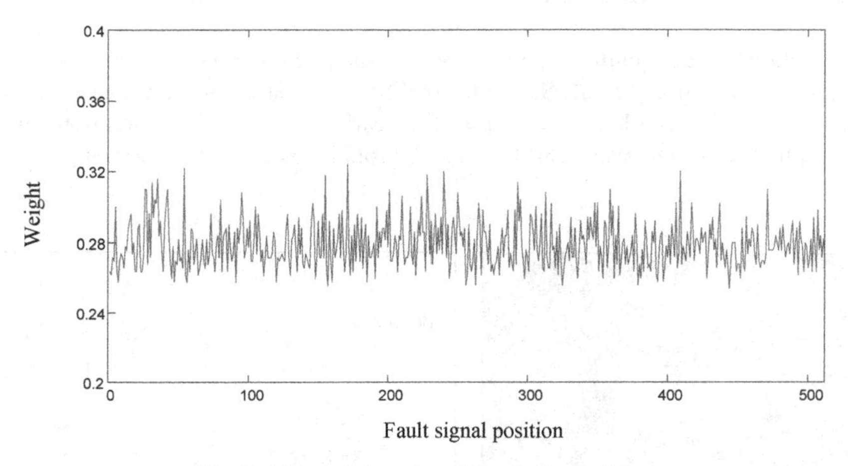

Fig. 9. The weight series of the fault condition

As we can see from Fig. 9, it's hard to see which part is more important for the fault condition directly. Because experiment data has more noise impact. Therefore, it's necessary to add the weights corresponding to each tooth. The experiment gear has 18 teeth. The points for each period can be calculated according to the sampling frequency and the rotating speed, the equation is given in Eq. (2).

$$Points\,for\,one\,circle\,of\,the\,gear = \frac{sampling\,frequence \times 60}{rotating\,speed} \tag{2}$$

It's 256 points by calculate the equation. Then we can calculate each gear has 14 points almost. Therefore, each tooth's weight can be gotten by accumulating the weight sum of each tooth and each period, which is shown in Fig. 10. To avoid the randomness of experiment, the experiment is implemented 20 times to get the final result.

From the result, we can find the tooth 1, tooth 2 and tooth 3 obviously have higher weights than other teeth. And the tooth 2 has the biggest weight. The result shows that

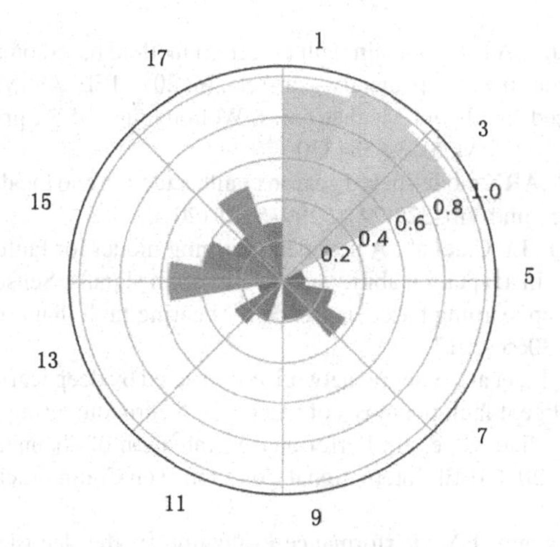

Fig. 10. The weights of each tooth

the proposed method can detect the fault tooth. And the fault tooth and two teeth around are obviously more important than other teeth for the diagnosis result.

5 Conclusion

In this paper, we proposed a method for gear tooth failure detection based on the designed CNN model. And the effectiveness of the proposed method is validated by the experiment signal. The validation result shows that the proposed method can effectively detect the fault area of the vibration signal and the fault tooth. The fault area detection can give instructions on failure mechanism and subsequent maintenance, which deserves research in future.

References

1. Lin, J., Zuo, M.J.: Gearbox fault diagnosis using adaptive wavelet filter. Mech. Syst. Signal Process. **17**(6), 1259–1269 (2003)
2. Liu, B., Riemenschneider, S., Xu, Y.: Gearbox fault diagnosis using empirical mode decomposition and Hilbert spectrum. Mech. Syst. Signal Process. **20**(3), 718–734 (2006)
3. Lei, Y., Han, D., Lin, J., et al.: Planetary gearbox fault diagnosis using an adaptive stochastic resonance method. Mech. Syst. Signal Process. **38**(1), 113–124 (2013)
4. Li, C., Sanchez, R.V., Zurita, G., et al.: Gearbox fault diagnosis based on deep random forest fusion of acoustic and vibratory signals. Mech. Syst. Signal Process. **76**, 283–293 (2016)
5. Liang, X., Zuo, M.J., Liu, L.: A windowing and mapping strategy for gear tooth fault detection of a planetary gearbox. Mech. Syst. Signal Process. **80**, 445–459 (2016)
6. Xue, S., Howard, I.: Torsional vibration signal analysis as a diagnostic tool for planetary gear fault detection. Mech. Syst. Signal Process. **100**, 706–728 (2018)
7. Kia, S.H., Henao, H., Capolino, G.: Fault index statistical study for gear fault detection using stator current space vector analysis. IEEE Trans. Ind. Appl. **52**(6), 4781–4788 (2016). https://doi.org/10.1109/TIA.2016.2600596

8. Hong, L., Dhupia, J.S.:A time-domain fault detection method based on an electrical machine stator current measurement for planetary gear-sets. In: 2013 IEEE/ASME International Conference on Advanced Intelligent Mechatronics, Wollongong, NSW, pp. 1631–1636 (2013). https://doi.org/10.1109/AIM.2013.6584330
9. Yang, M., Makis, V.: ARX model-based gearbox fault detection and localization under varying load conditions. J. Sound Vib. **329**(24), 5209–5221 (2010)
10. Zhang, W., Peng, G., Li, C., et al.: A new deep learning model for fault diagnosis with good anti-noise and domain adaptation ability on raw vibration signals. Sensors **17**(2), 425 (2017)
11. He, M., He, D.: Deep learning based approach for bearing fault diagnosis. IEEE Trans. Ind. Appl. **53**(3), 3057–3065 (2017)
12. Jia, F., Lei, Y., Guo, L., et al.: A neural network constructed by deep learning technique and its application to intelligent fault diagnosis of machines. Neurocomputing **272**, 619–628 (2018)
13. Lyu, W., Zhang, Z., Jiao, C., et al.: Performance evaluation of channel decoding with deep neural networks. In: 2018 IEEE International Conference on Communications (ICC), pp. 1–6. IEEE (2018)
14. Duan, Y., Lv, Y., Wang, F.Y.: Performance evaluation of the deep learning approach for traffic flow prediction at different times. In: 2016 IEEE International Conference on Service Operations and Logistics, and Informatics (SOLI), pp. 223–227. IEEE (2016)
15. Zhang, J., Wang, P., Yan, R., et al.: Deep learning for improved system remaining life prediction. Procedia CIRP **72**, 1033–1038 (2018)
16. Ren, L., Zhao, L., Hong, S., et al.: Remaining useful life prediction for lithium-ion battery: a deep learning approach. IEEE Access **6**, 50587–50598 (2018)
17. Xia, M., Li, T., Xu, L., et al.: Fault diagnosis for rotating machinery using multiple sensors and convolutional neural networks. IEEE/ASME Trans. Mechatron. **23**(1), 101–110 (2017)
18. Chen, Z.Q., Li, C., Sanchez, R.V.: Gearbox fault identification and classification with convolutional neural networks. Shock Vibr. **2015**, 1–11 (2015)
19. Jiang, G., He, H., Yan, J., et al.: Multiscale convolutional neural networks for fault diagnosis of wind turbine gearbox. IEEE Trans. Industr. Electron. **66**(4), 3196–3207 (2018)
20. Hu, R.F., Wang, L., Mei, X.Q., et al.: Fault diagnosis based on sequential pattern mining. Comput. Integr. Manuf. Syst. **16**(7), 1412–1418 (2010)
21. Cassel, M., Lima, F.: Evaluating one-hot encoding finite state machines for SEU reliability in SRAM-based FPGAs. In: 12th IEEE International On-Line Testing Symposium (IOLTS 2006), pp. 6. IEEE (2006)
22. Lin, J., Keogh, E., Lonardi, S., et al.: A symbolic representation of time series, with implications for streaming algorithms. In: Proceedings of the 8th ACM SIGMOD Workshop on Research Issues in Data Mining and Knowledge Discovery, pp. 2–11 (2003)
23. Kingma, D., Ba, J.: Adam: a method for stochastic optimization. In: Proceedings of 3rd International Conference on Learning Representations (2015)

Research on Satellite Fault Detection Method Based on MSET and SRPRT

Peng Sun(✉) and Guang Jin

National University of Defense Technology, Changsha, Hunan, China
875638381@qq.com

Abstract. Since the beginning of the 21st century, the increasing requirements of mankind for spacecraft technology have forced spacecraft technology to become more and more complex and increase investment. Most current fault detection methods only use single features and features or single fault detection data, and do not involve satellite fault monitoring under multi-parameter conditions. This paper proposes a satellite fault detection method that can be used in a multi-parameter state. The multivariate state estimation algorithm (MSET) is used to obtain the residual between the multivariate state and historical health data, and then the actual residual of the data to be measured is input into the sequential rank sum probability ratio test method (SRPRT) to test. This paper verifies the effectiveness of the combination of MSET algorithm and SRPRT algorithm through experiments, and finds the optimal parameters and accuracy relative to SPRT method.

Keywords: Fault detection · MSET · SRPRT

1 Background

Since the beginning of the 21st century, the increasing requirements of mankind for spacecraft technology have forced spacecraft technology to become more and more complex and increase investment. In such a system with relatively high complexity and relatively high investment, the reliability, safety and fault diagnosis technology of the spacecraft are forced to be on the agenda, which has become an important link restricting the development of the spacecraft. According to incomplete statistics, of the 764 spacecraft launched in 1990–2001, a total of 121 failed, accounting for 15.8% of the total spacecraft [1].

In the field of spacecraft on-orbit fault detection, the more mature engineering is the threshold detection based on the original telemetry data, and is currently actively exploring and applying detection methods based on feature quantities.. Fuertes et al. [2] analyzed the limitations of the threshold detection method of the CNES spacecraft condition monitoring and the monthly statistical feature monitoring method. In view of the shortcomings of the traditional fixed threshold detection method, D. DeCoste et al. [3] proposed an envelope learning and monitoring method based on error relaxation,

Q. Wu et al. (Eds.): WiSATS 2020, LNICST 358, pp. 33–45, 2021.
https://doi.org/10.1007/978-3-030-69072-4_4

which can continuously update and generate a tight upper and lower bound function envelope to reduce the rate of misdiagnosis and false alarm. Shan Changsheng et al. [4] pointed out that at present, the three main threshold abnormal methods based on telemetry parameter over-limit alarms include telemetry parameter threshold judgment, relative value judgment and associated diagnosis. Wang Weiwei et al. [5] pointed out that the abnormal state mutation can usually be detected in time using the threshold detection method, but there are also a considerable part of the satellite telemetry parameters that do not exceed the limit when the on-orbit abnormality occurs. Yang Tianshe et al. proposed a space system state symptom variable prediction model based on gray system theory [6], and a satellite fault diagnosis and prediction method based on knowledge [7]. Based on data mining and decision tree, Wang Xiaole et al. [8] selected the maximum gain rate information as the segmentation attribute, and obtained the optimal segmentation point by mining the data, and generated the fault diagnosis decision tree after pruning.

In summary, the more mature engineering in the field of rail fault detection is the threshold detection based on the original telemetry data, and is currently actively exploring and applying detection methods based on feature quantities. The current mainstream methods are regression tree, machine learning, Bayesian network, adaptive threshold, and gray system theory. However, most of the above methods only use single features and features or single fault detection data, and do not involve satellite fault monitoring under multi-parameter conditions.

2 MSET Algorithm

2.1 Basic Concepts

Some concepts related to MSET, including data matrix: observation matrix X_{obs}, Training data T, Memory matrix D, Residual training data L, Estimation matrix. X_{est}. For Observation matrix X_{obs}. The observation matrix defined by MSET, as shown in Fig. 1, contains n parameters and each parameter has m values. And n represents the number of monitoring parameters, m represents the number of time states. Each column of the matrix lists all parameter values from parameter X_1 to parameter X_n at the same time state t_i. Since each column contains all monitoring parameters of the system at the same time, it is called the system state.

When the fixed time is t_i, the system observation matrix X_{obs} is represented by a vector $X(t_i)$ or $X_{obs}(t_i)$ of length n, where n represents the number of system monitoring parameters.

$$X(t_i) = [x_{1i}, x_{2i}, ...x_{mi}]^T \tag{1}$$

When the fixed parameter is x_j, the system observation matrix X_{obs} is represented by a vector $X(x_j)$ or $X_{obs}(x_j)$ of length m, where m represents the number of system time states.

$$X_j = [x_{j1}, x_{j2}, ...x_{jm}] \tag{2}$$

Where X_{ij} is the observation value of parameter $j(j = 1, 2.......n)$ at time t_i.

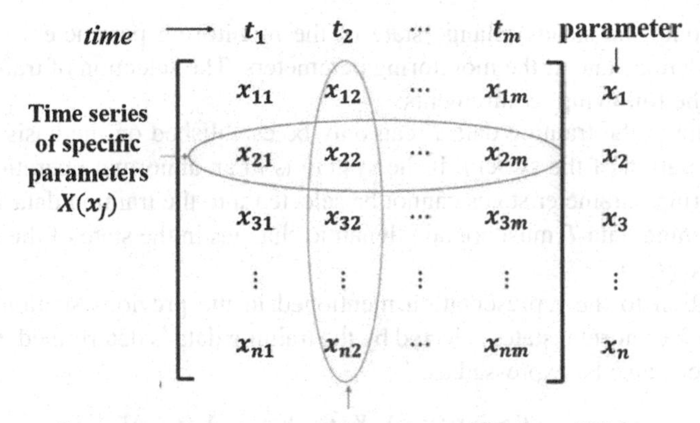

Fig. 1. The observation matrix defined by MSET

The training data T is a matrix consisting of a healthy historical state. The matrix format is defined as:

$$T = [x(t_i), ..., x(t_l), ...x(t_{i+k-1})] \tag{3}$$

Where k is the number of normal states selected for the training data, and this parameter is set by the user in advance.

The memory matrix D is a matrix selected from the training data T according to the corresponding rules. The number of states m is the number of states selected from the training data by the memory matrix. After the number of states m is determined, the memory matrix can be defined as:

$$D = [x_1, x_2, ...x_m] \tag{4}$$

The remaining training data L is the data state in the training data that is not selected by the memorized data. The relationship between T, D, and L is given by the following formula:

$$T = D \cup L \tag{5}$$

The estimation matrix X_{est} of the observation matrix X_{obs} and the estimation matrix of the remaining training data L are both estimates of the similarity measure calculated from the health data. The estimation matrix format is the same as the observation matrix format.

2.2 MSET Detailed Steps

Step 1: Acquiring new observation matrix based on actual telemetry data X_{obs}:
Step 2: Selects training data:
The training data T needs to include all health states of all monitoring parameters under the normal operating state of the system. The normal operating state of the system here

includes not only the steady change state of the monitoring parameters but also the normal degradation state of the monitoring parameters. The selection of training data T should meet the following requirements:

1. The state in the training data T can only be established on the basis of the normal operation of the system. If the system is in an abnormal operation state, all monitoring parameter states cannot be selected into the training data T.
2. The training data T must contain dynamic changes in the state of the monitoring parameters.
   In addition to the representation mentioned in the previous section, when the number k of normal states selected by the training data is determined, the training data T can also be expressed as:

$$T = [X(t_{1+i}), X(t_{2+i}), \ldots\ldots X(t_{k+i})] \tag{6}$$

Step 3: Constructs memory matrix D and generate residual training data. L:
When the number of states l is determined, a $n \times l$ memory matrix can be generated according to certain rules, where n represents the number of monitoring parameters and l represents the number of states selected in the memory matrix.
Referring to the existing research results, the memory matrix can be generated according to the following steps:

3. Number of states determined manually l.
4. Select the extreme state of each monitoring parameter included in the training data.
5. If the number of selected extreme state is less than the number of memory matrix states, the extreme state is added to the memory matrix, then calculate the vector of Euclidean norm of other data in the training data. After sorting, equidistant sampling is added to the memory matrix to complete the construction of the memory matrix.

Delete the state contained in the memory matrix from the training data to generate the remaining training data.
Step 4: Calculates healthy residuals;

When calculating the health residual, MSET is performed in two steps: calculating the estimated value L_{est} of all remaining training data L; calculating the health residual between the estimated value and the remaining training data. The calculation formula of L_{est} is as follows:

$$\mathrm{L}_{est} = \mathrm{D} \cdot \mathrm{W} \tag{7}$$

Where W is a weight vector, which represents a measure of similarity between the memory matrix and the current state. The weight vector W can be obtained by the following formula:

$$\mathrm{W} = \left(\mathrm{D}^T \cdot D\right)^{-1} (\mathrm{D}^T \cdot \mathrm{L}) \tag{8}$$

The calculation formula of L_{est} can be obtained by combining the above formulas:

$$\mathrm{L}_{est} = D \cdot \left(\mathrm{D}^T \cdot D\right)^{-1} (\mathrm{D}^T \cdot \mathrm{L}) \tag{9}$$

The difference between the estimated value and the actual value is the healthy residual. The formula is:

$$R_l = L_{est} - L \tag{10}$$

Step 5: Calculates actual residuals;

When calculating the actual residuals, MSET is also performed in two steps: calculating the estimation matrix X_{est} of the observation matrix X_{obs}; and calculate the actual residual between the estimated value and the observation matrix.

The calculation process of observation matrix X_{obs} is as follows:

$$X_{est} = D \cdot W^1 \tag{11}$$

Where W^1 is a weight vector, which can be obtained by the following formula:

$$W^1 = \left(D^T \cdot D\right)^{-1} (D^T \cdot X_{obs}) \tag{12}$$

Formula of X_{est}:

$$X_{est} = D \cdot \left(D^T \cdot D\right)^{-1} (D^T \cdot X_{obs}) \tag{13}$$

The actual residual is the difference between the estimated value and the actual value. The formula is:

$$R_x = X_{est} - X_{obs} \tag{14}$$

After completing the above steps, the fault detection process will compare the actual residual with the healthy residual to determine whether the current system is healthy.

3 SRPRT Algorithm

In the above chapters, a series of calculations are carried out to get the health residuals and the actual residuals. This section mainly introduces the basic principles and operation steps of the sequential rank sum probability ratio test (SRPRT) method.

3.1 SRPRT Nonparametric Test Principle

The core idea of non-parametric testing is to obtain as much necessary information as possible from actual data without assuming the overall distribution in advance. Among many non-parametric test methods, SRPRT only requires that the sample signal is continuous and symmetric about the median or mean, and the sample signal has lower requirements and is easy to implement. The input of the SRPRT method is the average and actual residual of the health residual calculated by MSET, and the output is directly set as a flag bit to judge whether the system is abnormal.

The SRPRT method is based on Wilcoxon symbol rank statistics, and the likelihood function becomes:

$$\Lambda(\mathrm{R}_n) = \frac{L(\mathrm{R}_n;\theta_1)}{L(\mathrm{R}_n;\theta_0)} = \frac{\mathrm{P}(\mathrm{W}_1, m)}{\mathrm{P}(\mathrm{W}_0, m)} = \frac{P_1}{P_0} \tag{15}$$

Special attention is needed when the actual residual is expressed as $R = [r_1, r_2, \ldots\ldots r_n]$, where n does not indicate the length of the actual residual, but the length of the test result.

The specific steps of the SRPRT method are as follows:

Step 1: builds statistical assumptions;

$$H_0 : \mu_0 = \mu,\ H_1 : \mu_1 = \delta \cdot \mu \tag{16}$$

Where μ is the average of the health residuals in the MSET result, and δ is the detection ratio, that is, when the actual residual of the parameter is greater than $1-\delta$ times the health residual, it is determined to be a fault.

Step 2: Under the assumption of H_i, the hypothetical mean μ_i is subtracted from each original residual sample r_j, namely:

$$\mathrm{r}_{ij} = \mathrm{r}_j - \mu_i, j = 1, 2, \cdots, n \tag{17}$$

Where i is the hypothetical serial number and j is the sample serial number; after the calculation, the new residual sample sequence $r_{i1}, r_{i2}, \ldots\ldots, r_{in}$.

Step 3: sets the sequence of new residual samples from the absolute value from small to large.

$$|\mathrm{r}_i^{(1)}| \le |\mathrm{r}_i^{(2)}| \le \cdots \le |\mathrm{r}_i^{(n)}| \tag{18}$$

The updated sample residual sequence is $r_1^{(n)}, r_2^{(n)}, \ldots\ldots, r_i^{(n)}$.

Step 4: Remove the samples with the absolute value of 0 among the above samples to generate rearranged samples. Let the number of remaining samples in the rearranged sample be m. Then, rank R is assigned according to the position of the remaining samples in the entire sequence. The rank assignment process can be expressed as:

$$\mathrm{R}(\mathrm{r}_i^{(k)}) = k \tag{19}$$

The function value of the sign indicating function Ψ is determined by the sign of the original values of the rearranged samples. The sign indicating function Ψ is constructed as follows:

$$\Psi(\mathrm{r}_\mathrm{i}^{(\mathrm{k})}) = \begin{Bmatrix} 1, \text{if } \mathrm{r}_\mathrm{i}^{(\mathrm{k})} > 0 \\ 0, \text{if } \mathrm{r}_\mathrm{i}^{(\mathrm{k})} < 0 \end{Bmatrix} \tag{20}$$

Among $\mathrm{k} = 1, 2, \cdots, \mathrm{m}$.

Step 5: Under the assumption of H_i, Wilcoxon symbolic rank sum statistics W_i^+ and W_i^- are discrete random variables subject to a certain distribution function, which can be calculated by the following formula:

$$\mathrm{W}_\mathrm{i}^+ = \sum_{\mathrm{k}=1}^{\mathrm{m}} \mathrm{R}(\mathrm{r}_i^{(k)})\Psi(\mathrm{r}_i^{(k)}) \tag{21}$$

When the test condition is small sample size ($m \leq 20$) constructing two sided test statistics:

$$\Lambda(R_n) = W_i^+ \tag{22}$$

Setting confidence is set toα, and the result is compared with the test time. $\Lambda(R_n)$ Critical value $t_{\alpha/2}$ and $\frac{n(n+1)}{2} - t_{\alpha/2}$:

When $\Lambda(R_n) \geq t_{\alpha/2}$ or $\Lambda(R_n) \leq \frac{n(n+1)}{2} - t_{\alpha/2}$ refuse H_0 and receive H_1, system failure, output fault flag bit 1;

When $\frac{n(n+1)}{2} - t_{\alpha/2} \leq \Lambda(R_n) \leq t_{\alpha/2}$ refuse H_1 and receive H_0, the system is normal, output fault flag bit 0.

When the test condition is large sample capacity ($m > 20$), calculated in two cases. $P(W_i, m)$:

When the absolute values of all samples in the sample sequence are different, The distribution of the statistic W_i is similar to the normal distribution of mean $T = \frac{m(m+1)}{4}$, variance $V_T = \frac{m(m+1)(2m+1)}{24}$, that is:

$$\frac{1}{\sqrt{2\pi V_T}} \exp\left[-\frac{(W_i - T)^2}{2V_T}\right] \approx N(0, 1) \tag{23}$$

Similarly, $P(W_i, m)$ can be calculated by the following formula:

$$P(W_i, m) = \frac{1}{\sqrt{2\pi}\sqrt{V_T}} \exp\left(-\frac{(W_i - T)^2}{2V_T}\right) \tag{24}$$

When there are samples (called sample groups) with the same absolute value and non-zero in the sample sequence, the variance V_T needs to be corrected. Let g be the number of sample groups composed of samples with the same absolute value, t_i is the number of samples contained in the i-th sample group. Then the variance V_T can be corrected according to the following formula:

$$V_T' = \frac{m(m+1)(2m+1)}{24} - \frac{1}{48}\sum_{i=1}^{g} t_i(t_i^2 - 1) \tag{25}$$

To sum up, the likelihood ratio function formula is:

$$\Lambda(R_n) = \frac{P(W_1, m)}{P(W_0, m)} = \frac{\frac{1}{\sqrt{2\pi}\sqrt{V_T}} e^{\left(-\frac{(W_1 - T)^2}{2V_T}\right)}}{\frac{1}{\sqrt{2\pi}\sqrt{V_T'}} e^{\left(-\frac{(W_0 - T)^2}{2V_T'}\right)}} \tag{26}$$

Step 6: Introduce the constants A and B (usually given by experts in the field), let A be the lower limit, B be the upper limit, and $0 < A < 1 < B$. Then it is determined by comparison that the hypothesis H_0 or hypothesis H_1 is accepted, and the sequential test scheme is constructed as follows:

1. If $\Lambda(\mathrm{R}_n) \leq \mathrm{A}$, accept assumptions H_0, the system is normal, and the output abnormal flag is 0;
2. If $\Lambda(\mathrm{R}_n) \geq \mathrm{B}$, acceptance assumptions H_1, the system is abnormal and the output abnormal flag is 1.
3. If $\mathrm{A} \leq \Lambda(\mathrm{R}_n) \leq \mathrm{B}$, it is impossible to make a decision. We need to continue sampling, add a subsequent set of data to recalculate and repeat the comparison process.

$$\mathrm{A} \cong \frac{\beta}{1-\alpha},\ \mathrm{B} \cong \frac{1-\alpha}{\beta}$$

Among them are the preset first type error probability and second type error probability, namely α is the false alarm rate (FAR) and β is the missing alarm rate (MAR), which can be 0.0001, 0.01, 0.015,0.02,0.05, and 0.1 in practical application.

3.2 SRPRT Experiment

In order to verify the effectiveness and accuracy of the SRPRT algorithm, a control experiment was designed according to the following method. The parameter M corresponds to the mean deviation of the fault data in the hypothesis in the algorithm from the normal data. The data used in the experiment are random data that follow the normal distribution with a mean value of 0 and a variance of 1. Therefore, the result of all algorithms determining a failure is an algorithm false alarm. The parameter FAR observation value is the number of algorithm false alarms divided by the total number of samples. The algorithm test method is to observe the false alarm rate as small as possible.

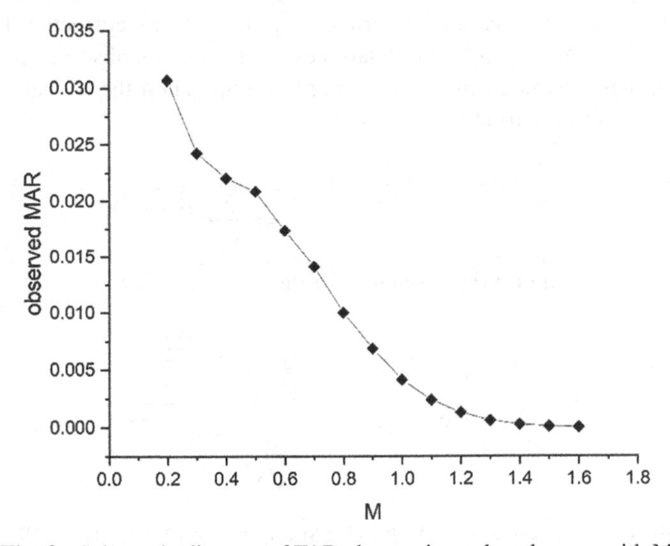

Fig. 2. Schematic diagram of FAR observation value changes with M

Experiment 1: verify the effect of the parameter M indicating the degree of mean shift on the experimental results. Set MAR = 0.1, FAR = 0.003, the number of samples is 100000, and observe the change law of FAR observation value with M (Fig. 2).

As shown in the above figure, the FAR observation value decreases with the increase of the mean value M of the abnormal data offset. The larger M is, the higher the data is judged as failure criterion, and the more difficult it is for the sample data to be judged as failure, which conforms to the original design assumption of the algorithm. M can be used as a confidence index to join the algorithm using process, which is convenient for adjusting the accuracy of the algorithm.

4 Example

In order to verify the effectiveness and accuracy of MSET and SRPRT, a set of control experiments were designed according to the following methods. The parameter M corresponds to the mean deviation of the fault data in the hypothesis in the algorithm from the normal data. The normal data used in the experiment are random data that follow the normal distribution with a mean of 0 and a variance of 1. The abnormal data use random data that follow a normal distribution with a mean of 0.8 and a variance of 0.01.

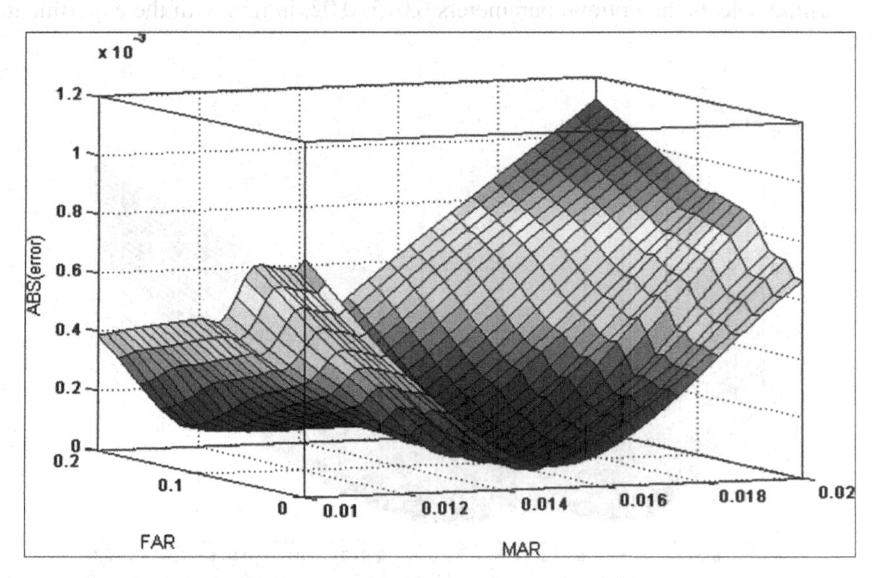

Fig. 3. Schematic diagram of failure rate error along with MAR and FAR

Experiment 1: Adjust the parameters and find the optimal MAR and FAR parameters. Change the MAR and FAR values and conduct multiple experiments to find the MAR and FAR corresponding to the smallest difference between the actual failure rate and the theoretical failure rate. Set the failure rate and add abnormal data to the normal data in proportion to the failure rate. Normal data and abnormal data run SRPRT algorithm separately. After the algorithm runs, the observed FAR is the number of abnormalities in normal data divided by the total number of normal data, and the observed MAR is the number of non-abnormalities in abnormal data divided by the total number of abnormal data.

As shown in Fig. 3, the X-axis and Y-axis respectively represent the theoretical values of MAR and FAR, and the Z-axis represents the absolute value of the difference between the actual measured value of the failure rate and the theoretical value of the failure rate. Therefore, the curved surface is similar to the parabolic surface, and the lower middle zone is the zone with the smallest failure rate error. When the measured failure rate is closest to the failure rate (the lowest point in the figure), the corresponding MAR and FAR are selected as the optimal parameters.

To clearly select the lowest point in the figure, project the three-dimensional map on the X-Z plane to find the lowest point of Z as shown in Fig. 4. In order to visualize the relationship between the Z value and size, make a straight line parallel to the Z-axis plane. It can be seen that the point in the red box on the right is lower than the lowest point in the valley on the left, so the area in the box is enlarged.

As shown in Fig. 5, there are two points in this area that have very similar values, so they are parallel to the X axis, and the point in the red circle on the right is slightly lower than the lower point on the left. Therefore, the lowest point takes MAR = 0.015 and FAR = 0.02, and the value of Z at this time is 4.59E-05, which is the lowest point, so the algorithm selects the optimal parameters 0.015, 0.02, in line with the experimental results.

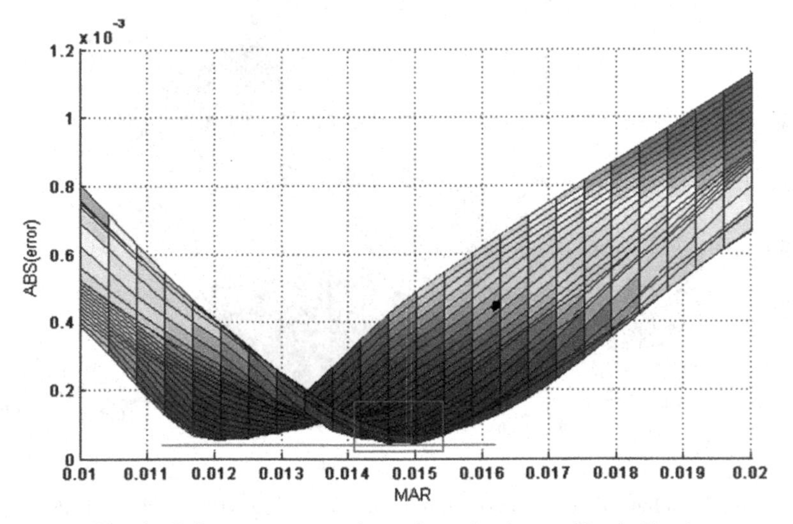

Fig. 4. Failure rate error schematic projection on X axis Z axis

Experiment Two

Experiment 2: The experiment case selects satellite attitude control system for fault detection. Compare the advantages and disadvantages of the existing MSET algorithm combined with SPRT algorithm and MSET algorithm combined with SRPRT algorithm.

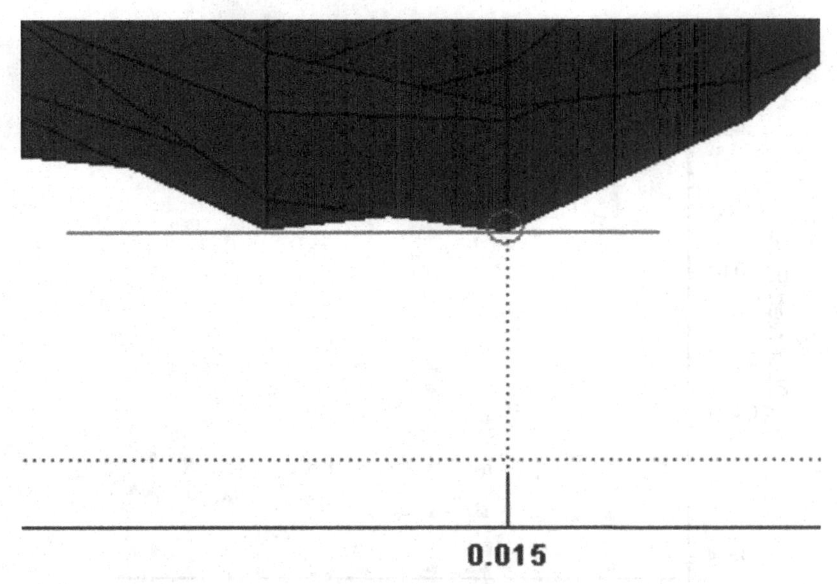

Fig. 5. Local sketch of failure rate error

All data are normal data, and the total sample data is 100,000, with a total of 19 parameters. According to the alphabetical order of English names, the parameters follow the normal distribution with mean values of 0, 1…18 and variance of 1. Since the mean value of the residuals after MSET calculation of 19 parameters is not 0, the mean value of variance needs to be shifted. For the SRPRT algorithm, the parameters M = 0.5, 0.8, 1.5 and MAR = 0.015 are set in the experiment. The parameters of the SPRT algorithm are the same as the SRPRT algorithm.

Since the FAR and FAR observation values are both small, in order to better display the relationship between the horizontal and vertical coordinates, the horizontal coordinate takes the logarithmic function of FAR to lengthen the distance between the horizontal coordinates. As shown in Fig. 6, MSET combined with SPRT algorithm under the conditions of FAR, M, are not as good as SRPRT algorithm. When M is unchanged, the FAR increases, and the FAR observations of the SPRT and SRPRT algorithms increase. However, when the FAR is greater than 0.001, the FAR observations of the SPRT algorithm increase significantly and are much larger than the FAR observations of the SRPRT algorithm. Generally speaking, the SPRT algorithm false alarm rate is greater than the SRPRT algorithm when M is unchanged, and the growth rate is extremely fast, which is obviously inferior to the SRPRT algorithm. When FAR is unchanged, M increases, and FAR fault detection values increase, which conforms to the algorithm design idea, and the SPRT algorithm performs well when M = 1.5; although the observed false alarm rate of both algorithms is smaller than the theoretical false alarm rate, the SPRT algorithm false alarm rate is still much higher than the SRPRT algorithm false alarm rate. Therefore, it can be proved that the SPRT algorithm is effective but not as accurate as the

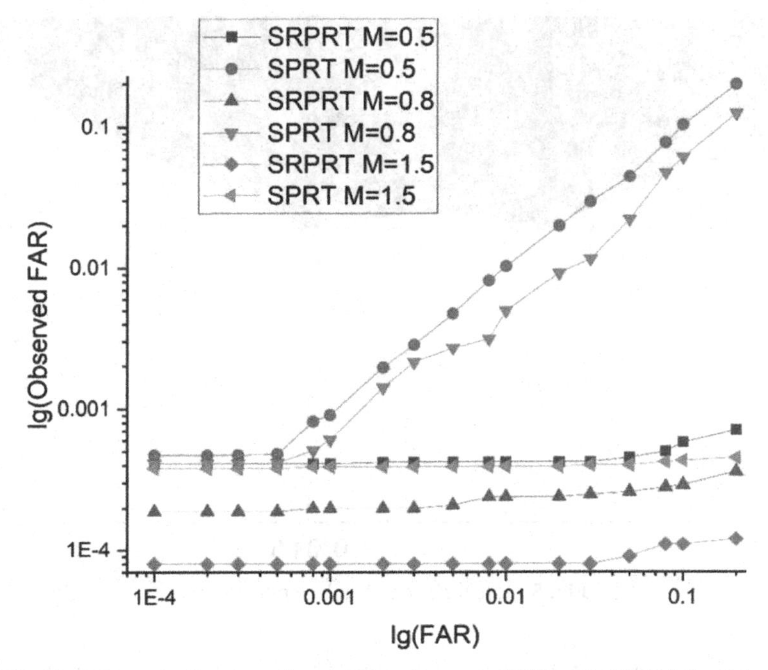

Fig. 6. Schematic diagram of comparison between SPRT and SRPRT algorithm

SRPRT algorithm. It also proves the effectiveness and accuracy of the SPRT algorithm from the side.

Moreover, because the SPRT method requires samples to follow a priori distribution with unknown parameters, satellite measured data may not necessarily meet this requirement. However, the sample signal required by the SRPRT method is continuous and symmetrical about the median or mean value, and the satellite measured data can be satisfied after adjustment. And the SRPRT algorithm has higher precision than the SPRT algorithm, so in this paper, the non-parametric method SRPRT is selected as the method of fault monitoring with the MSET method.

5 Summary

This paper proposes a satellite fault detection method that combines a multivariate state estimation algorithm with a sequential rank and probability ratio test method. This method can be used for satellite fault detection in multi-parameter states. First, the multivariate state estimation algorithm (MSET) is used to obtain the residual between the multivariate state and the historical health data, and then the actual residual of the data to be tested is input into the sequential rank and probability ratio test method (SRPRT) for testing. In terms of experiments, this paper firstly validates the effectiveness of SRPRT through experiments, and finally verifies the effectiveness and accuracy of the combination of MSET and SRPRT through the actual calculation examples of satellite attitude control system, and the superiority of combining MSET with SPRT.

The advantage of the algorithm in this paper is that it can be used for multi-parameter fault detection and can be used for satellite measured data. It is not necessary to be bound by theoretical research. The accuracy of the algorithm is significantly higher than the accuracy of the combination of the MSET algorithm and the SPRT algorithm. The disadvantage is that the running time of the algorithm is slightly longer than the SPRT algorithm, and it still needs to be improved in the future. Follow-up work will focus on comparing this algorithm with other fault detection algorithms such as regression trees, gray system theory, Bayes network in the performance of accuracy and algorithm operation efficiency, and to improve the weakness of the algorithm.

References

1. Huang, K., Liu, B., Huang, J., et al.: Overview of combat simulation technology. Syst. Simul. J. **16**(9), 1887–1895 (2004)
2. Fuertes, S., Picart, G., Tourneret, J., Chaari, L., Ferrari, A., Richard, C.: Improving spacecraft health monitoring with automatic anomaly detection techniques. In: SpaceOps Conference (2016)
3. DeCoste, D.: Automated learning and monitoring of limit functions. In: International Symposium on Artificial Intelligence, Robotics, and Automation in Space (1997)
4. Shan, C., Li, Y., Wang, L.: On orbit satellite abnormal alarm and fault diagnosis methods. J. Aerocraft Meas. Control **30**(3) (2011)
5. Wang, W., Peng, M., Liu, B., Liu, X.: Application of trend analysis in satellite orbit management. Spacecraft Environ. Eng. **29**(4) (2011)
6. Yang, T., Yang, P., Dong, X., Huang, Y.: Prediction method of spacecraft fault state based on grey system theory. Comput. Meas. Control **16**(9) (2008)
7. Yang, T., Yang, K., Li, H.: Knowledge-based satellite fault diagnosis and prediction method. Chin. Eng. Sci. **5**(6) (2003)
8. Wang, X., Zhang, Y., Yuan, Y., et al.: Knowledge mining method of satellite fault diagnosis based on decision tree. Electron. Des. Eng. **026**(3), 165–169

Satellite Mission Support Efficiency Evaluation Based on Cascade Decomposition and Bayesian Network

Ruixing Wang[1], Yuqing Li[1(✉)], Hailong Zhang[2], Fan Liu[2], and Mingjia Lei[1]

[1] Deep Space Exploration Research Center, Harbin Institute of Technology, Harbin 150080, China
bradley@hit.edu.cn

[2] China Xi'an Satellite Control Center, Xi'an 710043, China

Abstract. Aiming at the complexity of evaluation system construction is high due to the numerous and jumbled nodes of satellite mission support efficiency evaluation system and the difficulty in identifying the system hierarchy and the relationship between nodes, this paper proposes an evaluation method based on Cascade decomposition and Bayesian network. Firstly, establish a satellite mission support efficiency evaluation system based on Cascade decomposition. According to the basic information of satellite health status and environmental risk, the satellite mission is decomposed into multiple dimensions such as task level, attribute level, measure level and input level. Then, a method based on Bayesian network is designed to extract the experience knowledge, which can represent the complex expert experience mathematically. Finally, an example simulation analysis of earth observation mission is carried out, and the results show that this method can effectively and accurately complete the satellite mission support efficiency evaluation, and verify the validity and correctness of this method.

Keywords: Satellite · Efficiency evaluation · Cascade decomposition · Bayesian network

1 Introduction

With huge investment in the space industry and rapid changes in the situation of the space scene, the accuracy and timeliness of mission decision are highly required, Therefore, it is of great research value and practical significance to study how to build a satellite mission effectiveness evaluation system and accurately evaluate it, so as to provide effective technical support for mission command decision. When execute the satellite

This research was supported by the project: 2019001TJ20172A04097-4, the Key Laboratory Opening Funding of Harbin Institute of Technology of Deep Space Exploration Landing and Return Control Technology (HIT.KLOF.2018.076, HIT.KLOF. 2018.074), and the pre-research projects of equipment development department of China Central Military Commission (JZX7Y20190243001201).

Q. Wu et al. (Eds.): WiSATS 2020, LNICST 358, pp. 46–60, 2021.
https://doi.org/10.1007/978-3-030-69072-4_5

mission support efficiency evaluation, we need to carry out an effective and complete system for the specific mission of the satellite firstly. Then determine the support degree of the in-orbit satellite or satellites for the mission by the input of the existing quantifiable data of the satellite, finally using the support degree to provide effective technical support for the mission command decision.

In terms of satellite evaluation, there are many contents about satellite health evaluation or satellite subsystem health evaluation in the existing research results. For example, a health evaluation method based on the fuzzy variable weight principle and the improved analytic hierarchy process was proposed in literature [1], it can reflect the satellites in-orbit health more objectively. Literature [2] takes the health evaluation of the satellite power subsystem as an example, and carries out a study on the evaluation method based on the connection logic of satellite components. The evaluation is carried out from two dimensions: the capability of the satellite subsystem to complete the task and the risk accumulation to complete the task. Literature [3] proposed a multi-stage health evaluation method for in-orbit satellites based on reconfigurable degree for the health evaluation of in-orbit satellites. The introduction of reconfigurable degree solved the characterization of complex characteristics of satellite system such as high redundancy, high reliability and nonlinearity, and reduced the subjectivity of evaluation. Literature [4–7] adopted different evaluation systems and methods for different application scenarios, and carried out research on equipment system support effectiveness evaluation. Literature [8–11] studied remote sensing satellites, satellite remote sensing detection resource scheduling, index system construction and evaluation methods.

In conclusion, the current research on satellite evaluation is mainly focused on the health of satellite system, and less on the space mission support efficiency. Therefore, this paper proposes a Cascade decomposition method and combines the Cascade decomposition method with the Bayesian network, so as to provide a feasible method to determine the support efficiency of the satellite in space missions.

2 Problem Analysis

The satellite mission support capability refers to the capability of the satellite system according to the characteristics and requirements of the mission, while the satellite mission efficiency refers to the capability of achieving the specified use objectives under the specified conditions. Comparatively speaking, the mission support capability focuses on the capability of the satellite system, while the mission effectiveness pays more attention to the mission requirements.

Satellite system is a large and complex integrated system, including attitude and orbit control, temperature control, power supply, measurement and control, data management, payload and other subsystems, and each subsystem contains multiple components, which are composed of multiple sub-components. In space missions, the health of satellite systems, the performance of satellite systems, and the complexity of the space environment and external influences need to be taken into consideration. Comparatively speaking, it is easier to determine these contents. But how to determine the cause-and-effect dependence of the above indexes on the satellite mission support capability and efficiency, how to explain hierarchical decomposition, it just like a complex black-box between the input and output variables. How to effectively determine the specific content of black-box, that is the core of the research.

In practical engineering, satellite mission support efficiency is estimated in advance based on telemetry data and satellite design parameters before the implementation of space missions, which is of great practical significance to the cost control of mission completion and the effect of mission completion. In order to solve this problem effectively, this paper proposes a Cascade decomposition method, which is used to determine the network structure in the Bayesian network. The network parameters are learned from the sample data determined by the expert scoring method, and finally complete the evaluation process of satellite mission support effectiveness (Fig. 1).

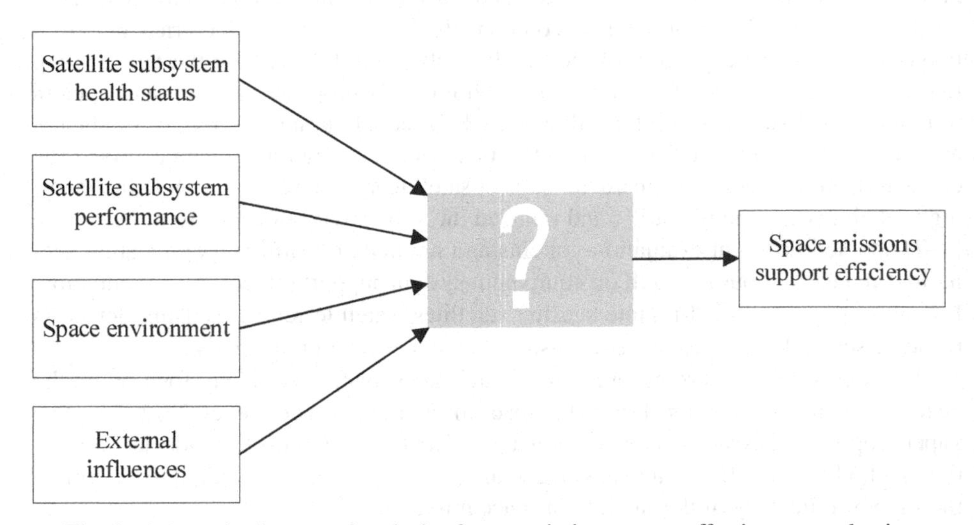

Fig. 1. Schematic diagram of analysis of space mission support effectiveness evaluation

3 The Construction of Mission Support Efficiency Evaluation System Based on Cascade Decomposition

The Cascade decomposition method is a step by step decomposition method, which provides a way to construct a satellite mission support effectiveness evaluation system.

3.1 Mission Decomposition

Mission Statement: In the process of mission decomposition, a brief statement is first made on the mission, in which the basic content and purpose of the mission are described and the actions and reasons to be taken are clearly defined. Who, what, when, where, and why should the mission statement include, but it doesn't have to be very detailed about the specifics of the mission. In short, the mission statement should be a clear and concise statement that states the content of the mission. Of course, before completing the mission statement, it is also necessary to present the mission to be performed in the form of a flow chart.

Desired Effect: In the process of mission decomposition, the desired effect of the mission is also crucial. In the process of drawing mission flowchart, the desired effect of the mission also needs to be clarified. On the one hand, in the process of clarifying the desired effect of the mission, the thinking and understanding of the mission will be deepened, which is of great benefit to the mission decomposition. On the other hand, after the mission is decomposed into tasks, it is an important test for the effectiveness and integrity of mission decomposition and an important standard to judge whether the decomposition is reasonable.

Task: In general, task can be thought as part of mission, where a mission consists of multiple tasks. If the mission statement is a further reflection and elaboration of the mission, then the determination of the task is another summary of the mission statement. A task is a mission flow with clear time or space boundary, its effectiveness depends on the extent to which it achieves the desired effect (Fig. 2).

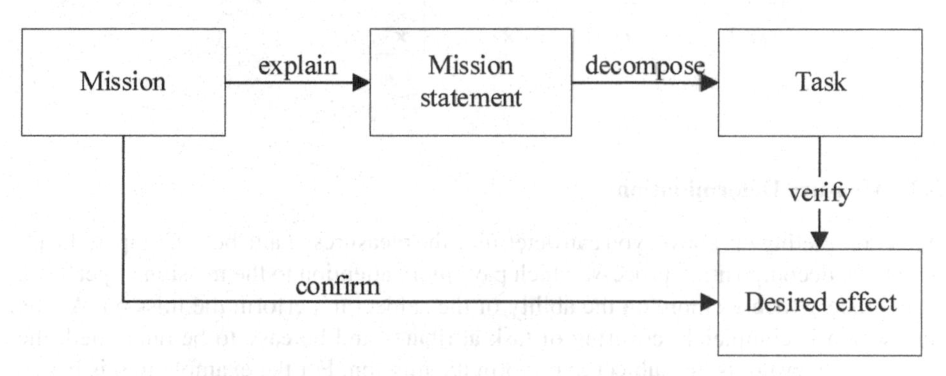

Fig. 2. Mission decomposition process

Therefore, the overall process of mission decomposition is summarized as follows: First of all, in the process of constantly clarifying the mission, draw the mission process completely and extract the mission statement and the desired effect. Then determine the tasks according to the mission statement. Finally, the validity criterion of task is whether the desired effect is well realized. If it is met, the mission decomposition is completed; otherwise, repeat the above procedures.

3.2 Task Decomposition

Timeliness: Time required to start or complete (e.g. response time).
Effectiveness: The quality of task completion.
Accuracy: The degree of accuracy with which a task is completed.
Reliability: Reliability of instruction and data transmission (e.g. anti-jamming capability).
Task attributes are different dimensions for evaluating task execution, such as accuracy of task completion and timeliness of task completion. The above-mentioned task attributes

are widely used in the evaluation process. As different dimensions of task evaluation, they play a crucial role in the decomposition process. Different tasks of the same mission have different dimensions of emphasis due to their different contents. Therefore, attribute is taken as the result of further decomposition of task. Its boundary is relatively clear, which can well guarantee the integrity and validity of decomposition. Of course, the attributes listed above cannot completely summarize all the tasks, but only serve as a reference example. When studying specific problems, the number and definition of individual attribute can be expanded and modified according to the characteristics of missions (Table 1).

Table 1. Mission – task - attribute cascading decomposition table

Task	Timeliness	Accuracy	Effectiveness	Reliability
Task 1	×	×	×	
Task 2	×	×		×
Task 3	×	×	×	

3.3 Measure Determination

After completing the above, you can determine the measures of attribute. Compared with the above decomposition process, which pays more attention to the mission to perform. This process focuses more on the ability of the subject to perform the mission. As the unit which is completely covering of task attributes and be easy to be quantified, the subject of measure is the subject to perform the mission. For the example in this paper, the subject of measure is the satellite to perform the space mission (Table 2).

3.4 Measure Decomposition

Measure is the hierarchy that connects the content of mission to the subject executing it. After a valid measure is determined, the measure should be decomposed. The results of measure decomposition, namely, the content of the input level, are the health degree of the mission executor, the performance of the mission executor, and the degree of external influence of the mission executor (Fig. 3).

Table 2. Mission – task – attribute - measure cascading decomposition table

Mission	Task	Attribute	Measure
Mission	1. Task 1	1.1 Attribute 1	Measure 1
			Measure 2
			Measure 3
		1.2 Attribute 2	Measure 4
		1.3 Attribute 3	Measure 5
	2. Task 2	2.1 Attribute 1	Measure 6
			Measure 7
		2.2 Attribute 2	Measure 8
			Measure 9
		2.3 attribute 3	Measure 10
		2.4 Attribute 4	Measure 11
	3. Task 3	3.1 Attribute 1	Measure 12
			Measure 13
			Measure 14
		3.2 Attribute 2	Measure 15
		3.3 Attribute 3	Measure 16

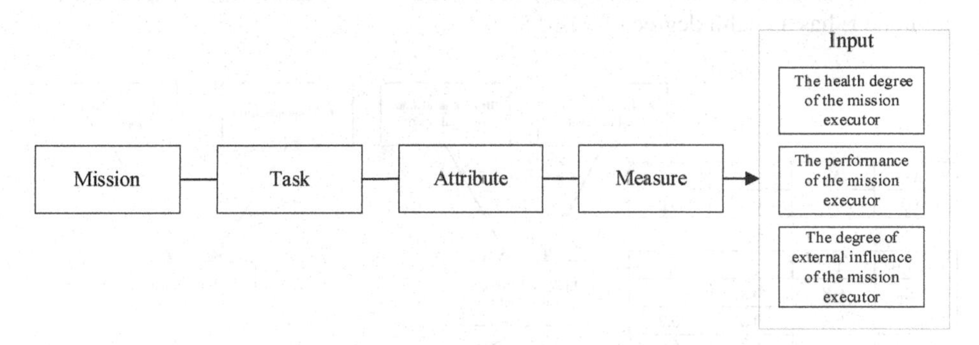

Fig. 3. Flow chart of Cascade decomposition method

4 Mission Support Efficiency Evaluation Based on Cascade Decomposition and Bayesian Network

4.1 Bayesian Network Construction in Mission Support Efficiency Evaluation

Bayesian network is a directed acyclic graph model based on probabilistic inference. It can represent the complex variable relationships in specific problem with a network structure. The network model reflects the dependence of variables in the problem domain and is suitable for the expression and reasoning of uncertain knowledge. A Bayesian network is composed of two parts, which correspond to the qualitative description and quantitative description of the problem domain respectively, Bayesian network structure and Bayesian network parameters. Bayesian network structure is the result of abstracted data instance and is a macroscopic description of the problem domain. Network parameters are the exact expression of the degree of association between variables and belong to quantitative description.

The Structure of Bayesian network is a directed acyclic graph (DAG), which consists of a set of nodes and a set of directed edges. Each node in the node set represents a random variable, which can be an abstraction of any problem and can be used to represent the phenomenon, part, state or attribute of interest, which has certain physical and practical significance. The other part of a Bayesian network is a set of local probability distributions that reflect correlations between variables namely network parameters, usually called a conditional probability table (CPT). This table lists all possible conditional probabilities for each node relative to its parent. Bayesian network takes the parent of node Xi as the condition, Xi is conditionally independent of any non-Xi child. The probability value represents the degree of association or confidence coefficient between the child node and its parent, and the probability of the node without parent is its prior probability.

For example, in Fig. 4, on the right is the Bayesian network structure of the satellite temperature control subsystem health evaluation, and on the left are part of Bayesian network parameters of the structure. Health status is divided into three levels, with high, medium and low health status represented by digital subscript 0, 1 and 2 respectively. So the conditional probability represented by $P(E_0|A_0,B_0) = 0.8$ means that under the condition that node A is low health (A_0) and node B is low health (B_0), the probability that node E has a health degree of 0 is 0.8.

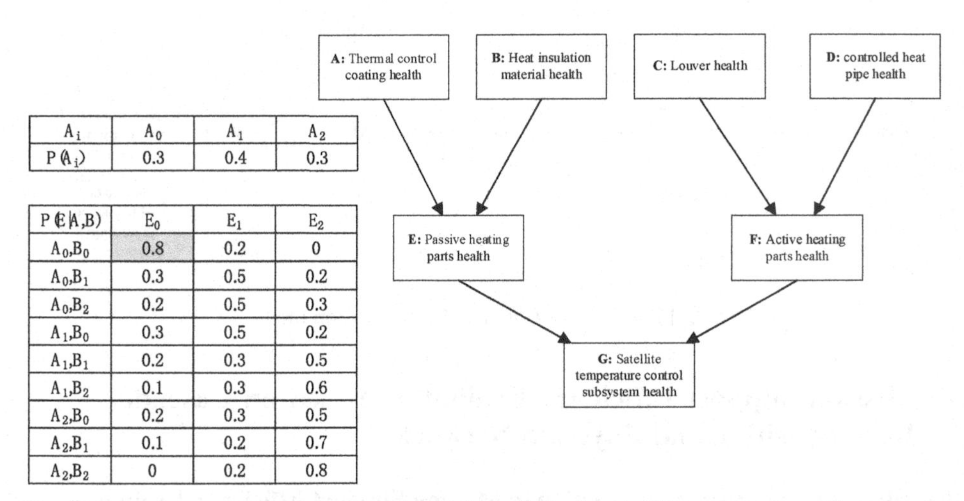

A_i	A_0	A_1	A_2
$P(A_i)$	0.3	0.4	0.3

$P(E\|A,B)$	E_0	E_1	E_2
A_0,B_0	0.8	0.2	0
A_0,B_1	0.3	0.5	0.2
A_0,B_2	0.2	0.5	0.3
A_1,B_0	0.3	0.5	0.2
A_1,B_1	0.2	0.3	0.5
A_1,B_2	0.1	0.3	0.6
A_2,B_0	0.2	0.3	0.5
A_2,B_1	0.1	0.2	0.7
A_2,B_2	0	0.2	0.8

Fig. 4. Bayesian network topology and partial conditional probability table of satellite temperature control subsystem health evaluation

Therefore, the construction of Bayesian network includes the following two parts:

(1) Determination of network topology;
(2) Determination of network parameters;

In general, there are three different ways to construct Bayesian networks:

(1) Domain expert determination method: In this way, the structure and parameters of Bayesian networks are defined subjectively, the variables in Bayesian network are determined by domain experts, and the structure and its distribution parameters of Bayesian network is determined by experts knowledge. The Bayesian network constructed in this way is completely under the guidance of experts. Because of the boundary of human knowledge, the network often has a great deviation from the physical truth, so the application scope of this method is very small.
(2) Complete sample learning method: In this way, domain experts define the node variables in Bayesian networks subjectively, and then learn the structure and parameters of Bayesian networks through a large number of training data. This method is entirely data-driven and highly adaptable. And advances in artificial intelligence, data mining and machine learning have made this method possible.
(3) Partial sample learning method: This method is a combination of the first and second methods. The variables in Bayesian networks are determined by domain experts, and the network structure is constructed by expertise, the parameters of the network are learned from the data by machine learning.

As for the research of satellite mission support effectiveness evaluation, due to the large number of nodes and the difficulty in determining hierarchical relationship, it is easy to have problems of missing nodes and wrong determination of causal relationship between nodes. Therefore, this paper adopts the method of Cascade decomposition. Under this decomposition framework, according to expert knowledge and past experience in this field, variables of satellite mission support effectiveness evaluation and its Bayesian network structure are determined in a more scientific way, thus the application of Bayesian networks in such problems is supported effectively. At the same time, this method can be used for the evaluation of mission support efficiency of other large complex systems.

Due to the characteristics of its application scenarios, satellite evaluation, satellite risk evaluation and satellite efficiency evaluation are mainly conducted by experts, therefore, the sample data of Bayesian network learning will also be determined by expert scoring, through learning, data distribution rules in samples are extracted to realize digital representation of complex expert experience.

4.2 Mission Support Efficiency Evaluation Based on Cascade Decomposition and Bayesian Network

The mission was decomposed step by step according to the Cascade decomposition method, and the hierarchical system after decomposition was taken as the Bayesian network structure of the evaluation problem, and the Bayesian network parameters were obtained by learning the sample data (Fig. 5).

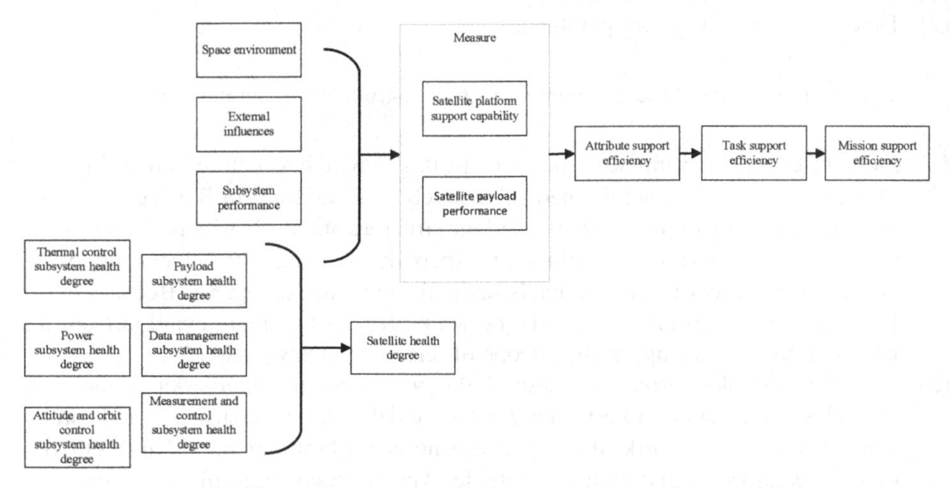

Fig. 5. Satellite support efficiency evaluation architecture

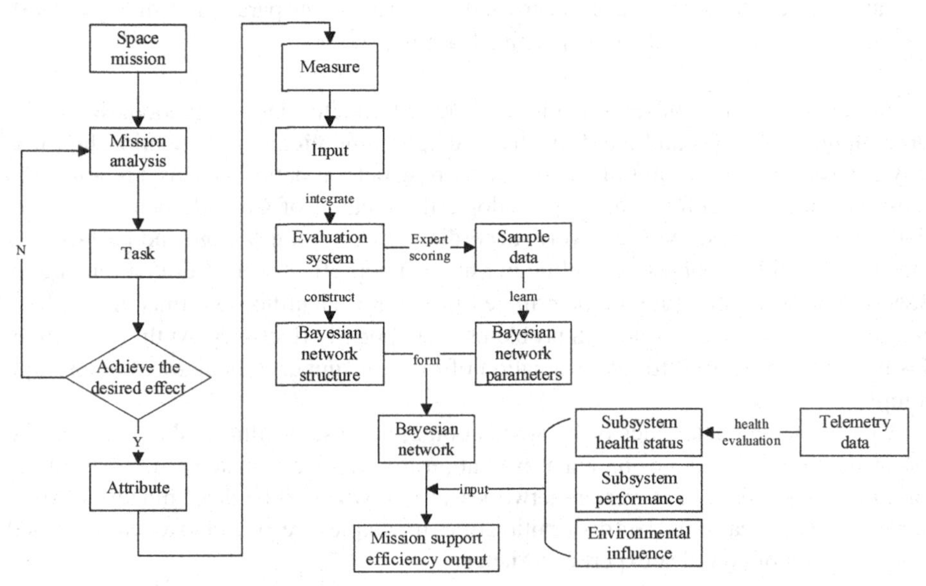

Fig. 6. Flow chart of satellite mission support performance evaluation based on Cascade decomposition and Bayesian network

On the basis of this evaluation method, the subsystem health degree, subsystem performance, space environment and external influence are taken as inputs, and the sequence of reasoning calculation is opposite to the decomposition process (as shown in Fig. 7). Finally, the evaluation results of each dimension support efficiency are obtained (Fig. 6).

5 Verification of an Example for Earth Observation Mission

5.1 Construction of the Earth Observation Mission Efficiency Evaluation System Based on Cascade Decomposition Method

The earth observation mission carried out by satellite is mainly used for space intelligence reconnaissance and information support, under the changeable situation, the importance of earth observation mission is self-evident. Therefore, it is of great significance to evaluate the support efficiency of the satellite in the earth observation mission to improve the space defense capability.

The earth observation mission flow is as follows: Submit imaging observation mission and requirements; Identify requirements attributes and priorities and generate candidate task sets; Plan the candidate task sets, allocation of satellite resources and determine the observation imaging time of the mission; According to the specific situation of the measurement and control department, convert the planning results into load control instructions; The satellite executes the relevant command, completes the observation mission, and obtains and transmits the data to the ground receiving station; Data processing and user submission.

Generally speaking, a complete earth observation mainly includes the following steps: First of all, the user requests for earth observation to the earth observation satellite management and control Center. Secondly, the management control center conducts demand analysis on the ground observation requirements submitted by users. Thirdly, the mission planning system is used to schedule the analyzed earth observation requirements. Then, form the satellite control commands, carry out earth observation, transmitted the observed information to the ground data processing center. Finally, return the final data to the user.

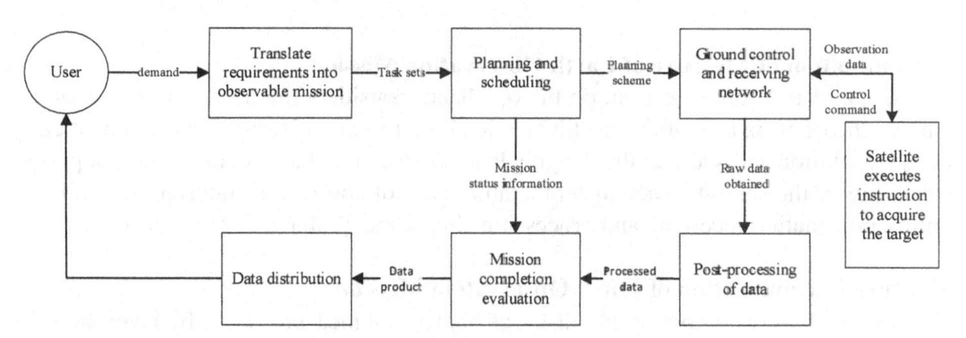

Fig. 7. Earth observation mission flow chart

Decomposition of Earth Observation Mission

Mission Statement: According to the mission scheduling of the management control center, a satellite or constellation in orbit observes a single or multiple ground objects during a specific time window, probe the state information of the observed point according to the mission requirements, then transmit the data to the ground control center, obtain space reconnaissance information and provide space information support.

Desired Effect: The satellite or constellation responds to the mission scheduling of the management center timely, fully implement the mission planning of the management control center, achieve the expected observation precision and observation period of the ground observation target, transmit the observation data to the ground data processing center timely and accurately.

Tasks: According to the above mission statement and the earth observation mission flow, the mission of earth observation was decomposed into three tasks: upload the control instruction, satellite observation and download observation data. By matching the tasks with the desired effect, it can be seen that the above three tasks achieve the accurate decomposition of the earth observation mission, so this decomposition is valid.

Task Decomposition of Earth Observation Mission

The mission of earth observation was decomposed into three tasks: upload the control instruction, satellite observation and download observation data. According to the characteristics of the task and the definition of attribute, decompose task into attributes as shown in the following table (Table 3).

Table 3. Earth observation mission - task - attribute Cascade decomposition table

Task	Timeliness	Accuracy	Effectiveness	Reliability
Upload the control instruction	×	×	×	
Satellite observation	×	×		×
Download observation data	×	×	×	

Determination of Measure of Earth Observation Mission

The scope of measure selection, on the one hand, considers the needs of the mission, namely the performance of the satellite payload. In the earth observation mission, it can be the resolution and width of the imaging load. On the other hand, considers the support capability of the satellite, such as temperature control ability, anti-interference ability, uplink information receiving and processing ability, etc. (Table 4).

Measure Decomposition of Earth Observation Mission

The mission was decomposed into tasks, attributes and measures layer by layer. In this example, measures were composed of satellite platform support capability and satellite payload performance. Finally, decompose the measure into the satellite subsystem health, the satellite subsystem performance and the safety degree of the space environment and external influence. The health of satellite subsystem is determined by the health telemetry data of satellite component. The performance of satellite subsystem is determined by

Table 4. Earth observation mission - task - attribute - measure Cascade decomposition table

Mission	Task	Attribute	Measure
Earth observation	1. Upload the control instruction	1.1 Timeliness	Satellite ability 1
			Satellite ability 2
			Satellite ability 3
		1.2 Accuracy	Satellite ability 4
		1.3 Effectiveness	Satellite ability 5
	2. Satellite observation	2.1 Timeliness	Payload performance 1
			Payload performance 2
		2.2 Accuracy	Payload performance 3
			Payload performance 4
			Satellite ability 6
		2.3 Effectiveness	Satellite ability 7
			Satellite ability 8
		2.4 Reliability	Satellite ability 9
			Satellite ability 10
	3. Download observation data	3.1 Timeliness	Satellite ability 11
			Satellite ability 12
			Satellite ability 13
		3.2 Accuracy	Satellite ability 14
		3.3 Effectiveness	Satellite ability 15

the design parameters of satellite. The safety degree of space environment and external influence are determined by the space forecast data.

So far, based on the theory of cascading decomposition method, the architecture of supporting efficiency evaluation system for satellite earth observation mission is completed (Fig. 8).

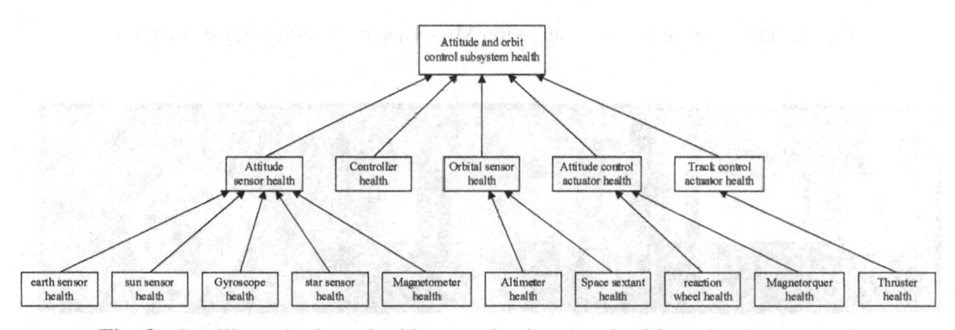

Fig. 8. Satellite attitude and orbit control subsystem health evaluation network

5.2 Efficiency Evaluation of Earth Observation Mission

In order to verify the feasibility and effectiveness of this method, Qt was used to develop a demonstration and verification software for earth observation mission efficiency evaluation method. The software includes input configuration interface, analysis method selection interface, expert scoring interface, expert scoring evaluation display interface and Bayesian network evaluation display interface.

First, the satellite subsystem health status, satellite subsystem performance status, space environment and external influence safety level are transformed to the dimensionless form properly and then filled into the input configuration interface. Then the expert scoring method is used to score the Bayesian network structure based on the Cascade decomposition method, each scoring result is saved in the Bayesian network evaluation sample file for the support efficiency evaluation of the earth observation mission. When there is some accumulation of sample data, Bayesian network method is used to learn the sample data, more accurate probabilistic relations between variables are extracted from quantitative evaluation with fuzzy boundary of domain expert knowledge. On this basis, the input of the input configuration interface is calculated step by step, and the evaluation results of each dimension of the satellite earth observation mission support efficiency are presented in the form of percentage ultimately.

Through the analysis of the above operation results, it can be seen that the mission support efficiency evaluation method based on Cascade decomposition and Bayesian network proposed in this paper, on the one hand, provides a systematic guidance for the establishment of a complex evaluation system for space missions, on the other hand, the more precise probability relationship between variables is extracted from the knowledge with fuzzy boundaries of domain experts through sample learning, guaranteeing the accuracy of this kind of uncertain knowledge inference. The effectiveness and feasibility of the method are verified by the simulation of an efficiency evaluation example for earth observation mission (Figs. 9 and 10).

任务支持效能输入

分系统健康度1	0.5	分系统健康度6	0.5	分系统能力1	0.5	分系统能力4	0.6
分系统健康度2	0.5	载荷性能指标1	0.5	分系统能力2	0.6	分系统能力5	0.5
分系统健康度3	0.6	载荷性能指标2	0.5	分系统能力3	0.5	分系统能力6	0.6
分系统健康度4	0.7	载荷性能指标3	0.6	环境指标1	0.7	分系统能力7	0.6
分系统健康度5	0.5	载荷性能指标4	0.6	环境指标2	0.6	分系统能力8	0.6

Fig. 9. The input of Earth Observation Mission support efficiency evaluation

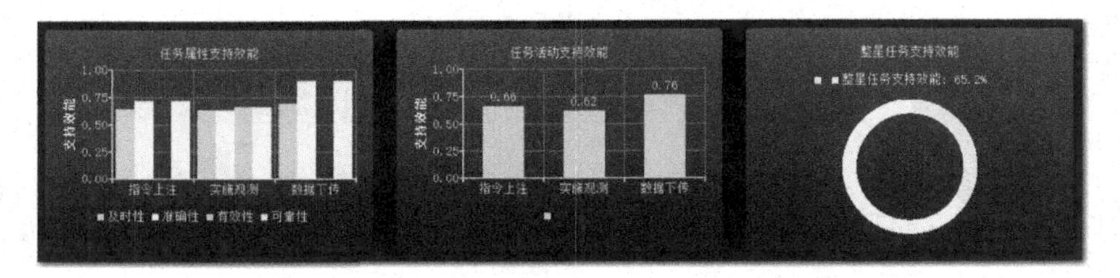

Fig. 10. The output of Earth Observation Mission support efficiency evaluation

6 Conclusion

Aiming at the problem of high complexity in the construction of satellite mission support efficiency evaluation system, this paper combines the Cascade decomposition method with the Bayesian network, decomposes the mission into tasks, attributes, measures and inputs step by step. In the process of stepwise decomposition, the object-mission in the problem is clarified constantly. Meanwhile, in the process of stepwise decomposition, more and more attentions are paid to the health degree and system performance of the subject-satellite. In the process of subject-object transformation, the relationship between subject and object in the research problem is deepened constantly, and finally the Bayesian network structure of the research problem is completed under the systematic guiding principle. Then, the most widely used expert scoring method for similar problems is adopted to generate sample data, and the probabilistic causal relationship between node variables presented in the form of network parameters is obtained by training and learning the sample data. Finally, the input data is converted into the result of mission support efficiency evaluation through reasoning calculation, so as to provide effective technical support for mission command decision-making. Of course, due to the limitations of personal experience, it is inevitable that there will be incomplete problems in the decomposition of the example for earth observation mission in this paper, but as a systematic decomposition method, the combination of Cascade decomposition and Bayesian network is indeed an effective method to solve the high complexity of satellite mission support efficiency evaluation. The research in the future will focus on improving this method, so as to further expand the scope of the application scenario of this method.

References

1. Li, X., Liu, Y., Li, G., Liu, R., Zhou, J.: Assessment of satellite health state based on fuzzy variable weight theory. Syst. Eng. Electron. **36**(03), 476–480 (2014)
2. Zhu, C., Dang, J., Zhang, M., Zahng, F., Zhuang, J.: Satellite health assessment method based on logic block diagram. Comput. Meas. Control **28**(02), 267–273 (2020)
3. Lu, Z., Jin, G., Yang, T., Wu, G., Lan, X.: Multi-level health evaluation method for on-orbit satellites based on reconfigurable degree. Syst. Eng. Electron. **40**(08), 1769–1776 (2018)
4. Li, J., Qin, G., Zhang, K., Zhang, H., Ji, X.: TT&C system operational effectiveness evaluation based on game theory. Fire Control Commend Control **44**(01), 105–109 (2019)
5. Liu, J., Sun, Y., Xing, R., Wang, H., Li, X.: Effectiveness evaluation of early warning satellite system for multi-missions. Aerospace Shanghai **36**(01), 10–15 (2019)
6. Liang, G., Zhou, X., Wang, Y.: Efficiency evaluation research on ground system of remote. Command Control Simul. **40**(05), 62–68 (2018)
7. Wang, J., Wang, K., Chen, J., Guo, J.: Research on weaponry system effectiveness evaluation based on task completion rate. Fire Control Commend Control **40**(11), 48–52 (2015)
8. Liu, F., Li, L., Meng, X.: Research on construction model of the capacity index system for remote sensing satellite system. Spacecraft Recov. Remote Sens. **38**(06), 40–45 (2017)
9. Peng, G.: Index system construction of information support capability evaluation of remote sensing satellite task-oriented. Command Control Simul. **41**(02), 15–19 (2019)
10. Xie, J., Wang, P., He, C., Cui, L., Cen, Z.: effectiveness evaluation for satellite remote sensing detect based on evidential theory. J. Sichuan Mil. Eng. **36**(02), 98–101 (2015)

11. Qin, P., Hao, S., Qin, G.: Research on evaluation method of contribution rate to SOS for remote sensing satellite application. Electron. Des. Eng. **27**(02), 70–73+79 (2019)
12. An, S., Long, J.: Model of satellite state evaluation based on bayers network. Trans. Beijing Inst. Technol. **30**(05), 548–551.

Importance Measurement of Parameters for Satellite Attitude Control System Fault Diagnosis Based on DBN

Mingjia Lei[1], Yuqing Li[1](✉), Guan Wu[2], and Junhua Feng[3]

[1] Deep Space Exploration Research Center, Harbin Institute of Technology, Harbin 150080, China
bradley@hit.edu.cn

[2] Key Laboratory for Fault Diagnosis and Maintenance of Spacecraft in-Orbit, Xi'an 710000, China

[3] National Key Laboratory of Astrodynamics, Xi'an 710000, China

Abstract. Efficient and accurate fault diagnosis of satellite attitude control system has an important role and significance to ensure the reliability of satellites in orbit. Recent researches on satellite fault diagnosis focuses on diagnosis methods, but less on the importance of telemetry parameters. Since the satellite itself is a highly complex nonlinear system, there are many types of telemetry parameters that can be used for fault diagnosis. The importance of different parameters has a greater impact on fault diagnosis. Aiming at the above problems, a new DBN-based parameter importance measurement method (PIM-DBN) is proposed by constraining the DBN network structure and fixing some part of weights during the update process. The proposed method can automatically solve the importance weights of the telemetry parameters by training network with the CD-K divergence algorithm. This method was applied to the fault diagnosis of the momentum wheel of a satellite with 10 telemetry parameters. In order to verify the effectiveness of PIM-DBN, three diagnosis method (SVM, ANN and DBN) were used to classify the data set. The accuracy of there methods above achieved 87.54%, 68.83% and 93.45% respectively with using the weighted data. These results show that the proposed importance measurement method is effective for the data-driven fault diagnosis field and health assessment field.

Keywords: Importance measurement · Deep belief network (DBN) · Satellite fault diagnosis · Attitude control system

---

This research was supported by the project: 2019001TJ20172A04097-4, the Key Laboratory Opening Funding of Harbin Institute of Technology of Deep Space Exploration Landing and Return Control Technology (HIT.KLOF. 2018.076, HIT.KLOF. 2018.074), and the pre-research projects of equipment development department of China Central Military Commission (JZX7Y20190243001201).

Q. Wu et al. (Eds.): WiSATS 2020, LNICST 358, pp. 61–73, 2021.
https://doi.org/10.1007/978-3-030-69072-4_6

1 Introduction

The satellite attitude control system is an important subsystem to guarantee the on-orbit operation and mission execution of the satellite. Therefore, it is of great significance to improve the health monitoring ability and fault diagnosis accuracy of the satellite attitude control system to ensure the reliability of the satellite [1, 2]. Generally, the satellite attitude control system has a variety of telemetry signals and a large amount of data, which provides a data basis for the attitude control system fault diagnosis and health assessment.

There are more and more studies on satellite health assessment. From the perspective of data, the current research can be divided into two categories: research on a single data source [3, 4] and research on multi-source data [5, 6]. With the deepening of research, the advantages of multi-source data in information expression completeness and accuracy are prominent. In recent years, the research on satellite fault diagnosis and health assessment gradually tends to focus on multi-source data.

With more and more various of telemetry parameters used for fault diagnosis and health assessment, the traditional methods based on threshold and expert system are limited in practical application. In order to make up for the shortcomings of traditional methods, many machine learning algorithms have been applied in the field of satellite fault detection [7, 8]. Although there are lots of researches on satellite fault detection methods, the importance of parameters used in fault detection is seldom studied. However, as the satellite system itself is a complex system with high coupling, there are intricate relationships between satellite telemetry data, and these relationships often have a great impact on satellite fault diagnosis results [9]. Hence, the importance of telemetry parameters in the process of satellite fault diagnosis can be analyzed to assist computers or field experts to make further judgment on satellite health status.

At present, the research on parameter importance measurement mainly focuses on two kinds of methods: based on physical model and based on data-driven. Considering the complexity of the satellite attitude control system, the data-driven method can be adopted to design the measurement method of parameter importance for the satellite.

In this paper, a parameter importance measurement method based on DBN is proposed to measure the abundance of satellite telemetry signals. This method enhances the number constraint of the underlying nodes and the connection weight constraint of DBN and trains the network based on the contrast divergence algorithm, and then obtains the parameter importance weight matrix based on RBM. The test on the satellite momentum wheel telemetry data set proves that this method can effectively improve the accuracy of fault diagnosis.

2 Parameter Importance Measurement Based on DBN (PIM-DBN)

2.1 Restricted Boltzmann Machine (RBM)

Restricted Boltzmann Machine (RBM) is a generative stochastic neural network that contains a visible layer and a hidden layer. Both the visible layer variable and the hidden layer variable of the network are binary variables, that is, their states are taken as $\{0,1\}$. The entire network is a bipartite graph. There is no mutual connection between neurons (nodes) on the same layer, and there is only mutual connection between neurons between adjacent layers. The connection between connectable neurons is bidirectional and symmetric, that is, the information can flow between the two connected neurons during the network training process, and the connection weight is independent of the direction. Usually the visible layer is used as the input layer of the data, and the hidden layer is the output layer of the generated data. Figure 1 shows the structure of the RBM.

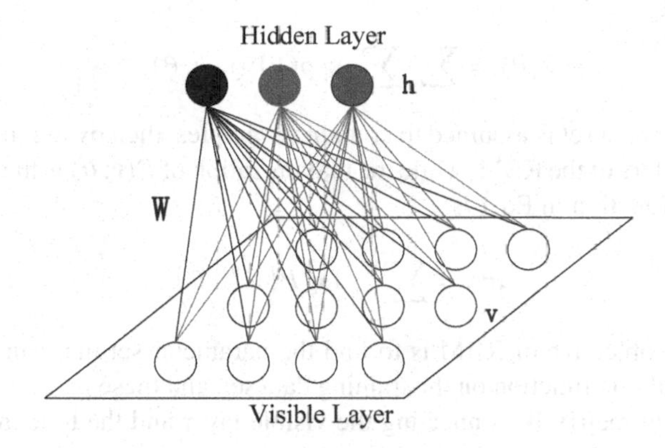

Fig. 1. The structure of RBM

Objective Function

RBM is an energy-based model, denoating its visible layer as V and hidden layer as h. In a Restricted Boltzmann Machine (RBM), visible element Vi is real number or binary number, hidden element hj is binary number, the energy expressions of visible variable V and implied variable h are shown in Eqs. (1) and (2):

$$E(v, h; \theta) = -h^T Wv - a^T v - b^T h \tag{1}$$

$$E(v, h; \theta) = -\sum_{ij} W_{ij} v_i h_j - \sum_i a_i v_i - \sum_j b_j h_j \tag{2}$$

Where θ is a parameter of RBM $\{W, a, b\}$, W is the weight between visible cell (visible node) and hidden cell (hidden node), a, b are the offset vector (bias) of visible cell and hidden cell respectively. The learning process of a RBM is to find the optimal value of θ in order to fit the given input data.

According to the joint allocation energy of V and h, the joint allocation probability of V and h can be obtained as shown in Eq. (3).

$$P(v, h; \theta) = \frac{1}{Z(\theta)} exp(-E(v, h; \theta)) \tag{3}$$

According to Eq. (2), the above equation can be further written as:

$$P(v, h; \theta) = \frac{1}{Z(\theta)} exp\left(\sum_{ij} W_{ij} v_i h_j + \sum_i a_i v_i + \sum_j b_j h_j\right) \tag{4}$$

The likelihood function of maximized observed data $P(v;\theta)$ is as shown in Eq. (5), which can be obtained from the edge distribution of h shown in Eq. (4).

$$P(v;\theta) = \frac{1}{Z(\theta)}\sum\nolimits_h exp\left(v^T Wh + a^T v + b^T h\right) \tag{5}$$

Where $Z(\theta)$ is a partition function, also known as a normalization factor, and $Z(\theta)$ is shown in Eq. (6).

$$Z(\theta) = \sum\nolimits_v \sum\nolimits_h \exp(-E(v,h;\theta)) \tag{6}$$

If the training data set is assumed to contain N samples, then by maximizing $P(v;\theta)$ to get the parameters of the RBM, while the maximization of $P(v;\theta)$ is the maximization of the objective function in Eq. (7):

$$L(\theta) = \sum\nolimits_{n=1}^{N} \log P\left(v^{(n)};\theta\right) \tag{7}$$

The learning objective of RBM is to find the parameter set that can maximize the logarithmic likelihood function on the training data set, and these parameter sets mainly include the weight matrix W connecting the visible layer and the hidden layer and the bias vector of the two layers.

RBM Training Method

According to Eqs. (2)–(7) and Gibbs sampling process, Eq. (7) can be further derived as

$$L(\theta) = \sum\nolimits_{n=1}^{N} (\log \sum\nolimits_h \exp\left(-E\left(v^{(n)}, h;\theta\right)\right) - \log \sum\nolimits_{v,h} \exp(-E(v,h;\theta))) \tag{8}$$

In order to sample effectively and efficiently, Hinton et al. put forward a new algorithm, that is, the CD(Contrastive Divergence) algorithm, whose basic thinking diagram is shown in Fig. 2.

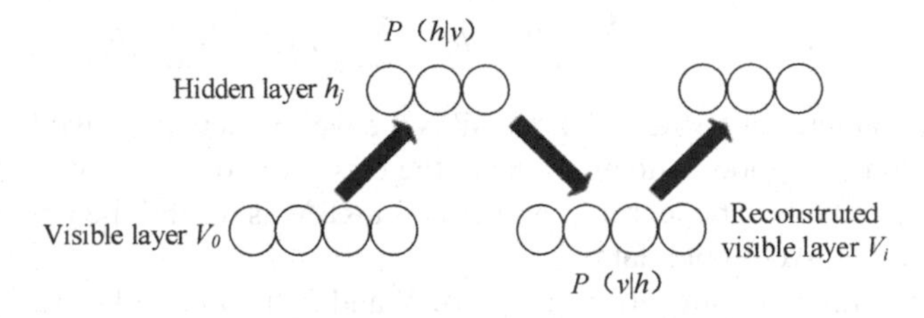

Fig. 2. Schematic diagram of basic idea of CD algorithm

After using the training data to initialize the visible layer where v_0, step on m (usually m = 1) Gibbs sampling. At the beginning of a contrast divergence algorithm, set the visible state of each node to a training sample, and use the Eq. (9) to calculate values of all the hidden layer nodes {0, 1}. When calculating all of the hidden layer unit of binary, according to the Eq. (10), the probability of each node of the visible layer being 1 is calculated, so as to obtain the first reconstruction of the visible layer. Then, the reconstructed visible layer is taken as the real model and put into the formula of RBM parameter update to calculate the updated RBM parameter.

$$P(h|v) = \prod_j P(h_j|v)P(h_j = 1|v) = sigmoid\left(b_j + \sum_i W_{ij}v_i\right) \tag{9}$$

$$P(v|h) = \prod_i P(v_i|h)P(v_i = 1|h) = sigmoid\left(a_i + \sum_j W_{ij}h_j\right) \tag{10}$$

The steps of training RBM with CD-K algorithm are as follows:
Step 1: Initialize

① Given training sample set X;
② Given the training period M, the learning rate η, and the parameter K of CD-k algorithm;
③ Specify Nk which is the number of cells in the hidden layer (Nv, which is the number of cells in the visible layer, is determined by the sample characteristic dimension);
④ Initialize the bias vectors a, b, and the weight matrix W;

Step 2: Training

⑤ Call CD-K (K, X, W, a, b) to calculate the network parameters variation ΔW, Δa, Δb;
⑥ Update parameters: $W_{ij} = W_{ij} + \eta \Delta W_{ij}$, $a_i = a_i + \eta \Delta a_i$, $b_j = b_j + \eta \Delta b_j$;
⑦ Repeat the above process ⑤–⑥ M times.

The flow of RBM algorithm is shown in Fig. 3.

2.2 Deep Belief Network (DBN)

Deep Belief Network (DBN) proposed by Geoffrey Hinton in 2006 is a generative model developed from logistic belief network. By training the weights among its neurons, the entire network is allowed to generate training data according to the maximum probability. Deep Belief Network (DBN) consists of multiple layers of neurons, which are divided into visible (dominant) neurons and hidden (recessive) neurons. Visible (dominant) neurons used to receive input data, hidden (recessive) neurons are used to implement feature extraction, which are also known as the hidden neurons characteristics detector (feature detectors). The top two layers of DBN structure are associative memory formed by undirected graph model. The other lower layers are connected by a directed connection between the upper and lower layers, forming a directed graph model. The hybrid model of deep belief network is shown in Fig. 4.

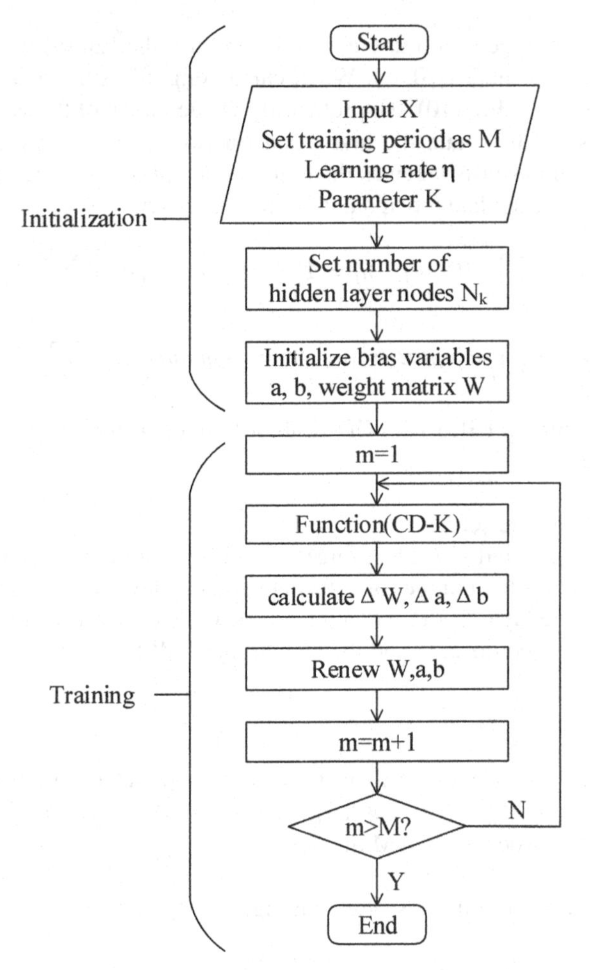

Fig. 3. The flow chart of training RBM with CD-K algorithm

DBN is essentially a stack of Restricted Boltzmann Machines, and the training process of DBN is carried out layer by layer. In RBM composed of two adjacent layers, the lower layer is the visible layer of RBM, and the data vector of the visible layer is used to infer the data of the hidden layer, and then the inferred hidden layer is used as the data vector of the next visible layer of RBM.

2.3 Parameters Importance Measurement Based on DBN (PIM-DBN)

The input data dimension is n, and the input layer node number of DBN network is n. This paper proposes a parameter importance measurement method based on DBN. By constraining the number of nodes and connecting weight matrix between the input layer and the first hidden layer of DBN, this method realizes the parameter importance

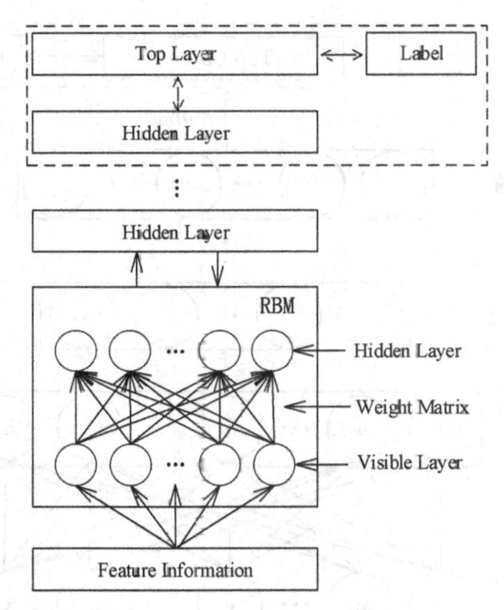

Fig. 4. Deep Belief Network (DBN) model structure diagram

measurement based on DBN structure and training method. The Eq. (11) and Fig. 5 represent the constraints.

$$\begin{cases} Node(InputLayer) = Node(HiddenLayer1) \\ w_{ij} = 0, (i \neq j) \end{cases} \quad (11)$$

Where $Node(InputLayer) = Node(HiddenLayer1)$ represents the number of nodes of input data equal to that of the first hidden layer of DBN; w_{ij} is the connection weight between the input layer node v_i and the hidden layer node h_j, and if $i \neq j$, then $w_{ij} = 0$.

The importance coefficient of input data $\{w_{11}, w_{22}, \cdots, w_{nn}\}$ can be obtained through network training. The parameter importance measurement method based on DBN is shown in the Fig. 6 as follows.

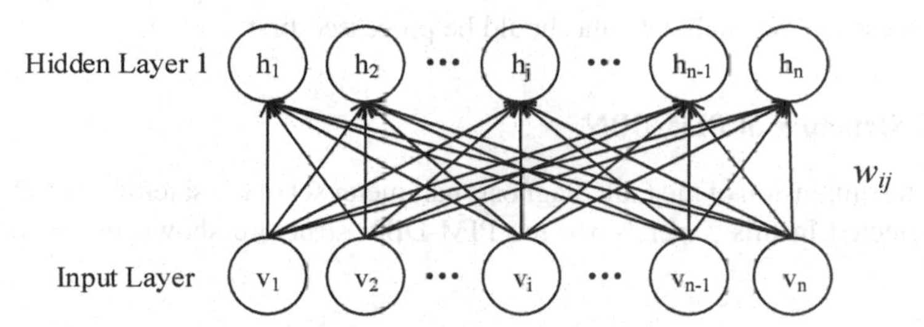

Fig. 5. The fix structure of the first RBM

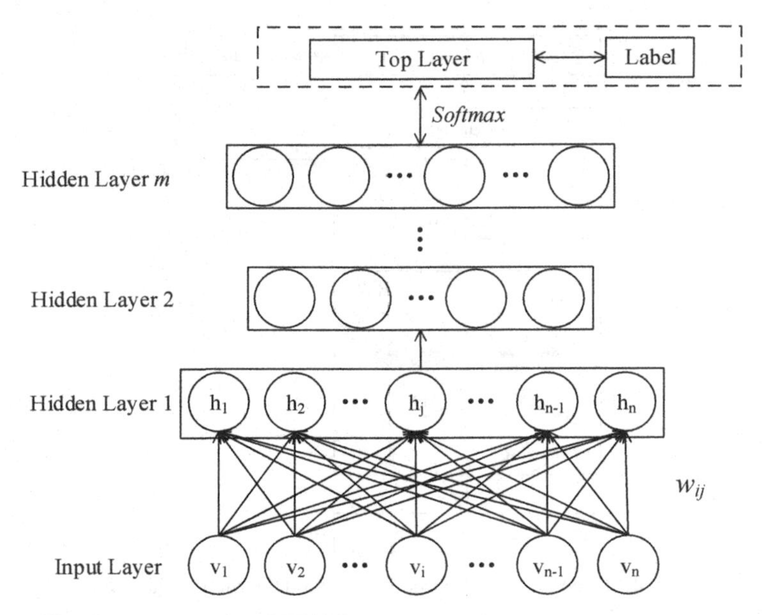

Fig. 6. The structure of DBN for parameters importance measurement

3 Fault Diagnosis of Attitude Control System Based on PIM-DBN

3.1 Parameter Set of Satellite Attitude Control System

There are many types of telemetry data for the satellite attitude control system. in this paper, 10 kinds of parameters are selected as the fault diagnosis parameter set: rotate speed; voltage; current; voltage/current; bearing temperature; case temperature; line temperature; axle temperature; friction moment; acceleration. Because satellite telemetry data often has some missing data and abnormal data noise, it is necessary to preprocess the original telemetry data. For the problem of large data noise, this paper uses median filtering to reduce noise; for the problem of missing data, the mean replacement method is used to supplement the data. In addition, to learn the importance of parameters, dimensionless and normalized data should be processed first.

3.2 The Structure of PIM-DBN

Because the dimension of the fault diagnosis parameter set of the satellite attitude control system selected in this paper is 10, the PIM-DBN structure shown in the Table 1 is designed.

Table 1. The structure parameter of PIM-DBN for satellite attitude control system

	Input layer	Hidden layer 1	Hidden layer 2	Hidden layer 3	Hidden layer 4	Hidden layer 5	Output layer
Number of nodes	10	10	64	128	64	32	N

Where N represents the number of categories of the sample data label.

3.3 Training Algorithm

PIM-DBN training algorithm is designed based on RBM training algorithm, and the specific process is as follows:
Step 1: Unsupervised pre-training

① Train the first restricted Boltzmann machine (RBM);
② The weight matrix W and offset vectors a, b of the first RBM are fixed, and then the state of the hidden layer neuron is used as the input vector of the second restricted Boltzmann machine. When the visible layer of RBM is the input layer, the weight matrix is $w_{ij} = 0, (i \neq j)$;
③ After the second RBM is fully trained, stack the second RBM on top of the first RBM;
④ Repeat the above three steps;

Step 2: Supervised fine-tuning of parameters

⑤ The output feature vector of top-level RBM is the input feature vector of fine-tuning BP network;
⑥ The final weight matrix W and the bias vector a, b are determined according to the error of label data and the calculated output result of fine-tuning BP network.

The flow chart of PIM-DBN algorithm is shown as follows (Fig. 7).

4 Analysis of Calculation Examples Based on Telemetry Data

4.1 Telemetry Data of Satellite Attitude Control System

This paper takes momentum wheel telemetry parameter of a satellite as an example to verify the effectiveness of the proposed method. The original telemetry parameters used in this paper are shown in Fig. 8.

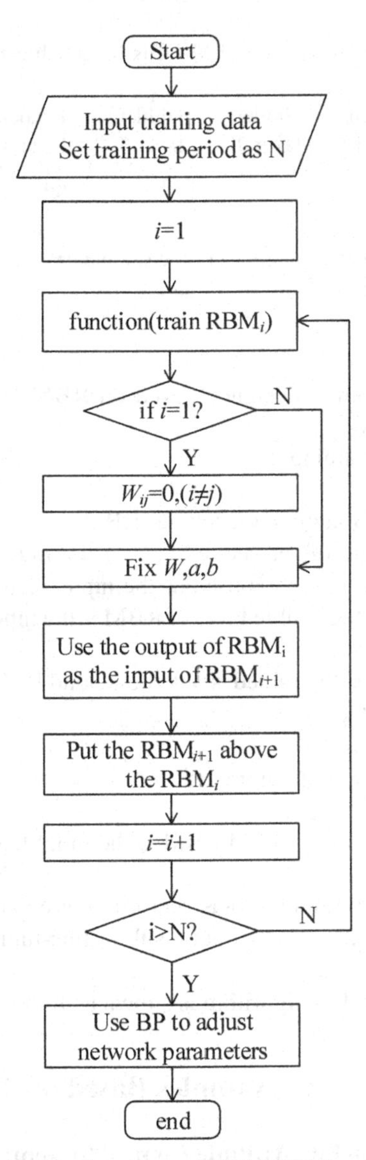

Fig. 7. The flow chart of PIM-DBN algorithm

In order to study the importance of the telemetry parameter of the momentum wheel in the fault diagnosis problem, momentum wheel telemetry data in a number of time periods are selected from the telemetry database, and the time periods include 6 modes: Acceleration Mode (Normal), Deceleration Mode (Normal), Stable Mode (Normal),

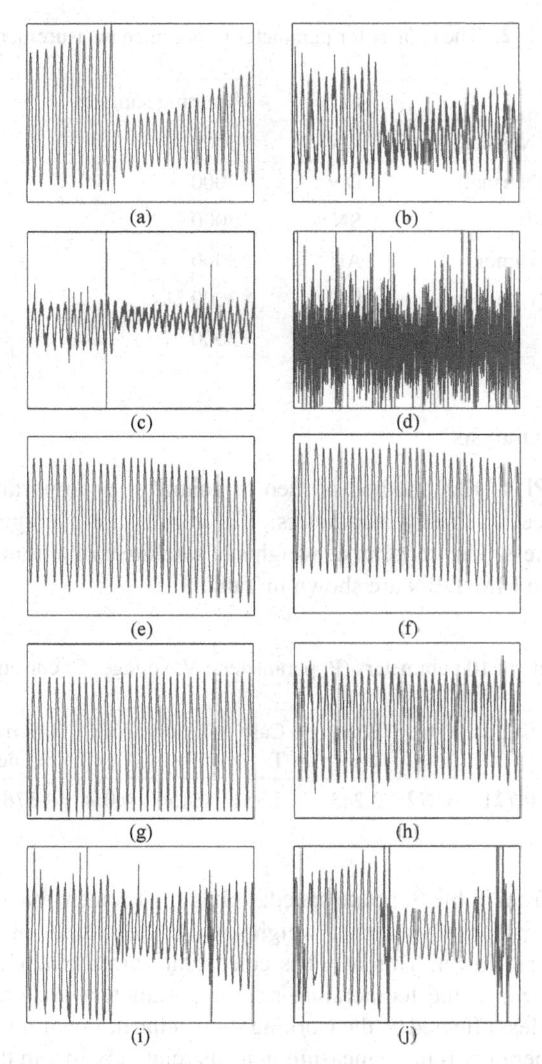

Fig. 8. Satellite momentum wheel telemetry data: (a) rotate speed; (b) voltage; (c) current; (d) voltage/current; (e) bearing temperature; (f) case temperature; (g) line temperature; (h) axle temperature; (i) friction moment; (j) acceleration

Acceleration Mode (Unnormal), Deceleration Mode (Unnormal) and Power Down, used for learning importance of parameters. The training set and testing set are shown in Table 2.

Table 2. The dataset for parameter importance measurement

State	Label	Training samples	Test samples
Acceleration Mode (Normal)	AN	3000	1000
Deceleration Mode (Normal)	DN	3000	1000
Stable Mode (Normal)	SN	3000	1000
Acceleration Mode (Unnormal)	AU	3000	1000
Deceleration Mode (Unnormal)	DU	3000	1000
Power Down	PD	3000	1000

4.2 Results and Analysis

In this paper, the PIM-DBN method is used to quantify the importance of the above 10 momentum wheel telemetry parameters:. The results are averaged by 10 trials to reduce the randomness. The importance weights of satellite momentum wheel telemetry parameters based on PIM-DBN are shown in Table 3.

Table 3. The weights of 10 parameters (P: parameters; V: voltage; C: current; T: temperature)

P	Rotate speed	V	C	V/C	Bearing T	Case T	Line T	Axle T	Friction moment	Acceleration
w	**0.635**	**0.798**	**0.721**	**0.872**	0.243	0.354	0.156	0.064	**0.578**	**0.697**

It can be seen from Table 3, rotate speed; voltage, current, voltage/current, friction moment and acceleration have higher weights,while the weight of the temperature-related parameters are lower. This result is consistent with the actual situation of the momentum wheel. Since the temperature-related parameters are greatly affected by lighting factors and less affected by the working state of the momentum wheel, the weight of the above 4 temperature remote measurements is relatively low in the fault diagnosis of the momentum wheel. On the contrary, the working state of the momentum wheel is closely related to its rotate speed, voltage, current, voltage/current, friction moment and acceleration, so the weight of the above 6 remote measurements is relatively high in the momentum wheel fault diagnosis.

In this paper, Support vector machine (SVM), Artificial neural network (ANN), DBN are used for fault diagnosis of the original data and the weighted importance data respectively. The results are averaged by 20 trials to reduce the randomness. The diagnostic accuracy is shown in Table 4. According to the data in Table 4, the accuracy of momentum wheel fault diagnosis based on DBN is higher than that based on SVM and ANN, and the fault diagnosis accuracy of the above 3 methods on the weighted original data is improved. The result shows that the parameter importance measurement method proposed in this paper can effectively improve the accuracy of fault diagnosis of satellite attitude control system.

Table 4. Comparison result of weighted data and raw data (%)

Methods	Mean accuracy	
	Weighted data	Raw data
SVM	87.54	76.34
ANN	68.83	53.64
DBN	93.45	82.79

5 Conclusion

This study presented a new DBN-based parameters importance measurement method. The main contributions of this study are proposing a new method PIM-DBN to calculate the importance of parameters and applying the PIM-DBN to the fault diagnosis field. The proposed method was tested on the telemetry data set of satellite attitude control system. In this paper, importance weights are learned for 10 types of telemetry data. The original data and weighted data are used for fault diagnosis based on SVM, ANN and DBN methods. All the method obtained higher accuracy by using weighted data. These results show the good potential of the proposed method in the data-driven fault diagnosis field and health assessment field.

References

1. Wang, D., Meng, L., Ye, P., et al.: Research of autonomous operation technology for deep space probe. Spacecraft Eng. **27**(6), 5–14 (2018)
2. Li, H., Dong, Y.: Intelligent development technology of satellite fault diagnosis system. Aerosp. Shanghai **34**(3), 52–59 (2017)
3. Ye, Z., Cheng, Y., Han, X., Jiang, B.: Fault location for attitude control systems of deep space exploration satellites. Control Theory Appl. **36**(12), 2093–2099 (2019)
4. Baldi, P., Castaldi, P., Mimmo, N., et al.: Combined singular perturbations and nonlinear geometric approach to FDI in satellite actuators and sensors. IFAC – PapersOnLine **50**(1), 7253–7259 (2017)
5. Jan, S.U., Koo, I.S.: Sensor faults detection and classification using SVM with diverse features. In: 2017 International Conference on Information and Communication Technology Convergence (ICTC), JejuIsland, Korea, pp. 576–578. IEEE (2017)
6. Ye, J., Zhen, C., Xuetao, W., et al.: A momentum wheel health ranking method based on fuzzy clustering model. Chin. Space Sci. Technol. **40**(3), 100–106 (2020)
7. Sheng, G., Wei, Z., Xu, H., et al.: Neural network-based fault diagnosis scheme for satellite attitude control system. In: 2018 Chinese Control and Decision Conference (CCDC). IEEE, Shenyang (2018)
8. Liu, Y., Yin, C., Hu, D., et al.: Communication satellite fault detection based on recurrent neural network. Comput. Sci. **47**(2), 227–232 (2020)
9. Du, Y., Budman, H., Duever, T.A.: Integration of fault diagnosis and control based on a trade-off between fault detectability and closed loop performance. J. Process Control **38**, 42–53 (2016)

An Optimized Timer-Based Passive Clustering Algorithm for Vehicular Ad Hoc Networks

Yang Lu[1,2](✉), Kai Liu[1,2], Tao Zhang[1], Xiling Luo[1,2], and Feng Liu[1,2]

[1] School of Electronics and Information Engineering, Beihang University, Beijing 100191, China
Ly517690205@163.com

[2] Hangzhou Innovation Institute, Beihang University, Hangzhou 310051, China

Abstract. In order to overcome the high mobility problem of nodes in vehicular ad hoc networks (VANETs), the clustering algorithm can effectively improve the overall communication performance. This paper proposes an optimized timer-based passive clustering algorithm (OTPCA) for VANETs. Vehicles can choose to actively leave the cluster or not join the cluster based on the communication environment and performance. The vehicle can choose to communicate directly with the road side unit (RSU) and force it to remain for a timer. After the timer expires, it is re-evaluated whether it is suitable to join a cluster, and then repeat the operation. This can effectively solve the problem of node state stuck and improve the average communication performance. Simulation results show that the proposed algorithm is better then the passive multi-hop clustering algorithm in terms of average communication delay and control information transmission ratio.

Keywords: VANETs · Clustering · Timer-based · Performance evaluation

1 Introduction

In typical highly dynamic networks such as vehicular ad-hoc networks (VANETs), the vehicles in the network generally have high mobility. Clustering can be considered as an effective approach to improve routing scalability and reliability. Based on the correlated spatial distribution and relative velocity, it groups vehicles to a cluster for distributing formation of hierarchical network structures.

Cluster-based routing technology is a method for solving routing problems in mobile ad hoc networks (MANETs) and VANETs. Clustering is to divide nodes into interconnected networks called clusters [1]. Each cluster has a cluster head (CH), which is as a coordinator in the interconnected network, and it can help the data transmission and communication between the vehicle and the cluster. The traditional passive cluster algorithm (PC) has many problems, such as the communication performance of the end nodes is poor and the control information packets occupy a large amount of channels during cluster maintenance [2–5].

Q. Wu et al. (Eds.): WiSATS 2020, LNICST 358, pp. 74–84, 2021.
https://doi.org/10.1007/978-3-030-69072-4_7

This paper proposes an optimized timer-based passive clustering algorithm (OTPCA) for vehicular ad hoc networks. It retains the characteristics of no contention and less control information overhead in passive clustering. At the same time, a vehicle can periodically evaluate its own communication role through a timer. Under the high-speed changing communication environment and topology, the vehicle can maintain an independent communication state based on the timer. Firstly, it reduces the cost of cluster maintenance. Secondly, it guarantees the communication performance of the node itself.

This paper is organized as follows. Section 2 briefly introduces passive clustering and its typical problems. Section 3 introduces the optimized timer-based passive clustering algorithm. Section 4 gives the comparison and analysis of the performance evaluation results. Section 5 proposes conclusion.

2 Typical Problems of Passive Clustering Algorithm

Passive clustering mainly solves the contradiction between cluster communication and routing communication that exists in active clustering. This contradiction will generate additional communication, thereby competing for bandwidth to increase the packet loss rate, and then cause normal communication. Passive clustering enables the two system to cooperate, reducing communication requirements and competition [6]. Some recent studies have optimized the transmission of shared data packets and control information sending and processing [7, 8]. And there is active and a hybrid (active–passive) clustering technique that try to solve this problem [9].

There are also some problems of the traditional PC algorithm.

Problem 1: Vehicles broadcast and share their own information by periodically broadcasting HELLO message packets, and choose to join the cluster through priority comparison. The worst node of communication performance is the cluster end node. When the network topology changes or clusters merge to increase the number of hops, the communication quality will become very bad, mainly reflecting the node communication delay is too large. Generally, after a node joins a cluster, it will maintain its cluster member identity until the cluster dies or out of cluster head communication range. This makes it difficult for vehicles to get out of this problem.

Problem 2: When cluster heads are choosed or replaced, most of them will set hysteresis threshold to ensure the stability of clusters [10, 11]. This will make small-scale car groups unable to form clusters. Multiple vehicles may not be cluster heads, but they frequently send out control information requests to join a cluster. At the same time, because there is no cluster head, the vehicles cannot get rid of the decision state. Not only will this cause excessive control information transmission and broadcast storms, but the vehicles will also fall into a state where they cannot communicate.

Problem 3: Because of the characteristics of VANETs high-speed changes, it will cause instability of the communication link between vehicles. This feature will cause the situation where the vehicle on the edge of the cluster communication repeatedly join and exit the same cluster frequently. The result is that the edge vehicle itself cannot stabilize the communication, and it also causes a lot of control information to contend for the channel.

3 Optimized Timer-Based Passive Clustering Algorithm

3.1 System Model

Multi-hop: The algorithm take the multi-hop cluster model. When the node chooses the best node to follow, it will evaluate the hop count of the node [12]. And the node will consider the node whose hop count after connection does not exceed the limit hops. Cluster member could connect to cluster head in 1-hop or multi-hop.

Priority neighbor following strategy: Through priority comparison, the nodes will follow the strategy of the node with the most stable link in the communication range to form an affiliation. This simple following strategy makes the model algorithm easy to implement. Usually traffic density and communication quality can effectively evaluate and predict the communication performance of nodes [13, 14]. We use *PRI* to represent the priority [5], the formula is as follows. The smaller the PRI_{ij} value is, the higher the node priority is.

$$PRI_{ij} = \alpha \cdot \frac{1}{N_{follow}(j)} + \beta \cdot ETX_{ij} + \gamma \cdot \frac{1}{LLT_{ij}} \quad (1)$$

where PRI_{ij} represents the priority of node j for node i, N_{follow} represents the following degree which depends on the number of followers and neighbors, $ETXij$ represents the the expected transmission count, and LLT_{ij} represents the expected link life time.

Communication routing: In this algorithm, in the entire network, the vehicles in the cluster member state cannot directly communicate with the RSU, and must communicate with the RSU through parent node and the cluster head which they belong to. The cluster head can communicate directly with the RSU or directly communicate with the members of the same cluster in the communication range. This will help to improve the integration of the cluster.

Passive: The algorithm uses passive communication technology. The vehicles do not need to through actively polling actively detect the nodes in the communication range. The node receives the information of the surrounding nodes by accepting the HELLO message packet and writes it into the information table. The node information written to the information table has an expiration date timer [15]. If the expiration date is exceeded, this information will be deleted.In this way, when the two nodes are out of the communication range and disconnected, the two nodes cannot immediately realize and react. After the information in the information table expires and is deleted, the node will not realize it. Although the node response will be delayed due to the validity period. However, the amount of control information sent by the nodes in the road network is reduced.

3.2 Cluster Head Selection

The cluster head selection is to solve how vehicles become cluster heads. Vehicles periodically send HELLO message packets to sense the communication environment and neighbors information [16]. Thus, through the priority neighbor following strategy in the system model, a general multi-hop network topology is constructed. Then, the vehicle with the best performance in the topology serves as the cluster head. The vehicle will not choose itself as a follower. So the vehicle with the best performance will also follow other vehicle first. Therefore, a recognized standard is needed to determine the cluster head. This algorithm uses the following degree [5] and the average mobility [17] to determine the cluster head. The larger the following degree and the smaller the average mobility, the more stable the vehicles and the more likely it is to become a cluster head.

$$CONDITION_{Be\ CH}(x) = \begin{cases} true & (N_{f\_x} > N_{f\_neighbors}) \wedge (AvgMobility_x < AvgMobility_{neighbors}) \\ false & Else \end{cases} \quad (2)$$

where N_f represent the following degree, and *AvgMobility* represent the average mobility.

3.3 Cluster Formation and Maintenance

The algorithm defines five communication states of vehicles in the road network [5]. Vehicles implement state switching through algorithms to match their own communication roles and complete their own communication tasks. The five communication states is defined as follow.The optimized timer-based passive clustering algorithm vehicle node state transition diagram is shown in Fig. 1, and OTPCA algorithm flow char is shown Fig. 2.

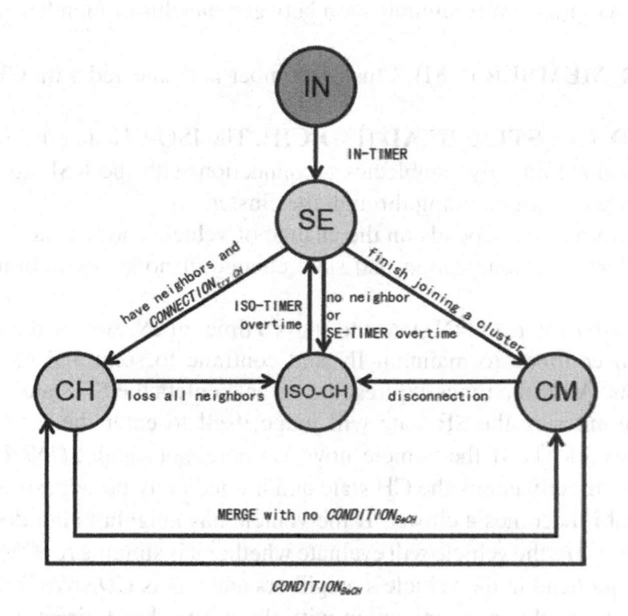

Fig. 1. OTPCA vehicle node state transition diagram

INITIAL (IN). IN is the initial state of the vehicle joining the road network, and receiving the HELLO packet of other vehicles to prepare for the SE.

STATE_ELECTION (SE). SE state will determine which state the vehicle enters.

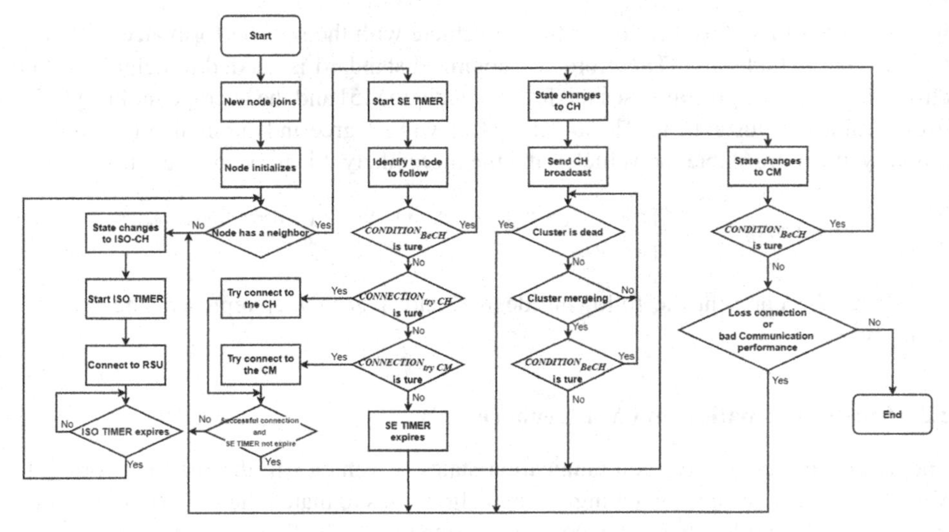

Fig. 2. OTPCA algorithm flow chart

CLUSTER_HEAD (CH). Cluster head state is similar to the role of traditional cluster head. It will manage communication between the cluster members and road side unit (RSU).

CLUSTER_MEMBER (CM). Cluster member is connected with CH in 1-hop or multi-hop.

ISOLATED_CLUSTER_HEAD (ISO-CH). The ISO-CH state is an independent node state. The node directly establishes a connection with the RSU to complete the communication task without going through the cluster.

The cluster formation depends on the change of vehicles node state. The algorithm realizes the orderly communication and state change of nodes by defining states and timers.

The vehicle first enters the IN state and starts a timer of IN. Before the timer expires, the vehicle will continue to maintain IN and continue to send and receive HELLO message packets. After the timer expires, the vehicle enters the SE state.

The vehicle entering the SE state will judge itself to enter the next state. And it will start a timer of SE. If the vehicle now has neighbors and $CONDITION_{BeCH}$ is ture, the vehicle directly enters the CH state and immediately broadcasts advertisement to announce that it becomes a cluster. If the vehicle has neighbors but does not satisfy $CONNECTION_{try\ CH}$, the vehicle will evaluate whether it is suitable for CM. At this time, if there is a cluster head in the vehicle's neighbors and meets $CONNECTION_{try\ CH}$, the vehicle will try to establish a connection with the cluster head directly. If there is no cluster head in the neighbors of the vehicle, but a vehicle in the neighbor that wants to follow meets $CONNECTION_{try\ CM}$, the vehicle establishes a multi-hop connection with the cluster head through the cluster member.

$$CONNECTION_{try\ CH}(x) = \begin{cases} true & N_{CH\ followers} < N_{\max\ members} \\ false & Else \end{cases} \tag{3}$$

$$CONNECTION_{try\ CM}(x) = \begin{cases} true & (N_{CM\ followers} < N_{\max\ members}) \wedge (Hop_{CM} + 1 \leq Hop_{\max}) \\ false & Else \end{cases} \quad (4)$$

where $N_{CH\ followers}$ represent the number of followers of the CH, $N_{CM\ followers}$ represent the number of followers of the CM, $N_{max\ members}$ represent the number of max members, HOP_{CM} represent the hop count between the CM and the CH, HOP_{CM} represent the allowed max hop count between the CM and the CH,

If the vehicle has no neighbors, it will enter the ISO-CH state. And if the vehicle does not leave the SE state after the timer SE expires, the node will also directly enter the ISO-CH state. This will solve the Problem 2. Multiple nodes that cannot be clustered due to $CONDITION_{BeCH}$ will enter ISO-CH state and normally communicate after the timer expires, without being stuck in SE.

Then nodes will switch between the three main communication states which are CM, CH and ISO-CH. Multiple nodes follow the following state transformation method to achieve cluster maintenance.

For the CH state, cluster merging may cause the node state to change from CH to CM. When two cluster heads enter communication range of each other, in order to avoid cluster group interference, the cluster groups will be merged. The node with poor performance will give up the CH state and become a follower of the other cluster head. At this time, the two clusters are merged, and the state of this vehicle will also change from CH to CM. In addition, when the CH loses all its followers, the cluster will die and the vehicle will enter the ISO-CH state.

For the CM state, when the vehicle meets CONDEION_CH compared to the following parent vehicle node, the vehicle will enter the CH state. When the vehicle is disconnected from the parent node, or when its communication performance is poor, the node will give up the CM state and enter the ISO-CH state. And this will solve Problem 1.

For the ISO-CH state, in the traditional algorithm, this state is triggered by parameter changes. It is redefined that this state is no longer triggered by whether or not vehicle nodes own a neighbor. Instead, there is an timer of ISO-CH, and the node state must maintains ISO-CH state during this timer. After the timer overtime, the state directly changes to the SE state to determine its next state. When the node is in the ISO-CH state, it still receives and sends HELLO messages packet. But the state change mechanism is no longer triggered. And nodes no longer sent join request packet to join a cluster. Nodes will communicate directly through RSU. This can effectively avoid the Problem 3. Besides, because when the SE state is changed to the ISO-CH state without neighbors, there only the decision is passed, no control information is sent, and the delay is very small. Therefore, a node that has been in an independent state for a long time under real road conditions can also maintain ISO-CH state for a long time. When there are no neighbors around the node, there is less chance of joining the cluster in a short time, and the timer can be set longer. On the contrary, there are some nodes around the node, but they cannot join clusters because of the algorithm limitation. This kind of node has chances to become a state that can join the cluster in a short time. And the timer can be set shorter.

4 Performance Evaluation

We used the SUMO version 0.30.0 traffic generator [12] and OMNeT++ 5.6 [13] in the simulation. We compared the communication performance between the OTPCA and the PMC algorithm.

The main VANETs simulation parameters setting is shown in Table 1. The vehicles speed is limited to 10 to 30 m/s, the transmission range of the vehicle is 200 m, and the IN TIMER of the vehicle is 10 s. The SE TIMER of the vehicle is set to 500 ms, which is to ensure that the node has a delay in the initial period of time in the cluster. The ISO TIMER of the vehicle is set to 20 s, which is to ensure the vehicle have good communication quality for a certain period of time, and also to allow the vehicle to enter a new communication environment after the timer expires to judge its next state again. This is to improve cluster stability, reduce cluster maintenance costs, and improve topology effectiveness. We compared PMC and OTPCA, and the three main performance indicators are: average transmission delay, Average CM duration and Cluster overhead. They can effectively evaluate communication performance of vehicles, cluster stability and channel occupancy.

Table 1. Simulation parameters

Parameter	Value
Simulation area size (m)	1000 × 1000
Simulation time (sec)	200
Number of vehicles	20–140
Transmission range (m)	200
MAC protocol	802.11p
Vehicles velocity (m/s)	10–30
Max hop	3
Max member	10
Number of lanes	Multi-lane
IN TIMER (sec)	10
SE TIMER (ms)	500
ISO TIMER (sec)	20
α, β, γ	0.3, 0.2, 0.5

Figure 3 shows the average transmission delay versus the number of vehicles. Usually the number of node hops has the greatest impact on communication delay. The OTPCA allows nodes give up the CM identity to become ISO-CH and communicating directly with RSU. Therefore, the transmission delay of such nodes is relatively low, thereby reducing the average transmission delay. It can be seen from the figure that the average transmission delay increases with the increase of the number of vehicles. In addition, it can be seen that the OTPCA algorithm is superior to the original PMC algorithm in average transmission delay. And the increase is more obvious in the case of medium traffic load. Because in the case of medium traffic load, the vehicles will encounter more problems. In the case of low traffic load, the increase is relatively small. Most nodes are always in the IN state or low-hop CM state. And most nodes have good communication performance, and most nodes will not actively leave the cluster. So the delay is low, and the difference is not obvious.

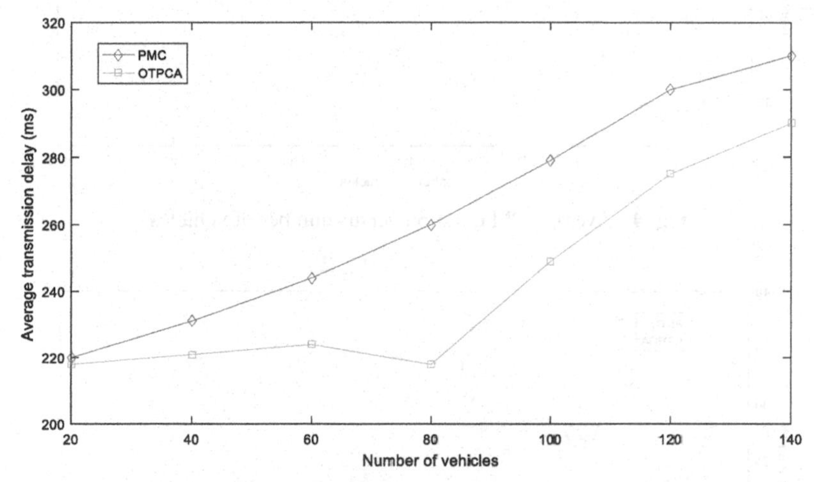

Fig. 3. Average transmission delay versus number of vehicles

Figure 4 shows the average CM duration and the number of vehicles. It can be seen from the figure that the OTPCA is smaller than the original PMC in the case of all the number of nodes situation. This is because the main idea of improving thinking is to maintain independent communication from the cluster. In some cases, the end node of clusters will voluntarily withdraw from the cluster, giving up the CM identity. Therefore, the average time for nodes to maintain CM will decrease. Similarly, in the case of medium traffic load, the CM duration is less. And the node has more opportunities to start the escape mechanism. This makes the average CM time of OPTCA lower. Compared with the PMC, the difference can be roughly estimated the extent to which the node actively exits the cluster. So the OTPCA also reduces the stability of the cluster. It is also more in the medium traffic load, and less in the low and high traffic load.

The Cluster overhead as the ratio define comes from [5]. The Cluster overhead as the radio is used to represent number of control packets spent in the cluster formation phase and the cluster maintenance phase with the total number of packets. The formula is as follows:

$$P_{overhead} = \frac{N_{contral\ packet}}{N_{all\ packet}} \times 100\% \tag{5}$$

Figure 5 shows the cluster overhead versus the number of vehicles. It can be seen from the figure that the cluster overhead increases with the increase of the number

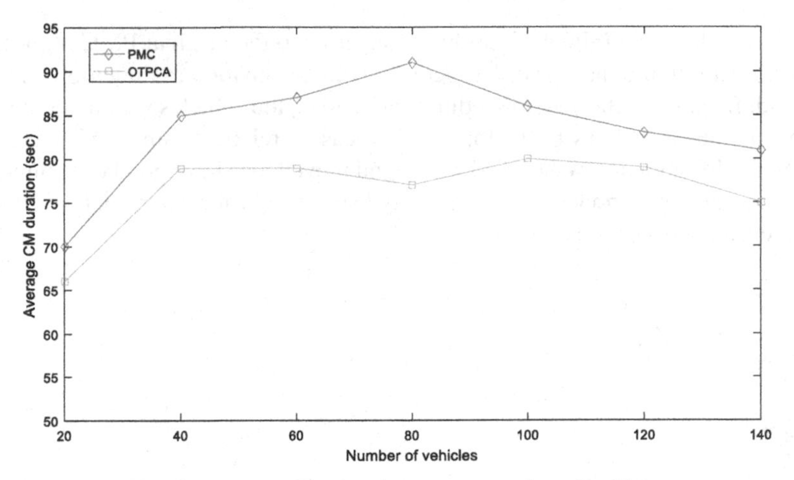

Fig. 4. Average CM duration versus number of vehicles

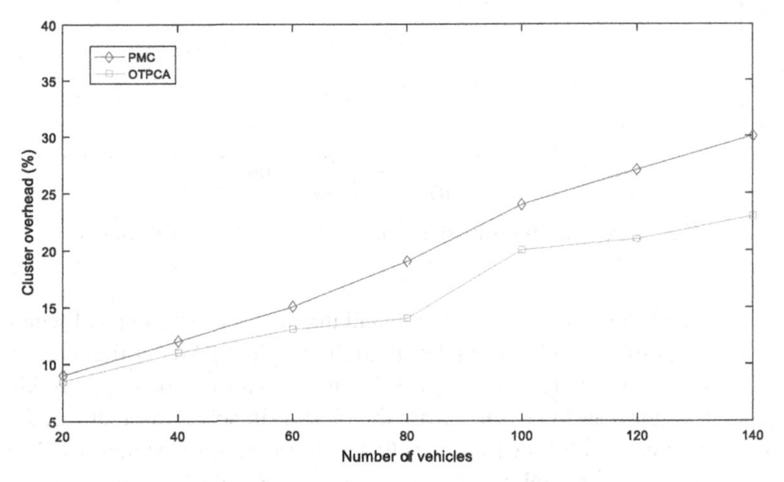

Fig. 5. Cluster overhead versus number of vehicles

of vehicles. This is because when the node density increases, the number of clusters and cluster heads increases, and there is interference between clusters. There are more cases of cluster maintenance and cluster merging, and more control information packets are sent.In addition, when the number of vehicles of the OTPCA increases, the cluster overhead gap gradually increases compared to PMC. In the case of the PMC algorithm, nodes preferentially maintain connections, so the overhead is large, especially in the case of large clusters caused by merging. However, usually the end node has a large proportion of control information packets due to the multi-hop situation. The OTPCA solves the end nodes, from CM to ISO, leaves the cluster, establishes and maintains the communication with RSU by themself. At the same time, due to the ISO TIMER, the node will not frequently change its own state, so as to avoid sending too many control information packets. Although the probability of collision is potentially increased, the overall control information transmission situation is better than the PMC for the channel.

5 Conclusion

The traditional PC algorithm lacks management of multi-hop nodes, and the communication performance of end nodes is poor. To solove these problems, an optimized timer-based passive clustering algorithm is proposed. Vehicles weighing their own communication performance can maintain direct communication mode with RSU or actively exit the cluster. The problems of PC is solved by timers based on passive technology. OTPCA evaluates and estimates the future communication performance of the node from various aspects to determine whether the node should continue to maintain the CM state or disconnect the link. When vehicles cannot join the cluster, OTPCA will make it preferentially maintain an independent state and maintain basic communication through the RSU. And evaluate the surrounding environment, set a timer to decide when to try to join the cluster. Finally, simulation results show that the OTPCA is better than the PMC in average communication delay and cluster overhead. This advantage works best at medium traffic load. At the same time, because of the mechanism, the average CM duration of the OTPCA is shorter than that of the PMC algorithm.

Acknowledgements. This work was supported by the National Key R&D Program of China under Grant No. 2016YFB1200100, and the National Nature Science Foundation of China under Grant No. 91638301.

References

1. Baker, D.: The architectural organization of a mobile radio network via a distributed algorithm. IEEE Trans. Commun. **29**(11), 1694–1701 (2003)
2. Taek, J.K., Mario, G.: Efficient flooding with Passive Clustering (PC) in ad hoc networks. SIGCOMM Comput. Commun. Rev. **32**(1), 44–56 (2002)
3. Senouci, O., Harous, S., Aliouat, Z.: Survey on vehicular ad hoc networks clustering algorithms: overview, taxonomy, challenges, and open research issues. International J. Commun. Syst. (5) (2020)
4. Wang, S.S., Lin, Y.S.: Performance evaluation of passive clustering based techniques for inter-vehicle communications. In: Wireless & Optical Communications Conference. IEEE (2010)
5. Zhang, D., Ge, H.: Zhang T,: New multi-hop clustering algorithm for vehicular ad hoc networks. IEEE Trans. Intell. Transp. Syst. **20**(4), 1517–1530 (2019)
6. Cooper, C., Franklin, D., Ros, M., Safaei, F., Abolhasan, M.: A comparative survey of vanet clustering techniques. IEEE Commun. Surv. Tutorials **19**(1), 657–681 (2017)
7. Abuashour, A., Kadoch, M.: Passive CH election avoidance protocol and CH routing protocol In VANET. In: 2018 IEEE International Conference on Internet of Things (iThings) and IEEE Green Computing and Communications (GreenCom) and IEEE Cyber, Physical and Social Computing (CPSCom) and IEEE Smart Data (SmartData), pp. 1753–1758 (2018)
8. Ghadi, F., Touil, A.: Efficient dissemination based on passive approach and dynamic clustering for vanet. Procedia Comput. Sci. **127**, 369–378 (2018)

9. Moore, G.L., Liu, P.: A hybrid (active-passive) clustering technique for VANETs. In: 2019 IEEE ComSoc International Communications Quality and Reliability Workshop (CQR). IEEE (2019)
10. Li, W., Tizghadam, A., Leon-Garcia, A.: Robust clustering for connected vehicles using local network criticality. In: Proceedings of the IEEE Internatiional Conference Communication (ICC), pp. 7157–7161, Ottawa, ON, Canada (2012)
11. Ghosh, R., Basagni, S.: Mitigating the impact of node mobility on ad hoc clustering. Wireless Commun. Mob. Comput. **8**, 295–308 (2008)
12. Ucar, S., Coleri Ergen, S., Ozkasap, O.: VMaSC: vehicular multi-hop algorithm for stable clustering in Vehicular Ad Hoc Networks. In: 2013 IEEE Wireless Communications and Networking Conference (WCNC), Shanghai, pp. 2381–2386 (2013)
13. Qureshi, K. N., Bashir, F., Abdullah, A. H.: Distance and signal quality aware next hop selection routing protocol for vehicular ad hoc networks. Neural Comput. Appl. **6**(4), 5916–5926 (2019)
14. Singh, R., Saluja, D., Kumar, S.: Reliability improvement in clustering based vehicular ad-hoc network. IEEE Commun. Lett. **24**, 1351–1355 (2020)
15. Bononi, L., Felice, M.: A cross-layered MAC and clustering scheme for efficient broadcast in VANETs. In: 2007 IEEE Internatonal Conference on Mobile Adhoc and Sensor Systems, MASS, pp. 1–8 (2007)
16. Souza, E.D., Nikolaidis, I., Gburzynski, P.: A new aggregate local mobility (ALM) clustering algorithm for VANETs. In: 2010 IEEE International Conference on Communications, pp. 1–5. Cape Town (2010)
17. Goonewardene, R.T., Ali, F.H., Stipidis, E.: Robust mobility adaptive clustering scheme with support for geographic routing for vehicular ad hoc networks. Intell. Transp. Syst. IET **3**(2), 148158 (2009)
18. The network simulator OMNeT++. https://omnetpp.org/. Accessed 10 June 2020
19. The Simulation of Urban Mobility (SUMO). https://sumo.dlr.de/docs/index.html. Accessed 10 June 2020

AODMAC: An Adaptive and On-Demand TDMA-Based MAC for Vehicular Ad Hoc Networks

Yaodong Ma[1,2](✉), Kai Liu[1,2], Xiling Luo[1,2], Tao Zhang[1,2], and Feng Liu[1,2]

[1] School of Electronics and Information Engineering, Beihang University, Beijing 100191, China
15257557503@163.com

[2] Hangzhou Innovation Institute, Beihang University, Hangzhou 310051, China

Abstract. To solve the high transmission collisions and channel resource wastage problems in unbalanced traffic conditions of VANETs, an adaptive and on-demand TDMA-based MAC (AODMAC) protocol is proposed. A dynamic frame is partitioned into equal slot sets according to the lane numbers, and each lane has its own disjoint time slot set for vehicles to access. The key operation of AODMAC is that it can adaptively adjust the size of slot set according to the different traffic density in each lane. Due to each lane can acquire its slot set on-demand, AODMAC can be efficient in both balanced and unbalanced traffic load scenarios. Before a vehicle can acquire a time slot, it should judge the traffic load of its lane. If the density has exceeded a threshold, the node should augment its slot set size from the other lane. Simulation results show that the proposed protocol outperforms VeMAC and MoMAC in terms of the transmission collision rate and channel utilization, especially in high traffic load and unbalanced conditions.

Keywords: VANETs · Adaptive MAC · On-demand · TDMA-based · Distributed

1 Introduction

Vehicular ad hoc networks (VANETs) is a special kind of mobile ad hoc networks (MANETs) which consist of a set of vehicles equipped with on-board units (OBU) and road-side units (RSUs), through V2V or V2R communications to realize a broad range of safety and non-safety applications [1]. Because of the special characteristics of VANETs, such as high mobility of the node, frequent change of topologies and different quality of service (QoS) requirements of different applications, to design an efficient and fair medium access control (MAC) protocol is a critical and challenging issue. However, we note that some characteristics can help us to develop MAC protocols, such as the sufficient power supply and the limited degrees of freedom in the nodes' movement constraint to the road topology.

Various MAC protocols have been proposed for VANETs. Literature [2] surveys the existing MAC protocols. In particular, the IEEE 802.11p [3] is the standard for Wireless

Q. Wu et al. (Eds.): WiSATS 2020, LNICST 358, pp. 85–98, 2021.
https://doi.org/10.1007/978-3-030-69072-4_8

Access in Vehicular Environment (WAVE). WAVE is operation mode which is used by IEEE 802.11p devices to operate in the dedicated short range communication (DSRC) band which is firstly coined by FCC. However, the IEEE 802.11p employs CSMA/CA-based distributed coordinated function (DCF) mechanism, which is a contention-based protocol. It performs well in the low traffic density as CSMA/CA can cover the topology changing in a sparse scenario. However, the access delay will grow to a significant level in the dense traffic condition. Moreover, the absence of RTS/CTS scheme in broadcast mode for efficient requirements will aggravate the hidden terminal problem, i.e., a collision occurs at a common neighbor node when other two senders cannot hear each other.

For the delay-bounded requirement in safety-related applications and throughput requirement in non-safety-related applications, time division multiple access (TDMA) based MACs have demonstrated their efficiency in VANETs. These protocols fall into three categories: centralized [4], cluster-based [5, 6] and fully distributed [7–12].

A fully distributed protocol is easy to deploy and its operational principle is relatively simple. Therefore, many distributed TDMA MAC protocols have been proposed. The ADHOC MAC proposed in [7] is a typical one. It operates in a frame-slot structure. By letting each vehicle reports its status within its transmission range in frame information (FI) periodically, ADHOC can support a reliable broadcast service without the hidden terminal problem. Moreover, in ADHOC, each node is guaranteed to access the medium at least once in a frame, which is suitable for the applications with delay-bounded. However, some limitations make ADHOC MAC inefficient. Firstly, due to node mobility, merging collisions may occur frequently. Secondly, ADHOC MAC is a single channel protocol that is not suitable for the seven DSRC channels.

Taking the problems encountered in ADHOC into consideration, Omar et al. proposed VeMAC in [8, 9]. VeMAC is a multichannel protocol with two transceivers and its main idea is to divide the frame into disjoint slot sets and then map these two sets to the vehicles on the opposite direction of road. Accordingly, (adaptive TDMA slot assignment) ATSA MAC in [10] further considers the unbalanced traffic load in opposite direction and it makes an adaptive classification of time slots, dynamically changes the frame length and adjusts the ratio of left slots and right slots according to the density of nodes. The results show that the ATSA can reduce the slot collisions, achieve the minimal time delay and maximum channel utilization compared with the ADHOC and VeMAC protocol. Similarly, A-VeMAC in [11] is based on VeMAC protocol, unlike VeMAC, which equally partitions each frame, the frame partitioning with A-VeMAC is not equal. Instead, it can adaptively vary with the vehicle traffic conditions in opposite directions. However, both VeMAC and ATSA protocols cannot solve the possible merging collision problem that the vehicles with different speeds in the same direction move together. A mobility-aware TDMA MAC (MoMAC) [12] is proposed to enhance the reliability of safety message exchange for safety applications. In MoMAC, the medium resource is assigned according to the underlying road topology and lane distribution on roads. With MoMAC, time slot collisions caused by vehicles' relative movements on multi-lane roads and merging together at intersections, can be relieved. However, two main limitations still exist in MoMAC. One is that under unbalance traffic load in different lanes, the slot sets assign scheme in MoMAC will cause slot wastage in sparse lanes and severe collisions in dense lanes. The other one is that MoMAC is a single channel protocol which cannot effectively use the seven channels. To solve the problems discussed before, it is necessary to design a multichannel MAC suitable for an unbalanced scenario, which motivates us to design this MAC protocol.

In this paper, we propose an adaptive and on-demand TDMA-based MAC (AODMAC) protocol for VANETs. A dynamic frame is partitioned into equal sets according to the lane numbers, and each lane has its own disjoint time slot sets for vehicles to access. The key operation of AODMAC is that it can adaptively adjust the size of the slot set according to the different traffic density in each lane. Due to each lane can acquire slot sets on-demand, AODMAC can be efficient in both balanced and unbalanced traffic density scenarios. Before a vehicle can acquire a time slot, it should judge the traffic load of its lane. If the density has exceeded the threshold, the node should augment its slot size from the other lane. Once the adjustment is completed, it will determine a set of slots that are available for the vehicle to reserve and randomly select one for reservation.

The remainder of this paper is organized as follows. Section 2 describes the proposed AODMAC protocol. Section 3 evaluates the performance of AODMAC. Section 4 concludes this paper.

2 AODMAC Protocol

In this section, we will demonstrate the proposed AODMAC protocol.

2.1 Preliminaries

In TDMA-based MAC protocols, access time is divided into consecutive frames consisting of a constant number of fixed duration time slots. The number of time slots per frame on control channel (CCH) is denoted by N. Every node (i.e. vehicle) is equipped with a global positioning system (GPS) receiver and thus can accurately determine its position and direction as well as its lane with the help of lane-level digital map. On the one hand, each node must acquire a time slot before transmission and can use it in all subsequent frames until a collision occurs or the node releases it. On the other hand, if a node gets a slot, it must transmit a packet during its time slot even if the node has no data to send. The reason is that the information in the header called frame information (FI) is necessary for other nodes to make decisions such as which time slot they can access on CCH and if the node should adjust the available slot set as discusses later.

In TDMA-based MAC protocols, all the neighboring vehicles in the communication range of a vehicle constitute the one-hop set (OHS) of the vehicle. In addition, the two-hop set (THS) of a vehicle refers to all the vehicles that can reach it in two hops at most. Figure 1 illustrates the notion of the OHS and THS.

There are two kinds of transmission collisions in the existing MAC protocols, i.e., *access collision* and *merging collision*. The access collision refers to two nodes in the same THS simultaneously access the same time slot; while the merging collision happens when the vehicles that occupy the same time slot in the different THS move to the same THS due to mobility or node activation. In VANETs, merging collisions can occur among vehicles in opposite directions as well as among vehicles in the same direction

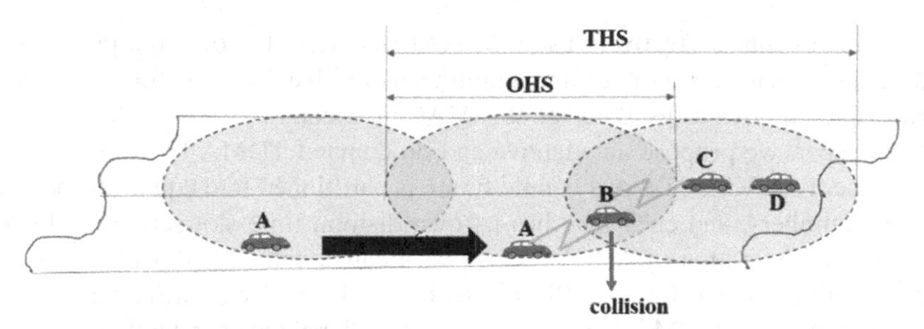

Fig. 1. Notion of OHS, THS and merging collision.

but different lanes due to acceleration or deceleration. For example, in Fig. 1, if vehicle A and C use the same slot and A moves to the THS of C, the collisions will happen at B.

These transmission collisions discussed above can be detected based on the FI that received from all the neighboring nodes in the OHS during the previous N time slots. Specifically, for node A, whenever it gets a new time slot or transmits a packet, it should passively listen to the channel for N successive time slots (not necessarily in the same frame), if the FI received from all its OHS (i.e. $y \in N_{CCH}(A)$)[1] indicate that $A \in N_{CCH}(y)$ [12], it means that there are no other vehicle occupies the same time slot in the THS; otherwise, the node may encounter a collision and all the collided nodes should release the slot and access a new one.

2.2 Design Overview

In accordance with MoMAC [12], disjoint slot sets map to the different lanes for vehicles to access. We denote the lane number l as follows. From the center lane to the margin, in the right direction, the number increases from 1; while on the left direction, the number decreases from -1. And a vehicle is assumed to move in a left (right) direction if it is moving from north/south to west (east). An example is illustrated as in Fig. 2.

Unlike MoMAC, the partitioning of each frame is not fixed. Instead, it can adaptively adjust according to the different traffic density in each lane. Due to each lane can acquire slot set on-demand, AODMAC can achieve efficiency in both balanced and unbalanced traffic density scenarios. Enhance the MoMAC, for the service channel, AODMAC employs the same access mechanism used in VeMAC.

2.3 Frame Structure

The initial frame structure in AODMAC is illustrated in Fig. 3, but it can be dynamically adjusted according to the traffic density in the lane when a vehicle needs to reserve a slot. Denote L as the number of lanes on a specific road, and each frame consists of N time slots, which are partitioned into L disjoint sets: $N_l(x), l = \pm 1, \pm 2, \ldots$, vehicles are allowed for reservation in set $N_l(x)$ when they are moving in the lane l. $|N_l(x)|$ denotes the size of the slot set that lane l maps to, and at the first beginning, $|N_l(x)| = \frac{N}{L}, l = \pm 1, \pm 2, \ldots$.

[1] $N_{CCH}(A)$ denotes the set of IDs of vehicle A's one-hop neighbors, which are updated by whether A has received packets directly on the channel during the previous N slots.

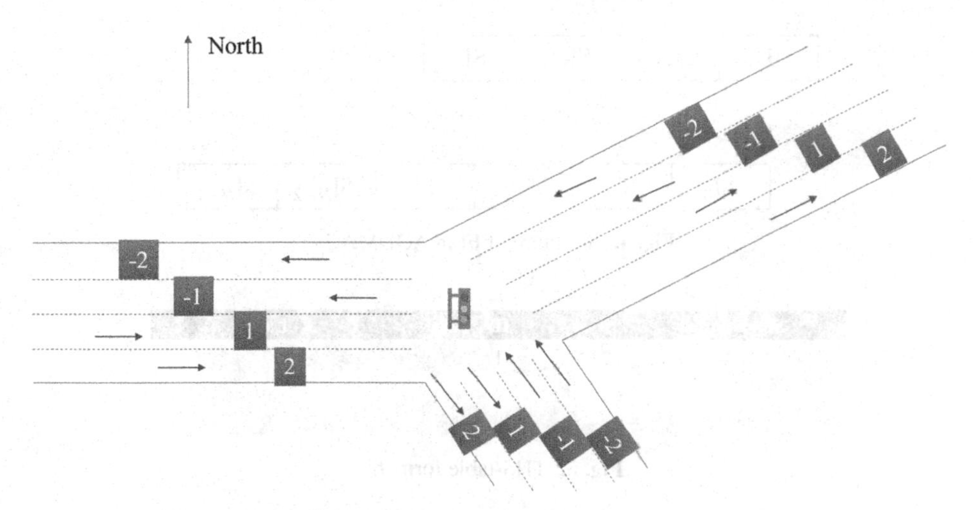

Fig. 2. An example of road topology and lane number.

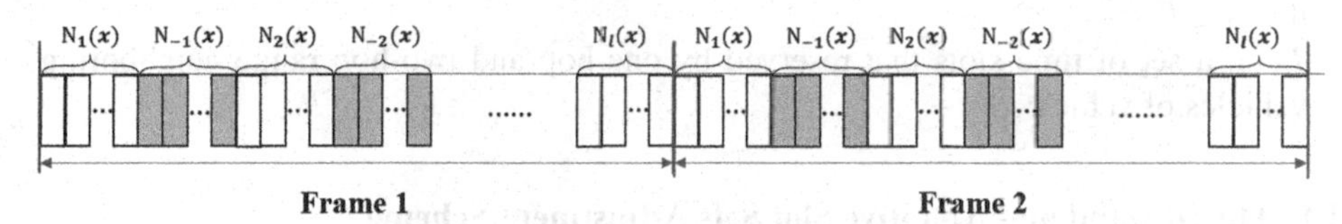

Fig. 3. Frame structure in AODMAC.

To facilitate time slot assignment in a distributed way, each vehicle needs to 1) maintain a THS-table including the information of its neighboring vehicles in one-hop and two-hops ranges as well as 2) maintain the frame information (FI). The structure of FI used in AODMAC is shown in Fig. 4 and the THS-table format is shown in Fig. 5. Note that $ID = 0$ and/or $Lane = 0$ means the slot is idle in a THS range. Specifically, for a vehicle, it generates/update its FI and THS-table on the basis of the information received from the previous N time slots and the process is as follows:

- Vehicle x will record its current ID, lane number and slot index into the FI's first three fields;
- According to the FI received from previous N time slots, the vehicle can record each FI's first three fields into the SI, and SI_k, $k \in [0, N-1]$ denotes the occupancy status of slot k including ID and lane number;
- Simultaneously, according to the FI received from previous N time slots, vehicle x can record each FI's SI field into THS-table, which denotes the two-hop range slot status.

With the above information, vehicle x can transmit the updated FI when the corresponding slot coming and decide the whole slot status in two-hops range which can be used for slot adjustment or collision detection. Therefore, for a certain node, the following sets are defined and will be used in the next section:

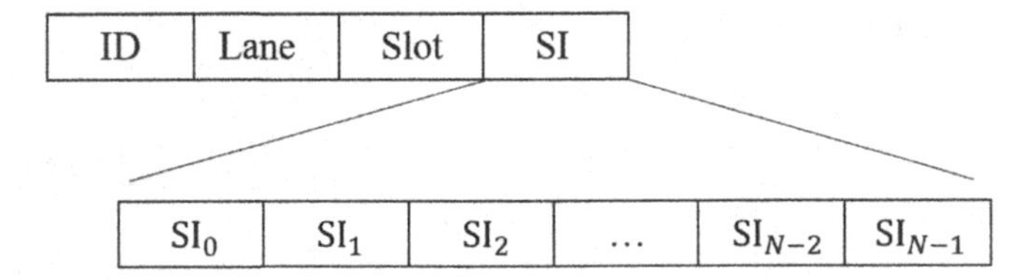

Fig. 4. Structure of FI in AODMAC.

Slot Number	ID	Lane
0	1	2
......	......	......
N-1	0	0

Fig. 5. THS-table format.

- $V_l(x)$: a set of one-hop and two-hop neighboring vehicles of vehicle x associated with the lane l.
- $T(x)$: a set of time slots that reserved by one-hop and two-hop range neighboring vehicles of vehicle x.

2.4 On-Demand and Adaptive Slot Sets Adjustment Scheme

In AODMAC, slot set size can be adaptively adjusted according to the traffic load in a specific lane. We define $D_l(x), l = \pm1, \pm2, \ldots$ as the traffic density in lane l which is calculated by vehicle x, and it can be derived as follows:

$$D_l(x) = \begin{cases} L, \frac{|V_l(x)|}{|N_l(x)|} < U_{min} \\ M, U_{min} \le \frac{|V_l(x)|}{|N_l(x)|} \le U_{max} \\ H, \frac{|V_l(x)|}{|N_l(x)|} > U_{max} \end{cases}, \tag{1}$$

where L, M and H denote the low, medium and high traffic density, respectively; U_{min} and U_{max} are the thresholds to classify the traffic load and the value are design parameters.

We define two kinds of vehicles in AODMAC, i.e., *reserved vehicle* and *non-reserved vehicle*. A reserved vehicle denotes that the vehicle has acquired a slot no matter from the initial slot set or the augmented slot set; A non-reserved vehicle denotes that the vehicle has not occupied a slot. Accordingly, the slot sets adjustment scheme can be divided into two cases:

For a Non-reserved Vehicle. As the flow chart shown in Fig. 6. Before a vehicle x in lane $\lambda, \lambda \in l$ can acquire a slot, it will first estimate $D_l(x), l = \pm1, \pm2, \ldots$ based on Eq. (1). If $D_\lambda(x) = L$ or $D_\lambda(x) = M$, then the size of $N_\lambda(x)$ needs not to be adjusted, and the vehicle will try to acquire a slot in $A_\lambda'(x)$, where

$$A_\lambda'(x) = \overline{T_\lambda(x)} \cap N_\lambda(x). \tag{2}$$

However, if $D_\lambda(x) = H$, it denotes the density of the lane λ is over the threshold, and hence the size of $N_\lambda(x)$ should be augmented. Then, vehicle x compares the $D_l(x)$, $l = \pm1, \pm2, \ldots$ to find if $D_l(x) = L$ exists; if true, vehicle x will give preference to select the nearest slot sets to augment, the reason is that we assume the closer the lane, the similar the movement of vehicles, which means the less probability of merging collisions will occur; if false, vehicle x will continue to find if $D_l(x) = M$ exists, similarly, vehicle x will give preference to select the nearest slot sets to augment. After adjusting the slot set, vehicle x can randomly access in set $A''_\lambda(x)$ derived as follows:

$$N'_\lambda(x) = N_\lambda(x) \cup A'_\mu(x), \tag{3}$$

$$A''_\lambda(x) = \overline{T_\lambda(x)} \cap N'_\lambda(x), \tag{4}$$

where $A'_\mu(x)$ which can be derived from Eq. (2) denotes that vehicle x finally decides to augment from the slot set μ.

If all the $D_l(x) = H$, vehicle x will not augment its set and acquire a slot in its initial set, and this case will give detailed solutions in our future work, i.e., to adjust the frame time to get a trade-off between the transmission delay and reliability.

For a Reserved Vehicle. When the slot of vehicle x coming, before it can transmit a packet, vehicle x should judge if the current using slot k belongs to its initial slot set. If not, it should calculate the $D_\lambda(x)$ (assume that vehicle is moving in the lane λ) to judge if $D_\lambda(x) = L$, if true, it means that the density of lane λ has turned from high to low, thus, to relieve the possible collisions, vehicle x should release the current slot and acquire

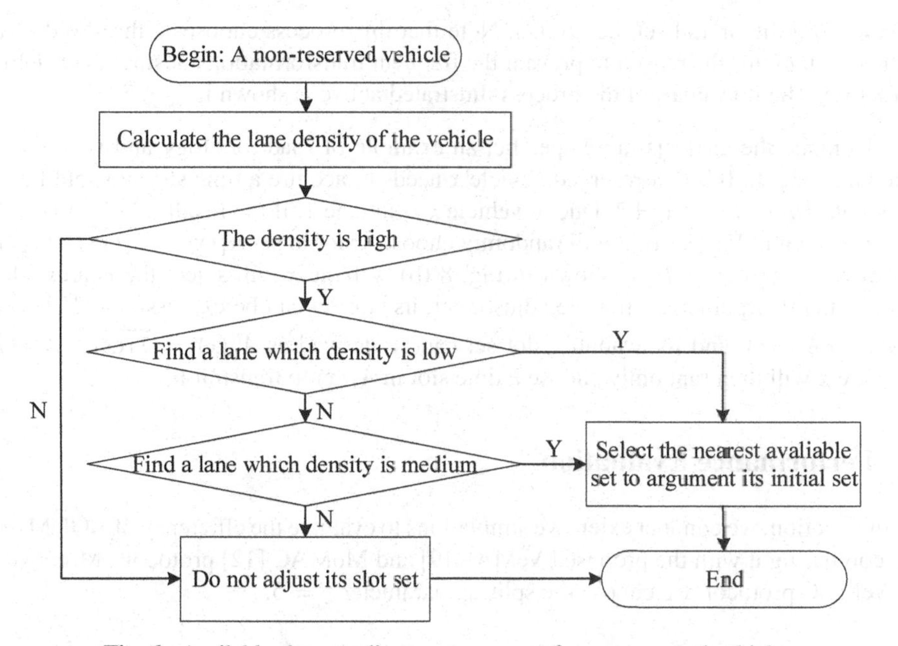

Fig. 6. Available slot set adjustment process of a non-reserved vehicle.

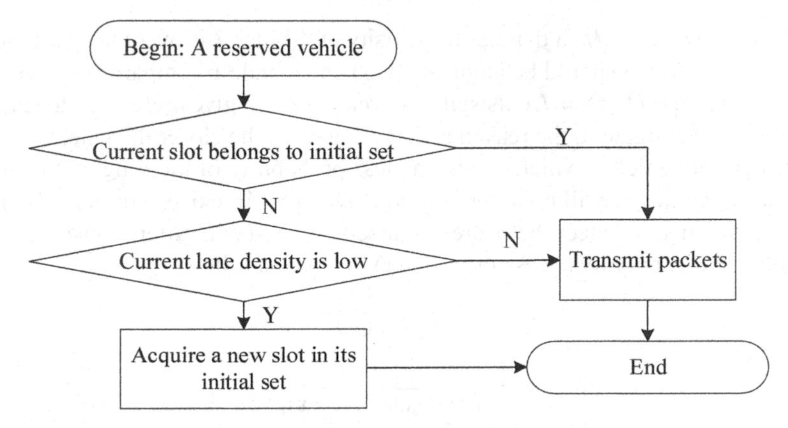

Fig. 7. Slot adjustment process of a reserved vehicle.

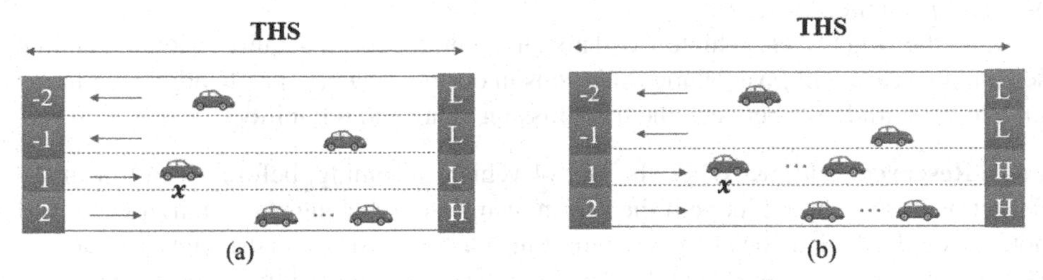

Fig. 8. An Example of the slot set adjustment scheme.

a new slot in its initial set, i.e., $A'_{\lambda}(x)$. Note that this process chooses a threshold of L rather than M for the reason to prevent the frequent transformation causing an unstable structure. The flow chart of the process illustrated above is shown in Fig. 7.

To make the analysis more specific, an example of road topology and vehicles is shown in Fig. 8. If a non-reserved vehicle x needs to acquire a time slot, it should first calculate $D_l(x), l = \pm 1, \pm 2$. Due to vehicle x is in lane 1, if the result of $D_1(x)$ is L or M, as shown in Fig. 8 (a), it will randomly choose a slot in set $A'_1(x) = \overline{T_1(x)} \cap N_1(x)$. However, if $D_1(x) = H$ as shown in Fig. 8 (b), vehicle x will select the nearest slot set $A'_{-1}(x)$ to argument. After the adjustment, its slot set can be expressed as $N'_1(x) = N_1(x) \cup A'_{-1}(x)$, and its available slot set can be derived as $A''_1(x) = \overline{T_1(x)} \cap N'_1(x)$. Vehicle x will then randomly choose a time slot in $A''_1(x)$ to transmit FI.

3 Performance Evaluation

In this section, we conduct extensive simulations to evaluate the efficiency of AODMAC by comparing it with the proposed VeMAC [9] and MoMAC [12] protocols. Moreover, in VeMAC protocol, we choose the split-up parameter $\tau = 5$.

3.1 Simulation Environment

We conduct network simulations through OMNeT++ 4.6 [13] and Simulation of Urban Mobility (SUMO) [14]. We consider three different traffic loads [9] in the highway scenario measured by the parameter

$$\eta = M \times \frac{2R}{L} \times \frac{1}{N}, \tag{5}$$

which is called THS occupancy, the parameter denotes the ratio of the number of slots required by a THS to the total number of slots available for a THS. In Eq. (5), M indicates the total number of vehicles on the road, R is the communication range, L is the length of the highway segment and N is the number of slots in a frame. Based on the THS occupancy, we denote high ($\eta = 0.85$), medium ($\eta = 0.5$) and low ($\eta = 0.2$) to mimic different traffic load in the highway, in each traffic load, we also consider two cases, i.e., balanced condition and unbalanced condition, thus by combining them, we get six different traffic conditions. Specifically, in the balanced condition, vehicles select any lane with the same probability, while in unbalanced condition, some lanes may exceed the capacity and others may be redundant.

In the simulation experiment, to mimic the real traffic environment, we consider a bidirectional 8-lane highway and each of the four lanes in one direction is given a speed limit of 60 km/h, 80 km/h, 100 km/h, 120 km/h, respectively. Moreover, vehicles also have different performance parameters, e.g., maximum velocity, acceleration and deceleration. Other simulation parameters are listed in Table 1.

Table 1. Simulation parameters

Parameter	Value
Highway length (L)	1 km
Lane width	3.2 m
Slot duration	1 ms
Slots/frame (N)	100
Transmission range (R)	300 m
Traffic conditions	High-Balanced/Unbalanced, Medium-Balanced/Unbalanced, Low-Balanced/Unbalanced
U_{min}	0.4
U_{max}	0.9
Simulation time	120 s

3.2 Performance Metrics

1. *Rate of transmission collisions.* Refers to the average number of transmission collisions per frame per THS.

2. *Channel utilization.* The ratio of the average number of time slots reserved by the vehicles to the total number of slots available for a THS.

3.3 Simulation Results

Figure 9 shows the transmission collision rate versus number of simulations in different traffic conditions. Firstly, in both conditions, no matter in balanced or unbalanced conditions, AODMAC protocol can achieve the minimum number of collisions and is more effective especially in high traffic load. Specifically, the mean value of transmission collision rate of AODMAC with unbalanced condition is 0.07, 0.29 and 1.41 in the low, medium and high traffic load, respectively, while the mean value in MoMAC is 0.31, 1.19 and 2.37, in VeMAC, the mean value is 0.09, 0.93 and 5.63. The main reason is that AODMAC can adaptively adjust the slot sets on demand according to the lane density. Secondly, in all three different traffic loads, the curves of unbalanced condition always have more violent fluctuations compared to balanced conditions in VeMAC and MoMAC, while it is more stable in AODMAC. This indicates that although in the same traffic load, different moving status or topology distribution (i.e., different simulation seeds in simulations) will matter a lot in VeMAC and MoMAC. Moreover, the transmission collision rate in MoMAC under unbalanced conditions shows worse performance than other protocols. It is mainly because MoMAC protocol is unable to cope with the surge of traffic load in some certain lanes. Lastly, both in balanced and unbalanced conditions, AODMAC shows similar curves that demonstrates the efficiency and stability of the protocol.

Figure 10 shows the channel utilization versus number of simulations in different traffic conditions. Firstly, in low traffic load, the performance of the three protocols are very close in balanced and unbalanced conditions respectively due to low contention. Secondly, based on the same condition, AODMAC always has a better channel utilization due to its lowest collision rate. Specifically, the mean value of channel utilization of AODMAC with unbalanced condition is 0.31, 0.64 and 0.66 in the low, medium and high traffic load, respectively, while the mean value in MoMAC is 0.30, 0.52 and 0.40, in VeMAC, the mean value is 0.30, 0.61 and 0.60. The main reason is that the adaptive slot sets adjustment in AODMAC is beneficial to take full advantage of the free slot as well as relieve the burden of the busy slot sets. Thirdly, the channel utilization will not monotonically increase with the traffic load due to the collision dramatically increasing when the number of vehicles is closing to slots in a THS. Moreover, when the traffic load is high, the performance of MoMAC will dramatically worse off, the reason is that excessive subdivision results in small size of each slot set and thus incur more collisions.

In summary, under balanced traffic conditions, the performance (transmission collision rate and channel utilization) with AODMAC is close to those with VeMAC and MoMAC when the traffic load is low. When the traffic load is high, the performance with AODMAC is better than that with VeMAC and MoMAC. Under unbalanced traffic conditions, the three protocols have close performance when the traffic load is low. With the traffic load increasing, the performance with AODMAC becomes significantly better than those with VeMAC and MoMAC.

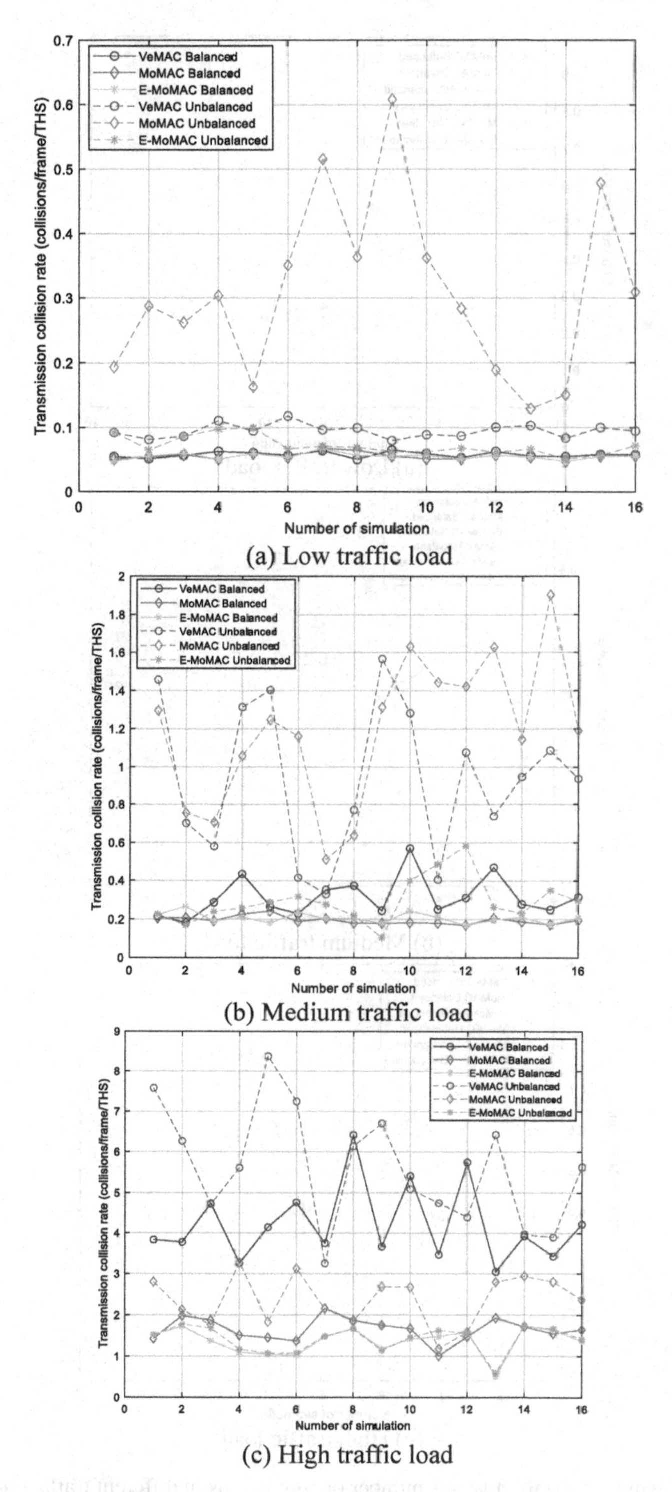

(a) Low traffic load

(b) Medium traffic load

(c) High traffic load

Fig. 9. Transmission collision rate versus number of simulations in different traffic conditions.

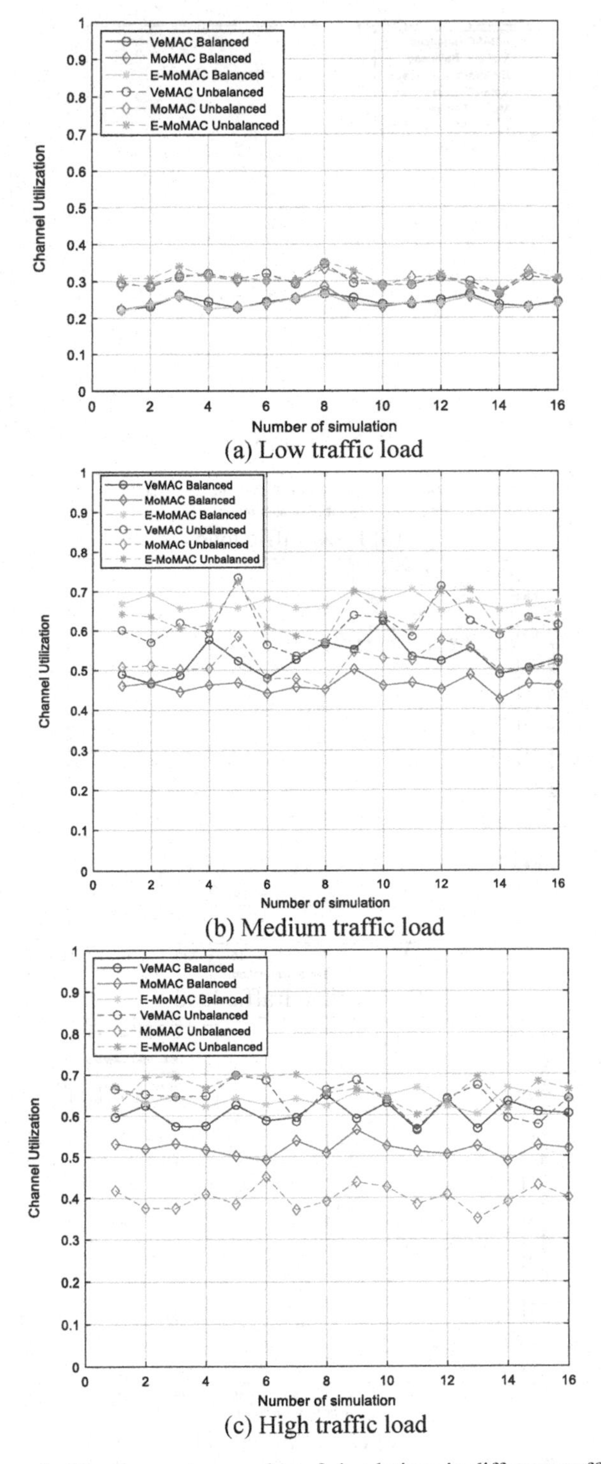

Fig. 10. Channel utilization versus number of simulations in different traffic conditions.

4 Conclusions

In this paper, in order to solve the high transmission collisions and channel resource wastage problems in unbalanced traffic conditions of VANETs, we propose an adaptive and on-demand MAC protocol for VANETs, named AODMAC. It is a fully-distributed MAC protocol based on the MoMAC. Its frame is partitioned into equal sets according to the lane numbers, and each lane has its own disjoint time slot sets for vehicles to access. In AODMAC, the partitioning of each frame is not fixed. Instead, it can be adaptively adjusted according to different traffic density in each lane. Due to each lane can acquire its slot set on-demand, AODMAC can solve the slot wastage problem in sparse lanes and the slot shortage problem in dense lanes. Thus, it is efficient in both balanced and unbalanced traffic density scenarios. Simulation results show that the proposed MAC protocol can achieve a better performance than VeMAC and MoMAC in terms of the transmission collision rate and channel utilization, especially in high traffic load and unbalanced condition. The results demonstrate the efficiency and stability of our proposed protocol.

Acknowledgments. This work was supported by the National Key R&D Program of China under Grant No. 2016YFB1200100, and the National Nature Science Foundation of China under Grant No. 91638301.

References

1. Cunha, F., et al.: Data communication in VANETs: protocols, applications and challenges. Ad Hoc Netw. **44**, 90–103 (2016)
2. Tambawal, A.B., et al.: Time division multiple access scheduling strategies for emerging vehicular ad hoc network medium access control protocols: a survey. Telecommun. Syst. **70**, 595–616 (2019)
3. Arena, F., Pau, G., Severino, A.: A review on IEEE 802.11p for intelligent transportation systems. J. Sensor Actuator Networks **9**(2), 22 (2020)
4. Zhang, R., Cheng, X., Yang, L., Shen, X., Jiao, B.: A novel centralized TDMA-based scheduling protocol for vehicular networks. IEEE Trans. Intell. Transp. Syst. **16**(1), 411–416 (2015)
5. Shahin, N., Kim, Y.-T.: An enhanced TDMA cluster-based MAC (ETCM) for multichannel vehicular networks. In: 2016 International Conference on Selected Topics in Mobile & Wireless Networking (MoWNeT), pp. 1–8. IEEE, Cairo, Egypt (2016)
6. Chaurasia, B.K., Alam, M.I., Prakash, A., Tomar, R.S., Verma, S.: MPMAC: clustering based MAC protocol for VANETs. Wireless Pers. Commun. **108**(1), 409–436 (2019)
7. Borgonovo, F., Capone, A., Cesana, M., Fratta, L.: ADHOC MAC: New MAC architecture for ad hoc networks providing efficient and reliable point-to-point and broadcast services. Wireless Netw. **10**(4), 359–366 (2004)
8. Omar, H.A., Zhuang, W., Li, L.: VeMAC: a novel multichannel MAC protocol for vehicular ad hoc networks. In: 2011 IEEE Conference on Computer Communications Workshops, INFOCOM WKSHPS 2011, pp. 413–418. IEEE, Shanghai, China (2011)
9. Omar, H.A., Zhuang, W., Li, L.: VeMAC: a TDMA-based MAC protocol for reliable broadcast in VANETs. IEEE Trans. Mob. Comput. **12**(9), 1724–1736 (2013)
10. Yang, W., Li, P., Liu, Y., Zhu, H.: Adaptive TDMA slot assignment protocol for vehicular ad-hoc networks. J. China Univ. Posts Telecommun. **20**(1), 11–25 (2013)

11. Chen, P., Zheng, J., Wu, Y.: A-VeMAC: an adaptive vehicular MAC protocol for vehicular ad hoc networks. In: 2017 IEEE International Conference on Communications (ICC), pp. 1–6. IEEE, Paris, France (2017)
12. Lyu, F., et al.: MoMAC: mobility-aware and collision-avoidance MAC for safety applications in VANETs. IEEE Trans. Veh. Technol. **67**(11), 10590–10602 (2018)
13. The network simulator OMNeT++. https://omnetpp.org/. Accessed 13 June 2020
14. The Simulation of Urban Mobility (SUMO). https://sumo.dlr.de/docs/index.html. Accessed 13 June 2020

Trajectory Design for 6-DoF Asteroid Powered Landing via Convex Optimization

Yingying Zhang(✉), Jiangchuan Huang, Yang Tian, and Hutao Cui

Harbin Institute of Technology, School of Astronautics, Harbin, China
zhangyyhit@hotmail.com, hjiangchuan@126.com,
{tianyanghit,cuiht}@hit.edu.cn

Abstract. In this paper, a trajectory design algorithm via convex optimization has been proposed for the 6-DoF asteroid powered landing problem. The main contribution is that the algorithm combines the time-optimal and the fuel-optimal trajectory optimization to give a fuel-optimal trajectory in the optimal flight time. First, two constrained nonconvex optimal control problems of the time-optimal and the fuel-optimal are proposed, then the original nonconvex continuous-time infinite dimensional problems are turned to convex discrete-time finite dimensional optimization problems through linearization and discretization of the nonlinear dynamics and the nonconvex state, control constraints. By developing the successive convexification, the final trajectory is achieved by solving a sequence of convex fuel-optimal sub-problems using the optimal flight time and the time-optimal trajectory given by solving the time-optimal optimization problem in successive manner. The validity of proposed algorithm of generating the fuel-optimal trajectory in the optimal flight time is verified through numerical simulations for landing on an irregular asteroid.

Keywords: Asteroid landing · Trajectory design · Time-optimal · Fuel-optimal · Successive convexification

1 Introduction

Landing vehicle on asteroids to obtain high resolution data and soil samples is becoming increasingly popular in recent years. In order to successfully complete the mission, the spacecraft must softly land at the intended landing site with pinpoint precision. Due to the irregular shape and high rotating speed of asteroids, as well as the communication delay from the Earth, the problem under investigation is to propose a reliable algorithm of fuel-optimal powered landing

Supported by the National Natural Science Fund of China [grant numbers 61503102, 61673057].

Q. Wu et al. (Eds.): WiSATS 2020, LNICST 358, pp. 99–115, 2021.
https://doi.org/10.1007/978-3-030-69072-4_9

trajectory design in finite time that can be rapidly computed onboard the vehicle without ground control.

The closed-loop control method for asteroid landing have been studied, including the method of tracking a predesigned cubic polynomials trajectory satisfying boundary conditions [8,9,21], the closed-loop guidance based on current state and the state of landing site [4,6,17]. Though the closed-loop control is widely used on real-time trajectory generation, the thrust constraint is not included in the control formulation. The trajectory design for asteroid landing has been posed as constrained optimal control problem, includes the indirect method and the direct method. The indirect method [5,19,20] combines the costate differential equations, the Pontryagin principle and the boundary conditions to find the optimal solution, and the method suffers from poor convergence performance. The direct method [7,10] suffers from low computation speed because the method solves the original optimal control problem by nonlinear programming (NLP). The two method are not suitable for real-time trajectory generation.

In order to improve the efficiency of trajectory optimization, the trajectory design problem is transformed into the convex optimization problem. The convex optimization problem gains the advantage of low complexity, the polynomial solution time and global convergence [14], which can be solved reliably and efficiently. The convex programming approach is first applied in powered descent guidance for Mars landing [2,3,15,16]. Especially in [15,16], the successive convexification are proposed and used for trajectory optimization of the fuel-optimal problem and free-final-time problem. The successive convexification is to solve the original non-covex optimization problem by instead solving a sequence of related convex sub-problems. In [18], convex optimization is used to rapidly generate time-optimal trajectories for asteroid landing. In [12], the successive convexification is used for fuel-optimal trajectory design for landing on irregularly shaped asteroids.

The convex optimization is well-developed and can be solved with custom solvers [11]. In this paper, we aim to propose a trajectory design algorithm that can generate a fuel-optimal trajectory in the optimal time via convex optimization. First, we formulate the time-optimal and the fuel-optimal nonconvex trajectory optimization problems, then we linearize and discretize the two problems to cast them into convex sub-problems. Lastly, we combine the time-optimal and the fuel-optimal trajectory optimization, and generate the trajectory by solving the fuel-optimal optimization problem via successive convexification using the solution of the time-optimal optimization problem solved in successive manner.

The paper is organized as follows: Sect. 2 presents the nonconvex continuous-time time-optimal and fuel-optimal trajectory optimization problems for asteroid landing, Sect. 3 presents the convexification and discretization for the two problems, and outlines the successive convexification framework, Sect. 4 presents the algorithm for generating the fuel-optimal trajectory in the optimal time and the simulation results, Sect. 5 concludes this paper.

2 Problem Formulation

2.1 The Dynamics

We consider the trajectory design problem as a optimal control problem of guiding the vehicle from the initial state to the landing site. The spacecraft is modeled as a rigid actuated by three reaction wheels and six identical thrusters rigidly mounting to its body axes with a feasible range of thrust magnitude. In order to describe the motion of the vehicle, we first define two coordinate frames: $\mathcal{F}_{\mathcal{L}}$ coordinate frame and $\mathcal{F}_{\mathcal{S}}$ coordinate frame. $\mathcal{F}_{\mathcal{L}}$ is the asteroid-fixed frame centered at the asteroid's center-of-mass $o_{\mathcal{L}}$, with its $z_{\mathcal{L}}$-axis pointing along the spin axis of the asteroid, its $x_{\mathcal{L}}$-axis pointing along the asteroid's maximum (minimum) inertial principal axis, and the $y_{\mathcal{L}}$-axis completing the right-handed system. $\mathcal{F}_{\mathcal{S}}$ is the vehicle-fixed frame centered at the vehicle's center-of-mass $o_{\mathcal{S}}$, with its $z_{\mathcal{S}}$-axis pointing along the the vehicle's maximum inertial principal axis, its $x_{\mathcal{S}}$-axis pointing along the vehicle's minimum inertial principal axis, and the $y_{\mathcal{S}}$-axis completing the right-handed system.

We assume the fuel of the vehicle depletes at a rate proportional to the magnitude of the thrust vector. Denoting the mass as $m(t)$, the control thrust as $\mathbf{T}_{\mathcal{S}}(t)$, the mass depletion is given by

$$\dot{m}(t) = -\frac{|T_{\mathcal{S},x}(t)| + |T_{\mathcal{S},y}(t)| + |T_{\mathcal{S},z}(t)|}{I_{sp} \cdot g_0} = -\frac{\|\mathbf{T}_{\mathcal{S}}(t)\|_1}{I_{sp} \cdot g_0} \tag{1}$$

where I_{sp} is the vacuum specific impulse, g_0 is the Earth's standard gravity constant.

Then we express the translational of the vehicle in the $\mathcal{F}_{\mathcal{L}}$ coordinate frame, given the position $\mathbf{r}_{\mathcal{L}}(t) \in \mathbb{R}^3$, the velocity $\mathbf{v}_{\mathcal{L}}(t) \in \mathbb{R}^3$ and the gravitation $\nabla U(\mathbf{r}) \in \mathbb{R}^3$, the translational motioncan be given by

$$\dot{\mathbf{r}}_{\mathcal{L}}(t) = \mathbf{v}_{\mathcal{L}}(t) \tag{2}$$

$$\dot{\mathbf{v}}_{\mathcal{L}}(t) = -2\boldsymbol{\omega}_e \times \mathbf{v}_{\mathcal{L}}(t) - \boldsymbol{\omega}_e \times [\boldsymbol{\omega}_e \times \mathbf{r}_{\mathcal{L}}(t)] + \frac{\mathbf{T}_{\mathcal{L}}(t)}{m} + \nabla U(\mathbf{r}) \tag{3}$$

where $\boldsymbol{\omega}_e$ and $\mathbf{T}_{\mathcal{L}}(t)$ are the rotating angular velocity vector of the asteroid and the control thrust expressed in $\mathcal{F}_{\mathcal{L}}$ coordinate frame respectively.

We use MRPs (Modified Rodrigues Parameters) $\boldsymbol{\sigma}_{\mathcal{S}/\mathcal{L}}(t) \in \mathcal{S}^3$ to describe the attitude of $\mathcal{F}_{\mathcal{L}}$ coordinate frame relative to $\mathcal{F}_{\mathcal{S}}$ coordinate frame. Given the inertia tensor$\mathbf{J} \in \mathbb{S}^3_{++}$, the angular velocity vector $\boldsymbol{\omega}_{\mathcal{S}}(t) \in \mathbb{R}^3$, the torque $\mathbf{M}_{\mathcal{S}}(t) \in \mathbb{R}^3$, the rotational motion can by given by

$$\begin{aligned} \dot{\boldsymbol{\sigma}}_{\mathcal{S}/\mathcal{L}}(t) &= \frac{1}{4}\mathbf{R}(\boldsymbol{\sigma}_{\mathcal{S}/\mathcal{L}})\boldsymbol{\omega}_{\mathcal{S}/\mathcal{L}}(t) \\ &= \frac{1}{4}\mathbf{R}(\boldsymbol{\sigma}_{\mathcal{S}/\mathcal{L}})\left[\boldsymbol{\omega}_{\mathcal{S}}(t) - \mathbf{C}_{\mathcal{S}/\mathcal{L}}\boldsymbol{\omega}_e\right] \end{aligned} \tag{4}$$

$$\mathbf{J}\dot{\boldsymbol{\omega}}_{\mathcal{S}}(t) = \mathbf{M}_{\mathcal{S}}(t) - \boldsymbol{\omega}_{\mathcal{S}}(t) \times [\mathbf{J}\boldsymbol{\omega}_{\mathcal{S}}(t)] \tag{5}$$

In Eq. (4), $\mathbf{C}_{\mathcal{S}/\mathcal{L}} \in SO(3)$ is the direction cosine matrix describing the attitude transformation from $\mathcal{F}_{\mathcal{L}}$ coordinate frame to $\mathcal{F}_{\mathcal{S}}$ coordinate frame, $\mathbf{R}(\boldsymbol{\sigma}_{\mathcal{S}/\mathcal{L}})$ and $\mathbf{C}_{\mathcal{S}/\mathcal{L}}$ are related to $\boldsymbol{\sigma}_{\mathcal{S}/\mathcal{L}}$ through the following relation

$$\mathbf{R}(\boldsymbol{\sigma}_{\mathcal{S}/\mathcal{L}}) = \begin{bmatrix} 1+\sigma_1^2-\sigma_2^2-\sigma_3^2 & 2(\sigma_1\sigma_2-\sigma_3) & 2(\sigma_1\sigma_3+\sigma_2) \\ 2(\sigma_1\sigma_2+\sigma_3) & 1-\sigma_1^2+\sigma_2^2-\sigma_3^2 & 2(\sigma_2\sigma_3-\sigma_1) \\ 2(\sigma_1\sigma_3-\sigma_2) & 2(\sigma_2\sigma_3+\sigma_1) & 1-\sigma_1^2-\sigma_2^2+\sigma_3^2 \end{bmatrix} \tag{6}$$

$$\mathbf{C}_{\mathcal{S}/\mathcal{L}} = \mathbf{E}_3 - \frac{4\left(1-\boldsymbol{\sigma}_{\mathcal{S}/\mathcal{L}}^T\boldsymbol{\sigma}_{\mathcal{S}/\mathcal{L}}\right)\left[\boldsymbol{\sigma}_{\mathcal{S}/\mathcal{L}}\right]^{\times} - 8\left(\left[\boldsymbol{\sigma}_{\mathcal{S}/\mathcal{L}}\right]^{\times}\right)^2}{\left(1+\boldsymbol{\sigma}_{\mathcal{S}/\mathcal{L}}^T\boldsymbol{\sigma}_{\mathcal{S}/\mathcal{L}}\right)^2} \tag{7}$$

where $\boldsymbol{\sigma}_{\mathcal{S}/\mathcal{L}} = [\sigma_1,\ \sigma_2,\ \sigma_3]^T$, $[\boldsymbol{\sigma}_{\mathcal{SL}}]^{\times} = \begin{bmatrix} 0 & -\sigma_3 & \sigma_2 \\ \sigma_3 & 0 & -\sigma_1 \\ -\sigma_2 & \sigma_1 & 0 \end{bmatrix}$ is the skew-symmetric matric.

With the direction cosine matrix, we can give the relation of control thrust $\mathbf{T}_{\mathcal{L}}(t)$ and $\mathbf{T}_{\mathcal{S}}(t)$, that is

$$\mathbf{T}_{\mathcal{L}}(t) = \mathbf{C}_{\mathcal{L}/\mathcal{S}}\mathbf{T}_{\mathcal{S}}(t) = \mathbf{C}_{\mathcal{S}/\mathcal{L}}^{-1}\mathbf{T}_{\mathcal{S}}(t) = \mathbf{C}_{\mathcal{S}/\mathcal{L}}^{T}\mathbf{T}_{\mathcal{S}}(t) \tag{8}$$

2.2 The State and Control Constraints

Since the asteroid is rotating and irregular-shaped, specific constraint must be imposed to avoid undesired collisions with the asteroid. Considering the possible complex terrain around the landing site, a glide-slope constraint that restricts the vehicle to fly in a cone with a cone angle of θ can meet the requirement of avoiding collisions, then the glide-slope constraint can be given by

$$cos\theta \le \frac{\left[\mathbf{r}_{\mathcal{L}}(t) - \mathbf{r}_{tf}\right]^T \mathbf{n}_{tf}}{\|\mathbf{r}_{\mathcal{L}}(t) - \mathbf{r}_{tf}\|} \tag{9}$$

where $\mathbf{r}_{tf}$ is the landing site position, $\mathbf{n}_{tf}$ is the normal vector pointing outside the asteroid, both of them are expressed in $\mathcal{F}_{\mathcal{L}}$ coordinate frame.

Furthermore, in order to fulfill the goal of pinpoint landing, we hope the optical camera on the vehicle can track the landing site during the landing process, therefore, a FOV constraint which keeps the landing site within the FOV (field-of view) of the vehicle is introduced. Given the FOV angle β, the installation position vector of vision sensor $\boldsymbol{\rho}_{\mathcal{S}}$, and the line-of-sight direction $\mathbf{d}_{\mathcal{S}}$, the FOV constraint can be given by

$$cos\beta \le \frac{\left[-\mathbf{C}_{\mathcal{S}/\mathcal{L}}(\mathbf{r}_{\mathcal{L}}(t) - \mathbf{r}_{tf}) - \boldsymbol{\rho}_{\mathcal{S}}\right]^T \mathbf{d}_{\mathcal{S}}}{\| - \mathbf{C}_{\mathcal{S}/\mathcal{L}}(\mathbf{r}_{\mathcal{L}}(t) - \mathbf{r}_{tf}) - \boldsymbol{\rho}_{\mathcal{S}}\|\|\mathbf{d}_{\mathcal{S}}\|} \tag{10}$$

Moreover, we must keep the mass of the vehicle always remains above the dry mass m_{dry}, the mass constraint is given as

$$m_{dry} \le m(t) \tag{11}$$

For the control constraint, the magnitude of thrust vector is constrained to lie within the interval $[T_{min}, T_{max}]$, while the magnitude of torque is constrained to less then M_{max}, thus the control can be given by

$$T_{min} \leq \|\mathbf{T}_{\mathcal{S}}(t)\|_{\infty} \leq T_{max} \tag{12}$$

$$\|\mathbf{M}_{\mathcal{S}}(t)\|_{\infty} \leq M_{max} \tag{13}$$

2.3 Problem Statement

For the trajectory design problem for asteroid powered landing, we can emphasize the problem as a nonconvex continuous-time free-final-time problem to achieve the trajectory of the optimal flight time t_f, the time-optimal cost function can be given by

$$\underset{t_f,\ \mathbf{T}_{\mathcal{S}}}{minimize}\ t_f \tag{14}$$

If the flight time t_f can be estimated in advance, we can emphasize the problem as a nonconvex continuous-time two-point boundary problem to achieve the fuel-optimal trajectory during the time interval $[0,\ t_f]$. Noted that the fuel consumption is the mass variation, so the fuel-optimal cost function is given by

$$\underset{\mathbf{T}_{\mathcal{S}}}{minimize} \int_0^{t_f} \alpha \|\mathbf{T}_{\mathcal{S}}(t)\|_1\, dt \tag{15}$$

where $\alpha = \frac{1}{I_{sp} \cdot g_0}$ is a constant.

Both the time-optimal optimization problem and the fuel-optimal optimization problem are subject to the dynamics in Eqs. (2–6), the state and control constraint in Eqs. (9–13), and the boundary conditions as below.

$$\mathbf{r}_{\mathcal{L}}(0) = \mathbf{r}_0,\ \mathbf{v}_{\mathcal{L}}(0) = \mathbf{v}_0,\ \boldsymbol{\sigma}_{\mathcal{S}/\mathcal{L}}(0) = \boldsymbol{\sigma}_0,\ \boldsymbol{\omega}_{\mathcal{S}}(0) = \boldsymbol{\omega}_0,\ m(0) = m_{init} \tag{16}$$

$$\mathbf{r}_{\mathcal{L}}(t_f) = \mathbf{r}_{tf},\ \mathbf{v}_{\mathcal{L}}(t_f) = \mathbf{v}_{tf},\ \boldsymbol{\sigma}_{\mathcal{S}/\mathcal{L}}(t_f) = \boldsymbol{\sigma}_{tf},\ \boldsymbol{\omega}_{\mathcal{S}}(t_f) = \boldsymbol{\omega}_{tf},\ m_{dry} \leq m(t_f) \tag{17}$$

where $[\mathbf{r}_0,\ \mathbf{v}_0,\ \boldsymbol{\sigma}_0, \boldsymbol{\omega}_0]$ is the initial state, $[\mathbf{r}_{tf},\ \mathbf{v}_{tf},\ \boldsymbol{\sigma}_{tf}, \boldsymbol{\omega}_{tf}]$ is the terminal state.

3 Convex Formulation

In the section, we develop convex formulation for the time-optimal and fuel-optimal nonconvex optimization problems. Since both the two problems are nonconvex continuous-time infinite dimensional optimization problems, we must cast the original problems into a convex discrete-time finite dimensional optimization problem through convexification and discretization, then the convex problem is used as the sub-problem solved in successive manner to draw the optimal trajectory.

3.1 Convexification

Since the non-convexity of the original problem is mainly caused by the non-linearity of dynamics and the FOV constraint, we take the way of linearization of dynamics and the FOV constraint to do convexification. First, we define the state vector $\mathbf{x}(t) = \left[\mathbf{r}_{\mathcal{L}}(t)^T,\ \mathbf{v}_{\mathcal{L}}(t)^T,\ \boldsymbol{\omega}_{\mathcal{S}}(t)^T,\ \boldsymbol{\sigma}_{\mathcal{S}/\mathcal{L}}(t)^T\right]^T \in \mathbb{R}^{12}$ and control vector $\mathbf{u}(t) = \left[\mathbf{T}_{\mathcal{S}}(t)^T,\ \mathbf{M}_{\mathcal{S}}(t)^T\right]^T \in \mathbb{R}^6$, so we the express the dynamics in Eqs. (3–6) to the as the vector-valued function by

$$\frac{d\mathbf{x}(t)}{dt} = X\left[\mathbf{x}(t), \mathbf{u}(t)\right] = \left[\dot{\mathbf{r}}_{\mathcal{L}}(t)^T,\ \dot{\mathbf{v}}_{\mathcal{L}}(t)^T,\ \dot{\boldsymbol{\omega}}_{\mathcal{S}}(t)^T, \dot{\boldsymbol{\sigma}}_{\mathcal{S}/\mathcal{L}}(t)^T\right]^T \tag{18}$$

Given a reference trajectory including the state, the control and the mass $\{\hat{\mathbf{x}}(t),\ \hat{\mathbf{u}}(t),\ \hat{m}(t)\}$, we can linearize Eq. (18) with first-order Taylor expansion directly for the fuel optimal problem. The linearized system for the fuel-optimal optimization problem can given as

$$\begin{aligned} \dot{\mathbf{x}}(t) &= \mathbf{A}(\hat{\mathbf{x}}, \hat{\mathbf{u}})\mathbf{x}(t) + \mathbf{B}(\hat{\mathbf{x}}, \hat{\mathbf{u}})\mathbf{u}(t) + \mathbf{C}(\hat{\mathbf{x}}, \hat{\mathbf{u}}) \\ \mathbf{A}(\hat{\mathbf{x}}, \hat{\mathbf{u}}) &= \frac{\partial X\left(\mathbf{x}, \mathbf{u}\right)}{\partial \mathbf{x}}\big|_{\hat{\mathbf{x}},\hat{\mathbf{u}}} \in \mathbb{R}^{12\times 12} \\ \mathbf{B}(\hat{\mathbf{x}}, \hat{\mathbf{u}}) &= \frac{\partial X\left(\mathbf{x}, \mathbf{u}\right)}{\partial \mathbf{u}}\big|_{\hat{\mathbf{x}},\hat{\mathbf{u}}} \in \mathbb{R}^{12\times 6} \\ \mathbf{C}(\hat{\mathbf{x}}, \hat{\mathbf{u}}) &= X\left(\hat{\mathbf{x}}, \hat{\mathbf{u}}\right) - \mathbf{A}(\hat{\mathbf{x}}, \hat{\mathbf{u}})\hat{\mathbf{x}} - \mathbf{B}(\hat{\mathbf{x}}, \hat{\mathbf{u}})\hat{\mathbf{u}} \in \mathbb{R}^{12} \end{aligned} \tag{19}$$

For the time-optimal optimization problem, since the flight time t_f is unknown, we cast Eq. (18) in terms of normalized trajectory time $\tau = \frac{t}{t_f} \in [0, 1]$. Applying the chain rule to the left side of Eq. (18), we can obtain

$$\frac{d\mathbf{x}(t)}{dt} = \frac{d\mathbf{x}(t)}{d\tau}\frac{d\tau}{dt} \tag{20}$$

We define the time dilation between τ and t as λ, where $\lambda \triangleq \frac{dt}{d\tau}$, so the Eq. (20) turns to

$$\dot{\mathbf{x}}(\tau) = \frac{d\mathbf{x}(\tau)}{d\tau} = \lambda X\left[\mathbf{x}(\tau), \mathbf{u}(\tau)\right] \tag{21}$$

Given a reference trajectory including the state, the control, the mass and the time dilation $\left\{\hat{\mathbf{x}}(t),\ \hat{\mathbf{u}}(t),\ \hat{m}(t),\ \hat{\lambda}\right\}$ for the time-optimal optimization problem, we approximate Eq. (21) by first-order Taylor expansion, the linearized dynamics for the time-optimal optimization problem can given as

$$\begin{aligned} \dot{\mathbf{x}}(\tau) &= \mathbf{G}_{\lambda}(\tau)\lambda + \mathbf{G}_{x}(\tau)\mathbf{x}(\tau) + \mathbf{G}_{u}(\tau)\mathbf{u}(\tau) + \mathbf{G}_{c}(\tau) \\ \mathbf{G}_{\lambda}(\tau) &= f\left[\hat{\mathbf{x}}(\tau), \hat{\mathbf{u}}(\tau)\right] \in \mathbb{R}^{12} \\ \mathbf{G}_{x}(\tau) &= \hat{\lambda}\frac{\partial f\left(\mathbf{x}, \mathbf{u}\right)}{\partial \mathbf{x}}\big|_{\hat{\mathbf{x}}(\tau),\hat{\mathbf{u}}(\tau)} \in \mathbb{R}^{12\times 12} \\ \mathbf{G}_{u}(\tau) &= \hat{\lambda}\frac{\partial f\left(\mathbf{x}, \mathbf{u}\right)}{\partial \mathbf{u}}\big|_{\hat{\mathbf{x}}(\tau),\hat{\mathbf{u}}(\tau)} \in \mathbb{R}^{12\times 6} \\ \mathbf{G}_{c}(\tau) &= -\mathbf{G}_{x}(\tau)\hat{\mathbf{x}}(\tau) - \mathbf{G}_{u}(\tau)\hat{\mathbf{u}}(\tau) \in \mathbb{R}^{12} \end{aligned} \tag{22}$$

By the definition of the time dilation λ, we can get $\lambda = t_f$, so the time-optimal cost function in Eq. (14) turns to

$$\underset{\lambda,\ \mathbf{T}_{\mathcal{S}}}{minimize}\ \lambda \tag{23}$$

For the glide-slope constraint and the FOV constraint, they can be expressed as the following equivalent form

$$\|\mathbf{C}_e\mathbf{x}(t) - \mathbf{C}_e\mathbf{x}_{tf}\| \leq \frac{\mathbf{n}_{tf}^T\mathbf{C}_e}{cos\theta}\left[\mathbf{x}(t) - \mathbf{x}_{tf}\right] \tag{24}$$

$$\|\mathbf{C}_{\mathcal{S}/\mathcal{L}}\mathbf{C}_e(\mathbf{r}(t) - \mathbf{r}_{tf}) + \boldsymbol{\rho}_{\mathcal{S}}\| + \frac{\mathbf{d}_{\mathcal{S}}^T}{cos\beta\|\mathbf{d}_{\mathcal{S}}\|}\left[\mathbf{C}_{\mathcal{S}/\mathcal{L}}\mathbf{C}_e(\mathbf{r}(t) - \mathbf{r}_{tf}) + \boldsymbol{\rho}_{\mathcal{S}}\right] \leq 0 \tag{25}$$

where $\mathbf{C}_e = [\mathbf{E}_3,\ \mathbf{0}_{3\times9}] \in \mathbb{R}^{3\times12}$, $\mathbf{x}_{tf} = \left[\mathbf{r}_{tf}^T,\ \mathbf{v}_{tf}^T,\ \boldsymbol{\sigma}_{tf}^T, \boldsymbol{\omega}_{tf}^T\right]^T$ is the terminal state.

For the fuel-optimal optimization problem, the glide-slope constraint in Eq. (24) is in the convex form of second-order cone, but the FOV constraint in Eq. (25) is nonlinear, so we linearize the left side of Eq. (25) by first-order Taylor expansion to make it convex, that we have

$$q(\hat{\mathbf{x}})'\,\mathbf{x}(t) + q(\hat{\mathbf{x}}) - q(\hat{\mathbf{x}})'\,\hat{\mathbf{x}}(t) \leq 0 \tag{26}$$

$$\begin{aligned}
q(\mathbf{x}) &= \|f(\mathbf{x})\| + \frac{\mathbf{d}_{\mathcal{S}}^T}{cos\beta\|\mathbf{d}_{\mathcal{S}}\|}f(\mathbf{x}) \in \mathbb{R}\\
q(\mathbf{x})' &= \frac{f(\mathbf{x})^T}{\|f(\mathbf{x})\|}f(\mathbf{x})' + \frac{\mathbf{d}_{\mathcal{S}}^T}{cos\beta\|\mathbf{d}_{\mathcal{S}}\|}f(\mathbf{x})' \in \mathbb{R}^{1\times12}\\
f(\mathbf{x}) &= \mathbf{C}_{\mathcal{S}/\mathcal{L}}\mathbf{C}_e\mathbf{x}(t) - \mathbf{C}_{\mathcal{S}/\mathcal{L}}\mathbf{C}_e\mathbf{x}_{tf} + \boldsymbol{\rho}_{\mathcal{S}} \in \mathbb{R}^3\\
f(\mathbf{x})' &= \mathbf{C}_{\mathcal{S}/\mathcal{L}}\mathbf{C}_e + \frac{\partial\left[\mathbf{C}_{\mathcal{S}/\mathcal{L}}\mathbf{C}_e\mathbf{x}(t)\right]}{\partial\boldsymbol{\sigma}}\mathbf{C}_\sigma \in \mathbb{R}^{3\times12}
\end{aligned}$$

where $\mathbf{C}_\sigma = [\mathbf{0}_{3\times9},\ \mathbf{E}_3] \in \mathbb{R}^{3\times12}$.

For the time-optimal optimization problem, the glide-slope constraint and FOV constraint share the same form in Eqs. (25) and (26), we just need replace t with τ.

For the control constraint, the left side of Eq. (12) $T_{min} \leq \|\mathbf{T}_{\mathcal{S}}(t)\|_\infty$ is nonconvex. Given $\hat{\mathbf{T}}_{\mathcal{S}}(t) \in \hat{\mathbf{u}}(t)$, we can use the following convex relation for the thrust constraint.

$$T_{min} \leq \frac{\hat{T}_{\mathcal{S},j}(t)}{|\hat{T}_{\mathcal{S},j}(t)|}T_{s,j}(t) \leq T_{max} \quad j = x, y, z \tag{27}$$

where $\mathbf{T}_{\mathcal{S}}(t) = \left[T_{s,x}(t),\ T_{s,y}(t), T_{s,z}(t)\right]^T$.

3.2 Successive Convexification

After convexification for the original problems, they have been turned to convex optimization problems. The convex problem can be regarded as a sub-problem solved in successive convexification process, so we can we indirectly solve the original nonconvex optimization problems by instead solving a sequence of related convex sub-problems, and the sub-problem in each iteration can be solved by second-order cone programming. First, we do discretization for the time-optimal and the fuel-optimal convex optimization problems.

For the fuel-optimal optimization problem, we discretize the time domain $t \in [0,\ t_f]$ into N equal intervals with the time increment Δt, the temporal nodes are

$$t_k = k\Delta t,\ k = 0, 1, 2, ..., N \tag{28}$$

We conduct the zero-order-hold control in each discrete time interval, and denote $\mathbf{x}(k) = \mathbf{x}(t_k)$, $\mathbf{u}(k) = \mathbf{u}(t_k)$, $m(k) = m(t_k)$. Denoting the ith iteration in the successive convexification by superscript i, we replace the reference trajectory $\{\hat{\mathbf{x}}(t),\ \hat{\mathbf{u}}(t),\ \hat{m}(t)\}$ with $i-1^{th}$ successive solution $\{\mathbf{x}^{i-1}(k),\ \mathbf{u}^{i-1}(k),\ m^{i-1}(k)\}$, then the discrete-time mass depletion and dynamics for the fuel-optimal optimization problem can be given by

$$m^{i-1}(k+1) = m^{i-1}(k) - \alpha\|\mathbf{T}_S^{i-1}(k)\|_1 \Delta t \tag{29}$$

$$\mathbf{x}^i(k+1) = \bar{\mathbf{A}}^i(k)\mathbf{x}^i(k) + \bar{\mathbf{B}}^i(k)\mathbf{u}^i(k) + \bar{\mathbf{C}}^i(k) \tag{30}$$

$$\begin{aligned} \bar{\mathbf{A}}^i(k) &= \phi_A(\Delta t) = e^{\Delta t \mathbf{A}(\mathbf{x}^{i-1}, \mathbf{u}^{i-1})} \\ \bar{\mathbf{B}}^i(k) &= \int_0^{\Delta t} \phi_A(\Delta t - \xi)\mathbf{B}(\mathbf{x}^{i-1}, \mathbf{u}^{i-1})\, d\xi \\ \bar{\mathbf{C}}^i(k) &= \int_0^{\Delta t} \phi_A(\Delta t - \xi)\mathbf{C}(\mathbf{x}^{i-1}, \mathbf{u}^{i-1})\, d\xi \end{aligned}$$

The discretized cost function for the fuel-optimal optimaization problem turns to

$$\underset{\mathbf{T}_S}{minimize} \sum_{k=0}^{N-1} \alpha\|\mathbf{T}_S^i(k)\|_1 \Delta t \tag{31}$$

For the time-optimal optimization problem, we discretize the normalized time domain $\tau \in [0,\ 1]$ into N equal intervals, the temporal nodes are

$$\tau_k = \frac{k}{N},\ k = 0, 1, 2, ..., N \tag{32}$$

Denoting $\mathbf{x}(k) = \mathbf{x}(\tau_k)$, $\mathbf{u}(k) = \mathbf{u}(\tau_k)$ and $m(k) = m(\tau_k)$, and replacing the reference trajectory $\left\{\hat{\mathbf{x}}(t),\ \hat{\mathbf{u}}(t),\ \hat{m}(t),\ \hat{\lambda}\right\}$ with $\{\mathbf{x}^{i-1}(k), \mathbf{u}^{i-1}(k), m^{i-1}(k), \lambda^{i-1}\}$, the discrete-time mass depletion dynamics for the time-optimal optimization problem can be given by

$$m^{i-1}(k+1) = m^{i-1}(k) - \frac{\lambda^{i-1}}{N}\alpha\|\mathbf{T}_S^{i-1}(k)\|_1 \tag{33}$$

$$\begin{aligned}
\mathbf{x}^i(k+1) &= \bar{\mathbf{G}}_x^i(k)\mathbf{x}^i(k) + \bar{\mathbf{G}}_u^i(k)\mathbf{u}^i(k) + \bar{\mathbf{G}}_\lambda^i(k)\lambda^i + \bar{\mathbf{G}}_c^i(k) \\
\bar{\mathbf{G}}_x^i(k) &= \bar{\phi}(\tau_{k+1} - \tau_k) = e^{(\tau_{k+1}-\tau_k)\mathbf{G}_x^{i-1}(k)} \\
\bar{\mathbf{G}}_u^i(k) &= \int_{\tau_k}^{\tau_{k+1}} \bar{\phi}(\tau_{k+1} - \xi) G_u^{i-1}(k)\, d\xi \\
\bar{\mathbf{G}}_\lambda^i(k) &= \int_{\tau_k}^{\tau_{k+1}} \bar{\phi}(\tau_{k+1} - \xi) G_\lambda^{i-1}(k)\, d\xi \\
\bar{\mathbf{G}}_c^i(k) &= \int_{\tau_k}^{\tau_{k+1}} \bar{\phi}(\tau_{k+1} - \xi) G_c^{i-1}(k)\, d\xi
\end{aligned} \tag{34}$$

The discrete-time state constraints and control constraints for both the fuel-optimal and the time-optimal optimization problems share the following relation.

$$\|\mathbf{C}_e\mathbf{x}^i(k) - \mathbf{C}_e\mathbf{x}^i(N)\| \leq \frac{\mathbf{n}_{tf}^T\mathbf{C}_e}{cos\theta}\left[\mathbf{x}^i(k) - \mathbf{x}^i(N)\right] \tag{35}$$

$$q\left[\mathbf{x}^{i-1}(k)\right]'\mathbf{x}^i(k) + q\left[\mathbf{x}^{i-1}(k)\right] - q\left[\mathbf{x}^{i-1}(k)\right]'\mathbf{x}^{i-1}(k) \leq 0 \tag{36}$$

$$T_{min} \leq \frac{T_{\mathcal{S},j}^{i-1}(k)}{|T_{\mathcal{S},j}^{i-1}(k)|} T_{\mathcal{S},j}^i(k) \leq T_{max} \quad j = x, y, z \tag{37}$$

$$\|\mathbf{M}_{\mathcal{S}}^i(k)\|_\infty \leq M_{max} \tag{38}$$

where $\mathbf{x}^i(N)$ is the terminal state.

In addition, in order to make the successive convexification work, we must ensure that the problem remains bounded and feasible throughout sequence iteration. Therefore, we introduce virtual control and trust regions.

The virtual control is used to eliminate the artificial infeasibility caussed by the linearization for the dynamics and the FOV constraint, we augment virtual control $\mathbf{V}_x^i(k) \in \mathbb{R}^{12}$ and $V_f^i(k) \in \mathbb{R}_+$ to the dynamics in Eqs. (30, 34) and constrains in Eq. (36), we can obtain

$$\mathbf{x}^i(k+1) = \bar{\mathbf{A}}^i(k)\mathbf{x}^i(k) + \bar{\mathbf{B}}^i(k)\mathbf{u}^i(k) + \bar{\mathbf{C}}^i(k) + \mathbf{V}_x^i(k) \tag{39}$$

$$\mathbf{x}^i(k+1) = \bar{\mathbf{G}}_x^i(k)\mathbf{x}^i(k) + \bar{\mathbf{G}}_u^i(k)\mathbf{u}^i(k) + \bar{\mathbf{G}}_\lambda^i(k)\lambda^i + \bar{\mathbf{G}}_c^i(k) + \mathbf{V}_x^i(k) \tag{40}$$

$$q\left[\mathbf{x}^{i-1}(k)\right]'\mathbf{x}^i(k) + q\left[\mathbf{x}^{i-1}(k)\right] - q\left[\mathbf{x}^{i-1}(k)\right]'\mathbf{x}^{i-1}(k) \leq V_f^i(k), \quad V_f^i(k) \geq 0 \tag{41}$$

The trust regions is to ensure the linearization can capture the nonlinearity of the original problems and keep the problem remain bounded, which make the trajectory not significantly deviate from the previous iteration. To do so, we first define the state deviation between the ith iteration and the $i-1^{th}$ iteration as

$$\delta\mathbf{x}_k^i = \mathbf{x}^i(k) - \mathbf{x}^{i-1}(k) \tag{42}$$

Then we introduce the following constraint

$$\left[\delta\mathbf{x}_k^i\right]^T \delta\mathbf{x}_k^i \leq \Delta_k^i \tag{43}$$

where $\Delta_k^i \in \mathbb{R}_+$ is the square of the trust region radius, the corresponding trust region center is located at $\mathbf{x}^{i-1}(k)$.

Adding the penalty term about trust regions and virtual control to the cost function in Eq. (23) and (31), we can obtain

$$\underset{\lambda,\ \mathbf{T}}{minimize}\ \ J^i[\lambda] = \lambda^i + W_x\|\mathbf{V}_x^i\|_1 + W_f\|\mathbf{V}_f^i\|_1 + W_\Delta\|\boldsymbol{\Delta}^i\|_1 \tag{44}$$

$$\underset{\mathbf{T}}{minimize}\ J^i[\mathbf{T}(k)] = \alpha\|\mathbf{T}^i\|_1\Delta t + W_x\|\mathbf{V}_x^i\|_1 + W_f\|\mathbf{V}_f^i\|_1 + W_\Delta\|\boldsymbol{\Delta}^i\|_1 \tag{45}$$

where $\mathbf{T}^i = \left[\mathbf{T}_\mathcal{S}^i(0)^T, \ldots, \mathbf{T}_\mathcal{S}^i(N-1)^T\right]^T$, $\mathbf{V}_x^i = \left[\mathbf{V}_x^i(0)^T, \ldots, \mathbf{V}_x^i(N-1)^T\right]^T$, and $\mathbf{V}_f^i = \left[V_f^i(0)\ , \ldots, V_f^i(N)\right]^T$, $\boldsymbol{\Delta}^i = \left[\Delta_0^i\ , \ldots, \Delta_k^i\ , \ldots, \Delta_N^i\right]^T$, W_x and W_f are the weight for virtual controls, W_Δ is the weight for the trust region.

3.3 Convex Sub-problem

In this section, we summarize the convex sub-problem which is solved repeatedly by the successive convexification method for the time-optimal and the fuel-optimal optimization problems. The summary of the convex subproblem is provided as below.

Problem 1. Convex discrete-time time-optimal convex optimization subproblem

$$\underset{\lambda,\ \mathbf{T}}{minimize}\ \ J^i[\lambda] = \lambda^i + W_x\|\mathbf{V}_x^i\|_1 + W_f\|\mathbf{V}_f^i\|_1 + W_\Delta\|\boldsymbol{\Delta}^i\|_1$$

subject to

$$m^{i-1}(k+1) = m^{i-1}(k) - \frac{\lambda^{i-1}}{N}\alpha\|\mathbf{T}_\mathcal{S}^{i-1}(k)\|_1$$

$$\mathbf{x}^i(k+1) = \bar{\mathbf{G}}_x^i(k)\mathbf{x}^i(k) + \bar{\mathbf{G}}_u^i(k)\mathbf{u}^i(k) + \bar{\mathbf{G}}_\lambda^i(k)\lambda^i + \bar{\mathbf{G}}_c^i(k) + \mathbf{V}_x^i(k)$$

$$\|\mathbf{C}_e\mathbf{x}^i(k) - \mathbf{C}_e\mathbf{x}^i(N)\| \le \frac{\mathbf{n}_{tf}^T\mathbf{C}_e}{cos\theta}\left[\mathbf{x}^i(k) - \mathbf{x}^i(N)\right]$$

$$q\left[\mathbf{x}^{i-1}(k)\right]'\mathbf{x}^i(k) + q\left[\mathbf{x}^{i-1}(k)\right] - q\left[\mathbf{x}^{i-1}(k)\right]'\mathbf{x}^{i-1}(k) \le V_f^i(k), \quad V_f^i(k) \ge 0$$

$$\left[\delta\mathbf{x}_k^i\right]^T\delta\mathbf{x}_k^i \le \Delta_k^i \qquad \|\mathbf{M}_\mathcal{S}^i(k)\|_\infty \le M_{max}$$

$$T_{min} \le \frac{T_{\mathcal{S},j}^{i-1}(k)}{|T_{\mathcal{S},j}^{i-1}(k)|}T_{\mathcal{S},j}^i(k) \le T_{max} \quad j = x, y, z$$

$$m^i(0) = m_{init} \quad \mathbf{x}^i(0) = \left[\mathbf{r}_0^T,\ \mathbf{v}_0^T,\ \boldsymbol{\omega}_0^T,\ \boldsymbol{\sigma}_0^T\right]^T \tag{46}$$

$$m_{dry} \le m^i(N) \quad \mathbf{x}^i(N) = \left[\mathbf{r}_{tf}^T,\ \mathbf{v}_{tf}^T,\ \boldsymbol{\omega}_{tf}^T,\ \boldsymbol{\sigma}_{tf}^T\right]^T \tag{47}$$

Problem 2. Convex discrete-time fuel-optimal convex optimization subproblem

$$\underset{\mathbf{T}}{minimize}\ J^i[\mathbf{T}(k)] = \alpha\|\mathbf{T}^i\|_1\Delta t + W_x\|\mathbf{V}_x^i\|_1 + W_f\|\mathbf{V}_f^i\|_1 + W_\Delta\|\boldsymbol{\Delta}^i\|_1$$

subject to

$$m^{i-1}(k+1) = m^{i-1}(k) - \alpha\|\mathbf{T}_{\mathcal{S}}^{i-1}(k)\|_1 \Delta t$$

$$\mathbf{x}^i(k+1) = \bar{\mathbf{A}}^i(k)\mathbf{x}^i(k) + \bar{\mathbf{B}}^i(k)\mathbf{u}^i(k) + \bar{\mathbf{C}}^i(k) + \mathbf{V}_x^i(k)$$

$$\|\mathbf{C}_e\mathbf{x}^i(k) - \mathbf{C}_e\mathbf{x}^i(N)\| \le \frac{\mathbf{n}_{tf}^T\mathbf{C}_e}{cos\theta}\left[\mathbf{x}^i(k) - \mathbf{x}^i(N)\right]$$

$$q\left[\mathbf{x}^{i-1}(k)\right]'\mathbf{x}^i(k) + q\left[\mathbf{x}^{i-1}(k)\right] - q\left[\mathbf{x}^{i-1}(k)\right]'\mathbf{x}^{i-1}(k) \le V_f^i(k), \quad V_f^i(k) \ge 0$$

$$\left[\delta\mathbf{x}_k^i\right]^T \delta\mathbf{x}_k^i \le \Delta_k^i \qquad \|\mathbf{M}_{\mathcal{S}}^i(k)\|_\infty \le M_{max}$$

$$T_{min} \le \frac{T_{\mathcal{S},j}^{i-1}(k)}{|T_{\mathcal{S},j}^{i-1}(k)|} T_{\mathcal{S},j}^i(k) \le T_{max} \quad j = x, y, z$$

$$m^i(0) = m_{init} \quad \mathbf{x}^i(0) = \left[\mathbf{r}_0^T, \mathbf{v}_0^T, \boldsymbol{\omega}_0^T, \boldsymbol{\sigma}_0^T\right]^T$$

$$m_{dry} \le m^i(N) \quad \mathbf{x}^i(N) = \left[\mathbf{r}_{tf}^T, \mathbf{v}_{tf}^T, \boldsymbol{\omega}_{tf}^T, \boldsymbol{\sigma}_{tf}^T\right]^T$$

where Eqs. (46) and (47) are the discrete boundary condition to be enforced in each iteration.

3.4 Algorithm

In this paper, we propose two problems, the time-optimal convex optimization problem and the fuel-optimal optimization problem. The fuel-optimal optimization problem is assumed to be a fixed flight time optimization problem, that means the algorithm should determine the optimal flight time t_f which yields minimum fuel consumption over the landing process. The algorithm for solving the time-optimal optimization problem can provide the estimation of the optimal flight time, so we combine the time-optimal optimization and the fuel-optimal optimization for trajectory design. First, we solve the convex discrete-time time-optimal optimization sub-problem (Problem 1) in the successive manner to give the optimal flight time λ and the time-optimal trajectory. The flight time for the fuel-optimal optimization problem is $t_f = \lambda$. Making the obtained time-optimal trajectory as the initial reference trajectory, then the fuel-optimal trajectory is achieved by solving the convex discrete-time fuel-optimal convex optimization sub-problem (Problem 2) through successive convexification. The algorithm is shown in Algorithm 1.

Algorithm 1. Algorithm for asteroid landing trajectory design

---

(i) **Initialization**
Input the vehicle parameters, the initial condition $\left[\mathbf{r}_0^T, \mathbf{v}_0^T, \boldsymbol{\omega}_0^T, \boldsymbol{\sigma}_0^T\right]^T$ and the terminal condition $\left[\mathbf{r}_{tf}^T, \mathbf{v}_{tf}^T, \boldsymbol{\omega}_{tf}^T, \boldsymbol{\sigma}_{tf}^T\right]^T$, the initial reference trajectory $\{\mathbf{x}^0(k), \mathbf{u}^0(k), m^0(k), \lambda^0\}$, the maximum iteration number N_{iter} and an acceptable state trajectory deviation ε_x.

(ii) **Successive Optimization Loop**

a) Calculate the coefficient matrices $\bar{\mathbf{G}}_x^0(k)$, $\bar{\mathbf{G}}_u^0(k)$, $\bar{\mathbf{G}}_\lambda^0(k)$, $\bar{\mathbf{G}}_c^0(k)$, $q\left[\mathbf{x}^0(k)\right]'$, $q\left[\mathbf{x}^0(k)\right]$ by using Eqs. (22, 26, 34), then compute $\mathbf{x}^1(k)$ and all the state constraints that $\mathbf{x}^1(k)$ needs to satisfy in Eqs. (35, 37, 38, 40, 41) with $\{\mathbf{x}^0(k), \mathbf{u}^0(k), m^0(k), \lambda^0\}$.

If $i \leq N_{iter}$ $(i \geq 1)$

If $\|\delta\mathbf{x}^i\|_\infty \geq \varepsilon_x$

(1) solve Problem 1 and compute $J^i[\lambda]$ by convex optimization
(2) store the successive solution $\{\mathbf{x}^i(k), \mathbf{u}^i(k), \lambda\}$ compute $m^i(k)$ by using Eq. (33).
(3) make $\mathbf{x}^i(k)$, $\mathbf{u}^i(k)$, $m^i(k)$, λ^i be the new reference trajectory $\hat{\mathbf{x}}(t)$, $\hat{\mathbf{u}}(t)$, $\hat{m}(t)$, $\hat{\lambda}$, then calculate the coefficient matrices $\bar{\mathbf{G}}_x^i(k)$, $\bar{\mathbf{G}}_u^i(k)$, $\bar{\mathbf{G}}_\lambda^i(k)$, $\bar{\mathbf{G}}_c^i(k)$, $q\left[\mathbf{x}^i(k)\right]'$, $q\left[\mathbf{x}^i(k)\right]$ by using Eqs. (22, 26, 34), and give $\mathbf{x}^{i+1}(k)$ and all the state constraints that $\mathbf{x}^{i+1}(k)$ needs to satisfy in Eqs. (35, 37, 38, 40, 41).
(4) return step (1) to compute $J^i[\lambda]$ and solve Problem 1.

else

Stop and compute $m^i(k)$, store $\{\mathbf{x}^i(k), \mathbf{u}^i(k), m^i(k), \lambda^i\}$

end

end

b) Make $t_f = \lambda^i$, calculate the coefficient matrices $\bar{\mathbf{A}}^0(k)$, $\bar{\mathbf{B}}^0(k)$, $\bar{\mathbf{C}}^i(k)$, $q\left[\mathbf{x}^0(k)\right]'$, $q\left[\mathbf{x}^0(k)\right]$ by using Eqs. (19, 26, 30), then compute $\mathbf{x}^1(k)$ and all the state constraints that $\mathbf{x}^1(k)$ needs to satisfy in Eqs. (35, 37–39, 41) with $\{\mathbf{x}^i(k), \mathbf{u}^i(k), m^i(k)\}$.

If $j \leq N_{iter}$ $(j \geq 1)$

If $\|\delta\mathbf{x}^j\|_\infty \geq \varepsilon_x$

(1) solve Problem 2 and compute $J^j[\mathbf{T}(k)]$ by convex optimization
(2) store the successive solution $\{\mathbf{x}^j(k), \mathbf{u}^j(k)\}$ and compute $m^j(k)$ by using Eq. (29).
(3) let $\mathbf{x}^j(k)$, $\mathbf{u}^j(k)$ and $m^j(k)$ be the new reference trajectory $\hat{\mathbf{x}}(k)$, $\hat{\mathbf{u}}(k)$ and $\hat{m}(k)$, then calculate the coefficient matrices $\bar{\mathbf{A}}^j(k)$, $\bar{\mathbf{B}}^j(k)$, $\bar{\mathbf{C}}^j(k)$, $q\left[\mathbf{x}^j(k)\right]'$, $q\left[\mathbf{x}^j(k)\right]$ by using Eqs. (19, 26, 30), and give $\mathbf{x}^{j+1}(k)$ and all the state constraints that $\mathbf{x}^{j+1}(k)$ needs to satisfy in Eqs. (35, 37–39, 41).
(4) return step (1) to compute $J^j[\mathbf{T}(k)]$ and solve Problem 2.

else

Stop and compute $m^j(k)$, output $\{\mathbf{x}^j(k),\ \mathbf{u}^j(k),\ m^j(k)\}$

end

end

4 Simulation Results

In this section, we present simulation results to examine our algorithm. The simulation is carried in MATLAB software using convex programming (CVX) and the solver SDPT3 4.0. We study the trajectory landing on asteroid 4769 Castalia. The diameter and density for the asteroid are 1.4 km and 2100 kg/m^3, the rotation period is 4.095 h, the GM is 94 m^3/s^2. The polyhedron gravitation method [13] is adopted to calculate the asteroid gravity using a shape model with 2048 vertices and 4092 faces the shape model data can be downloaded from [1]. The parameters for the vehicle are given in Table 1.

Table 1. The vehicle parameters

Parameters	Values
Initial moment of inertia	$\mathbf{J} = \begin{bmatrix} 2940 & 0 & 0 \\ 0 & 2758 & 0 \\ 0 & 0 & 1974 \end{bmatrix} \text{kg} \cdot \text{m}^2$
Mass of vehicle	$m_{init} = 1400$ kg $\quad m_{dry} = 1000$ kg
Thrust and Torque	$T_{min} = 2$ N $\quad T_{max} = 20$ N $\quad M_{max} = 0.2$ Nm
Vision sensor parameters	$\boldsymbol{\rho}_S = [0.9,\ 0,\ -1.0]^T \quad \mathbf{d}_S = [0,\ 0,\ -1.0]^T$
	$\beta = 25$ deg
Glide-slope	$\theta = 15$ deg
Vacuum specific impulse	$I_{sp} = 225$ s
Earth's standard gravity constant	$g_0 = 9.80665$ m/s^2

To start the successive convexification, we first do a simulation of the time-optimal convex sub-problem just considering the dynamics and convex control constraints with a reference state $\mathbf{x}_k^0 = \frac{N-k}{N}\mathbf{x}_0 + \frac{k}{N}\mathbf{x}_f,\ k = 0, 1, ..., N$, and use the obtained solution as the initial reference trajectory $\{\mathbf{x}^0(k), \mathbf{u}^0(k), m^0(k), \lambda^0\}$. The initial state and terminal state for the vehicle are given as follows.

$$\begin{aligned}
\mathbf{r}_0 &= [-237.554,\ -7.151,\ 1255.3]^T\ m \quad \mathbf{v}_0 = [1.423,\ 1.376,\ 0.698]^T\ m/s \\
\boldsymbol{\omega}_0 &= [0,\ 0,\ 0]^T\ rad/s \qquad \boldsymbol{\sigma}_0 = [0.1004,\ 0.0111,\ -0.3537]^T \\
\mathbf{r}_{tf} &= [0,\ 0,\ 289.3730]^T\ m \qquad \mathbf{v}_{tf} = [0,\ 0,\ 0]^T\ m/s \\
\boldsymbol{\omega}_{tf} &= [0.0001,\ 0.0001,\ 0.0005]^T\ rad/s\ \boldsymbol{\sigma}_{tf} = [0.0882,\ -0.0784,\ -0.3791]^T
\end{aligned}$$

Given the acceptable state trajectory deviation ε_x, when $\|\delta\mathbf{x}_k^i\|_\infty \leq \varepsilon_x$, the sequence iteration stops, and the solution of the last iteration is the optimal trajectory. We set $\varepsilon_x = 10^{-3}$, the simulation results of state and control, angle of glide-slope and FOV, mass depletion and the trajectories for the time-optimal optimization problem and the fuel-optimal optimization problem (using the simulation results of the time-optimal problem as the initial reference trajectory and the flight time) are given in Figs. 1, 2, 3, 4, 5, 6, 7, 8, 9 and 10.

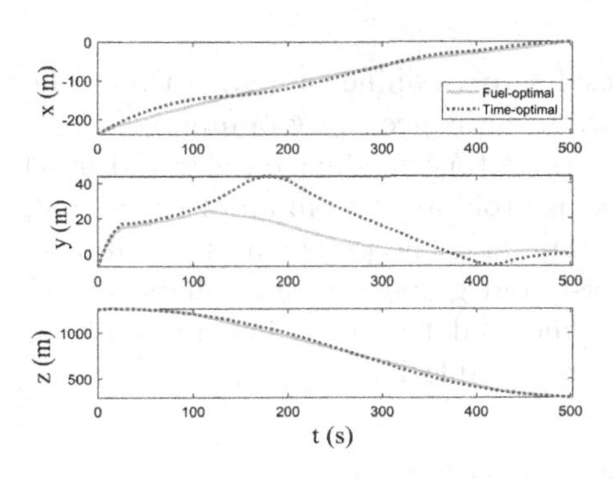

Fig. 1. The position $\mathbf{r}_{\mathcal{L}}$

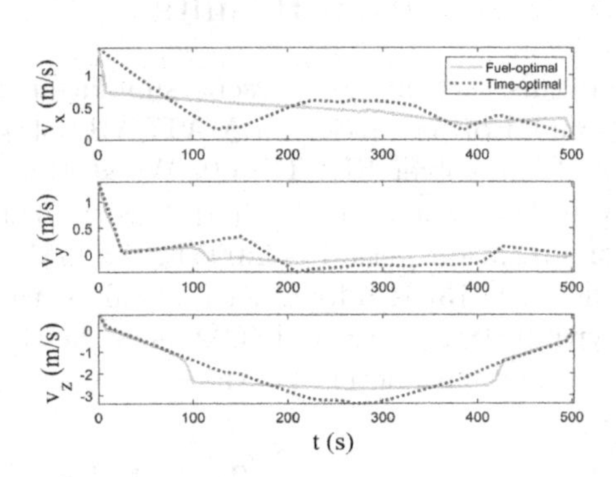

Fig. 2. The velocity $\mathbf{v}_{\mathcal{L}}$

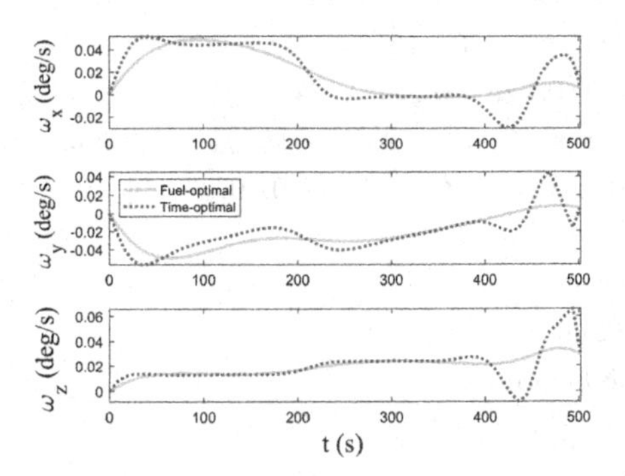

Fig. 3. The angular velocity $\boldsymbol{\omega}_{\mathcal{S}}$

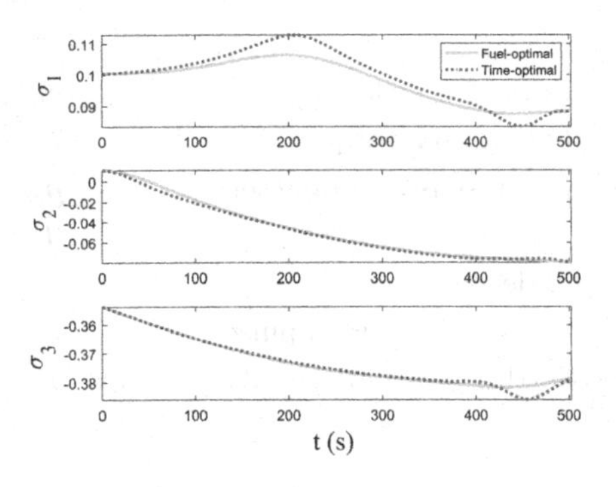

Fig. 4. The MRPs $\boldsymbol{\sigma}_{\mathcal{S}/\mathcal{L}}$

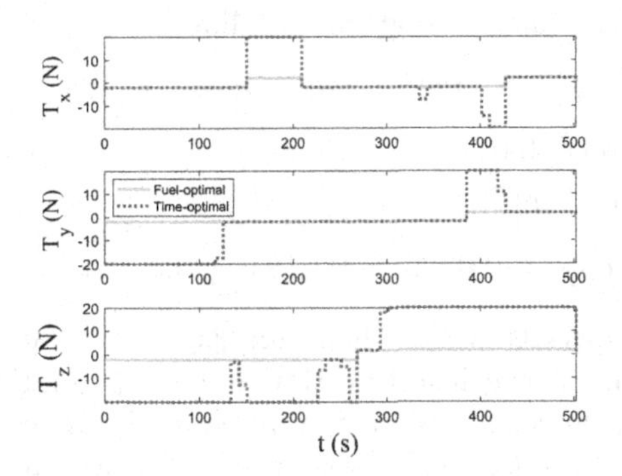

Fig. 5. The thrust $\mathbf{T}_{\mathcal{S}}$

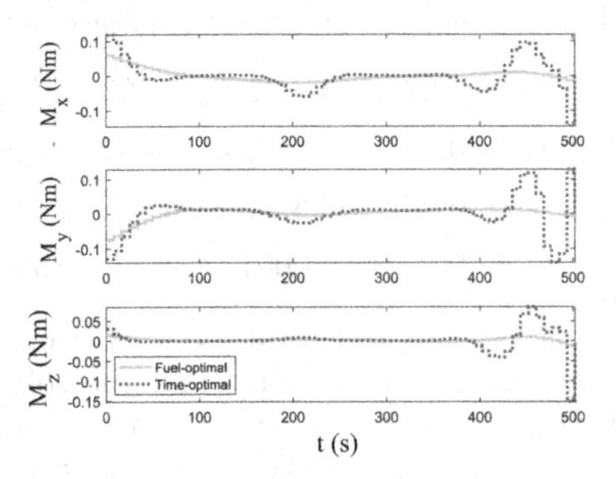

Fig. 6. The torque $\mathbf{M}_{\mathcal{S}}$

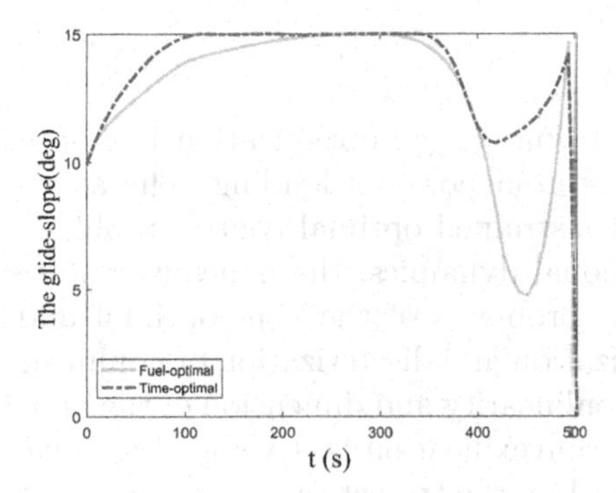

Fig. 7. The angle of the glide-slope

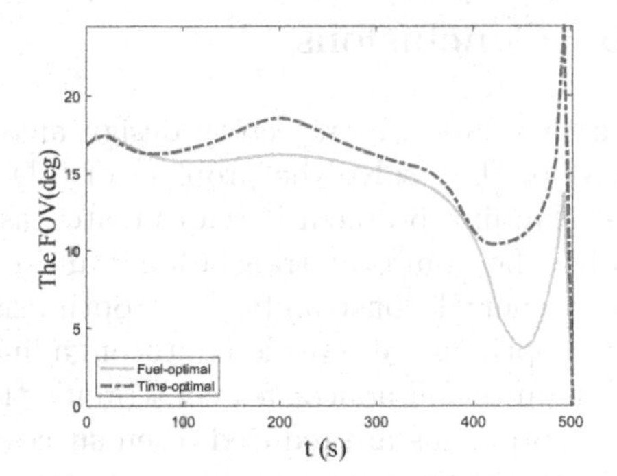

Fig. 8. The angle of the FOV

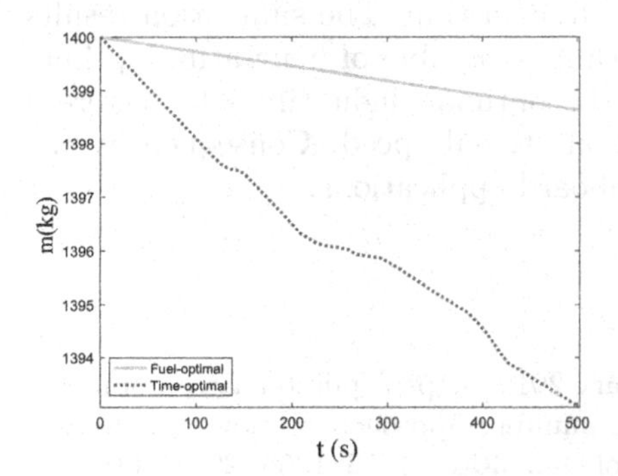

Fig. 9. The mass depletion

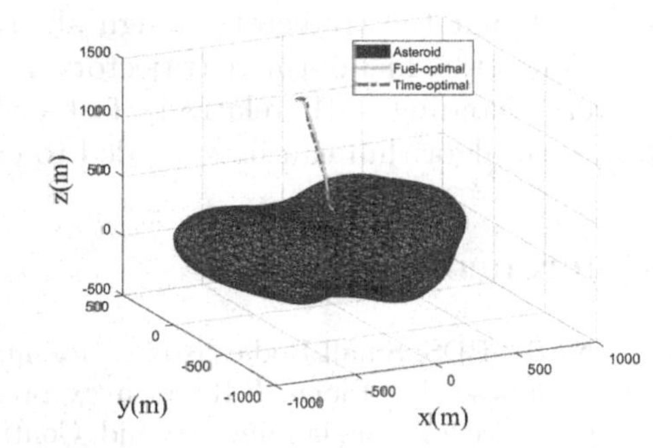

Fig. 10. The trajectory for landing on asteroid

For solving time-optimal optimization problem, the time dilation is $\lambda = 502.1388$, the iteration number is 7, the cut-off state deviation $\|\delta \mathbf{x}_k^i\|_\infty$ is 4.0920×10^{-6}, the CPU time is $78.1218s$. Making $t_f = \lambda$ and using the obtained time-optimal trajectory as the initial reference trajectory for solving fuel-optimal optimization problem, the iteration number is 4, the cut-off state deviation $\|\delta \mathbf{x}_k^i\|_\infty$ is 1.5202×10^{-4}, the CPU time is $56.4646s$, and the fuel-optimal optimization problem uses less fuel to obtain a more stable trajectory than that of the time-optimal optimization problem as can be seen from Figs. (1-10), the fuel consumption for the time-optimal optimization problem is $6.9303kg$ while the fuel consumption for the fuel-consumption optimization problem is $1.3654kg$. The simulation results indicate that the trajectory design algorithm combining the time-optimal and the fuel-optimal optimization problems solved by successive convexifcation is feasible and reliable, the calculation speed is relatively fast, which can be extended to onboard real-time calculation.

5 Conclusions

In this paper, a trajectory design algorithm via convex optimization has been proposed to solve the problem of 6-DoF asteroid powered landing. The asteroid landing problem is reformulated as a constrained optimal control problem, with the nonlinear translational and rotational dynamics, the nonconvex state and control constraints. Two optimization problems of the time-optimal and fuel-optimal are considered, through linearization and discretization of nonlinear dynamics and nonconvex constraints, the nonlinearity and dimension of the original problems are reduced, then successive convexification is developed to solve the two optimization problems. In the algorithm, the trajectory design combines the time-optimal and the fuel-optimal trajectory optimization, the trajectory is given by solving the fuel-optimal optimization problem via successive convexification using the flight time and time-optimal trajectory obtained by solving the time-optimal optimization problem in successive manner. Simulations are conducted in order to examine the proposed algorithm. The simulation results indicate that the trajectory design algorithm is capable of generating optimal solutions (the fuel-optimal trajectory in the optimal flight time) for asteroid powered landing with relatively fast computational speed. Consequently, the proposed algorithm can be extended to onboard applications.

References

1. NASA PDS: Small Bodies Node, 31 January 2019. https://pdssbn.astro.umd.edu/
2. Acikmese, B., Ploen, S.R.: Convex programming approach to powered descent guidance for mars landing. J. Guid. Control Dyn. **30**(5), 1353–1366 (2007). https://doi.org/10.2514/1.27553
3. Blackmore, L., Acikmese, B., Scharf, D.P.: Minimum-landing-error powered-descent guidance for mars landing using convex optimization. J. Guid. Control Dyn. **33**(4), 1161–1171 (2010). https://doi.org/10.2514/1.47202
4. Furfaro, R., Cersosimo, D., Wibben, D.R.: Asteroid precision landing via multiple sliding surfaces guidance techniques. J. Guid. Control Dyn. **36**(4), 1075–1092 (2013). https://doi.org/10.2514/1.58246
5. Gregory, L., Robert, B.: Optimal trajectories for soft landing on asteroids. Space Systems Design Lab., Georgia Inst. of Technology, AE8900 MS Special Problems Report (2017)
6. Hawkins, M., Guo, Y., Wie, B.: Zem/zev feedback guidance application to fuel-efficient orbital maneuvers around an irregular-shaped asteroid. In: AIAA Guidance, Navigation, and Control Conference, p. 5045 (2012), https://doi.org/10.2514/6.2012-5045
7. Hu, H., Zhu, S., Cui, P.: Desensitized optimal trajectory for landing on small bodies with reduced landing error. Aerosp. Sci. Technol. **48**, 178–185 (2016). https://doi.org/10.1016/j.ast.2015.11.006
8. Lan, Q., Li, S., Yang, J., Guo, L.: Finite-time soft landing on asteroids using nonsingular terminal sliding mode control. Trans. Inst. Measur. Control **36**(2), 216–223 (2014). https://doi.org/10.1177/0142331213495040

9. Li, S., Cui, P., Cui, H.: Autonomous navigation and guidance for landing on asteroids. Aerosp. Sci. Technol. **10**(3), 239–247 (2006). https://doi.org/10.1016/j.ast.2005.12.003
10. Lunghi, P., Lavagna, M., Armellin, R.: A semi-analytical guidance algorithm for autonomous landing. Adv. Space Res. **55**(11), 2719–2738 (2015). https://doi.org/10.1016/j.asr.2015.02.022
11. Mao, Y., Szmuk, M., Açıkmeşe, B.: Successive convexification of non-convex optimal control problems and its convergence properties. In: 2016 IEEE 55th Conference on Decision and Control (CDC), pp. 3636–3641. IEEE (2016)
12. Pinson, R.M., Lu, P.: Trajectory design employing convex optimization for landing on irregularly shaped asteroids. J. Guid. Control Dyn. **41**(6), 1243–1256 (2018). https://doi.org/10.2514/1.G003045
13. Werner, R.A., Scheeres, D.J.: Exterior gravitation of a polyhedron derived and compared with harmonic and mascon gravitation representations of asteroid 4769 castalia. Celestial Mech. Dyn. Astron. **65**(3), 313–344 (1996)
14. Stephen P., Lieven, V.: Convex Optimization. In: Cambridge University Press (2004)
15. Szmuk, M., Acikmese, B.: Successive convexification for 6-dof mars rocket powered landing with free-final-time. In: 2018 AIAA Guidance, Navigation, and Control Conference, p. 0617 (2018). https://doi.org/10.2514/6.2018-0617
16. Szmuk, M., Acikmese, B., Berning, A.W.: Successive convexification for fuel-optimal powered landing with aerodynamic drag and non-convex constraints. In: AIAA Guidance, Navigation, and Control Conference, p. 0378 (2016). https://doi.org/10.2514/6.2016-0378
17. Yang, H., Bai, X., Baoyin, H.: Finite-time control for asteroid hovering and landing via terminal sliding-mode guidance. Acta Astronaut. **132**, 78–89 (2017). https://doi.org/10.1016/j.actaastro.2016.12.012
18. Yang, H., Bai, X., Baoyin, H.: Rapid generation of time-optimal trajectories for asteroid landing via convex optimization. J. Guid. Control Dyn. **40**(3), 628–641 (2017). https://doi.org/10.2514/1.G002170
19. Yang, H., Bai, X., Baoyin, H.: Rapid trajectory planning for asteroid landing with thrust magnitude constraint. J. Guid. Control Dyn. **40**(10), 2713–2720 (2017). https://doi.org/10.2514/1.G002346
20. Yang, H., Baoyin, H.: Fuel-optimal control for soft landing on an irregular asteroid. IEEE Trans. Aerosp. Electron. Syst. **51**(3), 1688–1697 (2015). https://doi.org/10.1109/TAES.2015.140295
21. Zexu, Z., Weidong, W., Litao, L., Xiangyu, H., Hutao, C., Shuang, L., Pingyuan, C.: Robust sliding mode guidance and control for soft landing on small bodies. J. Franklin Inst. **349**(2), 493–509 (2012). https://doi.org/10.1016/j.jfranklin.2011.07.007

Multi-debris Removal in Low-Orbit Based on Swarm Intelligence Research on Optimal Guidance Method

Na Fu(✉), Tian-Jiao Zhang, Lai-Jian Zhou, Yan-Yan Zeng, and Chen Zhang

State Key Laboratory of Astronautic Dynamics, Xi'an Satellite Control Center, Xi'an 710049, Shaanxi, China

40365728@qq.com

Abstract. Low-orbit space debris removal path planning can be decomposed into optimization problems of debris removal sequences and optimization of transfer orbit design between debris. In this paper, a two-level planning model is established, and the corresponding group intelligent optimization algorithm is proposed. The upper-level optimization problem takes the debris removal sequence as the design variable, considers the task time constraints, and takes the minimum total task energy consumption as the optimization goal, and uses the discrete ant colony algorithm to solve the optimal debris removal sequence. The lower optimization problem takes the maneuvering time and impulse of the inter-debris transfer orbit mission as the design variables, considers the influence of the earth's non-spherical perturbation, and adopts the single-circle perturbation Lambert algorithm for the constraint processing method of terminal state satisfaction, and proposes a method based on continuous ant colony. Optimized path planning algorithm. Simulation results show that the strategy and algorithm proposed in this paper are efficient and feasible, which can save fuel to the greatest extent and maximize the benefits of space debris mitigation. The research results of this paper provide technical reserves for the follow-up exploration of the integrated design optimization of debris transfer orbits and debris removal sequences.

Keywords: Debris removal · Path planning · Swarm intelligence · Global optimization

1 Introduction

The continuous growth of space debris makes the space environment worse and worse, affecting the normal space activities of human beings. Especially for the near-Earth region [1–10], nearly 90% of the cataloged space targets are debris, and its distribution is relatively dense, which is prone to debris cascading collision effects. Figure 1 shows a schematic diagram of space debris. NASA scientist Kessler [9] pointed out that even if the mission spacecraft is no longer launched, the number of debris will continue to increase due to the mutual collision between the debris. This will seriously threaten the safe operation of spacecraft such as orbiting satellites and space stations. Therefore, low-cost and high-efficiency active debris removal is urgent and necessary [4–7].

Q. Wu et al. (Eds.): WiSATS 2020, LNICST 358, pp. 116–131, 2021.
https://doi.org/10.1007/978-3-030-69072-4_10

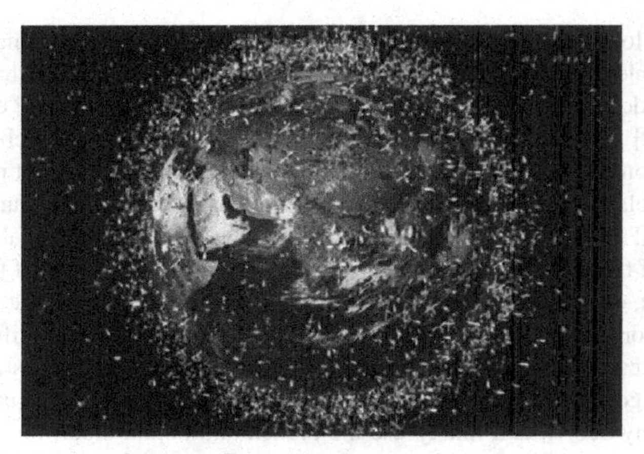

Fig. 1. Schematic diagram of space debris in Earth orbit

Since the orbital distribution of the most threatening debris may be scattered, making the cost of active debris removal missions high, consideration should be given to both the cost of removal and the benefits of removal. Decisions such as debris removal, optimization of debris removal timing, and optimal maneuvering strategy for spacecraft removal should be preferred. The collaborative optimization makes the low-orbit multi-debris removal path planning problem exhibit the characteristics of mixed integer nonlinear planning, and the continuous movement of space debris makes the energy consumption for the transfer of debris time-varying, which increases the difficulty of solving the problem.

In 1986, China included space debris research as one of the important space environmental factors facing manned spaceflight, and included it in the environmental protection plan. In 1995, China officially joined the IADC to carry out systematic research on space debris. Regarding the research on the space debris environment model, in the "Space Debris Environment Detector and Engineering Model Research" project during the 12th Five-Year Plan period, Harbin Institute of Technology undertook the establishment of a space debris environment debris environment model [3]. At present, the project has completed the investigation of modeling principles of typical space debris environment models at home and abroad, and compared and analyzed the typical space debris models published abroad. China carries out detailed analysis and research on foreign space debris generation event models, and establish a space debris orbit evolution model. The modeling method of the environmental engineering model of space debris in low-Earth orbit has been preliminarily established. China is still in the exploratory stage in predicting the future evolution of space debris environment and has not yet released a mature model or algorithm. Existing modeling methods and theoretical research also need to be improved, and there is a big gap with foreign countries. The establishment of China's autonomous space debris environmental engineering model requires the prediction of space debris environmental evolution.

At present, there are only a few articles on the optimal design strategy of multi-shard intersection. Barbee et al. [11] ignored the impact of J2 perturbation, considered a simplified two-body orbit transfer model, and described the removal path planning problem given a set of low-orbit debris to be removed as a static traveling salesman (Traveling Salesman Problem, TSP) problem, using order The optimization algorithm solves and compares the debris removal efficiency of different spacecraft loads and engine ratios. Cerf et al. [12] studied the clearance path planning of five low-orbit debris under the condition of considering J2 perturbation. By giving alternative drift orbit parameters to remove time-related factors, the branch and bound method was used to obtain the optimal Debris removal timing and corresponding orbit transfer path. Olympio et al. [13] studied the problem of the most energy-efficient removal of the five fragments of the solar synchronous orbit, discretized the possible start time interval of the task, the feasible time interval of the orbit transfer, and the allowable time interval of the orbit drift, determined the parameter combination for each group, and adopted The small thrust J2 perturbed the Lambert algorithm [15] to obtain the energy consumption of small thrust orbit transfer between any debris, and finally use the branch and bound algorithm to search for the optimal removal timing and removal path. From the publicly reported literature, the existing research usually performs two-body simplification and gives the debris removal time and calculates the corresponding transfer energy consumption, or discretizes the possible debris removal time and then conducts a grid search, and then models it as TSP Or solve its deformation model. However, due to the long period of debris removal tasks, usually in years, for the LEO debris removal task, the impact of J2 perturbation on the debris orbit cannot be ignored, and the two-body simplification is obviously unreasonable. However, the research based on grid search does not accurately estimate the optimal debris removal time and the corresponding energy consumption of orbital transfer, and its computational cost increases exponentially with the increase in the number of candidate debris. Supercomputer-assisted or manual correction is required to achieve the calculation It is difficult to generalize, so it cannot be used to solve the sequential removal path planning of large-scale candidate debris. In this paper, with the background of low-orbit multi-debris removal path design optimization as the background, a two-layer optimization framework is proposed: the upper layer optimization takes the order of debris removal as the design variable, considers the task time constraint, and takes the minimum total task energy consumption as the optimization goal, using the discrete ant colony algorithm Solve the optimal debris removal sequence; the lower-level optimization problem takes the maneuvering time and impulse of the inter-debris transfer orbit task as the design variables, considers the influence of J2 perturbation, and adopts the single-circle perturbation Lambert algorithm for the constraint processing method of terminal state satisfaction. A path planning algorithm based on continuous ant colony optimization.

2 Low Orbit Space Debris Removal Mission Scenes

2.1 Distribution and Evolution of Space Debris in Low Earth Orbit

There have been nearly 6,000 spacecraft launched into orbit in human history, most of which are distributed in low-Earth orbits below 2000 km in altitude and geosynchronous orbits at an altitude of about 36,000 km. Some man-made objects have returned to the atmosphere Falling and destroying, but most of them still remain in the earth's orbit. From the spatial distribution, most of them are distributed in the LEO area. And in the

LEO area, it is most distributed in an area of 8,000 km. Figure 2 shows the distribution of the number of space debris with the semi-major axis and the orbital inclination angle in December 2016. In the figure, the interval of orbital inclination is 2°, and the interval of semi-major axis is 100 km. It can also be seen intuitively from Fig. 2 that space debris is mainly concentrated in low-Earth orbits, synchronous orbits, and some mid-high orbit regions.

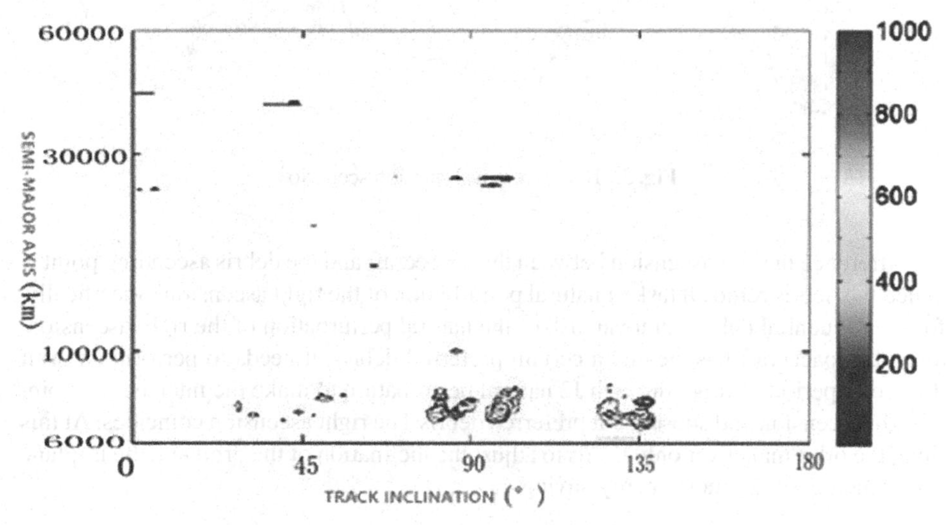

Fig. 2. Space debris distribution

2.2 Low-Orbit Space Debris Removal Mission Scenario

Currently, the generally accepted scenario for active debris removal is shown in Fig. 3. At the initial moment, a spacecraft carrying several debris removal devices is launched to a designated orbital position, usually coincident with the first preferred debris position. The clearing spacecraft meets with the first preferred debris. With the flight and release of the clearing device, the de-orbital removal of the debris is the responsibility of the clearing device, and then the clearing of the spacecraft departs, and the successive debris removal and removal of the preferred debris until the spacecraft propellant consumption is cleared After all or all of the preferred debris removal is completed, the sequential debris removal task ends.

Because the orbital distribution of the preferred debris may be scattered, if the clear spacecraft directly carries out pulse orbit transfer between the debris, it usually needs to consume more speed increments. Therefore, in order to ensure the successful completion of the sequential debris removal task, for the sequential debris removal task without orbit transfer time constraints, the influence of J2 natural perturbation on the right ascension of the ascending intersection point should be fully adjusted to adjust the orbital surface deviation, so as to effectively reduce the orbit transfer The purpose of energy consumption. In this paper, the debris removal task that uses only J2 natural perturbation to adjust

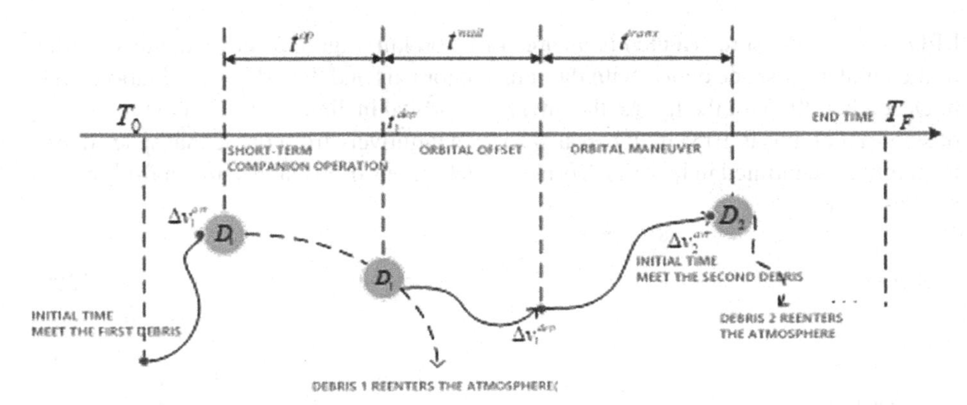

Fig. 3. Debris removal mission scenario

the difference in right ascension between the spacecraft and the debris ascending point is called the debris removal task of natural perturbation of the right ascension. Specifically, for the sequential debris removal task of the natural perturbation of the right ascension, after the spacecraft has cleared a certain preferred debris, it needs to perform an orbit drift for a period of time, through J2 natural perturbation to make the intersection point of right ascension and subsequent preferred debris The right ascension coincides. At this time, the orbit maneuver only needs to adjust the inclination of the orbit and the in-plane orbit change, so the most energy-saving.

3 Path Planning Model for Low-Orbit Space Debris Removal

The low-orbit space debris removal path planning problem has characteristics such as multi-minimum values, search space discontinuity, and multi-scale. Therefore, this section adopts the solution strategy of hierarchical modeling serial planning. The upper layer plan is used to determine the optimal removal order, and the lower layer plan is used to determine the optimal multi-pulse transfer path between two adjacent target fragments.

3.1 Upper Level Optimization Model

The goal of the upper-level planning problem is to determine the optimal removal order of the target debris, so that the total energy consumption of the orbital transfer of the debris removal by the spacecraft in order is minimized. Since the energy consumption of the spacecraft's orbital transfer between any two target fragments is determined by the lower layer planning, if the precise solution of the lower layer planning is used as the input for the upper layer planning, the solution algorithm has a high time complexity. In view of this, this paper designs a method for estimating the orbital energy consumption and time between target debris of a spacecraft that does not rely on lower level planning, to decouple upper and lower level planning, and to quickly determine the optimal removal order.

3.1.1 Energy Consumption and Time Estimation Method for Orbital Transfer Between Target Fragments

The energy consumption of orbital transfer between target debris is composed of the energy consumption of plane-free orbit change and the energy consumption of in-plane orbit change. This section makes full use of the impact of long-term perturbation of J2 on the right ascension of the ascending intersection point. After the spacecraft has cleared a debris, it drifts for a period of time. The natural ascension force causes the right ascension of the ascending intersection point to coincide with the debris of the debris to be met. At this time, the spacecraft and the debris to be removed have similar orbital inclination angles and the same ascension point of right ascension. Therefore, tracking spacecraft only needs to perform different plane orbit changing maneuvers and pulse adjustment camera movements with lower energy consumption to be able to locate with the debris to be removed.

The energy consumption of orbit changing in different planes is mainly used to adjust the inclination of the track, so it can be estimated by the following formula:

$$\Delta v_{inter} \approx 2v\sin(\Delta i/2) \quad (1)$$

Δv_{inter} is the estimated energy consumption for different plane orbit changes; v is the speed of the spacecraft before the orbit change; Δi is the estimated energy consumption for different plane orbit changes.

Among the orbital transfers between two coplanar elliptical orbits, the Homan transfer is the most energy-efficient double-pulse maneuver. Since the spacecraft's transfer time between debris is long enough, it is assumed that it can always be adjusted to the optimal phase to perform the Homan transfer before in-plane orbit transfer, so the in-plane between target debris is estimated by the energy consumption of the Homan transfer The energy consumption of track change is as follows:

$$\Delta v_{intra} \approx 0.5v\sqrt{(\Delta a/a)^2 + \Delta e^2} \quad (2)$$

Δv_{intra} Estimated energy consumption for in-plane orbit change; a, v the semi-major axis and velocity of the spacecraft before orbit change, respectively Δe is the difference in eccentricity between the two orbits.

3.1.2 Debris Removal Order Optimization Model

When the method described in Sect. 3.1.1 is used to estimate the spacecraft orbital transfer energy between two debris, the cleaning sequence optimization problem with the smallest total energy consumption can be abstracted as a classic TSP problem solution. The upper-level removal order optimization problem can be defined as searching for the shortest Hamilton path in the complete graph $G = <V, E>$, where V is the set of debris to be removed, $E = \{e_{ij} \mid d_i, d_j \in V\}$ is the set of edges G in the graph, $|V| = n$; and the length of the edge c_{ij} is set to the estimated energy of the spacecraft's orbital transfer between the two debris Consumption, the shortest Hamilton path in the figure G corresponds to the multi-debris removal sequence with the smallest total energy consumption.

x_{ij} is Boolean decision variable, used to characterize whether the spacecraft continuously removes debris d_i, d_j, if e_{ij} is in the shortest Hamilton Road, $x_{ij} = 1$; otherwise $x_{ij} = 0$.

The problem is modeled using the 0–1 integer programming model as follows:

$$\begin{aligned} \min \quad & \sum_{i=1}^{n}\sum_{j=1}^{n} c_{ij}x_{ij} \\ s.t. \quad & \sum_{i=1}^{n} x_{ij} \leq 1, j = 2, \ldots, n \\ & \sum_{j=1}^{n} x_{ij} \leq 1, i = 2, \ldots, n \\ & x_{ij} \in \{0, 1\}, \ \forall e_{ij} \in E \end{aligned} \tag{3}$$

3.2 Lower Level Optimization Model

On the basis of determining the optimal clearance order in the upper layer planning, the lower layer planning needs to optimize the precise path of the multi-pulse transfer between two adjacent debris according to the optimal clearance order.

3.2.1 Kinetic Model

Since spacecraft and debris are both in the vicinity of LEO orbit, only the gravitational effect of the earth is considered. The orbital dynamic equation of spacecraft under J2 perturbation described by the number of orbits is:

$$\begin{cases} \frac{da}{dt} = 0 \\ \frac{de}{dt} = 0 \\ \frac{di}{dt} = 0 \\ \frac{d\Omega}{dt} = -\frac{3}{2}\frac{nJ_2 \cos i}{(1-e^2)^2}\left(\frac{R_e}{a}\right)^2 \\ \frac{d\omega}{dt} = -\frac{3nJ_2[1-5\cos^2 i]}{4(1-e^2)^2}\left(\frac{R_e}{a}\right)^2 \\ \frac{dM}{dt} = n + \frac{3nJ_2[3\cos^2 i - 1]}{4(1-e^2)^{3/2}}\left(\frac{R_e}{a}\right)^2 \end{cases} \tag{4}$$

Number of orbits $E = (a, e, i, \Omega, \omega, M)$ represent the semi-major axis of the spacecraft orbit, eccentricity, orbital inclination, right ascension of the ascending intersection point, the perigee amplitude angle, and the meso point angle; J_2 is the second harmonic; R_e is earth radius.

3.2.2 Model of Spacecraft Transfer Path Planning Between Adjacent Debris

The spacecraft uses drift and four-pulse maneuvers to meet space debris. Taking the q path planning for the intersection with the first debris as an example, the lower-level optimization uses four maneuvers and the impulse as design variables:

$$y_q = \left(\Delta t_{q1}, \Delta t_{q2}, \Delta t_{q3}, \Delta t_{q4}, \Delta \mathbf{v}_{q1}, \Delta \mathbf{v}_{q2}, \Delta \mathbf{v}_{q3}, \Delta \mathbf{v}_{q4}\right)^T$$

Δt_{qi} is decision variable i for the moment of the second pulse maneuver $\Delta \mathbf{v}_{qi}, i = 1, 2, 3, 4$ is a four-pulse maneuver vector decision variable.

The path planning model for the intersection of spacecraft and debris is as follows:

$$\min \sum_{q=1}^{N} \sum_{i=1}^{4} |\Delta \mathbf{v}_{qi}| \tag{5}$$

$$s.t. \quad \mathbf{r}_s^+(t_{qi}) = \mathbf{r}_s^-(t_{qi}), \; q = 1, \ldots, N \; i = 1, \ldots, 4 \tag{6}$$

$$\mathbf{v}_s^+(t_{qi}) = \mathbf{v}_s^-(t_{qi}) + \Delta \mathbf{v}_{qi}, \; q = 1, \ldots, N \; i = 1, \ldots, 4 \tag{7}$$

$$\mathbf{r}_s^+(t_{q4}) = \mathbf{r}_q(t_{q4}), \; q = 1, \ldots, N \tag{8}$$

$$\mathbf{v}_s^+(t_{q4}) = \mathbf{v}_q(t_{q4}), \; q = 1, \ldots, N \tag{9}$$

$$t_{q1} \le t_{q2} \le t_{q3} \le t_{q4} \; q = 1, \ldots, N \tag{10}$$

$$\max_q t_{q4} \le \mathrm{T}_F, \; q = 1, \ldots, N \tag{11}$$

$$x_{q-1\,q} = 1, \; q = 2, \ldots, N \tag{12}$$

$\mathbf{r}_s^-, \mathbf{v}_s^-, \mathbf{r}_s^+, \mathbf{v}_s^+$, are the position and velocity vector of the spacecraft before and after the orbit change; $\mathbf{r}_q(t), \mathbf{v}_q(t)$ are the position and velocity vector of the No. q fragment at time t. T_F is the latest end of the total task for debris removal. Formula (5) is objective function, that is, the total energy consumption of the debris removal task is the smallest; formula (6) (7) are Pulse thrust model, that is, the spacecraft position vector does not change before and after the pulse is applied, and the velocity vector after the orbit change is the sum of the velocity vector before the orbit change and the pulse vector; formula (8) (9) are end state constraints for rendezvous tasks, In this paper, the single-circle J2 perturbed Lambert algorithm is used to meet the terminal constraints of each rendezvous task; formula (10) represents the time constraint of four-pulse orbit change; formula (11) indicates that the debris removal task needs to be completed within the specified time; formula (12) represents the spacecraft will meet the debris sequentially according to the optimal removal order.

4 Ant Colony Solving Algorithm

The low-orbit space debris removal path planning problem is essentially a mixed integer nonlinear planning problem, which is a NP difficult problem. With the increase of the number of debris to be removed, the traditional precise algorithm cannot find a feasible solution within an acceptable time, so this paper Use intelligent optimization algorithm to solve.

4.1 Classic Ant Colony Optimization Algorithm

Inspired by real ant foraging behavior, Professor M. Dorigo [14] first proposed a bionic evolution algorithm in 1991, called Ant Colony Optimization (ACO). The ACO algorithm is first used to solve the traveling salesman problem (TSP). It uses distributed feedback parallel computing, which is easy to merge with other algorithms and has strong robustness. In 2008, Sochi et al. [17–19] proposed ACO R, which uses the solution in the solution file as a pheromone. The pheromone is updated by the Gaussian kernel function. The algorithm directly extends the ant colony algorithm in the discrete domain to the continuous domain. Because of its global search, positive feedback, group optimization and distributed parallel computing and other characteristics, it has shown outstanding applicability when solving large-scale complex discrete combination optimization problems. Given the excellent performance of ACO in the field of discrete optimization, many scholars Expanding to the field of continuous optimization, with the rapid development of ant colony optimization algorithm, it has received more and more attention, and is used in various fields such as data mining and cloud computing.

This paper will improve a continuous ant colony algorithm, using ACO and continuous domain ACO (ACOR) to solve the upper and lower optimization problems. Due to the rich research results of the ACO algorithm, due to space limitations, this article will not repeat the details of the ACO solution, only the continuous domain ACO solution process is described (Table 1).

4.2 Feasible Solution Construction

At the beginning of each iteration, the ant adopts an incremental solution construction strategy to construct a feasible solution dimension by dimension. When constructing the decision variables of each dimension, the ant uses a two-stage sampling method to sample the Gaussian kernel function corresponding to the decision variables of the dimension. First, according to the weight parameters, a Gaussian sub-function is selected according to the probability; then, by selecting the Gaussian Box-Muller sampling of the sub-function completes the sampling of the Gaussian kernel function corresponding to the decision variable of this dimension.

Let T be the set of k n-dimensional elite solutions, and the second-dimensional decision variables of all elite solutions jointly generate a Gaussian kernel function G^i, where the Gaussian subfunction corresponding to the elite solution s_l is g_l^i; the objective function value of the elite solution s_l is $f(s_l)$, Its relative importance is w_l and the second-dimensional decision variable is s_l^i.

Table 1. ACO_R Solution process pseudocode

Continuous domain ant colony optimization algorithm ACO_R ( )
Initialization parameters, Pheromones;
while algorithm termination condition not met **do**
for each ant k **do**
Feasible solution construction;
end for
Local search;
Pheromone update;
end while
return Optimal solution s^*

The Gaussian kernel function of the i-to decision variable is defined as follows:

$$G_i(x) = \sum_{l=1}^{k} w_l g_l^i(x) = \sum_{l=1}^{k} w_l \frac{1}{\sigma_l^i \sqrt{2\pi}} e^{-\frac{(x-\mu_1^i)^2}{2(\sigma_1^i)^2}} \tag{13}$$

$$\boldsymbol{\mu}^i = \{\mu_1^i, \ldots, \mu_k^i\} = \{s_1^i, \ldots, s_k^i\} \tag{14}$$

$$\sigma_l^i = \zeta \sum_{e=1}^{k} \frac{\left|s_e^i - s_l^i\right|}{k-1} \tag{15}$$

$$w_l = \frac{1}{qk\sqrt{2\pi}} e^{-\frac{(l-1)^2}{2q^2k^2}} \tag{16}$$

$\zeta > 0$ is the convergence control coefficient. The ζ is smaller, the faster the algorithm will converge. Its function is similar to the pheromone evaporation coefficient in ACO. w_l can be seen as a Gaussian function with an expectation of 1, and a variance qk of. The smaller q is, the more inclined it is to use the optimal elite solution in the solution set to guide the optimization of this iteration, otherwise the tendency is to use any elite solution on average. The parameter q can be used to adjust the global search and local search preferences; l is the ranking of the elite solution s_l in the solution set.

4.3 Pheromone Update

Due to the difference in search space, ACOR cannot inherit ACO's pheromone setting and updating strategy, that is, setting pheromone for each candidate element and updating with a certain strategy. Instead, in the whole optimization process, a certain number of elite solutions are always saved, and the purpose of retaining historical search information is achieved by updating the Gaussian kernel function generated by the elite solutions.

5 Simulation Experiment and Data Analysis

The space debris generated by the disintegration of the Russian Cosmos-3M rocket body is used as an alternative debris removal. Due to the densest space vehicles in this area, and the large mass and volume of these space debris, the potential threat to the space environment is the greatest. Which will get a larger income. According to the cataloging information of the US Strategic Command Space Target Database [20, 21] 2017-1-1 at 00:00:00.000, the space debris of the Russian Cosmos-3M rocket body is distributed by the orbital inclination at 155 space debris at 82 deg (Recorded as 82-deg cluster) and 120 space debris (recorded as 74-deg cluster) with an inclination of 74 deg, the distribution is shown in Fig. 4. In this paper, four LEO debris with an orbital inclination angle of about 82° and the highest priority are selected from the Russian Kosmas 3M rocket disintegration debris library. The number of orbits of the debris to be removed is shown in Table 2. The constant parameters needed in the simulation are expressed as $R_e = 6378.137$ km, $J_2 = 1.0826 \times 10^{-3}$, $\mu_e = 398600.4418$ km^2/s^2. The ant colony algorithm parameter settings are shown in Table 3.

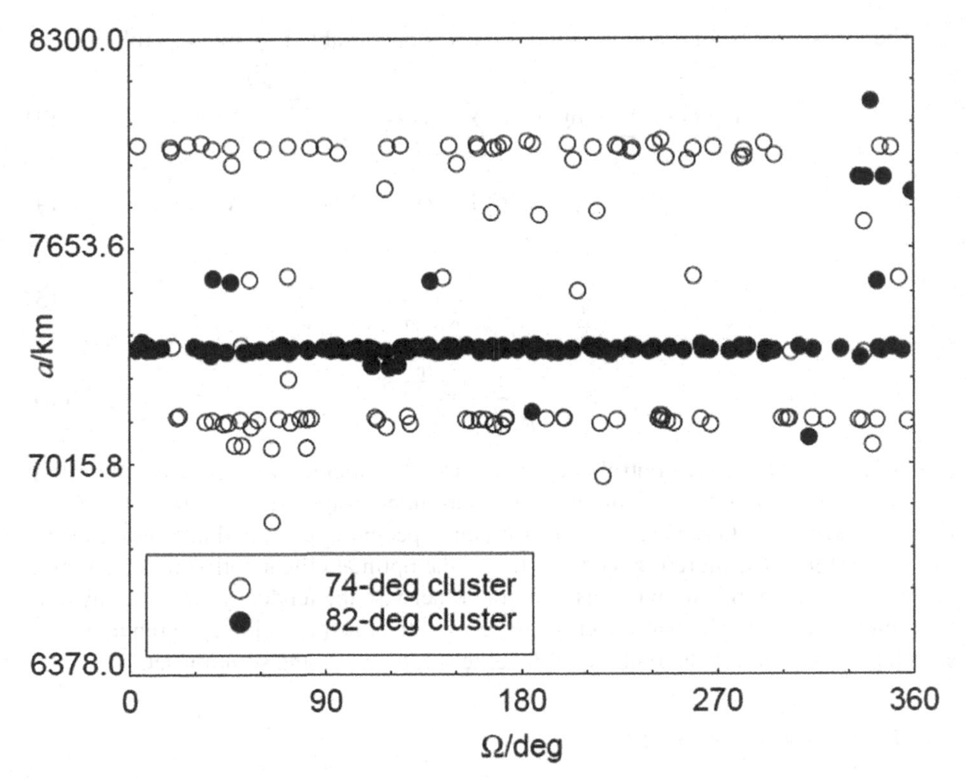

Fig. 4. Cosmos-3MRocket space debris distribution(2017-1-1 00:00:00.000)

Table 2. Track the number of initial orbits of spacecraft and target debris

Target no.	a (km)	e	i (deg)	Ω (deg)	ω (deg)	M (deg)
Clear spacecraft	7376.705	0.004	82.93	183.99	195.09	321.46
Debris 13302	7376.705	0.004	82.93	183.99	195.09	321.46
Debris 5907	7554.527	0.002	82.97	178.76	80.99	138.64
Debris 10138	7364.144	0.002	82.94	189.24	8.79	167.40
Debris 12139	7117.959	0.051	82.95	207.28	113.16	330.25

Table 3. Ant colony algorithm parameters

Parameters	Identifier	ACO	ACO_R
Population size	N	100	20
Maximum evolutionary algebra	MAX_cycle	300	200
Pheromone evaporation coefficient	ρ	0.95	/
Heuristic information, pheromone weight	a, b	3,5	/
Elite solution set size	$N_{archive}$	/	100
Convergence control parameters	ζ	/	0.65
Global search and local search preferences	q	/	10^{-4}

5.1 Upper-Level Planning Results

Based on the spacecraft orbit transfer energy consumption prediction method proposed in Sect. 2.1.1, discrete ACO is used to obtain the optimal debris removal sequence, removal time interval, and orbit transfer energy consumption as shown in Table 4. The optimal debris removal sequence is (13302, 5907, 10138, 12139), the total estimated speed increment is 407.606 m/s, and the total task time is 177.66 d.

Table 4. Debris removal sequence, estimated energy consumption and schedule for each segment

Clear sequence	Estimated transfer energy consumption (m/s)	$t^{op} + t^{wait} + t^{trans}$ (d)
13302 → 5907	88.912	83.516
5907 → 10138	95.101	74.754
10138 → 12139	223.593	28.156

5.2 Lower-Level Planning Results

According to the optimal removal order obtained in the previous section, this section gives the optimal transfer path between the debris of the spacecraft based on the ant colony optimization algorithm section by section. To further test the performance of the algorithm proposed in this paper, Table 5 compares the solution results of ACOR and Differential Evolution (DE) [22]. Figure 5 shows the process of the optimal intersection orbit and orbit height change, where the maneuver time is Refers to the time used by the spacecraft orbital maneuver.

Table 5. Comparison of spacecraft clearance trajectory optimization results

Clear sequence	ACO_R			DE		
	Energy consumption (m/s)	Drift time (d)	Maneuver time (d)	Energy consumption (m/s)	Drift time (d)	Maneuver time (d)
13302 → 5907	**87.22**	83.04	0.77	87.66	83.73	0.04
5907 → 10138	**93.79**	73.55	0.42	100.63	73.05	0.95
10138 → 12139	**187.49**	27.66	0.51	192.86	27.81	0.36

Comparing Tables 4 and 5, it can be seen that no matter the energy consumption is transferred or the interval time is clear, the difference between the exact solution and the estimated value is small, which verifies the effectiveness of the estimated method. It can be seen from Table 5 that the algorithm proposed in this paper is better than the differential evolution algorithm. As can be seen from Fig. 4, the spacecraft intersection fragmentation process is multi-turn transfer, so there are many local optimal solutions, and the optimal results are obtained through calculation examples. Compared with drawing, it shows that ACOR can find the optimal solution that is similar to the estimated solution, which fully verifies the excellent performance of ACOR.

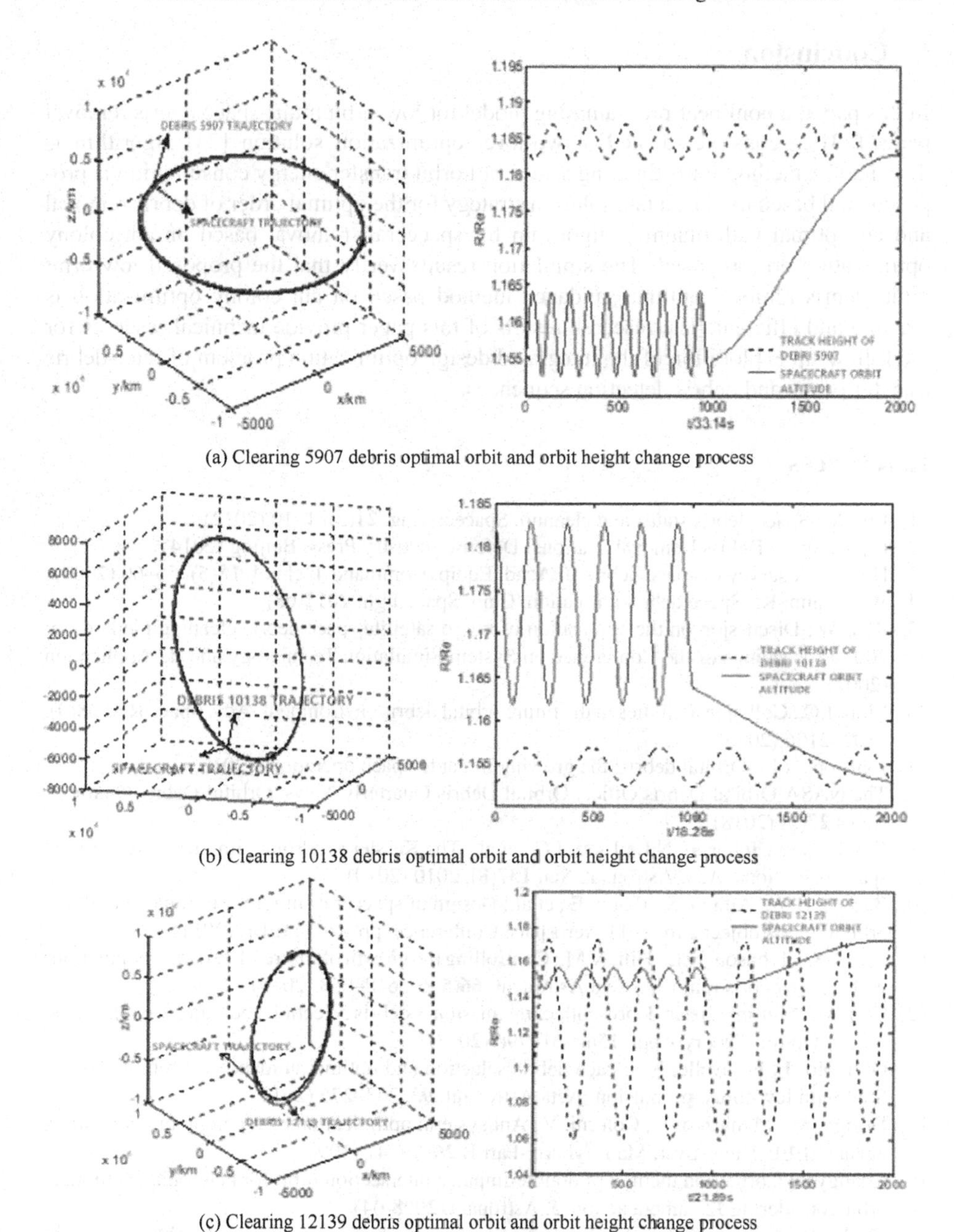

(a) Clearing 5907 debris optimal orbit and orbit height change process

(b) Clearing 10138 debris optimal orbit and orbit height change process

(c) Clearing 12139 debris optimal orbit and orbit height change process

Fig. 5. Optimal orbit and orbit height change process

6 Conclusion

In this paper, a nonlinear programming model for low-orbit multi-space debris removal paths [23] is constructed, and a two-level optimization solution [24] algorithm is designed. A method for estimating spacecraft orbit transfer energy consumption is proposed, and based on this, a fast solution strategy for the optimal order of debris removal and an optimal path planning algorithm for spacecraft removal based on ant colony optimization are proposed. The simulation results verify that the proposed low-orbit multi-debris removal optimal guidance method based on ant colony optimization is feasible and efficient. The research results of this paper provide technical reserves for the follow-up exploration of the integrated design optimization problem of inter-debris transfer orbits and debris detection sequences.

References

1. Lin, X.: Space debris status and cleanup. Spacecr. Eng. **21**(3), 1–10 (2012)
2. Li, Y.: Space Debris Removal. National Defense Industry Press, Beijing (2014)
3. Huo, J.: A survey of space debris. J. Acad. Equip. Command Technol. **18**(5), 56–60 (2007)
4. Weidmann, K.: Space debris mitigation. Chin. Spaceflight **2012**(08)
5. Zhu, W.: Discussion on the application of micro satellite space debris cleaning method. In: 2007 Proceedings of the Conference on System Simulation Technology and Its Application (2007)
6. Liou, J.C.: Collision activities in the future orbital debris environment. Adv. Space Res. **38**(9), 2102–2106 (2006)
7. Johnson, N.L.: Orbital debris: the growing threat to space operations (2010)
8. The NASA Orbital Debris Office. Orbital Debris Quarterly News. Orbital Debris Quarterly News **22**(3) (2018)
9. Kessler, D.J., Johnson, N.L., Liou, J.C., et al.: The Kessler syndrome: implications to future space operations. Adv. Astronaut. Sci. **137**(8), 2010 (2010)
10. Barbee, B.W., Alfano, S., Pinon, E., et al.: Design of spacecraft missions to remove multiple orbital debris objects. In: 2011 Aerospace Conference, pp. 1–14. IEEE (2011)
11. Liou, J.C., Johnson, N.L., Hill, N.M.: Controlling the growth of future LEO debris populations with active debris removal. Acta Astronaut. **66**(5–6), 648–653 (2010)
12. Cerf, M.: Multiple space debris collecting mission—debris selection and trajectory optimization. J. Optim. Theory Appl. **156**, 761–796 (2013)
13. Olympio, J., Frouvelle, N.: Space debris selection and optimal guidance for removal in the SSO with low-thrust propulsion. Acta Astronaut. **93**, 263–275 (2014)
14. Dorigo, M., Maniezzo, V., Colorni, V.: Ant system: optimization by a colony of cooperating agents. IEEE Trans. Syst. Man Cybern.-Part B **26**, 29–41 (1996)
15. Changyan: Correction method of double-impulse intersection orbit for heteroplane elliptical orbit considering J2 camera action. J. Astronaut. **2008**(04)
16. Ge, H.: Pheromone-based adaptive continuous domain hybrid ant colony algorithm. Comput. Eng. Appl. **2017**(06)
17. Socha, K., Dorigo, M.: Ant colony optimization for continuous domains. Eur. J. Oper. Res. **185**, 1155–1173 (2008)
18. Socha, K., Dorigo, M.: Ant colony optimization for continuous domains. Eur. J. Oper. Res. **2006**(3)
19. Socha, K., Dorigo, M.: Ant colony optimization for continuous domains. Eur. J. Oper. Res. **185**(3), 1155–1173 (2008)

20. https://celestrak.com/
21. https://en.wikipedia.org/wiki/North_American_Aerospace_Defense_Command
22. Qin, A.K., Huang, V.L., Suganthan, P.N.: Differential evolution algorithm with strategy adaptation for global numerical optimization. IEEE Trans. Evol. Comput. **13**(2), 398–417 (2009)
23. Lin, M., Xu, M., Fu, X.: A parallel algorithm for the initial screening of space debris collisions prediction using the SGP4/SDP4 models and GPU acceleration. Adv. Space Res. **59**, 2398–2406 (2017)
24. Ferreira, J.C., Fonseca, C.M., Denysiuk, R., Gaspar-Cunha, A.: Methodology to select solutions for multiobjective optimization problems: weighted stress function method. J. Multi-Criteria Decis. Anal. **24**(3–4), 103–120 (2017)

Low-Orbit Satellite Solar Array Current Prediction Method Based on Unsupervised Learning

Guan Wu(✉), Jun Chen, Wei Zhang, Xing Hu, and Jing Zhao

Key Laboratory for Fault Diagnosis and Maintenance of Spacecraft In-Orbit, Xi'an 710000, China
784732554@qq.com

Abstract. With the continuous development of the space industry, the role of satellite become more and more important in China's national economic construction, disaster prevention and mitigation. Power system is one of the important sub-systems that directly impact the in-orbit safe and affection of satellites. Satellite solar array determine the current output of whole satellite. The paper shows the solar array current prediction method based on unsupervised learning which can solve the low-orbit satellite solar array current prediction problem. This method introduces the competition elements that establish the mapping relation between the historical data and the competition element, obtains the best sample through the competition between the competition elements in the prediction processes, the relation functions take the best sample data as the benchmark which can realize the prediction of solar cell array output. Through competition the information of temperature, earth reflection, conversion efficiency and attenuation factors in the sample data are introduced effectively, and the description of such factors in the prediction process is avoided. Through the actual data analysis, we realize the extrapolation of the one-year current mean error is not more than 0.4 a, and the maximum error is not more than 0.5 a. The prediction algorithm for the solar cell array of low orbit satellites without the mathematical description of temperature, earth reflection, conversion efficiency and attenuation factors can predict the reasonable introduction of the above factors.

Keywords: Current · Prediction · Reflection · Solar array

1 Introduction

In order to satisfy the needs of current voltage of the primary power in power system, the satellite solar array is usually composed of a series of photovoltaic cell patches in parallel. The output of Photovoltaic is impacted by temperature, solar incident intensity, space environment, earth light and so many other factors. In document 1, the max power of solar array output is described as:

$$P_{BOL} = S_0 * X * X_s * X_e * A_c * N * F_b * \eta * F_c\left(\beta_p \Delta T + 1\right)\cos\theta$$

Q. Wu et al. (Eds.): WiSATS 2020, LNICST 358, pp. 132–144, 2021.
https://doi.org/10.1007/978-3-030-69072-4_11

S_0 is the space solar constant, θ is the angle of the right amount of the normal sun sail, X is the correction factor for oblique shooting, X_s is the seasonal change factors, X_e is the earth albedo gain factor, A_c is the battery array nominal area, N is the total number of individual solar cells, F_b is the testing calibration of loss factors, η is the transfer efficiency, F_c is the combined loss factor, β_p is the power temperature coefficient, ΔT is the differences between operating temperatures and nominal temperatures.

In all the factors, only the solar incident intensity can describe by mathematics, the other factors are difficult to be described by accuracy mathematics mode. For example, solar array working temperature, in the document 2 the solar array temperature is determined by the following energy equation:

sunlight + earthlight +earth thermal radiation +the heat from the neighbor components of satellite = output electric power+ heat of radiation back to the space.

The equation is described the battery array temperature because it caused by the earth reflection, thermal radiation, self-dissipating heat and so on is difficult to describe the temperature of the battery array more accurately.

Thus, the prediction of solar array output has to consider many factors based on model method and some of the factors cannot express accurately by data method. It is difficult to calculate the output of low-orbit satellite solar array using a general method for the analytical parameters often different to suit different satellite solar array. This paper proposes a prediction method of low-orbit solar array current based on unsupervised learning to these problems shown above. The advantages of this method are best matching samples through the competition between layers and to calculate the result in form of output function with the best matching samples to obtain the output current of solar array which effectively avoid the impact factors such as earth light, temperature and the difference between different satellites analyze model. The low-orbit satellite solar array output can use the unify algorithm.

2 Algorithm Design

The basic idea of this algorithm is to sample the historical current telemetry data according to certain rules and slice the data to form different sample data. The sample data are cleaned according to the cleaning rules to form a pure sample. The mapping of the sample and the solar cell array output influence factors are established. Each sample corresponds to the influence factors according to the mapping relationship, and the influence factors form the competitive layers of the data. When the currents are predicted, the influence factors corresponding to the period which will be predicted are calculated as the input of the prediction. The matching degree of competitions and inputs between each competition element in the competition layers. The historical data which are mapped by the winning competition elements are the benchmark sample, and the benchmark sample are calculated according to the prescribed functional relationship to form the prediction data. At the same time, the differences between the predicted data and the actual data are calculated and introduced into the next stage of current calculation as the correction coefficients. The basic flow is shown in Fig. 1. In this algorithm, the key link is sample cleaning, because the sample purity directly affects the accuracy of the prediction data. It is necessary to establish reasonable cleaning rules for the sample data to ensure the purity of the sample data.

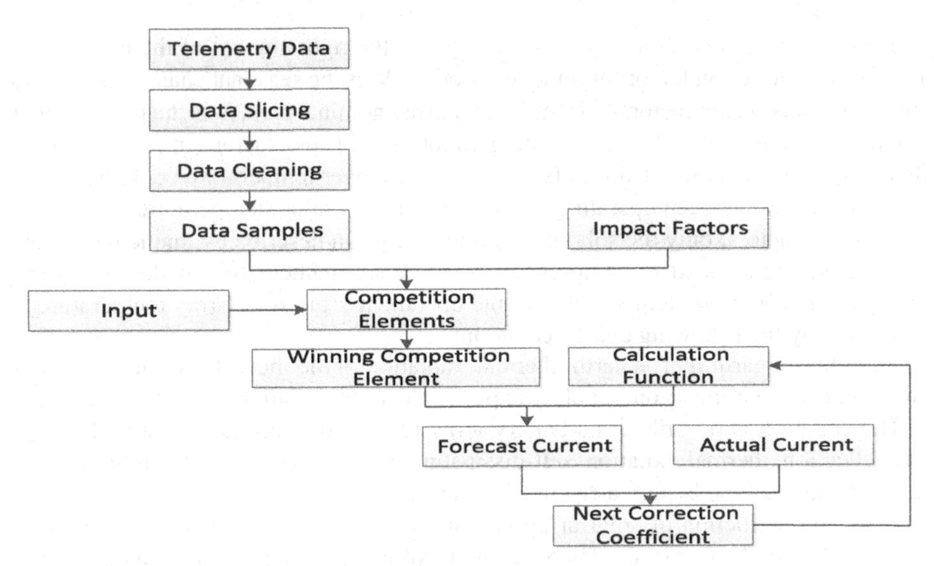

Fig. 1. Algorithm flow

2.1 Data Selection

In addition to the above factors, the output of satellite solar array is also affected by the working state and the working mode of the satellite. For example, in the side-swing mode, the relationship between the normal sail and the right amount of the sun is changed, and at the same time, it may cause the solar cell array shielding by the satellite body and the space-borne equipment. And the output of solar cell array will change. Because of the change of the load, the working point of the solar cell array is changed. According to the data analysis, the working point of the solar cell array of a remote sensing satellite is shifted to the right under the condition of load operation, resulting in the output current dropping about 0.5 a from the normal working point. In order to ensure the purity of sample data. different modes of sample data cause the output of its solar cell array change, which lead to the error in the prediction process. In the process of data selection, the data need to be cleaned to eliminate the interference of the satellite working state, working mode and so on.

The data of satellite battery array are extracted from the database which are combined with the satellite orbit cycle, and the ground shadow is taken as the starting time of the slice until the next point before the ground shadow, which is used as a slice of the satellite telemetry data. If there is no ground shadow, the data are extracted from the changing characteristics of the data and the satellite orbit cycle. the current data set as $I = (I_1, I_2, \ldots, I_n)$. Slice the I according to the rules of orbital period, illumination region, full illumination region, etc. To form different sets of slices $I_i'(i = 1, 2, \ldots, K)$ the current set corresponding to each slice $I'_i = (I'_{i1}, I'_{i2}, \ldots, I'_{ij})$.

Each current value of the satellite solar array output corresponds to each working state of the satellite. It is necessary to distinguish the satellite working state corresponding to the satellite current. There is only the expected state in the sample. for the undesired state in the slice, the fragment in the slice should be removed. for each data slice I'_i, the current data domain working state data needs to be aligned. Because of the telemetry sampling rate differences, the two are out of sync in time, so it is necessary to react to the satellite working state according to different parameters, so that the current output can be well approximated to the desired satellite working state. The corresponding cleaning rule set C = (C_1, C_2, ..., C_m) is established for slice I'_i,. If the corresponding state of each data in the I'_i satisfies the set c, all the data is selected as the element of the I'_i set. If there is a situation that the I'_{ij} and I'_{ij+k} does not meet the c, the data needs to be cleaned. the elements in the I'_{ij} to I'_{ij+k} does not meet the rules. if the time interval is greater than 5 min, this sample is culled; the time interval is less than or equal to 5 min, the data between the I'_{ij} and the I'_{ij+k} is culled, and the rest of the sample data is retained. After slice cleaning, the elements in the slice I'_i are output of satellite solar cell array in the desired state, and the purity of slice data is guaranteed.

2.2 Sample Establishment

For the clean satellite solar cell array current output is set as i'. The angle of incidence is calculated as:

$$\beta = \sin^{-1}(\cos \partial_s * \sin R_i * \sin(\Omega - \alpha_s) + \sin \partial_s * \cos R_i)$$

As shown above, Ω is the rising point of red longitude, α_s is the sun red longitude, ∂_s is the sun red latitude, R_i is satellite orbit inclination. The distance factor is calculated by the ratio of the current daily distance to the standard daily distance. The current daily distance is R_1, the standard distance is R_2, then the distance factor $R = R_1/R_2$. pi each R, β is defined as an impact factor P, and each impact factor P_i will correspond uniquely to the current sample I'_i, the impact factor P_i will map one-to-one with the sample I'_i to form a mapping f: $P_i \rightarrow I'_i$.

Make the R_i, β_i as a point P_i on the plane in three-dimensional space, the corresponding relationship between the P_i and the sample I'_i is shown in Fig. 2 below, and the corresponding elements of each sample are set as I'_I = (x_1, x_2, ..., x_k). the influence factor is defined on the Rβ plane, where point P_i mapped to the sample I'_i. the influence factor corresponding to the current period to be predicted is set as P_0 on the Rβplane. in this way, the most matching sample P_0 with the target point will be obtained and converted to the best match between the mapping influence factor P_i and the input influence factor on the Rβ plane. the point P_i on the Rβ plane is used as the competition element, and the matching degree between them. The P_0, and the winning point P_i in the corresponding sample will be used as the base sample to participate in the calculation of the predicted current.

2.3 Self Organization Mapping

The method based on Euclidean distance is used for the competition between points P_i on the Rβ plane. the euclidean distance between the j unit of the competition layer and the input influence factor P_0 is shown below.

$$d_j = P_0 - P_j = \sqrt{(\beta_j - \beta_0)^2 + (R_j - R_0)^2}$$

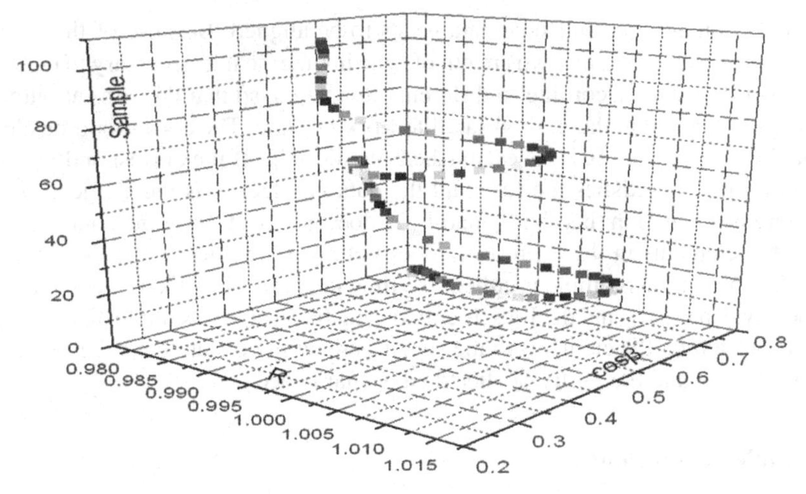

Fig. 2. The relationship of samples and parameters

To randomly select a competitive element P_j for any P_0, calculate its distance with the P_0 and write it as d_j the initial value of the competition. To the next unit of the competition layer, calculate its distance and write as d_{j+1}, if $d_j > d_{j+1}$, recorded as $d_j = d_{j+1}$, otherwise $d_j = d_j$, until the end of the competition, to obtain the minimum corresponding competition element is the winning unit.

According to the factors that affect the output of solar cell array described in reference 1, sample acquisition and cleaning proposes the best sample matching. we can make full use of the information of oblique correction factor, seasonal change factor, earth albedo gain factor, loss factor, conversion efficiency, power temperature coefficient and so on. The current value in the sample is highly similar to the above information contained in the current value of the target point to be predicted.

Mark the minimum distance unit after winning the competition as P_j, as the benchmark unit for data prediction. Take its corresponding data sample f:P → I'', $P_j \rightarrow I'_j = (x_1, x_2, \ldots, x_n)$ according to the mapping relationship between the unit and the sample. Each of the corresponding elements in the I'_j will serve as a reference element for the current to be predicted. The predicted current is recorded as the calculation function f(x), then the predicted current value $I_a = f(x) * I'_j$.

3 Example Verification

3.1 Competition of Competition Elements

Two typical satellites with low orbit are selected for verification, which are recorded as S1 and S2 respectively. Two satellites were selected to slice the measured data of solar cell array in 2019, and more than 400 slices were formed. The cleaning rules for the above slice formation are.

c = (pose control state, load state, shunt state, load current). after cleaning, the number of S1 is 483, and the number of S2 is 409. Each sample is taken as a mapping unit, and the sample data time is 2019 to each sample, calculate its corresponding influence factors pi, define the pi on the rβ plane, and the S1 and S2 samples correspond to their influence factors one by one to form a mapping relationship. Select four different dates for s1 and S2 to predict current in 2020, that is, give four different inputs in the rβ plane of s1 and S2. The input parameters p the S1 and S2 input points are (0.984477, 0.613864), (0.991789, 0.686474), (1.011244, 0.984914), (0.990069, 0.973689), (0.985539, 0.966172), (1.012402, 0.973927). In the competition layer the influence factors compete with each other to match the input and the unit with the smallest distance win. Specific competition results are shown in Table 1 below.

Table 1. Result of competition

Input P_0	Label	S1	S2
Day1	The minimum distance	0.007566	0.064538
	The winning competition units	P_3	P_{317}
Day2	The minimum distance	0.006646	0.017800
	The winning competition units	P_{35}	P_{317}
Day3	The minimum distance	/	0.019589
	The winning competition units	/	P_{287}
Day4	The minimum distance	/	0.008997
	The winning competition units	/	P_{213}

After competition, winning competition units P_3, P_{35} of S1 win in day1, day2, winning competition units P_{317}, P_{317}, P_{287}, P_{213} of S_2 that win in day1 to day4. The corresponding samples of these units contain the factors that affect the output of the solar cell array most closely to the actual factors, and will obtain the right to participate in the current calculation.

3.2 Current Prediction

Table 1 shows that the predict current of satellite S1 and S2 are the sample i'3, i'35 and the sample i'317, i'317, i'287, i'213, respectively the corresponding elements of each sample are extracted separately and participate in the current calculation. To establish the calculation function.

$f(X) = \frac{\cos\beta}{\cos\beta_i} * \frac{R_i^2}{R_2^2} * K$, where k is the correction coefficient and the ratio of the actual value to the theoretical value in the previous stage. The predicted current is $I_a = f(X) * I'_j = \frac{\cos\beta}{\cos\beta_i} * \frac{R_i^2}{R^2} * K * I'_j$, The elements in the sample I'_j are calculated according to the function $f(X)$ to form a set of current I_a, and the elements in the set I_a are the predicted current values.

Using the above method, the S1 and S2 satellites are calculated to formulate the output current prediction of the solar array at any date, and the current values are shown in Fig. 3, 4, 5, 6, 7 and Fig. 8 below.

The satellite S1operates in different orbital positions, the angle between the solar cell formation line and the solar vector is constantly changing. At the same time, the

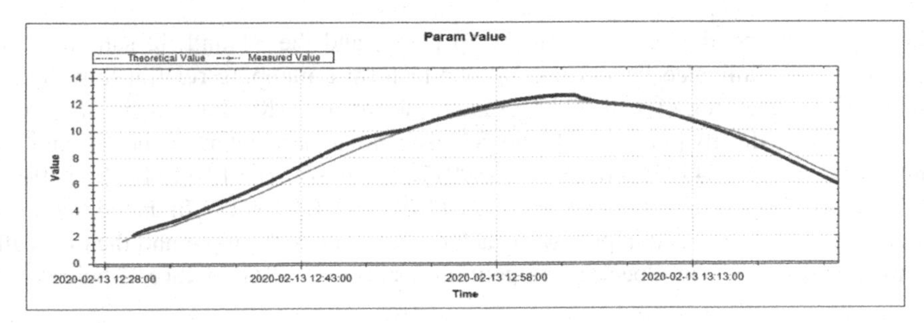

Fig. 3. S1 satellite current forecasting and actual results day1 (extrapolation for 1 year)

output of the satellite solar cell array is basically cosine curve due to the influence of the incident angle, the temperature of the battery array, the conversion efficiency and so on. Because the above factors are included in the sample information and are basically consistent with the state to be predicted, the predicted data can well reflect the actual state after competitive calculation. It can be seen from the Fig. 3 and Fig. 4 that the predicted value is in good agreement with the actual value. The predicted data can well track the output state of the battery array at different orbital positions, track the influence of the earth light on the output of the solar cell array, and reflect the current change of the satellite due to the change of incident conditions.

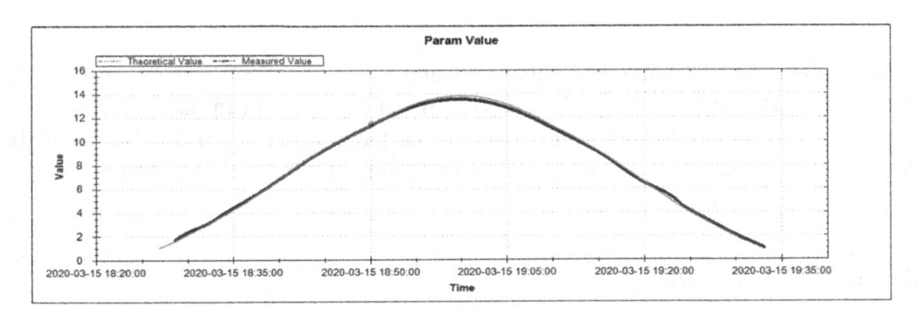

Fig. 4. S1 satellite current forecasting and actual results day2 (extrapolation for 1 year)

Figure 5, 6, 7 and 8 reflect the consistency between measured and predicted data from satellite S2. satellite S2 track solar mode for conventional solar cell arrays. the deviation of its solar cell formation line from the solar vector will remain within a certain range of requirements. in addition to the influence of incident angle, conversion efficiency, sail temperature and other factors during the operation of the satellite, there are also different orbital positions from the relationship between the solar cell formation line and the earth changes, it is can be known that in its output being affected by the earth albedo. Earth albedo is difficult to express mathematically, for the Earth albedo information is contained in the sample data, the predicted data can reflect the trend influencing of different factors on the output of solar array such as Earth albedo and so on.

Figure 7 predicts that there is no satellite shadowing process, because the shadowing data does not meet the cleaning rules c, and its data is cleaned during the sample

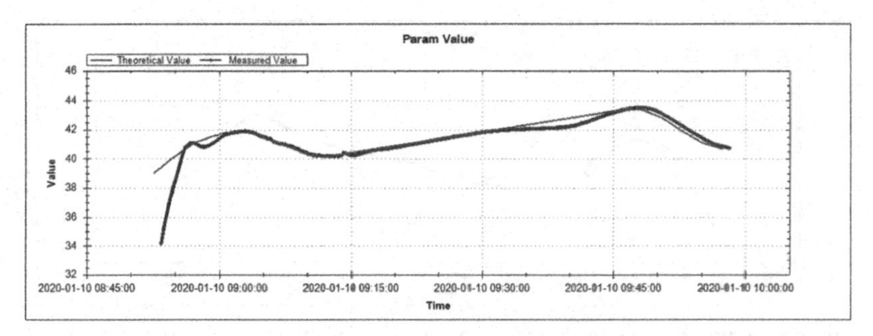

Fig. 5. S2 satellite current forecasting and actual results day1 (extrapolation for 1 year)

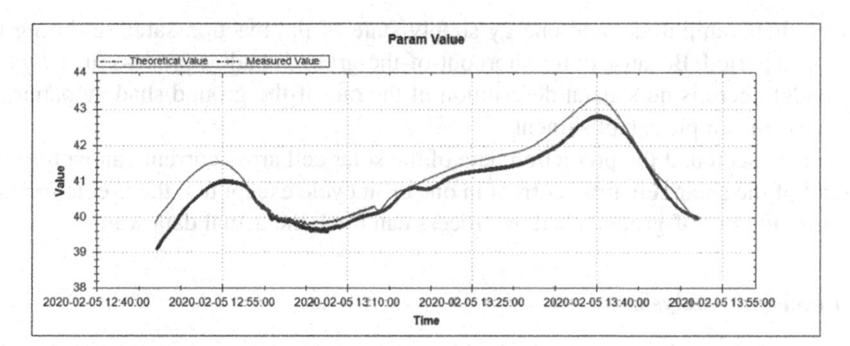

Fig. 6. S2 satellite current forecasting and actual results day2 (extrapolation for 1 year)

establishment. Through the actual data analysis, the satellite s2 due to the change of the satellite load, the working point of the solar cell array shifts to the right, which results in the phenomenon that the output of the solar cell array drops about 0.5 a. compared with the normal operation. If the sample data is not cleaned in model it will cause the prediction data to appear concave points, which will lead to prediction error.

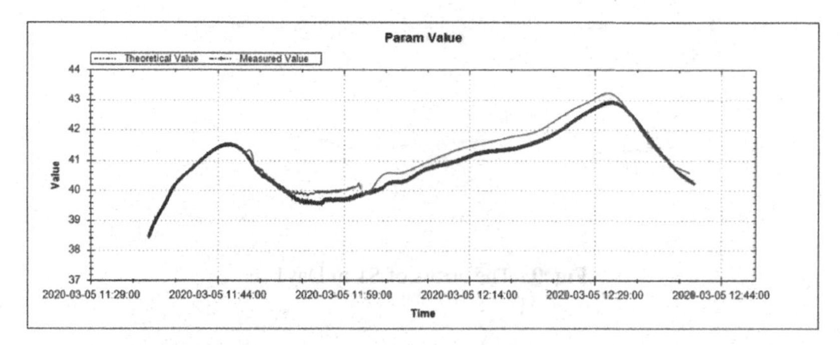

Fig. 7. S2 satellite current forecasting and actual results day3 (extrapolation for 1 year)

In one orbit period, after the satellite is completely out of the ground, the predicted current can be basically consistent with the measured data on the key information such

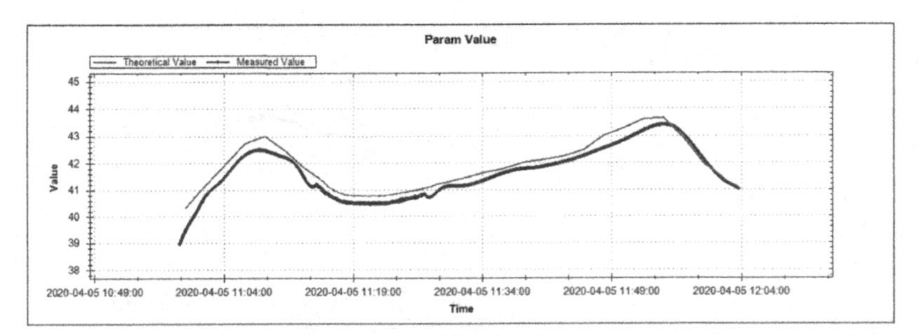

Fig. 8. S2 satellite current forecasting and actual results day4 (extrapolation for 1 year)

as curve shape amplitude, and energy supply state of the reaction satellite during the whole orbit period. Because of the short out-of-the-ground shadow process (usually tens of seconds), there is no special description of the out-of-the-ground shadow pattern in the process of sample establishment.

It can be seen that the prediction data of the solar cell array current can well reflect the trend of the solar cell array current in one orbit cycle except that the prediction data of the satellite out-of-ground shadow process can track the actual data well.

3.3 Precision Analysis

Analysis of the error between prediction data and measured data of satellite S1 is shown in Fig. 9 and Fig. 10. The error calculation method is to calculate the difference between the measured data and the predicted data frame by frame. The difference value is defined as absolute error, which can reflect the real-time tracking ability of the predicted data to the measured data. Where the day1 prediction error is approximately 0.7 a, that exceeds the expected result. The correction coefficient is calculated k, and the coefficient k is introduced into the calculation of day2. The absolute error of day2 is less than 0.5 a that is in line with the expectation.

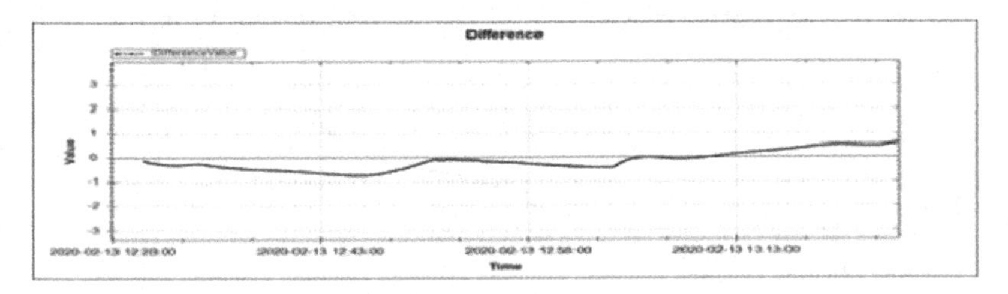

Fig. 9. The errors of S1 in Day1

An analysis of the error between prediction data and measured data of satellite s2 is shown in Figs. 11, 12, 13 and 14. In Fig. 11, Fig. 12 and Fig. 14, the error exceeds 0.7 a means satellite are part os its out-of-ground process. After the satellite is completely out of the ground, the predicted data can track the actual data well. The error

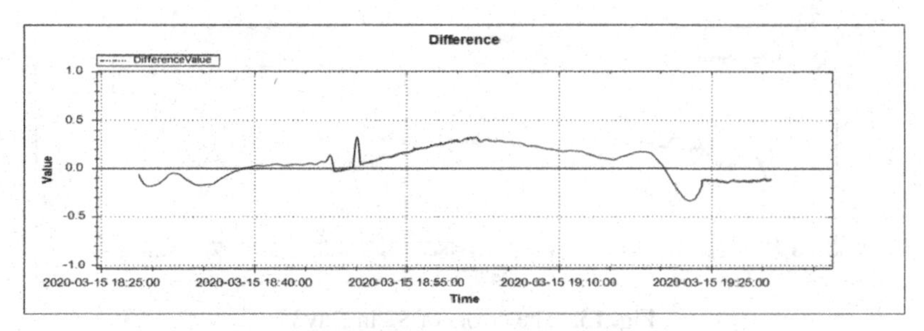

Fig. 10. The errors of S1 in Day2

can be controlled at about 0.5 a. The energy supply of satellite solar array is mainly concentrated in the light region. We need to pay more attention to the output current prediction of satellite in the sun illumination region. The process of entering or leaving the ground shadow, the output of solar cell array has little effect on satellite energy cannot be considered in prediction analysis.

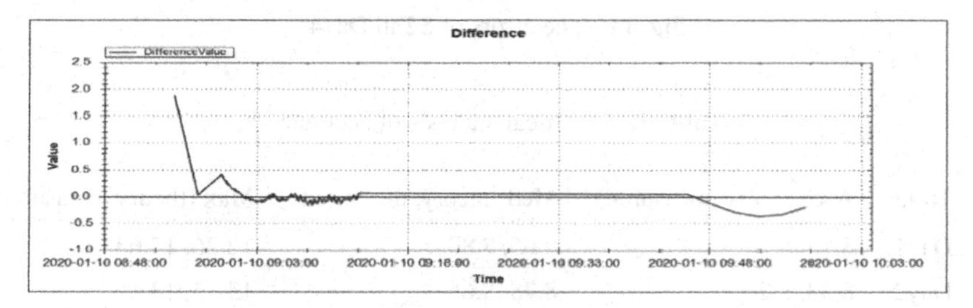

Fig. 11. The errors of S2 in Day1

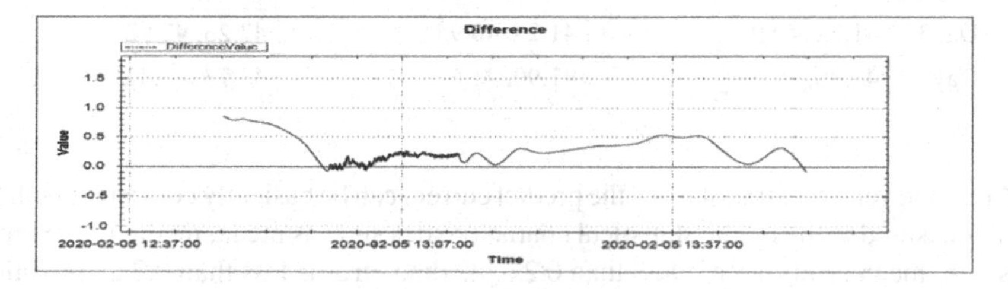

Fig. 12. The errors of S2 in Day2

The predict data and the measure data are statistically analyzed from three aspects: mean, median and maximum. The results are shown in Table 2 below. The main reason for selecting these three parameters is that the mean value can reflect the power supply capacity of the solar array in one orbital period, the median can reflect the central characteristic of the output current of the battery array in one orbital period, and the maximum value reflects the output characteristic of the battery array under the influence of the earth albedo. These three parameters are basically able to characterize the consistency between the predicted data and the actual data.

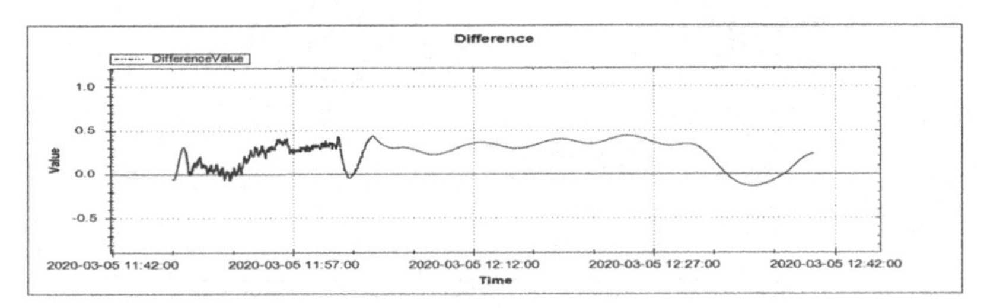

Fig. 13. The errors of S2 in Day3

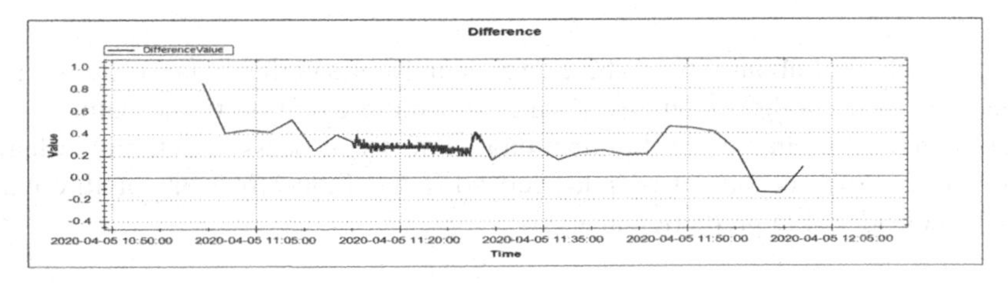

Fig. 14. The errors of S2 in Day4

Table 2. Statistical analysis of accuracy

Sat	Time	Ave (theory, measured)	Med (theory, measured)	Max (theory, measured)
S1	Day1	8.18, 8.16	8.65, 8.80	12.26, 12.63
	Day2	8.33, 8.23	8.78, 8.66	13.85, 13.55
S2	Day1	40.79, 41.47	40.89, 40.95	43.32, 43.52
	Day2	41.19, 40.89	41.13, 40.85	43.32, 42.84
	Day3	41.22, 40.94	41.24, 40.95	43.23, 42.92
	Day4	41.98, 41.65	41.90, 41.67	43.73, 43.42

After one year of extrapolation, the predict current can be basically consistent with the actual measured value on the statistical characteristics such as mean, median, maximum and so on. mean error of S1 is less than 0.2 a, median error is less than 0.2 a, maximum error is less than 0.4 a.. mean error of S2 is less than 0.4 a, median error is less than 0.3 a, maximum error is less than 0.5 a. In the above statistical characteristics, the mean value reflects the stability part of the output of the satellite solar cell array, which is generally the output state of the solar cell array after the earth shadow is basically constant, the working point is stable, and the earth albedo influence is small. The median value describes the central position data characteristics of the battery array output current data, reflecting the centralized trend of the data. The small median error can indicate that the prediction is in good agreement with the actual data in the trend of the data set. The maximum value mainly reflects the effect of the earth albedo on the output of the solar cell array, and the small error of the maximum value indicates that the predicted data can track the effect of the earth albedo well.

It can be seen from the above precision analysis that the method can be consistent with the measured data in absolute error and statistical characteristic error, and the long period prediction results can well reflect the change of the actual solar array current. It can be used in the prediction of the power supply capacity of the satellite solar array.

4 Conclusion

In this paper, the output of satellite solar cell array is predicted by unsupervised method. After one year of extrapolation, the accuracy and variation trend can keep good agreement with the measured data. This method can predict the output of solar cell array based on the historical data by establishing historical sample data and introducing competition elements. In the process of current prediction, the purity of sample data is the key to predict accurately. To establish pure samples, the appropriate sample cleaning rules must be selected. In the process of sample cleaning, it is necessary to fully consider the influence of satellites output of the solar cell array. Pure sample data information can reflect the output of solar cell array in different working states and working modes. The pure sample data information in different factors which can describe the effects of the output of the satellite solar cell array, the different factors in the current change. If the sample is not clear and clean, and the information of satellite working state is introduced, it will inevitably cause a large difference between the predicted data and the actual data. compared with the analytical model, we make full use of such a huge amount of influence factors contained in the historical output telemetry data of solar cell array that do not need to establish the model of temperature, earth albedo, conversion efficiency and other factors in the actual calculation process. through sample cleaning, competition between competing elements, the reasonable introduction of the above factors is realized. According to the actual situation of different satellites, this method can realize the unity of the algorithm. In the process of practical application, the mapping relationship between the output current and the influence factor can be formed by establishing the database of the output of the solar array output of different satellites. Through the precision analysis, it can be seen that the long-period extrapolation can meet the demand of low-orbit satellite solar array output prediction in terms of absolute error and statistical error. According to the demand of high-orbit satellite current prediction, adaptive modification is made in data sampling, cleaning and calculation.

References

1. Shanghai Space Power Research Institute: Physical Power Technology, Science Press, September 2014
2. By Memphis r Patel. Translated by Han Bo, Chen Qi, Cui Xiaoting. Spacecraft Power System. China Aerospace Press (2013)
3. Yang, T., Jing, G., Fan, H., Zhao, G.: Satellite In-Orbit State Detection and Health Management Technology. Defense Industry Press (2018)
4. Zhao, G., Li, Y., Xu, M., Yang, T.: Satellite Fault Diagnosis Technology and Application in Orbit. Defense Industry Press (2018)

5. Liu, H., Liu, D., Li, Q.: Nonlinear prediction of chaotic time series based on support vector machine. Syst. Eng. Theory Pract. **25**(9), 94–99 (2005)
6. Zhang, J., Hu, S.: Prediction of chaotic time series based on multiple kernel learning support vector regression. J. Phys. **57**(5), 2708–2713 (2008)
7. Chen, T.C., Han, D.J., Au, F.T.K., et al.: Acceleration of Levenberg-Marquardt training of neural networks. **3**, 1873–1878
8. Cai, M., Cai, F., Shi, A., et al.: Chaotic time series prediction based on local-region multi-steps forecasting model. In: Advances in Neural Networks-ISNN, 2004: International Symposium on Neural Networks. Part II, Dalian, China, vol. 8, pp. 418-423P (2004)
9. Liu, F., Zhao, L., Mehmood, S., Zhang, J., Fei, B.: A modified failure envelope method for failure prediction of multi-bolt composite joints. Compos. Sci. Technol. **83**(28), 54–63 (2013)
10. Jiang, Q., Xie, J., Ye, J.: Mathematical Model. Higher Education Press, Beijing (2003)
11. Yetai, F.: Error Theory and Data Processing. Machinery Industry Press, Beijing (2004)

Anomaly Detection Method Based on Granger Causality Modeling

Siya Chen(✉), G. Jin, Sun Peng, and Lulu Zhang

National University of Defense Technology, Changsha, China
2280526009@qq.com

Abstract. Satellites are very expensive to manufacture and require high reliability. Monitoring a large amount of telemetry data during the satellite orbit operation, the telemetry data are an important data source for analyzing the internal correlation of the satellite system and detecting anomalies. Telemetry data is in the form of time series, and there may be mutual influence and correlation between these time series. Due to the diversity of its influence and association forms, it is necessary to establish an effective model to determine the association relationship between them in order to detect anomalies on this basis and identify the cause of anomalies. In this paper, we use Granger causality model to analyze correlation between time series of telemetry data and establish a causality model. Detecting anomalies according to the causality which under normal circumstances and find out the cause of the anomalies. The case study shows that our method is effective.

Keywords: Granger analysis · Causal relationship · Anomaly detection · Satellites

1 Introduction

There has been a lot of work on association analysis for time series. Most researches use time series correlation coefficient to determine whether there is a correlation. For example, Pearson correlation coefficient [3] and Spearman correlation coefficient. When the time series have different change patterns or the correlation has a lag relationship, these methods cannot reflect the correlation well [1]. By extracting relevant features of time series and then calculating the correlation coefficient, but when the time series is very long, it may be difficult to give the fluctuation relationship of the time series accurately [2]. For time series of the same length, move to calculate the correlation coefficient to determine whether they have lag correlation, and find out the lag time. In addition to the correlation coefficient method, [4] Try to find out the influence structure diagram (SIG) when the time series is abnormal, and find the influence relationship between the time series. The time series anomaly is calculated by the skewness of the data in the sliding window relative to the distribution of the entire time series, but cannot recognize anomalies caused by some historical data. In addition, there are many statistical models used to calculate the relevance of time series [5–7], but they are aimed at specific time series and are not applicable.

Q. Wu et al. (Eds.): WiSATS 2020, LNICST 358, pp. 145–151, 2021.
https://doi.org/10.1007/978-3-030-69072-4_12

Some researchers use Granger causality models for anomaly detection [10]. A graphical model to study Granger causality in multivariate time series is proposed to detect anomalies. The model calculates a "relevant anomaly" score for each variable through the Granger graphical model, which can provide information about the possible causes of anomalies. [11] proposed an improved Granger-Lasso algorithm, which is applicable to a wider range of heterogeneous time series [14]. The use of Granger causality test for alarm correlation is applicable to alarms based on anomalies, but there is no analysis method for the causes of anomalies.

In general, much work has been done on time series anomaly detection, but it still faces many challenges, including:

(1) The influence relationship of time series is diverse, and it may be related in trend, shape, or pattern. At present, there is lack of more general models and methods to accurately determine the relevance of time series.
(2) For anomaly detection based on telemetry data, due to the huge amount of data, the current real-time nature of many anomaly detection methods is difficult to meet the requirements.

This paper proposes a method of time series association analysis and anomaly detection based on Granger causality model. The main work is as follows:

(1) Use the Granger causality model to discover whether there is a correlation between time series. This correlation is diverse, including trend correlation, time correlation, pattern correlation, and so on.
(2) Improve the Granger causality model to reduce the time complexity of the calculation, so that it can quickly produce results for large amounts of data.
(3) Quickly find out the cause of anomalies based on the Granger causality model.

The experimental analysis on the telemetry data of the space bridge shows that the method in this paper has a good performance on anomaly detection and anomaly detection.

2 Granger Causality Model

2.1 Correlation Analysis of Time Series

Clive W. J. Granger proposed the Granger causality model [13] in 1969 to analyze the correlation between economic variables. After years of development, Granger causality model has been applied to many other fields, and many improved methods have been proposed. The Granger causality model relies on the variance of the best least squares prediction.

Given two time series $\{X_s, i = 1, 2, 3, \ldots, t\}$, $\{Y_s, i = 1, 2, 3, \ldots, t\}$, t is the length of the time series, ε_{1s} is the white noise. p and q are the maximum lag periods of time series Y and X, respectively.

The test steps of Granger causality model are as follows:

① First verify whether X is the Granger cause of Y change. This test requires the estimation of the following regression model:

$$Y_s = \sum_{i=1}^{p} \alpha_i Y_{s-i} + \sum_{i=1}^{q} \beta_i X_{s-i} + \varepsilon_{1s} \tag{1}$$

$$Y_s = \sum_{i=1}^{p} \alpha_i Y_{s-i} + \varepsilon_{1s} \tag{2}$$

Equation (1) is called an unconstrained regression model (u), and Eq. (2) is called a constrained regression model (r).

② Propose the null hypothesis of the test: $H_0 : \beta_1 = \beta_2 = \ldots = \beta_q = 0$, That is, X is not the Granger cause of the change of Y.

③ Calculate the sum of squared residuals of Eq. (1) and Eq. (2) RSS_u, RSS_r.

④ Construct F statistics, n is the sample size:

$$F = \frac{(RSS_r - RSS_u)/q}{RSS_u/(n-p-q-1)} \sim F(q, n-p-q-1) \tag{3}$$

⑤ Test the null hypothesis, if $F \geq F_\alpha$, then $\beta_1, \beta_2, \ldots, \beta_q$ are not significantly zero, then the null hypothesis should be rejected, that is, X has an effect on Y; otherwise, the null hypothesis is accepted, that is, X has no effect on Y.

⑥ Swap the positions of X and Y, and test whether Y is the Granger cause of the change of X in the same way.

From the above, we can see that if the variables are interrelated, for both tests, we should reject the null hypothesis, that is, under the condition that contains the past information of the variables X and Y, effect of prediction on Y is better than the prediction effect made by Y's past information alone for Y, and the same is true for X. Therefore, we can determine whether there is a correlation between time series through a simple observation of the results.

Verifying the relationship between the two time series by using Granger Causality Model. For two time series, there may be four cases:

(1) The first case is that X is the Granger cause of the change of Y, but Y is not the Granger cause of the change of X. We can say that X has a unilateral effect on Y.
(2) The second case is that Y is the Granger cause of the change of X, but X is not the Granger cause of the change of Y. We can say that Y has a unilateral effect on X.
(3) The third case is that X is the Granger cause of the change of Y and Y is also the Granger cause of the change of X. we can say that X and Y are related to each other.
(4) The fourth case is that X is not the Granger cause of the change of Y and Y is also not the Granger cause of the change of X. We can say that X and Y are independent of each other, and there is no influence relationship.

If the past information of variables X and Y is included, the prediction effect of variable Y is better than the prediction effect of Y by past information of Y alone, that is, variable X helps to explain the future change of variable Y, It is considered that the variable X has an influence on the variable Y. The Granger causal correlation model relies on the variance of the best least squares prediction using all the information at certain points in the past, whether X and Y are trend correlations, shape correlations, or pattern correlations. All can be verified by Granger causality test.

2.2 Anomaly Detection

If there is a correlation between time series, then when they are in a normal state, if conduct Granger causality test, the result of the test is the case (3), that is, the two variables affect each other. For real-time monitoring, these variables are monitored in real time through a sliding window. Once it is found that the time series are not related to each other, an abnormality can be detected.

The prerequisite for Granger causality test is that the time series must be stable, otherwise false regression problems may occur. Therefore, before the Granger causality test, we should use the unit root test should test the stationarity of the time series of each indicator. The ADF test is used to check whether there is a unit root in the sequence: if the sequence is stationary, there is no unit root; otherwise, there will be a unit root. Therefore, the null hypothesis of the ADF test is that there is a unit root. If the statistical significance of the test is less than the three confidence levels (10%, 5%, 1%), then there are 90%, 95%, and 99% to reject the null hypothesis. If the data is unstable, differential processing is necessary until the data is stable.

Then use the processed data to test Granger causality. Take a sliding window of length T to detect time series that have been determined to influence mutually. By moving the window, conduct Granger causality test on each pair of time series of length T. Once it is found that the result of the test is not the case (3). That is, if there is no relationship that affects each other, an abnormality occurs, and an alarm is immediately issued to further determine the cause of the abnormality.

2.3 Analysis of Exception Causes

When the Granger causality model test is carried out through the sliding window and an abnormality is found, the cause of the abnormality is determined by analyzing the test results. If the test result is the case (1), X has an impact on Y, but Y has no impact on X,we can judge that X is abnormal, because at this time X appears a fluctuation different from the normal state, and the state of Y is still the same as in the normal state; if the test result is the case (2), Y has an impact on X, but X has no impact on Y. We can judge that Y is abnormal, because at this time Y has fluctuated differently from the normal state, and the state of X is still the same as in the normal state. If it is the case (4), further discussion is needed, which is the content of future research.

3 Case Study

In order to verify the effectiveness of the method in this paper, two sets of related time series X_1, X_2 are taken. As shown in Fig. 1, it can be seen that the time series X_1 and X_2 are related.

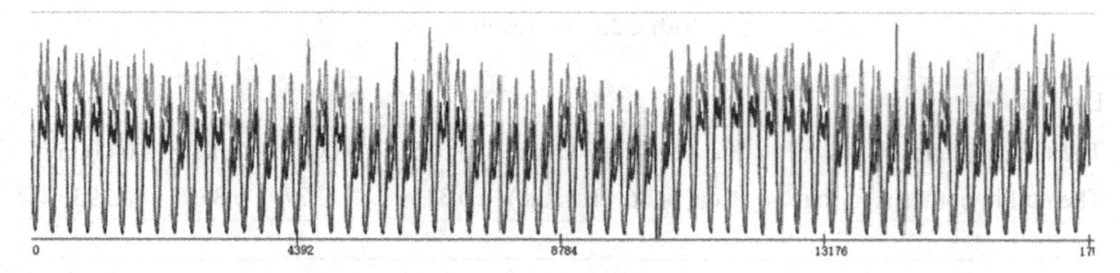

Fig. 1. Time series X_1, X_2

By conducting Granger causality test for X_1, X_2. The results show that X_1 and X_2 have a mutually influential relationship, which is very consistent with the actual situation, which can explain that the Granger causality model is effective in judging the correlation of time series.

When X_1 or X_2 is abnormal, take a sequence of time, and use sliding window to detect anomalies. When we move the sliding window, the result of Granger causality test during the abnormal time is no longer the mutually influential relationship between X_1 and X_2, the result matches the true situation. it can be concluded that even in the case of a large amount of data, the method in this paper can detect anomalies in time.

In order to verify whether the cause of the abnormality can be detected, firstly take the time series of X_1 is abnormal but X_2 is normal, and the results of Granger causality test are shown in Table 1. It can be concluded that the result of the test is that X_1 has an effect on X_2, but X_2 has no effect on X_1, and it is judged that X_1 is the cause of exception, which is in line with the actual situation.

Table 1. Test result 1

Lag	1	2	3	4
The null hypothesis: X_2 has no effect on X_1 (P value)	0.2051	0.6559	0.1987	0.2017
The null hypothesis: X_1 has no effect on X_2 (P value)	0.0052	0.0001	0.0000	0.0000

Then take the time series where X_2 is abnormal but X_1 is normal, and the result is shown in Table 2. It can be seen that the result of the test is that X_2 has an effect on X_1, but X_1 has no effect on X_2, and it we can judge that X_2 has an abnormality, which is in line with the actual situation. It follows from this that the method in this paper is effective in determining the cause of anomalies.

Table 2. Test result 2

Lag	1	2	3	4
The null hypothesis: X_2 has no effect on X_1 (P value)	0.0056	0.0005	0.0006	0.0005
The null hypothesis: X_1 has no effect on X_2 (P value)	0.3131	0.5377	0.3537	0.2956

4 Conclusion

This paper attempts to use the Granger causality model to determine whether the time series are correlated, based on the found relationship to monitor in real time, find anomalies in time, and further determine which variable caused the anomaly when the anomaly occurs. The case study shows that the proposed method in this paper is effective. In future work, we will further study how the related variables affect each other, as well as the analysis of the influence of one variable on other related variables when abnormal.

References

1. Su, Y., et al.: CoFlux: robustly correlating KPIs by fluctuations for service troubleshooting. In: Proceedings of the International Symposium on Quality of Service, IWQoS 2019 (2019)
2. Sakurai, Y., Papadimitriou, S., Faloutsos, C.: BRAID: stream mining through group lag correlations. In: Proceedings of the ACM SIGMOD International Conference on Management of Data, pp. 599–610 (2005)
3. Cohen, J.: Statistical Power Analysis for the Behavioural Sciences (1988)
4. Oliner, A.J., Kulkarni, A.V., Aiken, A.: Using correlated surprise to infer shared influence. In: 2010 IEEE/IFIP International Conference on Dependable Systems and Networks (DSN), pp. 191–200. IEEE (2010)
5. Hamao, Y., Masulis, R.W., Ng, V.: Correlations in price changes and volatility across international stock markets. Rev. Financ. Stud. **3**(2), 281–307 (1990)
6. Lütkepohl, H.: Forecasting with varma models. In: Handbook of Economic Forecasting, vol. 1, pp. 287–325 (2006)
7. Harris, R.I.D.: Using Cointegration Analysis in Econometric Modelling. Prentice Hall, Upper Saddle River (1995)
8. Fan, J., Yao, Q.: Nonlinear Time Series: Nonparametric and Parametric Methods. Springer (2008)
9. Shanbhag, S., Wolf, T.: Accurate anomaly detection through parallelism. IEEE Netw. **23**(1), 22–28 (2009)
10. Qiu, H., Liu, Y., Surahmanya, N.A., et al.: Granger causality for time-series anomaly detection. In: IEEE 12th International Conference on Data Mining, pp. 1074–1079 (2012)
11. Behzadi, S., Hlaváčková-Schindler, K., Plant, C.: Dependency anomaly detection for heterogeneous time series: a granger-lasso approach. In: IEEE International Conference on Data Mining Workshops, ICDMW, November 2017, pp. 1090–1099 (2017)
12. Saha, H., Liu, C., Jiang, Z., Sarkar, S.: Exploring Granger causality in dynamical systems modeling and performance monitoring. In: Proceedings of the IEEE Conference on Decision and Control (CDC), December 2018, pp. 2537–2542 (2019)

13. Granger, C.W.: Investigating causal relations by econometric models and cross-spectral methods. Econometrica **37**(3), 424–438 (1969)
14. Qin, X., Lee, W.: Statistical causality analysis of INFOSEC alert data. In: Vigna, G., Kruegel, C., Jonsson, E. (eds.) RAID 2003. LNCS, vol. 2820, pp. 73–93. Springer, Heidelberg (2003). https://doi.org/10.1007/978-3-540-45248-5_5

Research on a Management Control System in Space-Terrestrial Integrated Network

Teng Ling[1](✉), Li Shen[1,2], Xiaoting Wang[3], Leilei Wu[3], Zhou Hui[4], Yang Fei[4], Guangyang Wu[1], Hailong Hu[1], Lixiang Liu[1], and Changwen Zheng[1]

[1] Institute of Software Chinese Academy of Sciences, Beijing 100190, China
lingteng2016@iscas.ac.cn
[2] Space Engineering University, Beijing 101416, China
[3] Beijing Institute of Tracking and Telecommunications Technology, Beijing 100094, China
[4] Beijing Information Science and Technology University, Beijing 100192, China

Abstract. In order to improve the efficiency and stability of Space-Terrestrial integrated network resource management and control, a multi-element multi-domain network management protocol (MMMP) is proposed. Based on MMMP, Space-Terrestrial integrated network management and control system (STi-NMCS) is designed. By abstracting network management objects, the efficiency of network management is greatly improved. Experiments are carried by comparing the overhead and the success rate of network management between MMMP, simple network management protocol(SNMP) and common management information protocol (CMIP). The results show that by using MMMP rather than SNMP as well as CMIP, the Space-Terrestrial integrated network management system archives high success rate and low management overhead.

Keywords: Space-Terrestrial integrated network · Network management · Management integration

1 Introduction

Space-Terrestrial integrated network has a series of features such as broad coverage, flexible networking, none geographical restriction and so on. It has received the attention of many countries and institutions. At present, a Chinese satellite network is still in the experimental stage, single satellite telemetry and remote control is still the basic management mode of all satellites and the industry has not yet designed a mature network management and control system for the Space- Terrestrial integrated network. Under the background that satellite networking has become an important development trend [1–3], the research and

Supported by the National Key R&D Program "Research on Intersatellite Networking and Data Sharing Technology" (No. 2016YFB0501104).

Q. Wu et al. (Eds.): WiSATS 2020, LNICST 358, pp. 152–163, 2021.
https://doi.org/10.1007/978-3-030-69072-4_13

design of management and control system based on Space-Terrestrial integrated network has important application value and engineering significance.

Aiming at the characteristics of Space-Terrestrial integrated network, such as network heterogeneity, multi-information, high dynamic change of topology, complex and diverse management equipment, this manuscript proposes a multi-element multi-domain network management Protocol [4]. Based on this protocol, STi-NMCS is designed, which manages and processes network information from six aspects: platform management, node management, user management, resource management, performance management, security management, greatly improving the management efficiency of the Space-Terrestrial integrated network. The Space-Terrestrial integrated management and control system studied in this manuscript has the following characteristics:

- Referring to the telemetry and remote-control systems of various satellite platforms at home and abroad, a management and control system based on satellite network is designed, which can achieve the management and control objectives of "The whole network visible while anyone satellite visible, the whole network controllable while anyone satellite controllable".
- According to the characteristics of satellite communication environment, a multi-element multi-domain network management protocol is designed, which not only reduces the communication overhead of network management, but also ensures the efficiency and timeliness of management and control.
- Modular design and abstract mode are adopted to manage and control the objects of Space-Terrestrial, realize modular management of platforms, equipment nodes, network users, resources, performance and security, visually display the real-time status and situation of each module and strengthen the control system user friendliness and management effectiveness.
- The Space-Terrestrial network management and control system is designed based on modularization, which has strong expansibility and can add new management and control functions conveniently according to management requirements without increasing system management overhead.

STi-NMCS provides an integrated solution for the management and control of space information network. It provides a reference for solving the problem that China cannot manage and control all on-orbit satellites in real time and effectively because ground stations can't be built around the world casually, which makes certain research significance.

2 Analysis of Research Problems

Due to the extremely harsh conditions of satellite communication and the complexity of networking, the management and control of the Space-Terrestrial integrated network is the key to ensuring the effective operation of the integrated network. The complexity of the Space-Terrestrial integrated network management and control is mainly reflected in some aspects.

The first one is the complexity of the space network environment. Due to the high-speed operation of satellites in space orbit and the long distance between satellites, the channel is easily interfered by the space environment including temperature, radiation and other factors, resulting in excessive data transmission loss and excessive signal attenuation. Satellites and spacecraft orbiting the planets for high-speed rotating cloud motion, and link breaks are likely to occur between network nodes. In summary, the space network has the characteristics of high latency, high bit error rate, dynamic topology changes, and unstable communication links.

Secondly, the complexity of network management technology is an important feature of space networks. With the rapid development of computer networks, the network becomes more and more complex, and the structure level is more and more diversified. The specific performance is that the various protocols put into application in the industry are complex and diverse [5]. Usually, a network management system needs to support different functions, such as communication protocol, alarm monitoring, traffic management, task concurrency, fault detection and analysis, data interaction, etc. At the same time, it also needs to consider the network management technology when the architecture of the space network needs to be changed in the future. So, the complexity of network management technology is more obvious.

The complexity of space network equipment is another major feature. In the early days, each satellite platform was developed for a specific task. Due to the simplification and security considerations of application design, different satellite systems are independently designed and isolated from each other, arising a major problem that the difference in the satellite equipment of different constellations is significant. The real need for the development of space-integrated networks is to build these multi-heterogeneous networks into networks and make full use of space network resources. Therefore, how to manage complex and diverse space devices is a serious problem.

With the rapid development and gradual maturity of research on micro-satellite platforms at home and abroad in recent years, the conflict between management requirements and resource constraints will become more and more intense in the future when the number of satellites increases sharply. Due to Chinese special national conditions, it is currently impossible to establish stations on a global scale. Therefore, the construction of a satellite-based network management and control system has become an important solution. The goal is to achieve "The whole network visible while anyone satellite visible, the whole network controllable while anyone satellite controllable" with real-time and high-efficiency control of the Space-Terrestrial integrated network.

3 Network Management Protocol

3.1 Traditional Network Management Protocol

The satellite Space-Terrestrial integrated network management protocol is an improved model derived from the traditional ground network management protocol [6,7]. Although the satellite network management protocol is more complex

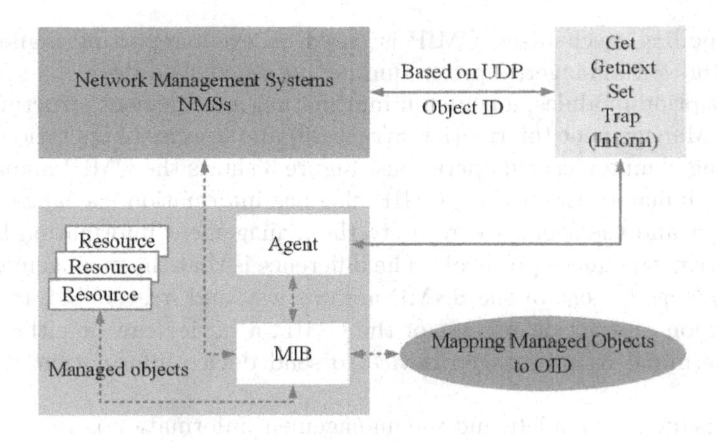

Fig. 1. Structure of simple network management protocol.

due to its specific network characteristics and special communication environment, it can be analyzed by analyzing the traditional terrestrial network management protocol [8,9]. The characteristics, development, application status and respective advantages and disadvantages of network management are more fully understood. In the modern network management system, it mainly includes four parts: Network Management System (NMS), Agent, Management Information Base (MIB) and Network Management Protocol (NMP) (Fig. 1).

Simple Network Management Protocol (SNMP) is proposed by Internet Engineering Task Force (IETF), while Common Management Information Protocol (CMIP) is proposed by International Organization for Standardization (ISO). Besides there are ANMP (Ad Hoc Network Management Protocol) [10], WMI (Windows Management) Instrumentation), CTL (Command-line interface), Netconf and so on. In these protocols, each implementation standard has its own application scenarios and advantages and disadvantages. For example, the SNMP protocol is applicable to TCP/IP networks, while CMIP originally originated from the telecommunication network, and the ANMP protocol is based on the improved SNMP protocol. A protocol for early Ad hoc network management.

SNMP is an application layer protocol based on UDP transmission. The SNMP management program does not need to establish a connection in advance during the interaction process with the agent of the managed device, so the communication overhead for the device system is low. The SNMP management program manages and monitors the managed devices of the entire network by polling, setting keywords, and monitoring pre-set special network events. The structure of the SNMP protocol is divided into Manager and Agent in Fig.Structure.

Another mature network management protocol is the Common Management Information Protocol (CMIP), which is a TCP-based connection-oriented application layer protocol, and is proposed by ISO for the management protocol in the terrestrial typical network framework. Unlike SNMP device management based on polling mechanism, CMIP is based on event reporting management. CMIP includes a Manager, a proxy running on a managed device, a set of protocol description modules, a common information management structure CMIS (Common Management Information Structure) and a series of operational primitives during communication operations. Figure 3 shows the CMIP management structure. Similar to the SNMP, CMIP also has information exchange between the manager and the agent according to the management information base and the respective agreement protocols. The difference is that the management party and the managed agent of the SNMP are one-way and irreversible. In a group of information interaction process of the CMIP, a device can be either a management terminal or a managed device to send device information through a proxy.

CMIP is highly complete and the management information is very complete. The device computing resources occupied by the CMIP are dozens of times that of SNMP. Therefore, the protocol has high performance dependence on the deployed devices and high device management overhead. CMIP runs a large number of processes while running network agents, so the burden of network agents increases dramatically.

3.2 MMMP

MMMP is a connection-oriented network management protocol in the application layer. In order to distinguish the transmission service from the lower layer to the connection, the transmission mode of the lower layer can be determined by the management entity through negotiation during the establishment of the connection. Therefore, the case that management information is blocked or delayed due to connection-oriented services of CMIP can be avoided. What‘s more, the case that management information is not reachable or discarded due to the completely connectionless services supplied by SNMP, which has an obvious impact on the notification of key events and the statistical calculation of indicator parameters.

In order to enable two MMMP management entities, i.e. management requesters and Agents, to communicate with each other, it is necessary to establish a management relationship between them, which involves the linkage mechanism of MMMP. The purpose is to establish management and application services, so as to make management activities more standardized and reliable. In the research on the structure of network management system, this manuscript organizes network management information and elements based on object-oriented method. Besides encapsulated attributes, the agents contain actions, parameters and announcements. Besides creating and revoking instances of agents, the Execute-service also specify some agents to execute corresponding actions.

Network managers keep query function for agents through Get-service, mainly to obtain the attribute values of agents; Set-service implements the modification service to agents which setting the attribute values of managed instances, including setting the attribute values to new ones or restoring default values; Inform-service, as an announcement of management information, can be either

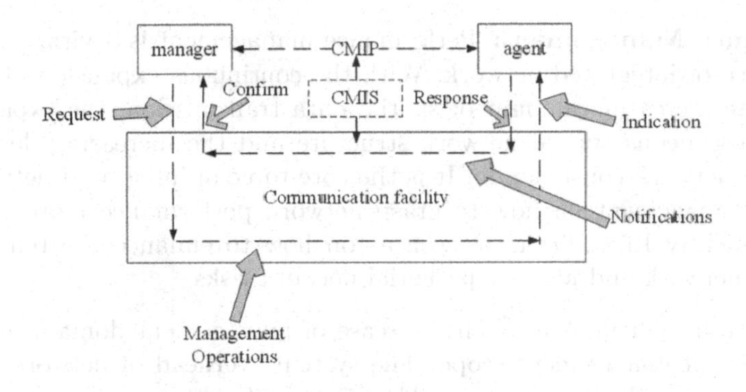

Fig. 2. Structure of common management information protocol.

from the management station to the agents, or vice versa. Cancel-service can be used to cancel a query operation or terminate an ongoing task, or to release the reserved resources; Resources-service and Mission-service can complete the corresponding resource and task management (Fig. 2).

3.3 Design of STi-NMCS

The integrated network management and control system is designed in the space information network. Because satellites are in high-speed orbit from hundreds of kilometers to thousands of kilometers, it is unrealistic to maintain the normal operation of satellites by means of on-the-spot maintenance. It is necessary to manage the status of satellites by remote and select the corresponding solution. Therefore, how to monitor the real-time status and parameters of the network as well as satellites and how to manage users in the space network are of particular importance. This manuscript divided the management and control system into the series modules including platform management, resource management, performance management, user management, node management and security management.

Platform Management: Platform management refers to the intuitive representation of the state of the Space-Terrestrial integrated network, including the whole network topology, the location of whole network equipment, the user list and the application list, analyzing the whole network state from different levels.

Resource Management: Resource management in integrated network includes computing resource management, network resource management and storage resource management, which contains the following aspects such as streaming table of LEO satellite, available bandwidth, real-time bandwidth, bandwidth utilization, packet loss rate, number of forwarding packets, forwarding packet rate and so on. Resource management is a very important part of integrated network management. It serves space tasks directly and provides available resource in physical layer, link layer and network layer for the scheduling of tasks.

Performance Management: Performance management is a vital part of the maintenance of integrated network. With the continuous expansion of network services, the increasing amount of spatial data transmission, the expanding of Multi-heterogeneous spatial network structure and the increasing demand for integration network construction, It is the core topic of integrated network performance management on how to grasp network performance more efficiently and conveniently In addition, as well as on how to enhance the reliability of integrated network and identify potential network risks.

- Define Management Areas. The increase of management domain means the expansion of management scope. The system overhead of network management system will also increase. Therefore, different management domains should be reasonably divided according to the specific functions of different modules.
- Select Performance Indicators. Network performance parameters are indicators to evaluate the performance of integrated network management and control system. These indicators directly reflect the network status and predict the trend of network development to a certain extent. The performance indicators selected in this manuscript include aspects such as satellite node routing information, link current bandwidth, traffic tracking, during of service response, bandwidth utilization, network bottleneck detection and so on.
- Analysis of historical performance data. It is limited to manage the performance of integrated networks by manual or regular means, which can neither accurately analyze, nor meet the needs of the rapid growth of the volume. In this way, analyzing on historical performance data is an extremely important research content. The conclusion can be drawn through the analysis of historical performance data. Computing with the current real-time status and parameters can provide more comprehensive and accurate services for the integrated network management system.
- Visual display. By making full use of real-time state and parameters, visualization technology is used to display the state of spatial network in real time and intuitively, which provides an intuitive reference for network administrators to carry out network analysis and expand new services.

User Management: An important challenge is how to manage users in the integrated network. There is no way to predefine the users and the tasks performed by users except for dynamic management technology. The difference between network management technology and network management users is very obvious that technology and physical information of satellite nodes can be clearly defined, but users in space network are a dynamic and complex concept. The prediction of users in space network is compared with real-time satellite state and space network parameters. Predictions are much more complex. User management generally includes a very important part of the specification of user behavior in integrated network. Users with different priorities have different levels of operation rights and instruction levels. Tasks with different priorities have different scheduling orders and scheduling modes.

Node Management: Node management mainly includes real-time operational data, measurement and control data of each satellite platform. By analyzing the node list, device parameters, node real-time status and network management mode, the operation status of the single satellite platform is visually displayed, which provides administrators with management and operational basis.

Security Management: Security management is mainly oriented to the integration of network management and control under network anomalies or specific situations. In this manuscript, fault management, authority management and regional resistance are included in the scope of security management. Privilege management mainly aims at setting the privileges of system administrators and commanders. STi-NMCS displays the information within the privileges and effectively avoid the leakage of sensitive information. Regional denial refers to a function that denying access of services in a particular region with specific states.

3.4 Modeling of MMMP

Space-Terrestrial integrated network has these characteristics' rapid changes in topology, limited transmission bandwidth, high link error rate, large transmission delay, and vulnerability to external interference. We pay attention to the following evaluation indicators: packet loss rate, delay, throughput. We can evaluate the performance of the protocol by substituting typical parameters of different protocols.

Packet loss rate is defined as the ratio of the number of lost packets to the number of packets transmitted during a certain period of time.

$$R = 1 - \prod_{i=1}^{n} \left(1 - \frac{L_t}{C_t}\right) \tag{1}$$

where R is the packet loss rate, L_t is the number of packets lost in time t, C_t is the number of packets transmitted in time t, n is the number of paths the packet passes.

The delay of end-to-end transmission mainly consists of transmission delay, propagation delay and routing delay. The routing delay is composed of processing delay and queuing delay. The total delay of the link is

$$T = \sum_{i=1}^{n} \left(\frac{L}{B_i} + \frac{D_i}{V} + P_i + Q_i\right) \tag{2}$$

where T is the end-to-end delay, L is the packet length, B_i is the i-th path bandwidth, D_i is the spatial distance of the i-th path, and V is the transmission speed of the signal in space, which can be approximated as the constant C, P_i is the processing delay of the data packet in the i-th router, and Q_i is the queuing delay of the data packet in the i-th router.

Throughput represents the maximum rate of information transfer without losing packets.

$$\rho = \frac{L}{\Delta T} = \frac{L}{\frac{L}{B} + T} = \frac{\sum_{i=1}^{n} L_{pi} \cdot 8}{\sum_{i=1}^{n} L_{pi} \cdot 8/B + T} \tag{3}$$

Where L is the total length of the data packet, L_P is the packet length of a certain protocol, n is the number of data packets, each byte is 8 bits, and ΔT represents the measurement time, which is composed of processing time and inherent delay.

4 Experimental Evaluation

Based on Qualnet simulation platform, this manuscript constructs a Space-Terrestrial integrated network with 100 LEO satellites. On the basis of this simulation platform, the management and control system for integrated network is designed and completed. The efficient control and management of network resources, network performance and network equipment are realized. As shown in Fig. 3.

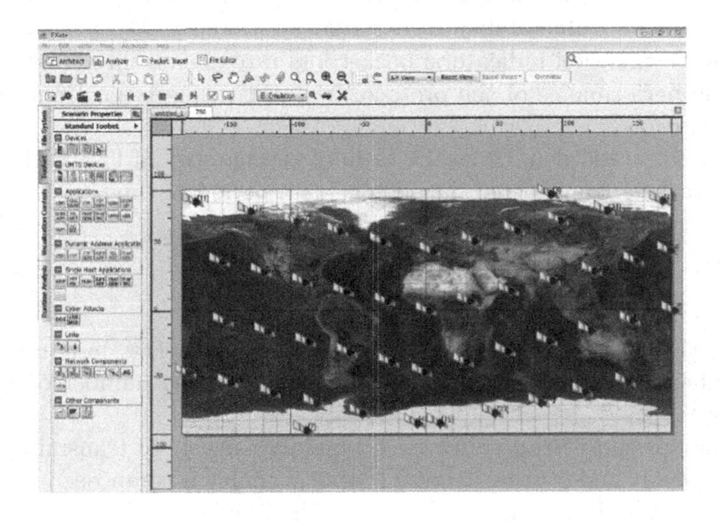

Fig. 3. Real-time topo of the Space-Terrestrial integrated network.

Figure 4 shows the control interface of the management and control system designed and implemented in this manuscript, which can query and respond to network status according to different network management objectives, and can manage and monitor typical network dynamic indicators and real-time parameters in real time.

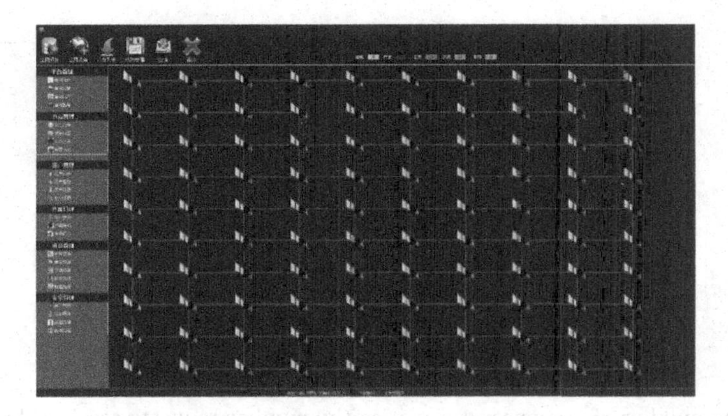

Fig. 4. The control panel of management control system in the Space-Terrestrial integrated network.

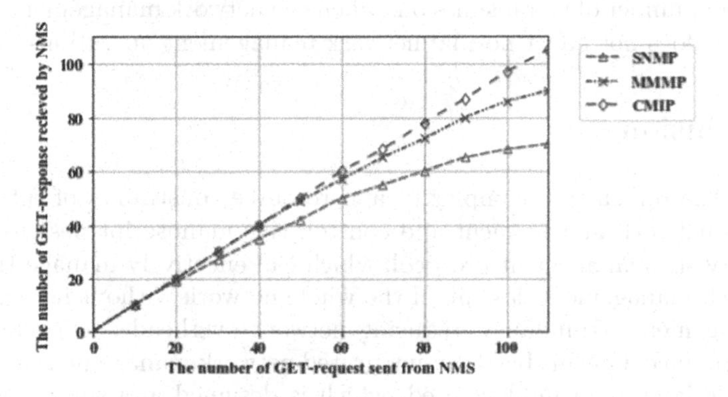

Fig. 5. The number of responses received varies the number requests sent by NMS.

Figure 5 shows the relationship between the number of GET data responses received by SNMP, MMMP and CMIP network management system (NMS) and the number of GET operation instructions sent by NMS. From the analysis, it can be seen that the CMIP protocol represented by the green line has less packet loss and can fully respond to the basic management operations of the management side. Obvious packet loss, because SNMP is for connectionless data transmission; red line represents the MMMP protocol also has packet loss, but not obvious, basically able to respond to the management operation of the management side.

Figure 6 shows the relationship between the number of response data sent by agent of SNMP, MMMP and CMIP protocol and the number of GET instructions received. The agent of CMIP protocol frequently carries out data retransmit operation, which is more obvious when the overhead of management is large. SNMP protocol does not carry out data retransmissions, because it's based on UDP data transmission without reliability of data transmission. MMMP protocol

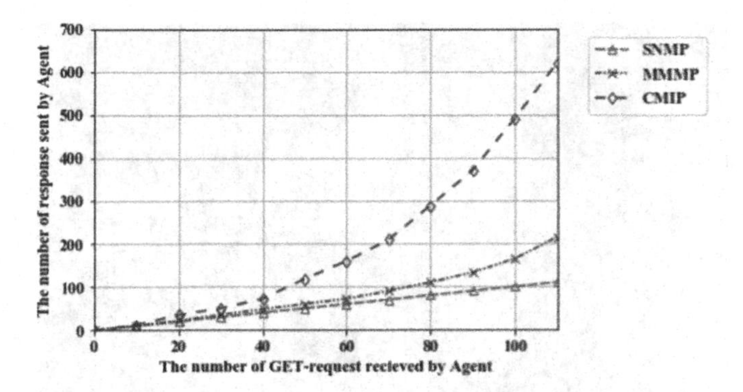

Fig. 6. The number of responses sent varies the number requests received by Agent.

has a certain number of retransmissions when the network management overhead is large, but does not affect normal network management operations.

5 Conclusion

In view of the difficulties, complexity and resource constraints of future space integration network management and control, this manuscript designs a multi-domain network management protocol, which can effectively manage the equipment in each management domain of the whole network without increasing network management redundancy, reducing network overhead and ensuring real-time performance. On this basis, an integrated network management and control system is designed and implemented, which is designed and summarized from six aspects: platform management, user management, performance management, security management, node management, business management and so on. The simulation results show that the Space-earth integrated management and control system designed in this manuscript has good comprehensive performance and efficiency, which has important support significance for the construction of the Space-earth integrated network, especially for the Space-earth integrated management and control.

References

1. Buchen, E.: Small satellite market observations (2015)
2. Shaw, G.B., Miller, D.W., Hastings, D.E.: A generalized analysis methodology for distributed satellite systems. In: van der Ha, J.C. (ed.) Mission Design & Implementation of Satellite Constellations. SPTP, vol. 1, pp. 33–49. Springer, Dordrecht (1998). https://doi.org/10.1007/978-94-011-5088-0_4
3. Ajibesin, A.A., Bankole, F.O., Odinma, A.C., et al.: A review of next generation satellite networks: trends and technical issues. In: IEEE AFRICON 2009. IEEE (2009)

4. Ling, T.: Research on management architecture in software-defined space information network. University of Chinese Academy of Sciences, Beijing (2019)
5. Bianchessi, N., Cordeau, J.F., Desrosiers, J., et al.: A heuristic for the multi-satellite, multi-orbit and multi-user management of earth observation satellites. Eur. J. Oper. Res. **177**(2), 750–762 (2007)
6. Case, J.D., Fedor, M., Schoffstall, M.L., et al.: Simple network management protocol (SNMP) (1990)
7. Stallings, W.: SNMP, SNMPv2, and CMIP: The Practical Guide to Network Management. Addison-Wesley Longman Publishing Co., Inc., Boston (1993)
8. Jiang, Y., Pan, C., Li, H., et al.: Resource management and mission management based on satellite network. J. Mil. Eng. **25**(5), 595–599 (2004)
9. Jiang, Y., Pan, C., Wang, G.: Research on compatibility of MNMP with SNMP and CMIP. Minicomput. Syst. **26**(10) (2005)
10. Chen, W., Jain, N., Singh, S.: ANMP: ad hoc network management protocol. IEEE J. SAC **17**(8), 1506–1531 (1999)

A Review of Fault Detection and Diagnosis of Satellite Power Subsystem

Bo Sun[1], Weihua Jin[2(✉)], Zhidong Li[1], and Lei Zhang[1]

[1] Beijing Institute of Spacecraft System Engineering, Beijing 100094, China
[2] Research Center of Satellite Technology,
Harbin Institute of Technology, Harbin 150080, China
wh.jin@hotmail.com

Abstract. This paper reviews the state of the art in fault detection and diagnosis in satellite power subsystem. Different algorithms are compared, and some examples are given. Finally, the existing problems and the future development trend are given.

Keywords: Fault detection · Diagnosis · Model-base · LSTM · FTA

1 Introduction

With the rapid development of industrial technology and new generation information technology, intelligent manufacturing has become the main focus of competition in the world. In 2010, the German cabinet passed the 2020 high tech strategy formulated under the auspices of the German Federal Ministry of education and research and put forward "Industry 4.0". General Electric of the United States put forward the concept of "Industrial Internet" in 2012. In 2015, Keqiang Li put forward the grand plan of "Made in China 2025" for the first time when he made the "government work report" at the national two sessions [1], it can be seen that the major manufacturing countries in the world are strategically deploying a new round of industrial revolution at the national level.

In recent years, there has been a climax of satellite launch in the world. In 2019 alone, 103 launches have been carried out worldwide, with a total of 505 payloads on board. Among them, China carried out 34 space launches in 2019, becoming the country with the largest number of space launches in the world for two consecutive years. So far, China is operating more than 300 satellites. Satellite power system plays an extremely important role in all subsystems of satellite. The failure of power system often leads to disastrous consequences of the whole satellite. According to historical data statistics, the ratio of on orbit failure of power system is the highest (35%) of all subsystems. The satellite power supply system is responsible for the generation, storage, transformation, regulation and distribution of satellite electric energy. It is an important symbol of the life knot of the satellite and the development level of space technology, and the basic guarantee for the safe and reliable operation of the satellite. According to NASA's Golan

Q. Wu et al. (Eds.): WiSATS 2020, LNICST 358, pp. 164–174, 2021.
https://doi.org/10.1007/978-3-030-69072-4_14

Research Center, from 1990 to 2006, there were 64 power system failures only reported by commercial and scientific scientists. In addition, the power system is global and typical in all satellite sub-systems. The state of power system will also affect or constrain the functional behavior of other sub-systems, thus directly affect the mission capability of the satellite. For example, in order to detect a specific area, a satellite needs to lock the area by means of a sudden orbit, side sway, etc. the energy supply in the process of side sway maneuver directly affects the attitude adjustment of the satellite. At the same time, the normal operation of the visible light, multispectral, SAR and other high-power earth observation loads depends on the normal and stable operation of the power system.

In conclusion, the research on fault detection and diagnosis methods of satellite power system can improve the operation and maintenance support ability of the satellite. Not only that, because of the typicality of the power system, the technical route and research method adopted by the Research Institute of power system fault diagnosis and prediction can be extended to other subsystems, so as to comprehensively improve the health assurance and safety operation and maintenance capacity of China's satellites, which has important social, economic and military value.

2 Fault Detection of Satellite Power Subsystem

A large number of telemetry data are generated by satellites in orbit every day. These data are large-scale, multivariate time series data. Most of these data are in normal state, while the number of abnormal samples is very limited. Therefore, the challenge of fault detection is to model normal patterns and detect patterns that have not been found before, which may prompt machine failure. In the past, this was usually done by engineers with sufficient domain knowledge. However, in terms of time, this is usually expensive. Therefore, the fault detection method of satellite power system must have the ability to effectively complete this unsupervised task [2]. In recent years, the unsupervised fault detection method has achieved fruitful results. As shown in Fig. 1, the existing achievements can be divided into statistical based method, nearest neighbor rule-based method, clustering based method and deep-learning based method. From this point of view, the paper analyzes the research status of unsupervised fault detection methods.

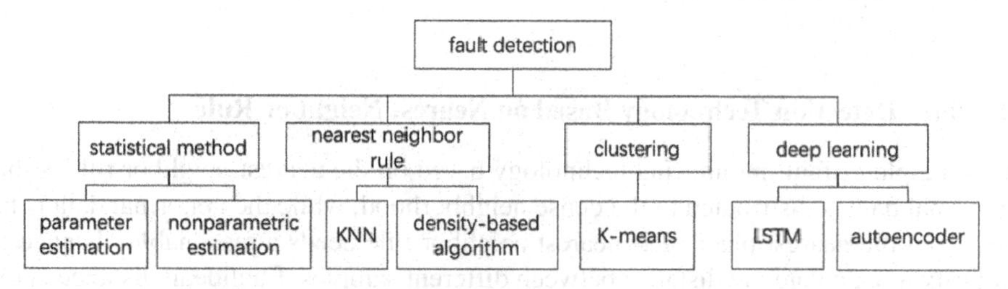

Fig. 1. Classification diagram of fault detection methods

2.1 Fault Detection Technology Based on Statistical Method

The principle of fault detection technology based on statistics is that the normal data appears in the high probability region of the random model, while the fault occurs in the low probability region of the random model [3]. This method uses normal data to train a statistical model, and then uses this statistical model to test data instances. When the probability value of the detected data instance belonging to this statistical model is relatively low, the data can be judged as abnormal. Both parametric and nonparametric estimation methods can estimate the parameters of stochastic models, which are described in detail below.

Parameter Estimation. As mentioned above, the parameter estimation assumes that the normal data is generated by a parameter distribution, which includes parameter 0 and probability density function f (x, 0). When the abnormal evaluation score of a test instance does not meet the probability density function, it can be determined that the instance is an abnormal value. In addition, statistical hypothesis test can also be used for outlier detection [4]. The original hypothesis of this test is that the sample is generated by the estimated distribution with parameters. If the statistical test does not meet the original hypothesis, it can be said that the sample of this test is an abnormal sample. Commonly used parameter estimation methods are based on Gaussian model [5], regression model [6] and mixed parameter distribution [7]. Yuhao Sun et al. [8] used the distance correlation coefficient to select the prediction variables and estimated the generalization error of the model to set a more reasonable prediction interval to detect the continuous fault of the data flow. Finally, the experiment verified that it can be used to detect the early fault of the satellite.

Nonparametric Estimation. In nonparametric estimation, the basic distribution is not assumed, and the information of random sampling itself is mainly used to judge the quality of estimators. The maximum score estimator method is a nonparametric estimation method. Using nonparametric statistical model for fault detection, the model structure is not defined by prior knowledge, but determined by the given data. Compared with parametric technology, this technology usually assumes less data, such as density smoothness [3]. The common nonparametric estimation methods are histogram-based methods [9] and kernel-based methods [10].

2.2 Fault Detection Technology Based on Nearest Neighbor Rule

The principle of fault monitoring technology based on the nearest neighbor rule is that the normal data is distributed in the dense neighborhood, while the abnormal data is far away from the nearest place. The nearest neighbor rule needs a reasonable distance or similarity to calculate the distance between different samples. Euclidean distance is the most commonly used method. Other methods include Mahalanobis distance and simple matching coefficient. Based on the nearest neighbor rule, fault monitoring technology can be roughly divided into two categories according to the calculation method of fault score: one is to take the distance from the sample to the K-th adjacent center as the fault score. The other is to calculate the relative density of each sample as the abnormal score.

KNN. K-nearest neighbor (KNN) algorithm is a relatively mature algorithm in theory. This method assumes that in the feature space, if most of the k-nearest samples near a sample belong to a certain category, then the sample also belongs to this category. Using this principle, we can distinguish the abnormal point from the normal point. This basic technology has been applied in fault detection. Byers et al. [11] have been used to detect mines from Landsat ground images since 1998. Guttomsson et al. [12] detected short circuit in large synchronous turbo generators. It is usually determined whether the test instance is abnormal by judging whether the abnormal score exceeds the threshold value.

Density-Based Algorithm. Density based fault detection technology estimates the density of each data sample neighborhood. A sample in a low-density cluster may be an exception if the sample in a high-density cluster is normal. Different from the distance-based clustering algorithm, the clustering result of the distance-based clustering algorithm is a spherical cluster, while the density-based clustering algorithm can find clusters of any shape. DBSCAN (density based spatial clustering of applications with noise) is a representative density-based clustering algorithm. It defines a cluster as the largest set of points connected by density, which can divide the area with enough high density into clusters and can find clusters of any shape in the samples with "noise".

2.3 Fault Detection Technology Based on Clustering

There are many similarities between fault detection based on clustering and nearest neighbor rule. For example, they all need distance measurement, and the choice of distance measurement method has a great impact on the results. The most difference between these two types of technologies is that the distance considered by clustering technology is the distance between each sample and its cluster center, while the distance from each sample point to its nearest neighbor is considered by the technology based on the nearest neighbor rule [3]. The fault detection technology based on clustering can determine whether a sample is abnormal in three cases: (1) normal samples are located in a cluster center, while abnormal samples are far away from any cluster center. (2) Normal samples are located in large and dense clusters, while abnormal samples are located in small and sparse clusters. (3) Normal samples are close to the nearest cluster center, while abnormal samples are far away from the nearest cluster center. The common clustering algorithm is K-means clustering.

K-means. The main principle of K-means clustering is to divide each sample into clusters represented by the nearest cluster center point given K initial cluster centers. After all samples are allocated, the center points of the cluster center are recalculated according to all samples in a cluster center (take the average value), and then the steps of allocating samples and updating the cluster center points are iterated Suddenly, until the change of clustering center is very small, or reach the specified number of iterations. The similarity evaluation index of K-means clustering algorithm is distance. The sum of error squares from sample points to clustering center is used as the evaluation index of clustering quality, and the sum of error squares function of overall classification is minimized by iteration.

2.4 Fault Detection Technology Based on Deep Learning

Artificial intelligence sprouted in the 1950s. After several peaks and troughs, it finally ushered in explosive development in the second decade of the 20th century. Artificial intelligence simulates the neurons of human brain based on artificial neural network. It is a kind of information processing method similar to human brain that can be realized by computer [13], and produces some intelligent behaviors, such as learning, reasoning, thinking, planning, etc. Deep learning is the only way to realize artificial intelligence. The concept of deep learning was put forward by Hinton et al. in 2006. By combining low-level features, it can form more abstract high-level representation of attribute categories or features to discover the distributed feature representation of data. This practical advantage of deep learning algorithm provides a high potential in practical application. In some cases, due to the lack of domain knowledge, the relevant input characteristics cannot be defined manually, and the extracted features may be too complex for engineers to code them. At this time, deep learning can be competent for this work. For example, in the task of object recognition, human beings can recognize objects intuitively, but they cannot easily derive a complete set of rules for the algorithm to recognize specific objects, which have invariance to the scale, direction or position in the image. However, the current object recognition model based on deep learning has surpassed the human eye in efficiency and accuracy. Because deep learning can abstract the high-level features of data, using this feature, normal data distribution can be obtained by training normal data first, when the sample does not belong to this distribution, it can be judged as abnormal. The commonly used deep learning models for fault monitoring are LSTM (long short term memory) and autoencoder.

LSTM. Sepp Hochreiter [14] found the problem of long-term dependence when studying the cyclic neural network, that is, when learning the sequence data, it can't learn the long-term information, and there will be the phenomenon of gradient disappearance and gradient explosion. In order to solve this problem, Sepp Hochreiter et al. Proposed a long-term and short-term memory network [15] in 1997. The long-term and short-term neural network is a special type of cyclic neural network, in which "gate" is added to each cyclic body to control the flow of information. The three gates are forgetting gate, input gate and output gate. The forgetting gate determines what information we will discard from the LSTM unit, the input determines how much new information we will add to the state of the LSTM unit, and the output determines what information we will output. This makes LSTM not only have the advantages of dynamic memory of cyclic neural network, but also have stronger adaptability in time series data analysis and can extract features of non-stationary parameters [16]. This characteristic makes LSTM outstanding in recognition and prediction. NASA uses the powerful non-linear modeling ability and automatic feature extraction ability of LSTM, takes remote control command and telemetry data as input at the same time, constructs LSTM model, and detects spacecraft anomalies with nonparametric dynamic threshold [17]. Li Hui et al. [16] used the LSTM model to train the parameters of satellite power system, taking the absolute value of the difference between the predicted parameter data and the actual parameter data as the model training target, using the parameter time series predicted by the model and the dynamic detection threshold generated by the model training error to detect the parameters, so as to realize the fault detection of satellite power system. Jingyi Dong et al. [18] used the strong nonlinear modeling ability of LSTM, combined with matrix norm to realize the multi-mode mining of remote control instructions, and through the construction and effective integration of multi LSTM prediction model, improved the adaptability of the model to the complex working conditions of spacecraft, and then effectively marked the anomalies in the telemetry data.

Autoencoder. Autoencoder is a neural network with the same input and learning objectives. It can learn the efficient representation of input data through unsupervised learning. Generally, autoencoder consists of encoder and decoder. The encoder transforms the input data into a fixed length high-order feature, which is generally much smaller than the input dimension. The high-order feature is used as the input of decoder to reconstruct the input sequence. Therefore, autoencoder can learn meaningful information to fully explain the characteristics of data. From encoder input sequence to sequence (sequence to sequence) model, this kind of model can monitor the fault by reconstructing the original sequence and compare the reconstruction results with the original input to find out the abnormal information.

Dechang PI et al. [19] break through the limitation of the traditional experience model, adopts the pure data drive model, on the basis of the variational automatic encoder, introduces the countermeasure network idea, uses the error of the reconstructed data and the original data to judge whether the satellite telemetry data is abnormal, and combines the week of the satellite orbit operation According to periodicity, a dynamic threshold determination method based on periodic time window is proposed to reduce the rate of misjudgment. Weihua Jin et al. [2] proposed a new stage training de-noising autoencoder (ST-DAE), which can train data characteristics in stages. Compared with the common autoencoder sparse autoencoder and de-noising autoencoder, this method has better reconstruction ability and outstanding performance in satellite power system abnormal monitoring.

3 Fault Diagnosis of Satellite Power Subsystem

Fault diagnosis methods can be divided into knowledge-based method, model-based method and data-driven method. The classification of fault diagnosis methods is shown in Fig. 2. For knowledge-based and model-based method, a priori knowledge is needed. The basic priori information in diagnosis is fault set and the relationship between symptom and fault. For data-driven methods, only a large amount of historical data is needed. There are many methods to convert these data into prior information in diagnosis, which can be used as a qualitative extraction process from historical data.

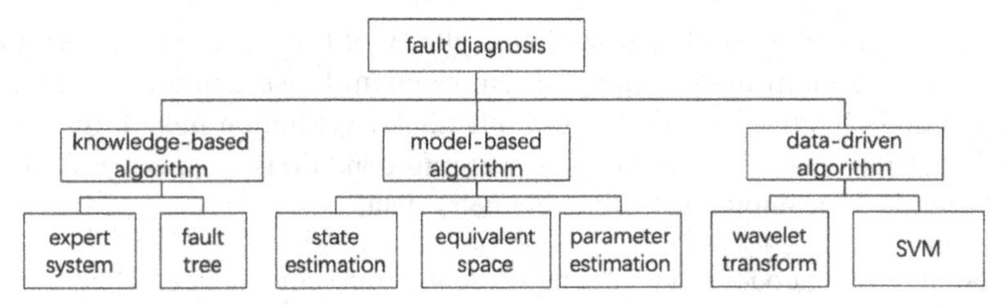

Fig. 2. Classification diagram of fault diagnosis methods

3.1 Fault Diagnosis Technology Based on Knowledge

Fault Diagnosis Technology Based on Expert System. The fault diagnosis method based on expert system constructs a knowledge base about the target object by inheriting the knowledge and experience of the experts in the field. The knowledge base is composed of abstract if-then rules [13]. In addition to the knowledge base, each expert system has an important part of "inference engine". According to some abnormal phenomena or fault field data, the inference engine calls the knowledge in the knowledge base and determines the fault step by step according to the inference steps [20]. Based on the expert system, Zheng Wei et al. [21] used neural network to expand the knowledge base, solved the "bottleneck" problem of knowledge acquisition in the expert system, and finally used the system to diagnose the satellite fault. Lian-xiang Jiang et al. [22] proposed the knowledge acquisition model of satellite fault diagnosis expert system to solve the bottleneck problem of establishing expert system. Firstly, a data discretization algorithm based on fuzzy set is proposed to discretize the decision table. Secondly, a rule extraction algorithm is proposed to extract production rules from decision table. Taking the satellite fault diagnosis expert system as an example, this paper illustrates how to extract effective rules. The operation parameters of the satellite power system are collected and discretized, which proves the correctness and validity of the knowledge acquisition model and the accuracy of fault diagnosis. Genqing Yang [23] proposed a design of knowledge base for Satellite Autonomous Fault Diagnosis Expert system. The resource knowledge base uses fault Petri net to describe the knowledge of satellite in detail, the position represents the state of component or system, and the transformation represents the evolution fault of component or system. In order to keep the consistency and correctness of knowledge base, the author proposes a verification algorithm of redundant rules.

Fault Diagnosis Technology Based on Fault Tree. Fault tree analysis (FTA) forms a complete fault analysis tree by building the logical relationship among the system, subsystems and components. Fault analysis tree is a deductive failure analysis method from top to bottom. According to the fault tree, we can infer from top to bottom, infer the components, causes, influence degree and failure probability of the failure [19, 24]. Jianing Wu et al. [25] analyzed the reliability of spacecraft solar array and determined the most critical subsystem of solar array. According to the working process of the satellite mechanical system, the FTA model is established, the logic expression of the top event is obtained by Boolean algebra, and the reliability of the solar array is calculated. Yi Yang et al. [26] analyzed the reliability of the solar array deployment mechanism by using the impact and hazard analysis (FMECA) and FTA. The main failure modes and their effects and hazards are described. A fault tree is established. The qualitative and quantitative analysis of fault tree is carried out. The probability of top event, structural importance and critical importance coefficient of different basic events are calculated. The suggestions for improving the reliability of the solar array are put forward, which provide the basis for the reliability design and structural improvement of the deployment mechanism of the satellite solar array.

3.2 Model Based Fault Diagnosis Technology

Fault Diagnosis Method Based on Quantitative Model. Quantitative model-based method, also known as analytical model-based method, is the earliest, most in-depth and most mature method of fault diagnosis. This kind of method makes full use of the knowledge synthesis of system structure, behavior and function to carry out reasoning diagnosis for the system. According to the different ways of generating residuals, analytical model method is divided into state estimation method, equivalent space method and parameter estimation method [27]. These three kinds of methods are developed independently. Generally, the parameter estimation method is more suitable for nonlinear systems than the state estimation method, while the equivalent space method is generally only suitable for linear systems [28].

State Estimation. The principle of state estimation is to evaluate the state of the system by constructing an observer or a filter to obtain the output of the system, and then compare the output value obtained with the output value of the real system to get the residual. In general, the residual signal of the system is usually very small or close to zero. On the contrary, if there is a fault in the system, the residual signal of the system should have obvious changes. The common state estimation methods are observer method and Kalman filter method. Wen Chen et al. [29] designed an iterative learning observer (ILO) to realize time-varying fault estimation and proposed a fault identification strategy based on ILO using learning mechanism to estimate fault instead of using the integrator commonly used in the classical adaptive observer. The stability of estimation error dynamics is established and proved. The experimental results show that the time-varying thruster fault can be diagnosed accurately. P. V. Sunil nag et al. [30] proposed a model-based nonlinear fault detection and diagnosis method. The global unscented Kalman filter (UKF) is applied to the fault diagnosis of LEO satellite. The results show that the spherical UKF can achieve better results without sacrificing the accuracy and saving the calculation amount. So, it is more suitable for real-time fault diagnosis.

Equivalent Space Method. The equivalent space method is to use the analytical mathematical model established by the system to construct the equivalent mathematical relationship between the input and output variables of the system. Through the mathematical relationship, it reflects the static direct redundancy between the input and output variables and the dynamic analytical redundancy between the input and output variables, to detect and separate faults. The main methods are equivalent equation method based on constraint optimization.

Parameter Estimation Method. The basic idea of parameter estimation method is to combine theoretical modeling with parameter identification. When using the significant change of parameters to describe the fault, the existing parameter estimation method can be used to detect the fault information, and then the system fault can be evaluated according to the deviation between the estimated value of parameters and the normal value. The fault diagnosis method based on the parameter estimation thinks that the fault will cause the change of the system process parameters, and the change of the process parameters will further cause a series of changes of the model parameters, Therefore, the fault diagnosis can be carried out by detecting the parameter changes in the model. With the development of the research, the fault diagnosis method based on parameter estimation has some new results. For example, the parameter estimation method based on fuzzy reasoning, the parameter estimation method based on neural network and the parameter estimation method based on image signal generator, etc., all of these methods improve the performance of fault detection and separation in varying degrees.

3.3 Data Driven Fault Diagnosis Technology

Wavelet Transform. Wavelet transform was first put forward by J. Morlet [31], an engineer who was engaged in oil signal processing in France in 1974. After gradual development, it can solve many problems that are difficult to be solved by using Fourier transform, so it is considered as a breakthrough development of Fourier analysis method. Compared with Fourier transform and window Fourier transform (Gabor transform), it is a local transform of time and frequency, so it can extract information from the signal effectively, and perform multi-scale analysis on the function or signal through the operation functions of scaling and translation.

According to the characteristics of multi-resolution analysis of wavelet transform, Wengao Lu [32] decomposed the telemetry data into four layers of wavelet. Through the analysis of the signal reconstructed by high frequency wavelet coefficients, the online real-time interpretation of telemetry data is realized, and the correctness and fault diagnosis efficiency of the method are verified. Wen Xin et al. [33] Based on the theory of wavelet neural network, combined with the problem of spacecraft fault detection and system reconstruction of the leader of spacecraft cluster, a fault diagnosis framework is constructed by combining wavelet neural network and neural network, and the feasibility is verified by simulation experiments.

Support Vector Machine (SVM). Support vector machine was first proposed by Cortes and Vapnik in 1995. It has many unique advantages in solving small sample, non-linear and high-dimensional pattern recognition, and can be extended to other machine learning problems such as function fitting. The support vector machine method is based on the VC dimension theory of statistical learning theory and the principle of structural risk minimization. According to the limited sample information, it seeks the best compromise between the complexity of the model (i.e. the learning accuracy of specific training samples, accuracy) and the learning ability (i.e. the ability to identify arbitrary samples without error), in order to obtain the best generalization ability.

Hong Yin et al. [34] proposed an improved support vector machine (SVM) based on hybrid voting mechanism (HVM-SVM) to solve the problem of large parameters, multiple faults and small samples in satellite fault diagnosis. A large number of experimental results show that the accuracy of fault diagnosis using HVM-SVM is improved. Mingliang Suo et al. [35] proposed a feature selection method based on Fuzzy Bayesian risk (FBR), which can automatically generate the optimal feature subset without preset feature number. A heuristic forward greedy feature selection algorithm based on Fuzzy Bayesian risk theory is designed. Then, a data-driven fault diagnosis strategy is designed by using FBR and SVM. Finally, numerical experiments on UCI data and satellite power system fault diagnosis are carried out to verify the superiority and applicability of this method.

4 Discussion

In the past decade, fault detection and diagnosis technology has developed rapidly, especially the model-based fault diagnosis technology has made great progress, which has a wide range of applications in spacecraft fault detection and diagnosis, but there are still many problems to be further studied and solved. With the rapid development of artificial intelligence, how to apply this new technology to fault detection and diagnosis, many people have made different attempts, but there are few applications in practice, which need further research and application.

References

1. Wang, J., Xiang, Y., He, Z.: Models and implementation of digital twin based spacecraft system engineering. Comput. Integr. Manuf. Syst. (2019)
2. Jin, W., et al.: Detecting anomalies of satellite power subsystem via stage-training denoising autoencoders. Sensors **19**(14), 3216 (2019)
3. Chandola, V., Banerjee, A., Kumar, V.: Anomaly detection: a survey. ACM Comput. Surv. **41**(3) (2009)
4. Lewis, T.: Outliers in Statistical Data, 3rd edn. Wiley, Hoboken (1994)
5. Shewhart, W.A.: Economic Control of Quality of Manufactured Product. Van Nostrand, New York (1931)
6. Abraham, B., Chuang, A.: Outlier detection and time series modeling. Technometrics **31**(2), 241–248 (1989)
7. Eskin, E.: Anomaly detection over noisy data using learned probability distributions. In: Proceedings of the Seventeenth International Conference on Machine Learning (ICML 2000), Stanford University, Stanford, CA, USA, 29 June–2 July 2000 (2000)
8. Sun, Y., Li, G., Zhang, G.: A satellite anomaly detection method based on distance correlation coefficient and GPR model. J. Beijing Univ. Aeronaut. Astronaut. 1–13
9. Eskin, E., Lee, W., Stolfo, S.: Modeling system call for intrusion detection using dynamic window sizes. Proceedings of Discex, vol. 1, p. 0165 (2001)
10. Dit-Yan, Y., Chow, C.: Parzen-window network intrusion detectors. In: Object Recognition Supported by User Interaction for Service Robots (2002)
11. Byers, S., Raftery, A.E.: Nearest-neighbor clutter removal for estimating features in spatial point processes. J. Am. Stat. Assoc. **93**(442), 577–584 (1998)

12. Guttormsson, S.E., et al.: Elliptical novelty grouping for on-line short-turn detection of excited running rotors. IEEE Trans. Energy Convers. **14**(1), 16–22 (1999)
13. Zhang, Y.: Research on Machinery Fault Diagnosis Method based on Deep Auto-encoder. Huazhong University of Science and Technology Wuhan (2019)
14. Schmidhuber, J.: Learning complex, extended sequences using the principle of history compression. Neural Comput. **4**(2), 234–242 (1992)
15. Hochreiter, S., Schmidhuber, J.: Long short-term memory. Neural Comput. **9**(8), 1735–1780 (1997)
16. Hui Li, et al.: Anomaly detection method of satellite power system based on LSTM model. J. Acad. Armored Force Eng. (3) (2019)
17. Hundman, K., et al.: Detecting spacecraft anomalies using LSTMs and nonparametric dynamic thresholding. In: Knowledge Discovery and Data Mining, pp. 387–395 (2018)
18. Dong, J., et al.: Spacecraft telemetry data anomaly detection method based on ensemble LSTM. Chin. J. Sci. Instrum. (7) (2019)
19. Dechang, P., Junfu, C., Zhiyuan, W.: A satellite anomaly detection method of an adversarial network autoencoder (2019)
20. Yang, Y.: Aero-engine Knowledge base construction for the fault diagnosis expert system. Shenyang Aerospace University (2013)
21. Zhang, W., Yang, X., Ge, N.: Design and implementation of satellite fault diagnosis system based on expert system and neural network. J. Yanshan Univ. **40**(01), 74–80 (2016)
22. Jiang, L., et al.: Knowledge acquisition model for satellite fault diagnosis expert system. In: Computational Intelligence, pp. 1–4 (2009)
23. Genqing, Y.: Design of knowledge base for satellite autonomous fault diagnosis expert system. Aerosp. Control (2009)
24. Ruijters, E., Stoelinga, M.: Fault tree analysis: a survey of the state-of-the-art in modeling, analysis and tools. Comput. Sci. Rev. **15–16**(03), 29–62 (2015)
25. Jianing, W.U., Shaoze, Y.: Reliability analysis of the solar array based on Fault Tree Analysis (2011)
26. Yang, Y., et al.: Failure analysis of deployment mechanism of a satellite solar array. In: International Conference on Reliability, Maintainability and Safety, pp. 931–937 (2011)
27. Shao, J.: Study on model-based fault diagnosis method and its application in aerospace. Harbin Institute of Technology (2009)
28. Cheng, Y., et al.: Model-based fault diagnosis methods: a survey. In: Proceedings of the 27th Chinese Control Conference (2008)
29. Chen, W., Saif, M.: Observer-based fault diagnosis of satellite systems subject to time-varying thruster faults. J. Dyn. Syst. Meas. Control Trans. ASME **129**(3), 352–356 (2007)
30. Nag, P.V.S., et al.: Model based fault diagnosis of low earth orbiting (LEO) satellite using spherical unscented Kalman filter. IFAC PapersOnLine **49**(1), 635–638 (2016)
31. Grossmann, A., Morlet, J.: Decomposition of Hardy functions into square integrable wavelets of constant shape. SIAM J. Math. Anal. **15**(4), 723–736 (1984)
32. Wengao, L., et al.: Method of satellite fault diagnosis based on wavelet transform. Foreign Electron. Meas. Technol. **37**(02), 30–33 (2018)
33. Wen, X., Shi, C., Fang, Z.: Fault diagnosis method of spacecraft based on wavelet neural network. Ordnance Ind. Autom. **38**(03), 49–54 (2019)
34. Yin, H., et al.: Satellite fault diagnosis using support vector machines based on a hybrid voting mechanism. Sci. World J. **2014**, 582042 (2014)
35. Suo, M., et al.: Data-driven fault diagnosis of satellite power system using fuzzy Bayes risk and SVM. Aerosp. Sci. Technol. **84**, 1092–1105 (2019)

Data-Driven Approach for Satellite Onboard Observation Task Planning Based on Ensemble Learning

Shuang Peng, Jiangjiang Wu, Chun Du, Hao Chen(✉), and Jun Li

College of Electronic Science and Technology, National University of Defense Technology, Changsha, Hunan, China
{pengshuang08,hchen}@nudt.edu.cn

Abstract. Onboard task planning can enhance the responsiveness of satellite to dynamic changes, which has attracted widespread attention. In this paper, the Satellite Onboard Observation Task Planning (SOOTP) problem is studied, and a data-driven onboard planning approach is proposed to decide the observation task to execute in real-time using machine learning techniques. In the approach, the satellite can learn how to make optimal decisions from the historical planning results. What is more, we design five types of features and employ three ensemble learning algorithms to solve the SOOTP. A comparison of the proposed method against two online searching algorithms indicates that the former has smaller profit gap and shorter response time, which verify the feasibility of our method.

Keywords: Satellite autonomy · Observation Task Planning · Data-driven onboard planning · Machine learning · Ensemble learning

1 Introduction

Onboard task planning has received extensive attention in recent years due to its rapid response capability to emergencies and dynamic changes (such as the arrival of new observation tasks [1], the unexpected resource level [2]), and it has become a research hotspot in the field of satellite task planning.

As shown in Fig. 1, the Autonomous Earth Observation Satellite (AEOS) orbits the Earth. It needs to decides whether to observe ground targets when passing over them (**observation** task) and download data when it passes over the ground station (**transmission** task). Energy is consumed when executing the observation tasks and transmission tasks, and is obtained only when the AEOS is in the sun. Memory is consumed when performing the observation tasks and is freed when performing the transmission tasks. In this paper, we assuming the used transmission tasks have already been determined from the ground in advance, so we only considering the Satellite Onboard Observation Task Planning (SOOTP) problem.

Q. Wu et al. (Eds.): WiSATS 2020, LNICST 358, pp. 175–184, 2021.
https://doi.org/10.1007/978-3-030-69072-4_15

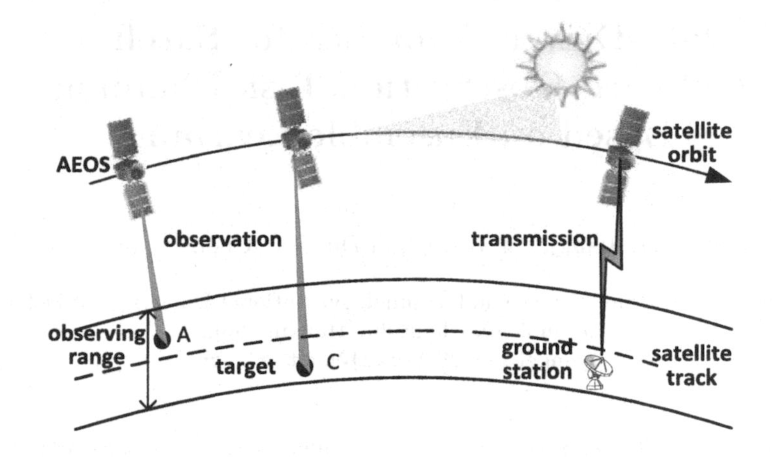

Fig. 1. Illustration of the satellite onboard tasks planning problem

The majority of existing studies solve the SOOTP problem with searching algorithms based on the rolling/continuous planning architecture [1]. In this architecture, the onboard planner only schedules the observation tasks in a short-term rolling planning horizon. As time goes on, the resource and tasks in the rolling planning horizon changes, it will trigger the scheduling process and repair the plan dynamically. For example, Chien et al. [2,3] considered the changes of observation tasks and unexpected resource level, and proposed an iterative repair algorithm. Beaumet et al. [4] used heuristic rules and iterated stochastic search algorithm to solve the problem. Li et al. [5] designed two heuristic rules of profit first and resource utilization first. The above researches mainly use heuristic methods to repair the plan in the rolling planning horizon. However, these repair strategies are relatively simple. There is still room for improvement in the optimization of plan.

With the rapid development of machine learning technologies, researchers try to combine machine learning methods with search algorithms to solve the SOOTP problem. They use machine learning methods to learn empirical knowledge from historical planning data to improve the performance of search algorithms. For example, Li et al. [6] used the neural network to compute the scheduling priority of user's requests, and combined it with the heuristic algorithm. Lu et al. [7] used a classifier to compute the probability of a task can be arranged and combined it with the greedy algorithm. The experimental results of the above studies indicate that the learning-based search algorithm is superior to the rule-based heuristic search algorithms. However, the optimization of these algorithms is limited by the architecture of the search algorithms, and the potential of the machine learning methods is not fully utilized.

In this paper, a new data-driven approach is proposed. It can use the machine learning method to solve the SOOTP problem without relying on any searching algorithms. The contribution of this study includes: 1) we propose a data-driven onboard planning framework, which can decide whether an observation task should be scheduled only through machine learning techniques; 2) we design five types of features for classification and use three ensemble learning methods to learn how to make a such decision; 3) Experiments results demonstrate that our approach can achieve smaller profit gap and shorter response time.

2 Problem Formulation

The objective of our problem is to maximize the total profit of the scheduled observation tasks without violating the constraints. The following is the notations we will use.

- $[Ta, Te]$: the planning horizon.
- M: the set of observation tasks.
- O: the set of orbits.
- M_o: the set of observation tasks in orbit $o, o \in O$. $\sum_{o \in O} M_o = M$ and $M_o \cap M_p = \varnothing (o, p \in O, o \neq p)$
- ta_i: the start time of task $m_i, m_i \in M$.
- te_i: the end time of task $m_i, m_i \in M$.
- p_i: the profit of task $m_i, m_i \in M$.
- e_i: the energy required to perform task $m_i, m_i \in M$.
- d_i: the memory required to perform task $m_i, m_i \in M$.
- Ts_{ij}: the setup time between tasks m_i and task m_j.
- $e(t), d(t)$: the energy level and data level at time t. The computation process can refer to Reference [8,9].
- E_{min}, E_{max}: the lower bound and upper bound of energy level.
- D_{min}, D_{max}: the lower bound and upper bound of memory level.
- $x_i \in \{0, 1\}$: the decision variable. $x_i = 1$ indicates task m_i is selected, otherwise not.

The mathematical model is as follows.

$$\text{Maximize} \quad \sum_{m_i \in M} x_i * b_i \tag{1}$$

$$\text{Subject to} \quad E_{min} \leq e(t) \leq E_{max} \tag{2}$$

$$D_{min} \leq d(t) \leq D_{max} \tag{3}$$

$$ta_j - te_i \geq Ts_{ij} * x_i * x_j \tag{4}$$

The objective (1) is to maximize the total profit. Constraint (2) restrict the scope of the energy level. Constraint (3) restrict the scope of the memory level. Constraint (4) requires the time interval between any two scheduled tasks should be greater than the setup time.

3 Data-Driven Onboard Planning Framework

To improve the responsiveness of AEOS, we propose a data-driven onboard planning framework, which using the machine learning techniques to decide whether an observation task should be performed. As illustrated in Fig. 2, the framework consists of offline learning and online decision-making.

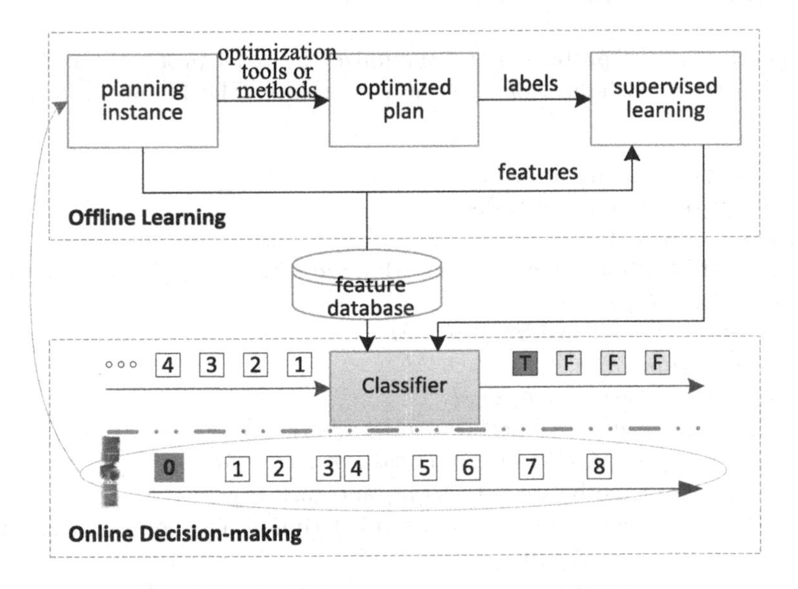

Fig. 2. Data-driven onboard planning framework

In the offline learning part, the onboard planning instance is optimized by the optimization tools or methods such as CPLEX solver. The label of an observation task is '1' if it is in the optimized plan, otherwise is '0'. Then we train the decision-maker (e.g., a classifier) to learn the decision rules for judging whether an observation task can be arranged. Details of offline learning can refer to Algorithm 1. Considering the limited computing power of the onboard computer, this part can be done on the ground.

In the online decision-making part, the decision-maker is employed to make decisions on the observation tasks one by one in chronological order. An observation task is selected if the output is 'true', otherwise it is discarded.

To train the decision-maker, the main problem we face is that how to construct a fixed-size length features to represent the observation task to be decided. Thus, we design five class of features based on the empirical knowledge and use them for classification. Before introducing these features, we first give the definition of group feature vector.

Definition 1. ***Group Feature Vector (GFV).*** *Let M_s be the subset of M, then the feature vector of M_s is represented by a six-tuple $GFV(M_s) = (n, dc, ad, ap, ae, am)$:*

Algorithm 1. Offline learning

Require: planning instance M, optimized plan P.
Ensure: classifier
1: $samples \leftarrow null$
2: **for all** task $m \in M$ **do**
3:     **if** $m \in P$ **then**
4:         $label(m) \leftarrow 1$
5:     **else**
6:         $label(m) \leftarrow 0$
7:     **end if**
8:     $feature(m) \leftarrow computeFeatures(m)$
9:     $samples \leftarrow samples \cup (feature(m), label(m))$
10: **end for**
11: $classifier \leftarrow Training(samples)$

- $n = |M_s|$: *the number of observation tasks in* M_s.
- $dc = \sum_{m_k \in M_s} \sum_{m_l \in M_s} b_{kl}/n^2$: *the degree of conflict between tasks.* ($b_{kl} = 1$ *if tasks* m_k *and* m_l *violate the constraint* (4), *otherwise is 0)*
- $at = \sum_{m_k \in M_s} (te_k - ta_k)/n$: *the average duration of observation tasks in* M_s.
- $ap = \sum_{m_k \in M_s} p_k/n$: *the average profit of observation tasks* M_s.
- $ae = \sum_{m_k \in M_s} e_k/n$: *the average energy required to perform observation tasks* M_s.
- $ad = \sum_{m_k \in M_s} d_k/n$: *the average memory required to perform observation tasks* M_s.

Let $m_i \in M_o$ be the observation task to be decided, then the following five group of features (i.e., totally 36 features) are computed.

1. state features $(e(ta_i), d(ta_i))$: the energy level and data level at the start time of m_i.
2. task features $(p_i, te_i - ta_i, e_i, d_i)$: the description of m_i.
3. local features $GFV(M_c)$: the GFV of task set M_c, where M_c is the set of observation tasks that conflict with m_i. It represents the degree of conflict of m_i with other observation tasks.
4. global features $GFV(M_o), \ldots, GFV(M_{o+k-1})$: the GFV of task sets $M_o, \ldots, M_{o+k-1}$. It is used to represent the distribution of the observation tasks in subsequent orbits, which can avoid the onboard planner making short-sighted decisions. k is set to 3 in this paper.
5. transmission features $GFV(M_t)$: the GFV of task set M_t, where M_t is the set of observation tasks before the next transmission task. It is used to represent the degree of competition between m_i and other observation tasks on memory resource.

Finally, we use three ensemble learning algorithms, including Extreme Gradient Boosting (XGBoost) [11], Gradient Boosting Decision Tree (GBDT) and Random Forest (RF) [12], to train the decision-maker in the framework.

Table 1. Data set

Scenarios	s100	s200	s300	s400	s500
Number of instance	120	120	120	120	120
Number of tasks in a instance	100	200	300	400	500

4 Experiment

4.1 Experimental Setting

In our experiment, the planning horizon was set as 24 h, and five scenarios with totally 600 planning instances are randomly generated. Details were shown in Table 1.

All experiments were run on a Windows 7 OS (Intel i7-4712M, 2.30 GHz, 8 GB RAM). All algorithms were implemented in Python except CPLEX. The decision-maker is implemented in Python's package such as scikit-learn [14] and xgboost [15].

To measure the performance of these algorithms, four statistics [10], include accuracy, response time, average profit and profit gap, were used.

4.2 Importance of Features

These three ensemble learning algorithms can calculate the importance of each feature while training the classifier. We use GBDT as the representative to test the impact of these feature on the performance of our method.

We first tested the effects of these five types of features on accuracy and profit gap (Fig. 3). The horizontal axis represents the planning scenarios and the vertical axis represents the accuracy or profit gap. In the legend, 'state', 'self', 'local', 'global', 'tran' represent the state features, task features, local features, global features, transmission features, respectively. In Fig. 3, we see that the accuracy increases with the use of more types of features, which proves the rationality of these five group of features. It is worth noting that the use of local features and global features results in a significant decrease in the profit gap. The local features and global features enable the AEOS to make more optimal decisions. To further improve the performance of this method, more attention can be paid to the design of these two types of features in the future. The remaining feature type combinations also show the same trend except the four feature type combinations listed in Fig. 3, and the results are no longer displayed here.

Next we analyzed the impact of each feature on the profit gap based on their importance. We sorted these features by their importance from large to small, then added each of them to a subset in order and tested the impact of the features in the subset on profit gap. The profit gap of GBDT under different number of features is shown in Fig. 4. In Fig. 4, the profit gap decreases as more features are selected. The profit gap is no longer is significantly reduced

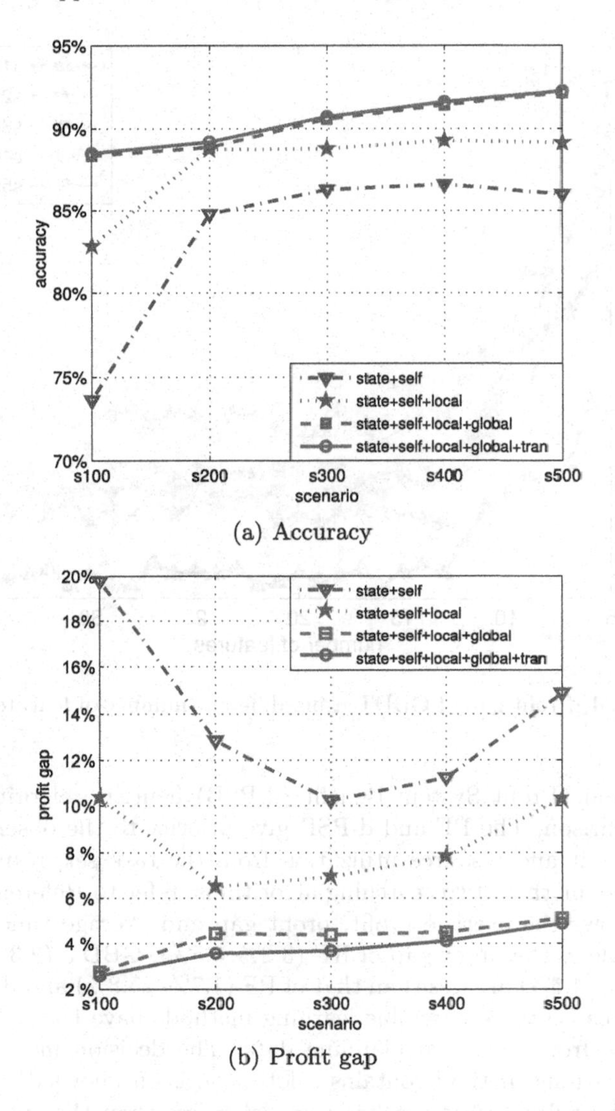

(a) Accuracy

(b) Profit gap

Fig. 3. Accuracy and profit gap of GBDT under different type of features

when the number of features in the subset exceeds 16. It indicates that only part of features have an important impact on the performance of our method. Finally, we choose the top 16 features for our framework. In feature engineering, different combinations of features can achieve different results, and we will do more analysis on the combination of features in the future.

4.3 Comparison

To verify the effectiveness of our approach, CPLEX [13] was used for baseline and two online planning algorithms: the Profit-based First (PF) heuristic algorithm

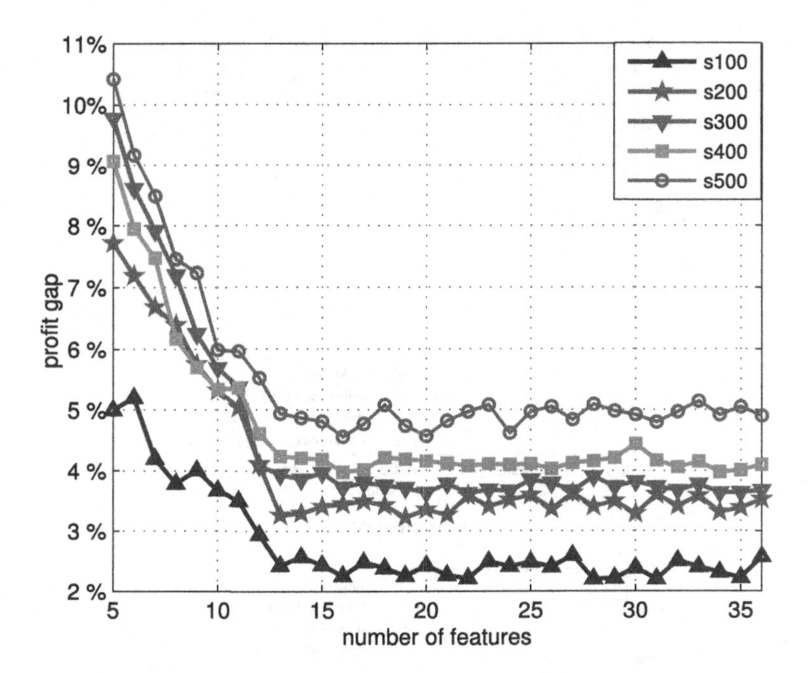

Fig. 4. Profit gap of GBDT using different number of features

and the Dynamic Profit System Benefit (d-PSB) heuristic algorithm [1] were used for comparison. The PF and d-PSB give priority to the observation tasks with higher profit and resource utilization from the task set, respectively. For more details about these two searching algorithms, refer to Reference [1].

Table 2 shows the average profit, profit gap and average time of six algorithms. In Table 2, the profit gap of RF (3.2%–6.5%), GBDT (2.3%–4.6%) and XGBoost (2.7%–4.6%) are less than that of PF (1.7%–25.8%) and d-PSB (5.8%–9.5%). It is because three ensemble learning methods have learned useful decision knowledge from historical planning data. The decision model learned by the machine learning method contains a lot of decision knowledge that cannot be expressed by rules and it is more comprehensive than the rules defined by humans. In contrast, the heuristic rules of d-PSB and PF are much simpler so that they are difficult to obtain optimal solutions. In addition, the response time of RF, GBDT and XGBoost are on the level of 10^{-4} or 10^{-3} s. Thus, RF, GBDT and XGBoost can quickly generate an feasible plan even if the computing power drops to one thousandth [1,5], which investigate the feasibility of the proposed method.

In these three ensemble learning methods, the profit gap and response time of GBDT and XGBoost is far less than that of RF, which indicate the boosting method is more suitable for our problem.

Table 2. Average profit, profit gap and response time of CPLEX, PF, d-PSB, RF, GBDT and XGBoost

Scenarios	CPLEX	PF	d-PSB	RF	GBDT	XGBoost
s100	1534	**1508 (1.7%)**	1445 (5.8%)	1486 (3.2%)	1500 (2.3%)	1493 (2.7%)
	3.4 s	0.4 ms	0.4 ms	5.5 ms	0.3 ms	0.3 ms
s200	2190	1976 (9.8%)	2011 (8.2%)	2070 (5.5%)	**2115 (3.5%)**	2113 (3.5%)
	42 s	0.5 ms	0.6 ms	4.8 ms	0.3 ms	0.3 ms
s300	2578	2148 (16.7%)	2359 (8.5%)	2436 (5.5%)	2482 (3.7%)	**2485 (3.6%)**
	174 s	0.5 ms	0.7 ms	4.6 ms	0.4 ms	0.4 ms
s400	2849	2235 (21.6%)	2583 (9.3%)	2697 (5.3%)	**2736 (4.0%)**	2732 (4.1%)
	438 s	0.5 ms	0.7 ms	4.3 ms	0.4 ms	0.4 ms
s500	3069	2277 (25.8%)	2778 (9.5%)	2870 (6.5%)	**2930 (4.6%)**	2927 (4.6%)
	1292 s	0.5 ms	0.8 ms	4.1 ms	0.5 ms	0.5 ms

5 Conclusion

In this paper, a data-driven onboard planning framework combining ensembles learning technology is proposed. It can solve the onboard observation task planning problem only through machine learning methods without rely on any searching algorithms. The experiments demonstrated that the proposed approach can achieve smaller profit gap and shorter response time.

In the future, we plan to use deep neural networks to automatically extract features and improve the performance of the decision-making model.

Acknowledgements. This work is supported by the Natural Science Foundation of Hunan Province under Grant 2020JJ4103 and National Natural Science Foundation of China under Grant 61806211.

References

1. Chu, X., Chen, Y., Tan, Y.: An anytime branch and bound algorithm for agile earth observation satellite onboard scheduling. Adv. Space Res. **60**(9), 2077–2090 (2017)
2. Chien, S., Knight, R., Stechert, A., Sherwood, R., Rabideau, G.: Using iterative repair to improve the responsiveness of planning and scheduling. In: International Conference on Artificial Intelligence Planning Systems, pp. 300–307 (2000)
3. Chien, S., Doubleday, J., Thompson, D.R.: Onboard mission planning on the intelligent payload experiment (IPEX) cubesat mission. In: International Workshop on Planning and Scheduling for Space (2013)
4. Beaumet, G., Verfaillie, G., Charmeau, M.C.: Feasibility of autonomous decision making on board an agile earth-observing satellite. Comput. Intell. **27**(1), 123–139 (2011)
5. Li, G., Xing, L., Chen, Y.: A hybrid online scheduling mechanism with revision and progressive techniques for autonomous earth observation satellite. Acta Astronaut. **140**, 308–321 (2017)

6. Li, C., Chen, Y., Causmaecker, P.D.: Data-driven onboard scheduling for an autonomous observation satellite. In: The 27th International Joint Conference on Artificial Intelligence, pp. 5773–5774 (2018)
7. Lu, J., Chen, Y., He, R.: A learning-based approach for agile satellite onboard scheduling. IEEE Access **8**(99), 16941–16952 (2020)
8. Spangelo, S., Cutler, J., Gilson, K., Cohn, A.: Optimization-based scheduling for the single-satellite, multi-ground station communication problem. Comput. Oper. Res. **57**, 1–16 (2015)
9. Peng, S., Chen, H., Li, J., Jing, N.: Approximate path searching method for single-satellite observation and transmission task planning problem. Math. Probl. Eng. **3**, 1–16 (2017)
10. Peng, S., Chen, H., Li, J., Jing, N.: Onboard observation task planning for an autonomous earth observation satellite using long short-term memory. IEEE Access **6**, 65118–65129 (2018)
11. Chen, T., Guestrin, C.: XGBoost: a scalable tree boosting system. In: The 22nd ACM SIGKDD International Conference on Knowledge Discovery and Data Mining, KDD 2016, pp. 785–794. ACM (2016)
12. Zhou, Z.: Ensemble Methods: Foundations and Algorithms. Taylor & Francis, Milton Park (2012)
13. CPLEX: IBM ILOG CPLEX optimization studio (2012). http://www-01.ibm.com/software/commerce/optimization/cplex-optimizer/index.html
14. https://scikit-learn.org/stable/
15. https://github.com/dmlc/xgboost

Analysis and Strategy Design for Quantitative Model-Based Fault Diagnosis

Yao Cheng[1(✉)], Yang Jin[2], and Jingyan Wang[1]

[1] Beijing Institute of Spacecraft System Engineering, Beijing 100094, People's Republic of China
chengyaohit@126.com

[2] College of Aeronautical Engineering, Civil Aviation University of China, Tianjin 300300, People's Republic of China

Abstract. This paper studies and analyzes quantitative model-based fault diagnosis method, and then presents a design of quantitative model-based fault diagnosis structural strategy. It can isolate the faults of actuator and sensor with reduced quantitative models. The strategy is proposed based on the analysis of traditional quantitative model-based fault diagnosis method. By redefining the analytical model-based method, the process of fault isolation is studied with the conception of support component. The effectiveness of the proposed strategy is also analyzed in the paper. Finally, the proposed structural strategy is applied for fault diagnosis of satellite attitude control system.

Keywords: Fault diagnosis strategy · Quantitative model · Fault isolation analysis

1 Instruction

Model-based fault diagnosis methods have been developed in two distinct and parallel research domains in the past few decades [1–4]. One comes from the field of automatic control which is known as fault diagnosis method based on quantitative model or analytical model [5–7]; another one comes from the field of artificial intelligence which is called fault diagnosis method based on qualitative model or qualitative reasoning [8–10]. These two methods are collectively referred to as fault diagnosis methods based on deep knowledge, and they have the ability to make up the shortage of fault diagnosis method based on shallow knowledge [11–13]. However, these two kinds of diagnosis methods have been developed independently. Qualitative model-based methods describe the system diagnosed according to system structure and function. They focus on the studies of diagnosis solving process such as conflict identification and candidate generation. However, the research of qualitative model-based method has certain significance for fault diagnosis of quantitative model-based method.

This paper studies the traditional quantitative model-based method by combining system structure information, and then provides a new fault diagnosis strategy for model-based method. By this study the fault diagnosis based on quantitative model is extended

Q. Wu et al. (Eds.): WiSATS 2020, LNICST 358, pp. 185–197, 2021.
https://doi.org/10.1007/978-3-030-69072-4_16

from single structure system to multiple structure system. The designed strategy can isolate the faults of actuator and sensor with a reduced number of quantitative models working at the same time.

In summary, the main contributions of this paper are as follows: a) traditional quantitative method-based fault diagnosis method and the existing problems are analyzed; b) object systems and quantitative model-based methods are redefined, and diagnosis solving process is studied; c) quantitative model-based fault diagnosis structural strategy using redundancy of system structure is presented.

2 Quantitative Model-Based Fault Diagnosis Method and Its Difficulty

2.1 The Traditional Quantitative Model-Based Fault Diagnosis Method

The traditional quantitative model-based method commonly concerns certain dynamic system as their diagnosis object. This object system is usually described by a set of differential equations in state-space form. It composes of actuator, sensor and process. And three types of faults are generally distinguished, that is, actuator fault, sensor fault and process fault. An actuator fault is a malfunction on certain control input of the system; a sensor fault is an abnormal variation in output measurements; process faults are changes in the inner parameters of the system that can affect the system dynamic.

In these methods fault diagnosis is typically achieved by constructing quantitative or analytical models which contain fault information. These quantitative models are constructed based on the principle of dynamic systems. The essence of these methods is to detect the consistency between the computed output of the quantitative model and the real measurement output of the system.

There are two kinds of diagnosis approaches for quantitative model-based methods, using fault-free model or faulty model. The first approach declare the fault if the behaviors of system and the model is not consistent. The second approach declare the fault if the system behavior is consistent with the model behavior under a particular fault scenarios. The schematic for quantitative model-based method is shown in Fig. 1.

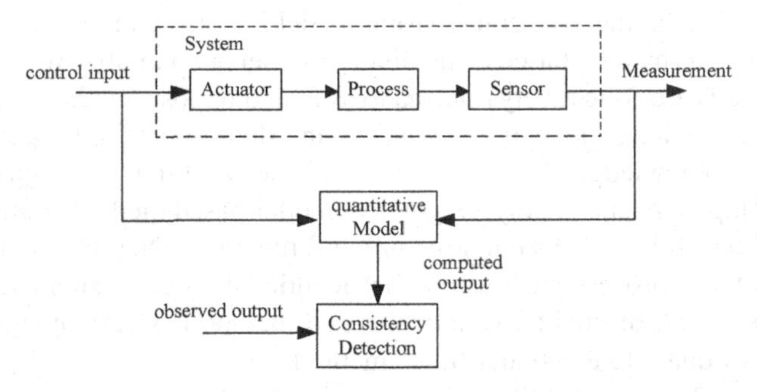

Fig. 1. The schematic for quantitative l model-based method

Faulty model-based approach need construct a particular pre-assigned fault model, and only the fault which can match the pre-assigned fault model can be detected. The drawback of this approach is all the likely fault should be taken into account, and the computational burden is large; however, the advantage is that the behavior of the fault can be estimated. Fault-free model-based approach uses nominal behavior of the system, and it can detect unknown fault. However, the behavior of fault cannot be further estimated by this approach.

Model-based methods usually generate a set of residuals to fulfill the fault isolation task. Each residual is designed to be sensitive to some faults and insensitive to other faults. According to the insensitive and sensitive relationships between residuals and faults, there are two kinds of strategies for residuals generation, namely the dedicated residual set and the generalized residual set. For the dedicated residual set, each quantitative model is driven by only one control input (or sensor output) and thus sensitive to only one actuator fault (or one sensor fault). For the generalized residual set, each quantitative model is driven by all control inputs (or sensor output) but one and thus sensitive to all actuator faults (or sensor faults) except one. The schematic of structured residual set is showed in Fig. 2 and 3.

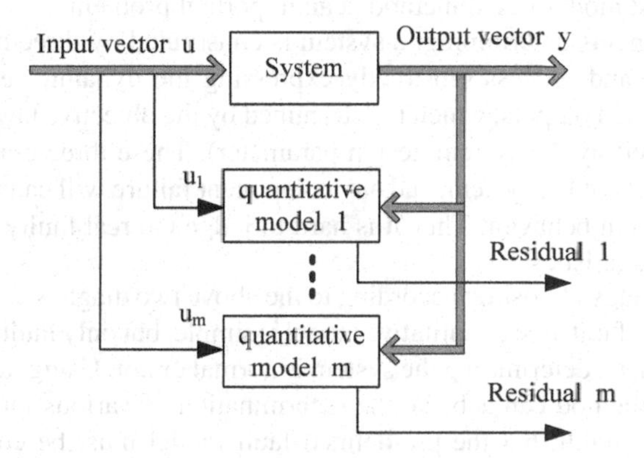

Fig. 2. The schematic of dedicated residual set

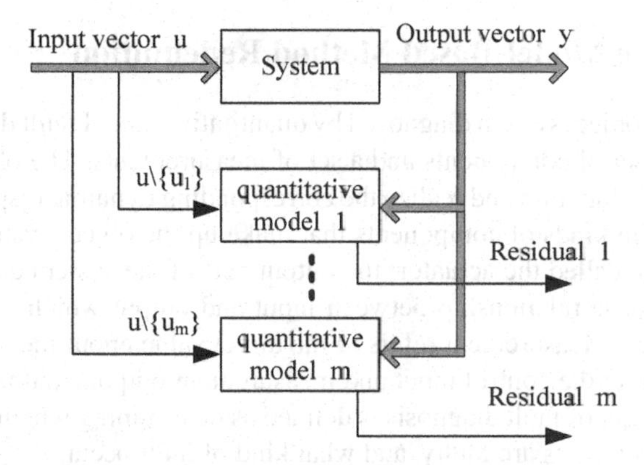

Fig. 3. The schematic of generalized residual set

In the dedicated residual set, simultaneous faults can be detected; however it needs more degrees of freedom to design such residual sets. In the generalized residual set, only a single fault can be detected, but it has more design degrees of freedom for achieving robustness against uncertainty of the system.

2.2 The Difficulty of the Quantitative Model-Based Fault Diagnosis Method

There are three difficult issues to be further study for quantitative model-based fault diagnosis methods:

1) Uncertainty processing: the accuracy of consistency detecting depends on the accuracy of the quantitative model. In quantitative model-based method, consistency detecting is achieved by residual which is a deviation between measurement of the real system and computed output of the model. In ideal case, the residual only reflects fault. However, the residual will be influenced by disturbance, noise and uncertainty of the system inevitably, which reduces the accuracy of fault detection. Thus, the study of robust model-based method is an important problem.
2) Faulty components determining: a system is constituted by three main parts: actuators, sensors and process (abstractly expressing the dynamic response between system inputs and outputs, which is determined by the objective laws of physics and may be affected by the system design parameter). These three components are all constituent parts of the system, and any component failure will cause the changes of the whole system behavior. Thus it is hard to judge the real faulty part that caused the fault characteristics.
3) Diagnosis strategy choosing: according to the above two diagnostic strategies, it can be seen that the fault-free quantitative model is simple, but only fault detection can be achieved, namely, determining the system is normal or not. Using faulty quantitative model-based method can achieve the determination of various faults by matching the pre-defined fault, but the pre-defined fault model must be constructed firstly which is usually complicated work. Thus effective combination of two diagnostic strategies is also worth discussing.

3 Quantitative Model-Based Method Redefinition

We define that the object system diagnosed by quantitative model fault diagnosis method is composed of a set of components and a set of measurements. The object system can achieve the specific function and realize the corresponding dynamic response from input to output. The three kinds of components that make up the object system are the input parts of the system called the actuator; the output part of the system called sensor; and the dynamic response relationship between input and output which is abstracted as a process component. Measurement refers to the direct value about the system operating conditions, including the control input and measurement outputs that the object system can observe. The task of fault diagnosis is defined as determining whether a fault occurs in the system, which parts are faulty, and what kind of fault occur.

An Analytical Redundancy Relation (ARR) is defined as a constraint deduced from system measurements, which is the basis for constructing analytical model. A residual is defined as the difference between outputs of real system and model corresponding to ARR. In order to further study the fault diagnosis process, the concept of ARR support is introduced. An ARR Support is defined as a set of components involved in the analytical redundancy relation, and the corresponding parts are called Support components for ARR. In traditional sense, ARR refers to the relationship between input and output of the system in normal situation. And the corresponding relationship between system input and output in a pre-defined fault condition is not included. The former is mainly used for FDI (fault detection and isolation), while the latter is used for the fault estimation. In the following, ARR in traditional sense and FDI based on the quantitative model are discussed first.

FDI based on quantitative models can be described in detail by the concept of ARR Support. Fault detection is defined as determining a certain subset of the support components set and one (corresponding to single fault situation) or some (corresponding to multiple faults situation) support components in this subset are faulty. Fault isolation is defined as determining a certain subset of the support components set, and all support components in this subset are faulty. The subset which has single component corresponds to single fault and which has multiple components corresponds to multiple faults. As fault diagnosis result comes from a subset of support components, the component set determines the maximum diagnostic granularity of FDI.

The fault symptom matrix (FSM) is defined as the binary relation matrix between the ARR support component and ARR, which can be deduced by the analytical redundancy relation. Assume that the total number of components in a system is m, and the number of analytical redundancy relation is n. thus, the FSM determines an $n \times m$ matrix denoted by d, which is a binary matrix composed with "0" and "1", the row of FSM corresponds to n ARR and the column of FSM corresponds to m components. If the i-th component is a support component of the j-th ARR, thus the element (j, i) in FSM is denoted by "1", otherwise it is denoted by "0". The i-th column of FSM is the fault feature vector of the i-th component, and two components can be isolated if and only if their fault feature vectors are different.

A multi-input and multi-output dynamic system S1 with three-input and three-output is showed in Fig. 4.

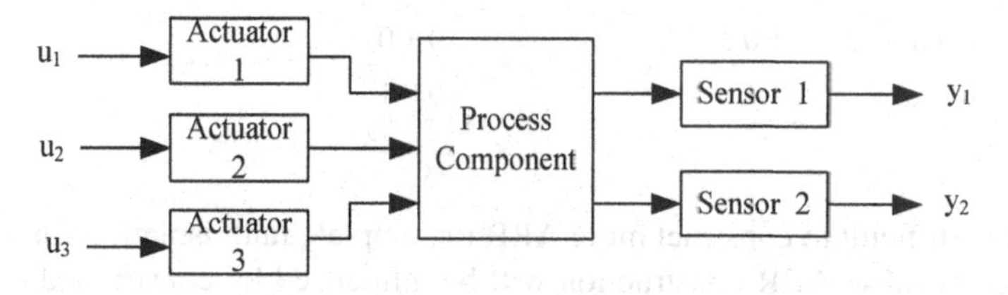

Fig. 4. Three-input and two-output system S1

In order to diagnose the actuator fault in S1, the strategies of dedicated residual set and generalized residual set are adopted, and the corresponding FSM is constructed in Table 1.

Table 1. Fault signature matrix for system S1

	Actuator 1	Actuator 2	Actuator 3	Process	Sensor 1	Sensor 2
ARR1	1	1	1	1	1	1
ARR2	0	1	1	1	1	1
ARR3	1	0	1	1	1	1
ARR4	1	1	0	1	1	1
ARR5	1	0	0	1	1	1
ARR6	0	1	0	1	1	1
ARR7	0	0	1	1	1	1

Where, ARR1 is constructed based on the constraint relationship between u1, u2, u3 and y1, y2, and its support components are actuators 1, 2, 3, sensors 1, 2 and process components. ARR1 can only be used to achieve fault detection, namely, determining whether the system is normal. ARR2, ARR3, ARR4 are the analytical redundancy relations constructed by using the strategy of generalized residual set within analytic model method. ARR5, ARR6, ARR7 are the analytical redundancy relations constructed by using the strategy of dedicated residual set. According to FSM, choosing ARR2-4 or ARR5-7 alone makes actuator 1, 2 and 3 have different fault feature vectors, as shown in Table 2. Thus it is easy to isolate the actuators fault by using the strategy of dedicated residual set or generalized residual set. However the sensor 1, 2 and the process components have the same fault feature vector which means that additional information is required to achieve fault isolation.

Table 2. Fault feature vector for system S1

	Generalized residual strategy	Dedicated residual strategy
Actuator 1	0 1 1	1 0 0
Actuator 2	1 0 1	0 1 0
Actuator 3	1 1 0	0 0 1

It is often difficult to construct more ARR to complete fault isolation for all support components, because ARR construction will be influenced by constrained conditions, as well as the specific distribution matrix of actuators and sensors. In addition, more analytical redundancy relations means that more quantitative models should be built and run in parallel, which will increase the burden of computation.

4 Fault Isolation Analysis

The traditional quantitative model-based method for FDI has been widely researched in constructing precise quantitative model and reducing disturbance influence so as to improve the sensitivity of fault detection. However, structure knowledge of complex systems is less considered into research for ARR generation. In the following, the strategy of ARR generation for quantitative model-based method is studied from the perspective of system hierarchy and subsystem division. And the problem of fault isolation for support components is researched. Usually, the complex system is composed of some different function modules, and each module can be viewed as a subsystem. The function of any subsystem is described through its input and output. These independent subsystems constitute the complex system according to its structural relationship.

Consider the following system S2 as shown in Fig. 5:

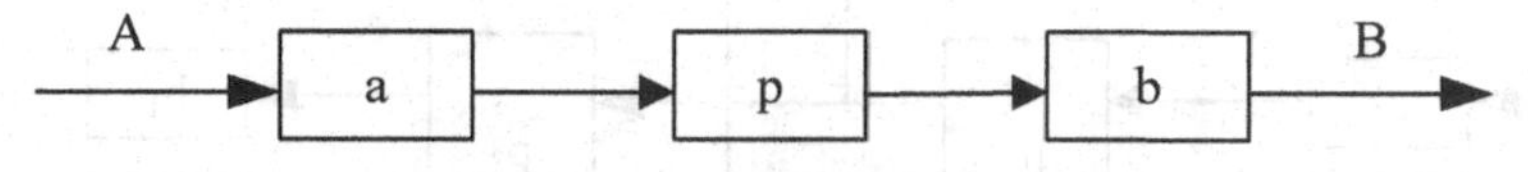

Fig. 5. The system S2 before the transformation

Where A is the control input of the system, B is the system output obtained by the sensor, *a* is the actuator, *p* the system process component, and *b* the sensor. If a new sensor *c* can be used to measure the intermediate process variables, the system can transform into a new form shown in Fig. 6. The process component *p* is abstracted as two process components *p*1 and *p*2 according to subsystem 1 and 2.

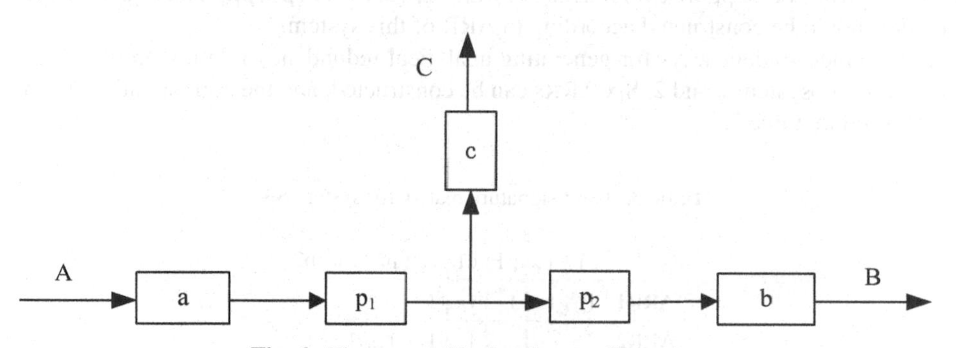

Fig. 6. The system S2 after the transformation

Through three measurements *A*, *B* and *C*, the original system can be divided into two subsystems, namely, the subsystem 1 with measurement *A* and *C*, and the subsystem 2 with measurement *C* and *B*. In subsystem 1, component *a* is the actuator of this subsystem, component *c* is the sensor of this subsystem, and *p*1 is the process component of subsystem 1. Since the input of *p*2 (i.e. the output of *p*1) is measured by the sensor *c*, the input information of subsystem 2 is obtained from measurement *C*. Thus, component *c* can be viewed as the actuator of subsystem 2, component *b* is the sensor of subsystem 2, and $p2$ is the process component of subsystem 2. After adding the new measurement C, the maximum diagnostic granularity is changed from the original components a, b, p to new components $a, b, p1, p2, c$, namely, an addition of measurement points is beneficial to obtaining more accurate diagnosis results.

Further expands the system discussed above into a multi-input and multi-output system S3, such as two-input and two-output system shown in Fig. 7.

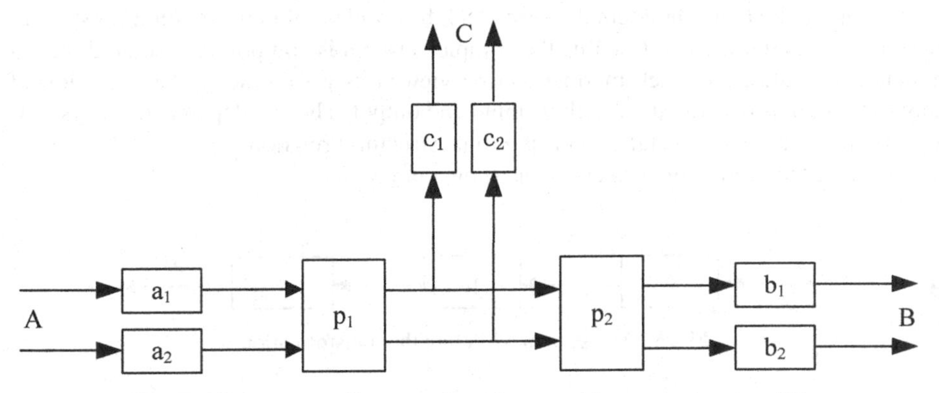

Fig. 7. The structure diagram of two-input and two-output system S3

It can be seen from Fig. 7 that in the two subsystems, support components for subsystem 1 are $a1, a2, p1, c1, c2$ and support components for subsystem 2 are $c1, c2, p2, b1, b2$. Fault detection and isolation for S3 is to determine the fault components from all support components $a1, a2, b1, b2, c1, c2, p1, p2$. Thus quantitative model should be constructed according to ARR of this system.

Two independent ways for generating analytical redundancy relation are provided based on subsystem 1 and 2. Six ARRs can be constructed, and the corresponding FSM is showed in Table 3.

Table 3. Fault signature matrix for system S3

	a1	a2	p1	c1	c2	p2	b1	b2
ARR1	1	1	1	1	1			
ARR2				1	1	1	1	1
ARR3	1	0	1	1	1			
ARR4	0	1	1	1	1			
ARR5				1	0	1	1	1
ARR6				0	1	1	1	1

In Table 3, ARR1 is a analytical redundancy relation constructed according to all of six components in subsystem 1; ARR2 is a analytical redundancy relation constructed according to all of six components in subsystem 2; ARR3 and ARR4 are analytical redundancy relations constructed according to subsystem 1 by the strategies of dedicated residual set or generalized residual set, and the corresponding support components are $a1, p1, c1, c2$ and $a2, p1, c1, c2$; ARR5 and ARR6 are analytical redundancy relations constructed according to subsystem 2, and the corresponding support components are $c1, p2, b1, b2$ and $c2, p2, b1, b2$.

According to the above FSM, the corresponding fault feature vectors can be easily obtained, and they are showed in Table 4:

Table 4. Fault feature vector for system S3

Component	Fault feature vector	Component	Fault feature vector
a1	1 0 1 0 0 0	p2	0 1 0 0 1 1
a2	1 0 0 1 0 0	b1	0 1 0 0 1 1
p1	1 0 1 1 0 0	b2	0 1 0 0 1 1
c1	1 1 1 1 1 0	c2	1 1 1 1 0 1

The fault components can be determined according to the differences of fault feature vectors. Due to components $p2, b1, b2$ have the same fault feature vector, the fault in $p2, b1, b2$ cannot be isolated in the current case, which means that some new analytical redundancy relations are required to solve this problem. Thus the final fault diagnosis result is {a1}, {a2}, {p1}, {c1}, {c2}, {p2, b1, b2}.

Six quantitative models (observers) should be constructed corresponding to the above six ARRs. If these six quantitative models run in parallel, the calculation amount of the fault diagnosis system will be large. Therefore, it is necessary to study the reasonable diagnosis strategy for diagnosis system to reduce the number of quantitative models in parallel.

5 Quantitative Model-Based Fault Diagnosis Structural Strategy

The fault isolation structural strategy based on quantitative model is proposed below, which achieve the fault diagnosis task in two stages. In the first stage, the fault is detected preliminarily; and in the second phase, the fault is isolated.

In the first stage, the quantitative model is designed respectively for each subsystem. This quantitative model is a fault-free model designed based on normal system, and its analytical redundancy relation contains all support components in the subsystem which corresponds to the above ARR1 and ARR2. According to fault symptom matrix determined by ARR1 and ARR2, $a1, a2, p1$ have the same fault feature vector [0, 1], $c1, c2$ have the same fault feature vector [1, 1], $p2, b1, b2$ have the same fault feature vector [0, 1]. Therefore, according to the quantitative model constructed by ARR1 and ARR2, the diagnosis results obtained are {a1, a2, p1}, {c1, c2}, {p2, b1, b2}.

In the second stage, a set of quantitative model is designed respectively for each subsystem. These analytical redundancy relations contain different support components from each other, which can be achieved by the strategies of dedicated residual set or generalized residual set. Analytical redundancy relations constructed based on subsystem 1 and 2 are ARR3,4 and ARR5,6 respectively. According to ARR3,4, the diagnosis result {a1}, {a2}, {p1, c1, c2} can be obtained; according to ARR5,6, diagnosis results {c1}, {c2}, {p2, b1, b2} can be obtained. Through the above analysis, fault diagnosis strategy is established in the following, which is showed in Fig. 8.

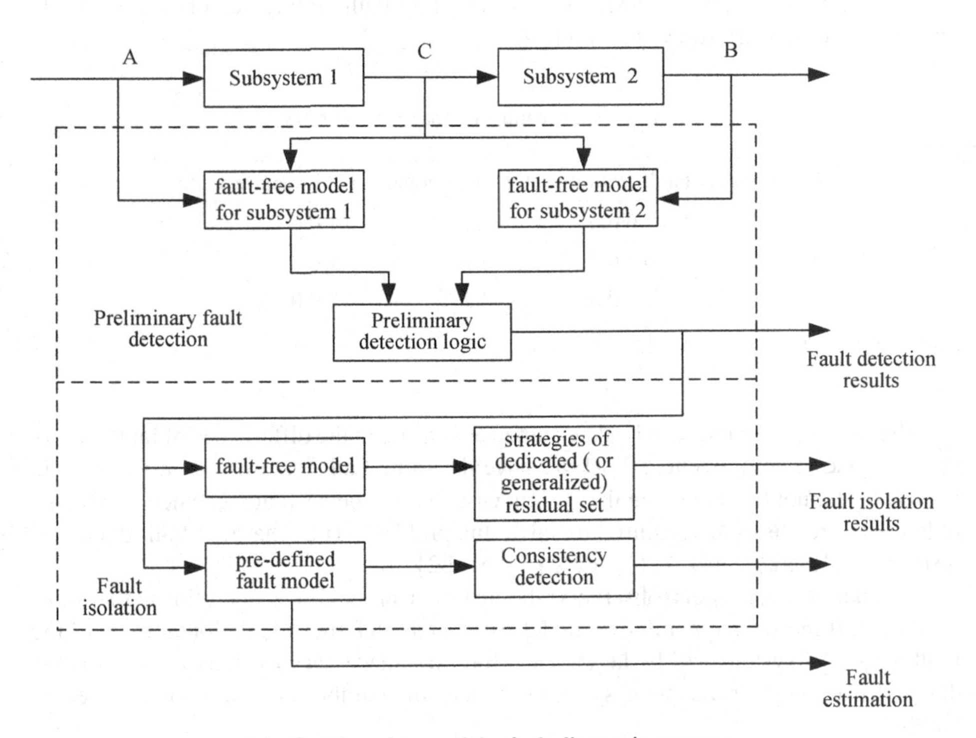

Fig. 8. The scheme of the fault diagnosis strategy

First of all, the two quantitative models designed in the first stage run in parallel. When there is a fault in the system, we will get diagnosis result {a1, a2, p1}, {c1, c2}, {p2, b1, b2}. Thus, preliminary fault detection can be achieved, and a subset which contains possible fault components can be obtained. According to the above detection result, fault isolation in the second stage is started. If the fault detection result is {a1, a2, p1}, the quantitative models corresponding to ARR3,4 are activated. As the result of {a1, a2, p1} ∩ {{a1}, {a2}, {p1, c1, c2}} is {a1}, {a2}, {p1}, the fault components $a1, a2, p1$ can be isolated. If the fault detection result is {c1, c2}, the quantitative models corresponding to ARR5,6 are activated. As the result of {c1, c2}∩{{c1}, {c2}, {p2, b1, b2}} is {c1}, {c2}, the fault components $c1, c2$ can be isolated.

It can be seen that by adopting the above diagnosis strategy, the final diagnosis result is the same as the six quantitative models run in parallel. However, due to adopting the hierarchical strategy, the detection and isolation of fault component is achieved step-by-step. Compared with no hierarchical diagnosis, the numbers of the quantitative model running in parallel at the same time is reduced, and the burden of computation is also reduced.

Remark. We limit the discussion of quantitative model-based FDI to fault-free model in the beginning. However, the diagnosis strategy proposed above is also suitable for pre-defined fault model. For ARR corresponding to pre-defined fault model, its support components is all of the components involved in ARR except the pre-defined fault components. In the research process for fault diagnosis by using FSM, ARR corresponding to pre-defined fault model is equal to the strategy of generalized residual set. All the components except the pre-defined fault components are all denoted by "1" in corresponding element of FSM. Using the method of pre-defined fault model may achieve deeper diagnosis for the fault component, such as application of adaptive technique which can estimate the time-varying characteristics of the fault.

6 Application of Fault Diagnosis Structural Strategy for Satellite Attitude Control System

A satellite attitude control system includes actuators, inertial sensors and direction sensors. Faults may occur in any one of these components, thus the primary task of satellite attitude control system fault diagnosis is to determine whether a fault occurs and the fault comes from which components. Although there are many researches on fault diagnosis for satellite attitude control system, they usually focus on particular part of components, such as actuators or sensors. Researches considering fault diagnosis for all parts of satellite attitude control system are few. In this section, Fault diagnosis structural strategy is used to discuss this problem.

The typical structure of the satellite attitude control system is shown in Fig. 9. The dynamics subsystem expresses the relationship between control torques and angular velocity, including the supporting component actuator 1, 2, 3, dynamics process, and gyro 1, 2, 3. Kinematics subsystem expresses the relationship between satellite angle and angular velocity, including supporting components gyro 1, 2, 3, kinematics process, and the star sensor. We consider that the attitude dynamics and kinematics of rigid-body satellites as laws of physics, thus process faults are ignored. However, both actuators and sensors faults can occur, and the diagnostic tasks are to isolate faults of actuator 1, 2, 3, gyro 1, 2, and the star sensor.

According to the proposed Structural isolation strategy, in the first stage, a fault-free model is designed according to the fault-free dynamics subsystem, which is referred to as the fault detection observer 1 (FDO1), and it is sensitive to all actuator and gyro faults. And another fault-free model is designed according to the fault-free Kinematics subsystem, which is referred to as the fault detection observer 2 (FDO2), and it is sensitive to all gyro and star sensor faults.

In the second stage, a bank of fault-free models based on the generalized residual set is designed according to the fault-free dynamics subsystem, which is referred to as the fault isolated observer group 1 (FDI1), it is insensitive to the specific actuator fault. And a bank of pre-defined fault models is designed according to the Kinematics subsystem

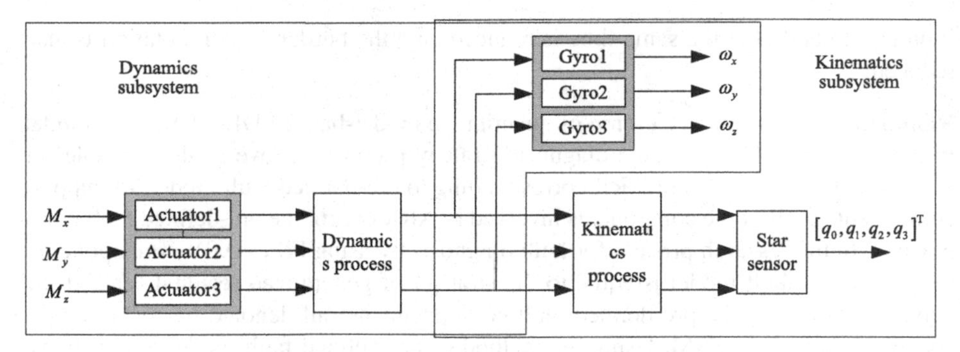

Fig. 9. The structure of the satellite attitude control system

with gyro faults, which is referred to as the fault isolation observer group 2 (FDI2), and it is insensitive to the specific gyro fault.

Thus the complete fault isolation logic is as follows:

Firstly, FDO1 and FDO2 run in parallel to detect whether there is a fault in the satellite attitude control system, and determine which part (actuator, gyro mechanism, star sensor) the fault comes from. It is assumed that r_{FDO1} is the residual evaluation function of FDO1 and $\overline{\varepsilon}_1$ is the corresponding fault detection threshold; r_{FDO2} is the residual evaluation function of FDO2 and $\overline{\varepsilon}_2$ is the corresponding fault detection threshold. The initial fault detection logic is as follows:

$$\begin{cases} r_{FDO1} \le \overline{\varepsilon}_1, r_{FDO2} \le \overline{\varepsilon}_2 \Rightarrow no\ fault \\ r_{FDO1} > \overline{\varepsilon}_1, r_{FDO2} \le \overline{\varepsilon}_2 \Rightarrow actuator\ fault \\ r_{FDO1} > \overline{\varepsilon}_1, r_{FDO2} > \overline{\varepsilon}_2 \Rightarrow gyro\ fault \\ r_{FDO1} \le \overline{\varepsilon}_1, r_{FDO2} > \overline{\varepsilon}_2 \Rightarrow star\ sensor\ fault \end{cases}$$

When the detection result is that the actuator has a fault, FIO1 is activated, which includes three fault isolation observers and $r_{FIO1-i}, i = 1, 2, 3$ is the residual evaluation function of the isolation observer designed to diagnoses the i-axis actuator fault, and $\overline{\varepsilon}_{1i}, i = 1, 2, 3$ is the corresponding threshold value, then

$$\left.\begin{array}{l} r_{FIO1-i} \le \overline{\varepsilon}_{1i} \\ r_{FIO1-j} > \overline{\varepsilon}_{1j}, \forall j \ne i \end{array}\right\} \Rightarrow \text{the i - axis actuator fault}, j, i = 1, 2, 3$$

When the detection result is that the gyro has a fault, FIO2 is activated, which also includes three fault isolation observers and $r_{FIO2-i}, i = 1, 2, 3$ is the residual evaluation function of the isolation observer designed to diagnoses the ith gyro fault, and $\overline{\varepsilon}_{2i}, i = 1, 2, 3$ is the corresponding threshold value, then

$$\left.\begin{array}{l} r_{FIO2-i} \le \overline{\varepsilon}_{2i} \\ r_{FIO2-j} > \overline{\varepsilon}_{2j}, \forall j \ne i \end{array}\right\} \Rightarrow \text{the ith gyro fault}, j, i = 1, 2, 3$$

Thus, the key components of the satellite attitude control system, including actuators, gyros and the star sensor, can be detected and isolated with the reasonable observer design.

7 Conclusions

In this paper, the traditional quantitative method-based fault diagnosis method is summarized and the difficulty of this method is analyzed. Furthermore, quantitative model-based fault diagnosis methods are redefined, and diagnosis solving process is studied. Finally, quantitative model-based fault diagnosis structural strategy which can isolate the faults of actuator and sensor with reduced analytical models is proposed and the corresponding analysis for diagnosis result is also presented.

References

1. Cordier, M.O., Dague, P., Lévy, F., et al.: Conflicts versus analytical redundancy relations: a comparative analysis of the model based diagnosis approach from the artificial intelligence and automatic control perspectives. IEEE Trans. Syst. Man Cybern. Part B Cybern. **34**(5), 2163–2177 (2004)
2. Pulido, B., González, C.A.: Possible conflicts: a compilation technique for consistency-based diagnosis. IEEE Trans. Syst. Man Cybern. Part B Cybern. **34**(5), 2192–2206 (2004)
3. Ding, S.X.: Model-Based Fault Diagnosis Techniques: Design Schemes, Algorithms and Tools. Springer, London (2012). https://doi.org/10.1007/978-1-4471-4799-2
4. Fijany, A., Vatan, F.: Method for the generation of analytical redundancy relations for system diagnostics: U.S. Patent 8,775,124 (2014)
5. Venkatasubramanian, V., Rengaswamy, R., Yin, K., et al.: A review of process fault detection and diagnosis: Part I: Quantitative model-based methods. Comput. Chem. Eng. **27**(3), 293–311 (2003)
6. Gao, Z., Cecati, C., Ding, S.X.: A survey of fault diagnosis and fault-tolerant techniques—Part I: Fault diagnosis with model-based and signal-based approaches. IEEE Trans. Ind. Electron. **62**(6), 3757–3767 (2015)
7. Xiao, C., Yu, M.: Model-based quantitative distributed fault diagnosis using system decomposition. In: Prognostics & System Health Management Conference, pp. 115–119 (2018)
8. Venkatasubramanian, V., Rengaswamy, R., Kavuri, S.N.: A review of process fault detection and diagnosis. Part II: Quanlitative models and search strategies. Comput. Chem. Eng. **27**(3), 313–326
9. Reiter, R.: A theory of diagnosis from first principles. Artif. Intell. **32**(1), 57–95 (1987)
10. Pantelides, C.C., Renfro, J.G.: The online use of first-principles models in process operations: review, current status and future needs. Comput. Chem. Eng. **51**(5), 136–148 (2013)
11. Marzat, J., Piet-Lahanier, H., Damongeot, F., Walter, E.: Model-based fault diagnosis for aerospace systems: a survey. Proc. Inst. Mech. Eng. Part G J. Aerosp. Eng. **226**, 1329–1360 (2012)
12. Frank, P.M.: Handling modelling uncertainty in fault detection and isolation systems. Palestine Explor. Q. **86**(2), 76–82 (2002)
13. Cheng, Y., Xiong, X., Wang, J.: Hybrid architecture for spacecraft diagnosis and its application. In: IEEE International Conference on Prognostics and Health Management, pp. 1–6 (2018)

A New Approach on Satellite Mission Planning with Revisiting Requirements

Yuyan Liu[1], Yuqing Li[1](✉), Pengpeng Liu[2], Xiaoen Feng[1], Feilong Jiang[1], and Mingjia Lei[1]

[1] Harbin Institute of Technology, Harbin 150001, China
bradley@hit.edu.cn
[2] Naval Research Academy, Beijing 10061, China

Abstract. With the development of space science and technology, the demand of observation mission increases. However, due to the limitations of the performance of platform or payloads and space environment of the remote sensing satellite, the observation ability is restricted, so it is necessary to carry out the mission planning. Aiming at the observation task of revisiting hot spots by remote sensing satellite, this paper firstly analyzes the practical constraints, and designs several functions about optimization targets. Secondly, the mathematical model was established. Thirdly, the algorithm to solve the problem was based on PBIL. Finally, to examine the performance of the algorithm, this paper creates simulation scenarios and test cases by means of STK, and obtains the initial simulation time window sequence. By comparing with the results of genetic algorithm, the effectiveness of the algorithm in solving the problem of multi-satellite revisit mission planning has been verified, which is better than the results of genetic algorithm.

Keywords: Satellite mission planning · Revisiting requirements · Population based incremental learning algorithm · Genetic algorithm

1 Introduction

Satellite mission planning is to generate a planning sequence for observation missions that satisfies various constraints based on limited resources. In addition, there is a need for repeated observation in hot spots to obtain effective local information. At the same time, the cost of satellites is relatively high, so the overall planning of limited satellite resources in order to achieve better mission requirements under certain resource conditions has become an urgent problem. Scholars from various countries have studied this problem from multiple perspectives.

This study was supported by the Key Laboratory Opening Funding of Harbin Institute of Technology of Deep Space Exploration Landing and Return Control Technology (HIT.KLOF. 2018.076, HIT.KLOF. 2018.074), and the pre-research projects of equipment development department of China Central Military Commission (JZX7Y20190243001201).

Q. Wu et al. (Eds.): WiSATS 2020, LNICST 358, pp. 198–209, 2021.
https://doi.org/10.1007/978-3-030-69072-4_17

Deng bao song and others summarized the current status and future trend of mission planning. They mentioned that satellite mission planning is a NP hard problem in theory. In the research and practice process, it is usually necessary to establish an effective constraint model based on specific tasks, in order to ensure the feasibility and reliability [1]. Scholars have made extensive studies on task planning from different perspectives, including overall problem analysis, algorithm implementation, software implementation, and analysis of different constraints. In the paper of Fatos Xhata et al., the genetic algorithm of STK is used to carry out multi-objective task scheduling [2]. There are also many ways to use intelligent algorithms to solve satellite mission planning problems. For example, in the paper written by Zhang Zhengqiang et al., neighborhood search algorithm was used. After the reasonable allocation of the target area, they comprehensively designed greedy random variable neighborhood search algorithm [3]. Song Yanjie proposed an improved genetic algorithm that could freely switch between global optimization and local optimization according to the population situation. In addition, he also proposed a task planning algorithm that could select a reasonable execution time for the improved mission sequence [4]. Hu Xiaoxuan et al. invented the method and system of multi-star emergency mission planning based on pointer neural network [5]. In many scholars' articles, it is often considered to improve the algorithm [4, 8] or combine the two algorithms [6] to solve the problem.

Based on the above analysis, the solving ability of the existing methods needs to be further improved, and the revisiting demand of hot spots is not fully considered. Therefore, based on previous studies and taking small satellites as the research object, this paper designed a population incremental learning algorithm to solve the problem of revisit mission requirements, and compared the results with the genetic algorithm, conducted simulation experiments on the multi-star time window sequence to verify the effectiveness of the algorithm.

2 Description of the Problem

2.1 Problem Overview and I/O

During the observation mission, the satellite carries a sensor as a payload to observe the earth and collect information, and then sends them down to the ground station. In the case of multi-satellite operation, the observation task is determined, the resource utilization rate is improved, and the observation effect is optimized.

The basic input elements of the question usually include the following aspects:

(1) satellite orbit parameters: the satellite's orbit is generally described by the orbit parameters (orbital altitude, orbital inclination, right ascension of ascending node and initial latitude argument);
(2) payload parameters: since the main problem in this paper is to use intelligent algorithm for revisiting mission planning, synthetic aperture radar (SAR) sensors that can work in the shadow area are selected uniformly to achieve the optimal value of observation efficiency. The power of the sensor and the field of view Angle;

(3) satellite platform parameters: power supply capacity, storage space capacity, data transmission time window, time for the satellite to enter the shadow area and light area, and angular velocity of the satellite's pitch axis and roll axis. At the same time, the satellite has the ability to swing and maneuver, which can improve the observation effect to some extent.
(4) Target: This paper selects the northern Indian Ocean region as an example. For remote sensing satellites, observation targets can be point targets or regional targets. In the subsequent revisiting mission planning, point targets are selected for specific analysis.

The basic output elements of the problem usually include the following two aspects: the first is the mission planning scheme, which can be represented by a structure, including the satellite number of the corresponding mission, the number of the ground target, the starting and ending time of the observation time window, and whether the window is selected or not. The second is the expression of observation effect, which mainly includes observation times, total observation time, mean revisiting time and mean variance of revisiting time.

2.2 Constraint Conditions and Optimization Objectives

The constraint conditions of the problem mainly include: time window conflict (A satellite can only observe one target at a time; In order to improve resource utilization, the same target can only be observed by one satellite at the same time), power constraints (satellite battery charging activities must be carried out when the circle of light period and meet the lap balance and depth of discharge shall not exceed 20%), storage and sufficient attitude adjustment time for observations.

Optimization objectives of the problem include: the satellite should ensure 100% coverage or observation of ground targets; Total observation times, total observation time, mean revisiting time and mean variance of revisiting time of the satellite to the ground target. Among them, the total number of observations and the total observation time are the primary objectives. In the optimization of the time window sequence, these two objectives are firstly optimized, and the average revisiting time and the variance of revisiting time are the secondary objectives. Based on the achievement of the first two objectives and then according to the secondary goals to optimize or take them as indicators to judge the quality of the results.

2.3 Simulation Constellation and Obtain

By analyzing and discussing the influence of orbit parameters (orbital altitude, orbital inclination, right ascension of ascending node and initial latitude argument) on the regional coverage, the constellation is finally determined. Considering the characteristics of small satellites, low-earth orbit is chosen for mission orbit, in the other word, the orbital altitude is less than 1000 km, so that the satellite has better observation results of the selected region. At the same time, the circular orbit is used for analysis, because the circular orbit has a uniform resolution for the ground target compared with the elliptical orbit. The target area is located in the North Indian Ocean area. The specific latitude and longitude were set as [0°N-20°N,58°E-70°E], the regional target resolution was set as 0.5°, the simulation time was set as 4 days, the sensor's field of view Angle was set as 25°, and the satellite adopted a two-body model. After experimental simulation and analysis, the specific parameters of the four satellites were finally selected as shown in the following table (Table 1):

Table 1. Simulation satellite parameters

Satellite number	Orbital altitude (km)	Orbital inclination (deg)	Ascending intersection right ascension (deg)	Initial latitude argument (deg)
1	600	20	0	360
2	600	20	90	330
3	600	20	180	120
4	600	20	270	180

Thirteen hotspots were selected in this region, and through STK analysis of visibility I finally obtained the initial sequence of 221 time Windows.

3 Design of Algorithms

3.1 Population Based Incremental Learning Algorithm

Incremental learning refers to a system that constantly learns new content from the outside world and updates the content learned. And population based incremental learning is based on a population, and regards the evolution of a population as a learning and updating process, and uses the acquired knowledge to guide the generation of the next generation of population, thereby producing a better solution of the fitness value results.

In the process of code design, it is possible to model the optimization process of population in genetic algorithm for processing and analysis. The main algorithm steps are as follows:

(1) chromosome coding

The sequences obtained in the previous chapter are first sorted by the initial time of the time window, then sorted by the satellite number, then according to whether the satellite time window is selected (1 means selected, 0 means not)to number them.Suppose there are 100 individuals in a population, and the initial sequence has n time Windows. Therefore, the chromosome pool matrix (Cmepool) is illustrated as follows:

$$Cmepool = \begin{bmatrix} 1101 & \nu & 1010 \\ \vdots & \ddots & \vdots \\ 1001 & \nu & 1110 \end{bmatrix}_{100*n} \tag{1}$$

(2) generation initial population

When using the genetic algorithm to calculate, it is necessary to first generate an initial population for subsequent optimization selection. A random pool matrix containing only 0 or 1 is directly generated by the random function, which is the initial population.

(3) fitness evaluation function

Before the fitness evaluation, eliminating the conflicts first. The conflict includes: satellite time window conflict, ground station time window conflict, attitude adjustment time conflict, energy constraint conflict and storage constraint conflict. If there is a conflict, the relevant time window will be removed randomly and then check conflict constraint again.

The fitness calculation function adopts two schemes. The first is to use the total observation time as the output variable to be optimized, that is, to traverse all the selected time windows and calculate the total observation time as corresponding chromosome's fitness value. The second is to take the total number of observations as the output variable to be optimized, that is, to traverse all the selected time windows and calculate the number of observations as corresponding chromosome's fitness value.

(4) population learning process

The population learning process is inseparable from the design of the learning process. The initial learning probability matrix is set as following formula.

$$p_1 = 0.5 * ones(1, 221) \tag{2}$$

Where ones() is a function of MATLAB that can generate all 1 matrix.

Then the population will improve the learning probability matrix according to a certain learning rate (α).

$$p_2 = (1 - \alpha)p_1 + \alpha p_{new} \tag{3}$$

Where p_{new} is a chromosomal gene with better fitness in the previous generation population.

Then design a mutation function for the learning probability matrix to increase the diversity of the population and avoid falling into a local optimal solution. The mutation probability is 0.1 and the mutation size is 0.2. The mutation formula is as follows:

$$p = p_2 * (1 - 0.2) + randi([01], 1) * 0.2 \tag{4}$$

Where randi() is a built-in pseudo-random integer function generated by MATLAB.

According to this learning probability, the next generation of population is generated.

Realizing the Algorithm

MATLAB programming is adopted to realize the algorithm. The main steps are designed according to the previous section, and the flow chart is as follows (Fig. 1):

Since the learning rate has a great influence on the evolution of the algorithm, analyzing the impact of the learning rate on the simulation, finally the learning rate is selected as 0.75 in this paper.

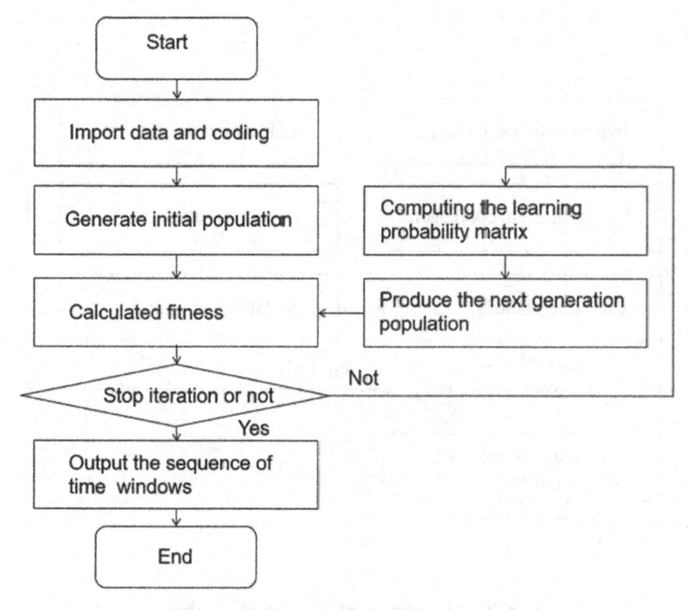

Fig. 1. Flow chart of population incremental learning algorithm.

3.2 Genetic Algorithm

The difference between genetic algorithm and population incremental learning algorithm design is how to generate the next generation. The population based incremental learning algorithm is based on a well-adapted individual performing directed learning to generate the next generation. And genetic algorithm generate the next generation through the selection operator (according to the proportion of the probability which is proportional to the individual fitness, operator determines whether the individual into the mating pool and it also adopts elite reserved strategy), the crossover operator (random selection of two individuals for single-point crossover to obtain offspring, Choose the best two of the four individuals) and mutation operator (with the possibility to carry out mutations of some chromosomal genes to increase the diversity of individuals) to produce (Fig. 2).

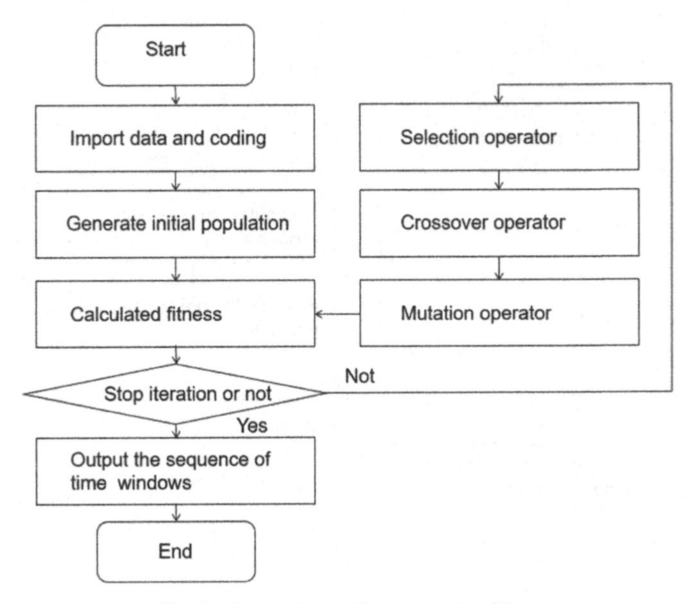

Fig. 2. Flow chart of genetic algorithm.

4 Examples and Analysis

4.1 PBIL Algorithm Simulation Examples

The learning rate (α) is 0.75, the number of iterations was 100, and the population size was 100, the mutation probability and the size of the mutation value were selected as shown in formula (4) above. The fitness is calculated according to the total observation time (example1) and observation times (example 2), and the fitness results were shown as follows (Fig. 5):

In the calculation result based on the total observation time as the fitness, the optimal solution is individual 1. In this last generation, the individual 3 has the lowest average revisiting time and individual 4 has the lowest mean variance of revisiting time. And in the result calculated according to the total observation time as the fitness, the optimal solution is individual 2, in the last generation, individual 5 has the least average revisiting time and individual 6 has the lowest mean variance of revisiting time.

It can be seen from Fig. 3 and Fig. 4 that it is feasible to apply PBIL to the satellite mission planning problem, and it can achieve convergence within a certain iteration range with a good convergence result. In the initial iterations, population's fitness rose rapidly, due to the huge role of directional learning which can make the whole population evolution towards the direction of the optimal fitness. While the later iteration process mainly relies on the effect of mutation to pull the population's fitness, and the upward space of the fitness decreases, so compared to the initial iterations the evolution process is relatively slow. The highest and lowest fitness of each generation are rising in fluctuation, because there is a certain probability of producing genes inconsistent with the overall learning direction. Such mutant genes can not only increase the population diversity to a certain extent, but also lead to the fluctuation of individual fitness in the population.

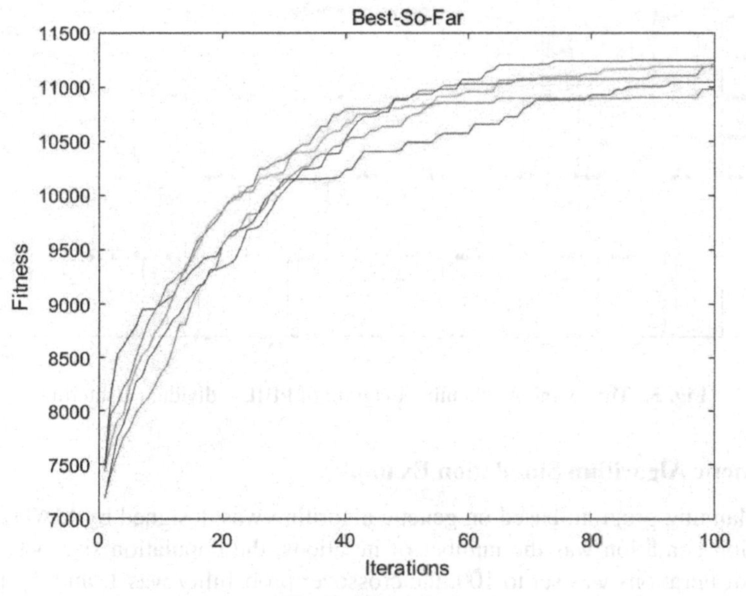

Fig. 3. Example 1

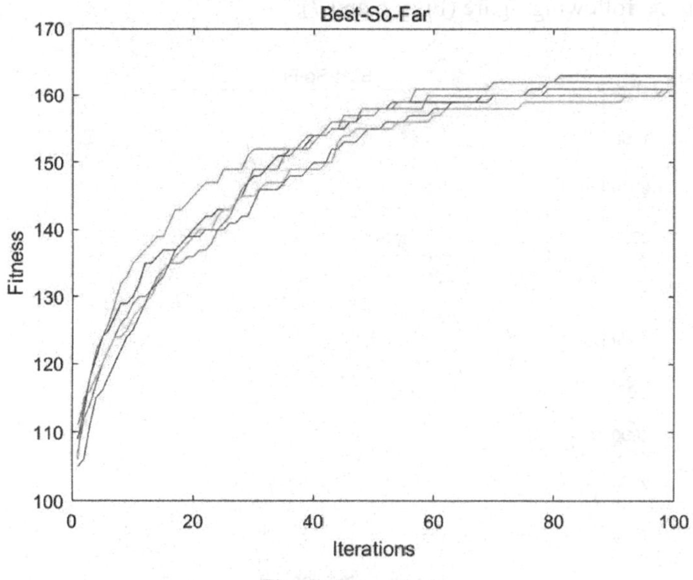

Fig. 4. Example 2

According to the previous section, the six individuals' data of the PBIL algorithm are as follows:

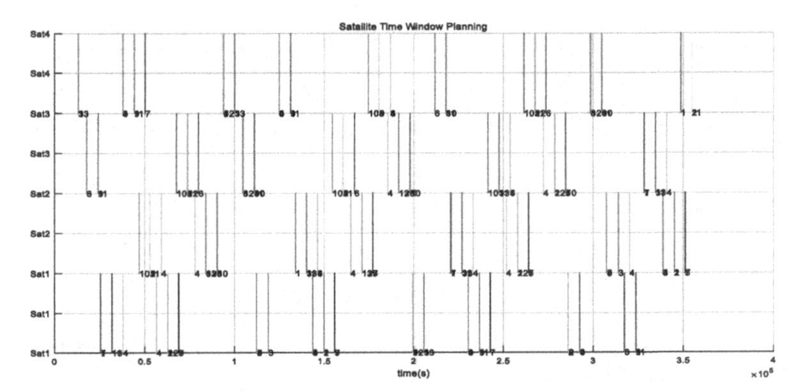

Fig. 5. Time window planning diagram of PBIL individual 1 satellite

4.2 Genetic Algorithm Simulation Examples

A task planning program based on genetic algorithm was designed by MATLAB. The termination condition was the number of iterations, the population size was 100, the number of iterations was set to 100, the crossover probability was 1, and the mutation probability was 0.1. The fitness function was calculated according to the total observation time (example 3) and the total observation times (example 4). And the simulation results are shown in the following figure (Figs. 6 and 7):

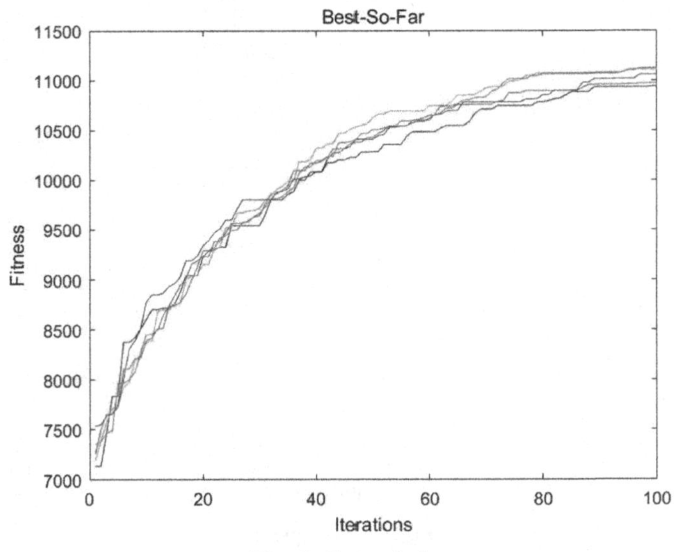

Fig. 6. Example 3

It can be seen from the above figures that the use of genetic algorithm can also achieve convergence with a good convergence value.

According to the previous section, the six individuals' data of the genetic algorithm are as follows:

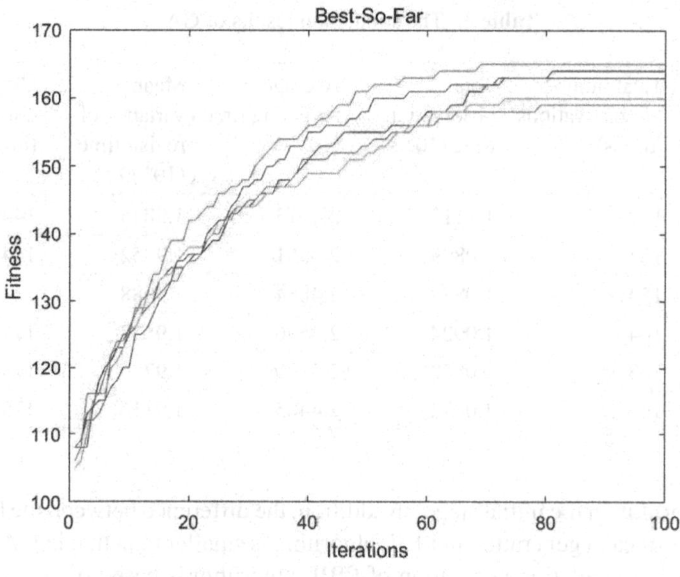

Fig. 7. Example 4

4.3 Comparison and Analysis

Convergent Value

Comparing PBIL and GA individuals in Table 2 and Table 3, the result of the two algorithms has little difference. This shows that both algorithms can achieve the desired convergence results as long as there are enough iterations.

Table 2. The simulation results of PBIL.

Individual code	Total number of observations (times)	Total observation time (10^4 s)	Average revisiting time (10^4 s)	Mean variance of revisit time (10^4 s)	CPU computation time (s)
P1-1	162	1.2141	2.4513	2.0641	560.7
P1-2	157	1.0744	2.4150	2.0575	561.0
P1-3	160	1.0980	2.4331	2.0305	560.9
P2-1	163	1.0744	2.4475	2.0996	576.5
P2-2	161	1.0613	2.4464	2.0984	576.7
P2-3	160	1.0527	2.4468	2.0953	576.8

Iteration Times of the Same Fitness

By comparing the number of iterations corresponding to the same fitness in the four graphs, the genetic algorithm has more iterations than the population based incremental

Table 3. The simulation results of GA.

Individual code	Total number of observations (times)	Total observation time (10^4 s)	Average revisiting time (10^4 s)	Mean variance of revisit time (10^4 s)	CPU computation time (s)
G1-1	157	1.1117	2.4913	1.9845	1442.3
G1-2	155	1.0899	2.4851	1.9852	1442.6
G1-3	154	1.0877	2.4854	1.9688	1442.6
G2-1	164	1.0924	2.4596	1.9537	1794.5
G2-2	163	1.0852	2.3870	1.9730	1794.8
G2-3	163	1.0874	2.4485	1.9116	1794.7

learning algorithm in the initial stage. In addition, the difference between the highest and lowest values of each generation in PBIL algorithm is smaller than that in GA algorithm.

Because the population generation of PBIL algorithm is based on a specific learning probability with strong orientation, which can make the individuals in the whole population iterate in a clear optimization direction. While the genetic algorithm needs to drive the population to change optimally through two ways: elite retention strategy and choosing two excellent ones from parents and two children. So, the orientation is relatively weak.

CPU Computing Time
Comparing PBIL and GA individuals 1 and 2 in Table 2 and Table 3, it is obvious that the genetic algorithm takes more than twice as long as the computing time of PBIL. This is because the genetic algorithm needs to pass three steps including selection, crossover, and mutation, when generating the next generation. What's more in the process of crossover the fitness function is called to increase the calculation time. While the population based incremental learning algorithm only needs to determine a learning probability matrix to generate the next generation.

All in all, the population incremental learning algorithm is superior to the genetic algorithm in terms of number of iterations required, and CPU computing time.

5 Conclusion

Aiming at the problem of multi-satellite remote sensing mission planning, reasonable modeling was carried out after analyzing its input and output and constraints and optimization objective. This paper used the population incremental learning algorithm and genetic algorithm to optimize the time window series. Taking 4 small satellites to observe 13 regional hotspots as an example Simulation. The calculation examples show that it is reasonable and effective to use this method to solve similar problems. It also shows that the performance of the population incremental learning algorithm is superior to the genetic algorithm.

It should be pointed out that this paper only achieved research results in a certain aspect, and the research on observation constraints is not sufficient. Other more complex constraints will be further considered in the future, and the algorithm will be further optimized for the actual application.

References

1. Baosong, D., Zhipeng, M., Yi Yujiang, Yu., Ye, Z.X.: Research on mission planning of earth observation satellite. Comput. Measur. Control **27**(11), 130–139 (2019)
2. Xhafa, F., Sun, J., Barolli, A., Biberaj, A., Barlli, L.: Genetic algorithms for satellite scheduling problems. Mob. Inf. Syst. **8**(4) (2012)
3. Zhang, Z., Guo, J., Ruan, Q.: Remote sensing satellite mission planning algorithm for regional target. Radio Eng. **39**(09), 40–43 (2009)
4. Song, Y., Wang, P., Zhang, Z., Xing, L., Chen, Y.: Improved genetic algorithm for multi-star task planning. Control Theory Appl. **36**(09), 1391–1397 (2019)
5. Hu, X., et al.: Method and system of multi-star emergency mission planning based on the needle neural network. CN110599065A, 20 December 2019
6. Zheng, Z., Guo, L., Gill, E.: swarm satellite mission scheduling & planning using hybrid dynamic genetic algorithm. Acta Astronaut. **137**, 243–253 (2017)
7. Wu, G., Liu, J., Ma, M., Qiu, D.: A two - phase scheduling method with the consideration of task clustering for earth observing satellites. Comput. Oper. Res. **40**(7) (2013)
8. Li, Y., Wang, R., Xu, M., Cui, H., Wang, H., Xu, R.: Research on a class of multi-resource measurement and control scheduling problem based on improved genetic algorithm. J. Aerosp. **33**(01), 85–90 (2012)
9. Zhang, Q.: An improved incremental learning algorithm based on group. In: Technical Committee on Control Theory, Chinese Association of Automation. Proceedings of the 26th China Control conference. Technical Committee on Cotrol Theory, Chinese Association of Automation, Professional Committee of Control Theory of China Automation Society, pp. 3273–3276 (2007)

Satellite Telemetry Anomaly Detection Based on Gradient Boosting Regression with Feature Selection

Zhidong Li[1(✉)], Bo Sun[1], Weihua Jin[2], Lei Zhang[1], and Rongzheng Luo[1]

[1] Beijing Institute of Spacecraft System Engineering, Beijing 100094, China
lizhidongcas@163.com
[2] Research Center of Satellite Technology,
Harbin Institute of Technology, Harbin 150080, China

Abstract. A data-driven satellite telemetry data anomaly detection method is proposed. The gradient boosting regression algorithm combined with feature selection, including feature scoring and recursive lowest-score feature elimination, can automatically mine the correlative telemetry variables through iterations and establish a nonlinear regression model for their functional association, which can be used as a health baseline for anomaly detection of telemetry data. This method requires no expert to specify correlative telemetry variables based on domain knowledge beforehand. It has the advantage of self-adaption for satellite operating conditions, which can overcome the problem of functional association altering under different operating conditions caused by orbit or sunshine condition changes. The validity and effectiveness of the method is verified by the telemetry data of the power subsystem.

Keywords: Anomaly detection · Satellite · Gradient Boosting · Feature selection

1 Introduction

The on-orbit satellite will generate a large number of telemetry data, which can reflect its on-orbit healthy state. Anomaly detection of telemetry data is important for the reliability and security of satellites.

With the development of AI and machine learning, data-driven methods are mainly used in anomaly detection nowadays, which include (1) one-class classification such as SVDD [1], OC-SVM [2], (2) statistical method such as Gaussian Mixture Model [3], (3) prediction based method such as LSTM network prediction [4], (4) supervised multi-class classification. For one-class classification and mixed Gaussian model, although it has strong universality, it has poor interpretability and unable to locate the cause of the problem further when an anomaly occurs. Prediction based method cannot handle the unpredictable telemetry variables. Moreover, due to the influence of conceptual drift, the prediction error will be accumulated gradually, affecting the accuracy of anomaly

Q. Wu et al. (Eds.): WiSATS 2020, LNICST 358, pp. 210–219, 2021.
https://doi.org/10.1007/978-3-030-69072-4_18

detection. For supervised classification, it is necessary to rely on experts to provide labels.

In engineering practice, single–variable-threshold method is often adopted. The upper and lower threshold values are set for a single telemetry variable. It is considered abnormal when the telemetry value exceeds the threshold. This method is simple and easy to use. Still it does not take into account the association between the various telemetry, nor does it take into account the impact of different satellite operating conditions on telemetries. For example, when telemetry violates certain constraints of consistency or does not conform to relevant rules in a particular context, it should also be judged as abnormal. However, the telemetry variables may not exceed their thresholds at the time. Therefore, multiple telemetry variables should be considered synergistically to achieve anomaly detection through joint analysis. When the telemetry variables deviate from their normal behavior pattern, also known as health baseline deviation, anomalies are considered to occur. When the satellite is in orbit, the change of orbit position and sunshine condition will lead to the satellite in different operating conditions, and the functional association between telemetry variables are usually different under different operating conditions. Multiple telemetry variables collaborative anomaly detection methods usually need to identify the operating conditions first, and then call the condition associated model to deal with the anomaly detection. However, the identification of operating conditions itself will introduce additional errors, and it is also difficult to achieve crisp segmentation of operating conditions during their transition. Moreover, expert knowledge like the functional hypothesis is usually needed when establishing a telemetry functional association model.

To solve the above problems, this paper uses a gradient boosting regression algorithm to automatically learn the nonlinear complex functional association model by data-driven manner, which is self-adaptive to the change of telemetry association altering caused by the change of operating conditions. Also, a novel feature selection method, which combines feature importance scoring through gradient boosting regression model training process and recursively lowest-score feature elimination, can automatically mine telemetry variables with the association through multiple iterations without domain knowledge. The method is characterized by high interpretability, high accuracy, and intelligence.

2 Problem Description

Data-driven anomaly detection requires first preparing training datasets, usually the historical telemetry data of satellites in orbit. Then, an anomaly detection model is learned from the training dataset through a data-driven manner. Finally, the trained anomaly detection model is used for anomaly detection for new on-orbit telemetry data.

A telemetry dataset containing N telemetry variables is represented as dataset = $\left\{\vec{X}_1, \vec{X}_2, \vec{X}_3, ..., \vec{X}_N\right\}$. $\vec{X}_k$ indicates the Kth telemetry variable, which is a vector with the timestamp and can be represented as $\vec{X}_k = [x_{k1}, x_{k2}, x_{k3}, ..., x_{kP}]^T$, and x_{kp} indicates the value of the Kth telemetry variable at time p.

We propose a novel anomaly detection method that can automatically mine the telemetry with correlation from the dataset and establish the association model. Taking

$\vec{X}_1$ as an example, we first mine the telemetry variables correlated to $\vec{X}_1$, assuming that the results are $\vec{X}_2$ and $\vec{X}_5$. Then take $\vec{X}_1$ as the dependent variable and take $\vec{X}_2$ and $\vec{X}_5$ as the independent variable. The regression model $\vec{X}_1 = f_1^*\left(\vec{X}_2, \vec{X}_5\right)$ stands for the association between correlated variables can be established through learning from the training dataset.

When we performing the anomaly detection, the regression model $f_1^*(\cdot)$ is used to receive newly on-orbit telemetry data, and the expected value of x_{1p} at certain time p is obtained. The expected value is represented as $\hat{x}_{1p} = f_1^*(x_{2p}, x_{5p})$. The regression error between the true value and the expected value of telemetry is represented as $\varepsilon_1 = x_{1p} - \hat{x}_{1p}$.

Anomaly detection criteria can be set by statistical methods or expert knowledge based on regression errors. For example, telemetry data may be considered abnormal if the regression errors exceed the limit one or more times in a given time period.

Similar to $\vec{X}_1$, anomaly detection can be applied to other telemetry data in the same way.

3 Anomaly Detection Algorithms

The training method of $f^*(\cdot)$ based on the gradient boosting regression algorithm is first introduced and then the feature selection method.

3.1 Gradient Boosting Regression

Gradient boosting regression algorithms is used to construct an association model $f^*(\cdot)$ through ensemble learning from the correlated telemetry variables. The algorithms take the regression tree as base model to jointly construct $f^*(\cdot)$. Assuming $f^*(\cdot)$ is composed of k regression tree models [5] $\{f_1, f_1, f_3, \ldots, f_K\}$. In these tree structures, leaves represent continuous regression values and branches represent conjunctions of features that lead to those values. Overall regression value $\hat{y}_i$ equals to the sum of the regression results of all base models.

$$\hat{y}_i = \sum_{k=1}^{K} f_k(x_i),\ f_k \in F \tag{1}$$

F is the functional space, x_i is the input of the based model.

The objective function to be optimized is given by

$$\text{obj} = \sum_{i=1}^{n} l\left(y_i, \hat{y}_i^{(t)}\right) + \sum_{i=1}^{t} \Omega(f_i) \tag{2}$$

The left part $\sum_{i=1}^{n} l\left(y_i, \hat{y}_i^{(t)}\right)$ is the training loss, and the right part $\sum_{i=1}^{t} \Omega(f_i)$ is the regularization term. $\Omega(\cdot)$ is model complexity of regression tree.

XGboost library is used for training the regression model. We give a brief review of XGboost training process in the following sections. People who are interested in XGboost can refer to [6].

Model training process of XGboost can be seen as additive training. In the training process, the new tree model is constantly being added. We write the prediction value at step t as $\hat{y}_i^{(t)}$. Then we have

$$\hat{y}_i^{(t)} = \sum_{k=1}^{t} f_k(x_i) = \hat{y}_i^{(t-1)} + f_t(x_i) \tag{3}$$

$f_t(x_i)$ is the new tree model at step t. And the objective function at step t becomes

$$\text{obj}^{(t)} = \sum_{i=1}^{n} l\left(y_i, \hat{y}_i^{(t-1)} + f_t(x_i)\right) + \sum_{i=1}^{t} \Omega(f_i) \tag{4}$$

Mean-Squared-Error (MSE) is used as the loss function, the objective becomes

$$\begin{aligned} \text{obj}^{(t)} &= \sum_{i=1}^{n} \left(y_i - \left(\hat{y}_i^{(t-1)} + f_t(x_i)\right)\right)^2 + \sum_{i=1}^{t} \Omega(f_i) \\ &= \sum_{i=1}^{n} \left[2\left(\hat{y}_i^{(t-1)} - y_i\right) f_t(x_i) + f_t(x_i)^2\right] + \sum_{i=1}^{t} \Omega(f_i) \end{aligned} \tag{5}$$

Taylor expansion of the loss function is taken up to the second-order, we obtain

$$\text{obj}^{(t)} = \sum_{i=1}^{n} \left[l\left(y_i, \hat{y}_i^{(t-1)}\right) + g_i f_t(x_i) + 1/2 h_i f_t^2(x_i)\right] + \sum_{i=1}^{t} \Omega(f_i) \tag{6}$$

The g_i and h_i are defined as

$$g_i = \partial_{\hat{y}_i^{(t-1)}} l\left(y_i, \hat{y}_i^{(t-1)}\right) \tag{7}$$

$$h_i = \partial^2_{\hat{y}_i^{(t-1)}} l\left(y_i, \hat{y}_i^{(t-1)}\right) \tag{8}$$

After all the constants are removed, the specific objective at step t becomes $\sum_{i=1}^{n} \left[g_i f_t(x_i) + 1/2 h_i f_t^2(x_i)\right] + \Omega(f_t)$. This is the optimization goal for the new tree. The computation of g_i and h_i can refer to [6].

It can be seen that the objective function decreases gradually with the increase of the number of base models in the training process. An intuitive understanding is that each base model is good at different aspect and try to *complement* each other. Therefore, the method is self-adaptive to the operating conditions.

3.2 Feature Selection

Although gradient boosting regression can construct $f^*(\cdot)$, we must know which telemetry variables are correlated with each other beforehand. For example, we must know $\vec{X}_2$ and $\vec{X}_5$ correlated to $\vec{X}_1$, then we can construct an association model $\vec{X}_1 = f_1^*\left(\vec{X}_2, \vec{X}_5\right)$. This correlation usually provided by some domain experts. If we have no domain knowledge, we should mine the correlated telemetry variables first.

We proposed a novel feature selection method, which can automatically mine the correlated telemetry variables without domain knowledge. It includes (1) feature scoring and (2) recursively lowest-score feature elimination.

For feature scoring, the telemetry variables in the dataset are taken as features, and the feature importance degree can be scored through the training process of gradient boosting regression. Construction of gradient boosting regression tree model work top-down by choosing a feature at each step and optimized its split. The score of each feature can be defined as the number of times a feature is used to split the data across all trees. For example, after constructing $\vec{X}_1 = f_1^*\left(\vec{X}_2, \vec{X}_5\right)$, the score of feature $\vec{X}_2$ and $\vec{X}_5$ can be obtained.

Table 1. Computational process of Recursively feature elimination algorithm

Recursively feature elimination algorithm	
step 1	Take $\vec{X}_1$ as dependent variable. Take $\vec{X}_2, \vec{X}_3, \ldots, \vec{X}_N$ as independent variables. Initialize $\vec{X}_1$_correlated as $\vec{X}_2, \vec{X}_3, \ldots, \vec{X}_N$.
step 2	Learn $\vec{X}_1 = f_1^*\left(\vec{X}_1\text{\_correlated}\right)$ from the dataset. Inclemently record $\vec{X}_1$_correlated and regression error as key-value pairs.
step 3	Compute all the feature scores in $\vec{X}_1$_correlated.
step 4	Update : Eliminate the feature from $\vec{X}_1$_correlated that has the lowest score.
step 5	If no feature in $\vec{X}_1$_correlated, go to step 6, else return to step 2.
step 6	According to all the key-value pairs, compute the best $\vec{X}_1$_correlated based on a utility function self-defined, which takes into account the regression error and the number of features.

Feature scores combined with recursively lowest-score feature elimination can be used to mine correlated features. For example, if we want to mine the variables correlated to $\vec{X}_1$ from the dataset $\left\{\vec{X}_1, \vec{X}_2, \vec{X}_3, ..., \vec{X}_N\right\}$.The computational process of the recursively feature elimination is as shown in Table 1:

By using the utility function, we can obtain the best $\vec{X}_1$_correlated that the number of features in $\vec{X}_1$_correlated is smaller, and the regression error is low. If the regression error maintains large enough during the whole recursively feature elimination algorithm, then the dependent telemetry variable has no correlated variable.

Other features in the dataset can be applied feature selection to mine its correlated variables in the same way as $\vec{X}_1$.

4 Experimental Results and Analysis

The satellite power subsystem is taken as an example to verify the anomaly detection method. The application scope of the method is not limited to the power subsystem. For satellite, power subsystem is responsible for power supply to whole satellite, and it has great significance.

The subsystem is mainly composed of solar array panels, lithium battery pack, power conditioning controller (PCU), main bus, and so on. In the sunshine area, the solar array panels usually supply power for the whole satellite and charge the battery pack. Under the condition of the high-power loads, the solar array and battery pack are combined to supply the whole satellite. In the shadow area, the solar array panels have no output power, and the whole satellite is powered by the battery pack. PCU controls the operating mode of the subsystem through the internal main error voltage MEA feedback. The charging and discharging behavior of the battery pack are coordinated controlled by MEA and the battery error voltage BEA.

Table 2. Description of telemetry data

Telemetry name	Distribution	Data type
MainBusVoltage	Main bus	Voltage
MainBusCurrent	Main bus	Current
−Y_solarCurrent	−Y_solarArray	Current
+Y_solarCurrent	+Y_solarArray	Current
−Y_BatVoltage	−Y_battery	Voltage
+Y_BatVoltage	+Y_battery	Voltage
−Y_charging	−Y_battery	Current
−Y_discharging	−Y_battery	Current
MEA	PCU	Voltage
−Y_BEA	PCU	Voltage
+Y_BEA	PCU	Voltage

A set of key telemetry variables of the power subsystem is taken as the dataset, as shown in Table 2.

Power subsystem telemetry data curves are shown in Fig. 1. MainBusVoltage, +Y_solarCurrent, +Y_BatVoltage, −Y_BEA, and +Y_BEA are not shown in the figure because there are too many variables.

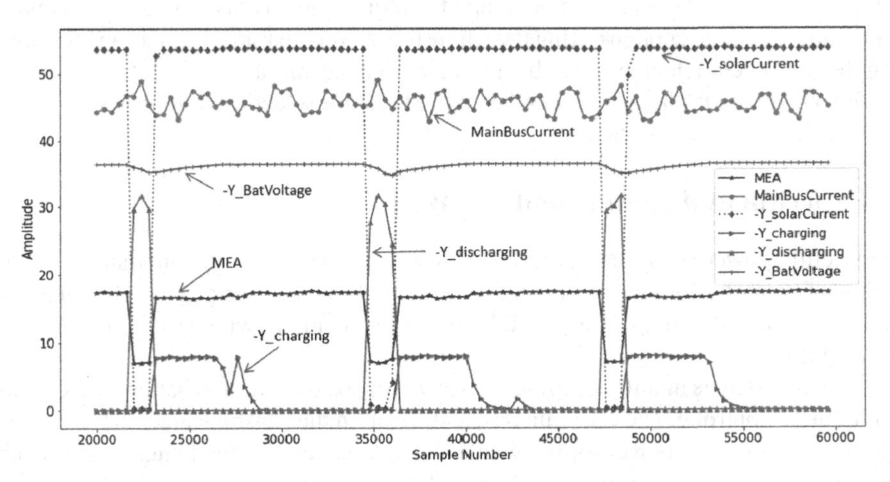

Fig. 1. Display of the satellite power subsystem telemetry data

From Fig. 1, it is shown that the telemetry curves show some correlation, and show different pattern under different operating conditions.

Take MEA as an example to verify the effectiveness of the method. Other telemetry variables can be handled in the same way.

MEA correlated telemetry variables are mined by the feature selection algorithm. The results are shown in Table 3. Due to a large number of process steps, the second and third feature elimination results were not shown.

From Table 3, it is shown that regression errors in the 9th and 10th elimination round is 0.3410 and 0.0350, which is much bigger than errors in the preceding round. Considering regression errors and the number of features, it is easy to know that the correlated telemetry variables to MEA are −Y_solarCurrent, MainBusCurrent and −Y_BEA. This feature selection result complies with expert's expectations. MEA and its correlated telemetry variables are shown in Fig. 2.

MEA is taken as dependent variables. −Y_solarCurrent、MainBusCurrent and −Y_BEA are taken as independent variables. The association model $f^*(\cdot)$ is constructed through gradient boosting regression algorithms learning from the training dataset. The true value and regression value of MEA are shown in Fig. 3.

It is shown that the regression value is very close to the real value, indicating that the regression model has high accuracy.

The regression error can be used as input of the anomaly criterion. The regression error is shown in Fig. 4.

Table 3. Results of feature selection

Error feature /Score/	1st 0.0652	4th 0.0663	5th 0.0646	6th 0.0660	7th 0.0664	8th 0.0649	9th 0.3410	10th 0.035
MainBusCurrent	0.314	0.3370	0.337	0.338	0.336	0.363	0.430	–
−Y_solarCurrent	0.292	0.343	0.320	0.342	0.350	0.455	0.570	1
−Y_discharging	0.105	–	–	–	–	–	–	–
−Y_BEA	0.081	0.0959	0.090	0.117	0.199	0.182	–	–
+Y_solarCurrent	0.079	0.118	0.134	0.120	0.114	–	–	–
+Y_BEA	0.066	0.0559	0.073	0.183	–	–	–	–
−Y_charging	0.048	0.050	0.045	–	–	–	–	–
−Y_BatVoltage	0.007	0.00	–	–	–	–	–	–
+Y_BatVoltage	0.007	–	–	–	–	–	–	–
MainBusVoltage	0.00	–	–	–	–	–	–	–

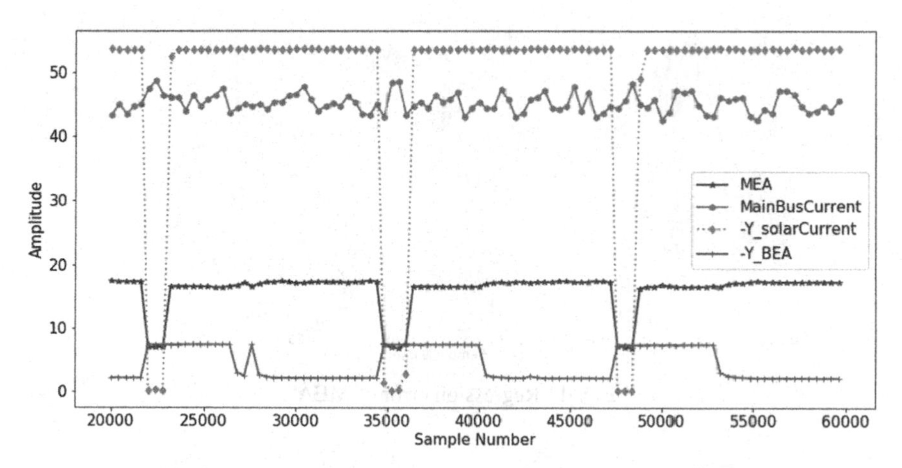

Fig. 2. Display of MEA and its correlated telemetry variables

From Fig. 4, It is shown that the regression error is small, and the threshold of anomaly criteria of regression error can be constructed by using statistical methods or based on expert experiences.

After artificial injecting some faults of MEA in the test dataset, anomaly detection result is shown in Fig. 5.

From Fig. 5, It is shown that the anomaly detection method proposed in this paper can detect anomalies effectively.

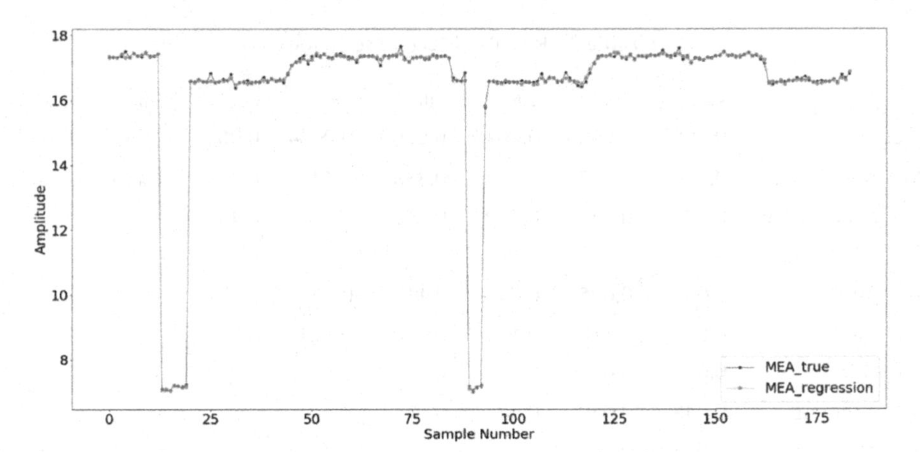

Fig. 3. True value and regression value of MEA

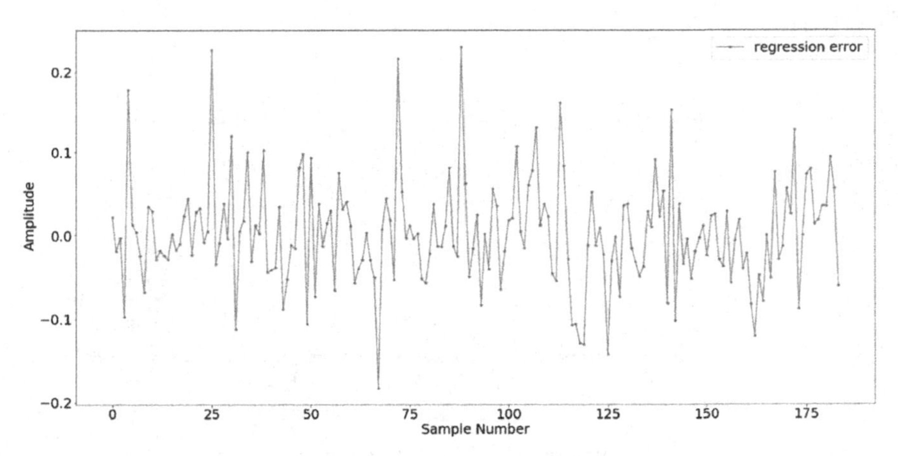

Fig. 4. Regression error of MEA

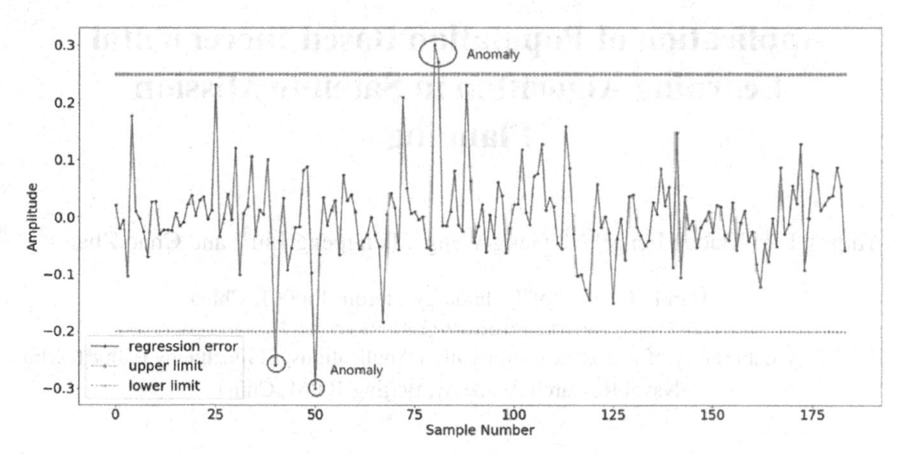

Fig. 5. Anomaly detection result

5 Conclusion

This paper proposes a new anomaly detection method. A gradient boosting regression algorithm is used to automatically learn the nonlinear complex functional association model by data-driven manner, which is self-adaptive to the change of telemetry association altering caused by the change of operating conditions. Also, a novel feature selection method, which combines feature importance scoring through gradient boosting regression model training process and recursively lowest-score feature elimination, can automatically mine telemetry variables with the association through multiple iterations without domain knowledge. The method is characterized by high interpretability, high accuracy, and intelligence. The validity and effectiveness of the method is verified by the telemetry data of the power subsystem.

References

1. Zhao, Y., Wang, S., Xiao, F.: Pattern recognition-based chillers fault detection method using support vector data description (SVDD). Appl. Energy **112**, 1041–1048 (2013)
2. Zio, E.: A support vector machine integrated system for the classification of operation anomalies in nuclear components and systems. Reliab. Eng. Syst. Saf. **92**(5), 593–600 (2007)
3. Laxhammar, R., Falkman, G., Sviestins, E.: Anomaly detection in sea traffic-a comparison of the gaussian mixture model and the kernel density estimator. In: 2009 12th International Conference on Information Fusion, FUSION 2009. IEEE, pp. 756–763 (2009)
4. Malhotra, P., Vig, L., Shroff, G., et al.: Long short term memory networks for anomaly detection in time series. In: Proceedings. Presses universitaires de Louvain, p. 89 (2015)
5. Liaw, A., Wiener, M.: Classification and regression by randomForest. R News **2**(3), 18–22 (2002)
6. Chen, T., Guestrin, C., XGBoost: a scalable tree boosting system. In: Proceedings of the 22nd ACM SIGKDD International Conference on Knowledge Discovery and Data Mining, pp. 785–794. ACM (2016)

Application of Population Based Incremental Learning Algorithm in Satellite Mission Planning

Yuqing Li[1], Xiaoen Feng[1(✉)], Gang Wang[2], Pengpeng Liu[3], and Chao Zhang[2]

[1] Harbin Institute of Technology, Harbin 150001, China
fengxiaoen0923@163.com
[2] CETC Key Laboratory of Aerospace Information Applications, Shijiazhuang 050081, China
[3] Naval Research Academy, Beijing 10061, China

Abstract. Considering the increasing demand for earth observation missions, aiming at the centralized cooperative mission planning problem of remote sensing satellites, analyzing the constraints in the operation of satellites while considering the load and platform operation, and establishing a reasonable mathematical calculation of satellite missions model. The population incremental learning (PBIL) algorithm is used to solve the satellite mission planning problem. The binary coding method of the traditional PBIL algorithm is improved to the real coding method, and the value matrix correction method is improved. The computational efficiency of PBIL algorithm based on real number coding is verified by numerical examples. The performances of genetic algorithm and PBIL algorithm in solving satellite mission planning problems are compared and analyzed.

Keywords: Satellite mission planning · PBIL algorithm · Earth observation · Remote sensing satellite

1 Introduction

With the development of space technology and the popularity of satellite applications, the number and types of Earth observation satellites are increasing, which are playing a quite important role in the fields of economy, military and people's livelihood. Facing the growing demand for large-scale and diversified tasks of users from all walks of life, satellite mission planning for constellation coordination has become a hot research issue at home and abroad.

Satellite mission planning refers to the process that the satellite control department allocates satellite payloads and ground control resources according to satellite missions

Supported by the Open Fund Project of CETC key laboratory of aerospace information applications (SXX18629T022), and the Key Laboratory Opening Funding of Harbin Institute of Technology of Deep Space Exploration Landing and Return Control Technology (HIT.KLOF. 2018.076, HIT.KLOF. 2018.074), and the pre-research project of equipment development department of China Central Military Commission (JZX7Y20190243001201).

Q. Wu et al. (Eds.): WiSATS 2020, LNICST 358, pp. 220–232, 2021.
https://doi.org/10.1007/978-3-030-69072-4_19

and routine maintenance needs, and satisfies various constraints, with maximizing the benefits of satellite missions during the satellite in-orbit operation [1, 2].

Obviously, satellite mission planning involves not only satellite payload resources, but also ground management resources to ensure their normal operation. It can be seen that there are many constraints in satellite mission planning. Therefore, reasonable and effective modeling methods and efficient mission planning methods are of great significance for describing and solving satellite mission planning problems.

As for the algorithm of the satellite mission planning problem solving, due to the NP characteristics of mission planning problems, most of the current researches use heuristic methods to solve the problem, mainly including tabu search [3], ant colony algorithm [4], genetic algorithm [5, 6], particle swarm algorithm [7, 8] and so on.

These heuristic optimization method is easy to implement and widely used. Arezoo Sarkheyli [3] applied the new tabu search algorithm to solve the problem of low-orbit satellite mission planning by considering the priority of the task and satisfying the time and resource constraints. However, the limiting factors are considered only include coverage rate, data storage capacity and battery capacity in that paper.

Zixuan Zheng et al. [6] used the improved genetic algorithm (GA) to solve the satellite mission planning problem, and proposed a Hybrid Dynamic Mutation (HDM) strategy, which overcomes the early convergence and long calculation time to some extent. But the simulation model used by it did not adequately consider the constraints, and only the constraints of satellite data transmission are considered.

However, in the face of complex large-scale satellite mission planning problems, in addition to the adequate consideration of the constraints of the model, the computational complexity and computational speed of the algorithm are also important aspects to achieving efficient and timely satellite mission planning.

Baluja, the professor of Carnegie Mellon University in the United States, proposed an evolutionary algorithm based on Population Based Incremental Learning (PBIL) [9]. The basic idea of the algorithm is to regard the evolution process as a learning process. The knowledge, also called the probability of learning, which is obtained by learning, to guide the generation of offspring. This probability is the accumulation of information throughout the evolutionary process, and it will be better to guide the resulting offspring (compared to GA's parental genetic recombination and single parent Gaussian variation of EP and ES), which results in faster convergence and better results.

In this paper, the following research work is completed for the satellite collaborative mission planning problem: (1) Under the condition of considering load and platform operation, the constraints of satellite operation are analyzed, a reasonable mathematical model of satellite mission planning is established, the optimization goal of satellite mission planning is proposed. (2) The Population Based Incremental Learning (PBIL) algorithm is used to solve the satellite mission planning problem. Combining with the characteristics of the mission, the binary coding method of the traditional PBIL algorithm is improved to the real coding method, and the correction method of value probability matrix is also improved. The satellite mission planning model based on PBIL algorithm is established and it is verified by numerical examples. (3) The computational efficiency of PBIL algorithm based on real coding is verified. And the performances of genetic algorithm and PBIL algorithm in solving satellite mission planning problems are compared and analyzed by numerical examples.

2 Terminology and Mathematical Statement

2.1 Problem Description and Basic Assumptions

The satellite cooperative mission planning problem can be described as that M satellites cooperatively observe R targets in a planning cycle, so that the objective function is optimal. The final output of the mission planning is mainly the allocation scheme of the observation mission. For a satellite, the distribution result can be expressed as a six-element array as follows:

$$[m, r, ST_{rm}, ET_{rm}, D_{rm}, V_{rm}]$$

Where $S = \{S_1, S_2, \ldots, S_m, \ldots S_M\}$ is the satellite collection, and m is the number of m-th satellite; $T = \{t_1, t_2, \ldots, t_r, \ldots t_R\}$ is the target collection, and r is the number of the r-th target; ST_{rm}, ET_{rm} are the start time and end time of the satellite S_m observing the target t_r;.D_{rm} is the duration of the satellite S_m observing the target t_r; V_{rm} is the benefit of the target t_r observed by the satellite S_m.

Considering the actual satellite system, some reasonable simplifications and basic assumptions for the satellite collaborative mission planning problem are made as follows:

(1) The target is a regional target, and the observation of the target by the satellite requires a certain image scanning time, that is, the observation activity has a certain duration.
(2) The satellite resources involved in mission planning are the satellites with side-swing capability carrying only one spaceborne remote sensor.
(3) The satellite needs to maintain a stable attitude during the execution of the observation mission. After completing the task, it needs to adjust the posture so that the observation task for the next target can be performed smoothly. From the start of the attitude adjustment to the stable attitude of the satellite, the time taken for this process is the satellite attitude adjustment time (also called the attitude maneuver stabilization time).

2.2 Constraints

Task Time Constraint. A satellite can only observe one target at a time, that is, each satellite-borne remote sensor can only perform one observation task at any time. The task start time and end time for each target t_r shall be within its corresponding visible window time range.

Data Storage Constraints. Due to the limited storage space on the satellite, the data size between the two missions of the satellite cannot exceed the capacity of the storage device.

Energy Constraints. Mainly consider two energy conflicts: the discharge depth of the battery for each discharge activity cannot exceed 20%; the satellite must achieve the energy balance of the circle during each illumination ground period, that is, the discharge energy of the battery pack during the grounding can be fully replenished during the subsequent illumination period.

2.3 Objective Function

In this paper, the optimization goal is to maximize the benefits, the objective function Q_1 is as shown in Eq. (1).

$$Q_1 = \max\left(\sum V_i x_i\right), i \in I \tag{1}$$

V_i—The benefit of observing the target t_i.
x_i—Whether the target t_i is selected for observation. If it is, $x_i = 1$, otherwise $x_i = 0$.

3 PBIL Algorithm Based on Real Number Coding

3.1 Encoding

When using the traditional PBIL algorithm for satellite mission planning, binary coding is often used, as shown in Fig. 1.

Each bit of the chromosome represents a time window corresponding to a target, and its value is 0 or 1, which indicates whether the time window is selected to arrange the observation task. The length of the chromosome is the number of visible time windows for all satellites toward all targets.

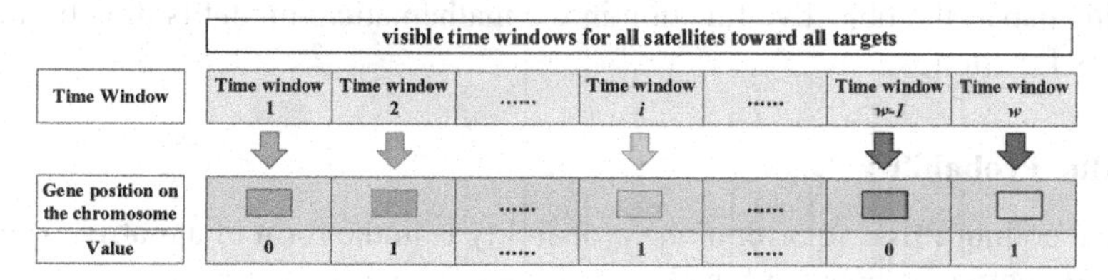

Fig. 1. Binary coding method of PBIL algorithm

However, in the actual satellite mission planning process, the number of satellites in a constellation and observation targets will be large, the planning interval will be long, and the number of visible time windows for the target will be correspondingly larger. If the binary coding method is used, the chromosome will be so long that it will take a long time for each bit of the chromosome to do the constraint collision check, which will result in very low algorithm efficiency.

To enhance the computational efficiency of the algorithm, a real number encoding method is used in this paper, as shown in Fig. 2.

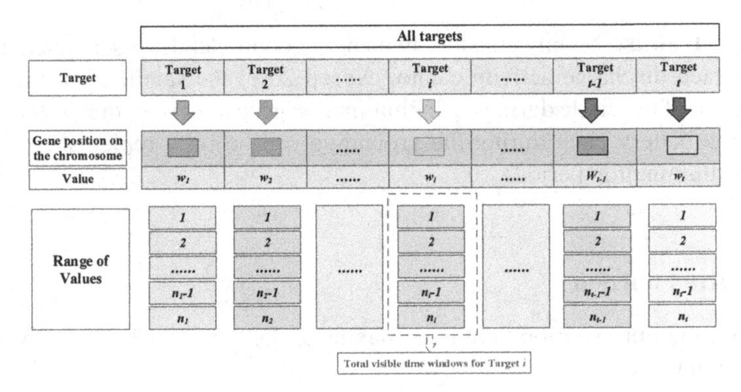

Fig. 2. Real coding method of PBIL algorithm

In the real number coding method, each bit of chromosome represents a target. For one target i in the overall target set I, it corresponds to the i-th bit of the chromosome.

Assuming that the total number of visible time windows for the target i is n_i, and each time window is numbered, corresponding to 1 to n_i.

If the value of the i-th gene position of the chromosome is w_i, one of the natural numbers from 1 to n_i, it means that the time window w_i of target i is selected to complete the observation task of this target. Thus the mapping relationship between chromosomes and problem search space points is established.

3.2 Fitness Function

In the PBIL algorithm, the fitness function represents the direction of evolution. It determines which individual will be chosen to learn and generate the probability of value to guide the generation of offspring. Generally, different fitness functions can be established according to different optimization goals.

In this paper, the objective function in the mathematical model is directly taken as the fitness function.

3.3 Value Probability

In the real coding PBIL algorithm, the probability is in the form of a matrix. The initial probability matrix is shown in Fig. 3.

A column of the probability matrix corresponds to a gene position of a chromosome, in other word, corresponds to an observation target. For the target i in the overall target set I, it has n_i observable time windows in total. This means that the value of the i-th gene position of the chromosome has n_i selections.

The matrix P is the probability of value selections in the algorithm. The j-th row of the i-th column of the probability matrix P represents the probability of selecting the j-th value of the i-th gene position. The probability matrix P is initialized as shown in Eq. (2), which to ensure that each value of each gene position has the same probability at the beginning of evolution.

$$P_{ij} = 1/n_i \tag{2}$$

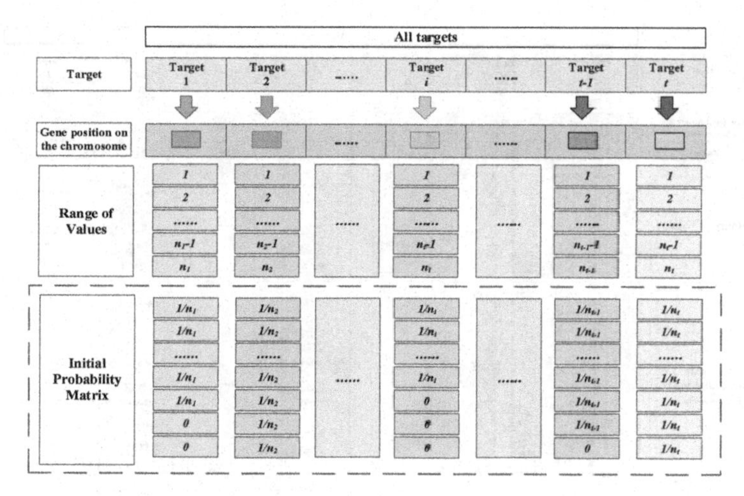

Fig. 3. The initial probability matrix

Among the newly generated populations of each generation, the individual *A* with the highest fitness value is selected for learning, and the probability matrix is updated, which will guide the population to update.

After the optimal individual *A* is generated, the update formula of the probability *P* is as shown in Eq. (3).

$$P_{ij} = P_{ij} + X\,(X \text{ is a constant, and } j = A_i) \tag{3}$$

Obviously, the probability of the j-th value of the i-th gene position is increased. In order to keep the sum of the probabilities of all the values of the i-th gene position to be 1, it is necessary to normalize the probability of them. The normalization formula is as shown in Eq. (4).

$$P_{ij} = P_{ij}/(X + 1)(1 \leq j \leq n_i) \tag{4}$$

Take the probability matrix update of the second-generation as an example. The update of probability matrix is shown in Fig. 4.

As the evolution process progressing, the probability of each value will deviate differently from the initial probability. And the offspring generated according to the probability update will be more likely to be highly adaptable.

3.4 Population Update

The update of the population is under the guidance of the probability matrix taking. With the real number coding, the way of population update is slightly different from that with the binary coding.

Similar to the roulette selection strategy, the probability of *n* different values of the same gene position is sequentially accumulated to obtain *n* cumulative probabilities. Then a random number *r* between 0 and 1 is generated.

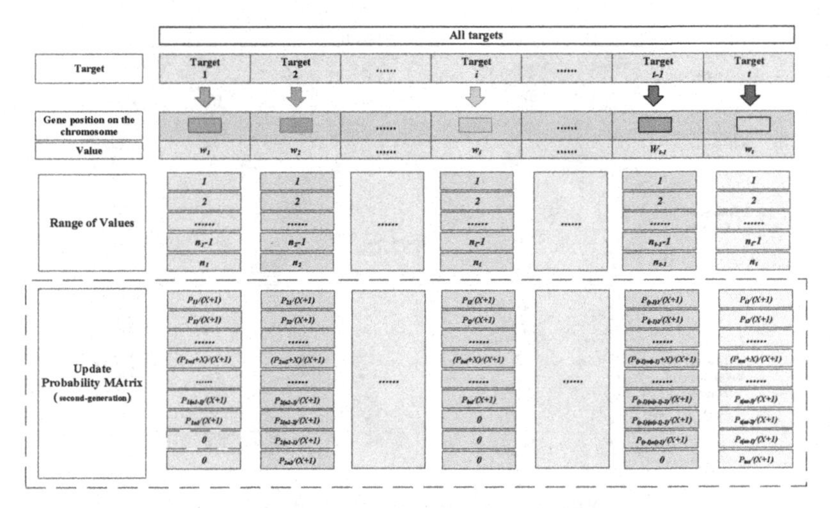

Fig. 4. The probability matrix update of the second-generation

The value corresponding to the smallest cumulative probability of the cumulative probability greater than r is the value of the genetic position. In this way, new individuals generation and population update can be completed.

3.5 End Condition

In this paper, the end condition is the number of evolutions determined by some numerical experiments, in which the population fitness value is not significantly improved in the late stage of evolution and the algorithm stops when the population completes these iterations. Usually the number of iterations will be related to the size of the population. The larger size of population is, the larger number of iterations is, and vice versa.

3.6 Algorithm Steps

The algorithm flow chart shown in Fig. 5.

Step 1. Encode each task according to the real number encoding method, and initialize the probability matrix.

Step 2. According to the above update method, use the probability matrix to guide the generation of the new population.

Step 3. According to the constraints in the mathematical model, each of the genetic positions of each chromosome in the population, that is, each task, is checked for conflict. A task that does not pass the conflict check will be abandoned, that is, the value of this gene position of the chromosome will be set as zero.

Step 4. The fitness value of each individual is calculated to obtain the best individual with the highest fitness value.

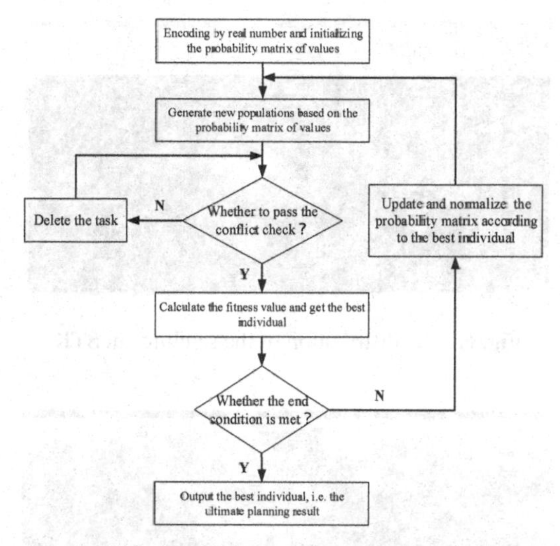

Fig. 5. The algorithm flow chart of PBIL algorithm

Step 5. If the end condition is satisfied, shift to Step 6. Otherwise, according to the best individual generated in the previous step, update and normalize the probability matrix and shift to Step 2.

Step 6. The algorithm ends. Obtain the best individual and output the corresponding mission planning scheme.

4 Numerical Examples and Results

In this paper, the model and algorithm proposed for satellite cooperative mission planning are verified by numerical examples as follows. By designing typical examples and solving them, the results are compared and analyzed, and the performance and efficiency of the PBIL algorithm for solving the satellite cooperative mission planning problem are verified.

4.1 Simulation Scenario

(1) **The satellites**

In this paper, the number of satellites is set to 10, and remote sensing satellite models S1 to S10 are established in STK and the distribution of the satellites in STK is shown in Fig. 6.

(2) **The targets**

A number of observation target points are randomly established globally using the MATLAB program and randomly assigned to each target a benefit value. The distribution of the targets in STK is shown in Fig. 7.

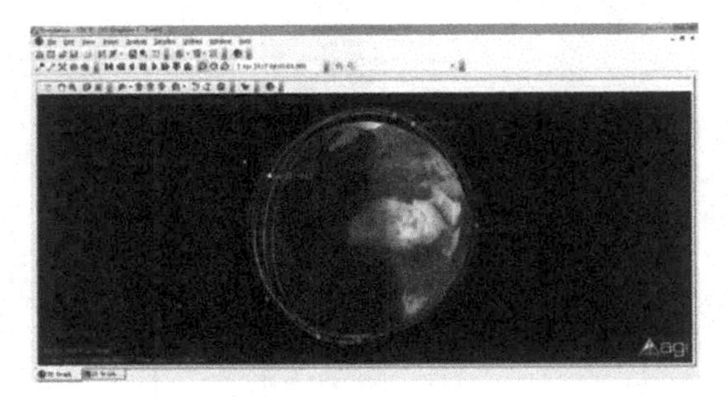

Fig. 6. The distribution of the satellites in STK

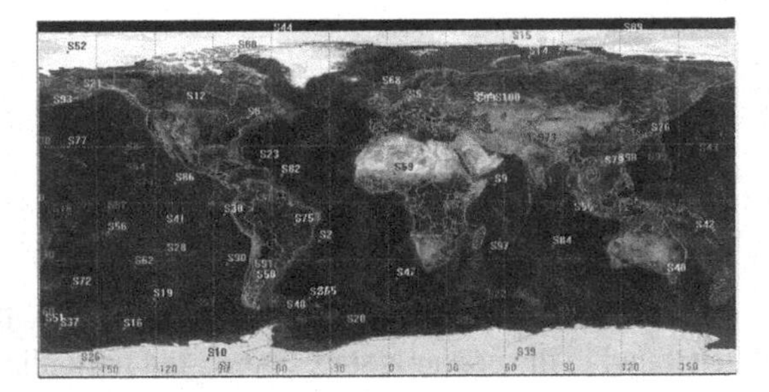

Fig. 7. The distribution of the targets in STK

(3) **The ground stations**

After the targets are observed by the satellites and the information is obtained, the data will be temporarily stored in the onboard device. When communication conditions permit, the data will be passed back to the ground station. In this paper, 12 ground stations are set up to simulate the completion of digital missions. The distribution of the ground stations in STK is shown in Fig. 8.

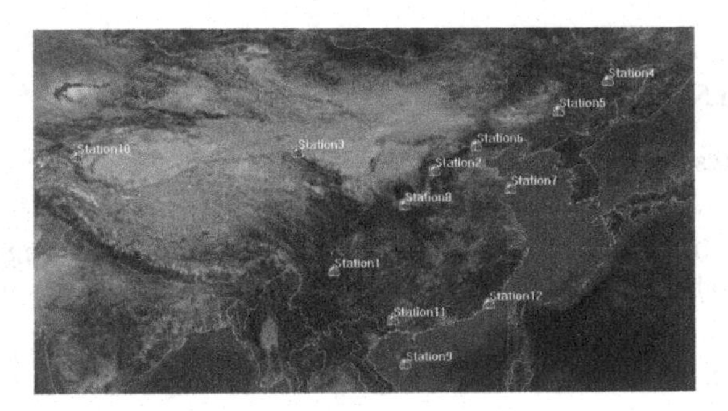

Fig. 8. The distribution of the ground stations in STK

4.2 Typical Results of Satellite Mission Planning Based on PBIL Algorithm

The average results of the 10 experiments are shown in Table 1, and one of the typical results is shown in Fig. 9.

Table 1. The statistical results of the comparison experiments

Simulation scene settings		Average optimal fitness value	
Objective function	Number of targets	Average optimal fitness value	Average running time (s)
$Q_1 = \max(\sum V_i x_i), i \in I$	50	7436	7046

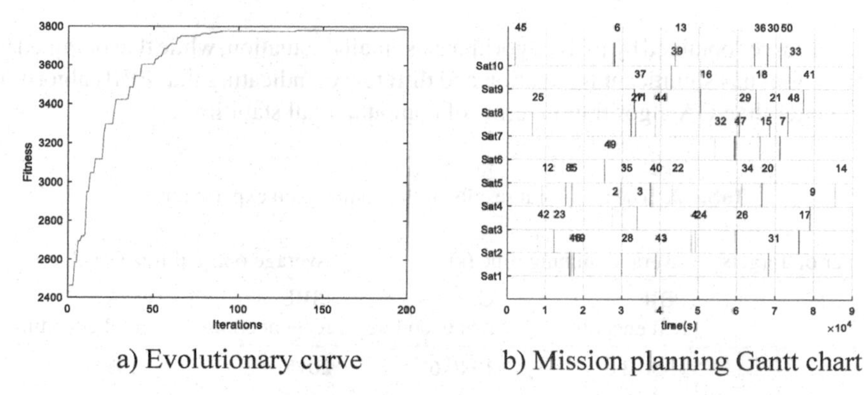

a) Evolutionary curve b) Mission planning Gantt chart

Fig. 9. The typical simulation results of PBIL algorithm

As shown in the Table and figure above, it can be seen that PBIL algorithm can effectively solve multi-satellite mission planning problem. As the evolution curve shown in Fig. 9a), it converges around generation 80 and has a high computational efficiency.

4.3 Analysis of Algorithm Performance

According to the optimization goal in Sect. 2.3, the comparison experiments of genetic algorithm and PBIL algorithm for solving satellite mission planning are respectively carried out. The Evolutionary curves of 10 consecutive simulation experiments for 50 targets are shown in Fig. 12, and the statistical results of computing power for different target quantities are shown in Table 2 and Fig. 13. All the data as follows are the average of the results of 10 consecutive simulation experiments.

As can be seen from the figure above, under the same conditions to solve the satellite mission planning problem, the PBIL algorithm converges rapidly around iteration 80, while the GA algorithm converges after iteration 100, indicating that the PBIL algorithm has faster computational performance than the GA algorithm. At the same time, comprehensive analysis of the evolution curve of 10 simulation experiments shows that the

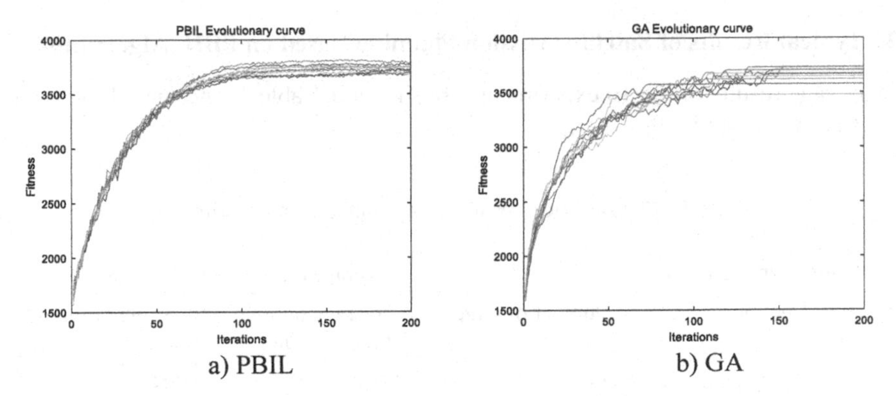

Fig. 12. The evolutionary curves of the comparison experiments

evolution curves obtained by PBIL algorithm has small fluctuation, while that obtained by GA algorithm has significant fluctuation and difference, indicating that PBIL algorithm is also better than GA algorithm in terms of computational stability.

Table 2. The statistical results of the comparison experiments

Number of Targets	Average running time (s)		Average optimal fitness value	
	PBIL real encoding	GA real encoding	PBIL real encoding	GA real encoding
25	550.2	1340.6	2015	1993
50	857.2	2113.5	3779	3635
75	1135.3	3197.2	5623	5446
100	1563.2	3718.7	7436	7046

As shown in the table and the figure above, through the quantitative comparative analysis of calculation running time and optimal fitness value, it can be seen that the running time of PBIL algorithm is obviously much shorter than that of genetic algorithm, where the computational efficiency is almost doubled, and most of the optimal fitness values are slightly higher than that of genetic algorithm.

Therefore, considering algorithm stability, computational efficiency and optimization quality, etc., PBIL algorithm is superior to genetic algorithm in solving satellite mission planning problem to some extent.

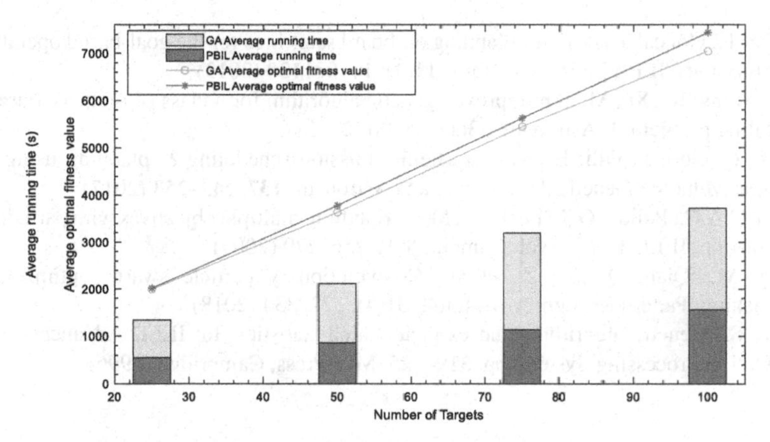

Fig. 13. The statistical results of the comparison experiments

5 Conclusions

In this paper, a quantity of theoretically analysis and numerical experiments have been done to find a better method to solve the satellite collaborative mission planning problem.

First of all, the constraints of satellite operation are analyzed and the abstract practical problems are transformed into mathematical problems. The mathematical model of satellite mission planning is established and the optimization goal of satellite mission planning proposed.

Secondly, the PBIL algorithm based on real coding is proposed for solving satellite mission planning problem. The key point of the algorithm is the real coding method and the update of the probability matrix, which is different from the traditional binary coding method. The PBIL algorithm is implemented, and the feasibility and effectiveness of the algorithm for solving satellite mission planning problems are verified by numerical experiments.

Furthermore, the performances of PBIL algorithm and genetic algorithm are compared for the same satellite mission planning scenario. According to the result data of numerical experiments, it can be seen that when solving the satellite mission planning problem, in terms of the algorithm efficiency, solution quality, and task completion rate, the PBIL algorithm based on real coding is superior to the genetic algorithm in the same situation.

References

1. Karapetyan, D., Minic, S.M., Malladi, K.T.: Satellite downlink scheduling problem: a case study. Omega **53**, 115–123 (2015)
2. Wu, K., Zhang, D.X., Chen, Z.H., et al.: Multi-type multi-objective imaging scheduling method based on improved NSGA-III for satellite formation system. Adv. Space Res. **63**(8), 2551–2565 (2019)
3. Sarkheyli, A.: Using an effective tabu search in interactive resources scheduling problem for LEO satellites missions. Aerosp. Sci. Technol. **29**, 287–295 (2013)

4. De, N.K.F., Goncalves, V.F.M.: Planning on-board satel-lites for the goal-based operations for space missions. IEEE Latin Am. Trans. **11**(4), 1110–1120 (2013)
5. Li, Y., Wang, R., Xu, M.: An improved genetic algorithm for a class of multi-resource range scheduling problem. J. Astronaut. **33**(1), 85–90 (2012)
6. Zheng, Z., Guo, J., Gill, E.: Swarm satellite mission scheduling & planning using Hybrid Dynamic Mutation Genetic Algorithm. Acta Astronaut. **137**, 243–253 (2017)
7. Coello, C.A.C., Pulido, G.T., Lechuga, M.S.: Handling multiple objectives with particle swarm optimization. IEEE Trans. Evol. Comput. **8**(3), 256–279 (2004)
8. Cheng, M., Qian, Q., Ni, Z., et al.: Co-evolutionary particle swarm optimization for multitasking. Pattern Recogn. Artif. Intell. **31**(4), 322–334 (2018)
9. Baluja, S.: Genetic algorithms and explicit search statistics. In: IEEE Advances in Neural Information Processing System, pp. 319–325. MIT Press, Cambridge (1996)

A Dynamic Modified Routing Strategy Based on Load Balancing in LEO Satellite Network

Li Shen[1](✉), Yuanqin Wang[1], Lixiang Liu[2], Shuaijun Liu[2], Dapeng Wang[2], Yuanyuan Fan[2], Huanren Zhou[2], and Teng Ling[2]

[1] Space Engineering University, Beijing 101416, China
337928671@qq.com
[2] Institute of Software Chinese Academy of Sciences, Beijing 100190, China

Abstract. A dynamically modified load balancing routing strategy, named Dynamic Modified routing table based on Load Balance (DMLB) was proposed in this manuscript for the problem of congestion and packet loss, which was caused by uneven distribution of business traffic in the low earth orbit (LEO) satellite network. Different from the traditional routing protocol for the satellite, the strategy forms a kind of fast forwarding through the steps of geographical location-based traffic prediction, calculation of the entire network routing forwarding table based on weighted shortest path and dynamic correction of load balancing based on priority. These lead to an efficiently updated routing protocol. Simulation results show that the proposed DMLB strategy has better load balancing capabilities and smaller rerouting convergence time, ensuring the reliability of delay-sensitive service transmission, reducing link management overheads, and saving on-board computing resources.

Keywords: LEO network · Routing strategy · Dynamic-static combination algorithm · Load balancing

1 Introduction

With the growth of various types of communication services, terrestrial communication networks have been unable to meet the exploding traffic demands. Satellite network have broken the limitations of traditional geographical environment and can provide Internet access services for any users in the world [1]. The features that low transmission delay and small size of user terminals have become a new direction for the development of communications infrastructure in the future [2]. In April 2020, satellite Internet was included in the list of "New Infrastructure Construction" by China and has broad development prospects [3].

Satellite network is a part of the Internet based on satellite communications. By deploying a certain number of satellites in space to provide broadband Internet access services for ground or air users, the development of this system began in the 1980s, based on "Iridium" constellation supported by Motorola. Recently, companies such as

Q. Wu et al. (Eds.): WiSATS 2020, LNICST 358, pp. 233–244, 2021.
https://doi.org/10.1007/978-3-030-69072-4_20

SpaceX and Amazon have begun to lead the construction of new satellite constellations [4]. In June 2020, the ninth part of Starlink was finished and the number of satellites in orbit reached to 540. Encouraged by relevant policies, China has launched a number of LEO satellite constellation plans since 2017. Constellations represented by Hongyun, Hongyan and Xingyun have successively launched demo satellites.

As a key technique to enable worldwide service, the routing protocol have been attracted much attentions. Scholars [5] proposed a method to reduce the frequent switching of network connections for LEO satellite constellations. But they restrict more high-priority services and affect the QoS service quality. Scholars [6–8] proposed Many typical methods of load-balancing routing protocol.One of them called LBRD for satellite networks based on geographic location as a routing strategy using neighbor notification to adjust the load. This method effectively reduces the delay caused by congestion and data packet loss rate. The traffic in the network needs to be recalculated every time according to the demand, so the resource consumption is large and there is no relatively fixed routing table, which affects the communication efficiency. Scholars [9] proposed a route update method based on source route multicast for the problem of topology changes in the snapshot route in the software-defined network architecture. This method can avoid loops generated during the satellite network update process, reduce the convergence time and network overhead. But when a link is suddenly congested or malfunctions, the packet loss rate increases significantly. Scholars [10] proposed an improved algorithm based on the traditional routing protocol OSPF for the problem of the cost and stability of the intra-domain routing protocol in the integrated network of heaven and earth. This algorithm introduces the topology prediction function, which combined with the neighbor state, reducing the flooding and calculation overhead and improving in order to stabilize the operation. The convergence is completed quickly. However, when the topology changes, the entire network still needs to be calculated. There is a problem of packet loss during convergence and no load balancing method is involved. Scholars [11, 12] proposed new network architectures, communication protocols and evaluation methods for mobile ad hoc networks, and scholars [13–15] gave better load balancing strategies for dynamic resource allocation, especially access links. Scholars [16, 17] apply deep reinforcement learning to the resource allocation of satellite communications, explore the relevance of different time slices, convert the system state into pictures, extract features, and then identify and make decisions.

Aiming at the problem of load balancing in LEO satellite network, this paper proposes a dynamically modified load balancing routing strategy. This strategy predicts the traffic distribution in advance according to the distribution of ground users, and fits the traffic distribution to the link weights. The weighted link weights are used to calculate the optimal path. The priority is used as the goal to interact with the neighbor status information. The load is adjusted, and the routing table is dynamically modified to ensure that subsequent packet forwarding can inherit the current optimal state. When the link state is congested again, the previous steps are looped to form a fast query, efficient update dynamic and static combined route protocol.

The rest of the paper is organized as follows: Sect. 2 describes the system model for LEO satellite network. Section 3 presents the dynamically modified load balancing routing strategy. Section 4 describes the simulation parameters and results analysis. Section 5 concludes the paper.

2 System Model

The LEO satellite network system is mainly composed of three parts: satellite, ground station and user terminal. The user terminal initiates the Internet access request and reaches the ground station through the inter-satellite link between the satellites. The ground station serves as a gateway to access the Internet. When transmitting service information to the user through the inter-satellite link the two user terminals serve as a group, by which users can communicate with each other. The routing strategy provides services for the path selection of IP data packets between the satellites. The data packets are transmitted hop-by-hop between the satellites by querying the next hop port from the source to the destination. The routing strategy plays an important role in the reliability of data transmission. Figure 1 shows the working principle of the system.

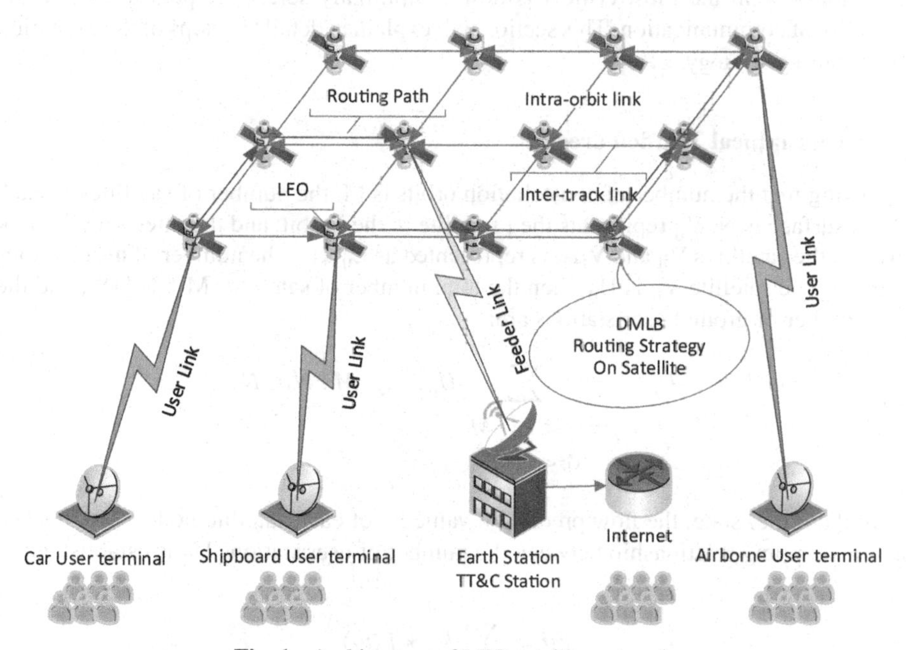

Fig. 1. Architecture of LEO satellite network

In LEO satellite network, the relationship between neighbors is relatively fixed with distributed topology and periodic inter-satellite links. But the distribution of ground users is uneven, and the distribution of business traffic is uneven, which is likely to cause traffic bursts. The resulting congestion and packet loss, while the surrounding network is not fully utilized. If the static time slice routing strategy is used on the satellite, the network will not be able to cope with the emergency situation. If the common dynamic routing strategy is adopted on the satellite, a large amount of link resources will be consumed when the network status is updated, and it will also be A large number of packets are lost and the re-routing time is long. If the self-organized load balancing route is adopted, although it can deal with burst traffic, for the scenario of simultaneous communication between multiple nodes, it will consume a lot of on-board computing resources and Produce a large delay.

3 Dynamically Modified Load Balancing Routing Strategy

This routing strategy is aimed at LEO satellite network and is used in a single-layer LEO satellite constellation that can be globally covered. A user link is established between the satellite and a number of ground stations, data transmission is performed between the satellite and the satellite through an inter-satellite link, and a feeder link is established between the satellite and the gateway station. The gateway station can be connected to the ground Internet. Therefore, the network can provide services for users to access the Internet or for direct communication between users and users.

Among them, the most critical is how to optimally select the path to ensure the reliability of communication. This section will explain in detail the steps of the execution of the routing strategy.

3.1 Geographical Traffic Forecast

Supposing that the number of constellation orbits is M, the number of satellites in each orbital surface is N, V_{ij} represents the j satellite in the i orbit, and the inter-satellite link between the satellites V_{ij} and V_{i+1j} is represented as $E_{ij,i+1j}$, The number of user stations accessing the satellite V_{ij} is U_{ij}, then the total number of satellites M * N [18], and the total number of ground user stations are:

$$U_{max} = \sum_{\substack{0 < i \leq M \\ 0 < j \leq N}} U_{ij},\ i,\ j,\ M,\ N \in N$$

In the initial state, the flow prediction value F_{ij} of each satellite node is established and the mapping relationship between the number of user stations U_{ij} is established:

$$Fij = \sum_{t=0}^{Umax} k_f * f(u_t)$$

Where ut is a specific user in U_{ij}, k_f is a predictive adjustment factor, and the node traffic prediction value is adjusted according to the user level and the type of transmission service.Generally it can be divided into 16 levels, with values ranging from 0 to 15. The distribution of users in different geographic locations is different. At the initial moment, each user station uij reports the area location information, user level, and service type waiting to be transmitted to the visible star with the longest connection time. The satellite obtains the traffic prediction value Fij (Fig. 2).

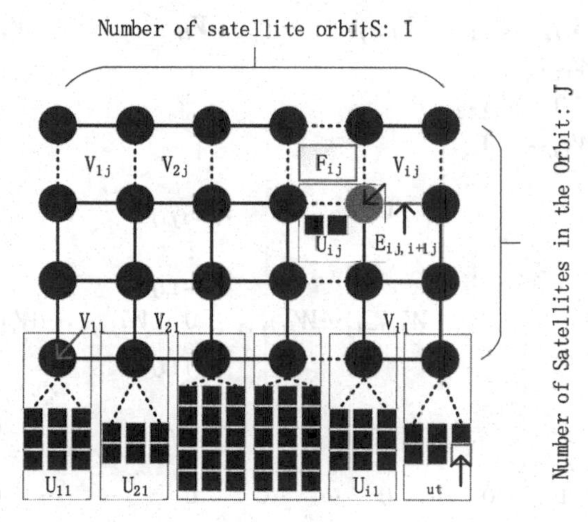

Fig. 2. Model of network topology

3.2 Calculation of the Weighted Shortest Path of the Entire Network Routing Forwarding Table

At the initial moment, in a M * N-scale network, satellite V_{ij} establishes 4 duplex links between common and different orbits, while the first orbit and the last orbit I do not establish a different orbit chain due to the opposite movement direction Road, so the total number of inter-satellite links is:

$$E_{max} = \frac{4 * M * N - 2 * N}{2} = (2M - 1) * N$$

Each link is divided into two channels, and each channel is equivalent to a directional edge. The weight W of the channel is proportional to the satellite traffic prediction value F_{ij}, the scale factor is k_w, and the weight of the directional edges V_{ij} to V_{st} is:

$$W_{ij,st} = k_w * F_{ij} = k_w * \sum_{t=0}^{Umax} k_f * f(u_t)$$

At the next moment, the satellite V_{ij} sends the obtained weight $\{W_{ij,i\pm1j\pm1}\}$ to the neighbor set $\{V_{i\pm1j\pm1}\}$, and obtains the directed edge weight of the neighbor set, add weights to the local matrix M_d, the matrix format is as follows (Fig. 3):

At the next moment, it is sent to the neighbor set $\{V_{i\pm1j\pm1}\}$ to continue to help V_{ij} diffuse its weights $\{W_{ij,i\pm1j\pm1}\}$, and at the same time V_{ij} receives and updates the weight table, after the time M + N, the satellite V_{MN} receives the link weight information of the satellite V_{11}, and the weight status of the entire network is unified.

At this time, according to the weight table and the Freud algorithm, the shortest path table between the stars is calculated, and the forwarding port is stored in the routing table. The path calculation continues through all satellite nodes in the order of the arrow, that is, when the satellite V_{ij} is the routing forwarding point, the calculation The weight sum of any two non-adjacent satellites is written into the shortest path table $\{D_{ij}\}$. At the

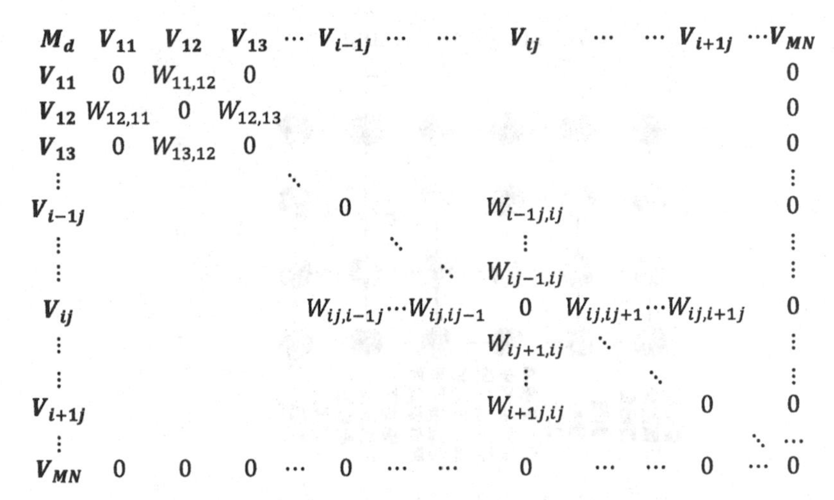

Fig. 3. Inter-satellite link weight storage matrix M_d

beginning, the weight sum is ∞. After iterative calculation, the weight table converges and forms Forwarding table $\{R_{ij}\}$. The definition of the forwarding table is: If the shortest path between V_{ij} and Vst is forwarded via V_{ij}'s P0 port, then in V_{ij}, port P0 is included in the next hop of the packet's destination as Vst, that is, when the packet is sent to Vst via V_{ij} At the time, after looking up the table, forward directly through P0 (Fig. 4).

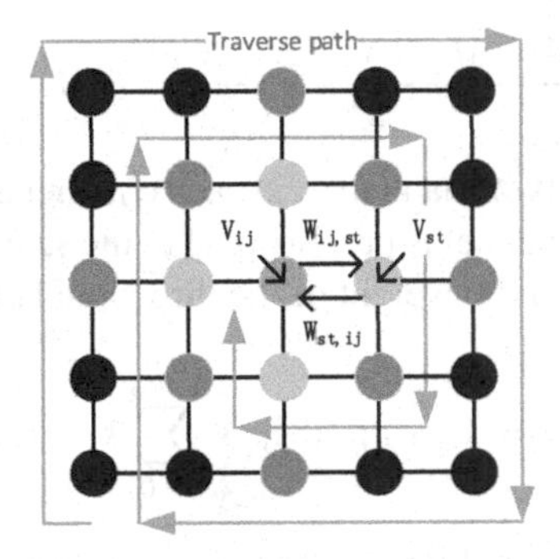

Fig. 4. Schematic diagram of satellite link weights and calculation traversal paths

3.3 Priority Load Balancing Dynamic Correction

After the routing status of the entire network is unified, IP data packets will be forwarded according to the routing table $\{R_{ij}\}$. As traffic increases, neighbor queues will be congested. Neighbor queues can be divided into 2N according to QoS level, and the average time per queue is The length is $\overline{q}_l$, l is the corresponding rank queue number, f(l) is the weight of the queue, and the maximum capacity of each queue is Qmax, then the load rate of the link in this direction is:

$$L_{ij,st} = \sum_{l=1}^{2^N}[f(l) * \overline{q}_l] / \left[\sum_{l=1}^{2^N} f(l)\right] * Q_{max}$$

If the load rate exceeds L_g or the single queue exceeds $\overline{q}_g$, it is considered that the path is congested. At this time, dynamic routing addressing is started, that is, the load rate L of other adjacent satellites is compared, and the smaller one is selected as the next-hop routing port. The local routing table is revised immediately, and subsequent IP data packets are forwarded according to the revised routing table until the next congestion occurs, and the above steps are recycled. At the same time, in order to avoid loops, it is forbidden to send data packets back to the sending port (Fig. 5).

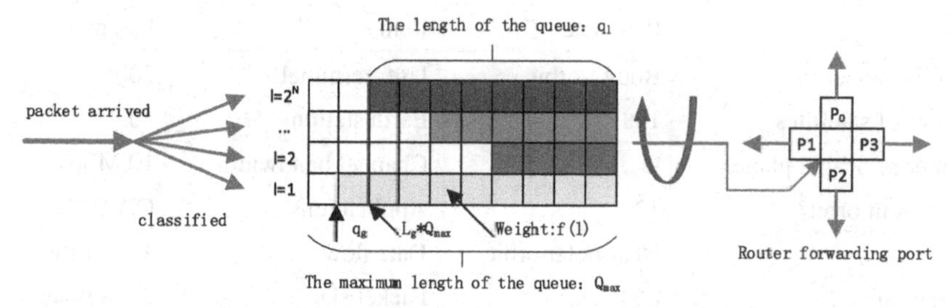

Fig. 5. Schematic diagram of Queue weighting and forwarding process.

4 Performance Analysis

Performance analysis adopts the network simulator EXata, which is developed by Scalable Networks Technologies of the United States. The simulation scenario is set according to the parameters of the low earth orbit constellation, including the global distribution of data streams, ground user terminals and gateway stations [19]. Three typical routing strategies, the static routing, OSPF and LBRD, are compared with the proposed DMLB routing strategy. Packet loss rate, rerouting time, throughput and average end-to-end delay are compared.

4.1 Simulation Platform

EXata standardized network simulator is selected as the simulation platform, where main functional modules are listed as Table 1.

Table 1. Composition and suppliers of simulation platforms

Functional module	Software	Company
Display control platform	Simulation testbed	ISCAS
Simulation engine	EXata 5.1	Scalable Networks Technologies
Development Platform	Visual Studio2010	Microsoft

4.2 Constellation Parameters and Scenario Settings

See Table 2 and Fig. 6.

Table 2. The parameters of LEO constellation, user station and link

Item	Parameter	Item	Parameter
Mobility model	Body2-orbit	User terminal	200
Number of satellites	108	Earth station	10
Number of orbital planes	9	Channel bandwidth	10 Mbps
Satellites in orbit	12	Applications	CBR
Track type	Near polar orbit	Data flow	1–10 Mbps
Inclination	86°	Packet size	2048 bytes
Constellation	Walker	Number of queues	3
Phase factor	4.5	Cache size	150000 bytes
Earth radius	6371 km	Queue scheduling	FIFO
Height of orbital planes	1000 km	Simulation time	60 s

4.3 Simulation results

(1) Packets loss rate due to link failure.

At the initial moment, each routing strategy has been configured and converged. At t = 20 s, a fault breakpoint is set in each forwarding link, and the packet loss rate is monitored. The static route cannot update the configuration information. It can only be forwarded along the original path, so the failure rate continues to increase. OSPF uses Hello packets to detect the status of neighbors. When a fault is detected, the entire network is updated. During the update, data packets are lost. After 27 s, the routing is

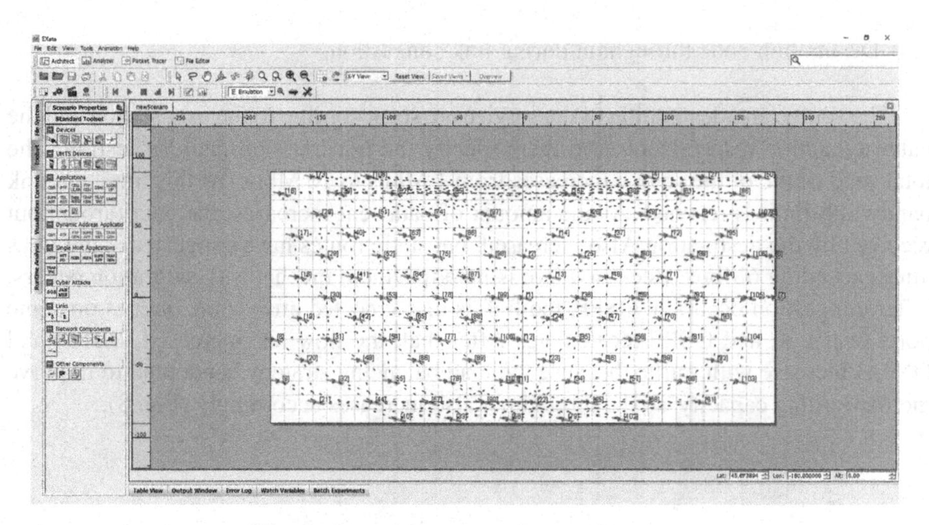

Fig. 6. Scenario topology diagram in EXata

updated and the packet loss rate decreases rapidly. LBRD only calculates the remaining paths after a link failure, so the path calculation is completed at 10 s, and the packet loss rate gradually decreases. From the simulation results, it can be seen that the packet loss rate of DMLB when the link fails has almost no obvious change. The reason is that after detecting the link failure, the satellite node starts dynamic calculation and only corrects the next hop, that is It can avoid the impact caused by link failure, and at the same time, replace the newly generated forwarding path with the original one to ensure that subsequent data can be forwarded in time after the arrival of subsequent data (Fig. 7).

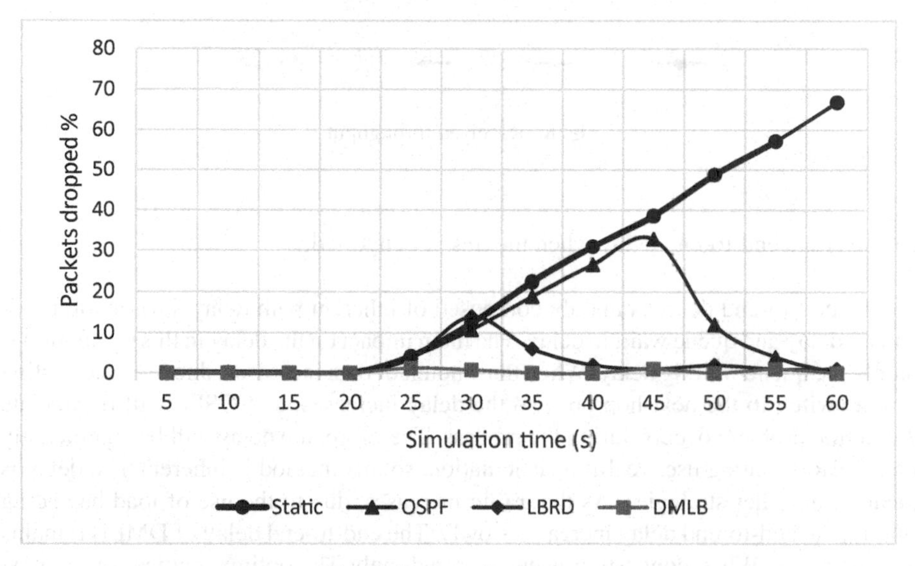

Fig. 7. Packets dropped rate

(2) Destination node throughput during link congestion.

The source and destination of the service are set according to the user station and the gateway station respectively. And then, specify the transmission path for testing. The total send traffic of the source increases from 1 Mbps to 10 Mbps. At this time, the link bandwidth limit is reached. As the amount of data sent increases, the data throughput received by the destination Also increased, but static routes have congested some links after exceeding 6Mbps. Because there is no adjustment mechanism, saturation occurs. After congestion occurs in OSPF, the link is disconnected after some queues on some ports overflow, and OSPF recalculates After that, the flow has increased. LBRD and DMLB increase with traffic, because the load balancing strategy is adopted to improve the forwarding capacity, so the throughput also increases accordingly (Fig. 8).

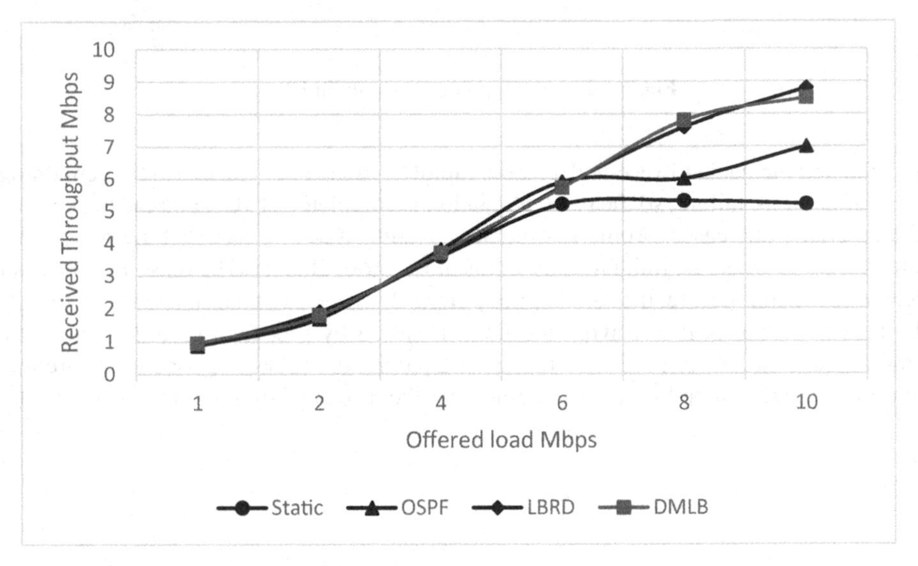

Fig. 8. Received throughput

(3) Average end-to-end delay when the link is congested.

The end-to-end delay is mainly composed of inherent path delay, information processing delay and queue waiting delay. The main impact on the delay in this simulation is mainly the queue waiting delay. When the amount of data increases, due to Static routing cannot switch to the next-hop port, so the delay increases, and OSPF will recalculate after a link problem occurs during the process. Therefore, the delay will be significantly jitter. LBRD routing uses real-time calculation, so this method is inherent The delay is greater than other strategies. As the traffic increases, due to the use of load balancing routing, the end-to-end delay increases slowly. The end-to-end delay of DMLB remains at a low value. When congestion is encountered, only The optimal choice for the next hop does not excessively change the original optimal path, so the delay is not increased.

At the same time, the queue adjustment mechanism in DMLB can reduce the delay caused by queuing. Therefore, as the amount of transmission from the source increases, DMLB Not particularly significant increase (Fig. 9).

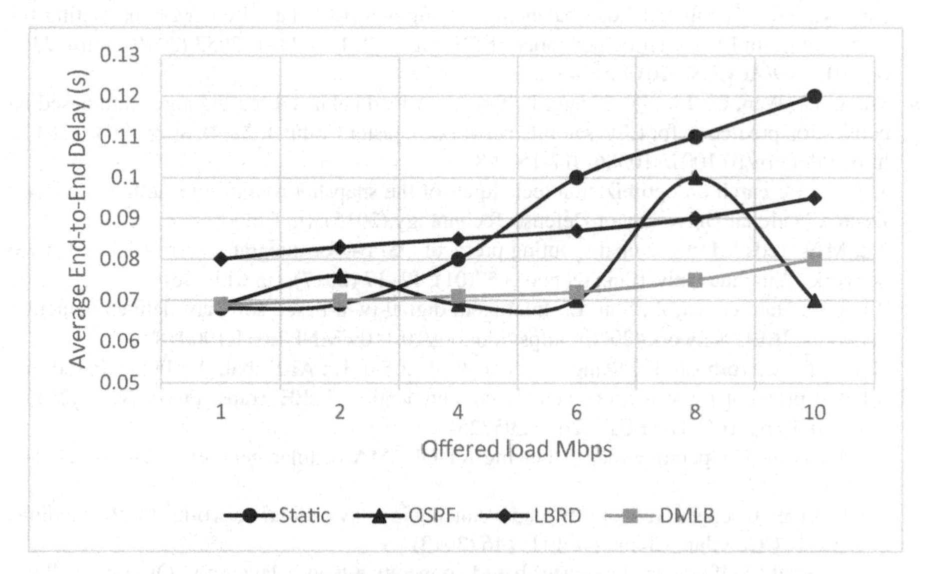

Fig. 9. Average end-to-end delay

5 Conclusion

This paper proposes a dynamically modified load balancing routing strategy for the low-orbit satellite Internet. This strategy uses traffic prediction based on the geographic location of the client, uses the weighted path length for calculation, and dynamically performs load balancing based on priority. Simulation results show that this strategy can be quickly and dynamically corrected to reduce the rerouting time and reduce the packet loss rate in case the link fails. What's more, the proposed DMLB routing strategy can ensure greater throughput and shorter end-to-end delay under the scenario of link congestion.

References

1. Liu, L.: Analysis of architecture and protocol of space-ground integrated information network. J. Chongqing Univ. Posts Telecommun. (Nat. Sci. Ed.) **30**(01), 9–21(2018). (in Chinese)
2. Cai, T.: Research on routing protocol of LEO satellite communication network. Master, Xidian University (2018). (in Chinese)
3. CCIDconsulting Homepage. https://www.mtx.cn/#/report?id=683916
4. Portilloa, I.D., Cameronb, B.G. (eds.): A technical comparison of three low earth orbit satellite constellation systems to provide global broadband. Satell. Netw. **2019**(07), 48–61 (2019). (in Chinese)

5. Wang, X. (eds.): A rerouting strategy in low earth orbit QoS satellite networks. J. Beijing Univ. Posts Telecommun. **2005**(01), 30–34 (2005). (in Chinese)
6. Chen, J.Z. (eds.): Load balanced routing protocol for double-layered satellite networks. J. Astronaut. **33**(06), 746–753 (2012). (in Chinese)
7. Liu, W., Tao, Y., Liu, L.: Load-balancing routing algorithm based on segment routing for traffic return in LEO satellite networks. IEEE Access 7, 112044–112053 (2019). https://doi.org/10.1109/ACCESS.2019.2934932
8. Wang, H., Wen, G., Liu, N., Zhang, J., Tao, Y.: A load balanced routing algorithm based on congestion prediction for LEO satellite networks. Cluster Comput. **22**(4), 8025–8033 (2017). https://doi.org/10.1007/s10586-017-1579-8
9. Zhu, T.: Research on optimization techniques of the snapshot routing in satellite networks. Doctor, National University of Defense Technology (2015). (in Chinese)
10. Xu, M.W. (eds.): I ntra-domain routing protocol OSPF+ for integrated terrestrial and space network. Tsinghua Univ. (Sci. Technol.) **57**(01), 12–17 (2017). (in Chinese)
11. Zhao, L., Han, G., Li, Z., Shu, L.: Intelligent digital twin-based software-defined vehicular networks. IEEE Network (2020). https://doi.org/10.1109/MNET.011.1900587
12. Hawbani, A., Torbosh, E., Wang, X., Sincak, P., Zhao, L., Al-Dubai, A.: Fuzzy based distributed protocol for vehicle to vehicle communication. IEEE Trans. Fuzzy Syst. (2019). https://doi.org/10.1109/TFUZZ.2019.2957254
13. Xu, L., et al: Cooperative load balancing for OFDMA cellular networks. Eur. Wirel. 1–7 (2012)
14. Xu, L., et al.: Cooperative mobility load balancing in relay cellular networks. In: Proceedings of IEEE ICCC, Xi'an, China, pp. 141–146 (2013)
15. Xu, L., et al.: Self-organising cluster-based cooperative load balancing in OFDMA cellular networks. Wiley Wirel. Commun. Mob. Comput. **15**(7), 1171–1187 (2015)
16. Liu, S., Hu, X., Wang, Y., Cui, G., Wang, W.: Distributed caching based on matching game in LEO satellite constellation networks. IEEE Commun. Lett. **22**(2), 300–303 (2018)
17. Liu, S., Hu, X., Wang, W.: Deep reinforcement learning based dynamic channel allocation algorithm in multibeam satellite systems. IEEE Access **6**, 15733–15742 (2018). https://doi.org/10.1109/ACCESS.2018.2809581
18. Jungnickel, D.: Graphs, Networks and Algorithms, 2nd edn. Springer, Heidelberg (2000). https://doi.org/10.1007/978-3-662-03822-2
19. Mohoric, M., Werner, M., Svigelj, A., et al.: Adaptive routing for packet-oriented intersatellite link networ ks: performance in various traffic scenarios. IEEE Trans. Wirel. Commun. **1**(4), 808–818 (2002)

International Workshop on Intelligent Satellites in Future Space Networked System

The Design and Implementation of Global Navigation Satellite System Remote Docking Test Platform

Wang Wei[1,3](✉), Chai Qiang[2], Gao Weiguang[1], Lu Jun[1], Shao Shihai[4], Bai Yu[2], Niu Jingyi[2], Feng Wenjing[5], and Li Shaoqian[3]

[1] Beijing Institute of Tracking and Communication Technology, Beijing 100094, China
15810266558@163.com
[2] GNSS System Engineering Center, China Academy of Aerospace Electronics Technology, Beijing 100094, China
[3] Shanghai Engineering Center for Microsatellites, Shanghai 201203, China
[4] National Key Laboratory of Science and Technology On Communications, University of Electronic Science and Technology of China, Chengdu 611731, China
[5] Beijing Institute of Spacecraft System Engineering, Beijing 100094, China

Abstract. The global navigation satellite system (GNSS) includes satellites of multiple types, ground facilities with multiple functions, and various user terminals. The docking test of multiple systems in ground is an important part for managing the design, construction, and deployment of the satellite navigation system. To achieve efficient parallel docking of multiple systems, this paper designs a platform for remote docking test. Specifically, the architecture, operating process, and functional performance of the docking test platform are designed according to the task and characteristics of the docking test for satellite navigation. Besides, some key techniques are also analyzed including the management of command and dispatch for multi-node system as well as the interconnection of remote fiber. This paper implements the effective interconnection between the simulation verification system and real engineering system, and realizes command control and timing scheduling with high-precision. The designed platform has the capability of full coverage test for signal and information projects, and the capability of remote docking test for multi-systems that work in parallel. By applying our platform, the docking efficiency can be improved, the docking cost can be reduced, and the implementation of high-density networking for satellite can be promoted.

Keywords: GNSS · Remote docking

1 Introduction

GNSS is a complex and large-scale system in aerospace engineering area. It consists of dozens of satellites, dozens of ground stations, some control centers, a management center (for inter-satellite link operations), and various user terminals. These components need to closely cooperate with each other in order to realize the centralized management

Q. Wu et al. (Eds.): WiSATS 2020, LNICST 358, pp. 247–258, 2021.
https://doi.org/10.1007/978-3-030-69072-4_21

between the satellite and the ground, and to provide high-precision and highly reliable positioning-navigation-timing (PNT) services for users. The satellite navigation system can provide various services as well as fast network deployment, and its design is usually very complicated.

To demonstrate the pre-designed schemes and protocol algorithms for the satellite navigation systems, supporting simulation systems are usually required. Some supporting simulation systems have been developed for the major satellite navigation systems in the world. The US GPS system has carried out many simulations and experiments in terms of positioning, operating modes, system control, and key algorithms. Such as GPS simulation system, satellite navigation software toolbox (NavTK) [1, 2], GIANT software [3–6], etc. The European Galileo system has attached great importance on the use of simulation software at beginning for overall design and system verification. Many hardware and software platforms are developed for constellation configuration demonstration, technical system design, navigation signal design, key indicator allocation, technical base evaluation, and performance indicator verification. For instance, Galileo system simulation software (GSSF) [7, 8], Galileo system test bed (GSTB) [9, 10], software simulation verification environment (GRANADA platform), and software simulation plan (Polaris plan) [11, 12].

GNSS will carry out the satellite-ground docking test in the initial and normal stages of satellite development. The major departments of the GNSS project will develop their own devices, and move their devices to the satellite plant to conduct docking tests for specific functions. The content of the test mainly includes: 1) verify the status between the interface of systems, including the signal format interface, signal level interface, and information layout interface for the satellite-ground devices; 2) verify the procedures of the information transmission and processing between the major systems, including the accuracy of the information transmission procedures between the satellite-ground transmission and between the satellite- satellite-ground transmission; 3) check the performance for the realization of key indicators such as anti-interference and delay.

The verification implementation of this docking mode is incomplete, which cannot represent the true state of the system. Besides, it cannot verify system-level functions such as inter-satellite links and autonomous navigation. As a result, it takes a lot of time to carry out on-orbit test after the satellite is in orbit, which wastes the effective life of the satellite. Once such on-orbit tests need to be repeated, the cost will be particularly huge, and the project construction may face high risks.

Therefore, in order to change the situation of long-term lack of a system-level test environment in the field of satellite navigation, this paper builds a system-level simulation system for satellite navigation system, which is multi-level flexible and can approximately represent the real state of the GNSS. In addition, the high-performance interconnection between the simulation test system and the real engineering system is achieved by the remote optical fiber. The presented simulation system can carry out the design verification of the system scheme, business processes, key technologies, inter-system interfaces, indicators, signal flows, information flows, and time flows under the state of the whole satellite navigation system. Using our simulation system can improve the docking efficiency, save the docking cost, and promote the implementation of high-density networking for satellite.

2 Architecture of Test Platform

The remote docking test platform for GNSS includes the space section, ground control section, and user terminal. These sub-systems represent the technical status of the project. To cooperate with the above sub-systems and improve the test scheme, environment segment simulation sub-system, control and comprehensive support sub-system, global system simulation software, performance evaluation software, information management system software are also inserted. The remote optical fiber system is added for connecting satellite plant signals to the system. The platform composition is shown below (Fig. 1).

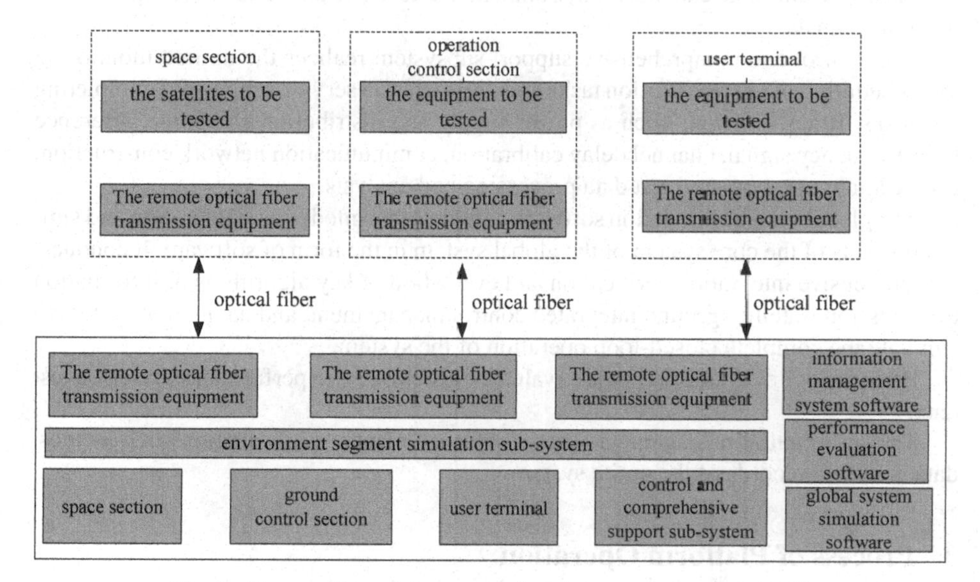

Fig. 1. Composition of the remote docking test platform of GNSS

The space segment subsystem represents the technical status of the GNSS, has the functions of satellite payload and platform control subsystem. It has the ability to parse commands between the ground operation control, measurement control, and inter-satellite link operation management systems. It is capable of inter-satellite data transmission and measurement, integrity monitoring and autonomous operation.

The ground control section forms a ground operation control network composed of a main control station, an injection station and a monitoring station, and realizes inter-system interfaces and business processes related thereto. It has functions such as navigation business processing, operation management and control, satellite-to-ground data transmission and measurement, etc. At the same time, it has functions such as constellation management in various space segment states such as constellation networking stage, constellation normal operation stage and constellation supplementary network stage.

The user terminal subsystem represents the technical status of typical application terminals. It has functions such as navigation and positioning, timing, and speed measurement based on the global system's downlink navigation signals. It verifies the signal system, system service performance indicators, and terminal algorithms.

The environmental segment analog subsystem is connected to the space segment subsystem, the ground control section and the user terminal subsystem in a matrix of multiple inputs and multiple outputs. It is responsible for multiple satellites and multiple stations on the ground. The radio frequency signals between multiple users and between satellites are superimposed with various dynamic characteristics such as various relative motions, transmission channels, environmental effects. It converts static signals into dynamic signals.

The control and comprehensive support subsystem realizes the unified monitoring and scheduling of test verification tasks and the operation service support for completing test tasks. It has functions such as power supply and distribution guarantee, reference time-frequency signal, channel delay calibration, communication network construction, test task management, and test data processing and analysis.

The global system simulation software completes the modeling, integration and simulation tests of the core system of the global system in the form of software. It conducts comprehensive integration verification and evaluation of key algorithms of information transmission, satellite-ground integrated control management, and navigation system to simulate the complete closed-loop operation of the system.

Performance evaluation software evaluates system service performance based on test data.

The information management system software manages information such as files, data, and task records of the entire system.

3 Process of Platform Operation

As a full-scale equivalent simulation system of GNSS, the test platform can operate independently, carry out simulation research and design verification of the core technology system of the system, and promote innovation and development. It can carry out comprehensive test verification of system operation control and interface between systems, confirm the technical status of the system, and support project construction. It can carry out the equivalent operation test of the system, support the abnormal or problem investigation of the GNSS, and ensure stable operation. On the other hand, the satellites to be tested and the ground test verification system are interconnected through the remote optical fiber and the radio frequency signal transmission technology by using the radio frequency signal remote transmission technology. The satellites to be tested in the test platform can be equivalent to one set of space segment satellite simulators, which are interchangeable with other satellite simulators of the space segment subsystem. Together with other subsystems in the test platform, the GNSS Equivalent Simulation Verification System is formed to carry out a multi-star multi-station system-level integrated docking test involving multiple real satellites.

4 Management of Comprehensive Control

The test platform is a large-scale test system with strong comprehensiveness, complex structure, wide professional coverage, and diverse test contents. It has the characteristics of "systematic", "authenticity", "completeness", and "flexibility". Therefore, it requires very high requirements for the comprehensive control of the system.

Comprehensive control management takes task planning management and operation control as the main line, based on test business and monitoring business, and uses delay calibration as a means. It designs the collection, transmission, storage and processing system of test data according to the standard of dynamic data management center. It builds the system network hardware and software platform according to the maximum equipment scheduling capability and task planning operation capability of full-speed operation. It can meet the needs of stable operation of the test platform, configurable tasks, easy integration, and flexible expansion. The comprehensive control management of the test platform is realized by the control and comprehensive support subsystem, including four parts: "time-frequency network subsystem", "test standard stator system", "software and communication subsystem", and "power supply and distribution subsystem". The time-frequency subsystem is responsible for generating high-precision 10 MHz, 1PPS, B code, NTP and other signals, providing a unified standard time and frequency signal for the entire test platform. The test calibration stator system is mainly used for high-precision equipment time-delay calibration of equipment in the space section and operation control section. The software and communication subsystem is responsible for the management control, business processing, data processing and system monitoring of the test platform. The power supply and distribution network subsystem, as an important part of the control and comprehensive support subsystem, provides a safe, reliable, and continuous power supply capability for the entire ground test verification system equipment. Among them, how to realize the high-precision time reference and time synchronization of the test platform and provide the test platform with high-precision, high-performance and high-stability time-frequency signals is the key to the operation of the test platform.

The time base of the test platform is controlled by the time and frequency subsystem of control and comprehensive support. The subsystem is controlled by atomic clock equipment, reference signal distribution equipment, space section time and frequency distribution equipment, ground control section time and frequency distribution equipment, user segment time-frequency interface, environment segment time-frequency distribution interface, monitoring hall time-frequency equipment, star-ground clock difference automatic measurement equipment, GNSS time traceability equipment (Fig. 2).

The working principle of the time-frequency subsystem is as follows:

(1) Atomic clock group equipment is a reference signal generation equipment: high-precision 10MHz, 1PPS, B code signals are generated by atomic clocks, time-frequency selection switches, digital clocks, and other equipment; the standard time is obtained through the coarse synchronization of the GNSS timing user machine based on the standard BDT; the counter records the time difference information of

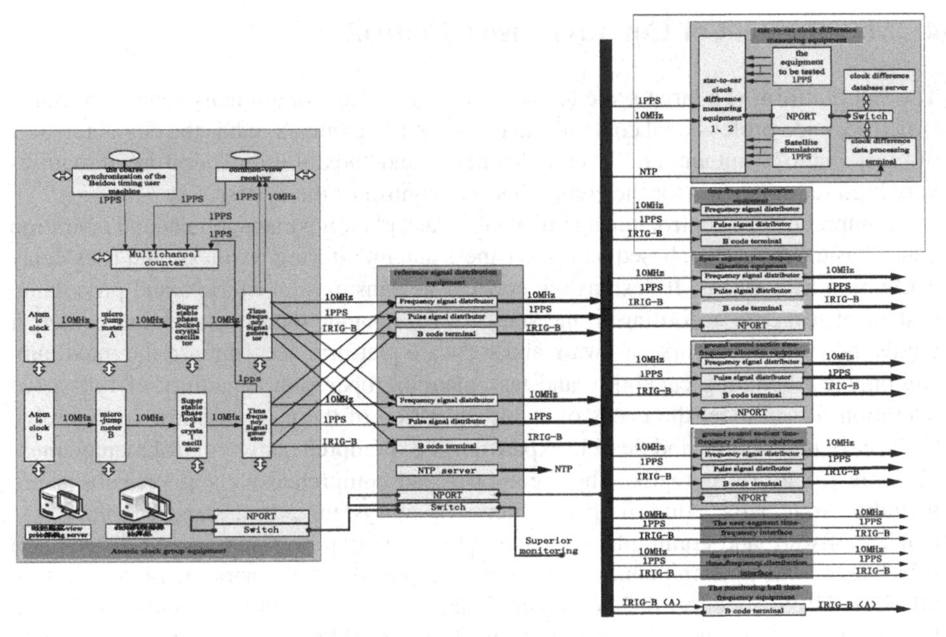

Fig. 2. The architecture diagram of time frequency subsystem.

two atomic clocks in real time; in addition, it also has the function of monitoring the integrity of the clock group equipment.

(2) The reference signal distribution device is a first-level distribution device for time-frequency reference signals: it receives high-precision 10MHz, 1PPS, and B code signals provided by atomic clock equipment; it realizes the multiplex distribution of reference 10MHz, 1PPS, and B code signals; it uses 10MHz, The B code and 1PPS signal generate the NTP time service signal.
(3) Space segment time-frequency allocation equipment, ground control section time-frequency allocation equipment are second-level allocation equipment: they realize the distribution of reference time-frequency signals; they provide high precision 10MHz, 1PPS, B code signal for space segment, ground control section, respectively.
(4) The user-segment time-frequency interface and the environment-segment time-frequency distribution interface are a set of 10 MHz, 1PPS, B code signals directly transmitted from the reference signal distribution equipment.
(5) The monitoring hall time-frequency equipment realizes the multi-channel distribution of the reference B code signal and provides multiple B code signals for the monitoring hall.
(6) Automatic measurement system for clock error.
The star-to-ear clock difference automatic measurement system is composed of three parts, including the star-to-ear clock difference measuring equipment, the clock difference data processing terminal, and the clock difference database server. The satellite-to-earth clock difference measurement equipment completes the clock difference measurement of 1PPS and the 1PPS of the integrated time and frequency

system sent by the satellite simulator or the satellite workshop of the Fifth Hospital. It simultaneously completes the comprehensive security local time reference and GPS and GNSS clock time measurement to provide support for time traceability. The clock difference data processing terminal completes the analysis, storage, and reporting of the clock difference data, and it controls the autonomous operation of the star-to-ground clock difference system. Clock difference database server completes the local storage of clock difference data.

(7) GNSS Time Traceability Subsystem.

The GNSS time tracing subsystem is composed of a common-view receiver, a micro-jump meter, a common-view processing server, and a clock control server. The GPS time of the time-frequency subsystem is traced to the GPS time through the GPS common-view receiver. Time-frequency subsystem GNSS time traces to GNSS time through GNSS timing user machine.

5 Transmission of Remote Interconnection

Through the remote optical fiber transmission system, the GNSS Satellite and the test verification system are distributed in different locations. The time and frequency reference is unified to realize remote interconnection transmission. Its principle is shown in Fig. 3.

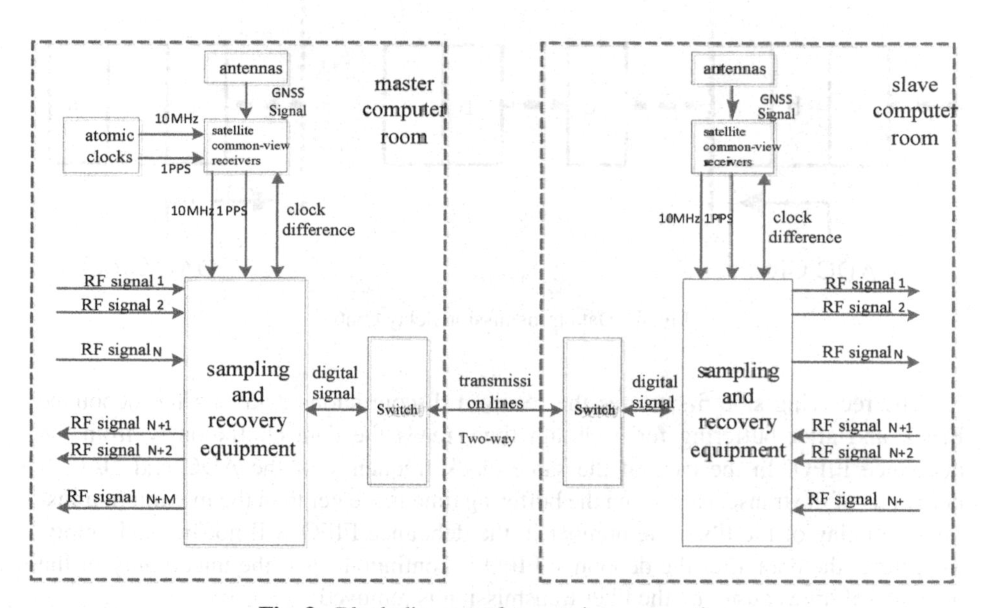

Fig. 3. Block diagram of remote interconnection.

The system includes sampling and recovery equipment in the master computer room, sampling and recovery equipment in the slave computer room, transmission lines (commercial data lines and switches at both ends), atomic clocks, satellite common-view receivers and antennas in the master computer room, satellite common-view receivers in the slave computer room, and antenna.

The transmitting side uses the analog-to-digital (A/D) converter of the sampling recovery device to convert the analog RF signal to be transmitted into a digital signal, and transmits it in the long-distance data line. The receiving sides uses the digital-to-analog (D/A) converter of the sampling recovery device to restore the received digital signal to an analog radio frequency signal to realize the long-distance transmission of the radio frequency signal [13, 14]. The 10MHz and 1PPS signals output by both ends are synchronized by the satellite common-view method; the sampling recovery equipment at both ends uses the 10MHz and 1PPS output from the satellite common-view receiver as their own reference clocks to maintain the consistency of the master and slave clock frequencies.

Due to the influence of the routing path, the transmission delay of the remote optical fiber fluctuates, so the data buffer needs to be removed at the receiving end to remove the uncertainty of the data arrival time. The schematic diagram is shown in Fig. 4:

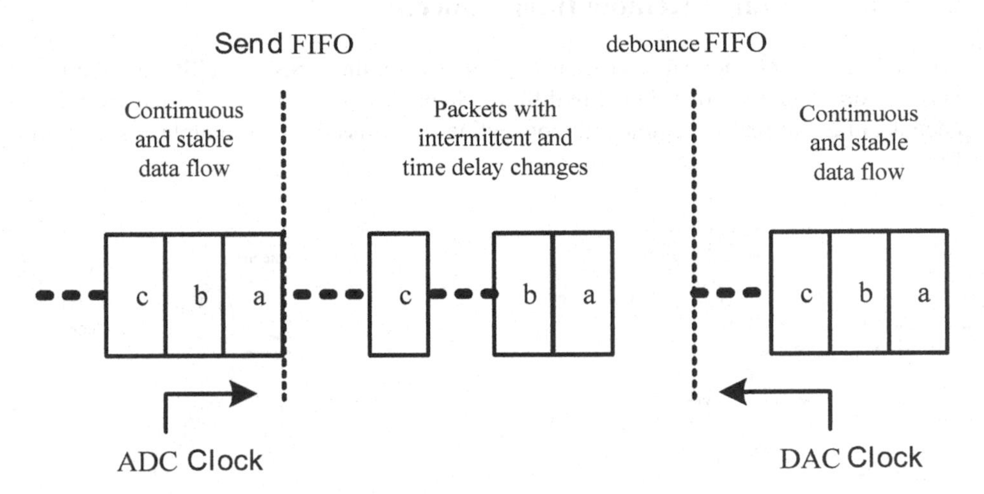

Fig. 4. Data transmission delay control

The receiving side first stores the received discontinuous data into the debounce FIFO, and after buffering for a certain time, reads the data continuously from the debounce FIFO. In the case of the same clock frequency of the ADC and DAC at both ends of the transceiver, when the buffering time is greater than the maximum transmission delay of the fiber, the number in the debounce FIFO will not be read empty. Therefore, the data after the debounce FIFO is continuous, and the uncertainty of the data arrival time caused by the fiber transmission is removed.

The delay of the data stream at both ends of the transceiver is determined by the time difference between the data transmission time and the reading time of the debounce FIFO. When the time difference is greater than the maximum transmission delay of the fiber, the data stream delay is not affected by the fluctuation of the fiber transmission delay. The time difference can be controlled by sending and receiving enable, as shown in Fig. 5:

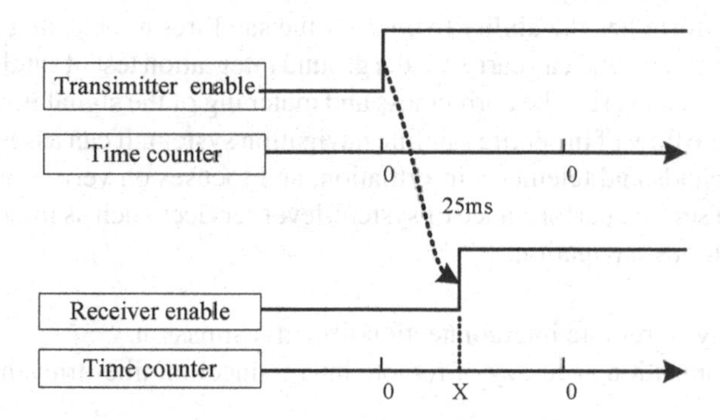

Fig. 5. Send and receive enable control

The time counters at both ends of the transceiver are counted by 10 MHz provided by the common-view satellite receiver, and cleared by 1PPS. Hence both ends of the transceiver use the same time reference. Set the delay between receiving enable and sending enable to 25 ms (greater than the maximum transmission delay of 20 ms between A and B). When the receiving time counter counts the corresponding value, enable the reading of the debounce FIFO. Therefore, the transmission delay of the off-site RF signal is $\tau = 25\text{ms} + \tau_{\text{d}} + \tau_a$, where τ_d is the delay introduced by digital circuits such as digital logic and digital-to-analog conversion at both ends of the transceiver, and τ_a is the delay introduced by analog devices such as RF channels and RF cables. τ_d and τ_a are two certain value that can be measured at a certain clock frequency and a certain temperature, hence the transmission delay accuracy of the RF signal is mainly determined by the accuracy of 25 ms. Notice that the accuracy of 25 ms is determined by 10 MHz and 1PPS, so the average value of the transmission delay of the RF signal is $\tau \pm 2ns$.

6 Implementation of the Test Platform

The GNSS remote docking test platform builds a multi-level flexible and controllable simulation test platform that approximately represents the real state of the GNSS. It can carry out simulation design and test verification that integrates all elements and the whole system. The test platform mainly has the following capabilities.

1) The test platform represents the overall technical status of the GNSS, and its composition and scale match the GNSS. It forms a system-wide test and verification environment for the entire system and configuration, which can cover the entire system's complete interfaces and business relationships (information flow, control flow, time flow).
2) The test platform has a flexible and controllable system architecture, and the hardware and software can be flexibly controlled and configured; it also takes into account

the mutually complementary verification methods of hardware verification and software simulation, and can be expanded and upgraded in time according to changes in needs and technology.

3) The test platform has the ability to connect the satellites to be tested in the satellite plant to the system, and can carry out the ground integration test of satellite navigation equipment. It can verify the correctness and matching of the signal flow, information flow, and time flow of the entire satellite navigation system. It can assess the accuracy of all commands and telemetry information, and focuses on verifying the operation process and service performance of system-level services such as inter-satellite links and autonomous navigation.

- Delay stability of remote interconnection fiber transmission.
- Time synchronization accuracy of remote interconnection fiber transmission.

Based on this platform, some tests were carried out, We verified the following performance: the correctness of the interface protocol between the satellite, ground control section and application verification; the matching, coordination and service performance of the integrated operation process of the satellite-satellite-ground; system basic intact function and process; onboard autonomous integrity monitoring functions and processes; Short message function and process; satellite-based enhanced information calculation, betting, broadcasting and user receiving functions and process; autonomous navigation function and process accuracy. And in the process of docking test, we found related problems such as autonomous navigation and basic integrity of the two networks. This platform improves the coverage of ground-level system-level test verification projects, reduces the pressure of satellite on-orbit networking testing, reduces the change of satellite on-orbit technical status, and accelerates the progress of satellite network access to provide service.

6.1 Performance of the Integrated Operation Process of the Satellite-Satellite-Ground

Mainly verify the correctness of operation control and measurement and control business information transmission on each network node and link of the whole system. The correctness of the integrated information flow function and process (Table 1).

6.2 System Integrity

Mainly verify the continuity test of various satellite monitoring data. The correctness of the processing function and process of the satellite's autonomous integrity is tested and verified. The continuity of intact monitoring data such as satellite carrier phase, signal power, satellite clock frequency/phase jump, on-board correlation value, etc. is verified. Realized the test of the basic integrity alarm process, and verified the alarm time and other indicators, which effectively supported the confirmation of the status of the satellite technical process (Fig. 6).

Table 1. Test results

Navigation message type	Expected injection state	Actual injection result	Expected comparison result	Actual comparison results	Compliance
Ephemeris parameters/ Star clock and group delay parameters/ Ionospheric model parameters/ Basic navigation information	Successful injection	Successful injection	Match correctly	Match correctly	Conform

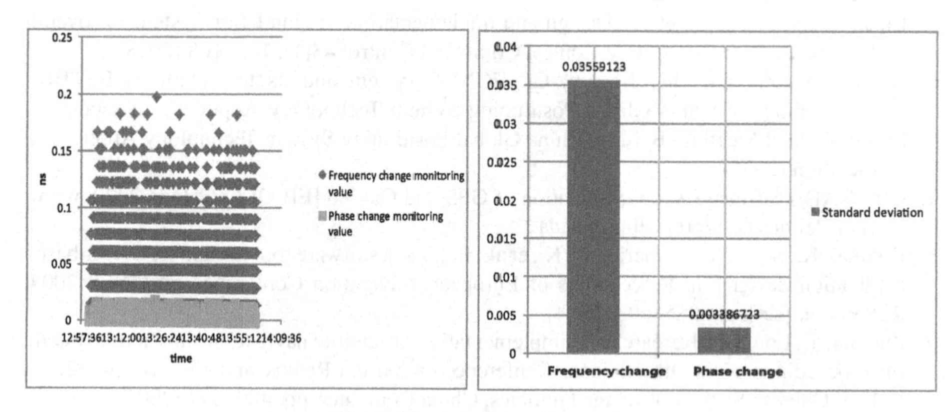

Fig. 6. System integrity results

7 Conclusion

The GNSS remote docking test platform builds a full-system, full-state, full-scale satellite navigation test verification system. It can provide four working modes: software, hardware, software-hardware collaboration, and virtual-real combination, and it integrates design verification, engineering docking, Equivalent operation and simulation test are all in one. At the same time, through the remote transmission technology of radio frequency signals, the satellites to be tested distributed in different locations and the ground simulation system are interconnected. A comprehensive docking test for parallel access of multiple real systems is carried out, which can effectively verify the correctness of the system-level service signal flow, information flow, and time flow for satellite navigation system inter-satellite links and autonomous navigation. This platform can fully expose the problem before the satellite is launched, and modify it in time to avoid the repeated technical status of the satellite in orbit and avoid improving the quality of the project construction. The construction quality of the project can be improved, the construction risk can be reduced, and the connection cost can be saved. This platform facilitates the implementation of satellite high-density networking launches.

References

1. Green, G.L., Hulbert, B.: An overview of the global positioning system interference and navigation tool (GIANT) [C]. In: Proceeding of the 13th International Technical Meeting of the Satellite Division of the Institute of Navigation (ION GPS 2000), Salt Lake City, ION, pp. 499–511 (2000)
2. Green, G.L., Gerteng: recent development for the global positioning system interference and navigation tool (GIANT). In: Proceeding of 2000 IEEE Aerospace Conference, Big Sky, pp. 547–554. IEEE (2000)
3. Secretan, H., Suard, N., De Mate, J.C., et al.: EGNOS system test bed status and achievements. In: Proceeding of ION on GNSS2001, Portland: ION, pp. 895–901 (2001)
4. GSSF: GSSF operations manual volume1: GSSFP2, OM. 001[EB/OL], 22 May 2005, 12 June 2020. https://www.gssf.info
5. Li, J., Kong, F., Li, Z., et al.: Design and implementation of simulation system for overall performance of spacecraft. Fire Control Command Control **43**(1), 165–168 (2018)
6. Jiulong, Y., Zhigang, D., Jingjun, G.: EGNOS system and its test platform ESTBIC. In: Proceedings of China Global Positioning System Technology Application Association Eighth Annual Meeting, Beijing, China Global Positioning System Technology Application Association (2005)
7. GRANADA Software Suite: Simulation of GPS and Galileo [EB/OL], 22 June 2020. www.elecnor-deimos.com/protfolio/granada
8. Gavinaj, K., Scardas, S., Sheridank, K., et al.: Polaris: a software tool to support GNSS-based application design. In: Proceedings of European Navigation Conference on GNSS 2004, Rotterdam: [s.n], pp. 985–993 (2004)
9. Zunhua, T., Long, Z.: Research and implementation of satellite navigation simulation system. In: Proceedings of the 4th National Conference on Virtual Reality and Visualization 2004, Dalian, Chinese Society of Image Graphics, China Computer, pp. 489–494 (2005)
10. Zunhua, T., Long, Z., Yan, J.: Research and implementation of a satellite navigation synthetic simulation platform. Comput. Eng. Sci. **29**(11), 145–148 (2007)
11. Wen, Y.: Analysis and Simulation Technology of Satellite Navigation System. China Aerospace Press, Beijing (2009)
12. Jun, Y., Li, F., Dexiang, M., et al.: An ACP approach of ground experimental verification for global navigation satellite system. J. Astronaut. **36**(2), 165–172 (2015)
13. Haijie, Y.: Design and Implementation of the Multi-Function Time-Frequency Transmission System. Beijing University of Posts and Telecommunications (2015)
14. Hong, S., Yingchuan, H.: Technology and realization of broadband RF signal transmission over linear optical fiber. Radio Eng. China **37**(4), 42–44 (2007)

Research on Distributed Beamforming Algorithm Based on Inter-satellite Link

Jianyun Chen and Yonggang Zhang(✉)

College of Intelligence Science and Technology, National University of Defense Technology, Changsha 410000, China
zzhangyonggang123@163.com

Abstract. The inter-satellite link load belongs to a system with limited power volume, and generally has low antenna gain and weak transmission capacity. Aimed at handling the problem that single-node inter-satellite link systems are often incapable of satisfying long-distance high-bandwidth communication requirements, the distributed beamforming algorithm is applied to the inter satellite design, in order to achieve higher inter-satellite link performance without increasing the inter-satellite link transmission power. This paper analyzes the feasibility and spatial beam pattern of distributed beamforming in inter-satellite links. The improved distributed beamforming algorithms that can be adapted to different channels change are proposed. In a flat stationary channel, the phase weight and correction factor are increased, when the random phase disturbance is 3°, the number of beam retransmissions is reduced by 800 times compared with the classical algorithm; In the time-varying channel, the feedback of the time-varying in-formation of the channel is increased, and the phase compensation is added to alleviate the influence of the dynamic change of the channel. Compared with the traditional algorithm, it can be adapted to the change of the time-varying channel.

Keywords: Distributed beamforming · One-bit feedback · Random perturbation

1 Introduction

Inter-satellite link refers to the communication link between satellites. Through the inter-satellite link, information transmission and precise measurement between satellites can be realized, and multiple satellites can be interconnected into space communication and measurement networks [1, 2]. The inter-satellite link load belongs to the power volume limited system, with low antenna gain and weak transmission capacity. When faced with the cooperative task of perceptual communication, the single node inter-satellite link system is often difficult to meet the requirements of long-distance and high bandwidth communication, and becomes the bottleneck of cooperative task. Multiple forwarding by multi-hop mode will inevitably lead to the increase of communication delay and can not be adapted to the scene with high real-time requirements; In addition, the forwarding by converging satellite node will put forward higher requirements for converging node

Q. Wu et al. (Eds.): WiSATS 2020, LNICST 358, pp. 259–270, 2021.
https://doi.org/10.1007/978-3-030-69072-4_22

resources, and make the whole inter-satellite network highly dependent on the converging node. In the face of complex environment, the damage of the converging node will lead to the paralysis of the whole network. Therefore, how to rely only on the coordination of the inter-satellite link nodes of the distributed satellite system to enhance the communication measurement capability of the inter-satellite network, to expand the scope of the inter-satellite link, and to improve the anti-interference ability is of great significance to the decentralized space-based system.

Distributed beamforming is independent of each other and the randomly distributed nodes randomly cooperate with each other to form a virtual antenna array which directly communicate with the target receiver through beamforming [3]. Distributed beamforming technology sends a common message and controls the phase of its transmission through multiple information sources at the same time, so that the signals can be constructively combined at the intended destination, and the antenna array with N array elements can obtain N^2 times of the radiant power gain. Distributed beamforming can increase the communication distance of nodes and enhance the communication range of nodes. Unlike multi-hop communication, it reduces the occurrence of problems in the safety and reliability of satellite long-distance communication.

In terms of distributed beamforming research, H. Ochiai first proposed the application of traditional beamforming theory to wireless sensor networks in 2005. Based on the above research results, M.I. Poulakis analyzed and discussed the application of beamforming theory in sensor network and satellite communication scenarios based on ideal environmental conditions [4]. Since 2004, with the support of the US Naval Research Office, DARPA and the National Science Foundation, the R. Mudumbai team at the University of California and the D.R. Brown II team at Worcester Polytechnic have conducted systematic research on distributed beamforming. The R. Mudumbai team's research achievement is mainly to propose a synchronization method based on closed-loop feedback: one-bit feedback synchronization scheme [5–7]. This synchronization scheme was proposed in 2005 [8]. In 2010, R. Mudumbai summarized the one-bit feedback synchronization method [9, 10], proposed a circuit prototype, and verified the algorithm experimentally.

The one-bit feedback algorithm proposed in this paper makes a simple iteration of the feedback from the satellite receiver to achieve satellite transmitter phase coherence, and shows that the process meets the requirements of distributed beamforming. The basic idea is as follows: each satellite transmitter randomly adjusts its phase in each iteration, while the receiver broadcasts a one-bit feedback in each iteration showing that its SNR is better or lower than before. If it is better than before, the transmitter maintains the phase disturbance, and if it is worse, the previous phase disturbance is eliminated. Repeat this random process until the transmitter converges to phase coherence.

2 Basic Model of Distributed Beamforming for Inter-satellite Links

Figure 1 shows the communication model of distributed inter-satellite link beamforming based on feedback control. It has N satellite transmitters, and all transmitters are frequency-locked to the reference carrier signal by using the master-slave architecture described in [6]. As a result, the carrier signals of all transmitters are at the same frequency f_c, without frequency offset. However, due to the unknown transmission delay in the master-slave architecture, there is an arbitrary phase difference between the satellite transmitters. The carrier signal of transmitter i is expressed as:

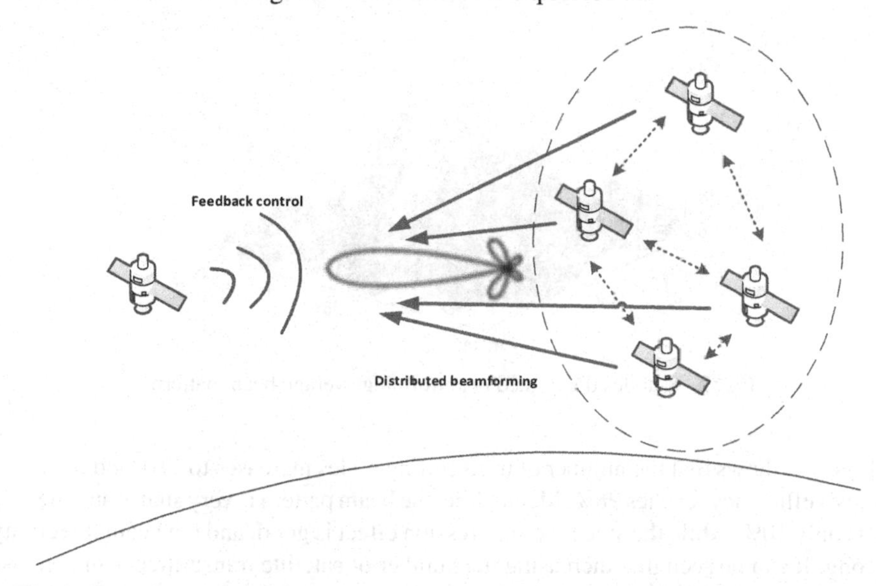

Fig. 1. Diagram of distributed interstellar link beam formation based on feedback control

$$c_i(t) = R\left(e^{j(2\pi f_c t + \varepsilon_i)}\right) \tag{1}$$

Where ε_i is the phase offset.

The modulated signal sent by transmitter i is expressed as:

$$s_i(t) = R\left(m(t)e^{j\theta_i}e^{j(2\pi f_c t + \varepsilon_i)}\right) \tag{2}$$

θ_i is the rotation angle of the modulated signal of the satellite transmitter i.

If the channel transmitted to the receiver is $h_i = a_i e^{j\varphi_i}$, the total received signal of the satellite receiver is:

$$r(t) = R\left(m(t)e^{j2\pi f_c t}\sum_{i=1}^{N} a_i e^{j(\varepsilon_i + \theta_i + \varphi_i)}\right) \tag{3}$$

The phase from transmission to reception is $\Phi_i = \varepsilon_i + \theta_i + \varphi_i$. The power of the received signal is expressed as:

$$S_r = \left|\sum_i a_i e^{j\Phi_i}\right|^2 \tag{4}$$

The transmitter adjusts its phase rotation θ_i so that the signals from all transmitters are coherently received at the receiving end, and the received power S_r is maximized. At this time, Φ_i is a constant value.

In order to visualize the effect of distributed beamforming, it is assumed that there are 8 transmitting nodes, distributed on a 100 * 100 m plane, and omnidirectional antennas are used, all of which have the same frequency of 1 GHz and the same phase, and are transmitted simultaneously (Fig. 2).

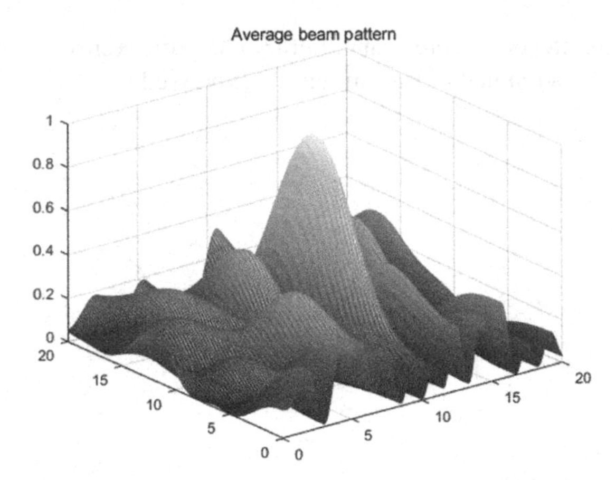

Fig. 2. 8-nodes distributed beamforming average beam pattern

Figure 3 shows that the number of transmitting nodes increases to 110, and the beam synthesis efficiency reaches 98%. Meanwhile, the beam pattern is very sharp, and the side lobe is only 10%, while the side lobe suppression effect is good, and the beam directivity is strong. It can be seen that increasing the number of satellite transmitters can increase the synthesized beam gain, but the number of transmitter nodes is determined. Therefore, it becomes the focus of this paper that how to improve the efficiency of beamforming and increase the communication distance of nodes by changing the phase of transmitter nodes, and increase the communication distance of nodes under a certain number of transmitter nodes.

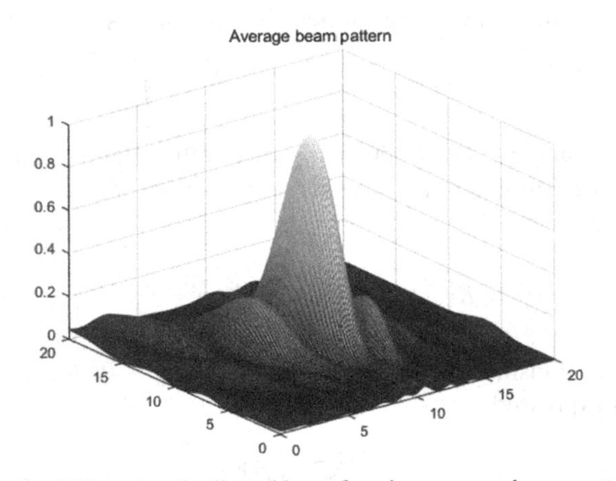

Fig. 3. 110-nodes distributed beamforming average beam pattern

3 One-Bit Feedback Distributed Beamforming Method and Feasibility Simulation

The net complex gain of the receiver is:

$$Y = \sum\nolimits_{i=1}^{N} a_i e^{j(\varepsilon_i + \theta_i + \varphi_i)} = \sum\nolimits_{i=1}^{N} a_i e^{j\Phi_i} \tag{5}$$

The amplitude Y $\geq$ 0 indicates the received signal strength (RSS), and $\Phi_i = \varepsilon_i + \theta_i + \varphi_i$ is the phase difference between the satellite receiver and the transmitter i signal. If the received carrier phases Φ_i are all equal, then:

$$Y = \left|\sum\nolimits_{i=1}^{N} a_i e^{j\Phi_i}\right| \leq Y_{max} \equiv \left(\sum\nolimits_{i=1}^{N} a_i\right), \text{ If and only } \Phi_i = \Phi_j \tag{6}$$

The purpose of the feedback control algorithm is to allow the transmitter i to dynamically calculate the optimal value of θ_i without knowing any φ_i or ε_i.

The classic one-bit feedback algorithm proposed in this paper only needs to add a random phase perturbation vector to the starting phase of each transmitter, and then after several iterations, the RSS finally reaches the optimal. First, a brief introduction to the classic distributed beamforming single-bit feedback algorithm is given as follows.

1) Each transmitter retains the best value of its current phase rotation $\theta_{best,i}(n)$. The receiving end measures the received signal strength Y of each time slot n, then the best $Y_{best}(n)$:

$$Y_{best}(n) = \max_{m \leq n} Y(m) \tag{7}$$

$$Y(m) = \left|\sum\nolimits_{i=1}^{N} a_i e^{j\Phi_i(m)}\right| \tag{8}$$

2) In the n + 1 time slot, each beamforming node transmitter generates random phase disturbance δ_i, subject to the probability distribution $f_\delta(\delta_i)$, so that: $\theta_i(n+1) = \theta_{best,i}(n) + \delta_i$,thereby:

$$\Phi_i(n+1) = \Phi_{best,i}(n) + \delta_i \tag{9}$$

Where $\Phi_{best,i}(n) = \varepsilon_i + \theta_{best,i}(n) + \varphi_i$ is the phase of the signal from the transmitter to the receiver, which corresponds to $\theta_{best,i}(n)$.

3) If the signal strength received by the feedback node satellite is stronger than the best received signal strength of the previous time slot, the satellite receiver will generate a single feedback bit and set it to "1", otherwise set it to "0", and then broadcast that feedback.
4) The receiver updates $Y_{best}(n+1)$, and the beamforming node transmitter updates the phase rotation $\theta_{best,i}(n+1)$, and maintains the phase disturbance δ_i when the feedback bit is "1", otherwise discards it.
5) Repeat the process in the next time slot.

The update process can be written mathematically:

$$Y_{best}(n+1) = \begin{cases} Y(n+1), & Y(n+1) > Y_{best}(n) \\ Y_{best}(n), & otherwise \end{cases} \tag{10}$$

$$\theta_{best,i}(n+1) = \begin{cases} \theta_{best,i}(n) + \delta_i(n), & Y(n+1) > Y_{best}(n) \\ \theta_{best,i}(n), & otherwise \end{cases} \tag{11}$$

The performance of the algorithm has a great relationship with the selected maximum random phase disturbance δ_i. The second step of the classic algorithm indicates that different phase disturbances have an effect on the final beamforming effect. Choosing the appropriate phase disturbance will help the algorithm to converge faster and the combined power efficiency becomes better. Suppose that there are 30 transmitting nodes with equal amplitude transmission power, the phase disturbance δ_i is subject to two-point distribution and uniform distribution, respectively.

1) The phase disturbance δ_i follows a uniform distribution. When $\delta_i = 30°, 10°, 5°$. The simulation results are shown in Fig. 4. The larger the phase disturbance δ_i, the faster the convergence speed, but the lower the final synthesis efficiency. Conversely, the smaller the phase disturbance δ_i, the slower the convergence speed, the higher the final synthesis efficiency. The reason is that the greater the phase disturbance, in the fourth step of the classic algorithm, the optimal received signal strength obtained by the destination receiver is difficult to be fine-tune to the maximum received strength.

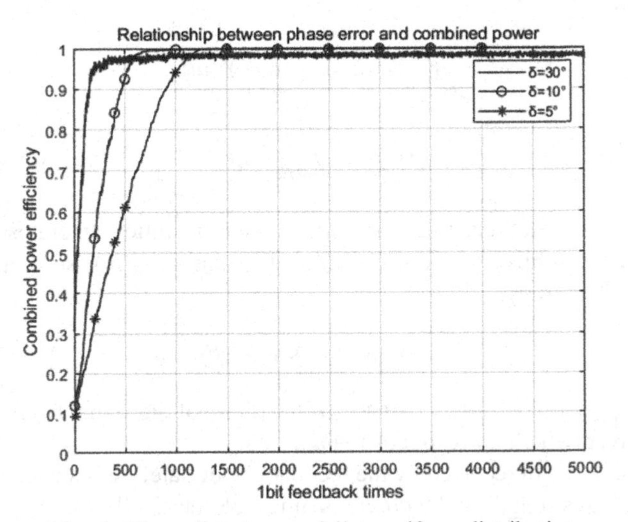

Fig. 4. Phase disturbances follow uniform distribution

2) The phase disturbance δ_i follows two points. Set the phase disturbance $\delta_i = 30°, 10°, 5°$. The simulation results are shown in Fig. 5, When the phase disturbance $\delta_i = 10°$, the two-point distribution only needs 550 iterations to converge to the optimal value, and the uniform distribution requires 800 iterations In order to achieve convergence,

the two-point distribution needs 800 iterations to converge to the optimal value when the phase disturbance $\delta_i = 5°$, and the uniform distribution requires 1100 iterations to achieve convergence, indicating that the smaller the phase disturbance, the greater the cost of uniform distribution and the slower the convergence rate.

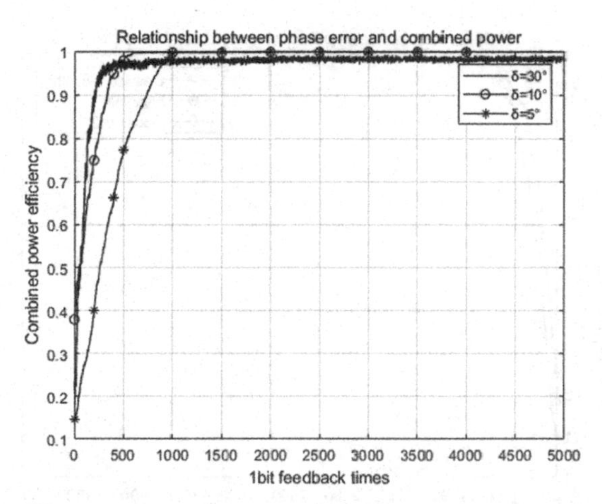

Fig. 5. Phase disturbances follow uniform distribution

In order to improve the adjustment speed of the algorithm and the stability of the channel change, we make certain improvements of the classic algorithm.

Improved algorithm 1: Improve the second step of the classic algorithm, so that the added random phase disturbance changes dynamically with the function convergence. At the beginning of synchronization, phase disturbances can be increased to speed up the convergence of the transmitting node. When approaching convergence, random phase disturbances can be reduced to make the convergence more stable and the synthesis efficiency higher.

Improved algorithm 2: The phase of the distributed beamforming node at the time slot n mentioned above is $\Phi_i = \varepsilon_i + \theta_i + \varphi_i$, After operating the phase, adding the phase weight and the correction factor $\tau_i(n)$, the initial n-slot beamforming phase is expressed as:

$$\Phi_i(n) = \varepsilon_i + \varphi_i + \theta_i(n) + \delta_i(n) + \tau_i(n) \tag{12}$$

When the phase disturbance added by time slot n is successful, that is $Y(n+1) > Y_{best}(n)$ satisfied, the initial n-slot beamforming phase can be expressed as:

$$\Phi_i(n) = \varepsilon_i + \varphi_i + \theta_i(n) + \delta_i(n) + \delta_i(n+1) + \left(1 + \frac{1}{R_D}\right)\tau_i(n) \tag{13}$$

When the phase disturbance of the n-slot fails, that is, $Y(n+1) \leq Y_{best}(n)$ is satisfied, the initial n-slot beamforming phase can be expressed as:

$$\Phi_i(n) = \varepsilon_i + \varphi_i + \theta_i(n) - \delta_i(n) + \delta_i(n+1) \tag{14}$$

Figure 6 shows the convergence process of the three algorithms when $\delta_i = 10°$: Initially, the improved algorithm 1 and improved algorithm 2 converge faster than the classic algorithm. After 500 iterations, the improved algorithm 2 has a better convergence rate than the classic algorithm and the improved algorithm 1. Finally, the combined power efficiency of the three algorithms is almost 100%.

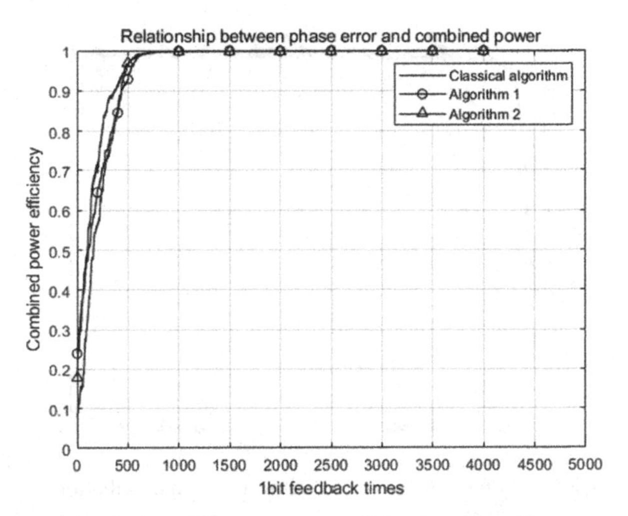

Fig. 6. $\delta_i = 10°$ convergence of the three algorithms

Figure 7 shows the convergence process of the three algorithms when $\delta_i = 3°$: it can be seen that the improved algorithm 2 is significantly better than the improved algorithm 1 and the classic algorithm. The combined power efficiency is almost 100%.

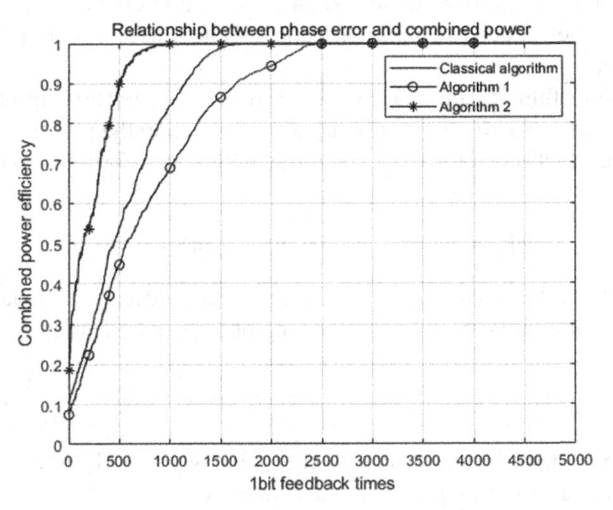

Fig. 7. $\delta_i = 3°$ convergence of the three algorithms

Figure 8 shows the convergence process of the improved algorithm 2 under different initial disturbance step sizes: the phase perturbation corresponding to the convergence speed from fast to slow is 30°, 10°, 5° and 3°, When the number of iterations is 900 The power efficiency is almost 100%, indicating the final value of the received signal strength is the largest.

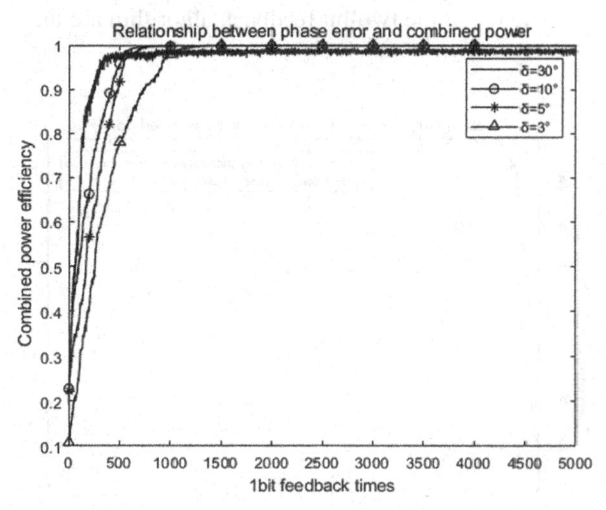

Fig. 8. Convergence process of the improved second algorithm under different δ_i conditions

The above simulation is assumed that the wireless channel from each transmitter to the receiver is static, and the phase synchronization convergence model. For such a channel, it can be proved that the single-bit feedback algorithm asymptotically converges to perfect coherence with probability 1. Once converged, the transmitter can use the optimal value $\theta_{best,i}$ obtained from the algorithm to maintain coherent transmission in subsequent time slots. But in actual situations, the channel phase response changes with time, for example. Due to the Doppler effect of moving scatterers. For such channels, channel changes will cause the transmitted signal to lose coherence over time: Even when the transmitter uses the same phase rotation $\theta_{best,i}$, the received phase $\Phi_{best,i}(n) = \varepsilon_i + \theta_{best,i}(n) + \varphi_i(n)$ will not remain unchanged due to the change of the channel phase response $\varphi_i(n)$. As a result, the received signal strength $Y_{best}(n) = \left|\sum_{i=1}^{N} a_i e^{j\Phi_{best,i}(n)}\right|$ decreases gradually. The one-bit feedback algorithm can be adjusted to dynamically adjust the transmission phase $\theta_{best,i}(n)$. The two-bit feedback algorithm adds feedback information, feeds back the time-varying information of the channel, and adds additional phase compensation to alleviate the adverse effects caused by the dynamic change of the channel, so that the receiving end node receives better quality of RSS.

The following will compare the convergence rate and the final value of the received signal strength of the time-varying channel simulation algorithm and the two-bit feedback algorithm at different channel drift speeds to better show the final stability of each algorithm.

The channel drift Δ_i of the three images is from small to large, and the time-varying channel is from weak to strong. When Δ_i is small, the combined power efficiency of the two algorithms can reach more than 95%; When Δ_i gradually increases, the convergence speed of the two algorithms also decreases, but the two-bit feedback algorithm is time-varying relative to the classic one. The advantages of the channel simulation algorithm are also reflected, especially when $\Delta_i \sim U\left(-\frac{\pi}{18}, \frac{\pi}{18}\right)$, the convergence speed and beamforming efficiency of the two-bit feedback algorithm are the best (Figs. 9 and 10).

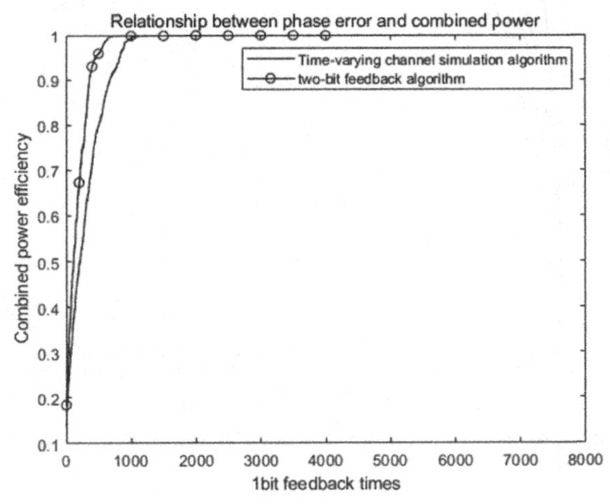

Fig. 9. The convergence process of the two algorithms when the channel drift is $\Delta_i \sim U\left(-\frac{\pi}{125}, \frac{\pi}{125}\right)$

The conclusion of the simulation comparison analysis is that two-bit feedback algrithmms proposed in this paper are suitable for distributed beamforming in time-varying channels. Compared with the existing algorithm, it can overcome the problem that the existing algorithm cannot converge due to channel drift, and has the advantages of fast convergence speed and large final value of received signal strength (Fig. 11).

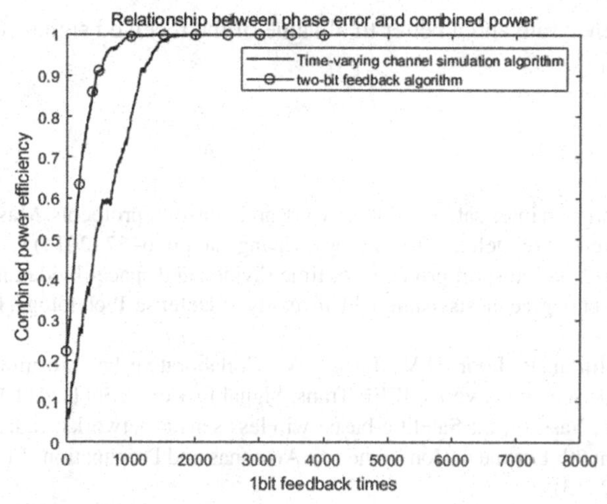

Fig. 10. The convergence process of the two algorithms when the channel drift is $\Delta_i \sim U\left(-\frac{\pi}{125}, \frac{\pi}{125}\right)$

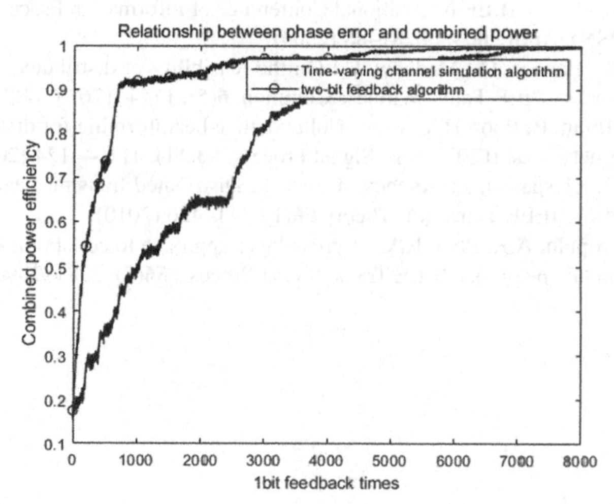

Fig. 11. The convergence process of the two algorithms when the channel drift is $\Delta_i \sim U\left(-\frac{\pi}{18}, \frac{\pi}{18}\right)$

4 Conclusion

This paper studies and analyzes the idea of using distributed beamforming in inter-satellite links from a theoretical perspective. This method can increase the satellite communication distance and improve the confidentiality of satellite communication. A single-bit feedback algorithm is proposed to solve the core problem of its implementation: carrier synchronization. Compared with other synchronization algorithms, the receiver has less feedback and strong scalability. For the stationary channel and the time-varying channel, the distributed beamforming algorithms designed separately have a faster convergence rate and a better final value of the received signal strength than the classic algorithm.

References

1. Wu, G.: Research on inter-satellite link network and transport protocols. Master degree thesis, National University of Defense Technology, Changsha, pp. 6–57 (2014)
2. Xu, P.: Research on transport protocols of time-divided and space-divided inter-satellite link network. Master degree thesis, National University of Defense Technology, Changsha, pp. 6–63 (2016)
3. Ochiai, H., Mitran, P., Poor, H.V., Tarokh, V.: Collaborative beamforming for distributed wireless ad hoc sensor networks. IEEE Trans. Signal Process. **53**(11), 4110–4124 (2005)
4. Poulakis, M.I., Vassaki, S.: Satellite-based wireless sensor networks: radio communication link design. In: 7th European Conference on Antennas and Propagation (EuCAP), pp. 2620–2624. IEEE (2013)
5. Mudumbai, R., Brown, D.R., Madhow, U., et al.: Distributed transmit beamforming: challenges and recent progress. Commun. Mag. **47**(2), 102–110 (2009)
6. Barriac, G., Mudumbai, R., Madhow, U.: Distributed beamforming for information transfer in sensor networks. In: IEEE International Conference of Information Processing and Sensor Networks (IPSN), April 2004, pp. 81–88 (2004)
7. Mudumbai, R., Barriac, G., Madhow, U.: On the feasibility of distributed beamforming in wireless networks . IEEE Trans. Wireless Commun. **6**(5), 1754–1763 (2007)
8. Ochiai, H., Mitran, P., Poor, H.V., et al.: Collaborative beamforming for distributed wireless ad hoc sensor networks. IEEE Trans. Signal Process. **53**(11), 4110–4124 (2005)
9. Mudumbai, R., Hespanha, J., Madhow, U., et al.: Distributed transmit beamforming using feedback control . IEEE Trans. Inf. Theory **56**(1), 411–426 (2010)
10. Dong, L., Petropulu, A.P., Poor, H.V.: A cross-layer approach to collaborative beamforming for wireless ad hoc networks. IEEE Trans. Signal Process. **56**(7), 2981–2993 (2008)

A Method for Performance Evaluation of the Low Earth Orbit Satellite Networks

Xuan Li(✉), Quan Chen, Lei Yang, Xianfeng Liu, and Lihu Chen

College of Aerospace Science and Engineering, National University of Defense Technology, Changsha 410073, China
lixuan366@163.com

Abstract. Low Earth Orbit satellite communication system has the characteristics of low latency and wide coverage, and is widely used in the non-terrestrial communication systems. But at the same time, the characteristic of its fast-changing topology also brings the complex problem of network performance evaluation. In this paper, we propose a Minimum Delay Maximum Capacity algorithm based on Minimum Cost Maximum Flow algorithm to evaluate the performance of the LEO satellite networks. We analyze the performance of several different constellation configurations based on the proposed algorithm.

Keywords: Low earth orbit satellite network · Delay and capacity · Minimum delay maximum capacity

1 Introduction

Low Earth Orbit (LEO) satellite communication system has the advantages of low latency and wide coverage which is widely used [1]. There are several LEO satellite communication systems such as Iridium system and Globalstar system in the early stage, and many newly proposed systems like SpaceX, Telesat, and OneWeb. However, due to the dynamic topological structure and expensive simulation computation cost, it is complex to evaluate the performance of these networks. The performance metrics of a network include bandwidth, delay, delay jitter and the packet loss rate. However, the common methods for performance evaluation of satellite networks, which need to run complex routing algorithms with specialized satellite network simulation platforms such as OPNET, NS-2, NS-3 and STK. When the number of satellite nodes is large, time consumption has increased dramatically. Therefore, this paper proposes an efficient method to calculate the capacity and delay by the Minimum Delay Maximum Throughput (MDMC) algorithm, which can reflect the performance of the network.

At present, many researchers have analyzed the satellite network performance. In [2], a dynamic routing scheme for time-variant topology environments is proposed, which transforms the dynamic topology into a series of static virtual topology. Then a satellite network topology based on virtual nodes is proposed. In the satellite network with virtual nodes, topology is stable and can be regarded as static [3]. Someone sets

Q. Wu et al. (Eds.): WiSATS 2020, LNICST 358, pp. 271–281, 2021.
https://doi.org/10.1007/978-3-030-69072-4_23

up a series of "snapshots" for the network changes over time. Within each snapshot, the satellite network topology is considered unchanged [4]. In [5], the Quality of Services (QoS) model of space system is established. Previous study uses a finite state automaton (FSA) to solve the difficulty arising from dynamic topology [6]. Since network with less delay has better performance. An asymmetric Discrete Time based Routing Algorithm (A-DTRA) is proposed to find the shortest path with least delay in a snapshot [7]. But A-DTRA ignores the effect of bandwidth. In literature [8], the capacity of the satellite network is expressed by time varying graph and established by "all-to-all" model which is simulated by STK. However, all the above studies depend on sophisticated routing algorithms, and the computation task is heavy. The Maximum Flow (MF) algorithm is a simple and effective method to evaluate network performance. The paper [9] proposes a Location-Based Multi-Service routing algorithm, and uses the MF algorithm to calculate throughput. In [10], capacity and throughput are optimized with an improved push-pull flow algorithm and MF algorithm is used to analyze the throughput. However, the MF algorithm can only evaluate the capacity performance of a satellite network without considering the effect of delay on the network simultaneously.

In this paper, to evaluate the performance of the satellite network, we propose a MDMC method based on Minimum Cost Maximum Flow (MCMF) to calculate the capacity and delay. First, we provide a short overview about LEO satellite networks and ISL topology characteristics. Then we construct the capacity and delay model. Finally we analyze several different satellite network constructions, and compare the difference of their performance by using MDMC.

2 LEO Satellite Network Model

2.1 Satellite Constellation

There are several common configurations of satellite network constellation, such as Walker Delta and Walker Star. This paper focuses on Walker Star Constellation. It consists N orbit planes, M satellites are evenly distributed in each plane with angular distance of $2\pi/M$. The orbits are all circular orbit with the same altitude. And the inclination of each plane is near 90°. The ascending nodes of the orbit planes are arranged at equal intervals along the equator in the range of π. The fixed offset angle between adjacent orbits is π/N. The nearest satellites in adjacent orbits differ in phase by Δw_f degrees from each other (phase offset is given by formula (1)) [11].

$$\Delta w_f = \frac{2\pi}{N \cdot M} \cdot F \tag{1}$$

F is the phase factor ranging from 0 to $N - 1$.

2.2 Satellite Network Model

Each satellite serves as a node in the network topology. The link between the satellites is inter satellite link (ISL), and between the satellite and the user is user data link (UDL) [1]. Finally, we build a satellite network topology.

Each satellite has a maximum of four point-to-point duplex ISLs, two of them are intra plane ISLs, and the others are inter plane ISLs. Because the relative velocity of the satellite over the polar region and the satellite on both sides of the reverse seam is too high, ISLs over polar regions and inter ISLs across reverse seam are closed [12] (the connection states of ISLs between satellites are presented in Fig. 1).

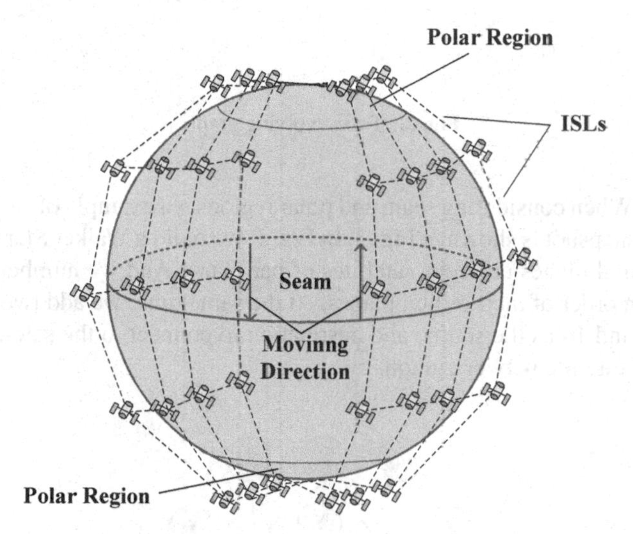

Fig. 1. Satellite network topology and ISLs.

The MDMC algorithm can analyze the network with single source and single terminal, while the LEO satellite network is the network with multi-source and multi-terminal. Thus, we need to introduce a virtual source and destination to solve this problem. The users on the ground dynamically connect with virtual source and destination under the full coverage.

2.3 Graph Model

The position of the satellites in the constellation changes over time, as a result, the topological structure of satellite network changes dynamically. We can use the temporal graph which is also called Time-Evolving Graph (TEG) [13] to show the dynamic changes of the LEO satellites networks. In Fig. 2, within a constellation period, period can be equally divided into K time intervals and the satellite network topology can be also divided into K different snapshots with the same time. A TEG can be expressed as $G(T_i, P_i)$, in which i is from 1 to K. We donate a snapshot as $P(S_j, E_j)$, where S means the Node Set of satellites and E means the Edge Set of ISLs, and j is from 1 to the number of total satellites.

Each snapshot is created dynamically, and the topology structure within the snapshot can be regarded as static. It can be found that, because of the symmetry of the constellation, the topology graph within the K snapshots is isomorphic. Therefore, we only need to select any snapshot for analysis to obtain the network topology of the entire

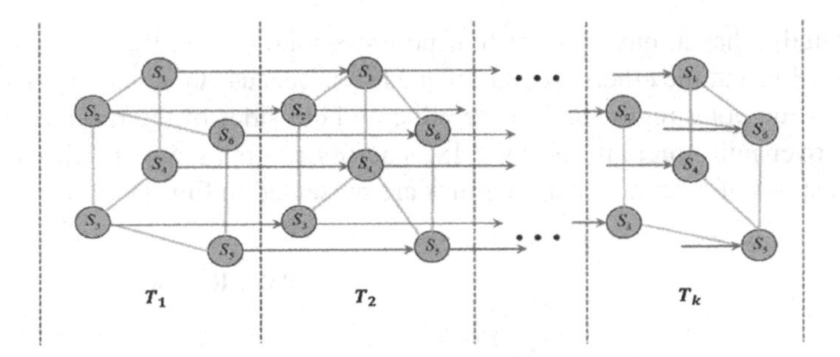

Fig. 2. Time-evolving graph.

constellation. When considering seam and polar regions, an example of satellite network topology in a snapshot is shown in Fig. 3. In Fig. 3, we build a Walker Star Constellation with three orbital planes and four satellites of per plane. And we number the satellites from 1 to 12 in order of their orbital planes. At the same time, we add two ground users numbered 13 and 14 as the source and destination to connect to the satellite randomly. Now we get a satellite network graph.

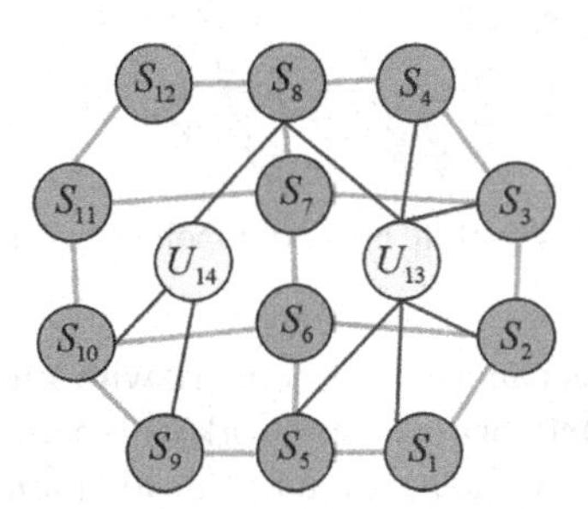

Fig. 3. Satellite network graph.

2.4 Delay and Capacity Evaluation Model

Delay Model. For the entire network, the total transmission path delay T_{total} includes the processing delay $T_{process}$, the propagation delay $T_{propagation}$, and the queuing delay T_{queue} [7]. The total delay between two adjacent nodes is given by

$$T_{total(i,j)} = T_{process(i)} + T_{propagation(i,j)} + T_{queue(i)} \tag{2}$$

The processing delay $T_{process(i)}$ between any two nodes is determined by specific hardware platform. When the hardware platform is determined, its value can be assumed fixed [14].

The propagation delay between node i and node j is formulated as

$$T_{propagation(i,j)} = \frac{d_{i,j}}{c} \tag{3}$$

$d_{i,j}$ is the distance between two adjacent nodes, and c represents the light speed.

The queuing delay $T_{queue(i)}$ depends on the specific traffic demand and node processing capability and is not considered in this paper. Therefore the total delay between two adjacent nodes is corrected to

$$T_{total(i,j)} = T_{process(i)} + T_{propagation(i,j)} \tag{4}$$

Capacity Model. Capacity is defined as bandwidth or throughput between any two nodes. And the capacity is divided into two categories. One is generated by the all ISLs. The capacity of ISL is identified as identical. The other one is from all the satellite-ground links (SGLs) which is from satellite to source or sink node. The link relationship between the satellite and the source or sink node is determined by the current coverage of satellite. The capacity of SGLs is regarded as infinite.

3 The Algorithm

3.1 Constructing the Topology Within a Satellite Snapshot

Using the virtual topology method, we divide the satellite period into K static snapshots. The performance evaluation algorithm is applicable for each snapshot. In each snapshot, we use the properties of LEO satellite to build network topology with capacity and cost. Besides, we add two virtual nodes as source and destination. Then, we calculate the visibility and distance between any two satellites, obtain the adjacency matrix and delay matrix, and combine them into capacity and delay expansion graph $G = \{V, E, Cap, Cost\}$, where V is vertex set, E is edge set, Cap is the capacity set of all edges in E, and $Cost$ is the delay set of all edges in E. Next, we describe the algorithm that generates the graph.

Algorithm 1. MDMC Graph Construction

1: **Input:** Satellite snapshot parameter *S*= <*N, M, h, inc, F, LatPLR*>
2: **Output:** Network topology with capacity and cost $G = \{V, E, Cap, Cost\}$
3: Construct the adjacency matrix *ISL* (*u, v*) and delay matrix *PLinkDelay*(*e*)
4: **repeat**
5: Initialize $i = 1$
6: **repeat**
7: Initialize $j = 1$
8: **if** (*i, j*) are not in polar region and not in seam
9: *ISL* (*u, v*) = 1
10: **end**
11: **until** $j = M$
12: **until** $i = N$
13: **repeat**
14: Initialize $i = 1$
15: Calculate the inter ISLs *PLinkDelay*(*i*)
16: **until** $i = M$
17: Calculate the intra ISLs *VLinkDelay*
18: **repeat**
19: Initialize $i = 1$
20: **repeat**
21: Initialize $j = i$
22: **if** *ISL*(*i, j*) = 1
23: Set $G(V_u) = i$, $G(V_v) = j$, calculate the capacity $G(Cap_{(u,v)})$
24: **if** $i = j$-1
25: $G(Cap_{(u,v)})$= *VLinkDelay*
26: **else**
27: $G(Cost_{(u,v)})$ = *PLinkDelay*(*i*)
28: **end**
29: **end**
30: **until** $j = M$
31: **until** $i = N$
32: Add virtual source node $v_{N \times M+1}$ and sink node $v_{N \times M+2}$
33: Extend $G = \{V, E, Cap, Cost\}$ to a digraph

3.2 MDMC Algorithm

The MDMC based on MCMF aims to calculate the minimum delay and the maximum capacity from source node to sink node. In a flow digraph, each edge has two attributes, the maximum capacity and the cost of per unit flow. The goal of the algorithm is to find a path from the origin to the destination, which minimize the cost under the condition of maximum flow. For example, in Fig. 4, the path with the minimum cost and maximum flow can be found by using MCMF.

The total minimum cost *minC* is formulated as

$$minC = min\sum\nolimits_{(u,v)\in E}\left[c(u,v) \times f(u,v)\right] \tag{5}$$

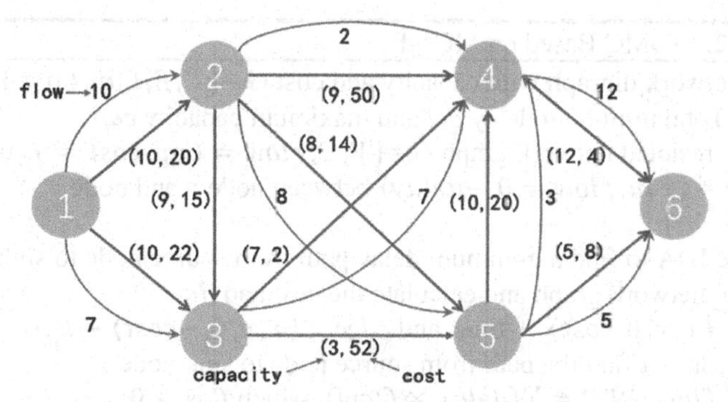

Fig. 4. An example of the flow network graph. The source is node 1 and the destination is node 6. The solution of the MCMF problem is highlighted by red arcs.

$c(u, v)$ is the cost of per unit of flow between two adjacent nodes, $f(u, v)$ represents the actual flow between two nodes, it must be less than the capacity, and $minC$ is the minimum total cost from source to destination. In MDMC, $c(u, v)$ is the delay between two adjacent satellites, $f(u, v)$ represents the throughput between two satellites, it must be less than or equal to the bandwidth, and $minC$ is the minimum Bandwidth-Delay Product (BDP) which is the minimum number of bits with maximum throughput from source to destination. Then the minimum delay $minD$ is given by

$$minD = \frac{BDP}{maximum\ Capacity} \tag{6}$$

maximum Capacity is the maximum throughput from source node to sink node in MDMC.

There are two main methods to solve MCMF. The one finds the path of minimum cost firstly, and then increases to maximum flow on the path. The other one finds the path of maximum flow firstly, then uses the negative circuit to cut the cost to minimum. In this paper, we use the first method.

For a given digraph with delay and capacity. Firstly, we construct a residual network by adding one inverted edge to every edge (see Algorithm 2). Next we use the Improved Dijkstra Algorithm (IDA) to find the minimum delay paths from source node to sink node in the residual network [15]. Then we calculate the flow in this path, we add flow to positive edge and subtract flow from inverted edge. Continuing operating the above steps until there is no path from source node to sink node. After that, we get maximum throughput and the minimum BDP. Finally, we use formula (6) to get the minimum delay. Certainly, the more capacity and the less delay means better performance for a given satellite network.

Algorithm 2. MDMC Based on MCMF

1: **Input:** Network digraph with capacity and cost $G = \{V, E, Cap, Cost\}$
2: **Output:** Total minimum delay *del* and maximum capacity *cap*
3: Construct residual network graph $G = \{V, E, flow = Cap, cost = Cost\}$, add the new $edge = \langle v, u, flow = 0, -delay \rangle$ between node u and node v
4: **repeat**
5: Use the IDA to find a minimum delay path from source node to sink node in residual network graph and calculate the *cost* and *flow*
6: $edge = \langle u, v, 0, cost \rangle + flow$, and $edge = \langle v, u, 0, -cost \rangle - flow$
7: **until** we can not find the path from source node to sink node
8: $cap = \sum flow$, $BDP = \sum(delay \times flow)$, which $flow > 0$
9: Output cap, $del = BDP/cap$

3.3 Time Complexity

When calculating the performance of giant constellations, algorithm with high time complexity will lead to a rapid increase in running time. Therefore, in this paper, a cost flow algorithm based on Dijkstra shortest path algorithm is modified to obtain an algorithm with low time complexity. The total time complexity of this algorithm mainly contains two parts. One is the construction of MDMC graph, the other one is MDMC. The first part is $O(M \cdot N)$. In a MDMC graph, the number of edges is a maximum of $2(N-1)M$ and the number of satellites is N. The most of the time for MDMC is spent finding shortest path by IDA. When we denote by C the maximum capacity of all edges, the number of executions of the IDA is $O(E \cdot log(C))$. And the complexity of IDA is $O(E \cdot log(E))$ by using Fibonacci Heap. Therefore, the total complexity is $O(E(E + NlogN)logC)$ [15].

4 Simulations and Discussion

In this section, we design three simulation cases. Each case studies one or multiple Walker Star Constellations. For anyone of these constellations, it consists N orbit planes, and each of plane is with M satellites. The orbit inclination (inc) of each plane is 90°. The range of the phase factor(F) is from 0 to 6. And the orbit altitude(h) is set from 800 km to 1500 km. The latitude of the polar region ($LatPLR$) is set as 70°. Finally, the capacity of each ISL is set as 100 Mbps and UDL is set as unlimited.

In the first scenario, we design and test two groups of constellation experiments. The first group of experiment contains 7 constellations, of which the number of orbit planes is set as 6, while the number of satellites of each plane is increased from 12 to 24 with 2 satellites of interval. The second group of experiment also compares 7 constellations, of which the number of satellites in each plane is set as 12, while the number of orbit planes is from 6 to 12. Other parameters are the same in both two groups.

In Fig. 5, we calculate the capacity and delay of each constellation by MDMC. From the two sets of results. As the total number of satellites increases, the capacity of both two groups of constellations also increase, but the delay of the most of constellation

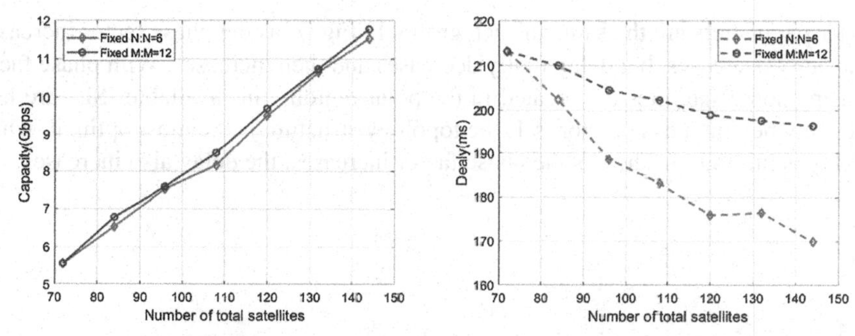

Fig. 5. The capacity and delay of the fixed number of orbit plane (FNOP) and the fixed number of satellites of each plane (FNSP).

decrease. Then we compare two sets of the results. When the total number of satellites is the same, the capacity of FNSP is higher than FNOP. However, the difference between delays is much greater than the difference between capacities. It can be explained as follows: As the total number of satellites increases, the number of ISLs is increasing, which lead to an increase in capacity and hop count. Especially the delay performance of FNOP is better than FNSP, because ISLs of FNOP is less affected by polar regions when the total satellites increase and can get better paths. In conclusion, as the total number of satellites increases, it is better to increase the number of satellites in the same orbit than to increase the number of orbits.

In the second scenario, we analyze the effect of orbit altitude on the performance of satellite network. The orbit altitude is divided into 8 groups from 800 km to 1500 km with 100 km interval. Other parameters are the same in each group. In Fig. 6, as the height increases, the capacity has little change, but the delay increases which results in degradation of the network performance. This result can be explained as follow: with the increase of orbit height, the topology of ISLs is unchanged, however the increase in distance of two adjacent satellites results in the increase of delay.

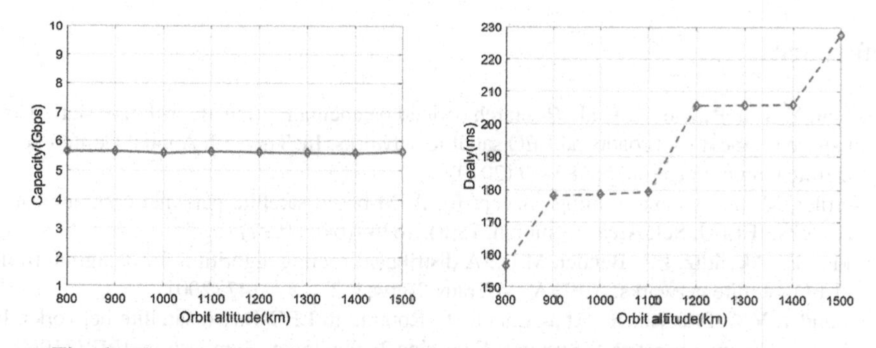

Fig. 6. The capacity and delay of constellations with the different orbit altitudes.

In the third scenario, we analyze the effect of phase factor on the performance of satellite network. According to formula (1), we set 6 groups of phase factor from 0 to

5. Other parameters are the same in each group. In Fig. 7, as the phase factor increases, the capacity decreases, but delay firstly decreases and then increases. With phase factor increasing some satellites are located in the polar region, thus available ISLs are less. However, when the phase factor is 1, the topology structure is the most optimal, which the delay is minimum. Then as the phase factor increases, the delay also increases.

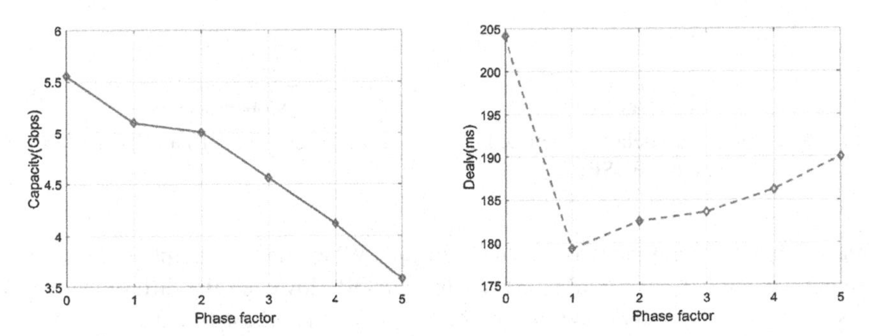

Fig. 7. The capacity and delay of constellations with the different phase factor.

5 Conclusion

This paper proposes an efficient algorithm MDMC for evaluating the performance of LEO satellite networks. Firstly, we build a fixed satellite topology. Then capacity and delay model are added into ISLs. Next, we use MDMC to evaluate network performance by calculating the minimum delay and maximum capacity. Finally, three different cases are set to study the difference of performance of constellation network. From the results, MCMD is appropriate to evaluate and compare the performance of LEO satellite networks.

References

1. Zhou, Y., Liu, P., Xie, Z., et al.: Research on load balancing routing algorithm in station area of space segment for broadband LEO satellite networks. In: The 15th Annual Conference of Satellite Communication, pp. 87–99 (2019)
2. Werner, M.: A dynamic routing concept for ATM-based satellite personal communication networks. IEEE J. Sel. Areas Commun. **15**(8), 1636–1648 (1997)
3. Ekici, E., Akyildiz, I.F., Bender, M.D.: A distributed routing algorithm for datagram traffic in LEO satellite networks. IEEE/ACM Trans. Netw. **9**(2), 137–147 (2001)
4. Gounder, V.V., Prakash, R., Abu-Amara, H.: Routing in LEO-Based satellite networks. In: Wireless Communications & Systems, Emerging Technologies Symposium. IEEE (1999)
5. Li, B., Zhang, C., Fu, Q.: Emulation of space communications system and research on QoS performance measurement. J. Grad. Sch. Chin. Acad. Sci. **25**(4), 530 (2008)
6. Chang, H.S., et al.: FSA-based link assignment and routing in low-earth orbit satellite networks. IEEE Trans. Veh. Technol. **47**(3), 1037–1048 (2016)

7. Li, W., Zhang, S., Shen, J.: research on asymmetric routing protocol for LEO satellite of space-based information network. Spacecraft Eng. **25**(1), 73–76 (2016)
8. Li, Y.: Research on the Structural Analysis and Performance Evaluation of the Integrated Space-Ground Network, Master, Xidian University (2018)
9. Liu, Q., Liu, N., Shi, H.: Location-based multi-service routing algorithm for LEO satellite networks. Comput. Simul. **32**(9), 95–98 (2015)
10. Liu, W., Liu, L., Tao, Y., et al.: Research on capacity and throughput of backhaul traffic in LEO satellite networks. Mob. Commun. **43**(7), 55–62 (2019)
11. Yang, X., Li, J.: Inter-satellite links analysis of walker constellation. J. Geodesy Geodyn. **32**(2), 143–147 (2012)
12. Li, N., Zong, P.: Opnet based simulation and optimization of routing protocols in LEO satellite networks. J. Spacecraft TT&C Technol. **32**(5), 408–413 (2013)
13. Zhou, D., Sheng, M., Wang, X., et al.: Mission aware contact plan design in resource limited small satellite networks. IEEE Trans. Commun. **65**(99), 2451–2466 (2017)
14. Tan, H., Zhu, L., Li, X., et al.: Routing optimization of low earth orbit satellite communication network. Comput. Simul. **32**(9), 80–85 (2015)
15. Plotkin, S.: Capacity scaling approach to the minimum cost circulation problem. https://web.stanford.edu/class/cs361b/files/cs361b-notes.pdf. Accessed 8 Aug 2020

A Practical Joint Coding-Modulation Mode and Frequency-Time Resource Allocation Approach in MF-TDMA Satellite Communication Systems

Heng Wang, Shijun Xie, Ganhua Ye(✉), Bin Zhou, and Yonggang Wang

The 63rd Research Institute, National University of Defense Technology, Nanjing, China
milsatcom@163.com

Abstract. In general, the problem of the resource management in the MF-TDMA satellite communication system can be divided into two phases: a timeslot calculation phase for each connection request and a timeslot allocation phase in the frame structure. In this paper, we propose algorithms to solve this two-phases problem. In the former phase, we first allocate each connection request on an appropriate carrier based on the traffic demand of each connection request, and next dynamically adjust the coding and modulation mode of each connection request, according to the channel condition and state of the system resource usage. Then we calculate the number of timeslots required to be assigned to each connection request. In the latter phase, we propose an algorithm called Best Fit (BF)-modified to allocate the timeslots in the MF-TDMA frame structure. Simulation results show that although the total traffic demands generated by all the connection requests are various, the timeslot is sufficiently utilized due to the dynamical adjustment of the coding and modulation mode. Moreover, the performance of the proposed (BF)-modified algorithm is better than that of the existing algorithm.

Keywords: MF-TDMA satellite communication system · Resource management · Dynamic coding and modulation adjustment · BF-modified algorithm

1 Introduction

The multi-frequency time division multiple access (MF-TDMA) technique is an efficient multiple access technique, since it has the most desirable feature of both the FDMA and TDMA technique [1]. Thus the technique has been employed in many satellite systems, such as EHF-SATCOM, IP-Star, DVB-RCS system and so on.

Figure 1 shows the configuration of the MF-TDMA satellite communication system. There are several terminals and one Network Control Center (NCC) in the system, and each terminal provides service to multiple connections, such as telephone, fax, IP data and so on. In this paper, the transponder in the satellite is assumed to be transparent.

Q. Wu et al. (Eds.): WiSATS 2020, LNICST 358, pp. 282–296, 2021.
https://doi.org/10.1007/978-3-030-69072-4_24

Thus MF-TDMA is employed as the access method for both the uplink and downlink. In addition, the terminal in the system supports multiple coding and modulation modes. In every frame, the terminals send connection requests to the NCC via the satellite, and then the NCC generates terminal burst time plan (TBTP) table and sends it to terminals. Upon receiving the TBTP table, each terminal reads the TBTP table to know what timeslots are assigned.

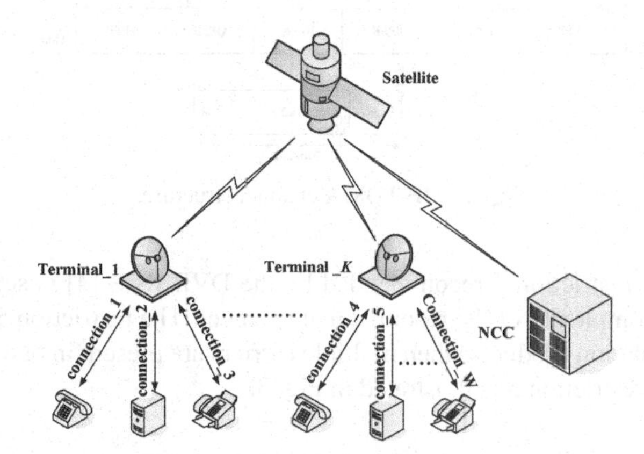

Fig. 1. Configuration of the MF-TDMA satellite system.

Figure 2 shows the frame structure of the MF-TDMA satellite communication systems. The frame is divided into carriers in term of the frequency, and each carrier is divided into timeslots in term of the time. Each timeslot consists of header, traffic and tail. The header consists of several symbols, which are used for bit synchronization. The tail is a period of free time, which is used for timeslot protection. The traffic is the time in which the terminal sends information. The length of each timeslot in different carrier is same or different, and different timeslots can adopt different coding and modulation modes. Thus it is flexible for us to manage the resource. However, it is the flexibility that introduces great difficulty to find the optimal solution for the resource management. To this end, in this paper we aim to find a considerable feasible solution to the problem.

In the practical MF-TDMA satellite communication system, the manager allocates each connection request in the appropriate carrier and timeslot, satisfying some basic restrictions given as follows [2, 3]:

1. A single terminal cannot be assigned more than the total timeslots in a carrier (It is supposed that only one transmitting and receiving system in each terminal).
2. A slot can't be assigned to multi-users.
3. The set of timeslots used by a terminal must be in the same carrier.
4. The set of timeslots used by a terminal to support a given single connection must be contiguous in one carrier.
5. A terminal can't use timeslots in different carriers that overlap in time.

The restriction 1 and 2 are easy to understand. The restriction 3 is imposed to simplify transmitting in the terminal, when the terminal can't hop from one carrier to another

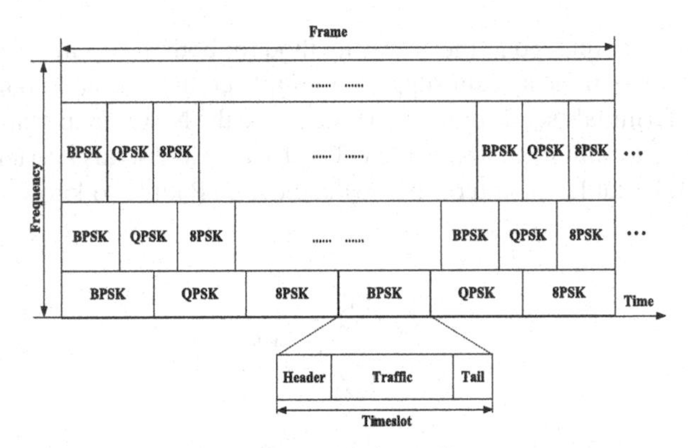

Fig. 2. MF-TDMA channel structure.

carrier fast. The restriction 4 recommended by the DVB-RCS [4] is set to reduce the computational complexity of the resource management. The restriction 5 is imposed to avoid intermodulation products when multiple carriers are present in one terminal at the same time. The restriction 5 is illustrated in Fig. 3.

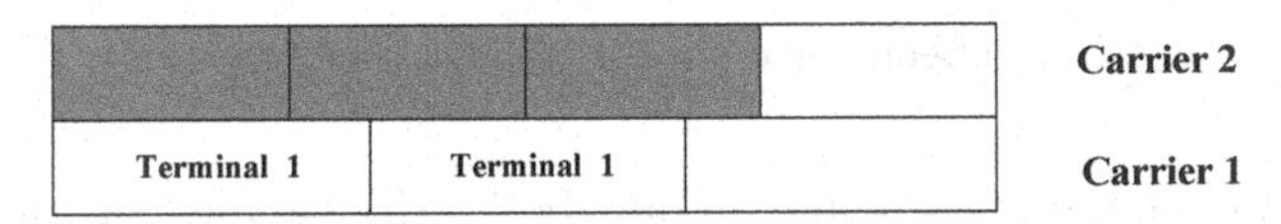

Fig. 3. An example of restriction 5.

As shown in Fig. 3, one connection from terminal 1 has occupied two timeslots in carrier 1, due to the restriction 5, the shadow timeslots in the carrier 2 can't be allocated to other connections from terminal 1, and only the white timeslots can be allocated to them.

Resource management in the MF-TDMA satellite communication system can be divided into two phases: a timeslot calculation phase and a timeslot allocation phase. The former phase calculates the minimum number of timeslots required to provide the desired level of bit error rate (BER) and data rate. The latter phase allocates the actual timeslots in the MF-TDMA frame structure. In the timeslot calculation phase, timeslots required to be assigned to each connection is determined by the modulation and coding mode and carrier symbol rate. In the existing studies [2] and [5], the modulation and coding mode of each connection request is only determined by the channel condition, regardless of state of the system resource usage. Motivated by the cross-layer design [6], we propose an algorithm which dynamically adjusts the modulation and coding mode according to the channel condition of each connection request and state of the system resource usage, taking into account the compromise between the system capacity and the terminal transmitting power. The proposed algorithm guarantees that the timeslot is sufficiently utilized, although the total traffic demands generated by all the connection requests are various. In addition, in the previous literature [2] and [3], the symbol rate of each carrier is assumed to be same. However, the assumption causes some problems.

When there are multiple connection requests from one terminal and the traffic demand of one connection request is high, the connection request will occupy many timeslots in one carrier. As a result, it is difficult to allocate timeslots in another carrier to the rest connection requests from the same terminal, due to the restriction 5. When the traffic demand of one connection request is low, it can't use one timeslot sufficiently and causes waste of the resource. To overcome the drawback mentioned above, in the MF-TDMA satellite communication system we studied in this paper, the symbol rate of each carrier is set to be various. Thus we encounter a new problem that how to choose an appropriate carrier for each connection request. We propose an algorithm to solve this problem.

As the carrier symbol rate and coding and modulation mode are given for each connection request, the timeslots number assigned to it is calculated. Then the next phase of resource management is allocating the timeslots in the frame structure. In [2], an algorithm called Reserve Channel with Priority (RCP)-Fit was proposed. To further improve the performance of RCP-Fit algorithm, the works in [3] proposed an algorithm called RCP-A. The effort of both the RCP-Fit and RCP-A algorithm is to get rid of impact of the restriction 3. However, as the development of the hardware, the restriction 3 can be ignored in the practical system. Thus advantage of the RCP-Fit and RCP-A algorithm is not obvious. To this end, the works in [7] proposed the Convergent Sequential-Fit (CSF) algorithm to reduce the computational complexity. In this paper, we also ignore the restriction 3, and propose a heuristic algorithm called Best Fit (BF)-modified algorithm, which outperforms the CSF algorithm.

The remainder of this paper is organized as follows. Resource management is formulated in the Section 2. The timeslot calculation and timeslot allocation phases are described in Section 3 and Section 4, respectively. Simulation results are provided in the Section 5. Finally, Section 6 concludes the paper.

2 Mathematical Formulation of the Resource Management in the MF-TDMA Satellite System

It is assumed that the MF-TDMA satellite communication system consists of K terminals X_i, $i \in \{1, 2,\ldots, K\}$, and W connections C_i, $i \in \{1, 2,\ldots, W\}$. The set of connections which are served by the terminal X_i is denoted by $\mathcal{N}_i$, and the terminal X_i supports V_i kinds of the coding and modulation mode. The frame consists of N carriers F_i, $i \in \{1, 2,\ldots, N\}$. The symbol rate and timeslot length of the i-th carrier are S_i and L_i, respectively. The length of the timeslot header and tail in the i-th carrier are Hi and T_i, respectively. The length of the frame is T_{frame}. Thus the timeslot number of the i-th carrier Y_i is $\lfloor T_{frame}/L_i \rfloor$, $i \in \{1, 2,\ldots, N\}$.

The traffic demand of the connection C_i is D_i. The coding and modulation mode assigned to the connection C_i is m_i. The bandwidth efficiency of the coding and modulation mode m_i is η_i. For the given bit error rate in the system, the corresponding threshold signal-to-noise ratio (SNR) per bit of the coding and modulation mode m_{ij} is $\left(E_b/n_0\right)^i_{th}$. If the connection C_i is assigned on the n-th carrier, it is denoted that $w^i_n = 1$. Otherwise, $w^i_n = 0$. Thus the number of timeslots required to be assigned to the connection C_i on the n-th carrier is calculated as follow:

$$a_n^i = \begin{cases} \left\lceil \frac{D_i \cdot T_{frame}}{\lfloor (L_n - H_n/S_n - T_n) \cdot S_n \cdot \eta_i \rfloor} \right\rceil, & w_n^i = 1 \\ 0 & w_n^i = 0 \end{cases} \tag{1}$$

Let b_n^i denotes the start timeslot allocated to the connection C_i on the n-th carrier, $1 \le b_n^i \le Y_n$. Since the timeslots used to support one connection must be contiguous in one carrier, the end timeslot allocated to the connection $e_n^i = b_n^i + a_n^i$. As a result, the start time p_i and the end time q_i of the duration for the connection C_i transmitting information are obtained as follows:

$$p_i = \left(b_n^i - 1\right)L_n \tag{2}$$

$$q_i = \left(e_n^i - 1\right)L_n \tag{3}$$

As mentioned above, there is no restriction 3 in the system we study here. Thus according to the system restrictions, we formulate the problem of the resource management in the MF-TDMA satellite communication system as follows:

$$\max_{w_n^i, m_i, b_n^i} \sum_{n=1}^{N} \sum_{i=1}^{W} w_n^i \tag{4}$$

$s.t.$

$$\sum_{n=1}^{N} \sum_{i=1}^{W} a_n^i \le Y_n \tag{5}$$

$$\sum_{n=1}^{N} w_n^i \le 1, \; \forall i \in \{1, \ldots, W\}, w_n^i = 0 \, or \, 1 \tag{6}$$

$$p_j \ge q_k \, or \, q_j \le p_k, \; \forall j, k \in \mathcal{N}_i, \; j \ne k \tag{7}$$

The function (4) represents that the objective of optimization problem is maximization of the number of connections which are accessed to the system simultaneously. The conditions (5), (6) and (7) imply the restriction 1, restriction 4, and restriction 5, respectively.

It is noted that the optimization problem is nonlinear integer programming with constrains, which is NP-hard. NP-hard problems mean that the problem cannot be solved in in polynomial time. Thus we require a prohibitive amount of computation to obtain an optimal solution requires [8]. However, in the practical MF-TDMA satellite communication system, the NCC must deal with all the connection requests in the time of a frame. Therefore, it is impossible for the NCC to find optimal solution of the problem. To this end, in this paper we propose an approach to obtain a considerable solution. The approach is divided into two phases. In the former phase, we calculate the number of timeslots, which are required to be provided to each connection request. For the optimization problem, it is meant that we search a considerable value for w_n^i and m_i. In the latter phase, we allocate the timeslots in the frame structure. It is meant that we assign a value to b_n^i.

3 Phase I: Timeslot Calculation

It is seen from (1) that the number of the timeslots assigned to each connection request is determined by the carrier symbol rate and coding and modulation mode assigned to it. Here we decomposed the problem of timeslot calculation into two sub-problems: carrier assignment and coding and modulation mode assignment. Both of the two sub-problems are solved in finite time according to the proposed algorithm.

3.1 Sub-problem One: Carrier Assignment

In the time of a frame, the NCC will receive many connection requests from different terminals. The traffic demands of the connection requests are various. To this end, we propose an algorithm to assign each connection request to the different carriers according to its traffic demand. Let $\mathcal{F}$ denotes the set of the carrier, $\mathcal{F} = \{F_1, F_2, \ldots, F_N\}$. S_{total} denotes the sum of the carrier symbol rates. $\mathcal{C}$ denotes the set of traffic demand of the request connection, $\mathcal{C} = \{\mathrm{C}_1, \mathrm{C}_2, \ldots, \mathrm{C}_\mathrm{W}\}$. $\mathrm{D}_{\mathrm{total}}$ denotes the sum of the traffic demand of the connection requests. Without loss of generality, it is assumed that the elements in the $\mathcal{F}$ and $\mathcal{C}$ are sorted in ascending order in term of the symbol rate and the traffic demand, respectively. The algorithm is described as the following steps:

Step 1: Began with the first carrier in $\mathcal{F}$ and the first connection request in $\mathcal{C}$, T connection requests are assigned to the first carrier, the sum of traffic demand of the T connection requests is $\sum_{i=1}^{T} D_i \leq D_{total} S_1 \Big/ S_{total} \leq \sum_{i=1}^{T+1} D_i$.

Step 2: Update the set of $\mathcal{F}$ and $\mathcal{C}$, $\mathcal{F} \leftarrow \mathcal{F}\text{-}\{F_1\}$, $\mathcal{C} \leftarrow \mathcal{C}\text{-}\{C_1, C_2, \ldots, C_T\}$. If all the connection requests have been assigned to the carriers, then terminate the algorithm. Otherwise, jump to step 1.

According to the above algorithm, the connection request with high traffic demand will be assigned on the high symbol rate carrier, thus the period for the connection transmitting data, which is calculated according to (1)-(3), will be smaller. Therefore, the adverse effect of the restriction 5 on other connection requests from the same terminal will be reduced.

3.2 Sub-problem Two: Coding and Modulation Assignment

Now the modern terminal supports multiple coding and modulation modes. According to 0, a flexible coding and modulation mode assignment to the connection C_i must satisfy the link budget equation given as follows:

$$[M^i] = [\left(\frac{C}{T}\right)^i] - [\left(\frac{C}{T}\right)^i_{th}] \geq \mathrm{CONSTANT} \tag{8}$$

$$\left(\frac{C}{T}\right)^i_{th} = \left(\frac{E_b}{n_0}\right)^i_{th} \cdot D_i \cdot k \tag{9}$$

where.

$[x] = 10\log(x)$,

M^i: link margin of the connection, which must be larger than a certain constant to guarantee the quality of the connection,

k: Boltzmann constant,

$(C/T)^i$: carrier-to-noise ratio of the total link, which is calculated as the following equations:

$$\left\{(C/T)^i\right\}^{-1} = \left\{(C/T)^i_{up}\right\}^{-1} + \left\{(C/T)^i_{down}\right\}^{-1} \tag{10}$$

$$\left(\frac{C}{T}\right)^i_{up} = \frac{EIRP^i_{ET}}{L^i_U} \cdot \left(\frac{G}{T}\right)_S \tag{11}$$

$$\left(\frac{C}{T}\right)^i_{down} = \frac{EIRP^i_S}{L^i_D} \cdot \left(\frac{G}{T}\right)^i_{ER} = \frac{EIRP^i_{ET}G_S}{L^i_U L^i_D} \cdot \left(\frac{G}{T}\right)^i_{ER} \tag{12}$$

where.

$(C/T)^i_{up}$: carrier-to-noise ratio of the uplink,

$(C/T)^i_{down}$: carrier-to-noise ratio of the downlink,

$EIRP^i_{ET}$: transmitting *EIRP* of the source terminal,

L^i_U: loss of the uplink, which consists of the rain loss, free space loss and other losses,

$(G/T)_S$: G/T value of the satellite receive system,

$EIRP^i_S$: the transmitting *EIRP* of the satellite,

G_S: gain of the satellite,

L^i_D: loss of the downlink,

$(G/T)^i_{ER}$: G/T value of the destination terminal.

Generally speaking, the bandwidth efficiency of the coding and modulation mode is higher, the power efficiency is lower. When the connection request adopts a higher order coding and modulation mode, the number of the timeslot assigned to the request is smaller, it is easy for the NCC to allocate the timeslots to the request. However, the transmitting power of terminal is higher. On the contrary, when the connection request adopts a lower order coding and modulation mode, the requirement of the transmitting power is lower. However, it is difficult for the NCC to assign enough timeslots for the request. To this end, we propose an algorithm to dynamically assign the coding and modulation mode to each connection request, taking into account a compromise between the system capacity and terminal transmitting power. The flowchart of the algorithm is described in Fig. 4.

The proposed algorithm dynamically assigns coding and modulation mode to the connection requests which have been assigned on the same carrier. At the beginning of the proposed algorithm, each connection request is assigned to the lowest order coding and modulation mode in order to save the transmitting power of the terminal. If the sum of timeslot assigned to the all the connection request is bigger than the total timeslots of the carrier, then the connection request with the biggest link margin is chosen to adopt the one order higher coding and modulation mode, which is most possible to support the higher coding and modulation mode. Therefore, the algorithm obtains a compromise between the transmitting power of each terminal and system capacity.

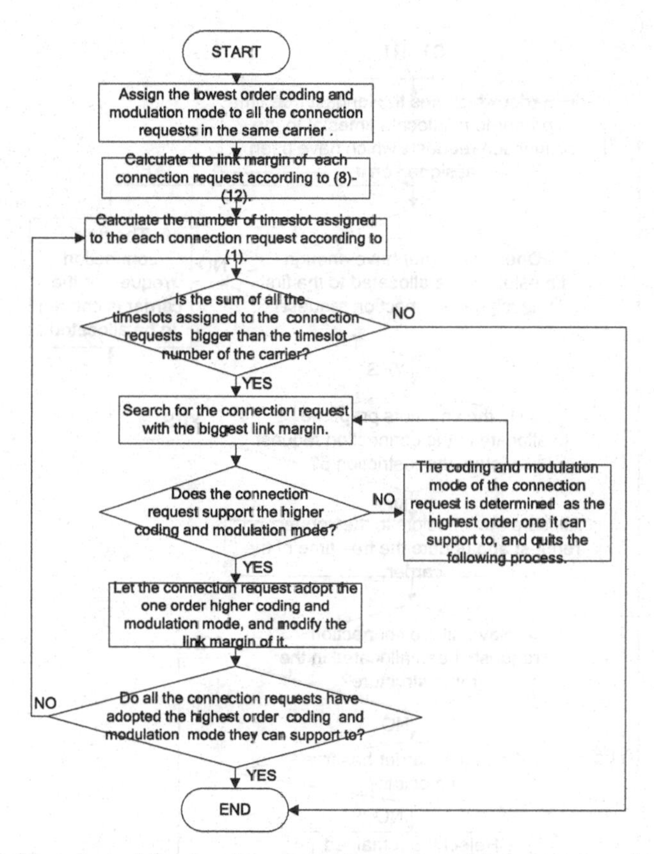

Fig. 4. Flowchart of the algorithm for coding and modulation mode assignment.

When the carrier and coding and modulation mode assigned to each connection are determined, the number of timeslots assigned to it is calculated according to (1). Then the next phase of resource management is allocating the assigned timeslots in the frame structure.

4 Phase II: Timeslot Allocation

In this section, we aim to solve the problem that how to allocate the calculated timeslots in the frame structure. The problem can be viewed as a variant of the bin-packing problem, which is NP-hard 2. As mentioned above, there is no restriction 3 in the system studied here. Thus the timeslot allocation problem is simpler than that of 2 and 3, and the advantage of the proposed RCP-Fit and RCP-A algorithm in above papers isn't obvious. To this end, we propose a heuristic algorithm called BF-modified algorithm, whose computational complexity is much lower than the algorithms mentioned in the above two papers. The process of the proposed algorithm is described as follows (Fig. 5).

In the algorithm, the carrier, which has the longest free time (free time means that the time hasn't been allocated to any connection request), is prepared to allocate timeslots

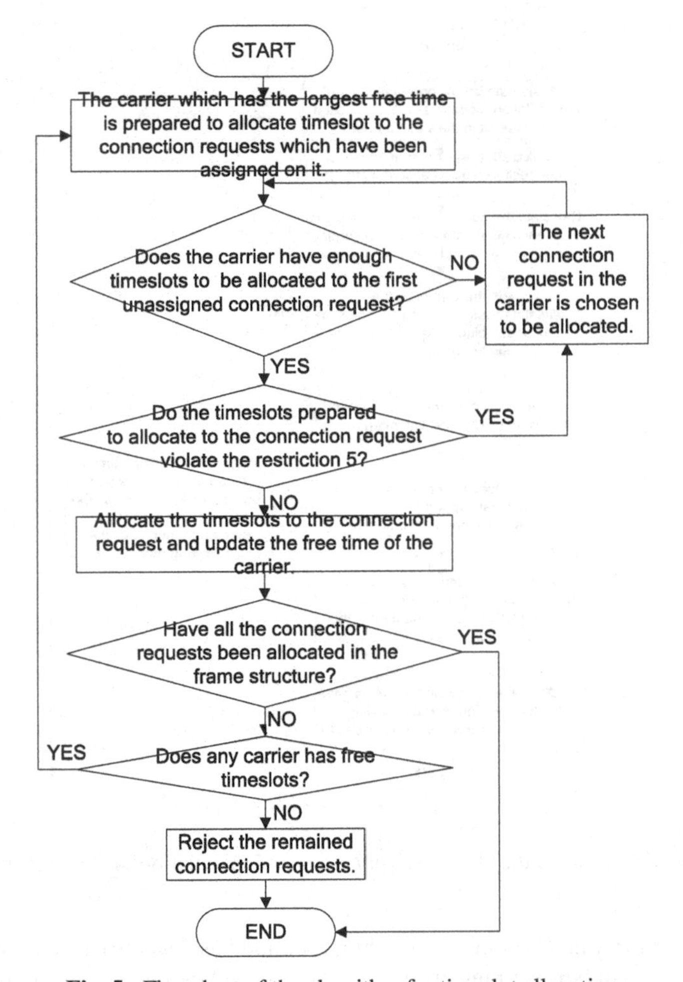

Fig. 5. Flowchart of the algorithm for timeslot allocation.

to the connection request. If there are no free timeslot or all the connection requests have been allocated in the frame structure, then the algorithm is terminated.

5 Simulation Results and Analysis

5.1 Simulation Parameter and Performance Measure

For the simulation, a MF-TDMA satellite communication system model is set up, the parameters of the system is given in Table 1.

The source and destination of each connection is randomly distributed among the twenty terminals. The traffic demand of the connection request is an exponential distribution with the mean value w.

To show the efficiency of the proposed approach, two measures are defined as follows:

Table 1. Parameters of the MF-TDMA system.

Frame length (ms)	110
Carrier number	4
Carrier symbol rate	64K, 2 × 64K, 4 × 64K,8 × 64K
Timeslot length in each carrier (ms)	10, 7, 5.5, 3
Timeslot header (symbol)	128
Timeslot tail (ms)	0.1
Terminal kind	6
Terminal number	20
Coding and modulation mode	BPSK (1/2),QPSK (1/2), QPSK (3/4),8PSK (3/4), 8PSK (7/8),16PSK (7/8)
Bit error rate	$e{-6}$
$(E_b/n_0)_{th}$(dB)	3,4.2,5.4,6.5,7.8,9.8
EIRP of each kind terminal (dBW)	76,68,64,60,48,43
G/T of each terminal (dB)	31,25,22,19,12.5,12

Traffic rejection ratio (**TRR**):

$$\sum_j D_j \Big/ \sum_{i=1}^{W} D_i, j \in \mathcal{R}$$

where $\mathcal{R}$ is the set of the rejected connection requests.
Timeslot utilization rate (**TUR**):

$$\sum_j A_j \Big/ \sum_{i=1}^{Z} A_i, j \in \mathcal{U}$$

where A_j is the number of symbol in the j-th timeslot, Z is total number of the timeslot, $\mathcal{U}$ is set of the used timeslots.

5.2 Efficiency of the Dynamical Adjustment of the Coding and Modulation Mode

In the phase of timeslot calculation, the coding and modulation mode of each connection is dynamically adjusted, depending on the total traffic demand generated by all the connection requests. The adjustment is clearly shown in the Fig. 6, where mode 1 and mode 6 represent the coding and modulation mode of BPSK(1/2) and 16PSK(7/8), respectively. It is seen that for the same number of the connection request, when the mean value of the traffic demand is larger, the occupation rate of mode 6 is higher. It means that when the traffic demand is higher, the bandwidth efficiency of coding and modulation

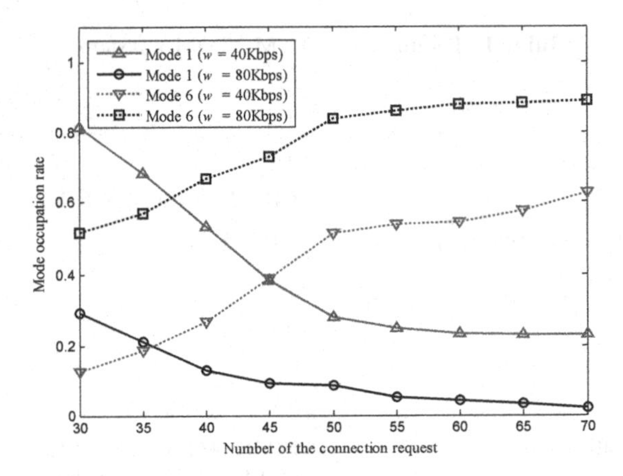

Fig. 6. Mode 1 and mode 6 occupation rate in term of the number the connection requests.

mode adopted by each connection request is higher. According to (1), the number of the timeslot assigned to each connection request is smaller, therefore, more connection requests are admitted to be accessed to the system. For the same reason, when the mean value of the traffic demand is same, the number of the connection requests is more, the bandwidth efficiency of coding and modulation mode adopted by each connection request is higher.

To show the advantage of the proposed dynamic adjustment of the coding and modulation mode, we compare it with the following two approaches:

1. Maximum Mode: All the connection requests adopt the maximum coding and modulation modes, which are calculated according to the link budget equation.
2. Minimum Mode: All the connection requests adopt the minimum coding and modulation.

For the simulations, the mean value of the traffic demand of each connection request is set to be 60 Kbps.

Figures 7, 8 and 9 show the comparison of the EIRP, timeslot utility rate and traffic rejection rate for the three approaches of the coding and modulation mode assignment, respectively. It is seen that when the traffic demands generated by all the connection requests are low, the approach of the maximum mode doesn't utilize the timeslot efficiently, causing a waste of the bandwidth and an unnecessary increase of the power. For example, when the number of the connection request is 30, the timeslot utility rate is only 47.13% and the total EIRP of the approach increases by 20.44%, compared with the approach of dynamic adjustment mode. On the contrary, the timeslot utility rate of the approach of the minimum mode is almost 100%, regardless of the total traffic demand. However, since the number of the timeslots which should to be assign to each connection request is high, the traffic rejection rate of the approach of minimum mode is the highest one among the three approaches. To overcome the drawbacks of the two approaches of the maximum and minimum mode, the approach of dynamic adjustment mode obtains a compromise between total transmitting power and the system capacity.

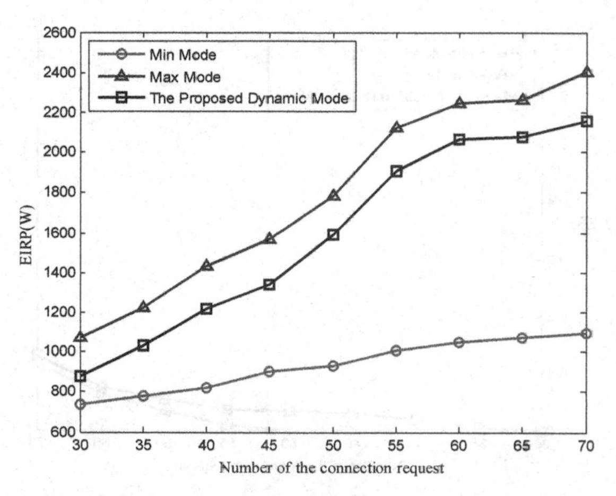

Fig. 7. Comparison of total EIRP of all the connection requests for the three approaches of the coding and modulation mode assignment.

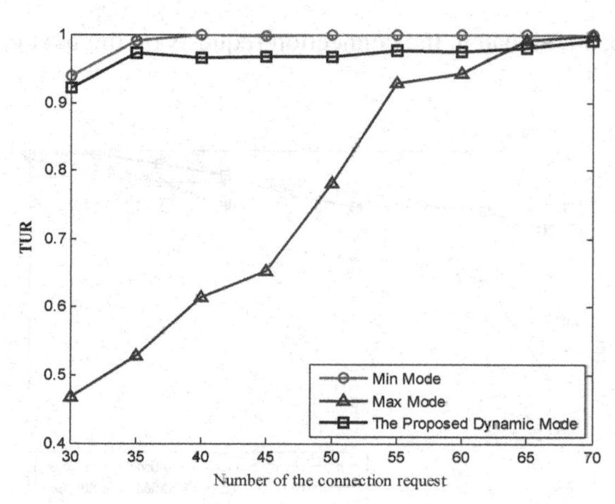

Fig. 8. Comparison of timeslot utility rate for the three approaches of the coding and modulation mode assignment.

It is noted that the total transmitting power of the approach is lower than that of the approach of maximum mode at the cost of traffic rejection rate slightly increases, and the traffic rejection rate of the approach is lower than that of the approach of minimum mode by the way of increasing the transmitting power.

5.3 Efficiency of the Proposed Timeslot Allocation Algorithm

To show the efficiency of the proposed BF-modified algorithm, we compare the proposed algorithm with the CSF algorithm proposed in 7. The CSF algorithm allocates the connection requests one carrier by on carrier. When all the connection requests on

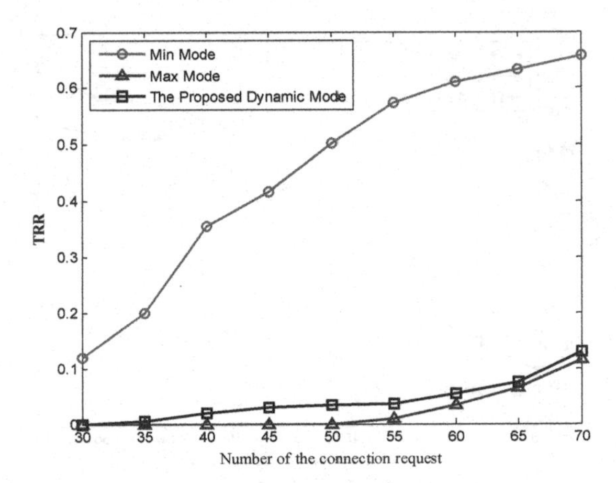

Fig. 9. Comparison of traffic rejection rate for the three approaches of the coding and modulation mode assignment.

one carrier have been allocated, the connection requests on the next carrier begin to be allocated.

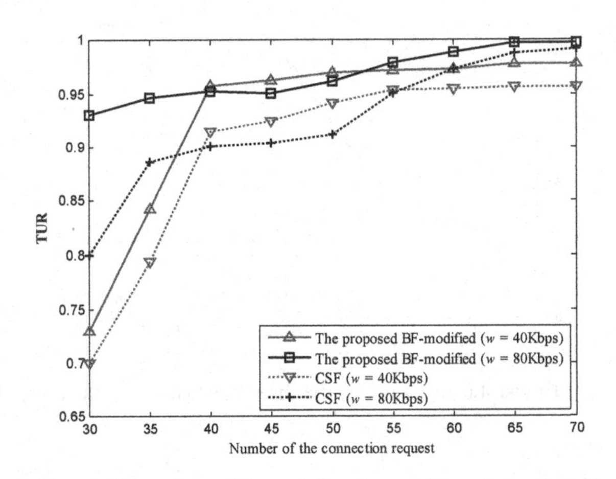

Fig. 10. Comparison of timeslot utility rate for the two timeslots allocation algorithms.

Figure 10 shows the timeslot utility rate (TUR) in term of the number of the connection request. It is seen that although total traffic demands generated by all the connection requests are various, the timeslot is sufficiently used due to the dynamical adjustment of the coding and modulation mode. In addition, the proposed BF-modified algorithm reduces the collision caused by the restriction 5, thus the TUR of the proposed algorithm is higher than that of the CF algorithm.

Figure 11 shows the traffic refused rate (TRR) in term of the number of the connection request. It is shown that the TRR of the proposed BF-modified algorithm is less than that of the CSF algorithm. For example, when the number of the connection requests is 55 and

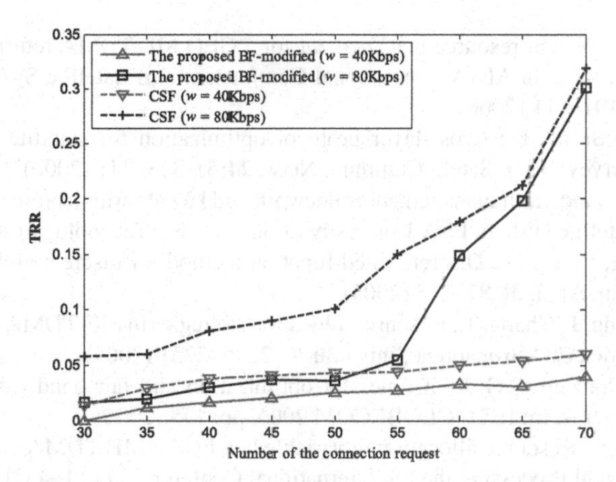

Fig. 11. Comparison of traffic refused rate for the two timeslots allocation algorithms.

the mean value of the traffic demand is 80 Kbps, the proposed BF-modified algorithm reduces the TRR by ten percent. Therefore, the proposed BF-modified algorithm supports more connection requests simultaneity, and it is more efficient than the CSF algorithm.

6 Conclusion

In this paper, we formulated the problem of the resource management in the MF-TDMA satellite communication system, and employed a practical approach to solve the NP-hard problem. The approach was divided into two phases: timeslot calculation and timeslot allocation. In the former phase, we proposed an algorithm to dynamically adjust the coding and modulation of each connection request according to the channel condition and state of the system resource usage. When the total traffic demand is high, a higher order modulation and coding mode is chosen for each connection request to admit more connection request. When the total traffic demand is low, a lower order modulation and coding mode is chosen for each connection request to save the transmitting power of each terminal. In the latter phase, we allocated the timeslots assigned to each connection request in the MF-TDMA frame structure, and we proposed an algorithm called BF-modified, which outperformed the existing CSF algorithm.

References

1. Dennis, R.: Satellite Communication. McGraw-Hill Education Co., New York (2001)
2. Park, J.M., Savagaonkar, U., Chong, E.K.P., et al.: Allocation of QoS connections in MF-TDMA satellite systems: a two-phase approach. IEEE Trans. Vehichular Technol. **54**(1), 177–190 (2005)
3. Dong, Q., Zhang, J., Zhang, T.: Channel management realization in MF-TDMA satellite systems. J. Electron. Inf. Technol. **31**(10), 2378–2384 (2009)
4. ETSI: Digital Video Broadcasting (DVB) Interaction channel for satellite distribution systems. EN 301 790 V1.5.1, France (2009)

5. Christian, K.: Efficient resource management for a GEO MF-TDMA return link with channel adaptation. In: 24th AIAA International Communications Satellite Systems Conference (ICSSC), pp. 101–111 (2006)
6. Giovanni, G., Sastri, K.: Cross-layer protocol optimization for satellite communications networks: a survey. Int. J. Satell. Commun. Netw. **24**(5), 323–341 (2006)
7. Shaodong, F.: Bandwidth management framework and key algorithms research in broadband multimedia satellite system, PLA University of Science and Technology (2011)
8. Ng, C., Zhang, L., Li, D.: Discrete filled function method for discrete global optimization. Comput. Optim. Appl. **31**, 87–115 (2005)
9. Dong, Q., Zhang, J., Zhang, T.: Resource allocation strategies in MF-TDMA satellite systems. Acta Aeronautica Et Astronautica Siniga **30**(9), 2245–2251 (2009)
10. Antoni, M., Gonzalo, S.G.:Joint time slot optimization and fair bandwidth allocation for DVB-RCS systems. In: IEEE GLOBECOM 2006, pp. 1–5 (2006)
11. Pan, X., Li, W.L: Resource allocation in variable bandwidth MF-TDMA satellite communications. In: Signal Processing the 8th International Conference, pp. 1–4 (2006)
12. Bejarano, J.M.R., Nieto, C.M., Piñar, F.J.R.: MF-TDMA scheduling algorithm for multi-spot beam satellite systems based on co-channel interference evaluation. IEEE Access **7**, 4391–4399 (2018)

Research on Intelligent Transmission of Space-Based Information

Tao Guan, Rong Lv(✉), Ganhua Ye, Wei Huang, Xin Ma, and Ruimin Lu

National University of Defense Technology, Nanjing, China
lvrong17@nudt.edu.cn

Abstract. Cognitive radio and artificial intelligence are hot research topics in the field of communication. This article discusses how to efficiently and reliably transmit space-based information from satellites to the ground. Related theories of cognitive radio and artificial intelligence are used to study the intelligent transmission of space-based information. This article also proposes ideas and strategies to improve the transmission efficiency and reliability of the satellite-earth data link. Several key issues including spectrum sensing and cognition, waveform reconstruction, the design of the intelligent decision engine, the massive data processing, spaceborne reconfigurable transmission platform, and signaling parameters synchronization were analyzed. The research results can provide help for real-time and reliable transmission of space-based information in the future.

Keywords: Space-based information · Cognitive radio · Intelligent data transmission · Communication system

1 Introduction

In this paper, the space-based information mainly refers to the data captured by satellite platforms (mainly by various sensors on the satellite). These kinds of information are mainly from the ground or the air targets, and stored in various forms (voice, text, image, etc.) for transmission to users. With the rapid development of space technologies [1], there are more and more satellites in the outer space, including the meteorological satellite, the remote sensing satellite, the imaging satellite, the communication satellite, the navigating satellite, etc. Furthermore, the future development of space-based information sensors will be accelerated in terms of resolution, transmission rate, and on-board processing capacity. As a result, the amount of the space-based data will increase exponentially. A large amount of space-based data needs to be transmitted from satellites to the ground, which brings high requirements for the capacity of the satellite-ground data transmission link.

The increase demand of the data transmission capacity will take up more frequency resources, but the frequency resources allocated by the ITU's Radio rules frequency division table are very limited. On the one hand, scheduled frequency resources limit the improvement of the satellite-ground data transmission capacity; on the other hand, the

Q. Wu et al. (Eds.): WiSATS 2020, LNICST 358, pp. 297–307, 2021.
https://doi.org/10.1007/978-3-030-69072-4_25

increasing number of satellites on orbit may also cause frequency interference to neighbor receivers. In such a complex electromagnetic environment, the wireless communication equipment is vulnerable to interference, including not only the natural interference and the man-made interference of docking receiver caused by overlapping frequency bands of nearby satellites, but also the malicious interference that may come from a hostile attacker. Therefore, the contradiction between the data-throughput demand of the space-based information and the transmission reliability of the satellite-ground data link becomes more and more serious. How to effectively avoid the interference spectrum, improve the reliability of the satellite-ground data link, and maximize the use of the limited and valuable frequency resources in a space-based system, need to be solved urgently.

According to the development of related techniques, there are three aspects deserves attention. First, in recent years, satellite communication technology has developed rapidly towards a direction of high throughput and high reliability. Through reuse of higher frequency band and multi-beam techniques, high-throughput communication satellites can make full use of frequency resources and significantly increase communication capacity [2]. Second, the software-defined satellite becomes a new developing trend. Through software-defined radio, software-defined payloads, software-defined data processing computers, software-defined networks and other means, different function modules of a satellite can be realized based on software. Then, a new satellite system with an open architecture is formed, which has re-definable function, reconfigurable software and reconfigurable hardware. Third, intelligent spectrum radio technology continues attracting attentions of the research field [3, 4]. In the literature, Haykin [5] defined the future intelligent radio as brain-empowered wireless communication. Then, related scholars carried out a lot of research, mainly focusing on understanding and prediction of the spectrum environment based on deep learning methods, intelligent decision-making of communication parameters based on spectrum situation, and dynamic spectrum access based on the deep reinforcement learning method (DRL) [6–8].

Based on deeply analyzing the aforementioned three aspects of related new technical trends, this paper studies an intelligent transmission strategy of space-based information. We propose a new idea to improve the efficiency and reliability of data transmission by combining the transmission subsystems of various types of satellites (e.g. the remote sensing satellite, the imaging satellite, the communication satellite, etc.) to form an integrated intelligent transmission system. In the rest of this paper, Sect. 2 analyzes the intelligent transmission strategy of space-based information. Section 3 discusses several critical issues for the design of an intelligent data transmission system. Conclusions are presented in Sect. 4.

2 Intelligent Transmission Strategy of Space-Based Information

Before we introduce the intelligent transmission strategy, we first review some basic methods to improve the capacity of the satellite-ground data link: 1) Expand the carrier frequency band. Raising the frequency band of the carrier can increase the transmission bandwidth, which is an effective way to improve the downlink data rate. For example, the available bandwidth of Ka band almost reaches 3GHz, and it has a great advantage over the lower X band. 2) Improve the communication waveform. Adopting higher-order modulation and demodulation types, more efficient coding and decoding schemes, is another effective way to improve the data rate between the satellite and the ground. Using high-order modulation (such as 8PSK, 16QAM) can achieve higher data rate in the same bandwidth. In addition, the variable code modulation schemes can also be used to improve the data link. 3) Increase the visibility time between the satellite and the ground. The data transmission time between the satellite and the ground can be prolonged by increasing the visibility time, which may indirectly improve the data transmission ability. On the one hand, this method can be realized by reasonably arranging the positions of the ground receiving stations in a larger area. On the other hand, the relay satellite can be used as a bridge between the satellite and ground receiving station.

The above basic methods have certain value for improving the transmission capacity of the satellite-ground data link. Each method has its own characteristics, but there are still some problems more or less. Raising the frequency band to the Ka band has the disadvantages of large transmission loss, easy to be affected by rain and snow, narrow beam width, and high requirements for acquisition and tracking of the ground equipments. Receiving high-order modulation signal requires higher signal-to-noise ratio and amplitude-frequency performance of the data link. Also, the structure of the receiving equipment may be more complex. If dealing with a static or slowly changing electromagnetic spectrum environment, these basic methods may work. Whereas, with the scarcity of frequency resources and increasing complexity of electromagnetic environment, only using fixed transmission modes is difficult to dynamically adjust with the changing environment. Their abilities to improve the transmission capacity of the satellite-ground data link are very limited. To solve this problem, a new transmission strategy is introduced as follows.

So far, the transmission subsystems of various types of space-based information systems are basically designed independently, and their transmission frequency bands are also divided in advance. Each system uses individual frequency band. In order to improve the overall transmission efficiency and reliability of the space-based information system, we could consider an overall design in such a way that the data transmission platform of each information system is designed in an unified scheme and the transmission frequency bands are planned as a whole to form a new integrated and intelligent transmission network to transmit the space-based information.

In order to achieve this goal, we need to design a data transmission system whose satellite-ground link has the ability of environmental perception and analysis, so that the data link has the ability of dynamic reconfiguration. In this manner, the onboard load is required to adjust the link transmission scheme corresponding to the interference environment. Cognitive radio techniques, which have the cognitive and reconstructive ability, can be employed. If the key techniques of the cognitive radio are introduced into the data transmission scheme, the system may have the ability of environmental perception, intelligent decision-making and link reconstruction, which will probably bring great benefits to the improvement of the satellite-ground data transmission ability in complex electromagnetic environment.

Cognitive radio was first proposed by Dr. Joseph Mitola in 1999 [4]. It is considered as a kind of radio that dynamically changes its parameters based on interactions with the external environment. Software radio is an ideal platform to realize it. Cognitive radio is an intelligent wireless communication system, which can use artificial intelligence techniques to learn from the radio environment. By changing the transmitting frequency, modulation and coding mode, transmission power and other working parameters, it can adapt to the change of wireless signal statistics, achieve highly reliable communication at any time and any place, and effectively use the spectrum resources [5, 9, 10].

Combining the cognitive radio with the space-based data transmission, and using theories and methods of artificial intelligence, the data transmission system will have the ability to learn, recognize and predict the spectrum environment, and then adaptively select the parameters and working methods to avoid interference spectrum more effectively. Such an intelligent data transmission technique may effectively improve the communication performance in a severe electromagnetic environment.

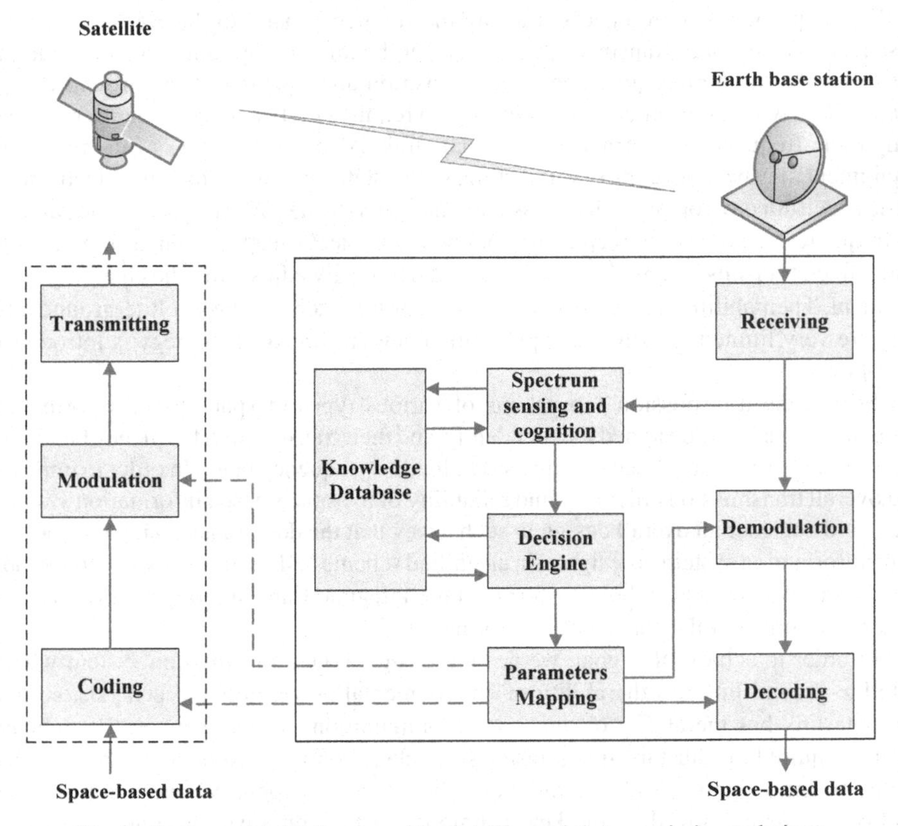

Fig. 1. Basic structural diagram of the intelligent data transmission technique.

Intelligent transmission of space-based information integrates the electromagnetic environment perception, the interference detection and identification, the dynamic spectrum allocation, the adaptive parameter configuration, and the intelligent decision engine into the conventional data transmission technique. A brief system structural diagram is shown in Fig. 1. Its working scheme can be summarized as follows. First, by establishing a cognitive model of the electromagnetic environment, the interference spectrum identification and the channel status identification can be realized at the ground receiving station. Second, it determines the optimal path of data transmission (using the path of the direct satellite-ground link or through a relay satellite) by analyzing the current type and amount of the data to be transmitted. Third, based on effective cases stored in the cognitive knowledge database, the intelligent decision engine dynamically determines the optimal transmission frequency bands using the reasoning and optimization methods in artificial intelligence, and adapts the transmission parameters (e.g. modulation type, coding scheme, transmission power, etc.) to reconstruct the transmission waveform. Finally, the communication parameters shall be updated synchronously with the satellite through some signaling parameters transmission channel, and then, the satellite carries out a new period of data communication based on its reconfigurable data transmission platform. The interference spectrum identification and the channel prediction module shall be optimized by continuously accumulating the spectrum sensing data and employing machine learning methods. Such an intelligent transmission technique will form an intelligent communication loop. On the one hand, it can avoid the interference spectrum. On the other hand, it can achieve the efficient use of available spectrum resources and achieve the efficient and reliable transmission of space-based information.

To realize the aforementioned intelligent data transmission system with reconfigurable parameters, it is necessary for the satellite's data transmission platform to be designed with a software-defined architecture [11]. As shown in Fig. 2, in a space-based system, the data transmission platforms of satellites for different applications (with different sensors) should be uniformly designed based on software communication architecture. This kind of data transmission platform has such capabilities including: 1) reconfigurable broadband RF front-end, so that the radio frequency part of the transmission platform covers a wide frequency band; 2) software-defined computing unit, so that the satellite can realize on-board spectrum sensing and interference identification; 3) software-defined parameters-managing unit, so that the satellite can change communication parameters as required; 4) software-defined storage unit, so that the satellite can efficiently allocate storage resources according to different tasks. With a uniformly-designed data transmission platform, the satellites for different applications could share a whole spectrum resource and actively adapt to the changing spectrum environment to ensure more efficient transmissions of space-based information.

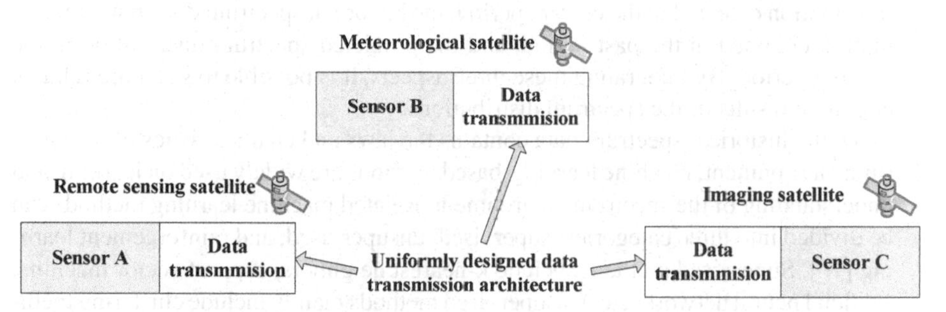

Fig. 2. Brief description of different satellites with uniformly designed data transmission architectures.

3 Key Issues of the Intelligent Data Transmission Technique

1) Spectrum sensing and cognition
Spectrum sensing and cognition is the premise and foundation of the cognitive ability of an intelligent transmission system [12–15]. It is an important way to estimate and predict the channel state. The process mainly involves modeling, detection, recognition and prediction of the interference signals. Common methods of interference signal detection include eigenvalue decomposition, cyclic spectrum detection, energy detection, etc. The main problem of the eigenvalue decomposition method is that the distribution of the interference spectrum cannot be analyzed. The main problem of the cyclic spectrum detection method is its high complexity for implementation. Since the interference detection should be able to detect the existence of interference and estimate the interference parameters, the energy detection algorithm has more advantages in this aspect. The frequency-based energy detection algorithm (e.g. the continuous mean elimination method) has the advantages of small influence to control parameters and low sensitivity to noise. To classify and identify the interference, we need to extract the features of the interference signal first. Different types of interference show different characteristics in time and frequency domains. We can classify them by extracting their features in different domains (e.g. single frequency component detection value, normalized 3dB spectrum bandwidth, spectrum flatness, etc.). By extracting the features that can reflect the interference characteristics of different categories, we can further use pattern recognition techniques to design a classifier, which use these features to classify and identify the interference types. Effective classifiers include support vector machine, extreme learning machine, artificial neural network, etc. To achieve effective interference recognition, we need to accumulate spectrum sensing data, use machine learning and big data analysis methods, and optimize the interference recognition and prediction model iteratively.
To effectively predict the channel state of a communication process, we should employ spectrum prediction techniques, which can estimate future distributions of the spectrum based on its current and historical data. Through predicting the spectrum information in the coming period, it can provide more reliable trend information for the decision engine and help to get more accurate parameter decision results. Three aspects of information are generally useful: the real time spectrum distribution information detected in the current period, the historical spectrum distribution information obtained in the past period, and the predicted spectrum distribution in the coming period. By integrating these three aspects, it is possible to get more reliable cognitive results of the spectrum distributions.
Since the historical spectrum data contains the laws and characteristics of the spectrum environment, machine learning-based methods are widely used on learning and understanding of the spectrum environment. Related machine learning methods can be divided into three categories: supervised, unsupervised, and reinforcement learning [16]. Supervised methods include k-nearest neighbors, support vector machine, artificial neural network, etc. Unsupervised methods mainly include clustering methods and principal component analysis-based methods. Two representative methods based on reinforcement learning are Q-learning and deep reinforcement learning.

The Q-learning has been used to find spectrum holes in the broadband spectrum based on achievable hardware resources [17]. DRL uses a deep neural network (DNN) to approximate the Q value table in the Q-learning algorithm. Due to the strong generalization ability of DNN, the DRL method is easier to mimic the internal laws of the spectrum environment. The DRL method treats the perception and the action as a unified solution optimization process, which will help to obtain a more suitable solution.

2) Data link waveform reconstruction
The waveform reconstruction is a key issue to realize the reconstruction ability of an intelligent transmission system. To realize it, we need to solve two main problems: dynamically allocating the spectrum and adaptively generating the parameters. The first one mainly uses the interference information obtained by the spectrum sensing module to determine the available frequency bands and select the most appropriate data transmission frequency bands. According to the processing results of the interference detection and identification, we can analyze and evaluate the interference level of different frequencies, determine the quality level of the available frequencies, evaluate the expected channel quality under special spectrum allocation rules, and formulate the optimal rule, so that the system can make the best use of the undisturbed or small interference frequency bands in the process of the whole data transmission. According to the data transmission performance requirements of the system, adaptively generating the parameters mainly deal with the modulation type (such as low-order modulation or high-order modulation type), the coding scheme (select coding scheme with different complexity according to the demand of bit error rate), the transmission power and other parameters of the data communication process.

3) Design of the intelligent decision engine
The intelligent decision engine is the core module of the intelligent transmission system. It uses decision-making optimization or learning and reasoning methods to give the optimal data transmission decision according to the historical experience and certain constraints, and then generates system parameters and reconstructs the link waveform according to the decision results. The learning and reasoning algorithm is the core algorithm for the decision engine. The genetic algorithm, reinforcement learning, case-based reasoning, neural network and other related algorithms in the field of artificial intelligence and machine learning can be used to design the intelligent decision engine. The key problem that the intelligent decision engine module needs to solve is a "multi-objective optimization" problem [9]. According to the objective decision criteria, the optimal solution will be searched and determined in a huge solution space.
It is an effective way to design the intelligent decision engine based on the case-based reasoning method. At this time, the decision engine needs the ability to store, analyze and make use of historical experience, which mainly includes two aspects: one is to perceive the external environment information through the cognitive and learning process; the other is to use the database to store and process knowledge data and dynamically adjust the communication parameters. By recording and storing the spectrum sensing result, the corresponding appropriate parameter-configuration result, and the evaluation result of the communication process, the case samples are

formed and the cognitive knowledge database is constructed. The cognitive knowledge database is a critical part of the intelligent decision engine. Through continuous communication tests, the cases in the knowledge database are constantly updated, which results in the fact that more effective communication decision cases are retained and the invalid decision cases are replaced. Then the whole intelligent decision engine is continuously optimized and updated to adapt to the changing spectrum environment and ensure more reliable data transmission. For an intelligent transmission system, the structure and organization of the knowledge database directly affect the response speed and execution efficiency of the decision engine. Designing a proper structure of the knowledge base will help to improve the performance of an intelligent communication system.

When the direct satellite-ground data transmission link is seriously interfered or the satellite beam does not cover the ground receiving station, the relay satellite can be used for indirect data transmission. Therefore, different from other communication techniques based on cognitive radios, the decision engine module of the space-based data transmission technology needs to weigh the path of the direct satellite-ground link and that of the transmission through the relay satellite according to estimating the channel state and predicting the capacity of different channels after spectrum sensing process, so as to obtain the optimal data transmission path.

4) Massive data processing

The proposed intelligent transmission technique needs to get a large amount of electromagnetic spectrum data to analyze the spectrum distributing and changing rules, so as to facilitate the intelligent decision engine to make decisions on the optimal communication parameters. The data to be processed can be divided into two parts: the first part is the spectrum sensing data, mainly including the spectrum distribution data in the relevant period; the second part is the cases data for decision-making of the communication parameters, mainly including the historical cases of the intelligent decision engine. Both the spectrum sensing and the case decision-making parts require a large amount of historical data. The decision engine needs to have the ability of self evolution to continuously accumulate data and optimize the core of the decision-making engine. Therefore, the development of the intelligent transmission technique requires the ability of high-speed storage, efficient retrieval and deep learning of massive data.

The main problem of massive data processing is to discover the laws of the data and mine the hidden information in the data [18]. The artificial intelligence-based technique is an important way to realize massive data analysis and processing. More attention should be paid to some effective methods in the research field, such as the deep learning-based data mining method and the computational intelligence-based distributed optimization method. In addition, how to take into account the real-time performance of the system as well as ensuring the effectiveness of data processing is another key issue. One potential way is to build a central data processing station as a supercomputing center on the ground, develop an integrated architecture based on the combination of cloud computing and edge computing [19], and make full use of various computing resources of the whole system. Furthermore, in order to further improve the real-time performance of the whole system, it can also make full use of the system's transmission gap period (idle period) to complete the calculation and processing of massive data. Last but not least, utilizing some predictive and pre-configured methods as auxiliary means may also be helpful for making decisions in advance.

5) The spaceborne reconfigurable transmission platform
In our concept, the data transmission subsystems of satellites for different applications should be designed with a unified architecture, that is, no matter in which application (e.g. remote sensing, imaging or navigation, etc.) the satellite is, its platform sensor load is different, but the structure of the data transmission subsystem is similar. This subsystem can be designed based on the "Software Communications Architecture", which has the ability of redefinition and reconfiguration [11]. Parameters of each satellite's data transmission subsystem, such as frequency band, communication waveform and data relay mode, are controllable and self-adaptive. In this way, different satellites' platforms of the whole space-based information system can adaptively select the best communication mode and parameters according to the electromagnetic spectrum environment, the transmitted data size, data type, timeliness requirements and other constraints. Then the ground control center can obtain the space-based data timely and effectively. This kind of satellite data transmission platform, which is based on software-defined architecture, puts forward higher requirements for effectively and reliably applying the software-defined radio technique to satellite platforms. Therefore, how to design the data transmission platform based on the software communication architecture for different types of satellites is a key challenge.

6) Reliable satellite-ground signaling parameters synchronization

Different from the conventional "parameter-fixed" data transmission architecture, an important change (or innovation) of the intelligent transmission technique is the need for signaling parameters interaction between both sides of a communication link. When the communication parameters are not suitable for the current electromagnetic spectrum environment, it is necessary to send the new parameters to the transmitter and receiver before applying new parameters for communication. It is necessary to establish a reliable signaling parameter transmission and synchronization mechanism between the satellite and the ground control center, so that each node of the communication process can synchronously update the parameters to complete the data transmission under new parameters. Reliable parameters transmission can be realized by designing a special channel, which needs low transmission rate, but high reliability, concealment and anti-interference performance. Some researchers have proposed a "transform domain communication" technique [9, 20], which improves the signal's concealment by constructing the basis function of analog noise. How to apply a similar low SNR but reliable communication technique to the signaling parameters transmission mechanism of the intelligent transmission system is another key challenge.

4 Conclusions

Based on discussions of space-based data transmission and cognitive radio technology, this paper studies an intelligent transmission strategy of space-based information and discusses how to improve the efficiency and reliability of the satellite-ground data link. With the development of space and information technologies, users' demand for obtaining space-based information based on satellite platforms is also growing. The contradiction between the real-time, efficient and reliable transmission of the space-based data and the insufficient data carrying capacity of the existing data transmission system is more and more prominent, and a new transmission strategy research is urgently needed. The intelligent space-based data transmission technique has potential advantages in interference spectrum avoidance and efficient utilization of the space spectrum resources. This "intelligent transmission" technique is trying to introduce the newly developed techniques in the field of communication and artificial intelligence into the transmission scheme of the space-based data. However, there are still many key issues to be studied to realize this technique. From a developing perspective, on the one hand, the evaluation of the effectiveness of this technique can be carried out by building a software simulation platform to simulate the complex interference environment between the satellite and the ground, and test its performance difference from the traditional techniques; on the other hand, after the relevant key techniques are mature and the key problems are solved, the proposed technique may be verified by an actual satellite-ground data communication test.

References

1. Wang, Z., Wang, D.: Research on transmission effectiveness of remote sensing data from LEO satellite-to-Earth at Ka-Band. Spacecraft Eng. **22**(1), 72–77 (2013)
2. Pang, L., Li, J., Feng, J.: Development of high throughput satellite: a survey and review. Radio Commun. Technol. **46**(4), 371–376 (2020)
3. Cheng, P., Chen, Z., Ding, M., et al.: Spectrum intelligent radio: technology, development, and future trends. IEEE Commun. Mag. 12–18 (2020)
4. Mitola, J., Gerald, Q., Maguire, J.R.: Cognitive radios: making software radios more personal. IEEE Pers. Commun. **6**(4), 13–18 (1999)
5. Haykin, S.: Cognitive radio: brain-empowered wireless communications. IEEE J. Sel. Areas Commun. **23**(2), 201–220 (2005)
6. Ali, A., Hamouda, W.: Advances on spectrum sensing for cognitive radio networks: theory and applications. IEEE Commun. Surv. Tutorials **19**(2), 1277–1304 (2017)
7. Huang, X., et al.: Intelligent cooperative spectrum sensing via hierarchical Dirichlet process in cognitive radio networks. IEEE JSAC **33**(5), 771–787 (2015)
8. Zhang, R., et al.: A learning-based two-stage spectrum sharing strategy with multiple primary transmit power levels. IEEE Trans. Sig. Process. **67**(18), 4899–4914 (2019)
9. Li, S., Cheng, Y., Dong, B., Tang, X.: Research on intelligent anti-jam communication techniques. Radio Commun. Technol. **38**(1), 1–4 (2012)
10. Guan, T., Lu, R., et al.: Research on intelligent transmission of satellite remote sensing data. In: Forum Conference on Satellite Application Technologies, Beijing, China, pp. 60–64 (2018)
11. Lv, Z., Lin, X., Xu, M., et al.: Design of an integrated payload architecture based on software defined radio. In: The 4th China High Resolution Earth Observation Conference, Wuhan, China, pp. 632–643 (2017)
12. Senthilmurugan, S., Venkatesh, T.G.: Optimal channel sensing strategy for cognitive radio networks with heavy-tailed idle times. IEEE Trans. Cogn. Commun. Netw. **3**(1), 26–36 (2017)

13. Bhattarai, S., Park, J.-M., Gao, B., Bian, K., Lehr, W.: An overview of dynamic spectrum sharing: ongoing initiatives, challenges, and a roadmap for future research. IEEE Trans. Cogn. Commun. Netw. **2**(2), 110–128 (2016)
14. Shafigh, A.S., Mertikopoulos, P., Glisic, S., Fang, Y.M.: Semi-cognitive radio networks: a novel dynamic spectrum sharing mechanism. IEEE Trans. Cogn. Commun. Netw. **3**(1), 97–111 (2017). https://doi.org/10.1109/TCCN.2017.2681081
15. Rahmanil, M.: Frequency hopping in cognitive radio networks: a survey. In: IEEE International Conference on Wireless for Space and Extreme Environments, Orlando, USA, pp. 14–16 (2015)
16. Qin, Z., Zhou, X., et al.: 20 years of evolution from cognitive to intelligent communications. IEEE Trans. Cogn. Commun. Netw. **6**(1), 6–20 (2020)
17. Li, Y., Jayaweera, S.K., et al.: Learning-aided sub-band selection algorithms for spectrum senseing in wide-band cognitive radios. IEEE Trans. Wireless Commun. **13**(4), 2012–2024 (2014)
18. Wang, W., Zhang, Z., et al.: Progress of big data analytics methods based on artificial intelligence technology. Comput. Integ. Manuf. Syst. **25**(3), 529–547 (2019)
19. Zhu, G., Liu, D., et al.: Toward an intelligent edge: wireless communication meets machine learning. IEEE Commun. Mag. 19–25 (2020)
20. Dillard, G.M., Reuter, M., Zeidiler, J.: Cyclic code shift keying: a low probability of intercept communication technique. IEEE Trans. Aerosp. Electron. Syst. **39**(3), 786–798 (2003)

Edge Computing Empowered Satellite-Territorial Networks: Service Architecture, Use Case, and Open Issues

Xianglin Wei, Rong Lv(✉), Shiyun Yu, Yongyang Hu, and Ruimin Lu

The 63rd Research Institute, National University of Defense Technology,
Nanjing 210007, China
lvrong17@nudt.edu.cn

Abstract. Satellite-assisted Internet of Things (IoT) communications, artificial intelligent (AI) empowered wireless communications have been expected as two of the key enablers for 6G visions, since they can help 6G achieve better intelligence, coverage in diverse scenarios besides faster transmission speed than 5G. A straightforward way to enable this vision is moving computation facilities onto the satellites using the edge computing paradigm. At its current state, existing satellite edge computing proposals only describes a rudiment of the satellite design with revealing the service architecture of the edge computing empowered satellite-territorial networks. In this backdrop, this paper presents a service architecture of edge computing empowered satellite-territorial networks, which is a layered structure contains two pools and five layers. To exhibit the benefit of the service architecture, two use cases are presented, in which a satellites-based spectrum sensing use case is detailed, and the numerical test results are given and analyzed. Finally, several open issues in implementing our proposed architecture are outlined.

Keywords: Intelligent satellite · Satellite network · Architecture · Use case

1 Introduction

The fifth-generation (5G) mobile networks, which are on the eve of their large-scale commercial operation in 2020, are promised to provide high bandwidth and low delay communication services for devices on the ground. However, for areas with scarce infrastructure, like rural area, mountain area, disaster-hit area, and aerospace, the service coverage is far from meeting the requirements. In this backdrop, satellite networks are treated as an import complement of territorial networks for providing 3D coverage and seamless service in the 6G vision. A satellite network could be utilized as the communication relay or space base station for providing services for ground or aerial end-user devices in the infrastructure-less areas. The inherent wide coverage characteristic of satellite networks is believed to be an important enabler for Internet of Everything (IoE). In the envisioned ubiquitous communication scenarios in the 6G, satellite communications are utilized in

Q. Wu et al. (Eds.): WiSATS 2020, LNICST 358, pp. 308–323, 2021.
https://doi.org/10.1007/978-3-030-69072-4_26

combination with aerial and terrestrial communications to support super IoT communications [1]. Moreover, satellite networks could be utilized in combination with aerial and territorial networks to form a Space-Air-Ground integrated networks (SAGINs) for supporting diverse applications [2, 3].

Therefore, satellite networks, and especially layered networked Low-Earth-Orbit (LEO) satellites, have attracted much attention from both the academia and the industry. Besides traditional LEO satellite communication systems, like Iridium, a few cheaper satellites adopting commercial off-the-shelf (COTS) components, called small satellites, have been growth rapidly. Starlink, a project of the SpaceX company, plans to launch nearly 12,000 satellites in the space, and has already deployed more than 482 satellites in the orbit by June 04, 2020. Amazon released its project, named 'Project Kuiper', in which 3,236 satellites will be launched in the next 10 years [4]. Several other technology majors are working on space-based internet projects, like FaceBook, Google, Samsung, and OneWeb. In academia, how to integrating satellite networks into territorial and aerial networks in the 6G era is a burgeoning research area [5, 6]. For the layered satellite networks composed of high orbit satellites, medium orbit satellites, and earth orbit satellites, software defined networking (SDN) network function virtualization (NFV) are chosen as the protocols to realize efficient network management in satellite-territorial networks (STNs) [7, 8].

These efforts could significantly extend the coverage area of the Internet service while promoting the flexibility of the STNs. However, the long latency, high mobility, and asymmetry properties of satellite communications may seriously degrade the network performance and user experience. Moreover, in existing proposals, the satellite constellation is mainly treated as a data transmission path in the space and it does not participate in the data processing of diverse applications. This hinder the reduction of the task response latency. To tackle this problem, one of the key points is to place computational facilities and algorithms, especially artificial intelligence (AI) algorithms, on the satellites to process data near the source. However, it is a non-trivial task to move the cloud up onto the satellite due to three factors:

- First, the payload of a satellite is usually very limited compared with a server at the territorial cloud data center.
- Second, the common tight-coupling design of the satellite payloads is not flexible enough to support agile service deployment.
- Third, the high mobility nature of satellites limits the service time of each satellite for an area.

Tackling these challenges require a clean-state design of the satellite payload as well as the satellite network service construction/usage. On the one hand, the design of satellite payloads should be intelligent, modularized, and reconfigurable. On the other hand, the satellite network should be service-oriented and should be transparent to the end-user devices. A few efforts have been made on this topic so far, which introduce edge computing and AI to alleviate the problem incurred by the limited on-board processing capability of the satellites. However, most existing works only focus on the network/software/hardware architectures from the communication or computation perspective, and none of existing works are service-oriented [5, 9–11]. Moreover, an instructive use case of edge computing-empowered STNs from the service perspective is still in absence.

In this backdrop, we aim to establish the service architecture of edge computing empowered STNs from the service-oriented perspective. The main works and contributions of this paper are fourfold: first, the layered architecture in the perspective of service is introduced for satellite edge computing; second, two instructive use cases of our service architecture is illustrated through satellites-based video transmitting relay and spectrum sensing; third, several open issues are analyzed to stimulate future researches in this area.

The remaining of this paper is structured as followers. Section 2 gives necessary research background and our research motivation. The service architecture of edge computing empowered STNs is introduced in Sect. 3. Section 4 presents motivating use cases, and the open issues are discussed in Sect. 5. Section 6 briefly summarizes our work in this paper.

2 Research Background and Motivation

2.1 Integrated Satellite Networks

Satellite networks are integrated with diverse network paradigms from different perspectives. Two typical proposals are STNs and SAGINs. STNs combine satellite networks with territorial networks to extend the service coverage while promoting service quality for IoT applications.

SAGIN is a new architecture aiming at extending the network coverage area to interconnect a huge number of IoT devices spread in diverse environments. Typically, a three-layer architecture, which contains space layer, air layer, and ground layer, is adopted to construct a SAGIN. In the space layer, a satellite network is established to provide long-range network service, and it may include satellites in different orbits; drones, balloons, and other unmanned aerial vehicles (UAVs) at different heights constitute the air-layer network; the ground-layer network refers to the territorial networks, like cellular networks, wireless sensor networks, etc. A few cross-layer wireless links are built between different layers to conduct traffic relay between heterogeneous wireless networks.

To tackle the complex management problem introduced by heterogeneous wireless network integration, software defined networking (SDN) [12] and network function virtualization (NFV) are widely accepted as the management framework for STNs and SAGINs. The controllers in SDN are usually implemented on the ground control stations (GCS) and high-orbit satellites, while low-orbit satellites and other air-layer platforms consist the data plane.

Incorporating satellite networks to territorial networks to support diverse services brings three main advantages. First, the satellites operate at high altitude have inherent advantage in its coverage area than any territorial or air networks. Second, the broadcast nature of satellite communications could greatly promote the transmission efficiency. Third, satellite transmissions are more robust than territorial or air networks, which could be easily affected by ground disasters, weather, etc. However, it is not straightforward to include satellite networks due to five main challenges. The first challenge lies into the heterogeneity between satellite networks and air/territorial networks in protocol, transmission speed, and management. Second, the long latency incurred by the space-ground-space data processing structure may fail the time-sensitive applications. Third, traditional satellites usually work in stand-alone fashion, and do not work as a satellite network. Fourth, traditional satellites' software and hardware are usually tightly orchestrated and coupled, and are hard to be reconfigured and reconstructed on demand. For instance, a navigation satellite cannot conduct earth-monitoring tasks due to the lack of proper cameras. Finally, compared with territorial communication stations, a satellite usually has limited payloads and could not support computation-intensive tasks.

To tackle one or two challenges mentioned above, a few proposals have been put forward. To shift intelligence on the satellite, in November 2019, China launched its first software-defined satellite, named Tianzhi 1, which carries a small-scale cloud platform to process its captured data locally rather than transmitting it back to the earth for processing [13]. Researchers at the Aerospace Corporation developed a project, named Space Cloud, in 2019 to demonstrate how Earth-based cloud computing and artificial intelligence can be moved into space for onboard processing, to enable satellites to detect and transmit only meaningful data to the earth [14]. Space Cloud is developed based on commercial available software and hardware components, including an Intel Movidius processor and Google's open-sourced Kubernetes tool. Denby et al. have introduced the concept of orbital edge computing (OEC) to address the limitations of a ben-pipe architecture. OEC supports edge computing at each camera-equipped earth-observing nanosatellite so that sensed data may be processed locally when downlinking is unavailable [15]. However, Denby et al. only focus on the operating models of OEC for nanosatellites without presenting an over-all service architecture overview, which is necessary for developing intelligent satellite systems.

2.2 Satellite Edge Computing

Cloud computing has achieved great success in the last decade, in which the computation facilities are centrally placed in the data centers, due to its nearly infinite computation capacity and bulk data process architecture. However, the centralized processing logic requires the service request and reply packets to be transmitted over the Internet, and this typically incurs a long delay and requires bulk transmission bandwidth. This will fail the service when the application is latency-sensitive or when the bandwidth is limited. In this circumstance, a new computing paradigm, called Edge Computing, in which data is processed where it originates, has emerged and attracted much attention in recent years. Compared with cloud computing, edge computing highlights the placement of computation devices at the network edge, and thus can greatly reduce the latency incurred by task offloading as well as relieve the burden at fronthaul/backhaul links. Moreover, computation at the edge server can better provide context-aware service and support device mobility.

For a satellite network, which usually has longer transmission latency and limited bandwidth, edge computing is a preferable computing choice due to the advantages mentioned above.

Zhang et al. have presented satellite mobile edge computing (MEC), in which a user equipment without a proximal MEC server can also enjoy MEC services via satellite links in STNs [5]. Wang et al. have proposed a cooperative offloading scheme in a double-edge satellite-terrestrial (DESTN) network [9]. In order to use the satellite Internet of Things intelligently, Wei et al. have proposed an application scheme of satellite IoT edge intelligent computing, and analyzes how edge computing and deep learning play a role in satellite IoT image data target detection [10]. A game-theoretic approach in satellite edge computing was proposed by Wang et al. to the optimization of computation offloading strategy [11]. Moreover, Wang et al. have proposed to transform the traditional satellite into a space edge computing node, which can dynamically load software in orbit, flexibly share on-board resources, and provide services coordinated with the cloud [16]. Denby et al. have presented orbital edge computing, in which nanosatellite constellations are equipped with computational devices to process the data when downlinking is not available [15].

2.3 Motivation

Simply introducing edge computing to the STNs cannot directly make them intelligent. To reveal the full potential of intelligent STNs for supporting diverse applications, we need to develop a service architecture for the edge computing-empowered STNs from the service-oriented perspective. Moreover, the whole process of a service call needs to be identified. Use cases should be given to reveal the application pattern of the service architecture. Finally, the open issues to realize this service architecture cannot be neglected.

Through establishing the service architecture, our work can benefit practitioners in this area from three aspects: first, it paves the way from physical resources to user access interfaces for service usage; second, system-level virtualization is implemented in the network through building several virtualized resource pools; third, the network could provide the satellite service in a transparent and intelligent way to the users without revealing the implementation details.

In the following, we first introduce our service architecture in Sect. 3, and detail its layers and key technologies; Sect. 4 gives two use cases of the service architecture; the open issues are discussed in Sect. 5.

3 Service Architecture Design

This section introduces our service architecture, which treats all the components of the STNs as resources to provide service to the end-user devices. The service architecture is illustrated first, then comes the introduction of each layer in the architecture.

3.1 Service Architecture

The design principles of the service architecture are threefold: first, it can composite, manage, and utilize all the available resources in an intelligent way, including sensing, computation, storage, and transmission resources; second, all the resources can be efficiently scheduled, managed, and utilized to construct diverse basic services for enabling the provision of composited services; third, users could access services easily through open and standardized interfaces, like APPs on the smartphones.

Based on these principles, our service architecture is shown in Fig. 1, in which two pools are contained, i.e. resource pool and service pool. The resource pool at the bottom of the figure consists of two layers:

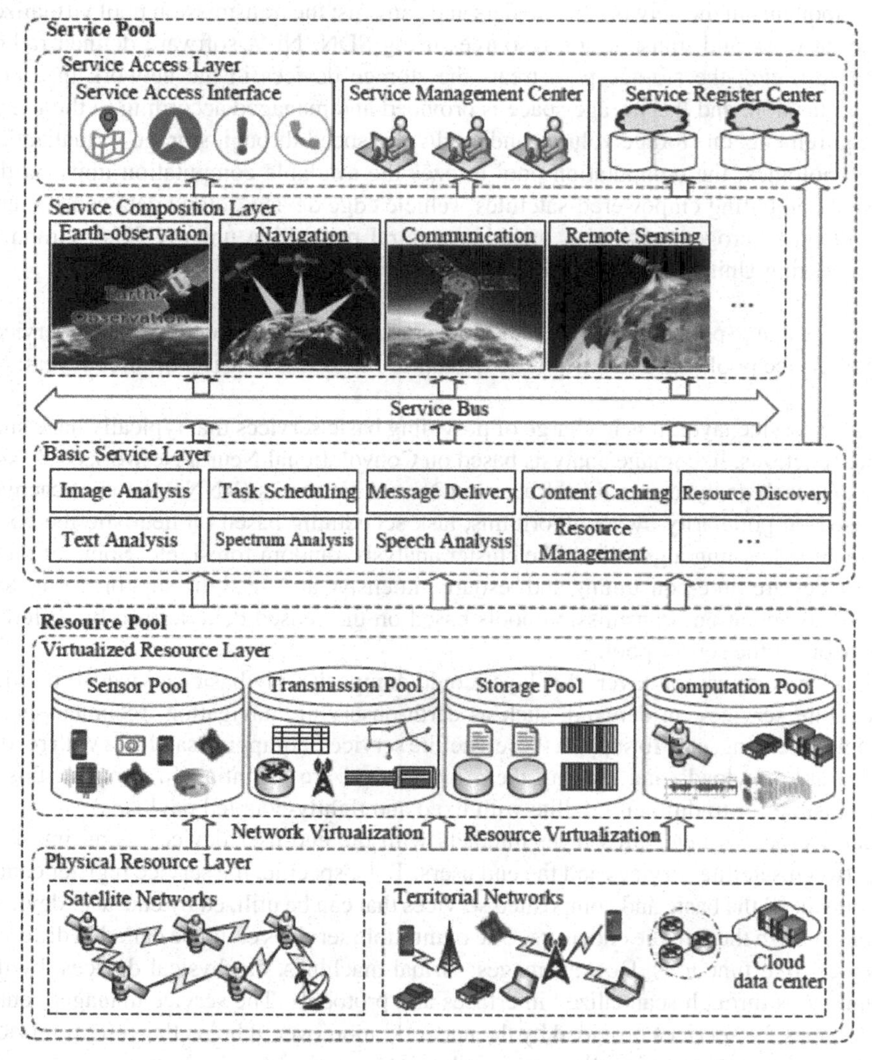

Fig. 1. Service Architecture of Edge Computing Empowered STNs.

- Physical resource layer: it contains all the physical resources in the STNs, like sensors equipped on the satellites, vehicles, and IoT devices; computation facilities located on satellite edge computing platforms, vehicle computation platforms [17], cloud data centers on the ground, and mobile devices with idle resources; storage disks installed on aerospace and ground platforms; transmission devices and links between diverse networked platforms; and other resources.
- Virtualized resource layer: the resources at the physical resource layer are virtualized into different resource pools at this layer. The sensor pool integrates all the sensing components in the network, e.g. radars and cameras; the transmission pool virtualizes the network and transmission resources using SDN, NFV, software defined radios (SDRs), etc.; the storage pool treats the storage devices in the network in a layered fashion, and the storage space is provided and managed according to the users' requirements on storage volume and read/write speed through storage virtualization technologies; the computation pool utilizes the available computation units on the edge computing empowered-satellites, vehicle edge devices, cloud data centers, etc. built on heterogeneous units, including central processing units (CPUs), Graphics Processing Units (GPUs), Field Programmable Gate Arrays (FPGAs), etc.

The resource pool serves as the underlying resources for constructing diverse services in the service pool, which is shown on the top of Fig. 1 and consists of three layers:

- Basic service layer: it is in charge of providing basic services that typically have simple functions, like image analysis based on Convolutional Neural Networks (CNNs), text/speech analysis based on Recurrent Neural Networks (RNNs), content caching based on popularity-aware algorithms, task scheduling based on heuristic methods, machine learning algorithms like cluster analysis, random forest, etc. Some of these services are time-consuming and resource-intensive and need the support from storage, computation, transmission pools based on the sensed data derived by different sensors at the sensor pool.
- Service composition layer: this layer could composite any basic services to provide satellite services on demand, such as earth-observing, navigation, reconnaissance, remote sensing, etc. To support these satellite services, equipping satellites with reconfigurable payloads and loading them on demand are essential. In contrast, this is infeasible for traditional satellite with fixed and tightly-coupled payloads.
- Service access layer: this layer interacts with the end-user devices as an interface between satellite services and the end users. To be specific, the service register center collects all the basic and composited services that can be utilized by end-user devices, and publish them to the end users. One or multiple services could be called in different styles, like functions, Docker images, virtual machines, or physical devices, by the end users through scandalized interfaces and protocols. The service manager center manages the services provided by the network; moreover, it holds the system service, like resource and service discovery, update, etc.

3.2 Service Provision Process

Under the framework established in Fig. 1, the service provision process of the network is shown in Fig. 2. First, a user initiates a service request to the service access layer in the service pool; the request is directed to the service access interface, and then is relayed to the service register center for service information. After receiving the response, a request is launched by the interface to the service management center, which resolves the request and delivers it to the service composition layer as well as the basic service layer. In the service composition layer, the request is analyzed and divided into several parts, and the corresponding resources are calculated; according to the results, service calls are initiated to utilize basic services. Based on all the received service requests, the basic service layer calculates the total needed resource, and starts a service monitoring thread. All the service requests then are directed to the virtualized resource layer to decide the resource requirements for different types of resources, i.e. sensing, transmission, storage, and computation. Finally, these mapped virtual resources are mapped back to their physical devices in the physical resource layer. The satellite networks reconfigure its functions and payloads and allocate the requested resources to this request; moreover, the territorial networks do the same things without reload its payload.

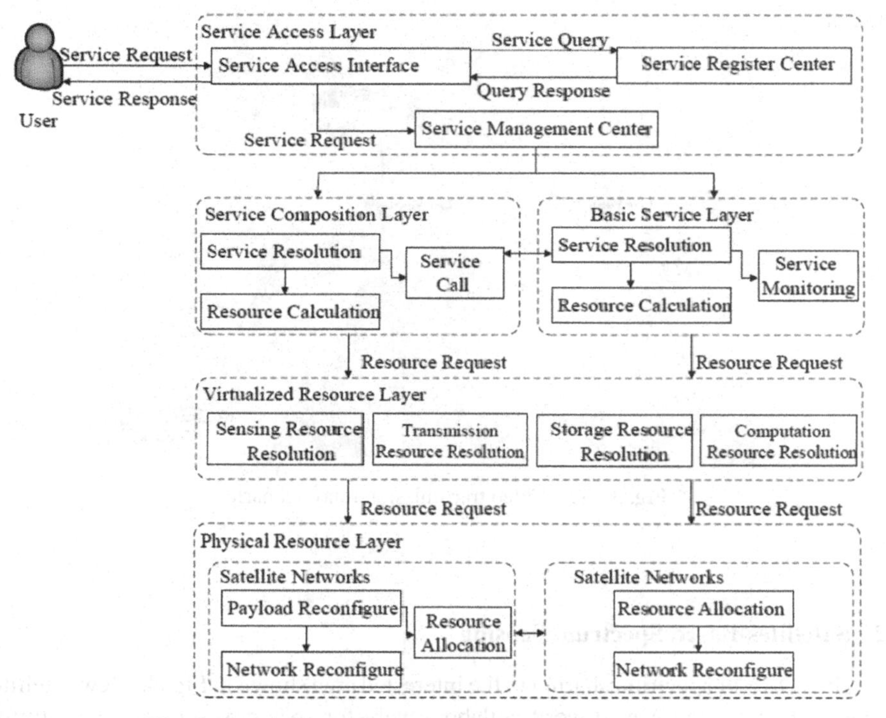

Fig. 2. Service provision process of the service architecture.

4 Use Case and Analysis

Edge computing empowered satellite networks could be utilized to support diverse applications as shown in Fig. 1. This section presents two typical use cases. In the first use case, a single edge computing empowered satellite is adopted as the communication and processing relay for video transmitting between a plane equipped with a camera that captures videos in some area. In the later use case, multiple satellites conduct collaborative spectrum sensing for dynamic spectrum access (DSA) in cognitive radio networks, to show the advantages of our service architecture.

4.1 Satellite as the Video Transmission Relay

In this use case, as shown in Fig. 3, an iSAT acts as the communication and processing relay between the plane-loaded cameras and the ground station for transmitting live videos. Here, several video processing functions could be conducted on the plane as well as on the iSAT. For example, video compressing using neural networks could be conducted on the plane to greatly reduce the size of the transmitted data; on the other hand, the iSAT could further alleviate the burden of the satellite links through conducting edge computing-based inter-video frame redundancy reduction between multiple video sources.

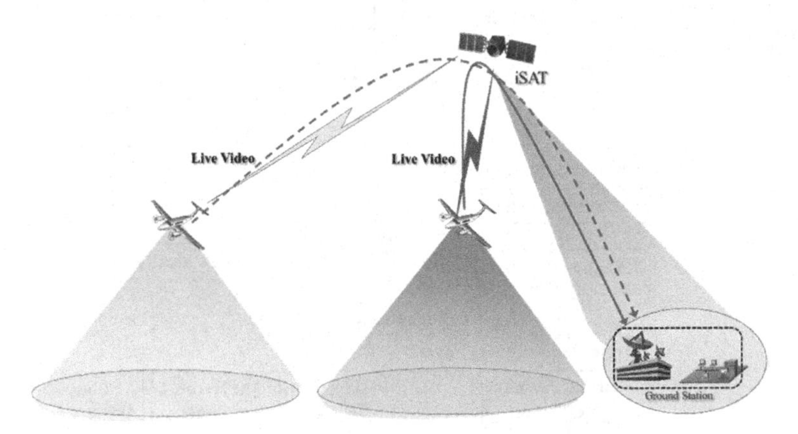

Fig. 3. The Video transmission relay scenario.

4.2 Satellites-Based Spectrum Sensing

To realize DSA or spectrum sharing in the interested area shown in Fig. 4, a few satellites flying over this area need to work collaboratively for spectrum sensing. An intuitive method to conduct satellite-based spectrum sensing is let the satellite collect the raw radio frequency (RF) data, and a ground facility is in charge of processing the RF data to derive the sensing results. To be specific, a satellite (take iSat3 as an example in Fig. 4) needs to receive radio frequency (RF) data first (①) after receiving the spectrum sensing task from the ground station, and then sends the data to the ground station directly or via a relay satellites (②). The ground station will offload the data to a cloud data center for processing (③), which processes the data and returns the results to the ground station (④). For the simplicity of description, this strategy will be referred as 'Raw-data back' in the following analysis.

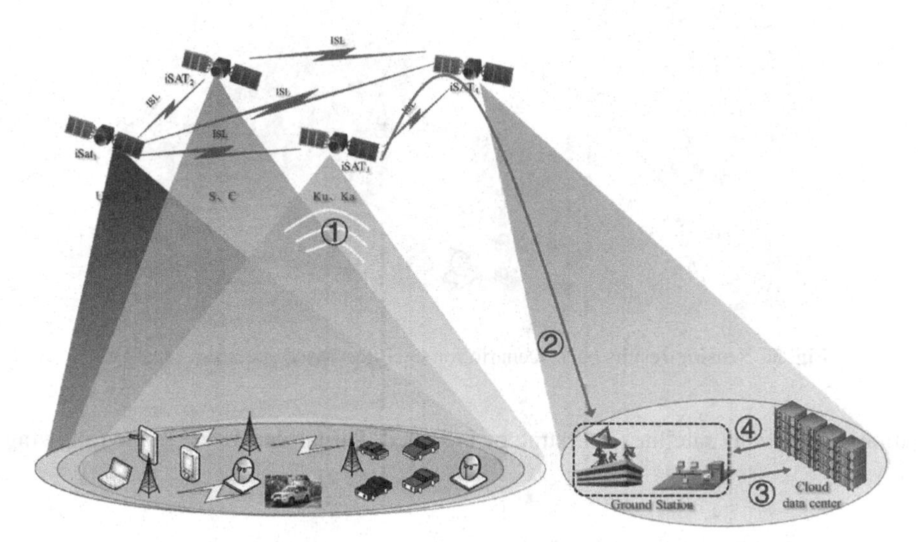

Fig. 4. Raw-data back scenario for satellites-based spectrum sensing.

After introducing edge computing-empowered intelligent STNs, spectrum sensing is a service in the service pool in our service-oriented architecture. The users can initiate the spectrum sensing service via an APP, and multiple satellites (e.g. 3 satellites in Fig. 5) will separately switch to spectrum sensing mode, and receiving RF data in different frequency bands (①). In Fig. 5, $iSat_1$ works at UHF and L bands; $iSat_2$ receives signals at S and C bands; $iSat_3$ conducts spectrum sensing at Ku and Ka bands. Through this band division, the cost and design complexity of the payloads on each satellite can be greatly reduced. Then, the received data is processed by the edge computing payload or edge server on each satellite (②) separately. Here, data processing contains the signal processing at multiple domains, including time domain, frequency domain, space domain, modulation domain, etc. In the time domain, the active times of each signal in this area can be derived; in the space domain, the transmitter of each signal may be located through the efforts of multiple satellites or the antenna array carried on one single satellite. Then, the sensing results will be derived on the aerospace without the intervention of the ground station. Note that, in order to tackle the challenges brought by the high mobility of the satellites, another satellite, i.e. iSate4 in Fig. 5, acts as the relay between satellites and the ground station to get the sensing results back (③). For the ease of presentation, this strategy is called 'Sensing-results back' in the following analysis.

Considering that a satellite may can only pre-process its sensed data due to its limited processing capacity. In this circumstance, it needs to send the reduced data to the ground

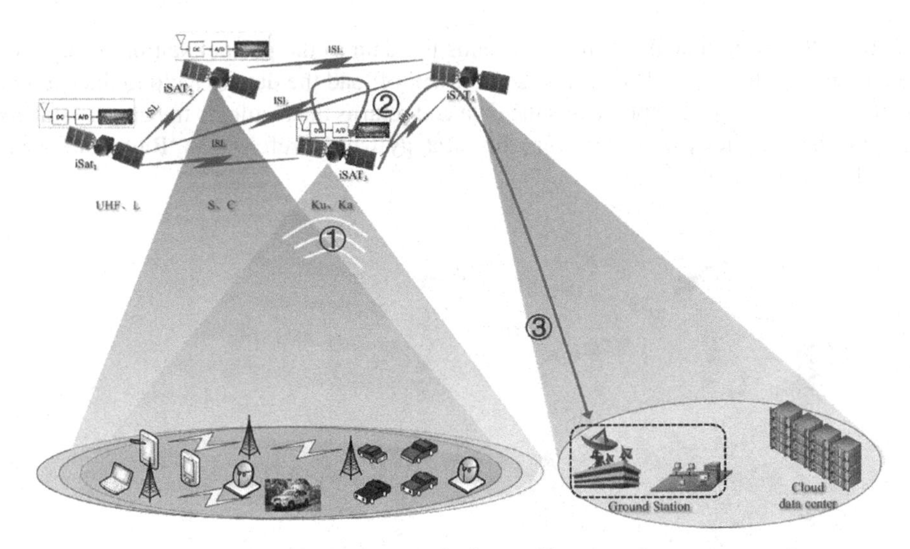

Fig. 5. Sensing-results back scenario for satellites-based spectrum sensing.

station via the relay satellite. This strategy is named 'Partial-data back' in the following analysis.

4.3 Numerical Results and Analysis

To highlight the different between different strategies illustrated above, we conducted a series of numerical tests. The parameter settings of our tests are as follows. The size of the raw data received at a satellite is S bits; the transmission bandwidth from the relay satellite to the ground station is B_{SG} bps; the bandwidth of an inter-satellite link is set to be B_{SS} bps; each sensed bit needs c_s processing cycles for deriving the sensing results; each sensed bit needs c_s processing cycles for calculating reduced data; to reduce p percent of each sensed bit, c_r processing cycles will be consumed; the processing frequency of the edge server on a satellite is f_e; the processing frequency of the server in the data center is f_c; the propagation delay from a satellite to the ground station is t_p; the bandwidth from the ground station to the cloud is B_{GC}. The default parameter settings are shown in Table 1.

The most important performance concern of spectrum sensing is the latency, which is defined as t_2 t_1. Here, t_1 is the time when the raw data is received by a satellite; t_2 is the time when the ground station gets the sensing results. The sensing results are very small in relative to the transmission bandwidth in the network. Therefore, we only consider the propagation delay between satellite and ground station while neglect the transmission time of the sensing results and the spectrum sensing message from the ground station to the satellites.

Table 1. Parameter settings.

Parameter	Default value	Parameter	Default value
S	100 Mb	p	0.5
B_{SG}	100 Mb	c_r	10
B_{SS}	100 Mb	f_e	2 GHz
B_{GC}	10 Gb	f_c	2 GHz
c_s	100	t_p	10 ms

The three processing strategies' latency could be calculated by:

$$t = \begin{cases} \frac{S}{B_{SS}} + \frac{S}{B_{SG}} + \frac{S}{B_{GC}} + \frac{S \times c_s}{f_c} + 2t_p, & Raw - data\ back \\ \frac{S \times p}{B_{SS}} + \frac{S \times c_r \times p}{f_e} + \frac{S \times p}{B_{SG}} + \frac{S \times p}{B_{GC}} + \frac{S \times c_s \times p}{f_c} + 2t_p, & Partial - data\ back \\ \frac{S \times c_s}{f_e} + 2t_p, & Sensing - results\ back \end{cases} \quad (1)$$

When S increases from 100 to 500 Mb, the three strategies' latencies are shown in Fig. 6. From Fig. 6, we know that introducing edge computing could reduce the sensing latency in the interested area under the parameter settings in Table 1. Transmitting the raw data back incurs long latency due to limited transmission bandwidths of satellite links. On the other hand, the sensing latency increases as the raw data size increases. This is a straightforward conclusion due to the fact that large data requires long processing latency as well as long transmission latency.

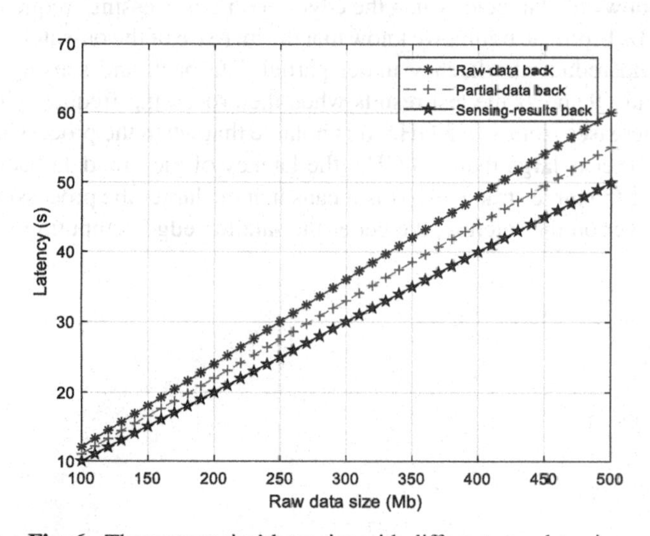

Fig. 6. Three strategies' latencies with different raw data size.

Figure 7 shows the test results when the transmission bandwidth between satellites increases from 100 to 500 Mb. The general observation is that the latency decreases slowly as the inter-satellite bandwidth increases for the Raw-data back and Partial-data back strategies due to the reduction of the data transmission delay in the aerospace. Moreover, the change of the bandwidth has no impact on the third strategy, i.e. sensing-results back, since no raw data transmission is needed. Note that we can draw similar observation when the bandwidth between a satellite and the ground station increases.

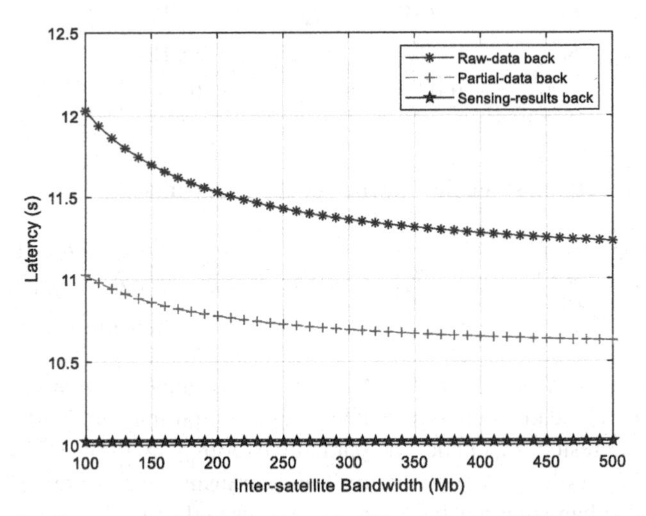

Fig. 7. Three strategies' latencies with different inter-satellite bandwidth.

Figure 8 shows the latencies when the edge server's processing frequency increases from 1 to 3 GHz. From the figure, we know that the increase of the on-satellite processing frequency could reduce the latency under partial-data back and sensing-results back strategies. Figure 9 shows the test results when the processing frequency of the server in the cloud increases from 1 to 2 GHz. It is notable that when the processing frequency in the cloud server is large than 1.3 GHz, the latency of the raw-data back will be the smallest among the three strategies. This means that the larger the processing frequency of the edge server on the satellite, the better the satellite edge computing is.

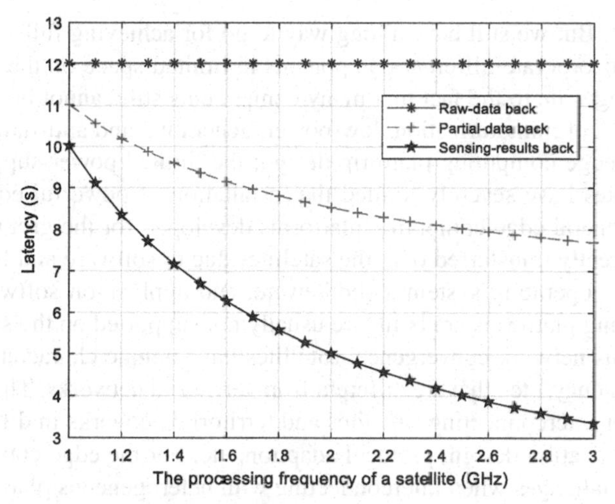

Fig. 8. Three strategies' latencies with different processing frequency of the edge server on a satellite.

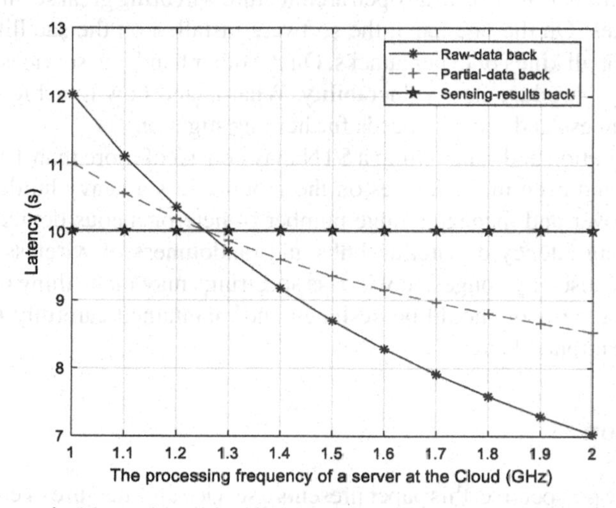

Fig. 9. Three strategies' latencies with different processing frequency of the server in the cloud.

5 Open Issues

To realize the full potential of our service architecture for the edge computing empowered intelligent satellite-territorial networks, the following open issues deserve further investigation in the future:

- Reconfigurable payloads design on the satellites: traditional satellites adopt tight-coupling design principle, which makes their payload fixed and hard-to-change on demand. In iSat architecture presented in [16], in which the payloads can be installed and configured as a service. iSat made an initial step for reconfigurable payloads in

the aerospace. But we still have a long way to go for achieving fully reconfigurable satellites to incorporate different components in limited space on the satellites. Part of the challenges lie to the fact that many components still cannot be integrated due to the hardness of miniaturization, low-power, generality, and anti-radiation design.
- Lightweight edge computing platform design: the limited power supply, and space on the satellites have severely limited the installation of powerful edge computing platforms. General edge computing platforms developed for the ground devices are hard to be directly transferred onto the satellites due to software and hardware compatibility. The operating systems, middleware, and application software, on which edge computing platforms are built, are usually not supported on the satellites.
- Heterogeneous network convergence: satellites have unique characteristics, such as bandwidth, latency, etc., that are different from territorial networks. This brings many challenges for interconnecting satellites and territorial networks in different aspects, including application design, protocol adaption, etc. For the edge computing part, it faces many challenges when interconnecting with heterogeneous platforms.
- Security issues introduced by the open architecture: traditional enclosed design of the satellites can ensure the security of the hardware and software on the satellites; however, the transformation to an open architecture will bring great security challenges to the satellites. On the one hand, the software installed on the satellites can not be fully tested for all kinds of cyber attacks. On the other hand, the services loaded on the satellites may introduce new vulnerability. What is and how to achieve the tradeoff between openness and security needs further investigation.
- Resource cognition and scheduling: a STN may consist of more than 10,000 satellites in the space and even more devices on the ground. It is a heavy burden for the network to discover and manage a huge number of heterogeneous devices in real time due to the long latency of satellite links and randomness of wireless transmission. Interference caused by congested wireless spectrums may make things worse. Therefore, the resource pool should be designed and maintained carefully to incorporate the above-mentioned factors.

6 Conclusion

From the service perspective, this paper presents a service architecture of edge computing empowered satellite-territorial networks, which is a layered structure contains two pools and five layers. In the resource pool, all the computation, storage, communication, and sensor resources in both satellite networks and territorial networks are organized into resource pools using virtualization techniques. The resources in the resource pool are utilized to construct diverse basic services, which are organized into composited services in the service pool. Moreover, a service access layer is provided for the users to access the service in a transparent fashion. To exhibit the benefits of our service architecture, two use cases, i.e. satellite-based video transmitting relay and spectrum sensing, are detailed with numerical analysis. Numerical results have shown that introducing edge computing could reduce the latency of the spectrum sensing under typical parameter settings. A few open issues several open issues in implementing our proposed architecture are outlined to stimulate further research in the future.

References

1. Zhang, L., Liang, Y., Niyato, D.: 6G visions: mobile ultra-broadband, super Internet-of-Things, and artificial intelligence. China Commun. **16**(8), 1–14 (2019)
2. Zhang, Z., et al.: 6G wireless networks vision requirements, architecture, and key technologies. IEEE Veh. Technol. Mag. **14**(3), 28–41 (2019)
3. Yang, H., Alphones, A., Xiong, Z., Niyato, D., Zhao, J., Wu, K.: Artificial intelligence-enabled intelligent 6G networks. arXiv:1912.05744 (2019)
4. Amazon moving Project Kuiper team to new R&D headquarters. https://spacenews.com/amazon-moving-project-kuiper-team-to-new-rd-headquarters/. Accessed 08 Aug 2020
5. Zhang, Z., Zhang, W., Tseng, F.: Satellite mobile edge computing: improving QoS of high-speed satellite-terrestrial networks using edge computing techniques. IEEE Network **33**(1), 70–76 (2018)
6. Saad, W., Bennis, M., Chen, M.: A vision of 6G wireless systems: applications, trends, technologies, and open research problems. IEEE Network **34**(3), 134–142 (2019)
7. Ferrús, R., Koumaras, H., Sallent, O.: SDN/NFV-enabled satellite communications networks: opportunities scenarios and challenges. Phys. Commun. **18**(P2), 95–112 (2016)
8. Sheng, M., Wang, Y., Li, J., et al.: Toward a flexible and reconfigurable broadband satellite network: resource management architecture and strategies. IEEE Wireless Commun. **24**(4), 127–133 (2017)
9. Wang, P., Zhang, X., Zhang, J., Wang, Z.: Performance analysis of task offloading in double-edge satellite-terrestrial networks. In: Liu, X., Cheng, D., Jinfeng, L. (eds.) Communications and Networking. ChinaCom 2018. Lecture Notes of the Institute for Computer Sciences, Social Informatics and Telecommunications Engineering, vol. 262, pp. 531–540. Springer, Cham (2019). https://doi.org/10.1007/978-3-030-06161-6_52
10. Wei, J., Cao, S.: Application of edge intelligent computing in satellite Internet of Things. In: 2019 IEEE International Conference on Smart Internet of Things (SmartIoT), Tianjin, China, pp. 85–91 (2019)
11. Wang, Y., Yang, J., Guo, X., Qu, Z.: A game-theoretic approach to computation offloading in satellite edge computing. IEEE Access **8**, 12510–12520 (2020)
12. Xu, S., Wang, X., Huang, M.: Software-defined next-generation satellite networks: architecture, challenges and solutions. IEEE Access **4**, 4027–4041 (2018)
13. Tianzhi-1. https://space.skyrocket.de/doc_sdat/tianzhi-1.htm. Accessed 08 Aug 2020
14. Experiment to Demo 'Cloud' Technology in Space. https://www.nationaldefensemagazine.org/articles/2019/6/13/experiment-to-demo-cloud-technology-in-space. Accessed 08 Aug 2020
15. Denby, B., Lucia, B.: Orbital edge computing: nanosatellite constellations as a new class of computer system. In: Proceedings of the Twenty-Fifth International Conference on Architectural Support for Programming Languages and Operating Systems (Asplos 2020), Lausanne, Switzerland (2020)
16. Wang, Y., Yang, J., Guo, X., et al.: Satellite edge computing for the internet of things in aerospace. Sensors **19**, 4375 (2019)
17. Tang, C., Zhu, C., Wei, X., Peng, H., Wang, Y.: Integration of UAV and fog-enabled vehicle: application in post-disaster relief. In: 2019 IEEE 25th International Conference on Parallel and Distributed Systems (ICPADS), Tianjin, China, pp. 548–555 (2019)

A Model-Driven Development Framework for Satellite On-Board Software

Junxiang Qin[1], Ninghu Yang[1(✉)], Yuxuan Wang[1], Jun Yang[1], and Jinliang Du[2]

[1] National University of Defense Technology, Changsha 410073, Hunan, China
qinjx163@163.com

[2] Xi'an Satellite Control Center, Xian 710000, Shanxi, China

Abstract. Traditional satellites are designed and developed according to specific functions, resulting in large size, high price and long development cycle. With the rapid development of small satellite technology, the satellite has higher and higher degree of modularization. Similar to smartphones, satellites can dynamically upload "Apps" in-orbit, achieving the transition from "function satellites" to "smart satellites". In view of the rapid, efficient and reliable development of on-board software, a model-driven software development framework and a development tool chain are proposed in this paper. To solve the problems of lack of standardized architecture in on-board software development, poor communication of various development stages, serious coupling of software and hardware, and low automation, the framework adopts unified architecture, standardized components, configurable integration and automatic code generation. The development tool chain provides a complete set of tools for entire on-board software development based on the model-driven framework. It improves the software reusability by decoupling software design from hardware platform and shortens the development period by automatically connecting the various development stages. Finally, this paper demonstrates and assesses the process of developing iSat-1, which is a CubeSat for function in-orbit defined experiment.

Keywords: Model-driven · Development tool chain · Satellite onboard software

1 Introduction

RADITIONALLY, how to design, build, test, and launch satellite is mainly "requirements-driven" [1]. In order to provide reliable telecommunications, broadcasting, remote sensing, meteorological services, navigation, positioning, etc. and sustain long-term operation in the hostile space environment, these satellites are usually bulky and expensive, need to be carefully qualified and tested, and take several years to develop. Therefore, after the satellite enters orbit, the technology used may lag behind the technical level for more than ten years.

Small satellites are dedicated to achieve a significant reduction in volume, mass, development time and cost by taking advantages of modern technologies (e.g., integrated circuits, digital signal processing, MEMS, and additive manufacturing) [2]. The

Q. Wu et al. (Eds.): WiSATS 2020, LNICST 358, pp. 324–350, 2021.
https://doi.org/10.1007/978-3-030-69072-4_27

development of small satellite will combine with rapid development model implemented by small agile teams [3] and typically use commercial off-the-shelf (COTS) to design and manufacture satellites. In recent years, small satellites have provided a low-cost platform for space missions and played an increasing important role in space exploration, technology demonstration, scientific research and education. Therefore, the rapid development of on-board software is more urgent [4, 5].

With the emergence of the small satellite constellation projects and the deep construction of the space information system, the production and application mode of small satellite will undergo profound changes. At the beginning of the 21st century, smart phones quickly replace the old mobile phones that were restricted to a few sets of tasks such as calling and texting. By dynamically installing “Apps”, smart phone can provide dedicated date for different users and accomplish specific tasks [6, 7]. In addition, various applications of smartphones can run on hardware produced by different vendors. Similarly, the on-board software is also can be developed in the form of “App”. The “App” is able to become a portable entity and run on various satellite hardware platform. This new pattern can bring the following benefits [8–12].

1) Enlarge the production scale of satellite. With the separation of software development and hardware production, satellite hardware can achieve large-scale general-purpose production like computers and mobile phones.
2) Enhance the ability of precision service. By uploading personalized “Apps” to satellites, it can provide users with fast and accurate customized services.
3) Accelerate the development of the satellite industry. Software is more flexible and reusable than hardware. It is easier to meet all kinds of new application scenarios and requirements by upgrading.

At present, some organizations have conducted related research. They hope to modularize the original on-board software and improve the platform independence, portability and reusability of onboard software. NASA’s Goddard Space Flight Center (GSFC) designed a multi-project core flight system called cFS for space rapid response [16, 17]. cFS is a component-based software production line and a platform-independent flight software environment with key feature including support for rapid assembly support for dynamic loading and integration, support for automated document generation and test cases. The CubeSat Laboratory of Vermont Technical College developed the reusable software package CubedOS for CubeSat [18]. CubedOS provides a robust software platform for the CubeSat’s mission, which simplifies the development of CubseSat flight software. It is similar to cFS. The difference is that CubedOS is written in SPARK and its key parts are verified to ensure its operational reliability. The Flight Instrument Reuse & Standardization Library (FIRSL) encapsulates the constantly updated device drivers and exposes the basic functionality of a common aerospace instrument. The framework uses an object-oriented approach to separate the conceptual operation of abstract devices from the physical devices in the real world. FIRSL provides a portable and unbound interface between applications and device controllers with high reusability, portability and extensibility [19]. In addition to the above projects, TERMA company built the on-board operation platform called OBOSS and P&P company built a reusable software framework using an object-oriented approach for AOCS [20].

In addition to the research on the modularization of on-board software, there is also the research on the software definition of satellite. It is inspired by software defined radio (SDR). At present, the standard software architecture of the SDR mainly includes Software Communication Architecture (SCA) and Space Telecommunications Radio System (STRS). In 2012, the International Space Station carried out three SDR payload for technical verification, which was developed by Haris. NASA researched on the use of cFS to implement STRS [21]. The "Eutelsat-quantum", designed by European Space Agency (ESA) and Eutelsat, is a software defined payload satellite [22]. It changes the parameters of the communication payload by software defined to achieve functional reconfiguration [20]. The satellite is expected to launch and conduct in-orbit experiments in 2019. The above projects are mainly to implement SDR on the satellite platform and do not achieve a totally software defined satellite. The Institute of Software, Chinese Academy of Sciences (ISCAS) organized the Software Defined Satellite Technology Alliance in 2017 [21, 22]. The alliance aims to create an open source platform-level software solution for satellites using common computing platform, creating the conditions for flexible software definition and expansion of satellite capabilities [23]. The first experimental satellite "Tianzhi-1" for verifying the technology was launched in November 2018.

The modular software projects and software defined satellite projects described above illustrate the growing importance of on-board software. On-board software will become the "soul" of the satellite, in the near future. At present, most of the development of on-board software is based on the method of embedded software development. It lacks theoretical methods and specific tools for on-board software development [24]. Many development tools can only be used on certain satellite platform. The model-driven software design method uses the model as a unified description of each stage of software development and ensures the consistency of each design stage through automation tools [25]. This method has been used in software development in many fields, such as automotive electronics [26], avionics [27], robotics [28], etc. But these work are not fit into the satellite on-board software. Therefore, we aim to solve the problem that adopts model-driven method to satellite on-board software.

With regard to this, the contribution of this paper has the following three points:

1) A model-driven framework for satellite on-board software is proposed to adopt unified architecture, standardized components, configurable integration and automatic code generation.
2) The meta-models of atomic components and composite components in the satellite software field are designed and the model conversion constraints are given. The engineering realization of the meta-model is given based on gmf.
3) The method and process of satellite on-board software development under model-driven framework are given, and the development tool chain is realized based on eclipse, which can provide complete development tools, management software, and analytical assessment reports to automate the design of software and enhance the consistency and maintainability of the development process.

This paper is organized as follows: Sect. 2 describes the transformation of satellite design patterns, analyzes the reasons for the change, and looks forward to the future development direction of satellites. In addition, an overview of the on-board software technology and software defined satellite projects is presented. Section 3 proposes a model-driven satellite software development framework, describing the development goals, architecture and development process of the framework. Section 4, based on the software development framework, proposes the corresponding software development tool chain, which provides a complete set of development tools for on-board software. Next, Sect. 5 demonstrates an application of the development tool chain with an instance of developing on-board software of a CubeSat named iSat-1 and assesses the development tool chain. Finally, Sect. 6 concludes the paper.

2 Related Works

2.1 The Transformation of Satellite Development Patters

The design concept of satellite has been slowly evolving since the launch of the first satellite for more than 60 years. In combination with the development trend of other electronic systems, such as computers, mobile phone, ATS (Automatic Test System), etc., they are all moving in the direction of increasing modularity [8].

Discrete Component Design Approach. At first, limited by the level of electronic devices, satellites use a discrete design approach. The hardware mostly uses discrete components and the software uses low-level languages, such as C or assembly language. This satellite function is simple and mainly completed by hardware. According to the mission, the satellite is decomposed into sub-systems, such as TM/TC (telemetry/telecommand) subsystem, AOCS (attitude and orbit control subsystem), PCDU (Power Conditioning and Distribution Unit), OBDH (On-Board Data Handling) subsystem, etc., and designed separately. All the sub-systems will be tested and integrated.

Since the satellite has just appeared in the world, there is no ready-made experience to learn from. This discrete design approach can meet the space task requirements well. However, it takes too much time, money and manpower to development a satellite. Moreover, the satellites designed in this way have a low degree of modularity. Each subsystem cannot be customized, replaced or upgraded throughout the life of the satellite.

Platform and Payload Design Approach. With the advancement of electronic devices, the satellite design gradually evolved into a common platform and payload design. By reusing the common platform and carrying different payloads, the satellite can perform a variety of space missions. The on-board software is also divided into platform software and payload software, which can be designed separately and exchange data though reserved interface.

However, due to the strong correlation between the platform and the payload, it has been proved by practice that the common platform has limited adaptability and can only satisfy several payloads with very close characteristics. Additionally, this development approach still does not change the feature that the function is too dependent on the hardware. The change of hardware electrical characteristic and interface parameter will cause the software to be unusable. The development of software always needs to wait until all the hardware design is completed and the interface functions are written. This is a waterfall development approach that is inefficient and time consuming. In general, satellites have a certain degree of modularity in this design approach. However, due to the tight coupling between the platform and the payload, only the same or similar functional modules can be replaced or upgraded.

Modular Design Approach. Based on the platform design approach, the modular design approach was discussed at the 19th Annual AIAA/USU Conference on Small Satellite held at the University of Utah in August 2005 [9, 10]. The approach divides the satellite into a series of standardized and generalized modules according to functions. Depending on the mission requirements, the developer of satellite can select and combinate these modules to develop satellites.

This method is proposed for many reasons. The level of embedded processors has increased. For example, the embedded processors (ARM) begins to be widely used in satellites. The embedded multi-tasking operating system (Vxworks, Linux) continues to mature. The in-depth application of object-oriented high-level programming language (C++, Java) makes software compatible with the difference of the various hardware platforms.

The satellite designed by the modular design approach has a structured mapping between the function and the actual components. The components can be connected to each other though standard interfaces. Through the standard interfaces, each module can be freely replaced or upgraded without damaging other parts of the system. This is very similar to a personal computer. Users can customize and upgrade quickly and easily according to their application requirements. However, for the current satellites, the interface between the modules are not fully standardized. It is not yet possible to achieve plug-and-play, raid customization and replacement of the modules like personal computer. The development of satellite modularization is advancing. Some new concept satellites, such as plug-and-play satellite (PnPSat) [11], Satlets [12], fractionated satellite [13], has been proposed. They tried to develop standardized interfaces to facilitate the modular manufacture of satellite. The degree and proportion of satellite modularization will continue to increase.

Software Design Approach. The development of ATS has gone through special-purpose instruments, bench-top building instruments, module-integrated instruments, and virtual instruments [14]. Similarly, after achieving a fully modular design, satellites will also move toward software design approach. The software design approach means that the functionality of the satellite will be defined by on-board software. The hardware only plays the role of providing basic platform.

Moreover, the next generation of satellite will also move toward networking. After fully implementing the modular design approach, the modularity of a single satellite has reached a peak. In order to adapt to more complex environments and implement more functions, it is necessary to expand a single satellite to the satellite network. This is consistent with the current development trends of Internet and Internet of Things. The distributed structure provides new capabilities to the system, and the concept of modularity will shift from static to dynamic [15].

In summary, after more than 60 years of development, the modularity of satellite is getting higher and higher. Satellite software has evolved from being part of the hardware to a major part of the satellite. Software has also evolved from highly customized to more flexible applications. Traditional embedded software development methods have not been well adapted to the new features of on-board software. Therefore, research on satellite software development methods and tools is needed.

2.2 The Research of On-Board Software Development Tools

On-board software is a complex high-tech system. Generally, it does not have a complete and friendly development environment as a general-purpose computer system. Developers usually use the command line to encode, compile, link, etc. Therefore, providing a development tool that is easy to grasp and use can effectively reduce the development difficulty of on-board software, improve the time-return rate of users and programmers, and shorten the development cycle.

Currently, most of the on-board software development adopts an embedded development environment based on a specific hardware platform, and there are not many development tools dedicated to satellite software. Some institutions and companies have conducted research on satellite development tools. The GenerationOne Flight Software Development Kit (FSDK), developed by Bright ascension, is a development environment for rapidly building a satellite software framework that allows the creation of task-specific spacecraft flight software using configurable off-the-shelf software components. It uses a component-based approach to software development that combines custom software components with previously validated library components to quickly develop reliable flight software for easy code reuse and easy integration of new features. In addition, it provides a more streamlined approach to testing and integration. OpenSatKit provides a complete, fast-deployed cFS-based development environment for onboard processors, reducing the cost of satellite software development, integration, testing and operation. The Safety-Critical Application Development Environment (SCADE) is a model-driven software development environment. It transforms Simulink models or UML models into SCADE models and provides detailed support for software requirements, enhancing traceability of software requirements. It also supports automated generation from models to code, as well as automatic generation and maintenance of documentation at all stages. NASA Operational Simulation for Small Satellites (NOS3) was developed by the JSTAR team. It allows multiple developers to simulate hardware models and test flight software.

In summary, most of the above satellite software development tools are based on specific tasks or specific software systems, such as cFS. SCADE is based on a model-driven architecture, but it is not a development tool for satellite software, and there are problems in the use of models. Therefore, we have proposed corresponding development frameworks and tools aimed at rapid development of software components and flexible deployment of software on heterogeneous hardware platforms.

3 A Model-Driven On-Board Software Development Framework

Given the advances in the hardware technologies software development in general is becoming an increasingly complex activity. However, the time for satellite development is getting shorter and shorter. At present, the degree of automation in the development process of on-board software in relatively low. Different methods and languages of description are used in each part of the development process. There is a lack of corresponding standard specifications. As a result, on-board software development is time-consuming, prone to human error, poor reusable, and unable to flexibly adapt to changes in task [29].

In order to fundamentally promote and standardize the further development of modeling technology, the Object Management Organization (OMG) proposed a new software development framework in July 2001, the model-driven architecture (MDA). MDA uses the modeling language as a programming language to take software development to a higher level of abstraction and ultimately to separate problem domains, business logic, and implementation platforms. It divides software development into three steps, corresponding to three types of models. They are computing-independent model (CIM), platform independent model (PIM) and platform specific model (PSM). CIM focuses on the system environment and requirements. PIM focuses on system operations and hides platform details. It usually describes in a platform-independent general-purpose modeling language. PSM focuses on the implementation details of a particular platform. MDA supports mapping CIM into PIM, PIM into PSM and PSM into implementation code. Therefore, MDA is independent of the specific platform and the particular software vendor, achieving standardized development.

This section proposes a model-driven on-board software development framework. The framework combines MDA with satellite domain. It uses a dedicated modeling approach for satellite applications to design satellite software system model. Through the formal verification of the model, the correctness of the design is ensured. Through the automatic model transformation, the consistency of the system design in each development stage is maintained. Through the automatic generation of code and documents, the efficiency of software development is improved.

3.1 The Target of Development Framework

The traditional satellite development process does not solve the communication challenge of each stage, which is mainly caused by two reasons. Firstly, all stages of on-board software development use different descriptions. Secondly, due to the different satellite functions, various satellites use different software architectures. In order to solve these problems, the targets of the framework are proposed: unified architecture, standardized components, configurable integration and automatic generation.

The unified architecture is the basis of collaborative development. However, the current satellite architectures and interfaces are different. On one hand, due to the different functions and structures of satellites, there is a lack of commonality between different components. For example, the AOCS is a typical real-time control system, while the TM/TC system is a communication system [30]. The sensor type and signal processing algorithm are completely different between the remote sensing payload and the communication payload. On the other hand, the entire satellite system is too large and complex. Therefore, the framework will design a unified software architecture to provide guidance for the design of on-board software.

The traditional on-board software development is a vertical design around the requirements of satellite. Whether it is application software or basic function software, it needs to be developed specifically. The complexity and urgent development period of satellite software requires cooperation among various departments to integrate new products with their respective strengths. Based on a unified architecture, the reuse of a large number of standardized components is a viable way to achieve this target. Therefore, the framework will use the low-coupling layered component model. For the key basic software component, performance optimization and formal verification are proposed. It is beneficial to the early detection of problems in system design.

The traditional on-board software is developed by manually code writing. With the advent of automated modeling, model transformation and automated generation have become important ways to improve the drawbacks of hand coding. However, it is continuously converted and refined from the top to the bottom based on the system model. The reusability between different projects is relatively low. Therefore, the framework will make full use of the unified architecture and standardized components. Through unified description files and configuration parameters, development of software components and personalized configuration of the operation environment can be implemented for different applications. It achieves a high degree of reuse of standardized components and decoupling of hardware platform and software development.

Automation is an important means to improve the efficiency of software development and eliminate human errors. There is a large number of hand-written code and documents in traditional on-board software development process. The modern model-driven design methodology is directly related to the display [31]. The framework will design a tool that is able to automatically generate code and documents based on the graphical models. It will improve the code quality and simplify the modification of system.

3.2 The Architecture of Development Framework

The model-driven on-board software development architecture is a model-centric software engineering approach. Through graphical modeling, a highly abstract model of complex system is constructed to characterize the hierarchical structure of the system and the associations between the layers. The developers have a better understanding of the internal entity of system, attribute, the relationship and evolution process between entities. Meanwhile, it also establishes a unified communication between experts and project teams in different fields [32]. By designing the model automatic conversion tools, the "automatic" design is realized. Therefore, the framework is a complete on-board software development solution, shown in Fig. 1.

3.3 Development Environment

The development environment is a model-based integrated development environment for on-board software, including the design tool, the configuration tool, the validation tool, the generation tool, and the test tool. These tools are based on virtual abstract connections and implement integration in a unified data exchange format.

An abstract connection of the entire on-board software components can be built in the design tool. To facilitate reuse and migration, software components are implemented

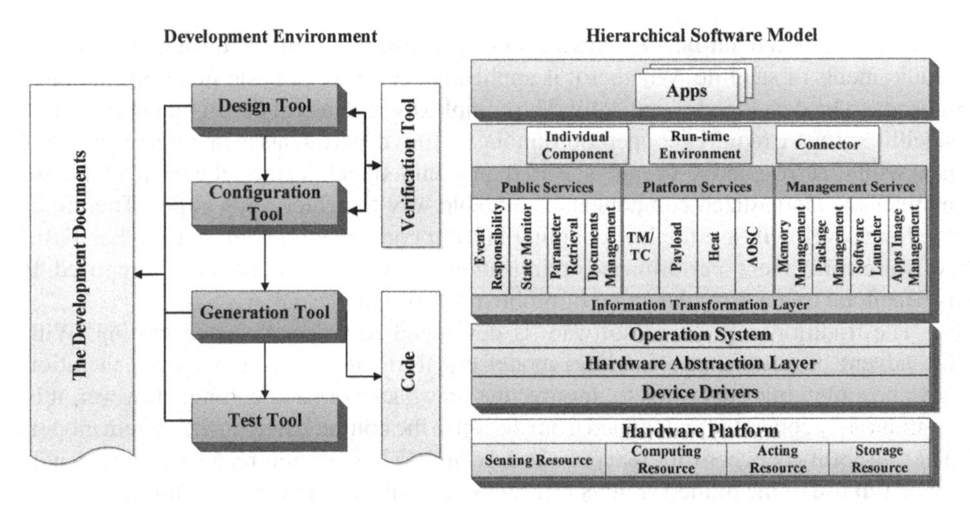

Fig. 1. Architecture of the development framework.

independently of hardware. They are designed with standardized interfaces that enable connections between components. The components also have fully defined ports through which you can define how and what types of data are exchanged.

The configuration tools used to connect the PIM and the PSM, achieving the mapping between software components and hardware platform. It uses the component description files as input and system description files as output. By analyzing the resources and structure of the entire system, the components are mapped to the hardware platform and related parameters are configured.

The verification tool is used to verify the models at every stage. Via the formal verification method, the correctness of the model design and model transformation is ensured.

The generation tool will automatically convert the models and associated configuration files into code. After that, the pieces of code are integrated and assembled to generate the complete code. After compiling and linking, the executable file will be obtained finally.

The test tool is used for testing the code. The generated code can be tested for functional correctness via simulation. It also can be tested the performance by hardware-in-loop testing.

Hierarchical Software Model. The operation environment is a software environment in which the on-board software runs. It is a modular hierarchical architecture, including hardware platform, operating system, system service and application.

The hardware platform contains all the hardware units of the satellite and abstracts the hardware devices into four categories of resources: computing resources, sensing resources, acting resources and storage resources. All kinds of resources are connected via standardized interfaces.

Operation system, hardware abstraction layer and device drivers are the key to realize software cross-platform operation. They can encapsulate and virtualize various hardware resources and provide a unified API for information acquiring, processing, storing and other specific functions.

The system service contains three parts. The information transmission layer defines a set of abstract information interaction patterns and types to realize communication between application components. In the middle, there are three service packages that provide public services, platform services and software management services. They are the main part of the system service. The top layer is the basic components of the application, including individual component, run-time environment and connector. The satellite can discover, start, stop, install, update and uninstall application at work by them. They provide support for on-board multi-application running and task reconfiguring.

There are various kinds of satellite "Apps" on the top layer. These "Apps" can be divided into two categories. The first category is the system "Apps". The satellite relies on these "Apps" to achieve the basic functions, such as TC/TM, AOCS, heat control, camera basic application, communication, etc. The other category is user "Apps", which can be developed freely by users. The satellite can use these "Apps" to extend functions. For example, users can develop an image recognition "App" to process an image taken by on-board camera directly and display the result to the user.

The On-Board Software Development Process. The process of on-board software development is usually divided into five steps: system requirements analysis, system design, system configuration, code generation, and system integration. These steps are all around the system model.

The system requirement model will be established in the system requirements analysis stage, which can describe the goal of the on-board software. It includes the demand modeling and the demand verifying. Based on the demand model, the system is specifically designed to find the solution to achieve all the requirements of the system in the system design stage. It includes system model design and system model verification. In the system configuration stage, the system model will be mapped with the specific hardware platform to generate the final models and configuration files. The implementation code will be automatically generated in the code generation stage based on the model and configuration files. The system integration is a unique task of on-board software development. It matches the software with the specific satellite through parameter configurations. It is also guided by the system model.

The detail flow of the on-board software development is shown in Fig. 2. It abstractly describes three steps of the development: software component design, system configuration and system test.

In the step of software component design, the developer will design a platform independent model for on-board software based on the system component library. There are two types of software components: Atomic Software Component (AtomicSC) and Composition Software Component (CompositionSC). AtomicSC is the elementary unit describing a function and communicates to others by relevant ports. CompositionSC is composed of AtomicSCs and can be nested. First of all, the system requirement model will be designed. Then the model will be confirmed and verified through model verification and modified based on the result of the verification. It is an interactive and iterative process. After that, the validated requirement model will be converted into a system model and designed in detail. Similarly, the well-designed system model also

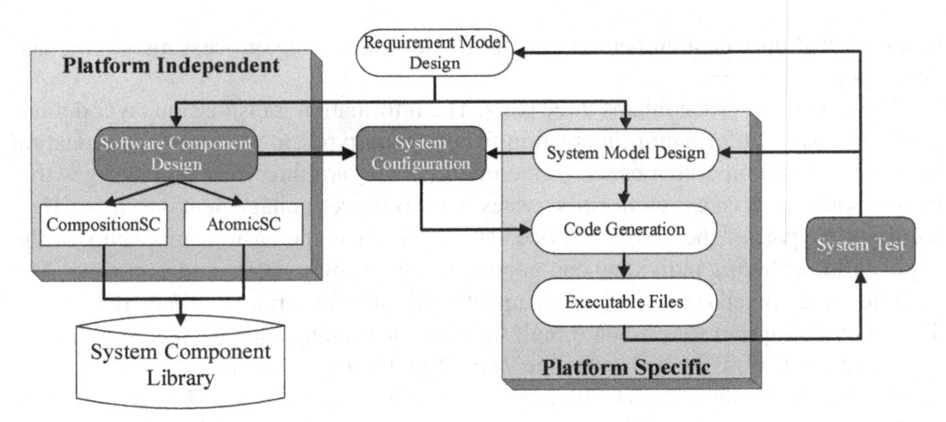

Fig. 2. The detail flow of the on-board software development.

needs to be verified. Based on the result, the developer corrects the system model or re-adjusts the design of the requirement model. Finally, the validated requirement model and system model are configured with specific target platform.

In the step of system parameter configuration, the platform independent model will be mapped to a specific hardware platform and parameterized in order to convert into platform specific model. After the configuration, the model will be transformed to generate the code with the software component in the system component library. Obviously, before the code is generated, the model will be verified to ensure that no errors occur during the configuration. After compiling and testing, the code can run on the hardware devices and become an "App".

The system test is also based on the model. The test process is to load the generated executable "App" into the test platform and execute the test case. It will test the function and performance of the development software. If the result of test cannot meet the requirements, it will return to the previous steps and begin a new round of iteration.

4 The Design of Development Tool Chain

Although there are a large number of integrated development environments for on-board software development, they are mostly based on traditional development process for specific satellite hardware platforms. The tools based on the MDA have the following challenges. Lack of tools for effectively composing satellite system form components. Lack of tools for configuring middleware. Lack of tools for automating the deployment of satellite component onto heterogeneous target platforms. Therefore, according to the framework proposed in Sect. 3, an on-board software development tool chain is designed in this section. On one hand, it develops on-board software in the form of components, achieving flexible combination and rapid construction. On the other hand, it decouples the development process of software and hardware, achieving the deployment of software on heterogeneous hardware platform.

The tool chain consists of the software component tool, the system configuration tool and the software test tool, integrated by a plug-in platform. The software component tool provides a graphical modeling environment. It can design software components and build system software models according to the on-board software meta-models. The system configuration tool can build the satellite hardware system model, establish a relationship with related software components and configure related parameter. The software test tool can simulate satellite operations according to the integrated STK kernel and realize the test of the software. The overall design of the development tool chain is show in Fig. 3.

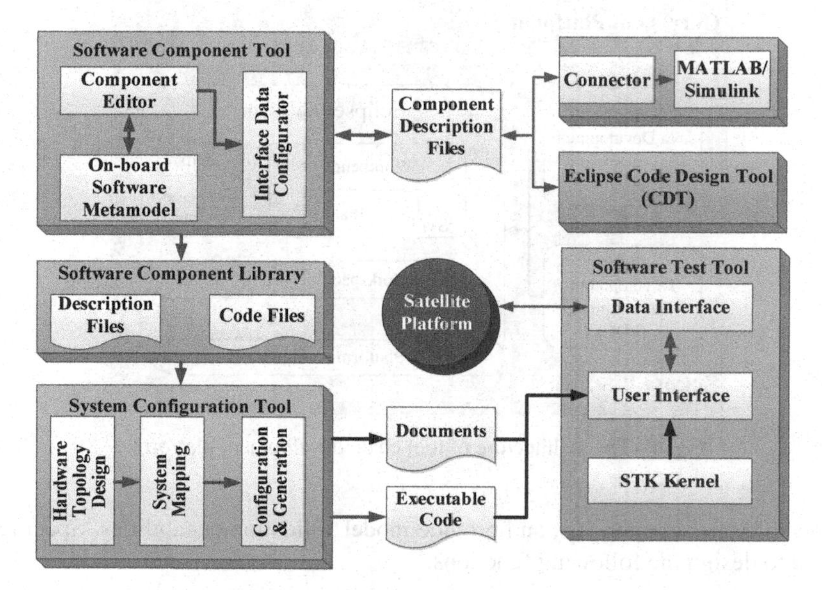

Fig. 3. The overall design of development tool chain.

In order to promote the development of the tool chain and improve the convenience of data interaction between tools, the tool chain adopts a unified Eclipse-based plug-in development platform, shown in Fig. 4. The platform is divided into three layers. The top layer is the application development platform that enables the development of specific functions of the tool. Currently, the tool chain contains three tools. The middle layer is the core tool platform, which includes the implementation of meta-model, model analysis, model comparison, basic project management, etc. The bottom layer is the Eclipse platform, which is a scalable open source multi-function system that integrates the program development platform, run time environment and application framework [33]. The tool chain integrates tools and related plug-ins in the form of plug-in on the Eclipse platform. In addition, the tool chain can dynamically call some mature software to assists the function, such as MATLAB/Simulink, C/C++ development tool (CDT), STK, etc.

4.1 The Design of Software Component Tool

The software component tool is the beginning of the development tool chain. Its mission is to provide a graphical modeling environment, complete the design and packaging of

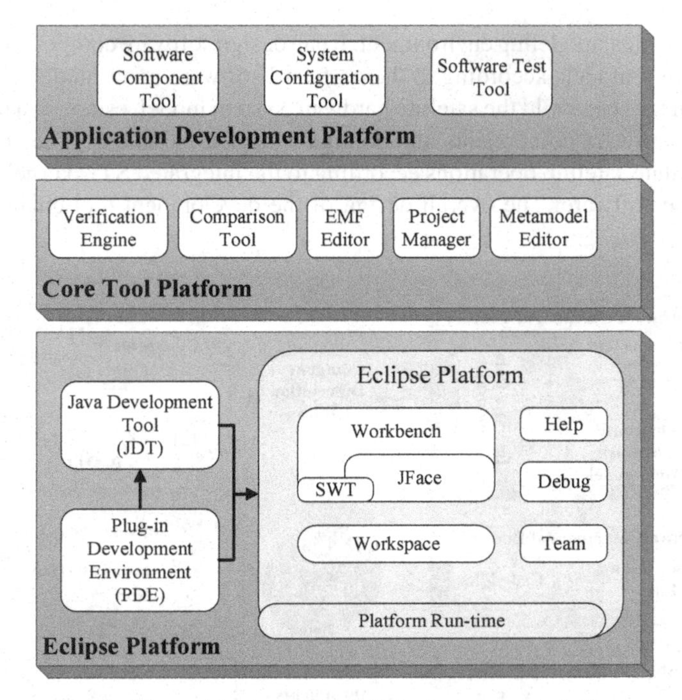

Fig. 4. The architecture of tool chain development platform.

satellite software components, and provide model validation capabilities. Specifically, we need to design the following functions.

1) Graphical software component modeling interface;
2) Configure the port and interface data of the software component;
3) Define the communication relationship between the various software components;
4) Internal behavior modeling and code generation;
5) Provide the software component model verification;
6) Establish a software component library, and provide functions such as component creation, saving, and searching.

The software component tool consists of three parts: the on-board software meta-model, the component editor and the interface data configurator.

A meta-model is used to describe the common elements of software component model. Although there is no uniform standardized architecture for on-board software now, we design the on-board software meta-model. The software components are divided into AtomicSC and CompositionSC, which are modeled by UML shown in Fig. 6. AtomicSC is the smallest implementation unit in satellite software, with a complete functional implementation. It communicates to others by relevant ports. The internal algorithm of AtomicSC is designed by calling MATLAB/Simulink. CompositionSC is used for presentation of top-level system. It can contain several AtomicSCs or CompositionSCs and support nesting. Regarding components, there are the following definitions:

$$\begin{aligned} C &= C_c \cup A_c \\ P &= P_p \cup P_r \\ I &= I_{cs} \cup I_{sr} \\ R &= R_a \cup R_d \end{aligned} \tag{1}$$

Among them, component C is a collection of CompositionSC C_c and AtomicSC A_c. And port P includes Provided ports P_p that are used to provide data or services and Required ports P_r that are used to request data or services. Interface I is make up of Client server interfaces I_{cs} and sending and receiving interfaces I_{sr}. Connector R contains associations R_a between internal components of a CompositionSC and associations R_d between internal components and CompositionSC. They have the following relationships:

$$\begin{aligned} R &\subseteq P \times P \\ R_a &\subseteq P_p \times P_r \\ R_d &\subseteq P_p \times P_p \cup P_r \times P_r \end{aligned} \tag{2}$$

Figure 5 shows the meta-model of the AtomicSC A_c. The meta-model defines the three components of the AtomicSC, namely interfaces, ports, and internal algorithms. As for the meta-model of composite components, as shown in Fig. 6. The meta-model also describes its components: connectors, ports, and AtomicSC.

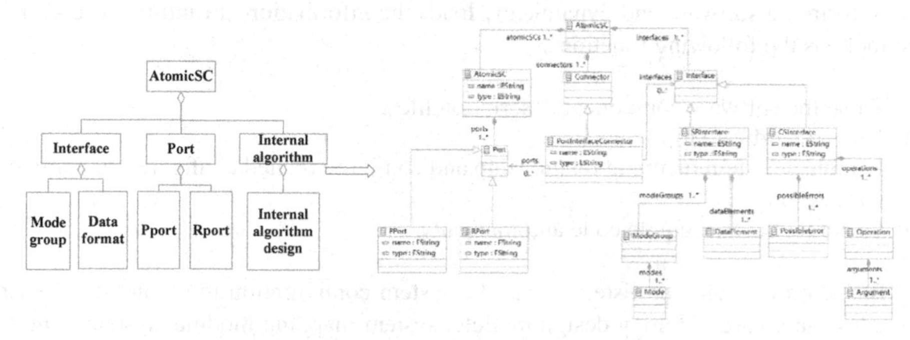

Fig. 5. The description of AtomicSC.

In addition, for CompositionSC, since it is a combination of AtomicSC, it should satisfy the following constraints:

$$\begin{aligned} & R_{pi} \subseteq P \times I \\ & R_{cp} \subseteq C \times P \\ & \forall i \in I \wedge \exists r_{pi}(p, i) \in R_{pi} \rightarrow \exists r_{cp}(c_t, p) \in R_{cp} \\ & \forall r_a(p_1, p_2) \in R_a \rightarrow \nexists r_{cp}(c_t, p_1) \in R_{cp} \wedge \nexists r_{cp}(c_t, p_2) \in R_{cp} \wedge p_1 \in P_p \wedge p_2 \in P_r \end{aligned} \tag{3}$$

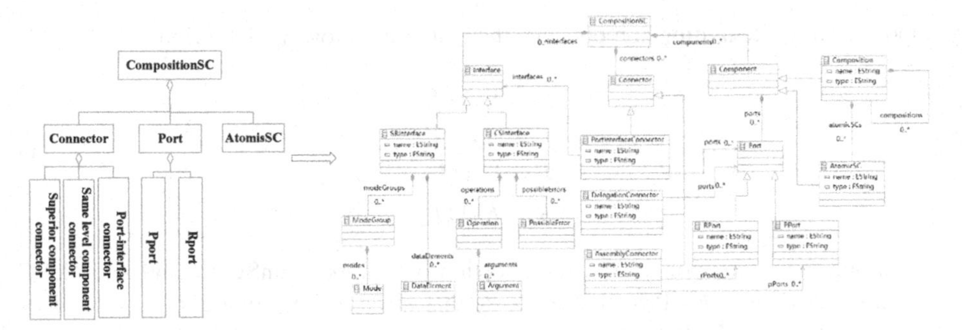

Fig. 6. The description of CompositionSC.

In other words, for CompositionSC, the nesting of components can only be inside the CompositionSC. The interface of the component must be connected to the corresponding port. When it comes to the internal nodes of the CompositionSC, the connection can only be from the P-type port to the R-type port. Constraints can avoid meaningless connections, leading to logical errors such as connections in the model.

4.2 The Design of System Configuration Tool

The system configuration tool is an intermediate part of the development tool chain, combining the software components with the hardware platform. The same software component requires different configuration parameters for different hardware platforms. The system configuration system separates the information related to the hardware implementation form the software and dynamically loads the information at runtime. Therefore, the tool has the following functions.

1) Parse the software component description files.
2) Design hardware topology.
3) Establish system mapping relationship and configure related configuration parameters.
4) Generate the executable code automatically.

Based on the function listed above, the system configuration tool consists of four modules: hardware topology design module, system mapping module, system configurator and code generator. The work flow is shown in Fig. 7. The software component description file is used as the input and the system configuration description file and executable code are the output.

Hardware topology design is the premise of system mapping and the basis of system configuration. It also uses GMF graphical modeling framework to build a graphical interface. According to the satellite architecture in Sect. 3, the developers will add and connect various processors and related peripherals. After that, the resource description files and topology description files, in the form of XML files, will be generated and saved for subsequent configuration.

System mapping module will establish a connection among the software component description file, the resource description file, and the topology description file. First of

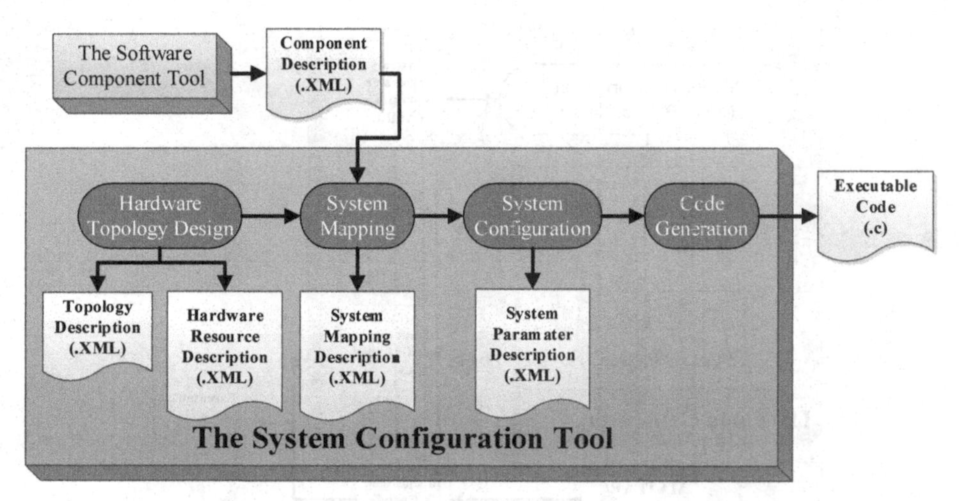

Fig. 7. The work flow of the system configuration tool.

all, through Java Document Object Model (DOM), the above three types of description files will be parsed. The internal modules and connection relationships of the hardware and software are loaded into the display. Then, the software components will be mapped to the corresponding hardware platform. In the mapping process, the processors are first mapped, then the sensors and actuators are mapped, and finally the ports of software components are mapped to the interfaces of the hardware.

The system configuration includes network configuration and parameter configuration. The network configuration is to configure the internal data transmission protocol of the satellite, achieving the requirements of different software components, such as data bandwidth, speed, reliability, etc. The parameter configuration includes interface parameters, such as interface type, data rate, data width, parity, etc. The priority of the software component, in order to realize the management and scheduling in the operation system.

The code generator can convert models and configuration files into executable code. It is based on the Velocity template engine. Firstly, the mapping between template and hardware is established. Then, the parameters in the XML files are converted to Java classes. Finally, the C code is generated. The specific process is shown in Fig. 8.

4.3 The Design of Software Test Tool

The test tool can load the generated description file and execution code on the hardware platform and simulate the running state of satellite by STK kernel to test the software. The tool has the following functions:

1) Input configuration document.
2) Test the software function.
3) Simulate satellite running state.

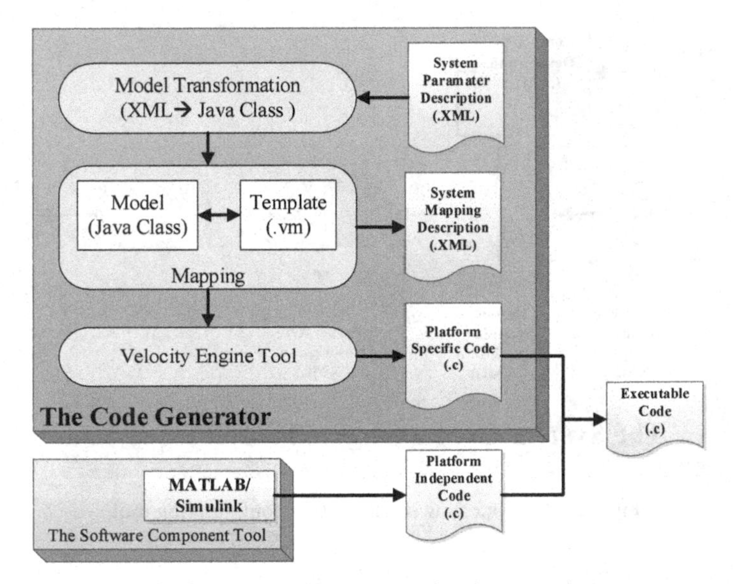

Fig. 8. The specific process of code generation.

Therefore, the software test tool consists of three parts: test files, user interface and STK kernel. The test files are mainly responsible for recording and managing the input and out files, including the software component description files, system configuration description files, the executable code, and hardware communication files. The software test tool can interact with the data of the above two tools freely. It parses the files through Java DOM, obtains all the software functions in the project, and displays them in the user interface.

A complete set of software test flow can be implemented through the user interface, including sending user instructions, loading configuration files, receiving and displaying the operation data, reconfiguring the software application. The software test tool can communicate with the satellite platform. Through the received data, the correctness, reliability and real-time performance of software can be tested. Users can test a function independently or design test cases to test the whole on-board software. The user interface is implemented by the Eclipse Standard Widget Toolkit (SWT).

The STK kernel is integrated in the software test tool. Through setting up the satellite scenarios, the overall running state, multi-task operation mode, software reconfiguration logic and resource consumption of on-board software can be tested. Embedding the STK into the Eclipse platform is mainly achieved through the Object Model, which calls the Object Model API to manipulate most objects and functions in STK. The Object Model provides STK secondary developer with methods for controlling and managing entities in STK scenarios, acquiring simulation data, analyzing, and calculating.

5 Application Case and Assessment

This section describes some actual software development cases which use the development tool chain presented in Sect. 4. The on-board software of a CubeSat named iSat-1, developed at the College of artificial intelligence of the National University of Defense Technology (NUDT). The iSat-1 is designed to experiment the software on-orbit definition.

5.1 The Development Tool Chain Platform

The development tool chain platform is showed in Fig. 9. The component editor includes sections such as toolbars, graphical editing interfaces, and other auxiliary views. The toolbar is a collection of tools, including interface configuration tools, system mapping tools, and testing tools in the system configuration. But the key part is the component designed that is relied on the graphical editing. The graphical editing interface consists of two parts: the drawing toolbox and the graphic editing area. The Drawing Toolbox provides tools for creating models under the current window. The graphic editing area is the area where graphics are created, edited, and displayed. Other auxiliary views provide some auxiliary functions for the component editor, such as providing outline views, property views, and so on.

The component editor is designed based on the Graphical Modeling Language (GMF) framework, which consists of a graphical development and a runtime environment. We develop the component editor by defining the domain model (Ecore model), the graphical definition model (gmfgraph model) for describing the domain model, the tool model (gmftool model), and the mapping model that associates the above models. The interface of the component editor is shown in Fig. 9. The user can quickly build the on-board software model in the graphical editor by a drag-and-drop manner. After completing the component editing, through the description file generator, the corresponding XML description file can be generated to provide a unified exchange format. It is convenient for developers to save and view model information.

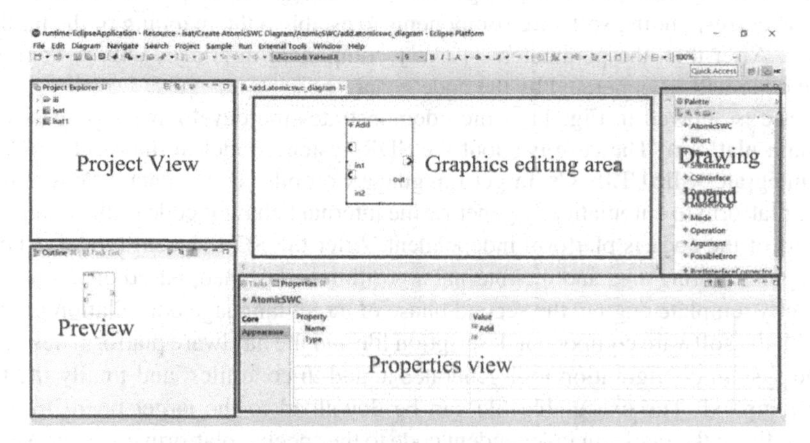

Fig. 9. The view of the development tool chain platform.

Another key work of component design is the data interface configurator. The data interface configurator realizes the design of the interaction relationship between software components through a visual configuration interface. It includes a data type editor and an interface type editor. The data type editor provides configuration of data structure and date semantic. The interface type editor completes the configuration of two communication modes of software components (send-receive mode and client-server mode). The output of the interface data configurator is the interface description file. The contents of the interface description file are: name, data type, content, description, and sending method.

5.2 The Test for the Framework

The functions of iSat-1 are divided into two categories. The one is the functions necessary to maintain satellite operations, such as TM/TC, heat control, AOCS, power control and housekeeping system. The other is the various applications implemented by satellite, such as SDR, remote sensing. All of these functions are first designed through software component tool, as shown in the Fig. 10. In the figure, every module is an CompositionSC, which contains some CompositionSCs and AtomicSCs. These AtomicSCs can be designed by developers themselves, or they can directly reuse existing component models. The reuse of software functions is achieved through the reuse of models. It improves the efficiency and quality of software development. Finishing the design of the software model, an XML file will be generated to describe the model and transform the information to the system configuration.

In order for the software to run on a specific hardware platform, a mapping of software components to the hardware platform is required through the system configuration tool. The iSat-1 uses two MCUs as power controller and OBC. The two are connected by an I2C bus. It also uses a Xilinx zynq SoC (ZYNQ 7020) as the processor of the SDR payload. The payload and the OBC are connected via Ethernet. It can be modeled by the system configuration tool, shown in Fig. 10. The software component description file is imported and combined with the hardware platform description file. These XML files will be parsed by the system mapping module. Through the drop-down menu, we can select the corresponding software components to establish the mapping of the hardware resource. After that, the parameters of every component interfaces will be configured and the code will be generated by the code generator.

A case is showed in Fig. 11, which demonstrates the development process of the tool chain platform. The case is about the SDR system model in the SDR SOC. This paper integrates SIMULINK's Target Language Compiler code generation tool on the Eclipse platform to automatically generate the internal behavior code of the component. This part of the code is platform independent. After the SDR system model is built in the Graphics editing area and the internal algorithm is designed, based on the principle of Velocity template engine, the second phase of target language compilation is carried out. With the software component description file and the hardware platform description file, the system configuration tool generates .c and .h code files, and finally the target file is compiled. The executable file can be download to the target board to test its function. From the platform independent code to the specific platform code, the Velocity template engine first maps the template, that is, the internal component code, to the hardware interface, and then reflects the configuration parameters in the code. All other components can be developed and executed in accordance with this process.

When the code is automatically generated, a code generation report can be generated to describe the related information of the code generation, such as the generated code

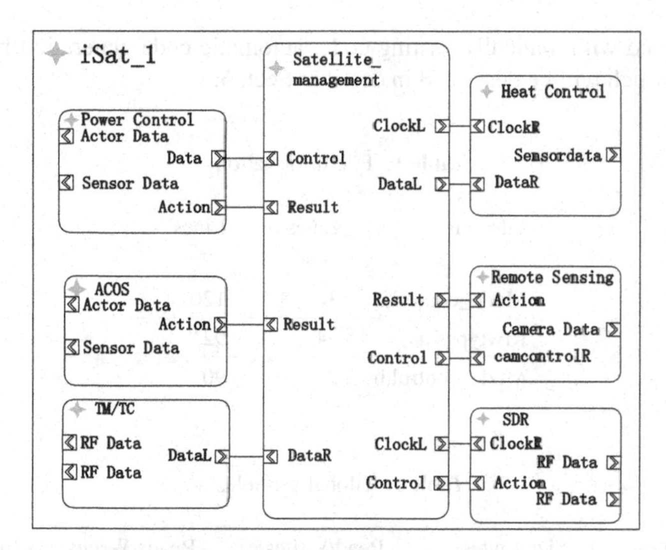

Fig. 10. The top model of the on-board software.

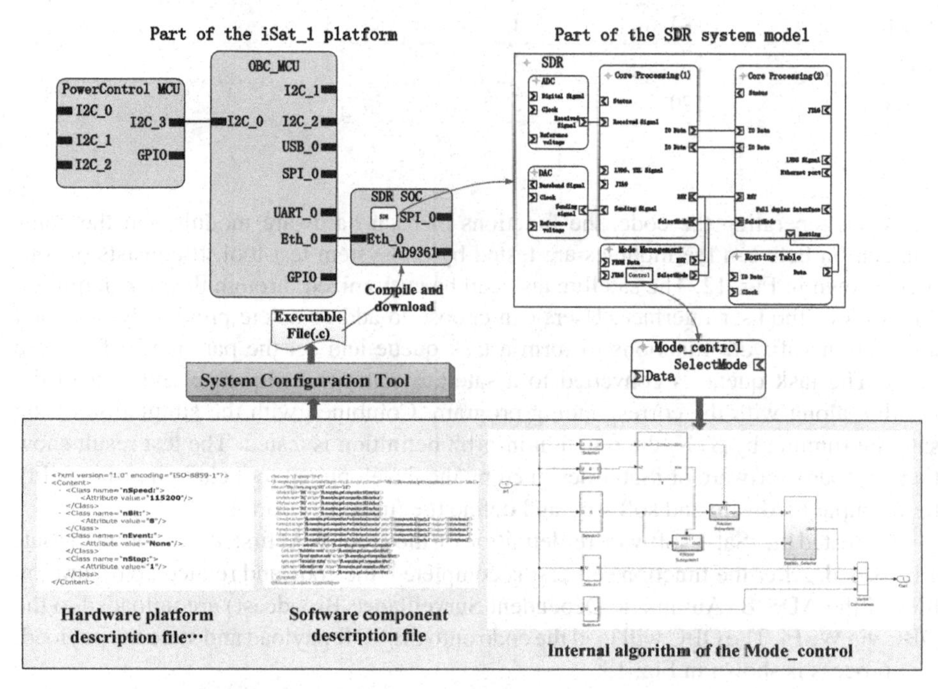

Fig. 11. Case of the development process of Mode_control

file information, as shown in Table 1, and the variable information that is displayed in Table 2. In addition, there are functional information and quality evaluation of the code. Compared with manually writing code, automatic code generation brings some advantages, which will be described in detail in Sect. 5.

Table 1. File Information

File name	Lines of code	Lines
Mode_control.c	36	120
Rtwtypes.h	34	92
Mode_control.h	27	90

Table 2. Global variables

Global variables	Size (bytes)	Read/Writes	Reads/Writes in a function
In1	284	1	1
Out1	284	1	1
add	2	1	1
Total	570	3	

After generating the code, the functions of each hardware module and the communication between the modules are tested by the system test tool. It consists of four parts shown in Fig. 12. The satellite task can be customized through the task definition windows of the user interface. Users can choose to add or delete previously designed application software functions to form a task queue and set the parameters for these tasks. The task queue is converted to a satellite command sequence and sent to the satellite along with the corresponding program. Combined with the simulation of the satellite running by STK, the function in-orbit definition is tested. The test result show that on-board software of iSat-1 designed by the development tool chain has the ability to decouple hardware and software and define the function in-orbit.

We tested the iSat-1 software re-definition on the ground. At first, the program of iSat-1 is loaded. After the function self-test is completed, the code and related configuration files of the ADS-B (Automatic Dependent Surveillance-Broadcast) are uploaded to the OBC via Wi-Fi. The OBC will load the code onto the SDR payload and stare the payload. The process is shown in Fig. 13.

The results of the experiment are displayed in the software test tool, shown in Fig. 14. As shown in the figure, iSat-1 consumes 3.9 s to complete the reconfiguration. The function of ADS-B is successfully executed. The nearby aircraft information is received and displayed. As a conclusion, the development tool chain can effectively support the development of on-board software in-orbit re-defined.

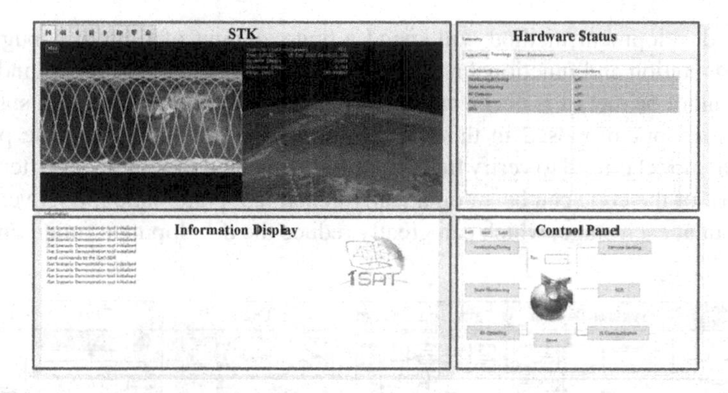

Fig. 12. The interface of the system mapping module.

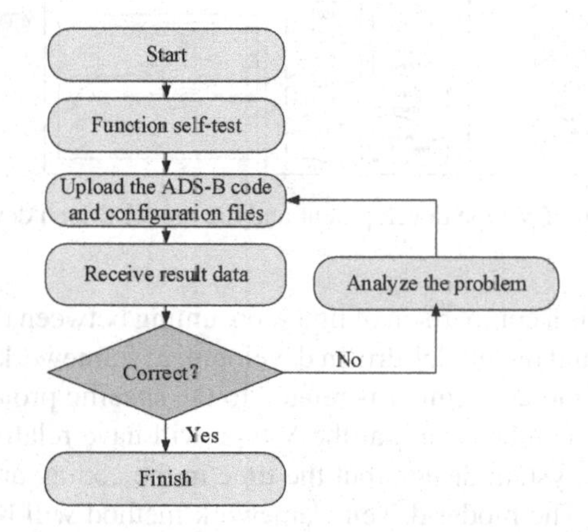

Fig. 13. The process of software re-definition experience.

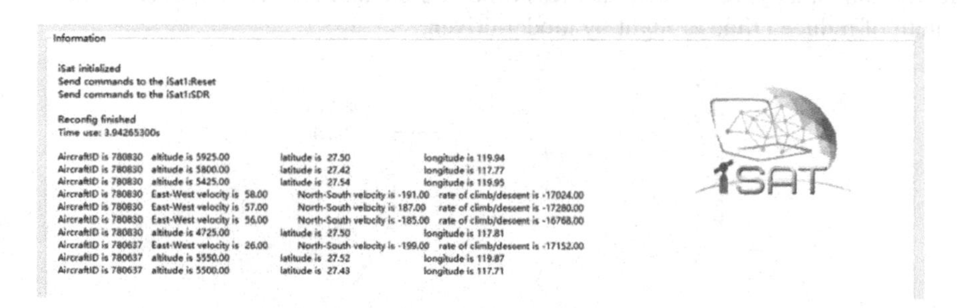

Fig. 14. The results of the experiment.

5.3 Assessment

Time-Consuming. The software development of traditional satellites is a long process. Traditionally, a waterfall-type (or V-type) development method is adopted, and the process from requirements, design, coding to testing is experienced. In the integration test phase, this development method will spend a huge amount of time in debugging the interface adaptation and functional requirements of each software. If it is found that the demands cannot be met, it is necessary to start over from the overall design stage.

The framework proposed in this paper is based on model-driven. The platform-independent model is used to verify functional demands at all design stage. After detailed design, most of the code can be automatically generated. Automatic model verification is carried out at each stage, which can greatly reduce the development time-consuming.

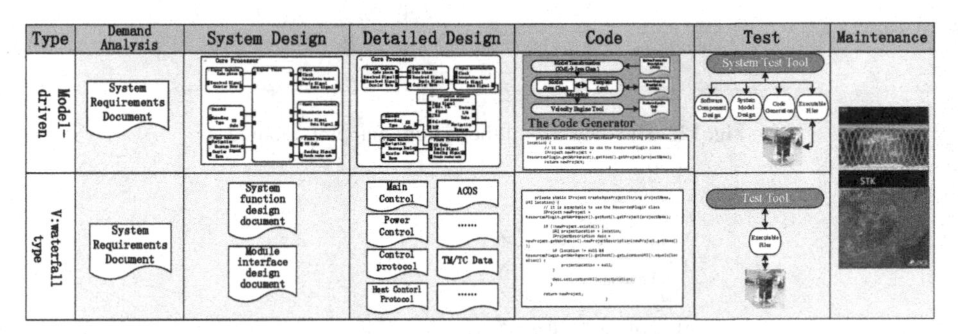

Fig. 15. Comparison of V-type development and the model-driven development process

The Fig. 16 below is a comparison of time-consuming between the traditional V-type development method and the model-driven development framework (MDF) proposed in this paper. Since the time-consuming is related to the specific project, the graph is just a trend comparison. It can be seen that the V-type will have relatively less time in the demands analysis and system design, but the time in the coding and testing phase will increase dramatically. The model-driven framework method will be a little bit more in system design and detailed design, because the system model needs to be constructed clearly and exactly, but it will take less time to code and test the software. This is the benefit of reduced time brought by model-driven.

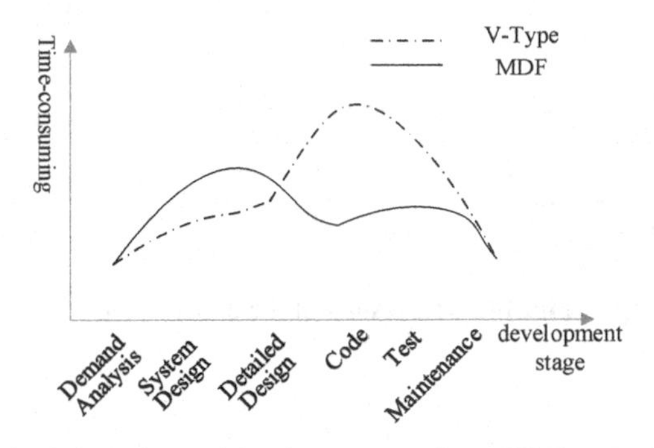

Fig. 16. Comparison of the time-consuming of V-Type and MDF

Software Reuse. The development tool chain encapsulates typical satellite software, including system models, CompositionSC and AtomicSC, which can be reused. This can reduce repetitive software development work and shorten the development cycle. According to the demands of navigation and remote sensing satellites, the design of the system models of the two satellites is shown in the Fig. 17 below. In these two types of satellites, most of the other software can be reused except for navigation software and remote sensing software. It is encapsulated as a general system model, which is benefit to improve the reuse of the system model. But it is worth pointing out that this does not mean that other software does not need to be changed, such as the Time_Processing component. Since navigation satellites require much higher time precission than remote sensing satellites, the design of this component is more complicated than remote sensing satellites. But this does not affect the reuse of other parts of the software.

For CompositionSC and AtomicSC, take the Mode_control unit in SDR as an example, as shown in Fig. 11. The Selector, if, if Action, Vector and other components in this component are reused. This type of component has a higher reuse ratio in internal behavior development, which reduces a lot of work for code development.

Characteristics and Limitations. Aiming at the software development of smart satellites, this paper proposes a model-driven framework and implements the development tool chain. The entire development process is shown in Fig. 15. The traditional satellite software development has been greatly changed, not only shortening the development cycle, but also increasing the reuse rate of satellite software, and improving the reliability of the software. However, the work of this paper has the following limitations and areas for improvement.

1) The development tool chain can only be developed for satellite application software and related drivers and operating environment, but does not support to develop the software of the operating system.
2) The proposed model-driven framework can be supported to analyze the satellite hardware structure design, thermodynamics, electromagnetic and so on, but the current work does not include this part.
3) In terms of testing, a more quantitative evaluation of software development performance, such as reliability, is also needed.

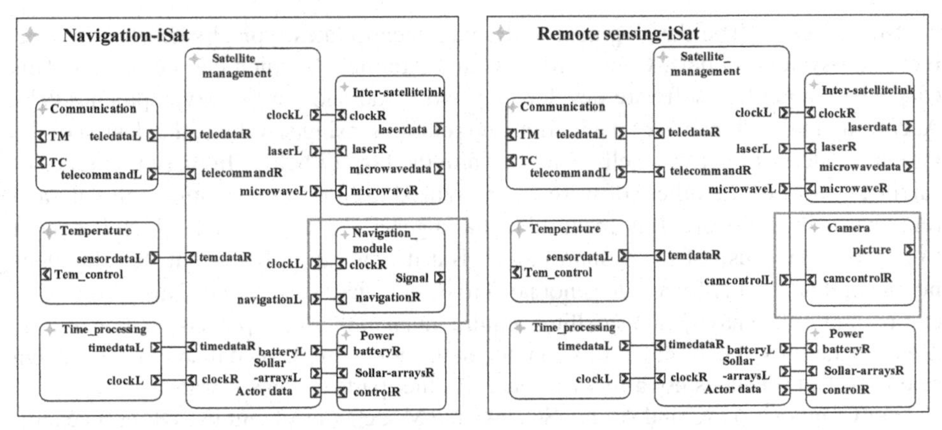

Fig. 17. System model of the Navigation and Remote Sensing satellite

6 Conclusion

Compared with the software development of other electronic systems, the development of on-board software is still in a more traditional stage. The on-board software development framework proposed in this paper are based on the model-driven software development method. The meta-models of AtomicSC and CompositionSC in the satellite software field are designed to build satellite software components. The work of the paper shifts the focus of on-board software from code writing to model designing. The entire software system will be divided into function modules, which are easy to be created, designed, reused and maintained. Therefore, the developers have more time to design software function, making the system more powerful and suitable.

It achieves the consistency of on-board software through using model as the unified description in each development stage. It also ensures the portability and reusability of on-board software development through standardized components. What's more, it decouples the software design from hardware platform and improves the platform independence through configurable integration. It improves the efficiency of software development through automatic transformation of models and automatic generation of code and documents.

Based on the development framework, a development tool chain covering all the stages of on-board software development is presented, facilitating software development engineers and testers. With the development tool chain, developers can design models graphically, configure parameters conveniently, and generate executable code automatically. What's more, the verified software component will be added to the component library, supporting software reuse and redeployment.

The framework and development tool chain have been used to develop the on-board software of iSat-1. The on-board software is developed in the form of "Apps" and independent of the hardware platform. Moreover, it supports to load software in-orbit, achieving the function software defined.

References

1. Laxmi, D.: Requirements engineering for software development process (2019)
2. Younas, M., Jawawi, D.N.A., Mahmood, A.K., et al.: Agile software development using cloud computing: a case study. IEEE Access **8**, 4475–4484 (2020)
3. Madry, S., Martinez, P., Laufer, R.: Innovative Design, Manufacturing and Testing of Small Satellites. Cham: Springer (2018). https://doi.org/10.1007/978-3-319-75094-1
4. Marmolejo-Saucedo, J.A.: Design and development of digital twins: a case study in supply chains. Mob. Netw. Appl. **25**(6), 2141–2160 (2020). https://doi.org/10.1007/s11036-020-01557-9
5. Gao, S., Sweeting, M.N., Nakasuka, S., Worden, S.P.: Issue small satellites. Proc. IEEE **106**, 339–342 (2018). https://doi.org/10.1109/jproc.2018.2805267
6. Sweeting, M.N.: Modern small satellites-changing the economics of space. Proc. IEEE **106**, 343–361 (2018). https://doi.org/10.1109/jproc.2018.2806218
7. Coelho, C., Koudelka, O., Merri, M.: NanoSat MO framework: when OBSW turns into apps. In: 2017 IEEE Aerospace Conference (2017). https://doi.org/10.1109/aero.2017.7943951
8. Heydari, B., Mosleh, M., Dalili, K.: From modular to distributed open architectures: a unified decision framework. Syst. Eng. **19**, 252–266 (2016). https://doi.org/10.1002/sys.21348
9. Kingston, J.: Modular architecture and product platform concepts applied to multipurpose small spacecraft. In: 19th Annual AIAA/USU Conference on Small Satellite (2005)
10. Young, Q.: Modular platform architecture for small satellites: evaluating applicability and strategic issues. In: 19th Annual AIAA/USU Conference on Small Satellite (2005)
11. Fronterhouse, D., Lyke, J., Achramowicz, S.: Plug-and-play satellite (PnPSat). In: AIAA Infotech@Aerospace 2007 Conference and Exhibit, July 2007. https://doi.org/10.2514/6.2007-2914
12. Barnhart, D., Hill, L., Turnbull, M., Will, P.: Changing satellite morphology through cellularization. In: AIAA SPACE 2012 Conference & Exposition, November 2012. https://doi.org/10.2514/6.2012-5262
13. Mccormick, D., Barrett, B., Burnside-Clapp, M.: Analyzing fractionated satellite architectures using RAFTIMATE: a Boeing tool for value-centric design. In: AIAA SPACE 2009 Conference & Exposition (2009). https://doi.org/10.2514/6.2009-6767
14. Zhao, X., Guo, M.: Design of software platform in general purpose automatic test system based on PAWS. In: 2011 International Conference on Electric Information and Control Engineering (2011). https://doi.org/10.1109/iceice.2011.5777911
15. Lafleur, J.: A Markovian state-space flexibility framework applied to distributed-payload satellite design decisions. In: AIAA SPACE 2011 Conference & Exposition, 2011. https://doi.org/10.2514/6.2011-7274
16. McComas, D., Strege, S., Wilmot, J.: Core Flight System (cFS) a low cost solution for SmallSats. NASA Technical reports Server (NTRS). https://ntrs.nasa.gov/search.jsp?R=20150018075. Accessed Aug 2015
17. Wilmot, J.: A core plug and play architecture for reusable flight software systems. In: 2nd IEEE International Conference on Space Mission Challenges for Information Technology (SMC-IT06), August 2006. https://doi.org/10.1109/smc-it.2006.7
18. Project Overview - CubeSat Lab (online database), August 2017. https://www.cubesatlab.org/CubedOS.jsp. Aug 2017
19. Mathur, D., et al.: An approach for designing reusable, embedded software components for spacecraft flight instruments. In: 11th IEEE Real Time and Embedded Technology and Applications Symposium. https://doi.org/10.1109/rtas.2005.7
20. Walter, A., Adilson, M.: Towards a pattern-based framework for satellite flight software using a model-driven approach. In: Brazilian Symposium on Aerospace Engineering & Applications, June 2017

21. Briones, J.C., Roche, R., Hickey, J., Handler, L.M.: Future standardization of space telecommunications radio system with core flight system. In: 34th AIAA International Communications Satellite Systems Conference (2016). https://doi.org/10.2514/6.2016-5720
22. Fenech, H., Sonya, A., Tomatis, A., Soumpholphakdy, V., Merino, J.L.S.: Eutelsat quantum: a game changer. In: 33rd AIAA International Communications Satellite Systems Conference and Exhibition, March 2015. https://doi.org/10.2514/6.2015-4318
23. The alliance was established in Chengdu on September 9, 2017 (online database). September 2017. https://www.sdsalliance.net/a/news/60.html. Accessed September 2017
24. France, R., Rumpe, B.: Model-driven development of complex software: a research roadmap. Future of Softw. Eng. (FOSE 2007) (2007). https://doi.org/10.1109/fose.2007.14
25. Li, H., Lu, P., Yao, M., Li, N.: SmartSAR: a component-based hierarchy software platform for automotive electronics. In: 2009 International Conference on Embedded Software and Systems (2009). https://doi.org/10.1109/icess.2009.54
26. Balasubramanian, K., et al.: Applying model-driven development to distributed real-time and embedded avionics systems. Int. J. Embedded Syst. **2**, 142 (2006). https://doi.org/10.1504/ijes.2006.014851
27. Schlegel, C., Steck, A., Lotz, A.: Robotic software systems: from code-driven to model-driven software development. Robot. Syst. Appl. Control Program. (2012). https://doi.org/10.5772/25896
28. Narumi, T., Takano, S., Kimura, S.: Development of high-performance compact on-board computer for micro/nano-satellites with software resource sharing framework. SICE J. Control, Meas. Syst. Integr. **10**, 10–15 (2017). https://doi.org/10.9746/jcmsi.10.10
29. Ziemke, C., Kuwahara, T., Kossev, I.: An integrated development framework for rapid development of platform-independent and reusable satellite on-board software. Acta Astronaut. **69**, 583–594 (2011). https://doi.org/10.1016/j.actaastro.2011.04.011
30. Dos Santos, W.A., Leonor, B.B.F., Stephany, S.: A knowledge-based and model-driven requirements engineering approach to conceptual satellite design. In: Laender, A.H.F., Castano, S., Dayal, U., Casati, F., de Oliveira, J.P.M. (eds.) ER 2009. LNCS, vol. 5829, pp. 487–500. Springer, Heidelberg (2009). https://doi.org/10.1007/978-3-642-04840-1_36
31. Tipaldi, M., Legendre, C., Koopmann, O., Ferraguto, M., Wenker, R., Dangelo, G.: Development strategies for the satellite flight software on-board Meteosat Third Generation. Acta Astronaut. **145**, 482–491 (2018). https://doi.org/10.1016/j.actaastro.2018.02.020
32. Süß, J.G., Pop, A., Fritzson, P., Wildman, L.: Towards integrated model-driven testing of SCADA systems using the eclipse modeling framework and modelica. In: 19th Australian Conference on Software Engineering (aswec 2008) (2008). https://doi.org/10.1109/aswec.2008.4483203
33. AUTOSAR - Enabling Innovation (online database), January 2019. https://www.autosar.org/. Accessed Jan 2019

Approximate Computing Based Low Power Image Processing Architecture for Intelligent Satellites

Zhixi Yang[1,2], Rong Lv[2(✉)], Xianbin Li[1], Jian Wang[1], and Jun Yang[2]

[1] National Innovation Institute of Defense Technology, Academy of Military Science, Beijing 100073, China
nudtyzx@163.com, lixianbincn@163.com, wangjian710108@126.com

[2] The 63rd Research Institute, National University of Defense Technology, Nanjing 210000, China
lvrong17@nudt.edu.cn, john323@163.com

Abstract. Approximate computing is an innovative circuit paradigm for lower power and real time image processing architecture within an intelligent satellite. Multiplication and addition are often fundamental functions for many image processing applications. Based on previous approximate compressor designs, a recursive type multiplier is first proposed. A reduced gate-level complexity full adder is then proposed. Extensive simulation results show that the proposed designs achieve significant reductions in area, power and delay compared with exact recursive multiplier and adders, as well as other approximate designs found in the technical literature. An image processing application is performed to further show that the performance of the proposed approximate designs for image processing achieves a very good accuracy (measured by the peak signal to noise ratio) as well as substantial reductions in power dissipation and delay.

Keywords: Approximate multiplier · Approximate adder · Low power · Real time · Image processing · Intelligent satellite

1 Introduction

The power consumption and processing speed are the major performance metrics for on-board image processing architectures within intelligent satellites. These architectures commonly rely on digital signal processing circuits and various design techniques are used to reduce their processing power. Approximate computing uses inexact or approximate processing circuits to produce meaningful results while provide an additional layer of power saving over conventional low-power design techniques. The simplified and approximate circuits operating at higher performance and/or lower power compared to their accurate logic counterparts [1], which has been extensively used for error resilient applications such as image processing [2].

Q. Wu et al. (Eds.): WiSATS 2020, LNICST 358, pp. 351–363, 2021.
https://doi.org/10.1007/978-3-030-69072-4_28

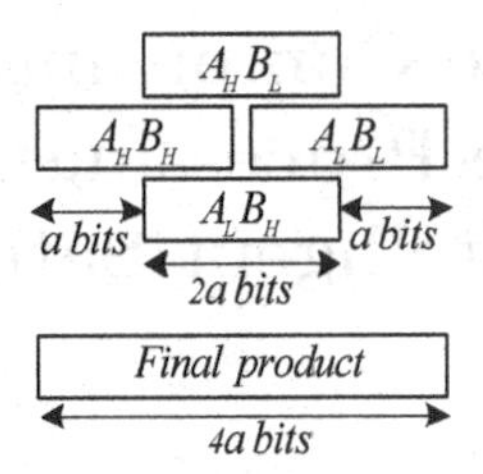

Fig. 1. Recursive multiplication by dividing multiplier and multiplicand into two parts.

Approximate circuits proposed starting from fundamental components such as multipliers and full adders [3,4]. A multiplier is designed either in the simple and popular array configuration [5,6] or in parallel column compression architecture [7,8]. The latter type of design is frequently used for high performance due to the shorter delay incurred by the compressors [9,10]. Different designs of a compressor lead to different architectures for the multiplier [11–14]. Several approximate schemes have been proposed as applicable to a multiplier [15–20]. In addition to these methods, several approximate compressors have been proposed for multiplication [21,22]. [23] uses the simple recursive multiplication technique which has also been used in this paper.

In terms of approximate adder design, [24] simplifies a single adder cell by removing transistors from a mirror adder (AMA). In this paper, multiplexer-based approximate adder designs are proposed and the multiplexer designs utilize transmission gates (TG) due to the low power dissipation than a conventional CMOS multiplexer.

An image processing application using previously proposed approximate compressors, multipliers [25] and TG based approximate adders are considered, the analysis and simulation results show that the proposed approximate designs for both the multiplier and adder are viable for approximate computing.

2 Proposed Approximate Designs

2.1 Approximate Multiplier Design

An alternative approach for designing a multiplier is to use recursive multiplication as shown in Fig. 1. Recursive multiplication splits input into two parts, i.e. $A_H(B_H)$ and $A_L(B_L)$; then perform multiplications as $A_H B_H$, $A_H B_L$, $A_L B_H$ and $A_L B_L$; finally four terms are added. The designs studied in this paper are shown in Table 1.

2.2 Approximate Adder Design

An alternative approach to implement complex logic is to use a logic network of switches, such as a multiplexer. Multiplexer logic can be accomplished by using either gate or transistor level designs. Conventional gate level multiplexers use

Table 1. Design features of approximate 8 × 8 multipliers.

Multiplier design	Features
M1-M3	Multipliers M1-M3 in [1]
M4-M6	ACCI1-ACCI3 [1] compressor based 4 × 4 multiplier for $A_L B_L$, $A_L B_H$, $A_H B_L$ only
Multiplier [2]	Lower 8 columns use compressors shown in [2]
Multiplier [3]	Inaccurate counter [3] based multiplier
Mul_Acc	Accurate compressor based recursive 8 × 8 multiplier

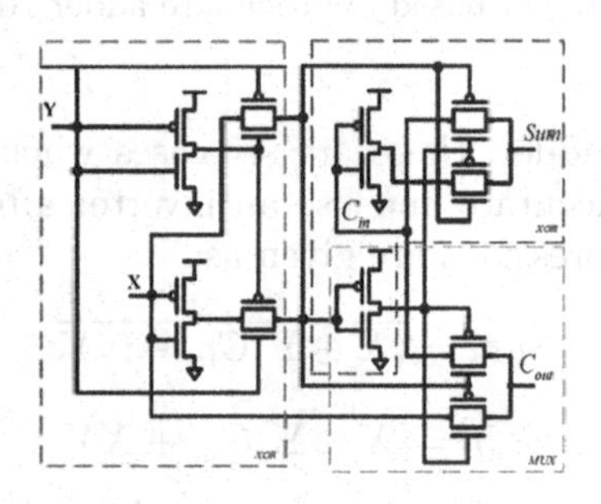

Fig. 2. TG based one bit accurate full adder.

complex gate structures, thus transistor level designs that include compounded logic and transmission gates are better alternatives.

[26] has shown that a TG based full adder exhibits good power and delay performance with a simpler circuit. Figure 2 shows an accurate TG-based full adder and this implementation is based on TGs and several inverters; the designs of approximate adders require either the removal of some modules, or changing signals for generating *Sum* or C_{out}. Moreover, in the proposed approximate adders, TG based multiplexers are frequently used due to the simple structure.

Figure 3 and Fig. 4 show the proposed approximate adders (denoted as APA1-2). The feature common is the modification of the first module XOR gate, so reducing the node capacitance and lowering the power dissipation by using only one conventional XOR gate for a reduction in delay and power.

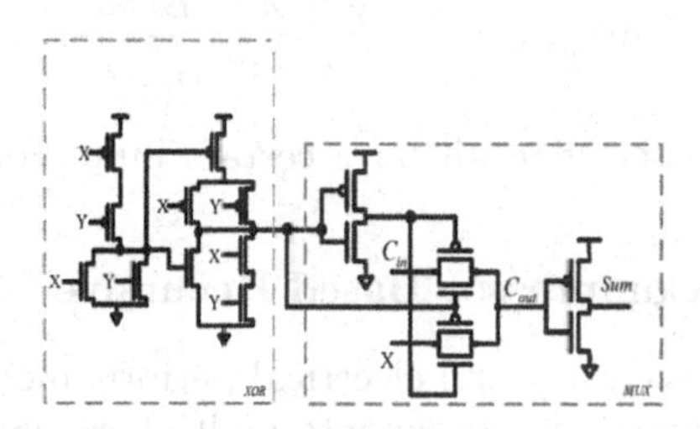

Fig. 3. TG based approximate adder APA1.

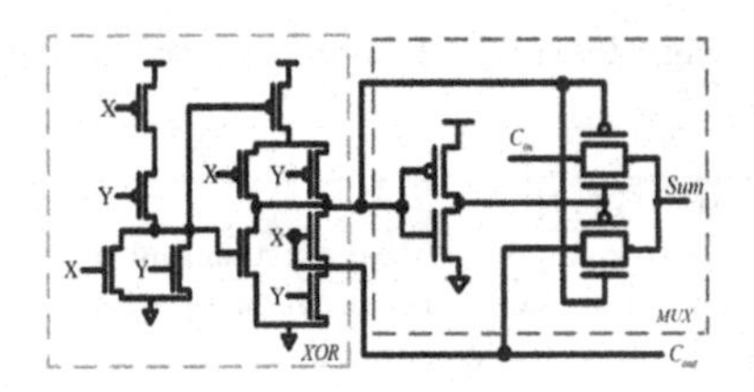

Fig. 4. TG based approximate adder APA2.

In one bit accurate adder, there are six cases when $Sum = \overline{C_{out}}$, thus an option is to keep C_{out} accurate and use an inverter after C_{out} to generate the Sum signal. Its logic expressions are given as:

$$Sum = \overline{(X \oplus Y)C_{in} + XY} \tag{1}$$

$$C_{out} = (X \oplus Y)C_{in} + XY \tag{2}$$

In APA1 the carry signal C_{out} is accurate while in APA2 C_{out} is modified. The error rate is four cases out of eight for combination of C_{out} and Sum, which is higher than APA1.

$$Sum = (X\overline{\oplus}Y)C_{in} + X\overline{Y} \tag{3}$$

$$C_{out} = X \tag{4}$$

3 Simulations Results

3.1 Metric for Approximate Design

Several metrics are introduced to quantify the effects of errors in an approximate design, including normalized error distance (NED) [2], pass rate (PR) [2] and accuracy of amplitude (Acc_{amp}) [22]. NED is defined as the mean absolute error over maximum value of the error. The pass rate is the ratio of the number of correct outputs over all outputs. Acc_{amp} is defined as:

$$Acc_{amp} = 1 - \frac{AbsoluteError}{|result_{correct}|} \tag{5}$$

$result_{correct}$ is the correct result for a certain input combination.

3.2 Approximate Compressor Based Recursive Multipliers

[25] has assessed both accuracy and electrical performance for M1-M3, hence in this subsection only recursive approximate multipliers using approximate compressors in [25] are simulated. The proposed approximate multipliers are simulated for an 8×8 recursive multiplication scheme. Delay, power consumption and area are investigated for these approximate designs compared to an exact multiplier using a recursive multiplication scheme with accurate compressors.

Table 2. Comparison of 8 × 8 multiplier for different approximate compressors based recursive multiplication.

Multiplier design	Power (uW)	Delay (ns)	Area (um^2)	NED (10^{-4})	PR (%)	Acc_{amp} (%)
M4	164.98	3.06	782.08	0.16	98.88	99.99
M5	165.67	2.92	775.84	1.56	89.7	99.86
M6	161.98	2.83	764.92	2.42	84.38	99.81
Mul_Acc	179.76	3.14	836.68	N/A	N/A	N/A

As discussed previously, A_LB_L, A_HB_L, A_LB_H utilize approximate compressor based multipliers, while an accurate 4 × 4 multiplier is used for A_HB_H.

The proposed approximate multipliers are simulated for an 8 × 8 multiplication Dadda tree. Delay, power consumption and area are investigated for approximate designs compared with an exact multiplier. Table 2 shows the comparison for these circuit based metrics and accuracy analysis. M6 has the least values for power, area and delay while a poor accuracy.

3.3 TG Based Approximate Adder

In this subsection, comparison with AMAs is presented for single APA in terms of accuracy and power, delay. Simulation is performed using Cadences Ultrasim simulator in STMicroelectronics 65 nm process, for which 1.0 V is used as the standard supply voltage (Vdd). A load of four standard Inverters is utilized, but its energy consumption is uncounted for in the evaluation of all adders. Inputs are provided by independent voltage sources. Since some inputs drive the outputs, the energy provided by the input signals is included in the simulation results. A comparison of each approximate design and the accurate full adder is pursued with respect to power consumption, delay and power delay product (PDP). All possible 64 transitions for different input combinations are considered for power and delay measurement. The delay is calculated from the input C_{in} to output C_{out} since it would propagate within a RCA; the value in the table is largest value under 64 transitions. AMAs in [24] are also included as a comparison reference. The NED is obtained by using an 8-bit RCA with all APAs. The results are shown in Table 3.

In terms of power, APA2 has the least power. AMA3 has the lowest value with 2.992uW within AMAs. However, AMA3 has a larger MED/NED than APA2.

In terms of delay, since APA2 is using input as output, the carry in-carry out delay is considered to be zero. For AMA1-3, they have similar delay within which AMA1 has largest delay; APA1 has the largest delay as more than 0.2 ns.

In terms of PDP which is the product of delay and power. Surprisingly APA2 has the least value as 0. The reason is obvious that the carry in-carry out delay is 0, thus there is no carry chain for APA2. While for AMAs, AMA4 has the least value. In a general conclusion, AMA4 is a better design within AMA4 with acceptable MED/NED and PDP.

Table 3. Simulation results for various approximate adders. Metrics of NED/MED are obtained by using an 8 bit RCA; power and delay is obtained for single approximate adder design.

Adder design	MED	NED	C_{out} delay (ns)	Power (uW)	PDP (fJ)
APA1	90.55	0.3537	0.206	3.971	0.794
APA2	63.99	0.25	0	2.883	0
AMA1	17.39	0.068	0.138	3.423	0.475
AMA2	90.55	0.3537	0.133	3.230	0.431
AMA3	74.31	0.2895	0.125	2.992	0.375
AMA4	33.12	0.1294	0.071	3.525	0.252

3.4 Comprehensive Comparison

This section discusses a new metric for a fair comparison by considering power dissipation, area and delay as well as accuracy. The Power, delay and area product (PDAP) is defined as:

$$PDAP = power * area * delay \tag{6}$$

The normalized PDAP for a group of designs is then defined as:

$$NPDAP_i = PDAP_i / max\{PDAP_j\} \tag{7}$$

where j denotes the design in the group with the largest value of PDAP; the design group includes M1_4, M2_6, M3_6, M4-M6, and the designs in [21] and [22]. The Normalized NED is defined in a similar manner, i.e.,

$$NNED_i = NED_i / max\{NED_k\} \tag{8}$$

Note that $NNED_i$ and $NPDAP_i$ relate to the same design i but the normalization is different, because the maximum values can occur in different designs (i.e. j and k). In this paper, the design of [22] has the highest value of PDAP and the highest value of NED. Figure 5 shows the NNED vs. NPDAP plot for approximate multipliers; so the design with the smaller NNED and NPDAP is the better design among the comparison set according to Pareto Front, i.e. nearest to the origin in Fig. 5. The best design is M6 with desirable position from origin.

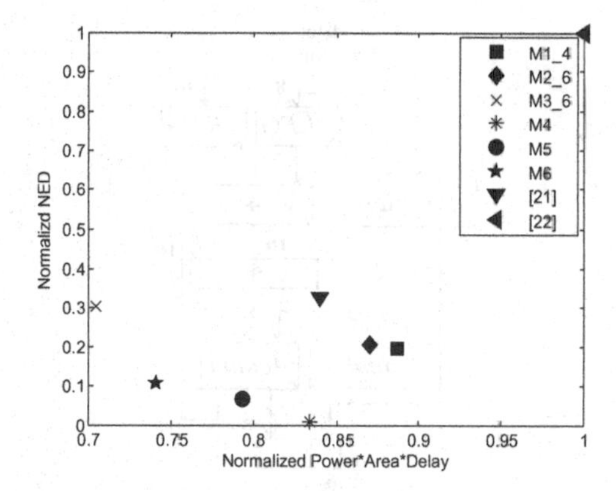

Fig. 5. Normalized NED vs. Normalized power*delay*area for approximate multiplier designs.

4 Image Processing Architecture Design

This section presents an image processing application using the proposed approximate multipliers, adders and approximate multipliers M1-M3 in [25]. An image sharpening algorithm is considered; image sharpening is functionally implemented in Verilog. The compressed image quality is measured by the peak signal noise ratio (PSNR).

The image sharpening is a Gaussian smoothing based image filter and the algorithm performs as [27]:

$$S(x,y) = \\ 2 \times I(x,y) - \frac{1}{273}\Sigma_{i=-2}^{2}\Sigma_{j=-2}^{2}G(i+3,j+3)I(x-i,y-i) \tag{9}$$

where I and S are original and processed image; G is a matrix given as:

$$G = \begin{pmatrix} 1 & 4 & 7 & 4 & 1 \\ 4 & 16 & 26 & 16 & 4 \\ 7 & 26 & 41 & 26 & 7 \\ 4 & 16 & 26 & 16 & 4 \\ 1 & 4 & 7 & 4 & 1 \end{pmatrix} \tag{10}$$

This algorithm is implemented in Verilog to build the whole architecture as shown in Fig. 6. Input and output signals are connected with registers. The components are identical apart from the multiplier and adder in Fig. 6.

Five images are selected for the sharpening algorithm executed using different approximate multipliers and adders; these images are selected, because they show features commonly found in multimedia applications; the corresponding PSNR and NED values are then measured.

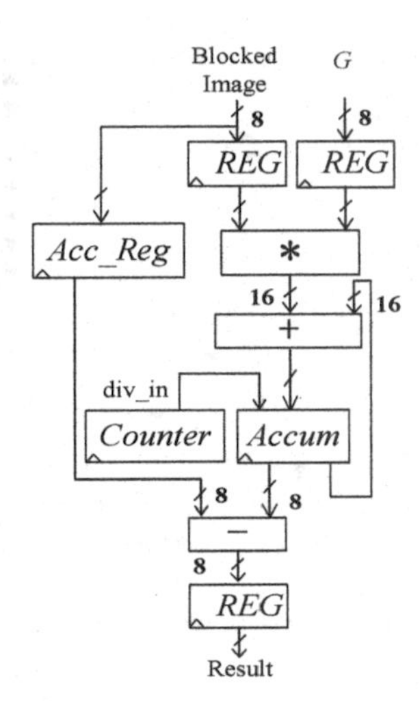

Fig. 6. Architecture of image sharpening algorithm.

4.1 Approximate Multiplier Based Image Sharpening

Two of the five processed images are shown in Figs. 7 and 8; also, the ranking of PSNR values are very close for those five images when processed by the same approximate design. When compared to the accurate results, all approximate designs (except the multiplier of [22]) produce images whose quality degradation is not perceived by human eyes. The images generated by the multiplier of [22] show areas of low quality (indicated by bold circles). For M4, for the example images, the PSNR is infinite, meaning no errors for M6 for the processed example images.

Table 4 also gives the NED and PSNR values for these two images. Table 4 shows that all approximate multipliers achieve PSNR values higher than 30dB; the approximate multipliers in [25] and proposed in this manuscript show a better image quality in terms of PSNR values than the two designs of [21] and [22]. The PSNRs of the output images generated by M2_6, M3_6 and M5, M6 reaches above 47dB, a high value that is acceptable by most applications.

4.2 Approximate Adder Based Image Sharpening

In this algorithm, addition is performed by the approximate adders proposed in this paper while for other operations, i.e., multiplication, subtraction and division all use accurate operations.

The sharpening algorithm executed using different approximate adders and the corresponding PSNR and NED values are then measured. For this algorithm, a 16 bit approximate adder is used, because the maximum possible sum is $255 * 273$, i.e. approximately $2^{16} - 1$. Case when lower 8 LSBs using approximate adders and higher MSBs using accurate adders are considered for the

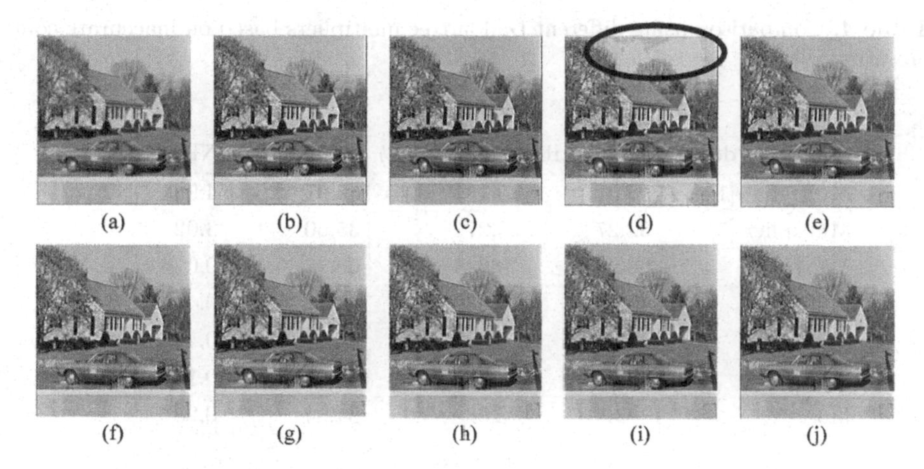

Fig. 7. Image sharpening results for Image 1: (a) original image, (b) using an accurate multiplier, (c) using multiplier of [21], (d) using multiplier of [22], (e) using M1_4, (f) using M2_6, (g) using M3_6, (h) using M4, (i) using M5, (j) using M6.

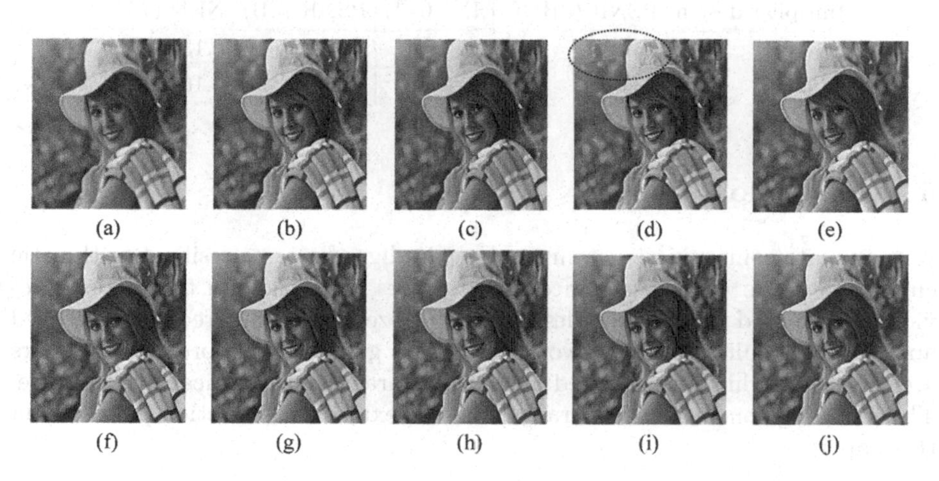

Fig. 8. Image sharpening results for Image 2: (a) original image, (b) using an accurate multiplier, (c) using multiplier of [21], (d) using multiplier of [22], (e) using M1_4, (f) using M2_6, (g) using M3_6, (h) using M4, (i) using M5, (j) using M6.

comparison. Table 5 shows the PSNR and NED for the example image, and it is easy to see when the approximate RCA with APAs has smaller NED, and then it would have better PSNR, i.e., image quality.

Table 4. Comparison using different Dadda tree multipliers based on inaccurate compressors for image processing.

	Image 1		Image 2	
Multiplier design	PSNR (dB)	NED (10^{-5})	PSNR (dB)	NED (10^{-5})
Multiplier [1]	35.61	5.18	35.97	4.90
Multiplier [2]	32.27	7.27	35.60	3.02
M1_4	66.06	0.029	66.17	0.029
M2_6	47.72	0.936	52.17	0.46
M3_6	47.98	0.892	52.31	0.44
M5	49.52	0.64	56.03	0.18
M6	49.35	0.68	54.84	0.23

Table 5. Comparison using different adders for image sharpening.

	Image 1		Image 2	
Multiplier design	PSNR (dB)	NED (10^{-4})	PSNR (dB)	NED (10^{-4})
APA1	45.31	0.136	45.39	0.132
APA2	43.09	0.17	43.37	0.16

5 Conclusion

Approximate computing is an innovative paradigm for error-resilient arithmetic circuits, because it offers significant advantages for design. In this paper, previously proposed compressor designs are utilized to design recursively based approximate multipliers and two transmission gate based approximate adders are proposed, which are assessed for both accuracy and electrical performance. The following conclusions are drawn from the extensive simulation presented in this paper:

(1) M4 has the least value of NED and best value of PS and Acc_{amp}, hence it has the best accuracy.
(2) By performing power delay and area product (PDAP) to indicate the utilization of resource and (PDAP vs. NED), M6 shows that it is a good candidate for approximate multiplication with lower power/area/delay and high accuracy requirements.
(3) When considering all metrics, generally M6 is the best approximate 8×8 multiplier.
(4) An image processing application by using design in [25] and proposed designs show that all proposed approximate multiplier design produce better quality images than the multipliers of [21] and [22] and M6 has the good image quality qualified by the PSNR while has the lower PDAP.

(5) The above proposed designs achieve lower power and faster processing speed than traditional image processing architecture, which can be potentially used in on-board in an intelligent satellite.

6 Discussion

This section discusses the relation of this paper to prior work. Compared to previously published work, this work extends the purely array based multiplier into recursively based multiplier. Recursive multiplier has flexible ability to adjust configuration of accurate and approximate computation, hence approximate multiplier with varying accuracy is easy to obtain. Moreover, only [23] has proposed recursive multiplier hence this work also extends this type of approximate multiplier designs. This paper also applies the designs to real image processing application compared to previous work [25]. The proposed image processing architecture could be used on-board within the satellites to achieve low power and high processing speed.

References

1. Han, J., Orshansky, M.: Approximate computing: an emerging paradigm for energy-efficient design. In: Proceedings of the ETS 2013: Proceedings of the 18th IEEE European Test Symposium, Avignon, France, May 2013, pp. 1–6 (2013)
2. Liang, J., Han, J., Lombardi, F.: New metrics for the reliability of approximate and probabilistic adders. IEEE Trans. Comput. **62**(9), 1760–1771 (2013)
3. Gupta, V., Mohapatra, D., Park, S.P., Raghunathan, A., Roy, K.: IMPACT: imprecise adders for low-power approximate computing. In: ISLPED 2011: Proceedings of the 17th IEEE/ACM International Symposium on Low-Power Electronics and Design, pp. 409–414 (2011)
4. Mahdiani, H.R., Ahmadi, A., Fakhraie, S.M., Lucas, C.: Bio-inspired imprecise computational blocks for efficient VLSI implementation of soft computing applications. IEEE Trans. Circuits Syst. I Regul. Pap. **57**(4), 850–862 (2010)
5. Kang, S.M., Leblebici, Y.: CMOS Digital Integrated Circuits. McGraw-Hill, New York (1999). ISBN 0-07-116427-8
6. Rabaey, J.M., Chandrakasan, A.P.: Digital Integrated Circuits, 2nd edn. Prentice Hall, Upper Saddle River (2003). ISBN 0-13-090996-3
7. Wallace, C.S.: A suggestion for a fast multiplier. IEEE Trans. Electron. Comput. **EC–13**(1), 14–17 (1964)
8. Dadda, L.: Some schemes for parallel multipliers. Comput. Arithmetic **34**, 349–356 (1965)
9. Bickerstaff, K.C., Swartzlander, E.E., Schulte, M.J.: Analysis of column compression multipliers. In: The Proceedings of 15th IEEE Symposium on Computer Arithmetic, Vail, CO, USA, June 2001, pp. 33–39 (2001)
10. Gahlan, N.K., Shukla, P., Kaur, J.: Implementation of Wallace tree multiplier using compressor. Int. J. Comput. Technol. Appl. **3**(3), 1194–1199 (2012)
11. Ma, W., Li, S.: A new high compression compressor for large multiplier. In: ICSIT 2008: 9th International Conference on Solid-State and Integrated-Circuit Technology, Beijing, China, October 2008, pp. 1877–1880 (2008)

12. Kwon, O., Nowka, K., Swartzlander, E.E.: A16-bitx16-bit MAC design using fast 5:2 compressors. In: Proceedings of IEEE International Conference on Application-Specific Systems, Architectures, and Processors, Boston, MA, USA, July 2000, pp. 235–243 (2000)
13. Chang, C.H., Gu, J., Zhang, M.: Ultra low-voltage low-power CMOS 4–2 and 5–2 compressors for fast arithmetic circuits. IEEE Trans. Circuits Syst. I Regul. Pap. **51**(10), 1985–1997 (2004)
14. Prasad, K., Parhi, K.K.: Low-power 4–2 and 5–2 compressors. In: Conference Record of the Thirty-Fifth Asilomar Conference on Signals, Systems and Computers, Pacific Grove, CA, USA, November 2001, vol. 1, pp. 129–133 (2001)
15. Swartzlander, E.E.: Truncated multiplication with approximate rounding. In: Conference Record of the Thirty-Third Asilomar Conference on Signals, Systems and Computers, Pacific Grove, CA, USA, October 1999, vol. 2, pp. 1480–1483 (1999)
16. Schulte, M.J., Swartzlander, E.E.: Truncated multiplication with correction constant [for DSP]. In: Workshop on VLSI Signal Processing VI, Veldhoven, Netherlands, October 1993, pp. 388–396 (1993)
17. Kulkarni, P., Gupta, P., Ercegovac, M.: Trading accuracy for power with an underdesigned multiplier architecture. In: Proceedings of the VLSID 2011: The Proceedings of 24th International Conference on VLSI Design, Chennai, India, January 2011, pp. 346–351 (2011)
18. Liu, C., Han, J., Lombardi, F.: A low-power, high-performance approximate multiplier with configurable partial error recovery. In: Proceedings of the DATE 2014: The Proceedings of IEEE Design and Test in Europe (DATE) Conference, March 2014, p. 95 (2014)
19. Kyaw, K.Y., Goh, W.L., Yeo, K.S.: Low-power high-speed multiplier for error-tolerant application. In: 2010 IEEE International Conference of Electron Devices and Solid-State Circuits (EDSSC), Hong Kong, China, December 2010, pp. 1–4 (2010)
20. Lu, S.-L.: Speeding up processing with approximation circuits. Computer **37**(3), 67–73 (2004)
21. Momeni, A., Han, J., Montuschi, P., Lombardi, F.: Design and analysis of approximate compressors for multiplication. IEEE Trans. Comput. **64**(4), 984–994 (2015)
22. Lin, C.H., Lin, I.C.: High accuracy approximate multiplier with error correction. In: Proceedings of the ICCD 2013: The 2013 IEEE 31st International Conference on Computer Design (ICCD), Asheville, NC, USA, October 2013, pp. 33–38 (2013)
23. Bhardwaj, K., Mane, P.S., Henkel, J.: Power-and area-efficient Approximate Wallace Tree Multiplier for error-resilient systems. In: Symposium ISQED 2014: 15th International Symposium on Quality Electronic Design (ISQED), Santa Clara, CA, USA, March 2014, pp. 263–269 (2014)
24. Gupta, V., Mohapatra, D., Park, S.P., Raghunathan, A., Roy, K.: IMPACT: imprecise adders for low-power approximate computing. In: Proceedings of the 17th IEEE/ACM International Symposium on Low-Power Electronics and Design, Fukuoka, Japan, August 2011, pp. 409–414 (2011)
25. Yang, Z., Han, J., Lombardi, F.: Approximate compressors for error-resilient multiplier design. In: Defect and Fault Tolerance in VLSI and Nanotechnology Systems (DFT), pp. 183–186 (2015)

26. Shams, A.M., Darwish, T.K., Bayoumi, M.A.: Performance analysis of low-power 1-bit CMOS full adder cells. IEEE Trans. Very Large Scale Integr. (VLSI) Syst. **10**(1), 20–29 (2002)
27. Lau, M.S., Ling, K.V., Chu, Y.C.: Energy-aware probabilistic multiplier: design and analysis. In: Proceedings of the 2009 International Conference on Compilers, Architecture, and Synthesis for Embedded Systems, Grenoble, France, October 2009, pp. 281–290 (2009)

International Workshop on Integrated Space and Onboard Networks (ISON)

The Design of a LEO Constellation Satellite Integrated Electronic System and the Reliability Analysis

Wu Ying(✉) and Xu Zhenlong

Beijing Institute of Spacecraft System Engineering, Mailbox 5142 Sub-Mailbox 367, 100094 Beijing, China
wy630628@163.com

Abstract. Targeting the needs of low-earth orbit (LEO) Internet constellations for the high performance, high reliability, and high functional density of satellite-borne integrated electronics, the study was implemented on domestic LEO mobile constellation satellite-borne integrated electronic technology. Upon benchmarking foreign advanced LEO mobile constellation satellite-borne integrated electronic products, we analyzed the architecture of the domestic ones, and proposed solutions based on domestic devices; For the requirements of long service life and high reliability, the reliability analysis was carried out on several working modes with the components and parts stress analysis method, and a reliability improvement plan was proposed on the basis of software and programmable devices. Finally, we obtained a design plan of a satellite-borne integrated electronic system for LEO mobile constellation applications. With the overall performance comparable to those of advanced foreign solutions, the processing performance trebling that of existing domestic satellite-borne computers, and the 10-year reliability of 0.99999, it meets the needs of domestic LEO mobile constellation services.

Keywords: Low-earth orbit (LEO) internet constellation · Integrated electronics · High performance · Reliability

1 Introduction

In recent years, with the development of satellite communication technology and the changes in the Internet application environment, in order to meet the globally growing demands for satellite broadband access and, especially, to solve the problem of Internet access in rural areas and other remote areas, satellite Internet has become an inevitable trend for the combination of satellite communication and Internet. Unlike satellite communication systems, satellite Internet serves Internet applications, uses a unified network layer as a bearing platform, and can work independently as a network system (an effective component of the Internet system). Promoted and supported by the Internet giants such as Google and Facebook, Space X, OneWeb and other innovative companies in the United States have planned to build their mobile constellation systems composed of small

Q. Wu et al. (Eds.): WiSATS 2020, LNICST 358, pp. 367–381, 2021.
https://doi.org/10.1007/978-3-030-69072-4_29

LEO satellites to actively seize new resources for space Internet access, consequently triggering a global upsurge [1–3].

The OneWeb satellite system, a LEO Internet satellite constellation system rapidly developing in recent years, is dedicated to providing terrestrial users with high-speed, broadband space-based access services. After the completion, the system will provide affordable network access for remote areas or areas with outdated Internet infrastructure, thus realizing the full coverage of the earth.

For the past few years, relevant Chinese institutions have also proposed development plans for LEO mobile constellations, such as the "Xingyun", "Hongyan" and "Hongyun" constellations. The study on the OneWeb and other foreign advanced LEO mobile constellation- related technologies might provide good references for the development of domestic systems.

Regarding the OneWeb constellation satellite platform, the electronic system developed by Airbus is used with the PureLine Amethyst centralized integrated electronic system as the core, which uses lots of automotive-grade devices to provide OneWeb satellites with an integrated high-performance, low-power consumption and low-cost solution featuring a computing performance of above 215 DMIPS and a reliability of above 99.999% [4].

In contrast, China's existing on-board computers and integrated electronic systems are characterized by the problems of low performance and large size. There is no integrated electronic system designed for LEO Internet constellation satellites, leading to the failure in meeting the developmental requirements of LEO satellite constellations [5, 6]. Besides, LEO Internet satellites are mass-produced small satellite platforms. Compared with large satellite platforms, their satellite-based integrated electronics pose requirements of higher integration, higher information fusion, and lower costs. There is still a certain gap between the domestic systems and the required. It is imperative to develop a satellite-based high-performance, high-integration and low-cost integrated electronic system for LEO Internet constellation satellite applications.

In order to meet domestic services and requirements for LEO Internet satellite constellations, an integrated electronic system for LEO Internet constellation satellite applications was designed in the paper upon the foundation of benchmarking foreign advanced products. With a new domestic high-performance processor and based on the modular design idea, the system is characterized by high performance and high integration. Besides, targeting the requirements for a long service life and a high reliability of the integrated electronics, components and parts stress analysis method was used to analyze the reliability under different working modes, and an on-orbit repair-based reliability improvement plan was proposed correspondingly.

2 Analysis on OneWeb Constellation Satellite Integrated Electronic Products

OneWeb constellation is one of the earliest and fastest-growing LEO Internet constellations in foreign countries. Its related technologies, especially the low-cost, high-performance satellite-borne integrated electronic technology, are worth of careful exploration to provide reference for domestic system design.

The core of the electronic system for the OneWeb constellation satellite platform is the PureLine Amethyst integrated electronic system designed by Airbus. The electronic system provides the satellite platform with the functions including on-orbit redundant computing and processing capabilities, TM/TC that satisfies CCSDS, GPS reception, secondary power distribution, attitude and orbit control sensors and actuator interfaces (incl. magnetic torque and solar array stepping motors), time and space partitioning of space software, etc. All Amethyst components have gone through irradiation experiments and are immune to latch-up, guaranteeing the LEO on-orbit service for 10 years. The block diagrams of the product appearance and functions are shown below (Fig. 1).

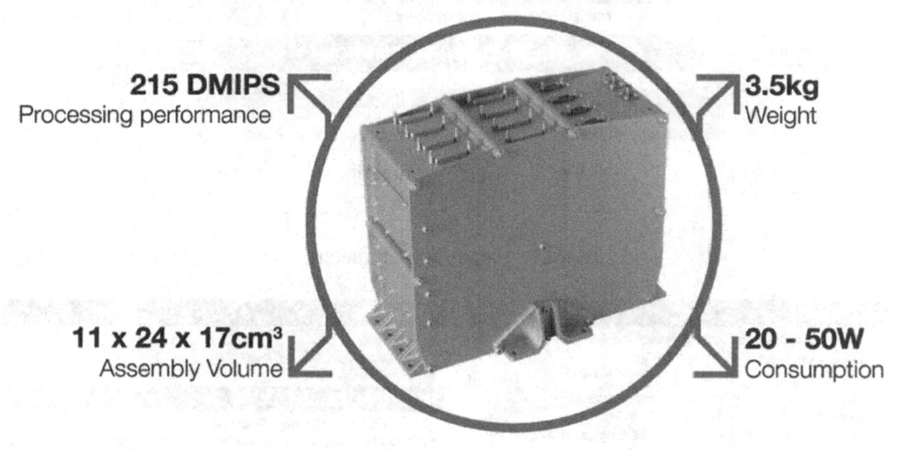

Fig. 1. Amethyst appearance

Amethyst adopts a dual-core automotive electronic-grade ARM processor as the core with 215 MIPS processing and floating-point processing capacities. Regarding the satellite bus, Amethyst uses CAN bus and Spacewire bus (for the latter, the bus communication rate is 200 Mbps) with the overall weight of 3.5 kg and the power consumption of 20~35 W (Fig. 2).

The specific parameters of Amethyst are shown in the following table (Table 1).

It can be seen from the above introduction that the Amethyst integrated electronics is composed of 4 modules in 2 categories, namely the core processing modules (active/standby) and the interface expansion modules (active/standby). Among them, a core processing module is mainly composed of a computer minimum system, a GPS and PPS (pulse per second), TM/TC interfaces, AES code function, a bus interface circuit (incl. CAN and SPW) and other functional circuits, while an interface expansion module is mainly composed of a RS422 interface, an analog acquisition interface, power supply control and distribution, a sensor, executive components and other functional circuits.

When designing the integrated electronic system for a domestic LEO constellation satellite platform, we can also draw on this idea and benchmark its technical parameters to meet the service needs.

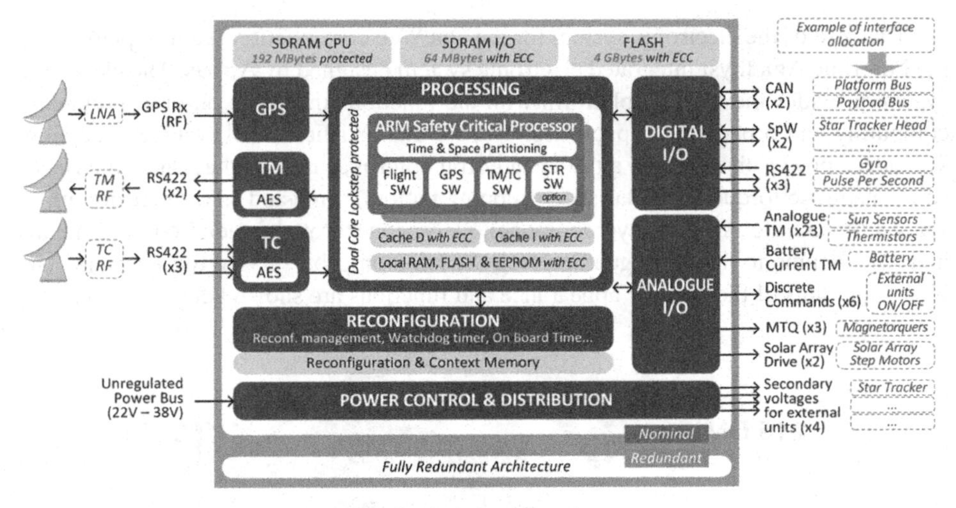

Fig. 2. Amethyst functions

Table 1. Amethyst parameters

FUNCTIONS

- Full Redundant On-Board Computer with reconfiguration
- GPS Receiver
- CCSDS TM/TC with TM/TC RF in option
- Interfaces with AOCS sensors and actuators, including Magnetorquers & Solar Array Step Motors
- Provides secondary voltages and discrete commands to external units

KEY FEATURES

- Single-point-of-failure-free centralized architecture
- Reconfiguration mechanism (50 scenarios)
- GPS Receiver: L1C/A, 10m accuracy in LEO
- CCSDS TM with ciphering & TC with deciphering (AES256)

PROCESSING

- ARM processor designed for safety critical applications, fully compatible with ARM ecosystem
- 215 Dhrystone MIPS & Floating Point Unit
- L1 Cache Instruction with ECC / L1 Cache Data with ECC
- Internal RAM, FLASH & EEPROM with ECC
- Time & Space Partitioning hosting several SW applications in a single core implementing RTEMS OS: Central Flight SW, GPS SW, TM/TC SW and STR SW (STR Head in option)
- Avionics delivered with Basic SW: BIOS, Boot SW
- JTAG / Ethernet links for SW development, trace and debug

MEMORY

- Volatile: 192MBytes SDRAM CPU with Error Detection
- Volatile: 64MBytes SDRAM IO with ECC
- Non Volatile: 4GBytes FLASH with ECC

BUDGETS

- Mass: 3.5kg
- Volume: 110 x 240 x 170mm³
- Power: 20-50W

INTERFACES

- Unregulated Input Power Bus 22-38V
- Secondary Voltages (regulated 5V) for external units (x4)
- GPS Rx LNA I/F
- CAN bus I/F (x2), SpaceWire I/F (x2), RS422 I/F (x8)
- Analog TM (x23), Battery Current TM (x1)
- Discrete Commands (x6)
- Magnetorquers I/F (x3) (L=2.7H; R=66Ω)
- Solar Array Step Motors I/F (x2) (22-38V, 290Ω, 260mH)

ENVIRONMENT / RELIABILITY

- Temperature: [-20°C; +60°C]
- Vibration level: // 18.3g Rms ⊥ 9.5g Rms
- Shock level: 1 000g (10 000Hz)
- EMI/EMC: tailored ECSS-E-ST-20-07C

RADIATION

- Latch Up Free parts
- ARM Processor in Dual Core Lockstep for error detection
- All memories protected with ECC (Reed Solomon or EDAC)
- Total Dose TID compatible with typical 10 years LEO

RELIABILITY

- Reliability better than 950 FIT (FIDES standard)
- Availability better than 99.999%

HERITAGE

- Airbus Space equipment quality legacy
- Automotive COTS process

3 The Design and Realization of a Domestic LEO Constellation Satellite Integrated Electronic System

An Internet satellite integrated electronic system is the core for whole-satellite information fusion and comprehensive decision-making. Considering the constellation requirements of high integration and miniaturization, an integrated solution with good expansibility and adaptability should be adopted as far as possible. Besides, the integrated electronics of foreign LEO constellations all use highly-integrated platform computers. Therefore, viewed from the perspective of optimizing the integrated electronics of the whole satellite overall, it is necessary to reduce the number of in-satellite computers.

3.1 Overall Architecture Design

Constellation satellite integrated electronics integrates traditional platform telemetry and tele-control units, a satellite house-keeping computer, business units, a control computer, a GNSS receiver, a star sensor circuit box, an array driver circuit box and other functions into a central management unit (CMU), which improves the system integration and information fusion, reduces the amount of whole-satellite computer systems, and minimizes resource requirements such as weight, power consumption and volume.

The topology of the whole-satellite integrated electronics with the CMU as the core is shown in the figure below (Fig. 3).

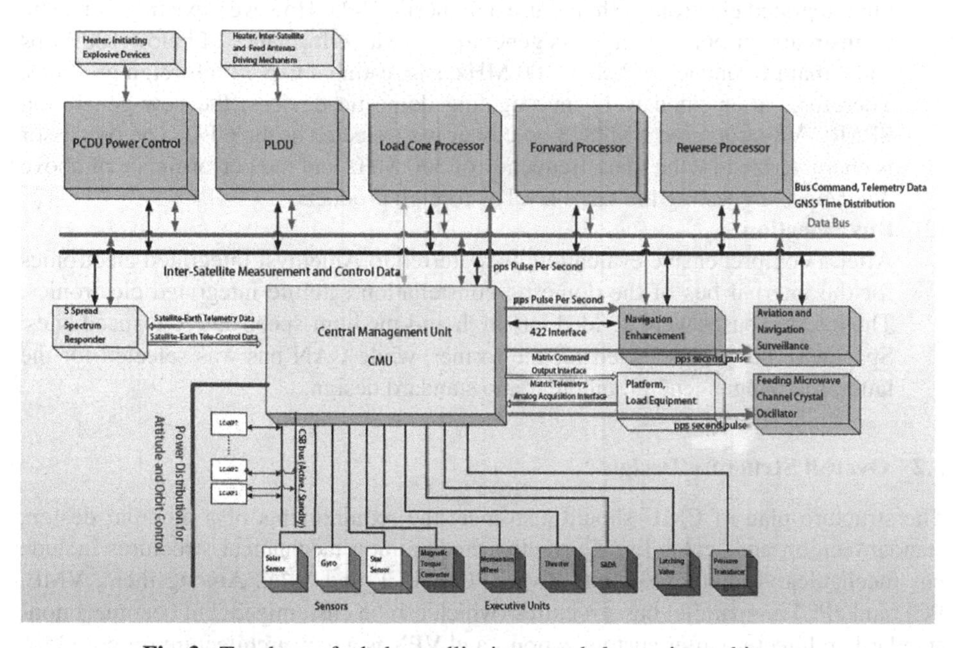

Fig. 3. Topology of whole-satellite integrated electronics architecture

The system uses CMU as the main control terminal, and the components are connected through data buses to build a distributed network system. Distributed data collection and command output, and centralized operation and control are realized through the data bus network, thereby improving the efficiency of system processing.

Based on the module division of Amethyst integrated electronic equipment, the above functional modules can also be divided into two categories—the core processing modules and the interface expansion modules. Among them, a core processing module includes two major functions—data management and tele-control, which specifically cover a CPU core system, time management, system buses, inter-satellite/satellite-earth measurement and control communications, measurement and control encryption and decryption, important data storage, and large-volume data processing. The core processing modules are divided into the active and standby machines configured in 2 panels with completely same functions. Among them, the satellite-earth tele-control and important data storage are processed with dual-machine hot backup, while the rest are processed with dual-machine cold backup. An interface expansion module includes command acquisition, load communication, sensor communication, attitude and orbit control drive, power distribution, GNSS and other functional modules.

(1) **CPU Selection**
The core issue for a core processing module is the selection of CPU. Amethyst uses a dual-core ARM processor with a performance of 215 MIPS. Considering from the perspective of independence and controllability, domestic constellation satellite integrated electronics should use a domestic CPU. However, existing domestic mainstream on-board computers generally have a performance of below 100 Mips and a main frequency of below 100 MHz, suggesting a gap with foreign products. Therefore, after extensively investigating domestic devices, the new-generation SPARC V8-structured BM3823 processor was selected as the CPU. The processor is characterized by the main frequency of 300 MHz and the performance of above 258 Mips, suggesting the same level as foreign products.
(2) **Bus Selection**
After a comprehensive evaluation, we referred to Amethyst integrated electronics for the internal bus of the domestic constellation satellite integrated electronics. The internal buses were divided into high-and-medium-speed and low-speed ones. Spacewire bus was selected for the former, while CAN bus was selected for the latter, realizing a general, modular and standard design.

3.2 Overall Structure Design

The structure plan of CMU should also meet the requirements of a modular design, standardization and scalability. Currently, the common mechanical structures include bus mechanical structures such as VME, PCI, cPCI, and VPX. Among them, VME, PCI, and cPCI are parallel bus structures (which can be customized, but become a non-standard architecture after customization), and VPX is a new architecture proposed for high-speed serial buses.

The buses used in the CMU are Spacewire serial bus and CAN bus, but it makes little sense to adopt a standard bus structure, since there are abundant non-standard signals such as power supply, command and telemetry transmitted between boards. In view of the large power consumption of a single board, the "cage drawer" structure was proposed. The schematic diagram of the whole-machine architecture is shown in the figure below (Fig. 4).

Fig. 4. Schematic diagram of the CMU structure

After detailed evaluation, the system weighed no more than 5 kg, and the overall power consumption was 20~50 W. Then, we finally obtained a domestic LEO constellation satellite integrated electronic system that can benchmark Amethyst integrated electronics and have similar overall performance.

4 Reliability Prediction Analysis on the LEO Constellation Satellite Integrated Electronic System

According to public information, the Amethyst on-board computer has the service life of 10 years, and the computer reliability at the end of the service is not less than 0.99999. In order to benchmark the Amethyst satellite-based computer, we set a same reliability requirement (not less than 0.99999 at the end of 10 years) on the domestic LEO constellation satellite integrated electronics.

In the following part, we will reversely infer the reliability requirements on the computer and modules based on the above requirement, and analyze the possibility of realizing the requirements.

The integrated electronic solution was provisionally determined to contain six functional modules, of which the active and standby processor modules accounted for one panel each, and the active and standby modules of the other five functions share a panel (the modules on a same panel are independent of each other). Accordingly, the on-board computer consists of seven panels. For the analysis convenience, it is assumed that the failure rates of all modules are the same, and the failure rates of the module does not change with time.

In order to facilitate the comparative analysis, the following several working modes were considered, including the dual-machine standby backup mode for whole machine switchover, the multi-machine parallel backup mode, the backup mode for module switchover, and the repairable dual-machine mode.

It was assumed that the failure probabilities of the system and the system components followed the exponential distribution; the failures of the system component were independent of each other; and the system components only had only two states– normal or failure, and there was no intermediate state [7].

5 The Dual-Machine Backup Mode for Whole Machine Switchover

We adopted the dual-machine backup working mode. It was assumed that the two single machine components were completely the same; a single machine is switched for a switchover; the reliability of the switchover control part is 1; and the internal modules of the on-board computer form a serial-and-then-parallel structure. The reliability model structure is shown as below (Fig. 5).

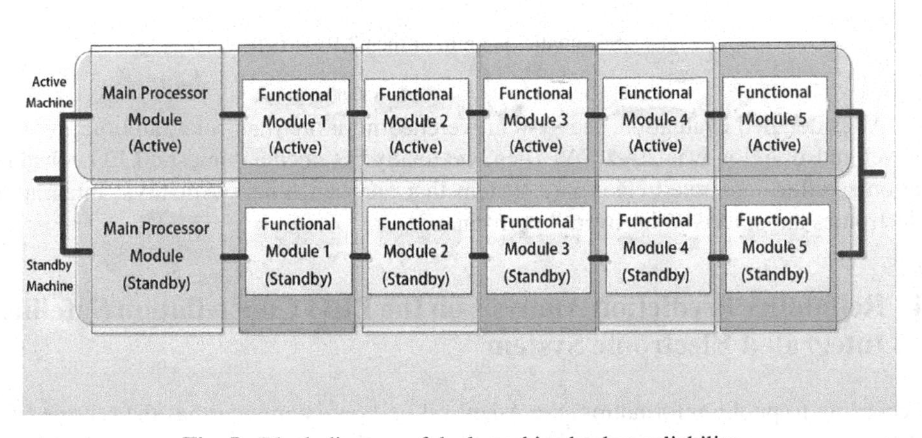

Fig. 5. Block diagram of dual-machine backup reliability

The formula below is to estimate the computer reliability under the dual-machine cold backup mode.

$$R(t) = e^{-\lambda t} + \lambda t e^{-\lambda t} \tag{1}$$

In the formula, $t = 10$ years $= 10 \times 365 \times 24 = 87{,}600$ h, and R(t) is not less than 0.99999. The results are shown in the following table (Table 2).

When the single machine failure rate is 0.00000005/h, it can be seen from the Table that the on-board computer under the dual-machine cold standby mode can meet the reliability requirements of not less than 0.99999 at the end of 10 years and not less than 0.999 at the end of 12 years.

Table 2. Calculated reliability in the service cycle under the dual-machine cold backup mode ($\lambda = 0.00000005/h$)

No.	Year	Day	Hour	Calculated reliability
1	0	0	0	1.0000000000
2	1	365	8760	0.9999999041
3	2	730	17520	0.9999996165
4	3	1095	26280	0.9999991374
5	4	1460	35040	0.9999984669
6	5	1825	43800	0.9999976053
7	6	2190	52560	0.9999965527
8	7	2555	61320	0.9999953092
9	8	2920	70080	0.9999938751
10	9	3285	78840	0.9999922505
11	10	3650	87600	0.9999904355
12	11	4015	96360	0.9999884303
13	12	4380	105120	0.9999862352
14	13	4745	113880	0.9999838502
15	14	5110	122640	0.9999812756

According to the model in Fig. x, the relationship between the failure rate of a single machine and the failure rate of every internal module is as below.

$$\lambda_{single-machine} = \sum_{i=1}^{6} \lambda_i = 6\lambda_{module} = 0.00000005 \quad (2)$$

It can be obtained that λ module = 0.0000000083. Correspondingly, the requirement on the module reliability at the end of 10 years is R module = 0.9993; and the requirement on the module reliability at the end of 12 years is R module = 0.9991.

In this case, excessively high requirements are posed on the module reliability, and are difficult to realize in reality.

5.1 The Multi-machine Parallel Mode

Based on the (1) description, a change was made to increase the number of parallels.

It was assumed that all functions of a single machine were all realized on one panel; a panel accounted for a single machine; and a satellite-based computer is composed of several same single machines. A switchover is based on a single machine, and the reliability of the switchover control part is 1.

For this case, the block diagram of the reliability model of the onboard computer is shown in the figure below (Fig. 6).

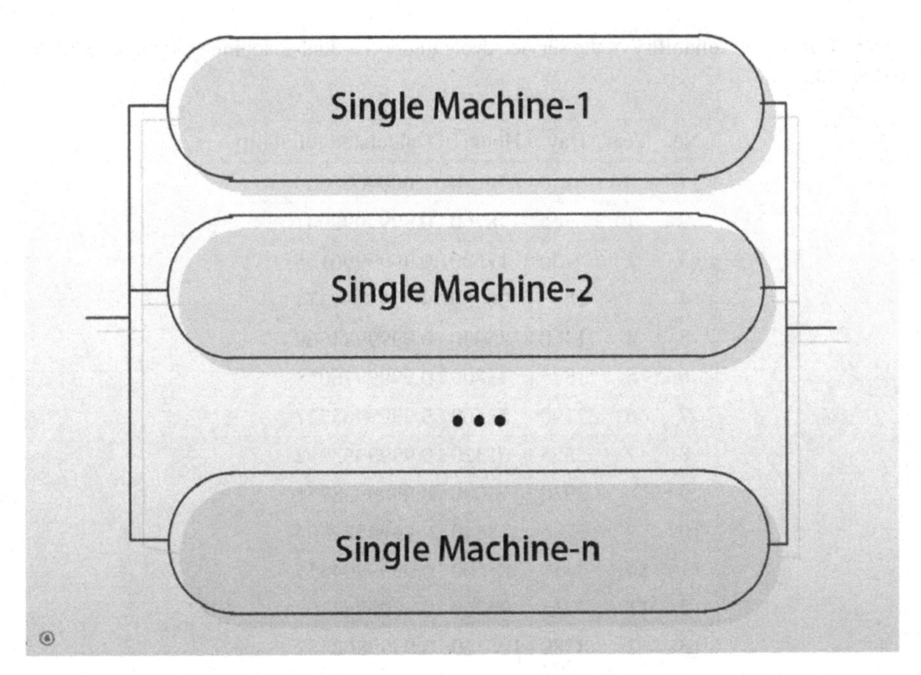

Fig. 6. Block diagram of the reliability under the multi-machine parallel mode

According to the model above, the relationship between computer reliability and module reliability is as the following.

$$R_{computer} = 1 - \left(1 - R_{single-machine}\right)^{n} \quad (3)$$

- When n = 3,

$$0.99999 = 1 - \left(1 - R_{single-machine}\right)^{3}$$

$$0.999 = 1 - \left(1 - R_{single-machine}\right)^{3}$$

Therefore, at the end of 10 years, the requirement on single machine reliability is $R_{single\text{-}machine} = 0.981$; and at the end of 12 years, the requirement on single machine reliability $R_{single\text{-}machine} = 0.9$;

- When n = 4,

$$0.99999 = 1 - \left(1 - R_{single-machine}\right)^{4}$$

$$0.999 = 1 - \left(1 - R_{single-machine}\right)^{4}$$

Therefore, at the end of 10 years, the requirement on single machine reliability is $R_{single\text{-}machine} = 0.944$; and at the end of 12 years, the requirement on single machine reliability $R_{single\text{-}machine} = 0.822$.

Under the multi-machine parallel mode, the on-board computer based on the existing technology can basically meet the reliability requirements of not less than 0.99999 at the end of 10 years and not less than 0.999 at the end of 12 years. However, under this mode, since the functions of a single computer are gathered on a single panel, the size of the panel would be too large; besides, multiple machines in parallel are required, and it is difficult to meet the service requirements in terms of volume and weight.

5.2 The Dual-Machine Mode for Functional Module Switchover

On the basis of the (1) description, the module cross-switch hot standby mode was adopted. A switchover is made for module, and the reliability of the switchover control part is 1.

The block diagram of the on-board computer reliability model is shown in the figure below (Fig. 7).

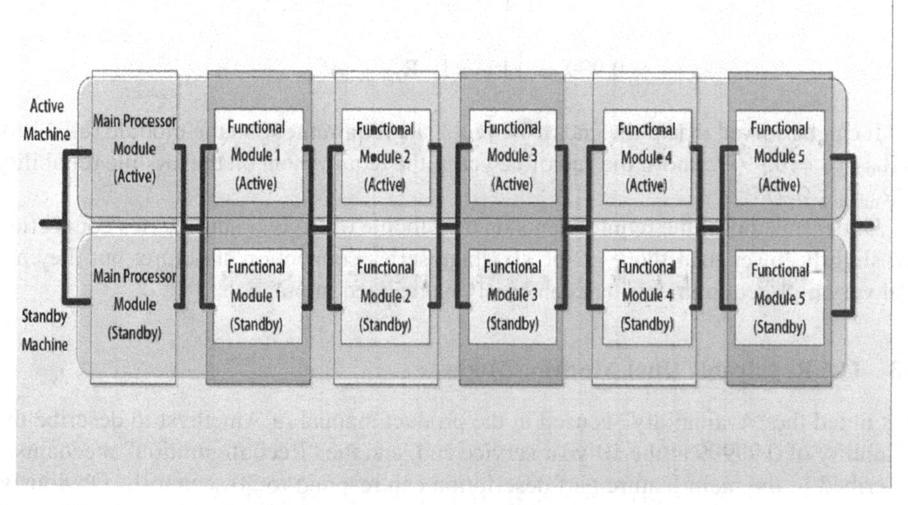

Fig. 7. Model of the reliability under the dual-machine module switchover mode

According to the model above, the relationship between the computer reliability and the module reliability is as the following.

$$R_{computer} = \left[1 - (1 - R_{module})^2\right]^6 \quad (4)$$

Bring in the relevant data, and obtain the followings.

$$0.99999 = \left[1 - (1 - R_{module})^2\right]^6$$

$$0.999 = \left[1 - (1 - R_{module})^2\right]^6$$

It can be solved that at the end of 10 years, the requirement on the module reliability is $R_{module} = 0.9987$; and at the end of 12 years, the requirement on the module reliability is $R_{module} = 0.987$.

The reliability of the two module are relatively high, and it is also difficult to realize them in practice.

- Under the same mode, refer to the structure of Amethyst (four panels and two-stage series connection).

The total number of modules was reduced to four (incl. 2 main processor modules and 2 functional modules), and every module accounted for a single panel. Then, the computer was composed of only four panels, and the series number was reduced to two. The above method was used to analyze the reliability requirements of related modules.

Bring in the relevant data, and obtain the followings:

$$0.99999 = \left[1 - (1 - R_{module})^2\right]^2$$

$$0.999 = \left[1 - (1 - R_{module})^2\right]^2$$

It can be solved that at the end of 10 years, the requirement on the module reliability is $R_{module} = 0.9977$; and at the end of 12 years, the requirement on the module reliability is R_{module} 0.977.

Under this mode, the requirements on the module of the two-stage series connection are slightly lower than those of the six-stage series connection structure, but they are still very high requirements that can barely be realized in practice.

5.3 The Repairable Dual-Machine Mode

It is noted the "Availability" is used in the product manual of Amethyst to describe the reliability of 0.99999 at the 10-year service end, and the "Reconfiguration" mechanism described in the main feature part description can respond to 50 scenarios. Obviously, Amethyst is a repairable on-board computer that uses reconfigurable technology. Such repairability is not only for the whole machine, but also likely for the local parts (such as channels, storage areas, specific area programmable logic, etc.) within a single machine under the situation of no affecting the operation of the single machine. Restricted by the space and weight of small satellites, an Amethyst computer has limited hardware resources. It is speculated that the technology is mainly based on software and programmable devices, and the hardware logic resource redundancy plays a supplementary role [8–10].

The on-board computer performs single-machine switchover mode, the reliability of the switchover control part is 1, and the internal modules of the computer form a serial-and-then-parallel structure. Because the service cycle is relatively long, the steady state availability of the computer can be used to characterize the reliability at the end of the service. It was assumed that both machines were in a normal state at the initial moment. The single machine failure rate is λsingle-machine, and the single machine repair rate is μsingle-machine.

The repair rate is calculated according to the reciprocal of the repair time. The repair time here is estimated according to the time of detecting a fault, isolating the fault, repairing the fault, and entering the ready-to-use state. According to the previous analysis, the repair is mainly carried out through software and programmable devices, and would not take long. In this paper, the repair time is estimated at 10, 30 and 60 min.

In the initial state, the two machines are powered on at the same time. When the active is faulty, it is switched to the standby machine. The original host performs online repair, and is then in the standby state after returning to the normal condition. The steady state availability of the computer is estimated with the following formula, and the target availability at the end of 10 years is 0.9999:

$$A = \frac{\lambda * \mu + \mu^2}{\lambda * \mu + \lambda^2 + \mu^2} = \frac{\frac{\lambda}{\mu} + 1}{\frac{\lambda}{\mu} + \left(\frac{\lambda}{\mu}\right)^2 + 1} = 0.99999 \quad (5)$$

It is solved that $(\lambda/\mu) = 0.00317$ (Table 3).

Table 3. Estimated module failure rates

No.	λ/μ	Repair time (h)	Repair rate (/h)	Sing-machine failure rate	Module failure rate
1	0.00317	0.167	6	0.0190200000	0.0031700000
2		0.5	2	0.0063400000	0.0010566667
3		1	1	0.0031700000	0.0005283333

It can be seen from the above Table that the module failure rates are relatively high. In other words, low requirements are posed on the module reliability. Under such module failure rates (0.00317, 0.0011 and 0.00053), if repairability is not considered, the module reliability will drop to below 0.205, 0.577 and 0.767, respectively, after 500 h, and the reliability of a module with a high failure rate decreases fast.

But after considering the repairability, on the premise of not exceeding $(\lambda/\mu) = 0.00317$, the availability of the computer at the end of 10 years and t 12 years can meet the requirements.

When the failure rate is constant, adopting advanced technology to reduce the repair time can contribute to a relatively high repair rate of the on-board computer, make it much higher than the failure rate, improve the availability at the end of the service, and thus improve the on-board computer reliability. Refer to the attached table below (Table 4).

Based on the above analysis, it can be seen that the LEO constellation satellite integrated electronics proposed in this paper cannot achieve the reliability requirements of

Table 4. The change of availability with repair rate (failure rate unchanged)

No.	Module failure rate	Single-machine failure rate	Repair time (h)	Repair rate (/h)	λ/μ	Availability at the end of 10 years
1	0.00317	0.01902	0.0167	60.00	0.0003170000	0.9999999000
2			0.167	6.00	0.0031700000	0.9999900000
3			0.5	2.00	0.0095100000	0.9999100000

0.9999 in 10 years and 0.999 at the end of 12 years with the conventional dual-machine cold backup approach. However, adopting the repair and reconstruction technology combining software and programmable devices and designing a multi-layer (single machines and modules) reconstruction strategy make the single machines repairable, consequently meeting the reliability requirements of not less than 0.99999 at the end of 10 years and not less than 0.999 at the end of 12 years for the integrated electronics and technically improving the integrated electronics to a level different from existing space computer.

6 Conclusion

Upon benchmarking foreign advanced LEO Internet satellite electronic system products, an integrated electronic system for LEO Internet constellation satellite applications is designed in the paper. By using a new domestic high-performance processor and adopting a modular design idea, the system is characterized by high performance and high integration. Besides, targeting the service requirements on long service life and high reliability of the integrated electronics, the reliability under different working modes was analyzed with the components stress analysis method, and a reliability improvement plan based on on-orbit repair was proposed. Finally, we obtained a design plan for a satellite-borne integrated electronic system for LEO mobile constellation applications. With the overall performance comparable to the those of advanced foreign solutions, it meets the needs of domestic LEO mobile constellation service.

References

1. Jiqiang, Z., Xiongfei, L.: Introduction of OneWeb system and domestic LEO internet satellite system. Space Electron. Technol. **6**, 1–7 (2017)
2. http://www.OneWeb.net/#solution[EB/OL]
3. Yingyuan, G., Niwei, W., Zhou, L.: The development research and construction suggestion of satellite internet constellations. J. CAEIT **14**(8), 875–881 (2019)
4. http://www.spaceequipment.airbusdefenceandspace.com/[EB/OL]
5. Panpan, Z., Tingyuan, G., Jianjun, G., Yong, S.: Plug-and-play on-board computer system design based on bm3803 processor. Spacecr. Eng. **22**(6), 92–96 (2013)
6. Xinsheng, W., Hanxu, S., Guodong, X., Zhihong, T.: Study on the on-board computer system based on ARM processor. J. Beijing Univ. Posts Telecommun. **28**(4), 23–26 (2005)

7. Hua, Y., Qun, L., Xinfa, Z.: Application of reliability technique in on-bard computer. Appl. Electron. Tech. **7**, 75–79 (2009)
8. Yuan, L., Zhaowei, S., Yi, S., Lei, X., Xiande, W.: FPGA pre-layout plan for reconfigurable on-board information processing system. J. Harbin Eng. Univ. **34**(7), 872–878 (2013)
9. Rui, C., Xinquan, Y., Wenfang, S., Yongfeng, L.: Design for on-orbit reconfigurable image processing devices. Space Electron. Technol. **1**, 61–65 (2017)
10. Zhengquan, J., Haichuan, Z., Shuangjian, X.: Construction of a local self-repairing system and the reliability analysis. J. Hebei Univ. Sci. Technol. **32**, 113–115 (2011)

Discussion on Design Method of Spacecraft Information Flow Based on SysML

Zheng Qi[1,2](✉), Xiuzhi An[1,2], Xiongwen He[1,2], Panpan Zhan[1,2], Yong Xu[1,2], Fang Ren[1,2], and Jiajin Li[1,2]

[1] Beijing Institute of Spacecraft System Engineering, CAST, Beijing 100094, People's Republic of China
qzqz365@126.com
[2] Institute of Telecommunication Satellite, CAST, Beijing 100094, People's Republic of China

Abstract. Aiming at the low efficiency of the traditional design method of spacecraft information flow based on text mode, combing with the method of Model Based System Engineering, this paper presents the design idea of spacecraft information flow modeling. Modeling of spacecraft information flow will speed up the process of the design phase of the spacecraft information system and ensure the reliability and traceability of information flow through model. Model Based System Engineering provides a new idea for the design of spacecraft information flow.

Keywords: MBSE · Information flow · Model

1 Introduction

Because the traditional spacecraft development mode is based on document and the spacecraft development is a system engineering involving multi-disciplinary integration, and designers from different fields focus on different problems, which leads to the problem on understanding and repeated iterations and modifications in the process of products design.

Model based system engineering (MBSE) has many advantages, such as reusability, no ambiguity, easy to understand, easy to copy and spread, etc. With the application in JSC, OSC and JPL related projects and successful application in the system design of CubeSat and Firesat, MBSE has gradually replaced the traditional document based system engineering and played an more and more important role [1, 2].

System modeling language (SysML) comes from unified modeling language (UML), an important embodiment of MBSE, and unifies the modeling language used in the field of system engineering design. SysML uses graphical symbolic language to create the model of the engineering field, instead of the lengthy text expression. SysML can give guidance in requirements expression, analysis, design, verification, validation and other stages of system engineering. With the emergence of SysML, although there are reliable

Q. Wu et al. (Eds.): WiSATS 2020, LNICST 358, pp. 382–391, 2021.
https://doi.org/10.1007/978-3-030-69072-4_30

and unified expression standards in the design phase and simulation phase of complex system represented by spacecraft, the research and expression standards of software design and simulation verification based on information flow are still in blank condition [3, 4].

How to apply the design method of SysML model to the design process of spacecraft information flow is the focus of this paper. This paper briefly analyzes the main process of spacecraft information flow design, the classification and application of SysML Meta model, and puts forward an idea of how to apply SysML Meta model to the design process of spacecraft information flow.

2 Spacecraft Information Flow Design Process

Information flow is a process of information transfer from source to sink with specified flow direction and format. The design of information flow includes the analysis of information requirements (to solve the problem of "what to transmit"), Information network design (to solve the problem of "where to transmit"), transmission protocol design (to solve the problem of "how to transmit"), information processing design (to solve the problem of "how to use") and information verification (to solve the problem of "how to verify"), the relationship of parts above is shown in the Fig. 1.

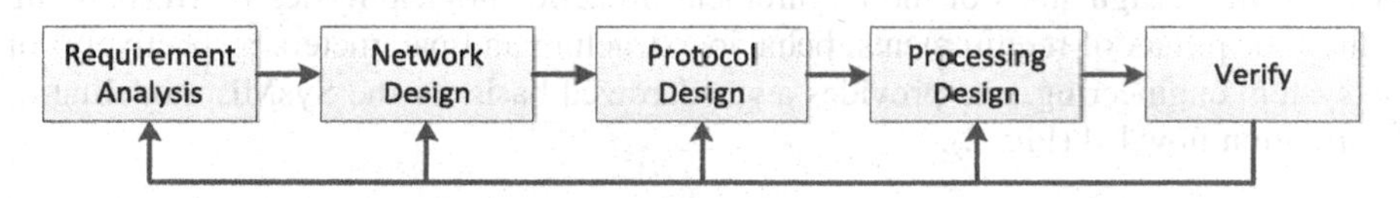

Fig. 1. Process of information flow design

(1) Requirement Analysis
In this stage, user requirements are used as input, information requirements are decomposed, and all functional and performance indicators required by the current information system are defined.
(2) Network Design
In this stage, it needs to know: 1) the source and destination of information in the current scenario; 2) the transmission medium between the source and the destination; 3) the complete information flow path from the source to the destination, and further determine the topology of the information transmission network.
(3) Protocol Design
In this stage, it is necessary to specify the transmission protocol used for information transmission, the internal implementation details of related protocols (Space Packet Protocol, etc.) and the message format related to the protocols.
(4) Processing Design
In this stage, it is necessary to make clear the process of information transmission through information network and after arriving at destination. The process depends on the purpose of the current information.

(5) Verify
In this stage, the test environment and test cases need to be defined. The test cases cover the complete design process of information flow: what information is sent from the source, the flow path of information in the network, whether the information received by the sink is complete and correct, and whether the processing results after the information is received are correct and reasonable. The results of information verification can provide confirmatory feedback for information requirement analysis, network design, protocol design and processing design.

The stage division of spacecraft information flow design process and the clarity of work content provide convenience for SysML modeling design and make the modeling objectives more clear.

3 SysML Modeling Method

3.1 MagicGrid Modeling Framework

The four pillars of MBSE model are requirements, behavior, structure and parameters. Starting from these four pillars, through the construction and iterative analysis of the MBSE system model, the MagicGrid system modeling framework realizes the synthesis of the design steps of the requirementsàfunctionàlogicàPhysics (corresponding to the four pillars of requirements, behavior, structure and parameters respectively) of the system engineering, and provides a standardized basis for the SysML modeling of information flow [5] (Fig. 2).

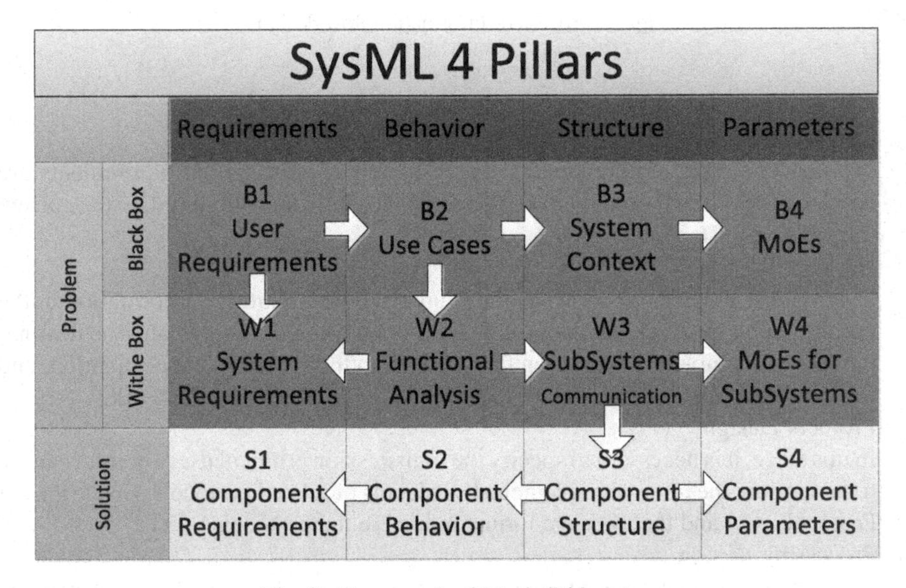

Fig. 2. Framework of MagicGrid system

3.2 SysML Model

SysML has nine kinds of diagrams (block definition diagram, internal block diagram, parameter diagram, package diagram, requirement diagram, use case diagram, activity diagram, sequence diagram and state machine diagram), which support three forms of system expression: requirement, structure and behavior. The requirement model emphasizes the traceability between requirements and the satisfaction of design to requirements; the structural model emphasizes the hierarchy of system and the interconnection between objects, including class and assembly; the behavioral model emphasizes the behavior of objects in the system, including their activity, interaction and state history. Besides, elements in diagrams are used to model as well.

The relationship is shown in the Fig. 3.

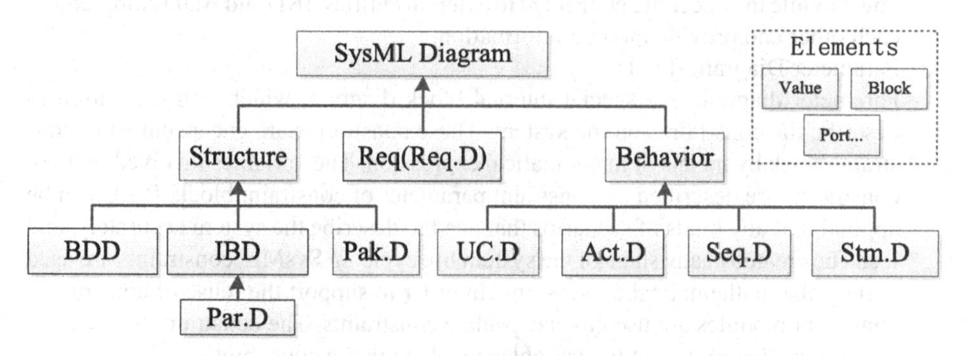

Fig. 3. SysML diagram

(1) Requirement Diagram (Req.D)
This diagram is used to represent text-based requirements and the relationship between requirements. The requirements table can clearly define each requirement of the system using the standard text description. A system requirement created by using a requirement diagram is a description of a system's functional or non-functional purpose (performance, etc.). The detailed definition of these requirements requires case analysis based on specific system application scenarios. The traceability between requirements and from requirements to system structure and behavior can be modeled by using the requirements diagram. According to the traceability, impact analysis can be carried out on the downstream. When the requirements change, the system structure and behavior that need to be modified can be found easily.

(2) Block Definition Diagram (BDD)
Block definition diagram is used to define the composition relationship between blocks and blocks. It can also be used to refine instances of blocks, including their configuration and value types. The structure attributes of a block mainly include parts, references, and values. The value attribute is defined by the value type of the feasible region, its quantization type and unit, etc. Value attributes can be associated with parameter constraints. Block behavior attributes include operation and

reception, which describe the behavior triggered by the block's response to external trigger.

(3) Internal Block Diagram (IBD)
The internal block diagram of SysML is the product of constraining and extending the composition structure diagram of UML. Internal block diagrams are closely related to block definition diagrams, and various elements can be displayed to illustrate various aspects of the system structure. The abbreviation of internal block diagram is IBD. IBD is created to specify the internal structure of a single module. As a supplement to BDD, IBD can represent the connection between component attributes and reference attributes, the event, energy and data types between the connections, and the services provided and requested through the connection. IBD represents how components of a module are combined to create valid instances and how module instances are connected to external entities. IBD and BDD complement each other and provide module information.

(4) Parameter Diagram (Par.D)
Parameter diagram is a special internal block diagram, which is mainly used to describe the constraints on the system. These constraints are encapsulated in constraint block by means of mathematical expression. The variables involved in these constraints are described by constraint parameter of constraint block. Par.D can be applied to many kinds of scenarios that need to describe the system accurately, and it can be created at any stage of the system life cycle. In SysML, constraints are used to describe mathematical expressions. In order to support the reuse of constraints, constraint modules are used to encapsulate constraints. The constraint module has parameters that represent the variables involved in the constraint.

(5) Package Diagram (Pak.D)
In SysML, package is the basic unit of model organization. Package and its contents are displayed on package diagram, which is used to organize model structure.

(6) Use Case Diagram (UC.D)
A use case diagram is a view that is composed of actors, use cases, boundaries and their relationships to describe system functions. Use case diagram is a model diagram of system functions observed by external users. Use case diagram is the blueprint of the system. The use case diagram presents some participants, use cases and their relationships. It is mainly used to model the specific requirements scenarios of the system and subsystem, so as to analyze the system functional behaviors needed to implement the requirements.

(7) Activity Diagram (Act.D)
Activity diagram is the modeling of the action sequence that constitutes the dynamic behavior of the system. It emphasizes the input, output, sequence and condition of a single activity, and provides flexible links between activities to describe the complex behavior of the system. In SysML activities, there are two kinds of flows: object flow and control flow; object flow connects the output pins of activities with the input pins of other actions, so as to promote the flow of tokens between actions; control flow specifies the execution sequence of activities. In order to assign behavior to a structure, SysML defines an activity partition, which usually represents a module or a component, and is responsible for executing actions within the activity partition.

(8) Sequence Diagram (Seq.D)
Sequence diagram of SysML is an extension of sequence diagram in UML. Sequence diagram is the dynamic behavior view of the system, reflecting the behavior and event sequence over time. In software engineering, sequence diagrams provide three kinds of information: the order of behavior execution, the execution structure of behavior and the triggering of behavior by structure, so the software system behavior created by sequence diagrams can be automatically transformed into the definition of source code. Sequence diagrams are useful in the early stages of a system's life cycle to illustrate the possible interactions between the system of interest and its environment's performers.

(8) State Machine Diagram (Stm.D)
State machine diagram, like activity diagram and sequence diagram, is a kind of behavior diagram, which is used to describe the dynamic view of the system. Unlike these two graphs, it focuses on the event driven state changes of modules in the system. The description object of state machine diagram is usually block, which can be any level module in the system structure level, such as system itself, subsystem or individual component, so it can be created at any point in the system life cycle. Because of its precise and clear behavior description, state machine diagram is very suitable to describe the final result of the design as the input of the subsequent development process.

The focus of this chapter is to clarify the function and application method of SysML Model, so as to prepare the model for modeling in the process of information flow design using SysML Model.

4 SysML Model and Information Flow Process Mapping

As shown in Fig. 4, the SysML modeling of spacecraft information flow design process is essentially how SysML diagrams and elements are applied to the information flow design process to match the static information and dynamic process in the design process.

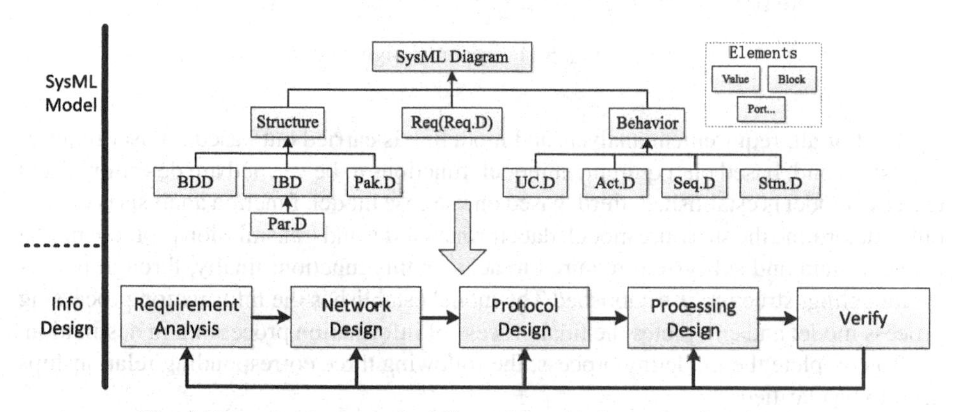

Fig. 4. Mapping between SysML model and information flow process

The Avoinics System is closely related to the information flow of spacecraft. The integrated electronic system involves the key factors related to the information flow, such as function, structure, data structure, transmission protocol and processing. Next, we will describe the process and method of SysML modeling from the perspective of integrated electronic system [6, 7].

4.1 Procedure Design

For the SysML modeling of spacecraft information flow, it is necessary to be familiar with the SysML modeling methodology, as well as the theoretical knowledge and engineering practice experience of electronic information system. Therefore, this paper adapts the modeling method according to the design characteristics of spacecraft information flow, and considers how to interface MBSE with spacecraft information flow design and simulation verification, such as the map of requirements, functions, behaviors and process, architecture, parameter constraints, etc. Based on the MagicGrid system modeling framework and the information flow design process, the information flow modeling process based on SysML model is designed as shown in the Fig. 5 [8].

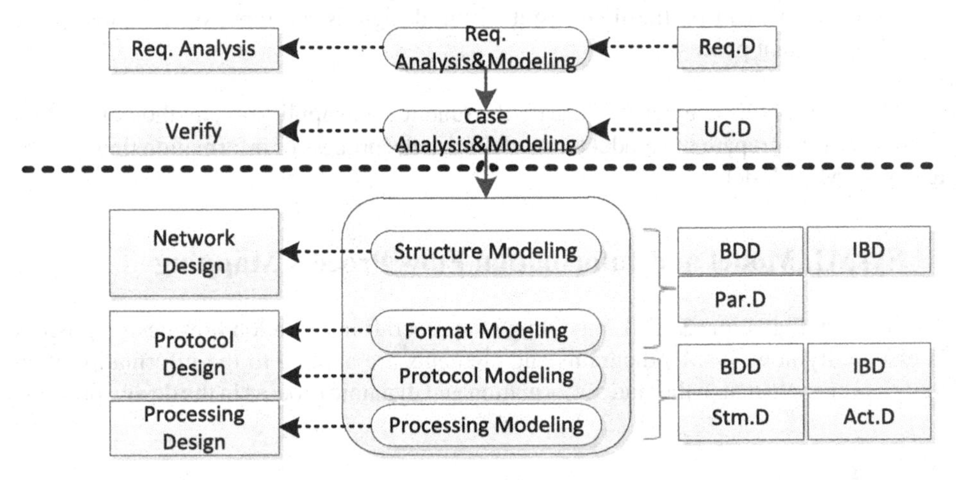

Fig. 5. Procedure design

First of all, requirement analysis and modeling is carried out based on user requirements; second, based on requirement model, functions to be verified are determined and use case model is established; third, based on use case model, function analysis is carried out to determine the structure model, data format model and transmission protocol model of the system and subsystem required to achieve this function; finally, through behavior modeling, structure is established The model establishes the information processing process model and completes the final process of information processing in destination.

To complete the modeling process, the following three corresponding relationships need to be clarified:

(1) Correspondence between information flow modeling process and MagicGrid system modeling process
1) Requirement analysis and modeling, use case analysis and modeling belong to the black box design stage of MagicGrid modeling process; 2) structure modeling, data format modeling, transmission protocol modeling and processing process modeling run through the gradual decomposition process of the whole satellite function and structure, and belong to the white box design stage and scheme design stage of MagicGrid modeling process.
(2) Correspondence between information flow modeling process and SysML Meta model
1) Use requirement diagram to analyze user requirements; 2) use case diagram to describe the Interaction scenario between user and system, and clarify the system functions that user needs to verify; 3) use block definition diagram and internal block diagram for structural modeling and data format modeling; 4) use activity diagram and state machine diagram for transmission protocol modeling and process modeling; 5) use parameters during structural modeling Figure for index constraints.
(3) Correspondence between information flow modeling process and information flow design process
Requirement analysis & Modeling corresponding information requirement analysis; 2) use case analysis & Modeling corresponding information verification demonstration. The verification demonstration here can only be described in terms of logic and function, and does not have bottom-level code compilation and operation and code level simulation. Other modeling tools are required to participate in this stage; 3) structure modeling corresponding information network design; 4) data format modeling and transmission Transport Protocol Modeling corresponds to transport protocol design; 5) processing process modeling corresponds to information processing design.

4.2 Modeling Ideas

(1) Requirements
The requirements of all stakeholders of information flow, which is all functions and performance that the system must meet, are reflected in the requirements diagram in the form of text.
(2) Use Cases
For all functions in information flow design, use case diagrams are used to build corresponding use case models, namely application scenarios. Information input and system environment must be included in the models. The system environment contains the current use case and the functions to be verified. This model can be understood as test case design in software testing.
(3) Structure
After completing the use case modeling, it needs to analyze the functions to be realized by the current use case, and the realization of the functions needs to be completed through the interaction between the functional entity and the entity.

(1) Entity modeling needs to use block. Among them, the nesting of entities (satellite à equipment à module) is also modeled by block and shown with BDD and IBD.
(2) In the IBD, the port and connector are added to the entity model to realize the data interaction between the entity block diagrams.

The entity model established by the BDD can be associated with the functions that need to be implemented or verified through the association matrix. Because entities may have multiple functions at the same time, the association matrix belongs to multi-to-multi association.
The parameter graph is used to constrain the parameters of the function module synchronously, so that the function must meet certain performance requirements on the premise of realization.
(4) Data Format
This part defines the format of information in different stages or different module structures in the process of transmission, and the visual representation of the model is block definition diagram.
The modeling of data format, like the modeling of the above entities, also has nesting, which is completed by block definition diagram.
(5) Transmission Protocol
This part defines which transmission protocols are used in different functional entities, and the information flow relationship between the protocols. The protocol itself is modeled by the block definition graph, the information processing within the protocol is modeled by the state machine graph, and the information flow between protocols is modeled by the internal block graph (input and output interfaces are added to the protocol model of the IBD).
(6) Process
This part defines the process of the information received by the sink. It uses activity diagram or state machine diagram to model, which belongs to the behavior modeling within the entity model.

5 Conclusion

Based on the analysis of the design process of Spacecraft information flow and the concept and structure characteristics of SysML Model, this paper proposes a SysML modeling design method of spacecraft information flow. This method provides a feasible solution to the problem of low efficiency in the requirement analysis and system design of spacecraft information flow based on text. At present, this method is only a prototype, still need more detailed and in-depth analysis and case verification, in order to better integrate the spacecraft information flow design process and SysML model, and improve the validity and reliability of spacecraft information flow design.

References

1. Hongtao, C., Yuchen, D., Jianhua, Y.: Basic principle of model-based system engineering. Aerosp. China (2016)
2. Shuhua, Z., Yue, C., Zheng, Z.: System design and simulation integration for complex mechatronic products based on SysML and Modelica, **30**(4), 728–738 (2018)
3. Lu, Z., Liu, X., Mao, Y.: Application practice of model-based system engineering method in satellite integrative system design, **27**(3), 7–16 (2018)
4. Kunsheng, W., Jianhua, Y., Hongtao, C., et al.: Research and practice of model—based systems engineering. Aerosp. China **11**, 52–57 (2012)
5. Yu, S., Li, M.: Model-based systems engineering and system modeling language. Comput. Knowl. Technol. **7**(31) (2011)
6. Han, F., Lin, Y., Fan, H.: Research and practice of model—based systems engineering in spacecraft development **23**(3), 119–124 (2014)
7. Yusheng, L., Yuqin, J., Shunting, G.: Model-driven modeling for system design of complex products: a survey. China Mech. Eng. **21**(6), 741–749 (2010)
8. Yifan, Z., Qun, L., Feng, Y., et al.: NASA. NASA Systems Engineering Handbook. Publishing House of Electronics Industry, Beijing (2012). (translated)

Data Management of Space Station Bus Network

Panpan Zhan[1(✉)], Xin Liu[1], Yating Cao[2], Lan Lu[1], Xiongwen He[1], and Yong Sun[1]

[1] Beijing Institute of Spacecraft System Engineering, Beijing 100094, People's Republic of China
panpan3210@qq.com

[2] Beijing Shenzhou Aerospace Software Technology Co., Ltd, Beijing, China

Abstract. Compared with other spacecrafts, there are many bus networks and many interactive data. Moreover, it has the bus network connection and data management functions among the three space station capsules, and the manned spaceships and cargo spaceships. Aiming at the problem of data management of space station bus network which can be combined and separated dynamically, through the design of multi-level bus networks and docking bus networks in the capsule, the data management solution is given from the system level. The process of telemetry management, telecommand management and interactive data management between subsystems are described in detail. Through the unified protocol design and routing management, the integrated networking and data communication between the spacecrafts are realized, which reduces the complexity and test difficulty of the system. This method has been tested and verified in the space station task, which not only ensures the reliability of docking and separation between the space station capsules, but also takes into account the flexibility and expansibility of data management.

Keywords: Space station · Data management · Rendezvous and docking · Bus network

1 Introduction

China's manned space projects are implemented in accordance with the "three-step" development strategy. The first step is to "start with a manned spaceship, launch several unmanned test spaceship and a manned spaceship" to solve the transportation problem between space and earth; the second step is to launch a space lab and realize rendezvous and docking. The third step is to "build a large space station" [1–3].

After more than 20 years of development, China has made remarkable achievements in manned space flight, manned rendezvous and docking, and has completed the first two steps, and is now in the third step of building a manned space station with Chinese characteristics [4]. The strategic goal of China's space station project is to build and operate the near earth space station, so that China will become a country that independently masters the long-term manned flight technology in near earth space, has the ability to carry out long-term scientific and technological experiments in near earth space and comprehensively develop and utilize space resources [5].

Q. Wu et al. (Eds.): WiSATS 2020, LNICST 358, pp. 392–400, 2021.
https://doi.org/10.1007/978-3-030-69072-4_31

Bus network data management belongs to the on-board data handle system, which is the key component of the space station. It is responsible for the bus communication management in each capsule and the bus communication management function between capsules of the space station. It plays an important role in the information communication and control of the space station. In the process of rendezvous and docking between each capsule of the space station and the transport spaceships (manned spaceships and cargo spaceships), the bus network data management is responsible for establishing the docking bus network among multiple spacecrafts, realizing the functions of telecommand, command transmission, telemetry data collection and control data transmission [6]. The complexity of the space station task brings challenge to the design of bus network data management between multiple spacecrafts.

2 Mission Characteristics

China's space station consists of kernel capsule, experimental capsule I and experimental capsule II. The three capsules form the basic configuration of the space station through rendezvous and docking and capsule transposition [5]. During the space station is in orbit, it performs rendezvous and docking with manned spaceship and cargo spaceship to form a combination, which realizes the transportation of people, goods and propellant fuel.

There are independent and combined flight modes between multiple capsules of the space station, and the mode of rendezvous and docking with multiple manned spaceships and cargo spaceships is complex. These tasks put forward the following requirements for the design of bus network data management of the space station:

1) Ensure the reliable transmission of information under the independent and combined flight mode of three capsules. It is required to continue to use 1553B bus network with high reliability as the main network to realize data flow control. Through the combination and separation of special docking bus, the other capsules' subnets and transport spacecraft subnets are integrated into the kernel capsule's subnets to realize the real-time synchronous exchange and collaborative control of Multiple Spacecrafts' information. Fast switching between independent flight mode and combined flight mode among the spacecrafts is achieved.

2) Requirements for integrated networking and data communication between the spacecrafts and within one spacecraft. During the space station is in orbit, there are at least five spacecrafts, including three capsules, a manned spaceship and a cargo spaceship, which need data communication at the same time. If the communication protocols and data formats are not unified, it will greatly increase the cost of protocol conversion and the difficulty of equipment realization. Therefore, it is necessary to design a unified communication protocol and data format to realize the integrated networking and communication among the spacecrafts.

3) Hierarchical management of multiple bus networks. According to the experience of the international space station, there are hundreds of electronic devices in a single capsule of the space station, and the maximum number of terminals in a single 1553B bus is 32. Therefore, it is necessary to manage multiple 1553B buses. The category of 1553B bus network includes the main bus network, combination bus between the three

capsules, docking bus with transport spaceships, and secondary bus networks within the subsystems.

3 Bus Network Design

The bus network is designed in a hierarchical way. The first level bus is used for the main control of the whole capsule, including the system bus in the capsule and the docking bus between the spacecrafts. The system bus in the capsule manages the main computer equipment of each subsystem. The docking bus manages the communications between the capsules and spaceships in combination mode. The second level bus is used to control and manage the equipment in each subsystem.

The design of the single capsule bus network of the space station is shown in Fig. 1. The onboard computer is the bus control terminal (BC) of the first level bus, which manages multiple docking buses and system buses. It is the control center of the whole network, responsible for the telecommand data, downlink data transmission and control of the whole capsule. In addition to connecting the equipment in the capsule, the docking bus is also connected with the docking bus of other capsules. The kernel capsule is connected with the experimental capsule I and experimental capsule II through the docking bus to form a combination, which form the whole space station. Each subsystem controller is connected to the first level bus as the remote terminal (RT) of the first level bus and the BC of the second level bus. It is responsible for receiving the telecommand data and instruction data from the central computer, forwarding them to the equipment in the subsystem through the second level bus, collecting the telemetry data, display data or control data in the subsystem, and transmitting them to the onboard computer. Onboard computer transmits the control data to other subsystem controllers, packages and frames all received telemetry data and then descend them to the ground.

The information combiner receives the whole capsule's telemetry data from the onboard computer, multiplexes the real-time telemetry, delay telemetry, bus monitoring data, etc., generates several virtual channel data units (VCDU [7]) and sends them to the ground through the physical channel.

After the space station is out of the TT & C area, the real-time telemetry is converted to delay telemetry. At this time, the onboard storage device stores the delay telemetry data of the capsule, and transmits the data after entering the TT & C area. According to the application of space lab [6], the capacity of onboard storage device needs to be designed above 1000 GB to meet the requirements of long-term use in orbit.

The docking bus network is divided into two levels. The first level is the docking bus in the capsule, which is used to establish the bus communication link after the kernel capsule forms a combination with the experimental capsule I and experimental capsule II. The second level is the special docking bus with the transport spaceship, which forms a combination with the manned spaceship and the cargo spaceship respectively, and then establishes the bus communication link. The docking bus network design of the space station is shown in the Fig. 2.

The kernel capsule is connected with the experimental capsule I and experimental capsule II through the docking bus. Before the docking, each capsule is in independent flight mode. The onboard computer, as the BC end of the docking bus, controls

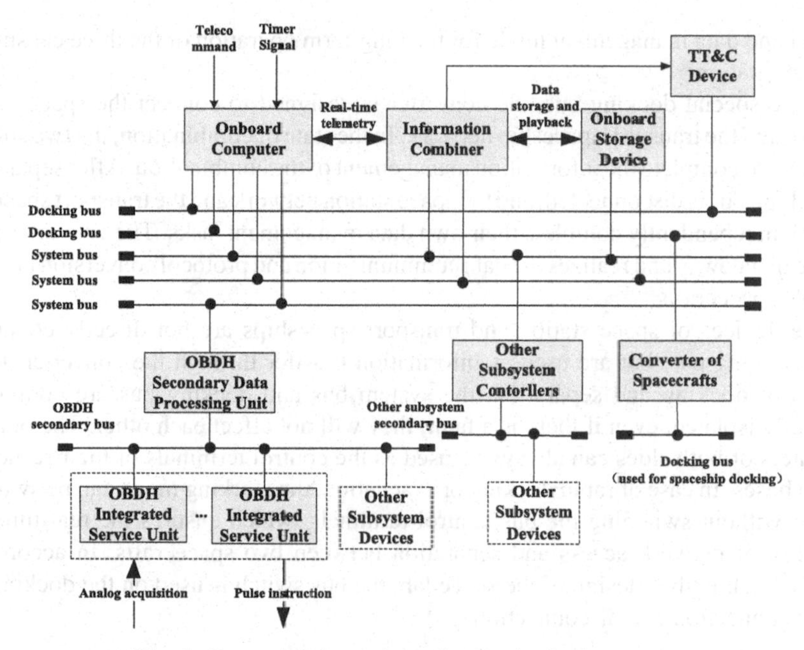

Fig. 1. Bus network topology diagram in single capsule

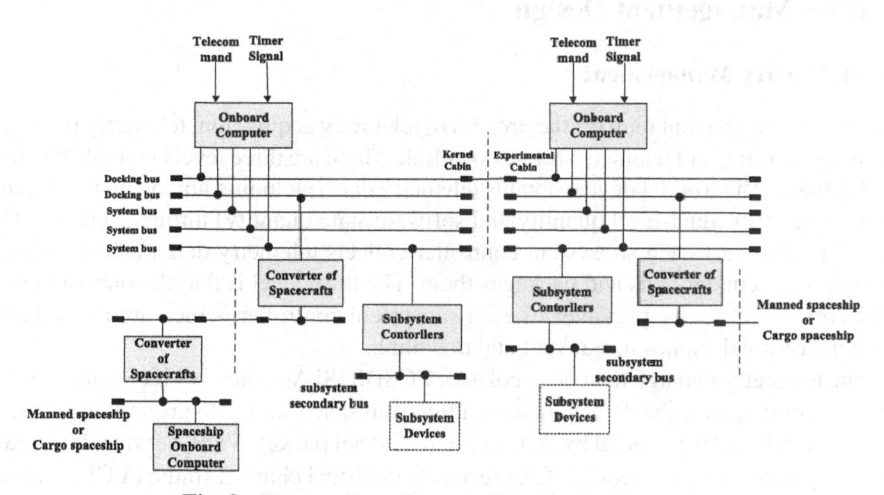

Fig. 2. Bus topology diagram of docking bus network

the data communication on the bus. After the docking, the independent flight mode is transformed into docking mode, and the onboard computers of experimental capsule I and experimental capsule II are transformed into RT terminals. The onboard computer of kernel capsule is still used as BC terminal to manage the data communication on the docking bus. The data management on the system bus is still in the charge of the onboard computer in each capsule. In this way, bus channels are established to ensure the interconnection of information between the three capsules, providing a reliable network channel and data management mode for the long-term operation of the three capsules in the space station.

In the special docking bus, the converter is designed to connect the space station network and the transport spaceship network. In the state of combination, the two subnets cooperate to complete the information management of the combination. After separation, the docking bus is disconnected, and the space station network and the transport spaceship network independently complete their own data management tasks. The converter plays the role of gateway and realizes the data communication and protocol conversion between multiple spacecrafts.

The devices of space station and transport spaceships are not directly connected to the docking bus, but are used as information transfer through the converter. In the process of docking and separation, the system bus and docking bus are completely physically isolated, even if there is a fault, they will not affect each other. The onboard computers of both sides can always be used as the control terminals of their respective system buses. In case of rapid docking or evacuation, the working mode can be switched quickly without switching the bus control terminals, which ensures the real-time and reliability of network access and separation between two spacecrafts. In accordance with the docking bus design of the space lab, the bus switch is used on the docking bus for bus connection and disconnection.

4 Data Management Design

4.1 Telemetry Management

Telemetry management realizes the process of telemetry acquisition, telemetry package, telemetry framing and telemetry frame downlink. There are three levels in total. The first level is that each terminal device obtains telemetry data (including analog quantity, temperature quantity, dual-level quantity and software state quantity) through sensors. The second level is that each subsystem controller collects telemetry data of the first level through the secondary bus and packages them. The third level is that the onboard computer collects telemetry packages of each subsystem controller, which are multiplexed to virtual channel frames to transmit and downlink.

The telemetry management protocol uses CCSDS [8] Advanced Orbit System (AOS) [7] protocol to realize the data communication from space station to ground. It uses four kinds of services [9] provided by AOS: virtual channel packet (VCP) service, bit stream service, virtual channel access (VCA) service and virtual channel frame (VCF) service.

As shown in Fig. 3, through the virtual channel packet (VCP) service, each subsystem controller encapsulates the telemetry data as EPDU [10] on the secondary bus, organizes them into EPDU packet sequences and sends them to onboard computer, which encapsulates all packets as MPDU and sends them to the information combiner for transmission in transfer frame data field. Through bit stream service, the continuous bit sequence, including image and voice data, is encapsulated as BPDU by information combiner and transmitted in transfer frame data field.

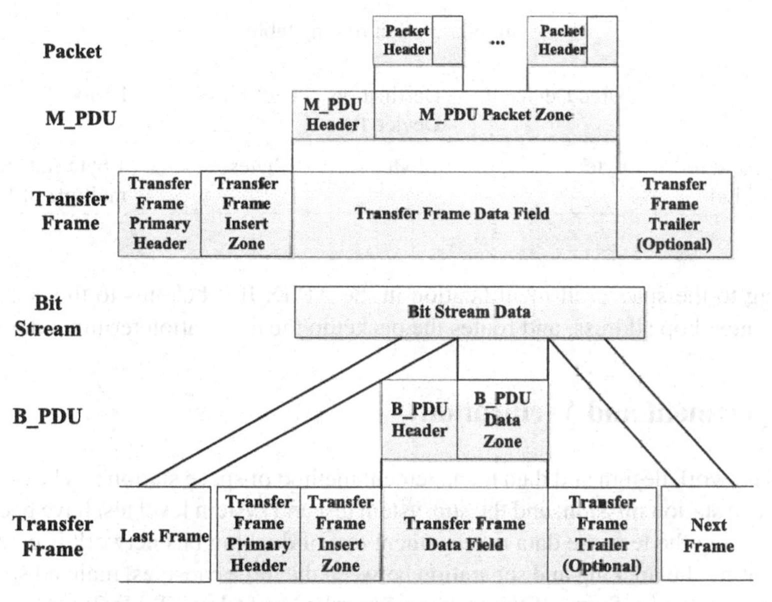

Fig. 3. Data processing process of VCP service and bitstream service

4.2 Telecommand Management

The telecommand management function uses CCSDS telecommand data link protocol [11] to realize the telecommand data receiving and forwarding function. The data format uses the standard data format of telecommand transmission frame, and the standard EPDU packet is used in the data field. After receiving the telecommand frame from the ground, the onboard computer processes the frame routing and packet routing respectively.

If the telecommand frame comes from the other spacecraft (other capsules or spaceships), the frame routing is performed and sent to the target spacecraft for processing. If it is the telecommand frame of other terminals in the capsule, it will be routed to the corresponding bus device according to the VCID. If it is a telecommand frame that needs to be processed by the capsule onboard computer, telecommand packet analysis shall be carried out, packet routing shall be carried out according to the APID of telecommand packet and distributed to the corresponding terminal equipment for processing.

4.3 Interactive Data Management Between Subsystems

The standard EPDU packet is used for data transmission among subsystems. APID is used to identify the spacecraft, the subsystem and the data type. The onboard computer routes the package according to the package routing table, and sends the EPDU packet to the destination device to support the data communication between the capsule and the spaceship. The main elements of the packet routing table are designed as follows Table 1:

The onboard computer searches the routing table according to the APID of the EPDU packet, and routes the packet to the onboard computer of the destination spacecraft

Table 1. Packet routing table

APID	Source Device ID	Destination Device ID	Packet Length	Period
2 bytes (valid for lower 11 bits)	1 byte	1 byte	2 bytes	1 byte (integer multiple of 50 ms)

according to the spacecraft identification in the APID. If it belongs to this spacecraft, finds the next hop address, and routes the packet to the destination terminal device.

5 Experiment and Verification

The bus network design and data management method of space station has been applied to the space station mission, and the subsystem test and system level test have been completed. During the test, the data management test of docking bus network is carried out by simulating the docking and separation between the three capsules, manned spaceship and cargo spaceship. Some of the tests are described as follows Table 2:

Through the system level test, it is found that the single capsule of the space station can realize at least six sets of bus network data communication and management functions, and the single bus data communication rate can reach about 300 kbps. Through

Table 2. Test results of data management of space station

Test Item	Test Content	Test Situation
Single capsule's data management test	Telemetry management	The telemetry acquisition, organization and downlink of all terminal devices on the bus in the capsule are tested
	Telecommand management	The telecommand, frame and packet forwarding and processing are tested
	Interactive data management between subsystems	Receiving, forwarding and processing of packets between subsystems are tested
Three capsules' data management test	Telemetry management	After the docking of the three capsules, the acquisition, organization and downlink of the telemetry in a capsule are tested, and the function of telemetry package framing between capsules are tested

(continued)

Table 2. (*continued*)

Test Item	Test Content	Test Situation
	Telecommand management	Telecommand frame forwarding, telecommand packet receiving and processing are tested
	Interactive data management between subsystems	Receiving, forwarding and processing of packets between capsules are tested
Data management test of docking combination of space station and spaceships	Telemetry management, Telecommand management, Interactive data management between subsystems	After the docking combination of the space station and the transport spaceships, the telemetry data of the spaceships collected by the space station through the converter, the telecommand data sent to the spaceships and the interactive data processing are Tested
Docking and separation data management test	Docking and separation data management of three capsules and spaceships	Through the repeated docking and separation process, the data communication and processing are correct, and the switching between independent flight mode and combined flight mode is realized

the frame and packet routing mechanism, the integrated networking and data communication between devices are realized, the data format is unified, the protocol conversion overhead is avoided, and the difficulty of system implementation and test is reduced. It supports the rendezvous, docking and separation functions among three capsules, manned spaceships and cargo spaceships. It realizes the safe, reliable and fast switching between independent flight and combined flight modes among the spacecrafts.

6 Conclusion

Space station bus network data management is an important part of the space station mission, which involves the information management between the three capsules of the space station, manned spaceships and cargo spaceships. It is also an important direction of the future development of the space field. The bus network data management method designed in this paper can support single capsule independent flight mode, three capsules docking flight mode, docking and separation flight mode with manned spaceships and cargo spaceships, which is safe and reliable. Through the unified protocol design and routing management, the function of integrated networking and data communication between spacecrafts and within spacecrafts is realized. This method has been tested and verified in the space station mission.

References

1. Jianping, Z.: Rendezvous and docking technology of human space flight. Manned Spaceflight **2011**(2), 1–8 (2011)
2. Zhi, S.: Technology achievements and prospect of china first rendezvous and docking mission. Spacecraft Eng. **20**(6), 11–15 (2011)
3. He, Y., Hong, Y., Mingsheng, B.: Spacelab technology summary and development stratagem. Manned Spacelight **15**(3), 10–17 (2009)
4. Yongzhi, W.: Implementing china's manned space station program and developing manned space industry scientifically. Manned Space **2011**(1), 1–4 (2011)
5. Zhonggui, W.: Challenges and opportunities facing TT&C and communication systems for china's manned space station program. J. Spacecraft TT & C Technol. **32**(4), 281–285 (2013)
6. Zhan, P., Lu, L., He, X., Wang, L., Sun, Y.: Data management software system design for spacelab. In: Jia, M., Guo, Q., Meng, W. (eds.) WiSATS 2019. LNICSSITE, vol. 280, pp. 320–328. Springer, Cham (2019). https://doi.org/10.1007/978-3-030-19153-5_33
7. Consultative Committee for space Data System: AOS space data link protocol. CCSDS 732.0-B-2. Recommended Standard, Issue 2. Washington D.C., USA: CCSDS Secretariat (2006)
8. Consultative Committee for space Data System: CCSDS 130.0-G-3 Overview of space communications protocols. Washington D.C., USA: CCSDS Secretariat (2014)
9. Heping, Z., Xiongwen, H., Chonghua, L., et al.: Space Data System. Beijing Institute of Technology Press, Beijing (2019)
10. Consultative Committee for space Data System: CCSDS 133.0-B-1 Space Packet Protocol. Washington D.C., USA: CCSDS Secretariat (2003)
11. Consultative Committee for space Data System: CCSDS 232.0-B-3 TC Space Data Link Protocol. Washington D.C.,USA: CCSDS Secretariat (2015)

A Space Network Oriented Spacecraft Software High-Reliability Maintenance Method

Liang Qiao[1(✉)], Ying Wu[1], Xiaoyi Zhou[2], and Lijun Yang[1]

[1] Beijing Institute of Spacecraft System Engineering, China Academy of Space Technology, Beijing 100094, China
owenqiao@126.com

[2] School of Computer Science and Engineering, Beihang University, Beijing 100191, China

Abstract. In order to improve the capability of on-demand customization and agile reconfiguration of space network, and to improve the scalability and reliability of space network, this paper proposed a method of spacecraft software in-orbit high-reliability maintenance method that is suitable for space network. This method is based on the electrical erasable memory of the onboard computer, uses various methods to improve the reliability, writes the reconfiguration data into the memory, and realizes the non-volatile reconfiguration of onboard software based on multiple granularities such as parameters, modules, processes or complete software. In addition, this method uses the hardware EDAC function to detect and correct errors in the memory during operation, which further improves the robustness. The in-orbit application and a large number of tests show that the method is suitable for on-demand customization of space network and can realize in-orbit reconfiguration of onboard software with high reliability.

Keywords: Space network · Spacecraft software · Software high-reliability maintenance

1 Introduction

Currently, there are more than 200 in-orbit satellites in China, most of which are designed for functional solidification. Also, these satellites are heterogeneous and difficult to connect to the Internet, resulting in the delay of information transmission, the difficulty of cooperation among satellites, the high complexity of ground operation and maintenance and the low efficiency of satellite application [1]. However, current satellite users have increasing demands for agile reconfiguration and on-demand customization of the space network. The existing space network does not have the overall design of software architecture based on the software definition, and it is difficult to make the dynamic deployment and in-orbit reconfiguration for several types of inter-satellite links and multiple network nodes, which makes the space network unable to exert the full effectiveness of the existing satellite system.

The spacecraft data management software acts as the brain of all satellite information on the satellite. It is not only responsible for the transmission, processing and autonomous

Q. Wu et al. (Eds.): WiSATS 2020, LNICST 358, pp. 401–409, 2021.
https://doi.org/10.1007/978-3-030-69072-4_32

task management within the satellite, between the satellites and the ground stations, or among the satellites through inter-satellite links, but also an important implementation carrier of space network routing, network protocols and antennas pointing calculating. The PROM (Programmable Read-Only Memory) chips, that are stable but can be programmed only once, are generally used for programming software on traditional satellites. The only way to reconfigure software is to remove the chip and reprogram the new software. Using programming-once PROM chips have better resistance to spatial radiation, but make software debugging difficult. Even worse, it is impossible to change the space network protocols after the launches of the satellites, and this programming method is not conductive to agile reconfiguration and on-demand customization of the topology and the protocols of space network. Another way to reconfigure spacecraft software is to change the data in RAM (Random Access Memory) directly as the software changes a little. But RAM is a kind of volatile memory. In the space environment, high energy particles often cause the computer to restart [2], resulting in the loss of software updates, which means disconnection from the network and loss of communication for space network node satellites. Therefore, in practical usage, this method also has many problems.

In traditional spacecraft computer design, in order to improve the reliability of satellite service, software and hardware are with integrated design, but integrated design also poses the problems of pattern rigidity, which has an essential counterpart and a deep diction with the future demand for flexibility and plasticity. In order to improve the flexibility and maintainability of the spacecraft software, some satellites, especially those connected to the space network or carrying the network protocol function, adopt non-volatile memory, such as flash [3] and EEPROM (Electrically Erasable Programmable Read-only Memory) [4], to program software with space network management module. Since updates to non-volatile memory will not be lost after a power failure, all or part of the new software version can be written to memory through telecommand channel. In this way, the non-volatile reconfiguration of onboard software can be performed based on multiple granularities such as parameters, modules, processes or complete software, which can achieve downward compatibility and upward evolution of space network. In academia, there are several discussions on the method of in-orbit maintenance of spacecraft software. Wang Zhanqiang et al. proposed a method on software on-orbit reconfiguration of space-borne processing equipment [5], which can adapt to the software in-orbit reconfiguration tasks related to software designed radio technology, but this method needs to be improved in reliability; Guo Zongzhi et al. proposed a method on spacecraft software refactoring scheme based on dynamic loading mechanism of module [6]. However, this method can only be used with VxWorks operating system, which lacks of universality.

In this paper, we propose a method of maintaining in-orbit spacecraft software orienting the agile reconfiguration of space network with high reliability. First of all, this paper introduces the basic process of software in-orbit maintenance based on non-volatile memory, which is suitable for agile reconfiguration of space network. Then, this paper introduces several key technologies to ensure the reliability of software in-orbit maintenance. Finally, the effectiveness of this method is illustrated by introducing the test results.

2 Basic Process of Software High-Reliability Maintenance for Space Network Agile Reconfiguration

Compared to common embedded software, there are three main differences in the in-orbit maintenance process of spacecraft software. Firstly, the TT&C ground station cannot connect the satellites at all time [7]. For instance, LEO satellites can connect with a ground station for a few minutes per circle. And it takes a long time to send and execute the reconfiguration telecommands of the entire space network protocol, so the whole reconfiguration process may be divided into several times. Secondly, the telecommand channel is a wireless channel, which has a relatively high error rate. Therefore, to improve the reliability of the reconfiguration process, there should be more reliable design. Thirdly, high energy particles in the universe can be projected into the sensitive area of semiconductor devices, resulting in Single Event Effect [8]. Program data stored in the memory may have a single-bit error or a double-bit error. Therefore, it is necessary to detect and repair errors continuously while the program running.

Taking into account the needs for maintenance of spacecraft software with space network function and the different characteristics from common embedded software, as shown in Fig. 1, the authors designs the maintenance process of in-orbit software suitable for agile reconfiguration of space network.

After starting the spacecraft onboard computer, the program data in the EEPROM is moved to the RAM and run in RAM. If the program has to be modified in orbit due to the updates of software parameters or the space network protocols, the data in RAM can be modified directly, but this method will cause data loss in case of power failure. If a permanent update is needed, it can be written with whole or part of the new version of the in-orbit software in EEPROM, by this way, the non-volatile reconfiguration of onboard software can be performed based on multiple granularities such as parameters, modules, processes or complete software. In order to resolve the high dynamic performance of space network and the relatively high bit error of the uplink channel, and to achieve the high reliability of the software maintenance process, the uplink telecommand instructions from the ground are temporarily stored in RAM. After receiving all instructions, the running software compare the check code attached to the instructions with the check code calculated from the data temporarily stored in RAM by same algorithm. If the verification is correct, the reconfiguration data is written to EEPROM.

To improve the reliability of the in-orbit software, to improve the reliability of its communication inter-satellite link and to reduce the impact of Single Event Effect, the EDAC circuit can be used for self-checking of EEPROM in the idle time of software running. In addition, another common method is Triple Modular Redundancy (TMR), that is to store the same data in three pieces of memory. When loading data, program is processed by a majority-voting system to produce a single output., but this method needs much more storage resources.

After the satellite was launched, when there are agile reconfiguration and customization requirements of the space network topology or protocols, the in-orbit maintenance method in this section can be used to reconfigure the spacecraft onboard software performing space network functions and detect and correct errors in memory.

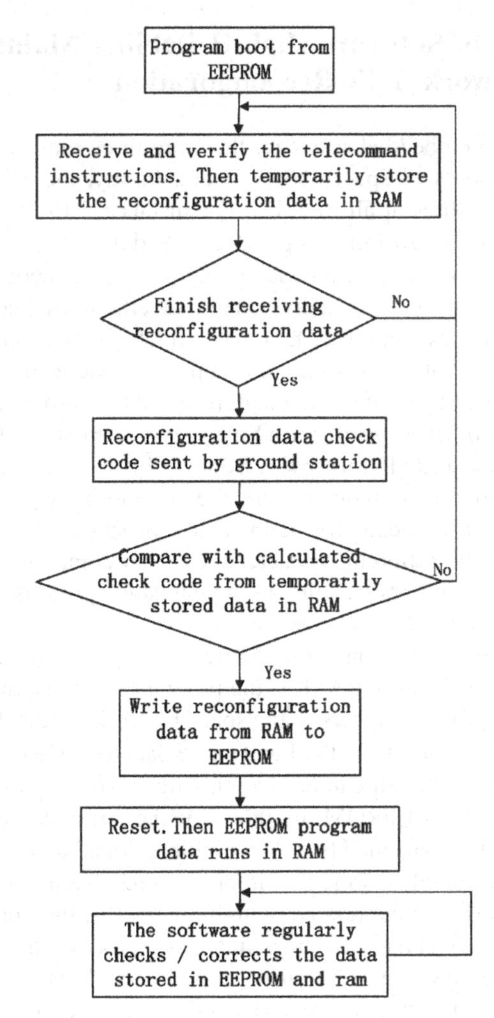

Fig. 1. The flow chart of in-orbit software high-reliability maintenance

3 Key Technologies of Spacecraft Software In-Orbit Maintenance

In this section, some key technologies of spacecraft software in-orbit maintenance adapted for agile reconfiguration of space network are discussed.

3.1 High Reliability EEPROM Data Maintenance

A single high energy particle in the universe can be projected into the sensitive area of semiconductor devices, causing Single Event Effect. Under this circumstance, program data stored in the EEPROM may have a single-bit error or a double-bit error, which could cause the software crash in severe cases. This is a fatal problem for spacecraft software that performs space network functions and could interrupt communications

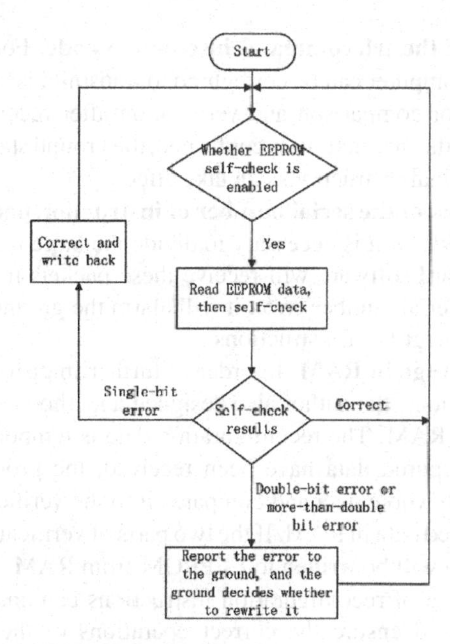

Fig. 2. The flow chart of EEPROM self-check and auto-correc

among satellites. As a result, the redundant design for EEPROM is very important for the reliability of the space network (Fig. 2).

It should be noted that when writing EEPROM, the tunnel oxide layer would withstand high voltage and high electric field, so the lifetime of the EEPROM is limited. To extend the lifetime of EEPROM and to prevent in-orbit failure of EEPROM, the frequency of self-detection of EEPROM should not be too high.

3.2 Reliability Design of In-Orbit Reconfiguration Telecommand Instructions

The TT&C ground station cannot maintain communication links with satellites at all time, and it also takes a long time to reconfigure the entire space network parameters and protocols, so the entire program may have to be divided into hundreds of instructions and be sent separately. Moreover, the data uplink channel is a wireless channel, which has a relatively high error rate. Therefore, to improve the reliability of the reconfiguration process, there should be more reliable design. In this section, the fault-tolerant design of reconfiguration instructions is of great importance to ensure the integrity and efficiency of reconfigured data and the implementation of space network functions.

The reliable design of the software in-orbit reconfiguration instructions mainly includes the following:

(1) Verification of the instruction format. Software checks the instruction fields according to pre-determined format including the instruction verification code format comparison, optional range of each field and the validity of the memory addresses to reconfigure, etc. The software will refuse to execute the telecommand instructions that unable to pass the format verification. Verification of the instruction format could prevent the instructions from appearing error codes in instruction uplink.

(2) Comparison of the telecommand instruction code. For small-scale and key changes, the onboard computer can be configured to transmit instruction code data back to the ground station for comparison and verification after receiving the instructions. Once the correctness of the instructions is confirmed, the ground station sends the confirm instruction and the original instructions can take effect.

(3) Continuity check of the serial number of instruction packets. To write a large amount of data to EEPROM, it is necessary to divide the large instructions into several packets. And the onboard software will receive these packets in sequence. In case of packets loss or packet serial number error, it will alarm the ground station by telemetry channel to ensure the integrity of instructions.

(4) Temporary storage in RAM. In order to further improve the reliability of the reconfiguration instructions, the author also designed a method to store temporarily the reconfiguration data in RAM. The reconfiguration data is temporarily stored in RAM. After all of the reconfigured data have been received, the ground station sends the verification code for the whole data and compares it to the verification code calculated from the temporary stored data in RAM. If the two parts of verification code are matched, the reconfiguration data will be written to EEPROM from RAM.

The reliability design of reconfiguration instructions can ensure the accuracy and completeness of data and ensure the correct operations of the space network after reconfiguration.

4 Engineering Design and Test Verification

At present, there are several satellites in orbit equipped with computer with non-volatile memory, which can realize space network oriented software in-orbit reconfiguration, and realize the on-demand customization of space network protocols. The typical computer architecture is shown as Fig. 3. Compared with the traditional method, that is programming program in PROM, the use of non-volatile memory, although losing the reliability within the tolerable range, improves software flexibility and achieve a balance between reliability and flexibility, which is very important for the rapid evolution of the current space network development. The CPU board of a high orbit satellite platform computer takes CPU as the core, and constitutes a complete computer system with other modules including memory, 1553B bus controller, high stability clock interface, etc. In the process of software running, the non-volatile reconfiguration of onboard software can be performed based on multiple granularities such as parameters, modules, processes or complete software. In the process of reconfiguration, the original program can still continue to run.

The authors constructed the test environment, and verified the in-orbit software reconfiguration method introduced in this paper. As shown in the Fig. 4, the test environment is composed of the main control computer, test client, LAN network, cables and test software to form a high-performance test system. The main control computer controls each test client, and all test data and test results can be displayed and processed on the main control computer.

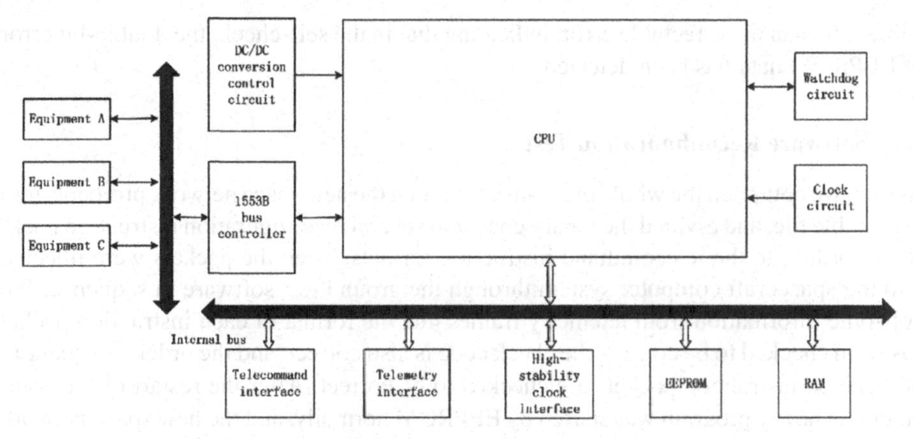

Fig. 3. A typical spacecraft computer architecture

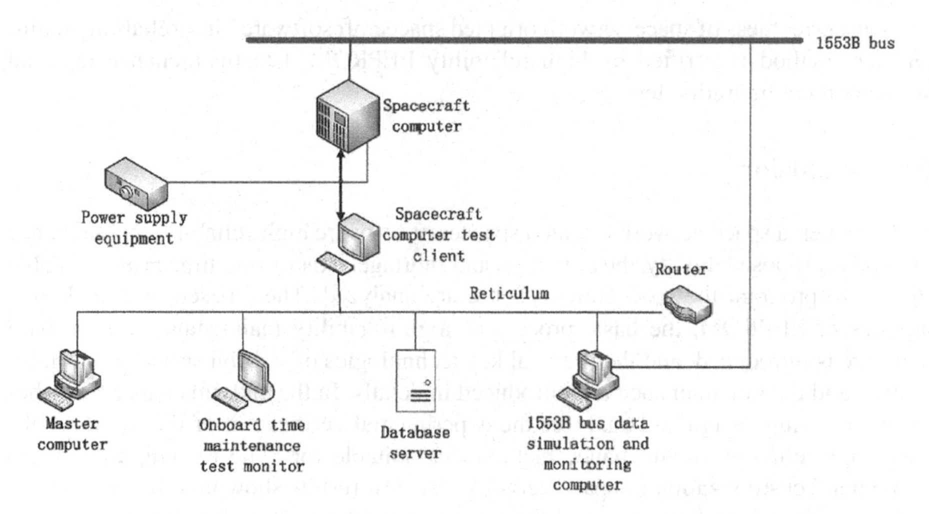

Fig. 4. Spacecraft software high-reliability maintenance test environment

4.1 High Reliability EEPROM Data Maintenance Test

Single-bit Error Test. Firstly, we wrote the data at an address within EEPROM address space as 0x55555555. With calculation, we got the EDAC check code as 0xed, then used the emulator to change the original data to 0x55555554. Next, we turned on the EEPROM self-check function. After a period of time, we read the data at that address, and found that the data became 0x55555555, which showed that in the self-check, the single-bit error of EEPROM data has been corrected automatically.

Double-bit Error Test. Firstly, we wrote the data at an address within EEPROM address space as 0x55555555. With calculation, we got the EDAC check code as 0xed, then used the emulator to change the original data to 0x55555556. Next, we turned on the EEPROM self-check function, after a period of time, the telemetry showed that that EEPROM address had an uncorrectable error, indicating that in the self-check, the double-bit error of EEPROM data has been detected.

4.2 Software Reconfiguration Test

At first, we compiled the whole program containing the new space network protocols into executable file, and divided the binary code into several reconfiguration instruction packets according to the telecommand instruction formats. Then the packets were injected into the spacecraft computer system through the ground test software in sequence. We got some information from telemetry frames that the format of each instruction packet has been checked to be correct, the check code is also correct, and the order and quantity of received instruction packets are checked to be correct. After the restart of the computer, the newly program was started by EEPROM normally, and the new space network protocols ran correctly, which proves the correctness of the software reconfiguration process.

The correctness of space network oriented spacecraft software high-reliability maintenance method is verified by high reliability EEPROM data maintenance test and software reconfiguration test.

5 Conclusion

In this paper, a space network oriented spacecraft software high-reliability maintenance method is proposed. Firstly, the limitation and shortage of using one-time programmable PROM to program the spacecraft software are analyzed. Then, based on the characteristics of EEPROM, the basic process of high-reliability maintenance for onboard software is introduced, and then several key technologies of in-orbit software reconfiguration and data maintenance are introduced in details. In the end, this paper describes the engineering design and analyzes the experimental verification of the in-orbit software high-reliability maintenance method that suitable for agile reconfiguration and on-demand customization of space network. The test results show that the method can realize in-orbit reconfiguration and data maintenance of spacecraft software, meet the design requirements, and improve the in-orbit maintainability and expansibility of space network.

References

1. Chien, W.C., Lai, C.F., Hossain, M.S., Muhammad, G.: Heterogeneous space and terrestrial integrated networks for IoT: architecture and challenges. IEEE Netw. **33**(1), 15–21 (2019)
2. Peng, C., et al.: Low-energy proton-induced single event effect in NAND flash memories. Nucl. Inst. Methods Phys. Res. **969**, 164064 (2020)
3. Choi, S., Oh, Y., Song, Y.-H.: A novel three-dimensional NAND flash structure for improving the erase performance. IEICE Electron. Express **16**(3), 20181016–20181016 (2019)
4. Chenguang, W., Wensheng, S.: Design and implementation of multi-state reboot recording system for embedded devices based on linux. Softw. Guide **18**(05), 125–129 (2019)
5. Zhanqiang, W., Shenghua, Z.: Research on software on-orbit reconfiguration of space-borne processing equipment. Space Electron. Technol. **1**, 7–13 (2013)

6. Zongzhi, G., Bin, L., Yulong, Z., Xiaoli, T., Chong, N.: Research on spacecraft software refactoring scheme based on dynamic loading mechanism of module. Comput. Meas. Contr. **19**, 126–9 (2018)
7. Qiao, L., Yan, H., Zhang, Y., Zhang, R., Jia, W.: Multilayer satellite network topology design technology based on incomplete IGSO/MEO constellation. In: Yu, Q. (ed.) SINC 2019. CCIS, vol. 1169, pp. 28–38. Springer, Singapore (2020). https://doi.org/10.1007/978-981-15-3442-3_3
8. Aerospace Research - Avionics; Findings from Institute of Space Systems in Avionics Reported (Heavy Ion Induced Single Event Effects Characterization on an RF-Agile Transceiver for Flexible Multi-Band Radio Systems in NewSpace Avionics). Defense & Aerospace Week (2020)

A Novel Protocol and Layered Implementation for Spacecraft Telecommand and Device Management

Lan Lu(✉), Xin Liu, and Xiongwen He

Beijing Institute of Spacecraft System Engineering, Beijing 100094, China
abbylulan@hotmail.com

Abstract. The application of CCSDS telecommand space data link protocol in the Chinese space field is still limited to intra-spacecraft communication recently, and the research on the standardized protocols and layered system architecture which is suitable for inter-spacecraft telecommand data forwarding is still insufficient. In this paper, we introduce a new protocol based on telecommand space data link protocol and a novel layered implementation of the protocol, which enables interpreting and forwarding uplink data, device management command and manual control command through unified protocols, processes and modules. Comparing to traditional protocol and implementation of spacecraft telecommand, the new protocol and corresponding implementation has great advantage in terms of standardization, flexibility and extensibility, and has been applied to a large spacecraft assembly.

Keywords: Protocol · Layered implementation · Telecommand · Device management

1 Introduction

With the emergence and development of various complex space missions, such as spacecraft rendezvous and docking [1, 2], more collaborative controls and data interactions between different types of spacecrafts and between devices within spacecraft are needed. Besides, the standardization of the inter-spacecraft and intra-spacecraft information exchanging interface is expected to be enhanced constantly. To meet above requirements, it is necessary to adopt standard protocols for command and data interaction within spacecraft data management system and design the system architecture for information interaction in modular, scalable and flexible way. At present, there are some applications of telecommand space data link protocol in the Chinese space field [3–8], but the research on modularized and layered system architecture design and implementation is still insufficient. In this paper, we propose a unified protocol and corresponding layered implementation for spacecraft telecommand and device management, which standardizes inter-spacecraft and inter-device interfaces. In the implementation, the telecommand space data link protocol are strictly followed, the interfaces between

Q. Wu et al. (Eds.): WiSATS 2020, LNICST 358, pp. 410–419, 2021.
https://doi.org/10.1007/978-3-030-69072-4_33

layers are clearly defined, and each layer can be independently expanded to meet the requirements for various types of collaborative controlling, information interaction, and system rebuilding in the large orbiting spacecrafts.

2 Unified Design for Telecommand and Device Management

2.1 Design

The data management system (DMS) in large-scale spacecraft assembly needs to process and forward commands from different sources. Typically, there are two types of commands:

1. uplink telecommands from N (N >= 2) physical channels which are from different telecommand systems.
2. manual commands and device-to-device commands from M (M >= 3) member spacecrafts in the spacecraft assembly.

The process of forwarding command includes multiple steps:

1. collecting command from bus.
2. storing, verifying and parsing data.
3. addressing and routing.
4. packing and delivering message.

In traditional design, for each source S, there is a unique data processor (DP) to forward commands from S. Assume the average complexity of DP is C_0, let C_1 denote the complexity of DMS in single spacecraft and let C_{all} denote the complexity of DMS in the whole spacecraft assembly. It is easy to know that

$$C_1 = (M + N) * C_0$$

$$C_{all} = M * C_1 = M * (M + N) * C_0$$

So C_{all} increases quadratically with M, which is the number of member spacecraft. Besides, each time when a new member spacecraft join the spacecraft assembly, the DMS in original M member spacecrafts are all required to be upgraded to support the new member spacecraft. Obviously, the design is not scalable and extensible, and is not suitable for DMS in large-scale spacecraft assembly.

The key problem in the traditional design is that the data structures used in different channels and sources are different, and thus make the DP not sharable. Be inspired by the observation, in following sections, we proposed a new design of DMS which can unify the data structures and make DP sharable, so that the complexity of DMS in the whole spacecraft assembly will not increase with the number of member spacecrafts. At the same time, the extensibility and scalability of DMS is improved significantly because the DMS in all existing member spacecrafts does not need to be upgraded when a new member spacecraft joins the spacecraft assembly.

There are some key challenges in the new design, for example,

1. There are 1 USB channel and several relay channels in a large-scale spacecraft assembly, and each channel has its own telecommand system. The length of telecommand frame, transmit rate and format of frame of each channel are significantly different. To ensure the DP for telecommand can be unified, the new design of data structure for telecommands must be adaptive to the characteristics of different physical channels. So, in this paper, we propose a new data structure for uplink telecommand that can improve the utilization of channel bandwidth and simplify system design:

   a. The telecommand frame of different channels is filled with variable-length transfer frames which share the same format.
   b. The variable-length transfer frames adapt to variable transmit rate of different channels.

2. Device-to-device command is the command sent actively from any device in assembly to other devices. Manual command is the command sent actively from astronaut to devices. In traditional design of DMS, those commands are often implemented as customized simple command in private format, which can't be addressed in larger scope and thus can't meet the needs of forwarding command multiple times among multiple spacecrafts. In this paper, we propose a new way of defining and implementing device management command that can support transferring any device-to-device command and manual command on the bus network in assembly:

   a. The structure of data frame is the same as telecommand transfer frame except the length of frames are different. So that the telecommand and device management command can be processed and forwarded in a unified way.
   b. To improve the utilization of system resource and reduce the overhead of bus, the length of frame for device management command is only the length of command data packet plus the length of frame primary header.

   In following sections, we will introduce the new design in detail.

2.2 Data Structure for Uplink Telecommand

Referring to the standard of telecommand space data link protocol, a transfer frame consists of frame primary header, frame data field and frame error control field, as depicted in Fig. 1. The frame data field contains one or more telecommand packets, which consists of packet primary header, packet secondary header, application data and packet error control field.

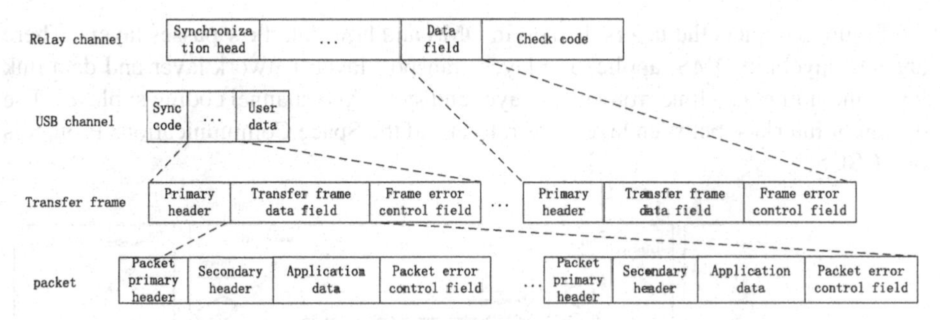

Fig. 1. Data structure of uplink telecommand

Several identifiers are put in the data structure to support command processing and forwarding. In the frame primary header, there are spacecraft identifier, which is used for distinguishing different spacecrafts, and virtual channel identifier (VCID), which is used for distinguishing different users in one spacecraft. In the packet primary header, there is application process identifier (APID) that is used for identifying a unique device.

Based on the layered data structure defined above, DMS can forward user data from different source and to different destination transparently, and thus significantly enhance the flexibility and scalability.

2.3 Data Structure for Device Management Command

To unify the process of uplink telecommand and device management command (DMC), we use the same data structure to represent DMC. As depicted in Fig. 2, the frame data field of DMC contains a command source packet and padding zeros, which are used for ensuring the size of transfer frame can reach the lower limit of size of transfer frame. The command source packet follows the same data structure as the telecommand packet.

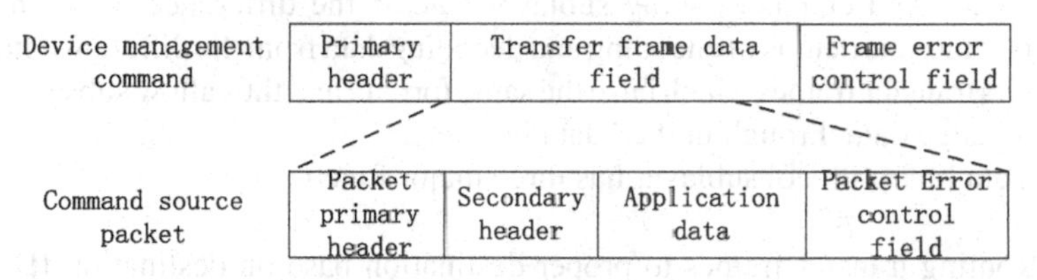

Fig. 2. Format of the device management command

2.4 Layered DMS Implementation Mechanism

Based on the data structure for uplink telecommand and DMC described in Sects. 2.2 and 2.3, in this paper, we propose a layered DMS implementation mechanism to simplify and unify the process of executing and forwarding uplink telecommand, device management command and manual command.

Figure 3 depicts the layers defined in DMS and how data flow passes layers. There are four layers in DMS: application layer, transport layer, network layer and data link layer, including data link protocol sublayer and sync. And channel coding sublayer. The design of interface between layers has referenced the Space Communications Protocols of CCSDS.

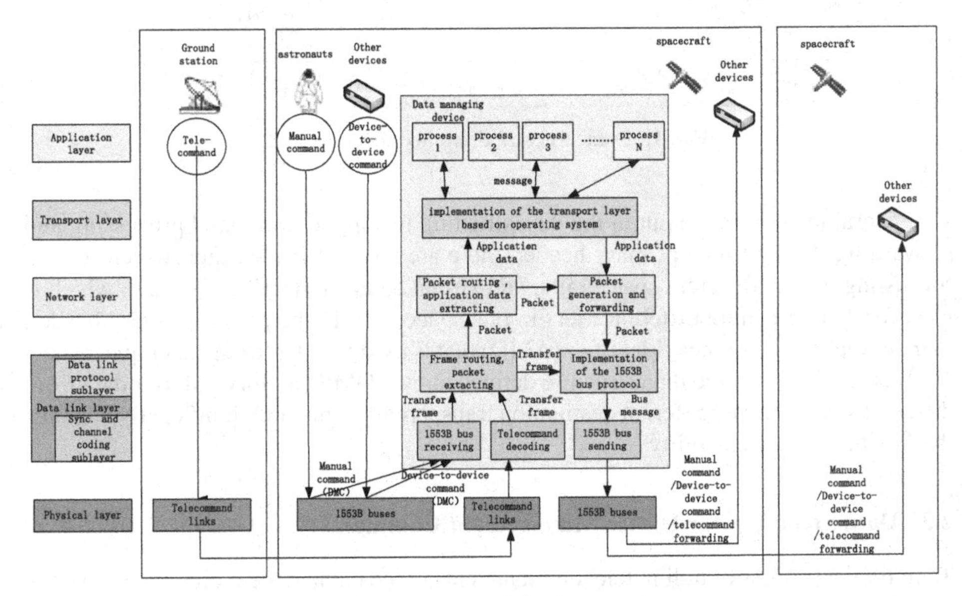

Fig. 3. Layered DMS implementation

The key functionalities of each layer are:

1. The sync. And channel coding sublayer shields the difference between physical layers, hides the details of encoding and decoding data from the different data sources, extracts transfer frames which have the same format, and thus allow subsequent layers to exchange data through unified data interface.
2. The data link protocol sublayer has three major functions:

   a. Routing transfer frames to proper destination base on destination ID stored in the transfer frame.
   b. Extracting packets from input transfer frame and sending to the network layer for processing.
   c. Implementation of the 1553B bus protocol.

3. The network layer has following major functions:

   a. Routing packets to proper destination based on destination ID stored in the packet.

   b. Extracting application data from input packet and sending to the transport layer.
   c. Generating packets and forwarding them to the data link layer.

4. The transport layer leverages the messaging mechanism provided by operating system to distribute application data to proper process and allows inter-process data exchanging.
5. The application layer consists of multiple application processes. It performs concrete data managing functions, such as telecommand, telemetry, program controlling, manual controlling, autonomous management, etc.

Taking a data managing device which adopts the new mechanism as example, the detailed process of parsing and forwarding data is:

1. Parsing process

   a. Data and commands from different uplink channels and from on-board data buses are processed by the sync. And channel coding sublayer, and the complete transfer frame is extracted accordingly.
   b. After received transfer frame, the data link protocol sublayer checks the spacecraft ID in the transfer frame.

      (1) If it is not the native spacecraft ID, the entire frame is forwarded directly to corresponding spacecraft for disposal.
      (2) Otherwise, the VCID in the transfer frame header is identified.

         i. If it is not the virtual channel frame that should be processed by this device, the entire frame is also forward directly to the remote terminal (RT) address corresponding to the VCID through the bus.
         ii. Otherwise, the integrity of frame is verified. The frame is dropped if verification fails. Otherwise, packets are extracted from the transfer frame and sent to the network layer.

   c. For each packet, the network layer checks the APID in the packet primary header.

      (1) If it is not the command that should be executed by the device, the entire packet is sent to the RT address corresponding to the APID through the bus.
      (2) Otherwise, the application data are extracted from the packet and sent to the transport layer.

   d. Based on the type of application data, the transport layer packs the application data into messages and distributes messages to proper processes in the application layer.
   e. The application process handles messages, generates new program-controlled commands, and transfers them to the upper layer through the output and forwarding process.

2. Output and forwarding processes

    a. Application data generated by the application process are sent to the network layer.
    b. The network layer wraps the application data, generates the command source package and sends it to the data link protocol sublayer. Besides, the network layer receives the command source packets from the parsing process and forwards them to the data link protocol sublayer.
    c. The data link protocol sublayer takes following steps to route and forward received transfer frames and packets.

        (1) Searching the frame routine table according to the VCID of the transfer frame or the APID of the packets.
        (2) Finding the appropriate physical address of the bus, converting the frame or the packet into a sequence of messages and forwarding it to the sync. And channel coding sublayer.

    d. The sync. And channel coding sublayer sends out the sequence of messages through the bus.

2.5 Comparison of Telecommand Implementation Mechanism

Compare to traditional telecommand implementation mechanism, the new layered implementation mechanism proposed in this paper has advantages on almost all aspects. Table 1 shows the result.

Table 1. Comparison of telecommand implementation mechanisms

	Layered implementation mechanism	Traditional implementation mechanism
Telecommand protocol	Follows telecommand space data link protocol	Follows PCM telecommand protocols, which are non-standard protocols
Multi-user support	Supports multi-user through segmentation Has good scalability	Supports multi-user through customized format Has no scalability
Inter-spacecraft telecommand forwarding	Has spacecraft identifier. Supports forwarding telecommand multiple times among multiple spacecrafts	Has no spacecraft identifier Supports forwarding telecommand only once between two spacecrafts
Inter-spacecraft telecommand forwarding features	Forwards entire frame directly, doesn't need to parse frame, has high efficiency and low delay	Needs to parse frame and strip header, has low efficiency and high delay
Device-to-device command forwarding	Supports forwarding device-to-device command multiple times among multiple spacecrafts	Supports forwarding device-to-device command only once between two spacecrafts
Manual command forwarding	Supports forwarding manual command multiple times among multiple spacecrafts	Supports forwarding manual command only once between two spacecrafts
Telecommand forwarding for new visiting spacecrafts	Can form new flow for data transmission dynamically by injecting the modified route table on board Doesn't need to upgrade software	Can't support, needs to upgrade software

Overall, the new mechanism has great advantages over the traditional telecommand implementation mechanism in terms of protocol standardization, system flexibility, scalability, and extensibility.

3 Application Validation

The layered implementation mechanism proposed in the paper for telecommand and device management has been applied to the DMS of a large spacecraft assembly. The assembly consists of three independently orbiting spacecrafts which are interconnected by the docking buses. Each spacecraft is equipped with a data managing device as the bus controller (BC) and all the three data managing devices have adopted the layered implementation mechanism. The bus topology and information flow are shown in Fig. 4.

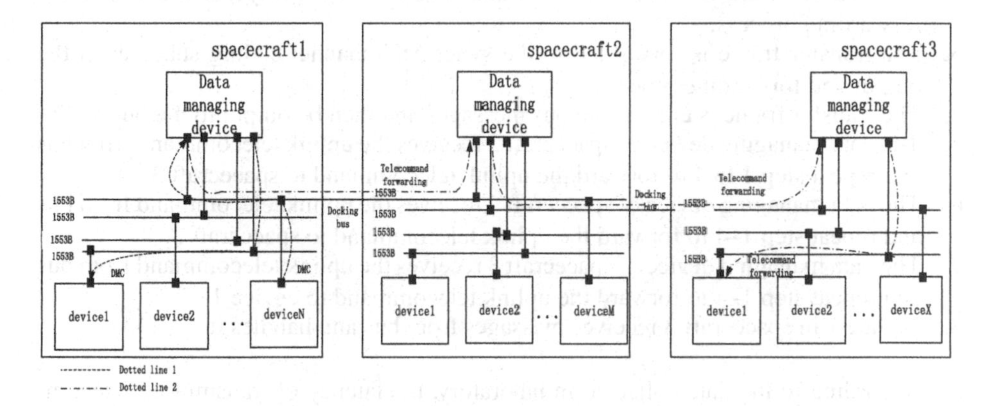

Fig. 4. The bus topology and information flow

We run the three data managing devices in laboratory and use simulator software to simulate RTs on the 1553B networks of the three spacecrafts. To verify the new mechanism can work correctly, we keep the volume of data transmitted among the three data managing devices and simulated RTs the same as the volume of data in real orbiting system. The average volume of data transmitted on each bus is about 200–300K bps.

The dotted line 1 in Fig. 4 shows the example data flow of transmitting the DMC from device N to device 1 within the spacecraft 1. The DMC issued by device N is collected by the data managing device firstly, and then is handled as below:

1. The DMC is decoded by the sync. And channel coding sublayer. A transfer frame is extracted and sent to the data link protocol sublayer in the parsing process.
2. One or more command source packets are extracted from the transfer frame and sent to the network layer in the parsing process.
3. The command source packets are transferred to the network layer in the output and forwarding process.
4. The command source packets are forwarded to the sync. And channel coding sublayer in the output and forwarding process.

5. The command source packets are encoded to bus messages and then be output to the bus.
6. Device 1 receives messages from bus and handles it.

According to the data collected in laboratory, the latency of transmitting DMC between two devices in the same spacecraft is about 20–80 ms.

The dotted line 2 in Fig. 4 shows the example data flow of transmitting telecommands from spacecraft 1 to device 1 in spacecraft 3 via spacecraft 2. The uplink telecommand is received by the data managing device of spacecraft 1 firstly, and then is handled as below:

1. The telecommand is decoded by the sync. And channel coding sublayer. A transfer frame is extracted and sent to the data link protocol sublayer in the parsing process.
2. The transfer frame is forwarded to the data link protocol sublayer in the output and forwarding process.
3. The transfer frame is forwarded to the sync. And channel coding sublayer in the output and forwarding process.
4. The transfer frame is encoded to bus messages and then be output to the bus.
5. The data managing device of spacecraft 2 receives the uplink telecommand from bus and repeat step 1 to 4 to forward the uplink telecommand to spacecraft 3.
6. The data managing device of spacecraft 2 receives the uplink telecommand from bus and repeat step 1–4 to forward the uplink telecommand to spacecraft 3.
7. The data managing device of spacecraft 3 receives the uplink telecommand from bus and repeat step 1–4 to forward the uplink telecommand to device 1
8. Device 1 in spacecraft 3 receives messages from bus and handles it.

According to the data collected in laboratory, the latency of transmitting telecommand between two spacecrafts is about 120–550 ms.

The result of application validation shows that the DMS adopted the layered implementation mechanism can forward DMC and telecommands among multiple devices and multiple spacecrafts steadily and reliably, and the latency of command transmission is low. It proves that the layered implementation mechanism can satisfy the needs of command transmission in large scale spacecraft assembly.

4 Conclusion

The layered implementation mechanism for telecommand and device management proposed in the paper has been successfully applied to a large spacecraft assembly. With the new mechanism, the commands for each spacecraft in the assembly can be injected through a unified physical channel and be transferred to the destination spacecraft in real time through the parsing process and the output and forwarding process. All devices connected to the on-board bus network of the assembly can send and receive commands mutually. All the manned ships, cargo ships and other visiting spacecrafts that will be docked with the assembly later can also interact with the on-board assembly seamlessly. On the basis, the complex networks of multi-ship, multi-cabin, multi-spacecraft assembly can be built finally, and the much more complex functions of the space information systems will be realized.

References

1. Zhu, R.: Rendezvous and Docking Techniques of Spacecraft. National Defense Industry Press, Beijing (2007)
2. Polites, M.E.: Technology of automated rendezvous and capture in space. J. Spacecr. Rocket. **36**(2), 280–291 (1999)
3. CCSDS 133.0-B-1 Space packet protocol. Blue Book Issue 1. CCSDS, Washington D.C. (2003)
4. CCSDS 232.0-B-3 TC space data link protocol. Blue Book Issue 3. CCSDS, Washington D.C. (2015)
5. CCSDS 231.0-B-3 TC synchronization and channel coding. Blue Book Issue 3. CCSDS, Washington D.C. (2017)
6. CCSDS 130.0-G-3 Overview of space communications protocols. Green Book Issue 3. CCSDS, Washington D.C. (2014)
7. Commission of Science, Technology and Industry for National Defense. GJB 1198. 7A-2004 Telemetry tracking command and data handling for spacecraft part 7: Packet Telecommand. Commission of Science, Technology and Industry for National Defense, Beijing (2004)
8. Yahang, Z., Siyang, Z.: A multilayer telecommand design based on the traditional telecommand system. J. Spacecr. TT&C Technol. **12**(31), 81–85 (2012)

Design of Distributed Satellite Data Management System with Wired /Wireless Interconnection

Yong Xu[1](✉), Lei Zhang[2], Ke Yin[1], Long Ji[1], Ling Tong[1], Zheng Qi[1], and Xiangyu Lin[1]

[1] Beijing Institute of Spacecraft System Engineering, Beijing 100094, China
andrexu@163.com

[2] Beijing Institute of Tracking and Telecommunication Technology, Beijing 100094, China

Abstract. A wired/wireless distributed on-board data management system is proposed in this paper, in which Distributed IO Modules are embedded in all kinds of on-board equipment that need to be measured and controlled, and provides interface services such as measurement and control, Low-speed serial data, 1-wire Temperature measurement, etc. The distributed information management device is used to replace the traditional integrated electronic centralized telemetry acquisition and control architecture to form a distributed satellite information acquisition and control network. The wireless Wi-Fi channel or a standardized control bus is used to replace hundreds or even thousands of analogy signal cable networks, which makes the external interface of satellite electronic equipment with different forms and functions standardized To be possible, it simplifies the process of field integration and assembly, and is an important support technology for the standardization and rapid assembly of electronic interface of satellite equipment.

Keywords: Wireless interconnection · Distributed · Satellite Data Management

1 Introduction

The traditional remote control and telemetry of satellite is centralized collection and control through the data handle subsystem. One or two stand-alone computers of the data handle subsystem or integrated electronic subsystem of the satellite platform provide hundreds or thousands of satellite analog data collection and transmission, so as to realize the monitoring of the operation status of satellite equipment on the ground [1]. At the same time, hundreds or thousands of tele-command pulse channels are provided for the control of many devices on the satellite [2]. At the same time, it also provides other low-speed data interfaces, such as ML, DS, UART interfaces, which are not connected to the whole satellite bus network.

The above-mentioned traditional mode is provided by one or two centralized devices, which results in a large number of cables to connect the discrete signal line and low-speed data line of centralized acquisition and control equipment to the electronic devices

Q. Wu et al. (Eds.): WiSATS 2020, LNICST 358, pp. 420–431, 2021.
https://doi.org/10.1007/978-3-030-69072-4_34

distributed in all corners of the satellite during the general assembly of the satellite electronic information system equipment [3]. As a result, the overall assembly and integration of the satellite is more complex, which is not conducive to the rapid production and test of the satellite; and the weight of the cable network that provides the connection for thousands of remote control and telemetry is much heavy, statistics show that the weight of the cable network has accounted for about 15% of the weight of the whole satellite.

In order to effectively solve this problem, this paper proposed a Distributed Satellite Data Management System Supporting Wired /Wireless Interconnection for satellite on orbit assembly, which adopts the Distributed IO module (DIO) to meet the measurement control and low-speed data interface requirements of satellite electronic equipment. The Distributed IO module is installed in each electronic equipment of the satellite. The relevant discrete telemetry signal interface and low-speed data telemetry interface are converted and packaged into standard data frame format by the distributed wireless measurement device in each electronic equipment. Multiple distributed wireless measurement and control modules form a distributed information network use wireless/wired interconnection interfaces, to pass the information to the satellite computer and send it to the ground. In turn, the uplink control instructions are received by the on-board computer and then transmitted to the distributed measurement and control system, and then sent to the corresponding distributed wireless measurement control module for instruction decoding or given through the low-speed data interface.

2 Distributed Satellite Data Management System

Distributed IO module is an important part of information system, which is embedded in the measurement and control signal equipment of spacecraft to provide IO signal interface services (Fig. 1).

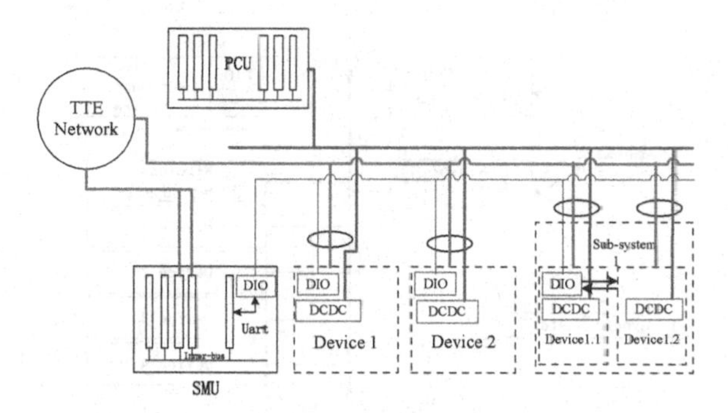

Fig. 1. Distributed Satellite Data Management System

As shown in the figure above, the distributed IO module, as a satellite micro neuron, can be used in a variety of flexible ways. That is to say, it can be embedded in each electronic device as the information acquisition and control node, or it can be installed

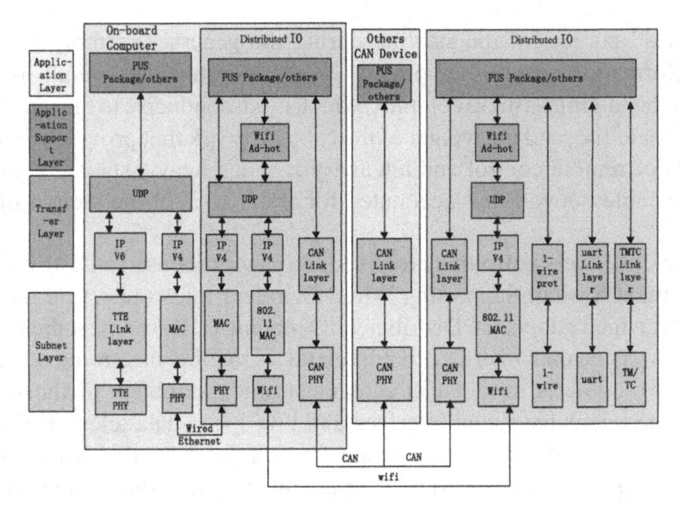

Fig. 2. Communication Protocol stack of Distributed Satellite Data Management System

on the whole satellite structure for acquisition and control of multiple small or passive devices (Fig. 2).

The peripheral topology of the DIO related system is shown in the figure below. The system includes two sets of buses. The first bus uses dio1 as the main uplink channel as the bridge from TTE to Can bus 1. The telemetry data is transferred and combined to dio1 according to APID, then sent to the on-board computer, and then sent to the software radio for downlink through TTE. In contrast to telemetry, the information flow of remote control data is also distributed according to the APID forwarding table saved in each distributed IO (Fig. 3).

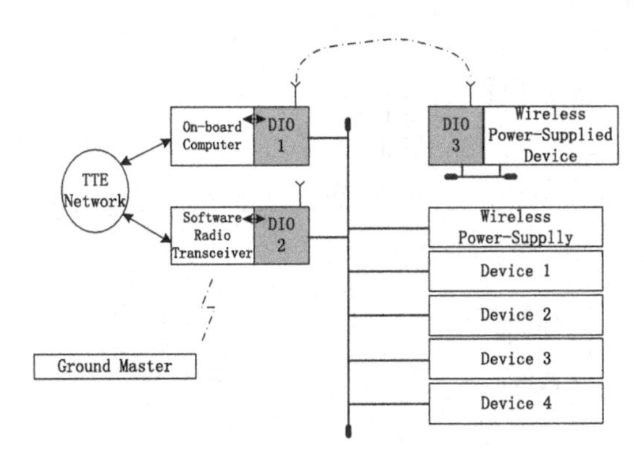

Fig. 3. The peripheral topology of the DIO related system

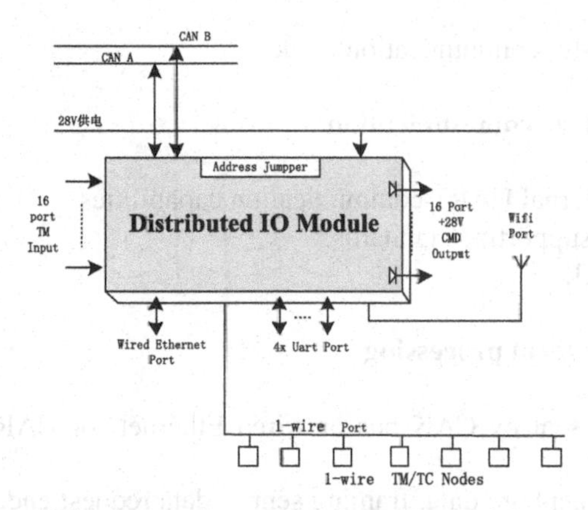

Fig. 4. Interface of distributed IO modules

3 Design of Distributed IO Modules

3.1 Interface Design of Distributed IO Modules

As shown in the figure above, the external interface of the distributed IO module includes a pair of Dual Redundant CAN bus interfaces, 28V control bus interfaces, 16 channels configurable analog quantity acquisition interfaces, 16 channels 28V pulse command output interfaces, 1-wire interfaces and 4 UART interfaces, Wi-Fi and wired Ethernet interfaces (Fig. 4).

3.2 Function Design of Distributed IO Modules

Distributed IO module has the following functions:

(1) Telemetry signal acquisition

- Support telemetry signal acquisition of temperature, 5V analog and switching value;
- Adopt telemetry acquisition interface sub card to adapt the above acquisition requirements according to the requirements;
- Acquisition frequency can be adjusted from 2Hz to 0.1Hz;
- Acquisition accuracy is 12bit.

(2) Pulse command output

- Output 28V positive pulse command;
- Command pulse width can be adjusted from 64ms to 1s (interval of 10ms);
- Command driving capacity 200mA;

(3) Control bus communication

- CAN bus bidirectional communication ability;
- Two way communication conversion from bus to wired Ethernet port;

- Support multi master communication mode.

(4) UART interface communication

- Provide 4-way external UART communication capabilities
- See baud rate for supporting standards;
- Adopt RS422 level;

(5) Data and protocol processing

- Analyze the data sent by CAN bus or wired Ethernet (or UART) bus to generate command signal;
- Acquisition of semaphore data, framing sent to data request end, can be fed back to can bus or wired Ethernet (or UART) bus;
- Receive the data of CAN bus and convert it to wired Ethernet (or UART) for sending;
- Receive wired Ethernet (or UART) data and convert it to can bus output;

(6) Wireless communication function

- Provide 1 channel of wireless transceiver;
- Acquisition signal can be sent to other equipment through wireless channel;
- Command data sent by other equipment can be received through wireless channel;

4 Software Design of Distributed IO Modules

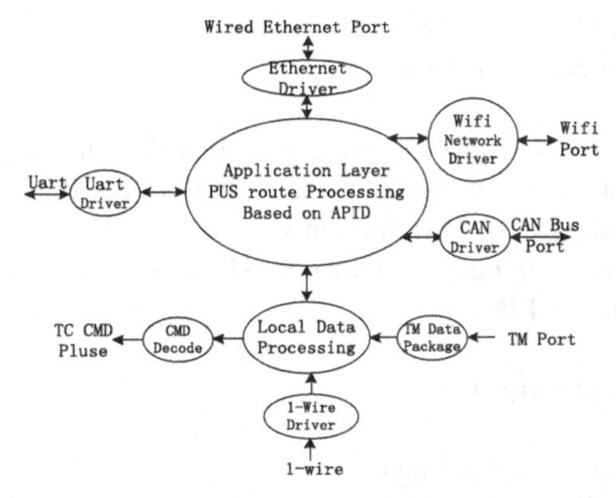

Fig. 5. Software Demands of Distributed IO Modules

The software requirement architecture of distributed IO is shown in the above image, including interface, processing, forwarding and other blocks. The following sections will make detailed requirements for the function points (Fig. 5).

4.1 PUS Route Processing Based on APID

The application layer software in DIO carries out data forwarding and local processing based on the destination APID [4] in pus package;

(1) If it is an APID processed locally, it will be forwarded to the local processing process. In the local processing process, the local business processing will be carried out.

(2) If the APID is not processed locally, it needs to be forwarded to other devices. The forwarded port and addressing parameters required for forwarding are obtained by querying "DIO APID data processing table" (Fig. 6). (Table 1).

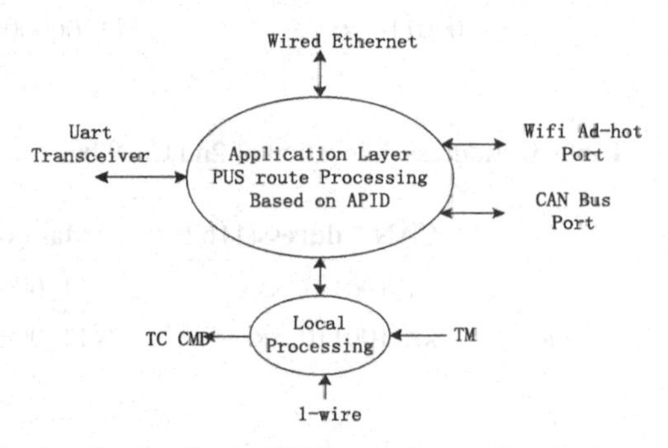

Fig. 6. Application Layer PUS route Processing Based on APID

Table 1. DIO1 APID data processing table

Destination APID	Process	Addressing parameter
0 × 402	wired Ethernet sending	IP = 192.168.2.1(general computer intranet)
0 × 541	Wi-Fi sends	IP = 10.74.1.3(Wi-Fi address of DIO)
…	…	…
0 × 583	can bus sends	can id = = xx_000100 (distributed peak regulator)

4.2 Communication Interface

(1) CAN Bus Interface [5]

It can be seen from the figure that there are two can buses in the system, namely the system can bus and the 1-to-1 local can bus in the wireless charger. The can addresses on both buses are assigned as follows (Table 2, 3):

(2) Wi-Fi Ad Hoc Bus Communication

Realize the Wi-Fi self-organizing communication between the devices on the satellite, support the wireless connection of the devices on the satellite, adopt 802.11 protocol standard, and the rate is not less than 1Mbps.

Table 2. Address Allocation of 1st CAN bus

CAN Devices	CAN **Address**(11bit)	Mask code (PJA1000)
DIO1	xx_000000_xxx	11_000000
DIO2	xx_000001_xxx	11_000000
Wireless Power-Supplly	xx_000010_xxx	11_000000
Device 1	xx_000011_xxx	11_000000
Device 2	xx_000100_xxx	11_000000
Device 3	xx_000101_xxx	11_000000
Device 4	xx_000110_xxx	11_000000

Table 3. Address Allocation of 2nd CAN bus

CAN Devices	CAN **Address**(11bit)	Mask code (PJA1000)
DIO3	xx_100101_xxx	11_000000
Wireless Power-Supplied Device	xx_100110_xxx	11_000000

(3) Wired Ethernet Communication

When the distributed IO module is placed inside the device, the data communication between the upper computer inside the device and the distributed IO is realized, supporting 10m/100Mbps wired Ethernet communication, which supports TCP/IP or UDP communication protocols. The data of application layer adopts pus communication protocol.

(4) UART Serial Communication

Adopt 3.3V power supply RS422 three wire serial port. The bus features are as follows: the camera remote control and telemetry function is realized by adopting bidirectional asynchronous serial communication interface. Communication rate: the baud rate of asynchronous serial communication is 115.2kbps.

Frame format: 1-bit start bit, 8-bit data bit, 1-bit stop bit. In the transmitted bit-stream, the standard serial digital communication protocol is adopted, with the low bit first and the high bit last. In multi-byte data transmission, the high byte is the first and the low byte is the last (Fig. 7).

4.3 Local Business Processing

According to the purpose APID of the pus package, the type of pus package distributed to the local service processing includes instruction decoding or 1-wire instruction.

(1) TC Command Decoding

The instruction data [6] is packaged in pus format and sent by the ground master. The data field content of PUS package is in the following format:

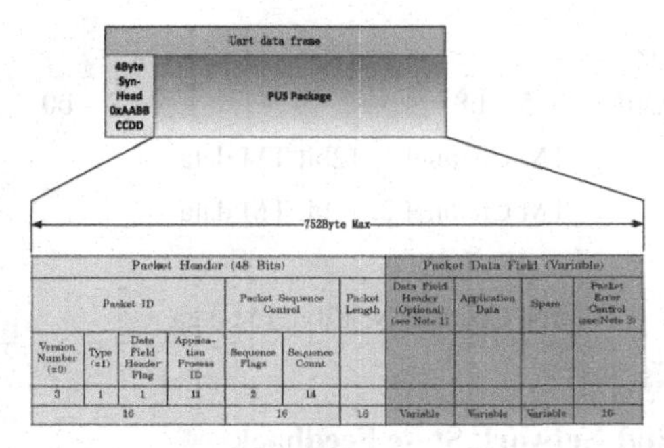

Fig. 7. Uart communication protocols

Word Order	b15 ~ b8	b7 ~ b0
1	DATA_TYPE(=0x00)	Reserve(=0x00)
2	LENGTH(=0x0050); means 80ms	
3	CMD_Index1	CMD_Index2
4	Reserve(=0x00)	Reserve(=0x00)

(2) Telemetry Acquisition Package

The telemetry acquisition data is packaged and sent to the application layer forwarding module by the pus package, and sent to the final ground master according to the destination APID. The data domain content of the pus package is in the following format:

Word Order	b15 ~ b8	b7 ~ b0
1	DATA_TYPE(0x01)	Reserve(0x00)
2	TM_Num(=0x0010)	
3	TM Channel 1, 12bit TM data	
4	TM Channel 2, 12bit TM data	
…	…	
18	TM Channel 16, 12bit TM data	

(3) 1-Wire Drive and Acquisition Packaging

The 1-wire Temperature is sent to the application layer forwarding module in a package of pus packets, which are sent to the final ground master according to the destination APID. The data field content of pus packets is in the following format:

Word Order	b15 ~ b8	b7 ~ b0
1	DATA_TYPE(=0x02)	Reserve(=0x00)
2	Number of TM data, TM_Num	

(*continued*)

(*continued*)

Word Order	b15 ~ b8	b7 ~ b0
3	TM Channel 1, 12bit TM data	
4	TM Channel 2, 12bit TM data	
…	…	
N + 2	TM Channel N, 12bit TM data	

(4) Local Machine and Network State Feedback

DIO, which is set as the main node, needs to report to the ground the current equipment connection on the CAN bus and Wi-Fi bus, and design the corresponding regular query and response mechanism to reflect the connection status of the equipment.

4.4 Other Functions

Support "APID data processing table" injection and update for the purpose of equipment replacement, fault repair and task migration. The software of multiple distributed IO modules is consistent. The differential can address, IP address, initial APID processing query table and other parameters are configured through the software header file.

5 Implementation Results

The system adopts the form of main board plus acquisition sub board, in which the main board is realized by the finished core board plus customized sub board, acquisition sub board completes telemetry signal acquisition and pulse command output, and the operating system is Linux or domestic embedded real-time operating system. The extended interfaces on the backplane include SPI interface for connecting wireless data transmission module and redundant ADC controller, multiple UART interface for RS-422 communication, one 10/100M adaptive Ethernet interface, two can interfaces, on-chip ADC interface and sufficient GPIO pins. In addition to the interface conversion, the baseboard also completes the conversion of external 28V power supply to the 5V power supply of the machine, and provides over-voltage, over-current and over temperature protection functions for the whole machine (Figs. 8, 9).

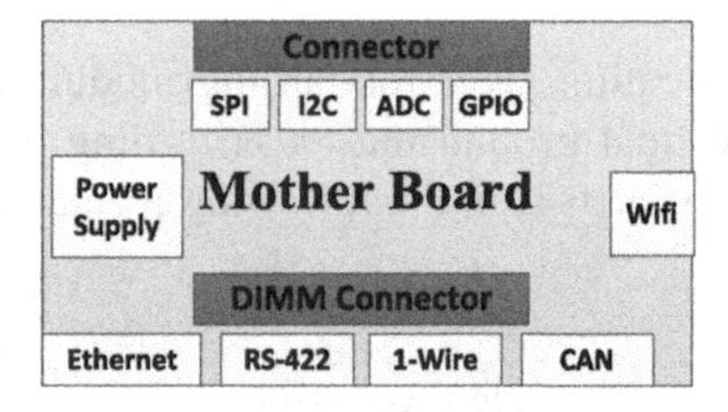

Fig. 8. Mother Board

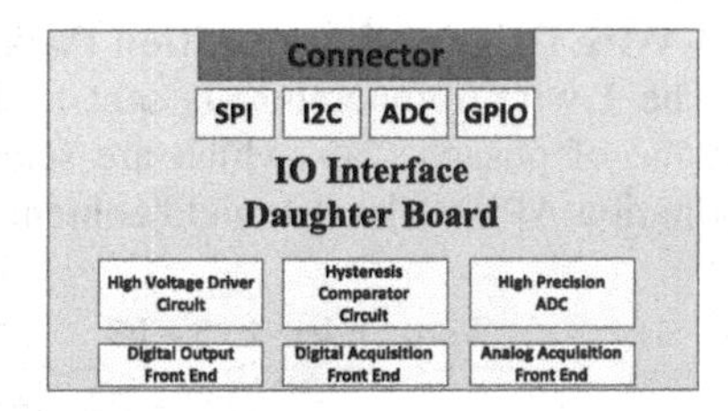

Fig. 9. IO Interface Daughter Board

The front-end of digital acquisition and the front-end of analog acquisition share the same input port. After filtering circuit, they are respectively input to comparator circuit and high-precision ADC circuit for digital and analog acquisition. The back end of the comparator circuit is connected with the input port of the IO expansion chip to collect 16 channels of digital signals in parallel, and the processor reads back the data through the SPI interface; the processor also configures and reads the parameters of the ADC chip through the SPI interface (Fig. 10, 11)

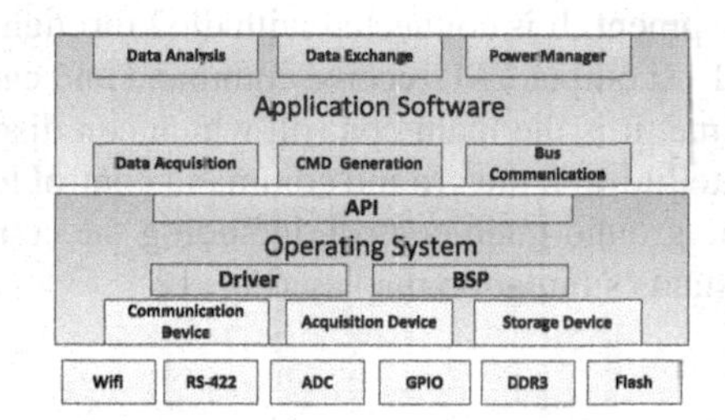

Fig. 10. Software Hierarchy Diagram

Fig. 11. Appearance of Distributed IO Modules

The output port of the IO expansion chip is the TTL input signal of the pulse instruction output circuit. After the high voltage drive circuit and the current limiting circuit composed of MOSFET, the 28V pulse instruction signal is generated.

The operating system abstracts the data transmission module, RS-422 interface, DDR3 and other interfaces, peripherals and memory into different types of devices and files, realizes the relevant device drivers, and forms the board level support package (BSP); on the operating system, the application software operates the abstract devices through the standard API provided by the operating system, and realizes data reading and interface cooperation The conversion and power management are discussed to realize the functions required by the system.

6 Design Results Analysis

To test the functional requirements of Distributed Satellite Data Management System, we build a test environment as shown in the following figure. The whole test environment includes: Test monitor computer: running test software, connecting with distributed IO main node (dio1/dio2) through Ethernet; three sets of distributed IO modules: dio1 as the main node and test upper computer through Ethernet, dio2, DIO3 as the slave node, dio1 and dio2 through Ethernet, dio1 and DIO3 through wireless Wi-Fi; can simulation card simulation load can equipment, It is connected with dio2 through CAN bus B. The load simulator can simulate load output TM, receive command and can data communication function; at the same time, it is the main control, which can display the data collected and processed on the satellite, and the ground command control load; it can also display the satellite status as the ground main control, including the command control switch, satellite operation and status simulation display (Fig. 12).

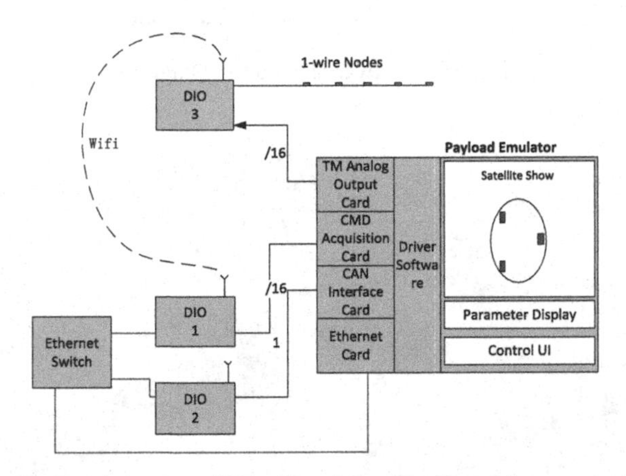

Fig. 12. Test environment of Distributed Satellite Data Management System

It is verified that the distributed satellite data management system based on wired/wireless interconnection can be embedded in all kinds of satellite equipment that need to be measured and controlled by spacecraft, and provide interface services such as measurement and control, Low-speed serial data, 1-wire Temperature Measurement and collection. The function, performance and technical index of the distributed module of the core equipment have been tested and meet the design requirements.

7 Conclusion

In this paper, a wired/wireless distributed on-board data management system is proposed, which is embedded in all kinds of on-board equipment that need to be measured and controlled, and provides interface services such as measurement and control, Low-speed serial data, 1-wire Temperature measurement, etc. The distributed information management device is used to replace the traditional integrated electronic centralized telemetry acquisition and control architecture to form a distributed satellite information acquisition and control network. The wireless Wi-Fi channel or a standardized control bus is used to replace hundreds or even thousands of analogy signal cable networks, which makes the external interface of satellite electronic equipment with different forms and functions standardized It simplifies the process of field integration and assembly, and is an important support technology for the standardization and rapid assembly of electronic interface of satellite equipment.

References

1. CCSDS. 132.0-B-1 TM Space Data Link Protocol. CCSDS, Washington (2003)
2. CCSDS. 232.0-B-1 TC Space Data Link Protocol. CCSDS, Washington (2003)
3. Black, R., Fletcher, M.: Honeywell International, Next generation space avionics: a highly reliable layered system implementation. IEEE (2004)
4. European Cooperation for Space Standardization: ECSS-E-70-41A Space Engineering: Ground Systems and Operations-telemetry and Telecommand Packet Utilization. ECSS, Noordwijk (2003)
5. ECSS. ECSS-E-ST-50–15C, CAN Bus Extension Protocol. ECSS, Noordwijk (2013)
6. CCSDS. 133.0-B-1 Space Packet Protocol. CCSDS, Washington (2003)

Research and Implementation of Real-Time Monitoring Technology of Space Constellation Network Status

Jiaxiang Niu(✉), Liang Qiao, Hongcheng Yan, Ruijun Li, Bo Zhou, and Sheng Yu

China Academy of Space Technology, Beijing 100094, China
niujx2014@163.com, owenqiao@126.com, yanhc519@163.com,
npulrj@163.com, 76176636@qq.com, yusheng86@outlook.com

Abstract. At present, the space network is booming. In the face of an increasingly large space network, how to monitor the network status with high real-time performance becomes increasingly important. This paper is directed to the space network, and proposes a highly real-time technology scheme for space constellation network status monitoring, which supports real-time acquisition of various types of space network status information. Based on the idea of the integration of the satellite and the ground, the design and implementation of both the satellite and the ground are carried out.

Keywords: Space network · Network management · SNMP · Satellite-ground integration

1 Introduction

Space network is a network constructed by satellites as nodes based on inter-satellite links. It is mainly for solving the information transmission problems of space platforms and serving for satellite communication systems. At present, the space network is booming, how to monitor and manage the network status with high real-time performance becomes increasingly important. The space network has the characteristics of continuous dynamic change and limited node resources. At present, the development of the space information network shows a trend of a sharp increase in the number of nodes, heterogeneous node types and diversified functional services. Therefore, real-time and rapid acquisition of space constellation network status information and the clear operating status of the space network are the foundation for the realization of the satellite space network communication function [1].

Currently, monitoring the status of the space constellation network by traditional telemetry has many disadvantages. For example, first, the huge amount of telemetry data on the entire network poses certain challenges for telemetry reception, storage, analysis, and observation; Second, telemetry information redundancy is a problem. It requires ground extraction before users can obtain information of interest; Third, for space network monitoring, after the initial acquisition of the space network status, the

Q. Wu et al. (Eds.): WiSATS 2020, LNICST 358, pp. 432–445, 2021.
https://doi.org/10.1007/978-3-030-69072-4_35

effective information required is the changed network status information, and it is not necessary to obtain all the space network status data; Fourth, telemetry resources are limited on the satellite, and a huge amount of network status information takes up too much telemetry resources. Therefore, it is of great significance to study the use of methods other than traditional telemetry to realize space network status monitoring.

2 Real-Time Monitoring Scheme of Space Constellation Network Status

Designing real-time monitoring scheme of space constellation network status needs to ensure compatibility and coordination of inter-satellite and satellite-ground communications, with good real-time performance. At present, the ground TCP/IP protocol stack is very mature, and has mature and complete supporting applications. Most of the satellites currently have embedded software environment, under which the lightweight TCP/IP protocol stack (LwIP) can run. LwIP is an implementation of the open source TCP/IP protocol stack. The main architecture and IPv4 kernel are mainly developed by C language and support IPv6. Its easy-to-clip and low memory characteristic makes it suitable for satellite applications [11, 12]. Simple Network Management Protocol (SNMP) is a network management protocol based on TCP/IP. It was proposed in 1988. With the rapid development of TCP/IP, SNMP network management technology has been rapidly promoted and applied [2]. In the field of network management, the SNMP protocol has the advantages of easy implementation and easy expansion, which makes it the most widely used network management framework at present, and has become the industry standard in the field of network management [6]. Based on the consideration of the integrated design of the satellite and the ground, the TCP/IP protocol stack is applied. And improve the simple network management protocol, which can ensure that the satellite and the ground can have good communication and can obtain the space constellation network status information with high real-time.

Therefore, the real-time monitoring scheme of the space constellation network status is: integrated design of the satellite and the ground, the IP protocol stack compatible with the ground is operated on the satellite, and the simple network management protocol (SNMP) in the LwIP protocol stack operated on the satellite is supplemented and improved to make sure it can run normally. The space network status information is managed by the satellite, and the ground obtains the network status information of each satellite node of the space network by using simple network management protocol commands. As shown in Fig. 1.

Specifically:

First, build an inter-satellite and satellite-ground communication network. Based on TCP/IP protocol stack, the inter-satellite and satellite-ground communication is implemented by using UDP communication protocol. In addition, through the inbound space constellation satellite node, the ground can communicate with any satellite in the constellation, which lays a foundation for the ground to obtain real-time network status information of any satellite node in the space network.

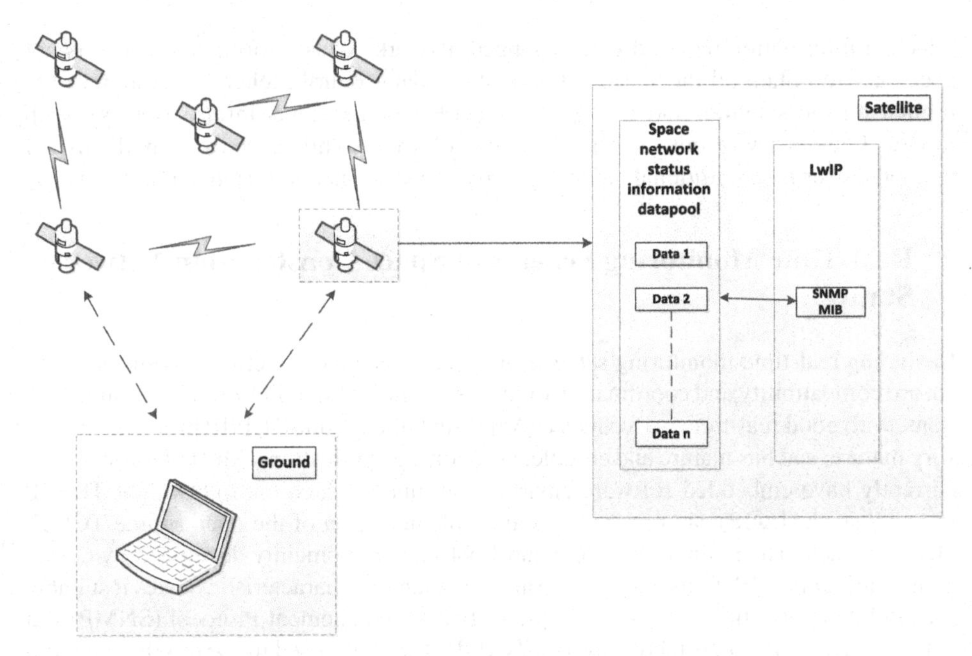

Fig. 1. Space network status real-time monitoring scheme

Second, complement and improve the Simple Network Management Protocol (SNMP), and ensure its normal operation under the LwIP protocol stack [10] to realize space network status monitoring. In the TCP/IP model, the SNMP protocol is located in the application layer, which relies on the transport layer UDP protocol for communication [4, 5]. In the process of space constellation network status monitoring, the management station and agent management model are adopted [7–9]. It is designed to realize the role of agent on the satellite and the role of management station on the ground in this paper. As shown in Fig. 2.

Management station: The management station is an entity that monitors the real-time network status. It is the issuer of commands related to the monitoring status of the entire space constellation network. It sends various management operation commands to the agent and provides space network monitoring personnel operation interface.

Agent: The agent is installed on the satellite node of the space network, monitors the working status of the satellite node where it is located, accepts management control commands from the management station, and reports the execution of the commands to the management station.

Based on the idea of integration of the satellite and the ground, the satellite part needs to be implemented: run the simple network management protocol (SNMP) under the LwIP protocol stack. The core components of SNMP are management information structure and identification (SMI) and management information base (MIB) [3]. All network devices that support SNMP maintain a MIB database that stores information about their operations. The management information base is a collection of management

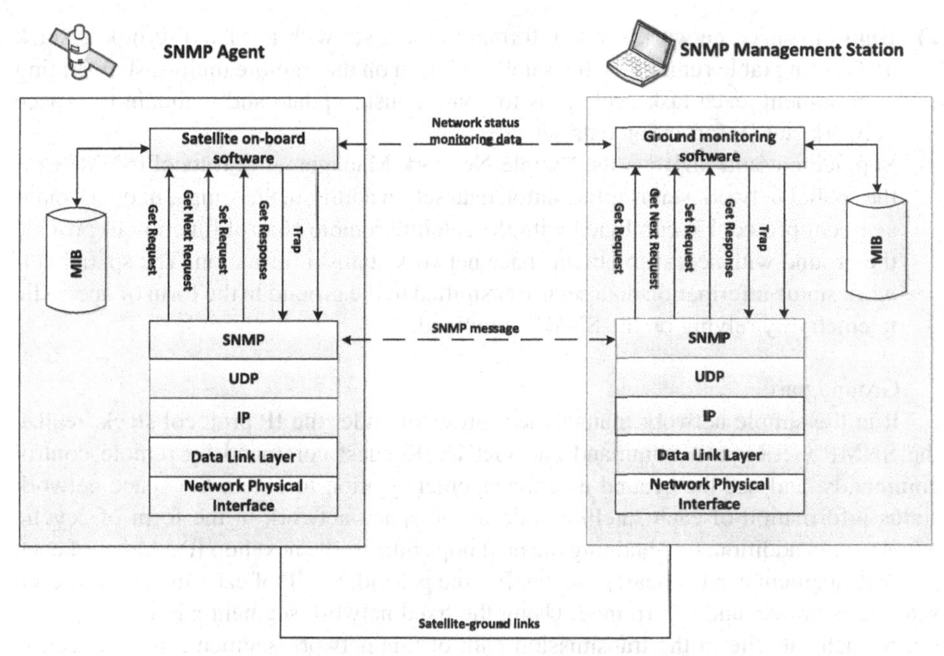

Fig. 2. Spatial network status real-time monitoring model

information. MIB uses SMI and ASN.1 to describe management information. The management information is established under the information tree defined by SMI (1.3.6.1). Each management information is a node of the management information tree and has a unique object identifier. By completing and improving the simple network management protocol, it can gather and manage all space network information on the satellite. Based on this scheme, the management information base corresponding to the satellite on-board network status information is defined and realized, and the network status information is obtained through the simple network management protocol and management information base. The ground part needs to be implemented: run the simple network management protocol under the IP protocol stack, and get the network status information of each satellite node in the space constellation network from the ground by the SNMP command. By interpreting the network status information, get the current space constellation network connection status.

3 Space Constellation Network Status Information Acquisition

3.1 Space Constellation Status Information Acquisition Design

Satellite part (each satellite node in the constellation):

1) Design and implement a space network status information data set, which contains device name, UDP send count, UDP receive count, routing information and other information data that can represent the current space constellation network status, including space constellation network connection status.

2) Bind the space network status information data set with the LwIP protocol stack and routing table running on the satellite. Based on the satellite multi-task operating environment, each task cycle runs to continuously update and maintain the space network state information data set.
3) Supplement and improve the Simple Network Management Protocol (SNMP) for the spatial network status information data set. In addition, the simple network management protocol is combined with the satellite remote control function to provide the ground with access to obtain space network status information. The spatial network status information data set is transmitted to the ground in the form of aperiodic telemetry by relying on the SNMP command.

Ground part:

Run the simple network management protocol under the IP protocol stack, realize the SNMP GetRequest command and GetNextRequest command by remote control commands, and use the ground as a management station to obtain the space network status information of each satellite node in the space network in the form of acyclic telemetry. In addition, by obtaining the next hop address, the next hop IP address of each network segment can be clearly known. For the ground, the IP of each interface of each satellite is known and determined. Using the fixed network segment address as a clue, query each satellite in the transmission path of this network segment, the connection relationship between the satellites can be clarified, and the spatial network connection can be obtained.

3.2 Realization of Space Constellation Status Information Acquisition

Satellite part:

First, the design of space network communication capabilities. Design the protocol stack and external interface to make the protocol stack run normally to achieve inter-satellite and satellite-ground communication. Use Netconn-API to realize the communication mechanism between LwIP protocol stack and the outside, and define the external interface through NETIF. Through the above two parts, the normal operation of the LwIP protocol stack and the communication with the outside are realized to ensure the normal communication in the space network, including inter-satellite and satellite-ground communication. The flow chart for defining the use of Netconn is shown in Fig. 3.

Second, the design of space network UDP communication. Follow the steps below to implement UDP communication under the LwIP protocol stack:

1) Create UDP communication thread (udptx_thread);
2) Initialize source IP, destination IP and transmission content;
3) Create Netconn;
4) Complete the binding of netconn and destination IP;
5) Call netconn_sendto to complete the message sending.

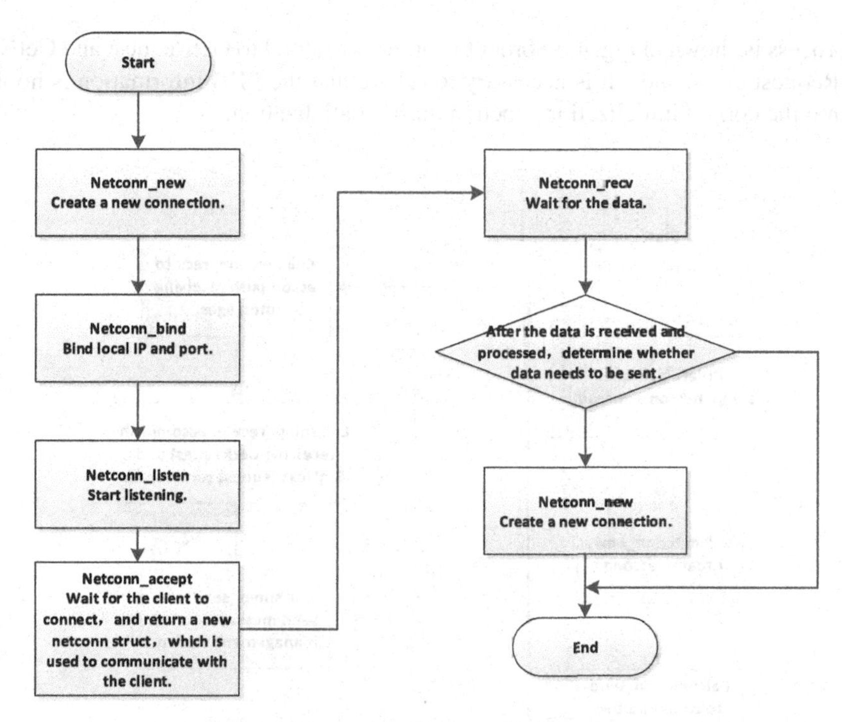

Fig. 3. Netconn implementation flow chart

Third, space constellation network status information acquisition:

1) Determine the required space network status information. as follows: DeviceName-the name of the device; UDPSendNum-the count of sending UDP messages; UDPReceiveNum- the count of receiving UDP messages; NextHopIP-the next hop IP in the routing table. The above information can be expanded as needed.
2) Bind the determined space constellation network status information with the LwIP protocol stack and routing table running on the satellite. Bind network status information such as DeviceName, UDPSendNum, and UDPReceiveNum in the space network status information data set to the LwIP protocol stack. Bind NextHopIP to the routing table. In the multi-tasking environment of satellite-based software, keep updating and maintaining the space network status information data set.
3) Add the space network status information data set to the management information database, and design the corresponding object identifier as follows:
   DeviceName-1.3.6.1.2.1.1.5
   UDPSendNum-1.3.6.1.2.1.2.2.1.17.
   UDPReceiveNum-1.3.6.1.2.1.2.2.1.11.
   NextHopIP-1.3.6.1.2.1.4.21.1.7
4) Determine the SNMP initialization method. Since the Netconn-API is used, an initialization method conforming to the API needs to be selected. The initialization

process is shown in Fig. 4. In order to correctly respond to GetRequest and GetNextRequest commands, it is necessary to ensure that the MIB information is hooked into the correct initialization function during initialization.

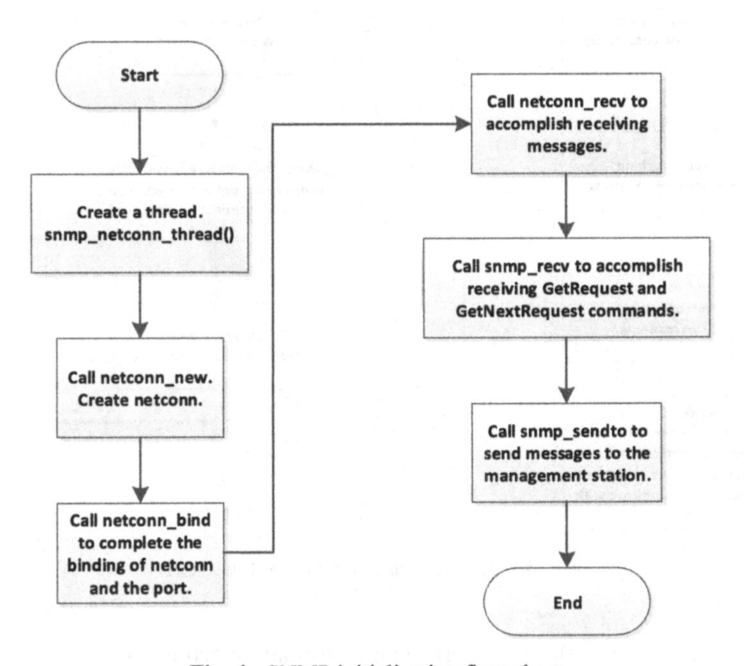

Fig. 4. SNMP initialization flow chart

5) Create a routing table. LwIP itself does not provide a routing mechanism, so the routing table needs to be implemented, including: establishment of the routing table, addition and deletion of routing table entries, access to the routing table, and hooking the completed routing table into the LwIP protocol stack. The specific design is as follows:

1) Determine the structure content of the routing table entry.
2) Implement the following functions to complete the routing table management function, including: add entry for routing table; remove a certain entry in the routing table; query an entry in the routing table according to the destination route and return its position in the routing table; query an entry in the routing table according to the destination route and return its Netif; query the next hop address of an entry in the routing table according to the destination route and return; get the current routing table.
3) Hook the created static routing table into the LwIP protocol stack.
4) The next hop address information class is implemented in the management information base, and the nexthop_static_route information is obtained by calling nexthop_static_route.

Ground part:

Use the ground IP protocol stack and C # for software implementation to ensure the normal operation of the SNMP protocol. The software flow chart of receiving UDP messages is shown in Fig. 5. Complete sending GetRequest command and GetNextRequest command, the specific implementation flow chart is shown Fig. 6 and Fig. 7.

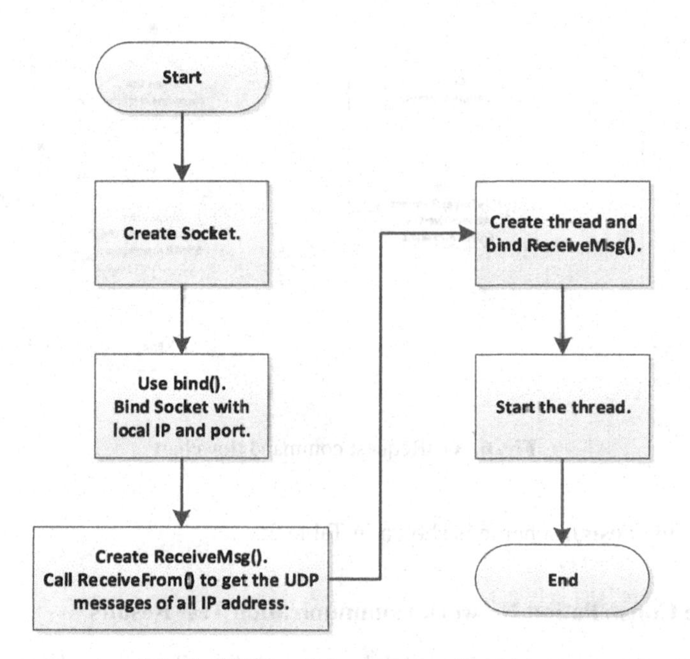

Fig. 5. UDP receiving software flow chart

4 Testing and Verification

4.1 Simulation Test Model and Environment

A simple network scenario is built using commercial shelf products to verify the research content of the paper. The constructed network scenario is shown in Fig. 8:

There are three satellites and a computer in the model. The three satellites communicating with each other simulate space network, a computer simulates ground monitoring equipment. In the above simulation test environment, three STM32 development boards are used to simulate three satellites, and a computer is used to simulate ground equipment. The three development boards are connected to each other through a serial port, and the development board 3 is connected to a computer through a network port. Table 1 shows the network interface configuration of each device:

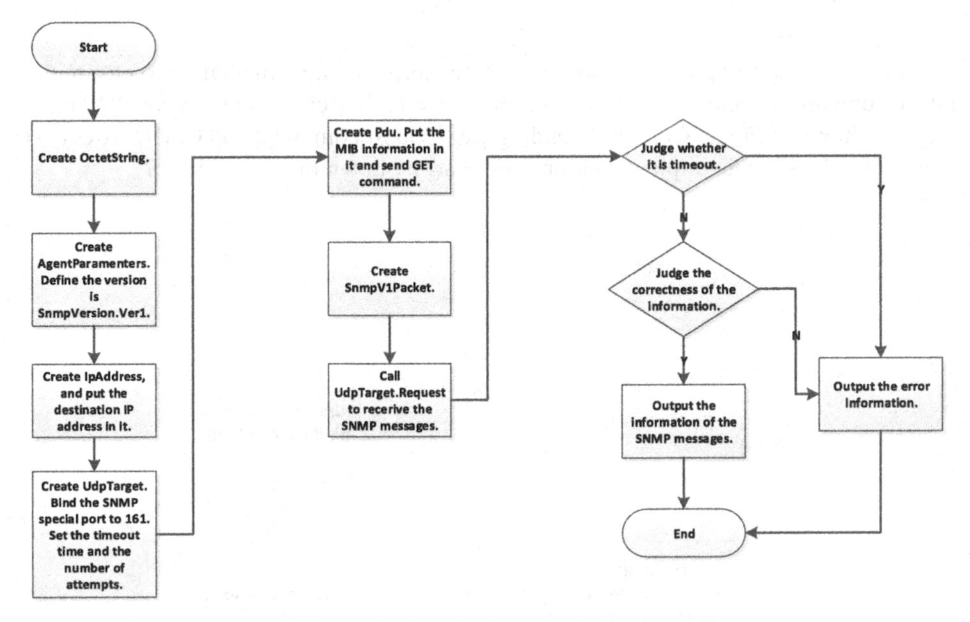

Fig. 6. GetRequest command flowchart

The routing design scheme is shown in Table 2:

4.2 Space Constellation Network Communication Test Results

According to the simulation test model established in Sect. 4.1, design satellite 2 (development board 2) to send UDP information, the destination address is the ground equipment (notebook computer), namely the source IP: 192.16.1.2, the destination IP: 192.168.0.4, the data content: Hello UDP.

The operation status of satellite 2 (development board 2) monitored by ground monitoring software is shown in Fig. 9. From the figure, we can see the operation status of the satellite on-board software, and the UDP transmission count is increasing.

4.3 Space Constellation Network Status to Obtain Test Results

According to the simulation test model established in Sect. 4.1, the ground equipment (notebook computer) and satellite 3 (development board 3) are directly connected via a network cable. To test the connectivity of the network, the GetRequest command and the GetNextRequest command are sent to satellite 1 (development board 1).

Destination IP: 192.168.3.1, device name (1.3.6.1.2.1.5) is obtained by the GetRequest command. The operation of ground monitoring software is shown in Fig. 10. UDP receive count (1.3.6.1.2.1.2.1.11) is obtained by the GetNextRequest command. The operation of ground monitoring software is shown in Fig. 11. UDP send count (1.3.6.1.2.1.2.1.17) is obtained by the GetNextRequest command. The operation of ground monitoring software is shown in Fig. 12.

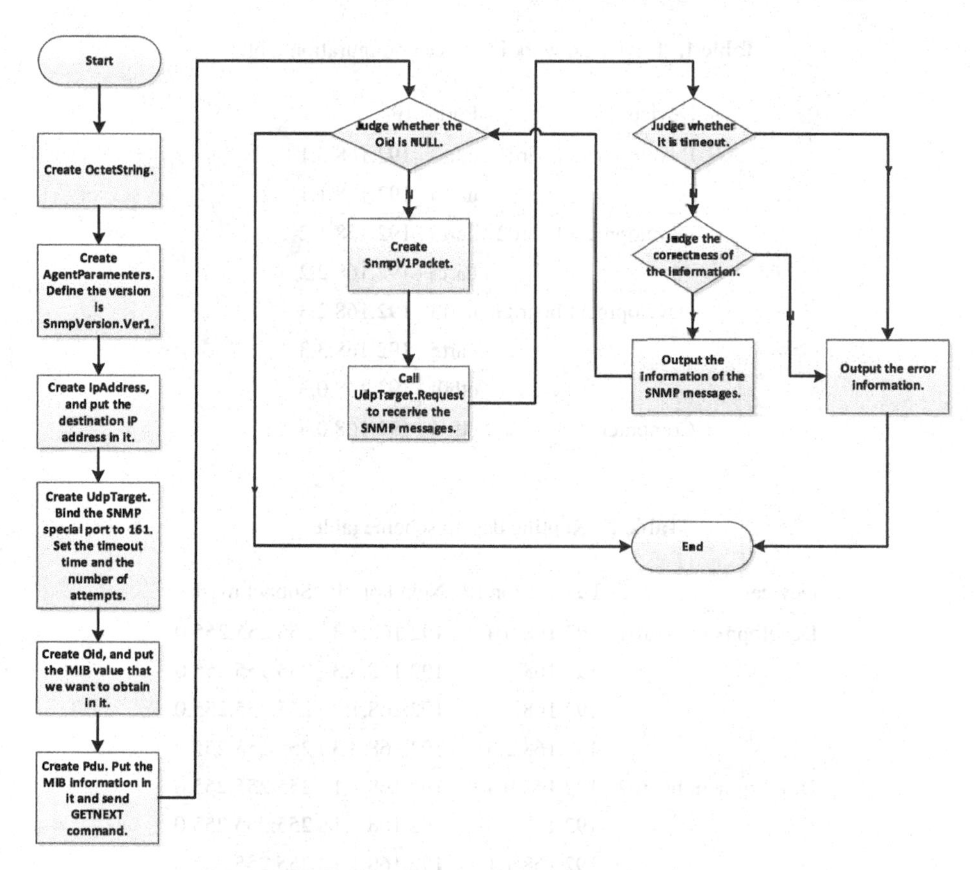

Fig. 7. GetNextRequest command flowchart

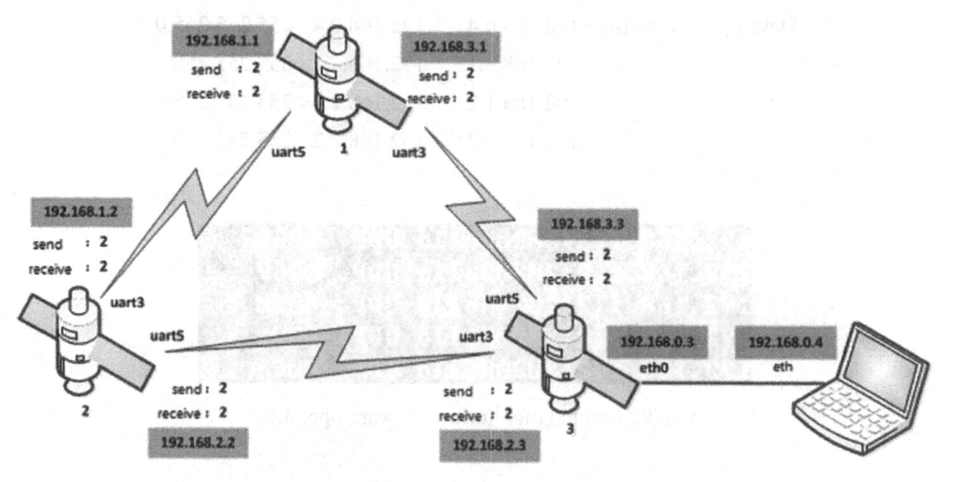

Fig. 8. Spatial network model

Table 1. Device network interface configuration table

Device	Port	IP
Development board1	uart3	192.168.3.1
	uart5	192.168.1.1
Development board2	uart3	192.168.1.2
	uart5	192.168.2.2
Development board3	uart3	192.168.2.3
	uart5	192.168.3.3
	eth0	192.168.0.3
Computer	eth	192.168.0.4

Table 2. Routing design scheme table

Device	Destination IP	Next hop IP	Subnet mask
Development board1	192.168.0.4	192.168.3.3	255.255.255.0
	192.168.3.3	192.168.3.3	255.255.255.0
	192.168.1.2	192.168.1.2	255.255.255.0
	192.168.2.3	192.168.3.3	255.255.255.0
Development board2	192.168.0.4	192.168.1.1	255.255.255.0
	192.168.3.3	192.168.1.1	255.255.255.0
	192.168.1.1	192.168.1.1	255.255.255.0
	192.168.2.3	192.168.2.3	255.255.255.0
Development board3	192.168.0.4	192.168.0.4	255.255.255.0
	192.168.3.1	192.168.3.1	255.255.255.0
	192.168.1.2	192.168.2.2	255.255.255.0
	192.168.2.2	192.168.2.2	255.255.255.0

```
192.168.1.2:2020Hello UDP. 0068
192.168.1.2:2020Hello UDP. 0069
192.168.1.2:2020Hello UDP. 0070
192.168.1.2:2020Hello UDP. 0071
192.168.1.2:2020Hello UDP. 0072
```

Fig. 9. Ground monitoring software operation

Space network connection status test:

According to the simulation test model established in Sect. 4.1, read the satellite on-board routing table, obtain the next hop address of the corresponding route and output it,

```
sysDescr(1.3.6.1.2.1.1.5.0) (OctetString): FQDN-unk
```

Fig. 10. Ground monitoring software to obtain the name of the device

```
1.3.6.1.2.1.2.2.1.11.1 (Counter32): 4068
1.3.6.1.2.1.2.2.1.11.2 (Counter32): 8
```

Fig. 11. Ground monitoring software to obtain UDP receive count

```
1.3.6.1.2.1.2.2.1.17.1 (Counter32): 0
1.3.6.1.2.1.2.2.1.17.2 (Counter32): 3300
```

Fig. 12. Ground monitoring software to obtain UDP send count

and get space network connection status. NextHopIP (1.3.6.1.2.1.4.21.1.7) is obtained by using the GetNextRequest command. The result of obtaining the information about NextHopIP of all satellites is shown as follows Table 3:

Table 3. The result of obtaining the information about NextHopIP.

Device	Result
Development board1	1.3.6.1.2.1.4.21.1.7.0.0.0.0 < IPAddress >: 192.168.3.3
	1.3.6.1.2.1.4.21.1.7.192.168.2.0 < IPAddress >: 192.168.1.2
	1.3.6.1.2.1.4.21.1.7.192.168.3.0 < IPAddress >: 192.168.3.3
Development board2	1.3.6.1.2.1.4.21.1.7.0.0.0.0 < IPAddress >: 192.168.1.1
	1.3.6.1.2.1.4.21.1.7.192.168.1.0 < IPAddress >: 192.168.1.1
	1.3.6.1.2.1.4.21.1.7.192.168.2.0 < IPAddress >: 192.168.2.3
Development board3	1.3.6.1.2.1.4.21.1.7.0.0.0.0 < IPAddress >: 192.168.0.4
	1.3.6.1.2.1.4.21.1.7.192.168.0.0 < IPAddress >: 192.168.0.4
	1.3.6.1.2.1.4.21.1.7.192.168.2.0 < IPAddress >: 192.168.2.2
	1.3.6.1.2.1.4.21.1.7.192.168.3.0 < IPAddress >: 192.168.3.1

From the table, satellite 1 (development board 1): the next hop address of the default route is 192.168.3.3, the next hop address of the 192.168.2.0 network segment is 192.168.1.2, and the next hop address of the 192.168.3.0 network segment is 192.168.3.3. Satellite 2 (development board 2): the next hop address of the default route is 192.168.1.1, the next hop address of the 192.168.1.0 network segment is 192.168.1.1, and the next hop address of 192.168.2.0 network segment is 192.168.2.3. Satellite 3 (development board 3): the next hop address of the default route is 192.168.0.4, the next hop address of the 192.168.0.0 network segment is 192.168.0.4, the next hop address of the 192.168.2.0 network segment is 192.168.2.2, and the next hop address of the 192.168.3.0 network segment is 192.168.3.1.

According to the information we have, the spatial network connection status of the entire space constellation shown in Fig. 8 can be obtained.

4.4 Test Results of the Ground Monitoring Software Platform

In order to monitor the network status and clarify the spatial network connection status, the following ground monitoring software platform is made to integrate the above functions, as shown in Fig. 13. Figure 13 show the state after the stand-alone "acquire" button.

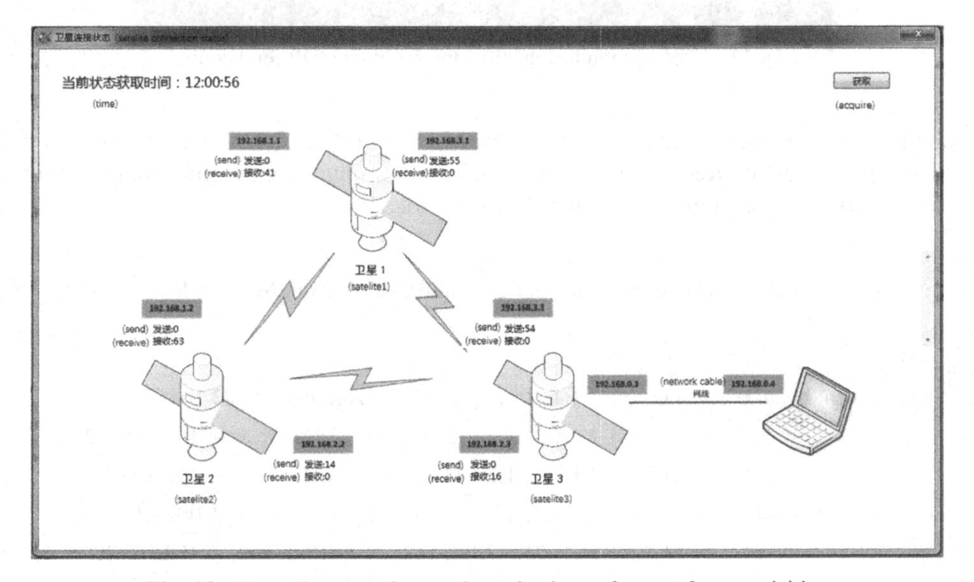

Fig. 13. State diagram of ground monitoring software after acquisition

5 Summary

Facing the booming development of space constellation networks, real-time monitoring of space constellation network status is increasingly important. Traditional reliance on telemetry for downlink space network status information has the shortcomings of poor real-time and poor autonomy. This paper proposes the idea of integrating the satellite and the ground, and runs the simple network management protocol under the satellite LwIP protocol stack. Under the premise of maintaining good compatibility with the ground, the realization of monitoring space network status information has high real-time and autonomously obtainable capabilities.

References

1. Wen, Y., Zhao, J., Wang, G.: A network management system applying to Integrated satellite information network. ACTA ARMAMENTARII **26**(2), 123–124 (2005)
2. RFCl 157. Simple Network Management Protocol
3. Blumenthal, W.: The User based Security Model for Vetsion3 of the simple Network Management Protocol (SNMP)
4. Lin, Z., Li, Y.: Improved SNMP-based network topology discovery algorithm and its implementation. J. Ocean Univ. Chin. **30**(5), 171–174 (2008)
5. Jiang, Y., Feng, Y., Wang, G.: The model of network management for satellite information network. J. Northeast. Univ. Natur. Sci. (Chin.) **23**(1), 15–18 (2003)
6. Stallings, W.: SNMP Network Management. China Electric Power Press, Beijing (2001)
7. Deng, H., Liu, G., Zhang, L.: Analysis and implementation of embedded SNMP agent. In: IFIP International Federation for Information Processing, pp. 96–102 (2011)
8. Huiping, H., Shide, X., Xiangyin, M.: Application of RFID and SNMP technology in highway electronic toll collection system. IEEE (2010)
9. Wang, C., Zhai, H.: Network Management Based on SNMP and B/S Mode, pp. 192–199. Springer, Berlin Heidelberg (2012)
10. Xin, X., Cao, Q.: Analysing and optimisng LwIP protocol stack-based UDP protocol. Comput. Appl. Softw. **14**, 13–17 (2011)
11. Zhang, Q., Lao, Z.: Analysis and improvement of light weight protocol stack LWIP. Comput. Eng. Des. **4**, 41–43 (2010)
12. Fu, X., Xia, Y., He, X.: Memory management of embedded LwIP stack. Appl. Electron. Tech. **9**(3), 0–33 (2006)

International Workshop on High Speed Space Communication and Space Information Networks

Complex-Valued Pipelined Recurrent Neural Network for Transmitter Distortions Compensation in High-Throughput Satellite Communication

Changzhi Xu[1,2](✉), Yi Jin[2], Li Yang[2], Li Li[2], Mingyu Li[3], and Zhenxin Cao[1]

[1] State Key Laboratory of Millimeter Waves, Southeast University, Nanjing 210096, China
sandy_xu@126.com, 274630851@qq.com

[2] Xi'an Branch of China Academy of Space Technology, Xi'an 710000, China
john.0216@163.com, 87701726@qq.com, lili_504@126.com

[3] Chongqing University, Chongqing 400044, China
myli@cqu.edu.cn

Abstract. With the continuous development of satellite communication system towards the direction of high frequency band, large capacity and high spectral efficiency transmission, the signals processed by these new technologies have many characteristics, such as ultra-high bandwidth and higher peak-to-average power ratio (PAPR), etc., which puts forward a great challenge for the spaceborne transmitter used in the satellite communication system. In view of the above requiremes, a novel digital predistortion (DPD) model based on complex-valued pipelined recurrent neural network (CPRNN) for joint compensation of wideband spaceborne transmitter is proposed in this paper. Once the CPRNN model is constructed, the complex-valued real time recurrent learning (CRTRL) algorithm is used for the CPRNN model training. Here, the CRTRL algorithm is derivated in detail based on the real-valued RTRL algorithm. The imperfect transmitters based on a GaN PA excited by the 400-MHz 64-amplitude/phase-shift keying (64APSK) signals was employed to verify the compensation performance of the proposed models. The simulation and experimental results show that the proposed CPRNN DPD model can achieve better linearization performance for the nonlinear transmitter with imperfect RF impairments.

Keywords: Digital predistortion (DPD) · Complex-valued pipelined recurrent neural network (CPRNN) · I/Q imbalance · Power amplifiers (PAs) · Satellite communication

1 Introduction

The inexorable pursuit of broadband satellite systems is motivating the transmission of broadband signals at symbol rates of multiple GHz(G) Baud rate. The high speed transmission demand of massive data promotes satellite communication to high frequency band, large bandwidth and high spectral efficiency. With the development of

Q. Wu et al. (Eds.): WiSATS 2020, LNICST 358, pp. 449–461, 2021.
https://doi.org/10.1007/978-3-030-69072-4_36

transmission direction, it is very important for nonlinear digital compensation of space-borne RF transmitter. The MAPSK/MQAM and other multicarrier modulation, FDMA/TDMA/CDMA and other new technologies are widely used in the Gbps Baud code rate wireless transmission technology. Without exception, the signals processed by these new technologies are characterized by multi-carrier, multi-level, ultra-high bandwidth and peak to peak ratio, etc. For the RF transceiver front end, the new requirements caused by these characteristics must be considered, such as high efficiency and high linearity of the transmitter, etc. At the same time, the RF transceiver front end must be realized in a smaller volume. Because of the important role of RF transmitter in satellite communication and its serious influence on communication signals, the design and research of RF transmitter has always been an important subject in the development of satellite communication. On the one hand, the transmitter excited by wide bandwidth signals will present stronger and deeper nonlinear memory characteristics. Meanwhile, the RF transmitter system is inevitably affected by the nonlinear distortion of the amplifier, the modulator in-phase/quadrature (I/Q) imbalance, and the local oscillator (LO) leakage, etc. In addition, these different nonlinear characteristics will interact with each other, which seriously degrade the performance of the satellite communication system [1]. Therefore, it is the core technology to solve the reliable transmission of satellite communication in the future by researching a new type of broadband efficient linear transmitter, which make the RF front-end of wireless broadband transmission work efficiently under the premise of meeting the strict linearity of the system.

Compared with the RF and IF predistortion, baseband digital predistortion (DPD) does not involve RF signal processing and has become the most widely used predistortion scheme [2, 3]. Common baseband digital predistortion implementations include lookup tables [4, 5] and polynomials [6]. Recently, various methods have been proposed to compensate the interaction distortion between the PA nonlinearity and I/Q imbalance in transmitter [7–11]. For example, Ref. [8] analyzed the interaction between PA nonlinearity and IQ imbalance in detail, and studied the influence of I/Q orthogonal modem imbalance on adaptive digital predistortion parameter estimation. Some estimation methods have also been reported, where the effect of unbalanced coupling between PA and I/Q is considered in the compensation process. In addition, a novel rational function based conjugate model is proposed for alleviating the joint nonlinearity of the transmitter [7]. Furthermore, the dual-input nonlinear model based on the real value Volterra series is proposed in [11], this model can contain nonlinear frequency-related cross terms between the I and Q branch, where the nonlinear characteristics of radio frequency modulator can be modeled and compensated. However, the shortcoming in the dual-input compensator is that the nonlinear characteristics of the PA can not be considered. In order to solve the joint compensation problem of wideband transmitter, the method of joint estimation and compensation of frequency-dependent nonlinear distortions of the transmitter is proposed for the first time in literature [12]. This method can compensate all the analog front-end damages of the wideband direct frequency converter transmitter in one step estimation method, and the digital predistorter parameters can be extracteded without adding any additional RF hardware.

In recent years, with the rising and development of the artificial intelligence theory, people have applied the artificial intelligence theory to the wireless communication system, such as the establishment of PA behavioral model and the research of predistortion technology. In the past decade, artificial neural networks (ANNs) have been successfully applied in the fields of radio frequency and microwave circuit design domain [13, 14]. Artificial neural networks can be arbitrarily close to any continuous nonlinear function, and this method can be applied to transistor-level modeling [15] or more abstract system-level modeling [16, 17]. Recently, some modified NN models have been proposed for jointly compensating the transmitter distortions and impairments [17–19].

In this paper, a complex-valued pipelined recurrent neural network (CPRNN) model for nonlinear compensation of the transmitter distortions and impairments is proposed. To compare the different model performance, the RVFTDNN model [13], the parallel Hammerstein (PH) model [12], and the proposed CPRNN model were used to model and compensate the nonlinear characteristics of the transmitter. The simulation and exterimental results show that the the proposed CPRNN model can give the excellent performance for joint compensation of transmitter.

2 Proposed CPRNN Model Structure

It is the first step of constructing the transmitter behavioral model accurately for designing digital predistortion compensation system, so it is necessary to capture the main nonlinear characteristics of transmitter as a whole. In the transmitter, the mirror interference of IQ direct transform modulator will generate self-interference phenomenon, which causes the mirror interference generated by the transmitter to be located on the carrier frequency and in the same frequency band as the expected signal. Therefore, the transmitter behavioral model should capture all kinds of nonlinear sources as much as possible. When the NN theory is applied to transmitter behavioral modeling, it is necessary to study the regression method which is different from traditional fixed-model-based parameter identification. Mennwhile, the complex neural network structure and the complex training algorithm should be used in the transmitter behavioral modeling [20]. Usually, the inputs, the weights, and the outputs of the proposed NN structure are all complex-valued, and the training algorithm should also be extended to the complex domain.

The fully connected recurrent neural network (FCRNN) model structure is given in Fig. 1, which is consisted of L neurons and L feedback nodes. In order to increasing the approximation ability of the input signal, the orthogonal function extension defined as "FE" is proposed for representing the complex nonlinear dynamic systems. The input and the expansion using nonlinear polynomial can be given as

$$\begin{aligned} U(n) &= [u(n-1), u(n-2), \ldots, u(n-J)]^T \\ &= U^r(n) + jU^i(n) \end{aligned} \tag{1}$$

$$\begin{aligned} U_{FE}(n) &= FE(u(n-1), u(n-2), \ldots, u(n-J)) \\ &= [U_{FE,1}(n), U_{FE,2}(n), \ldots, U_{FE,J}(n)]^T \\ &= U_{FE}^r(n) + jU_{FE}^i(n) \end{aligned} \tag{2}$$

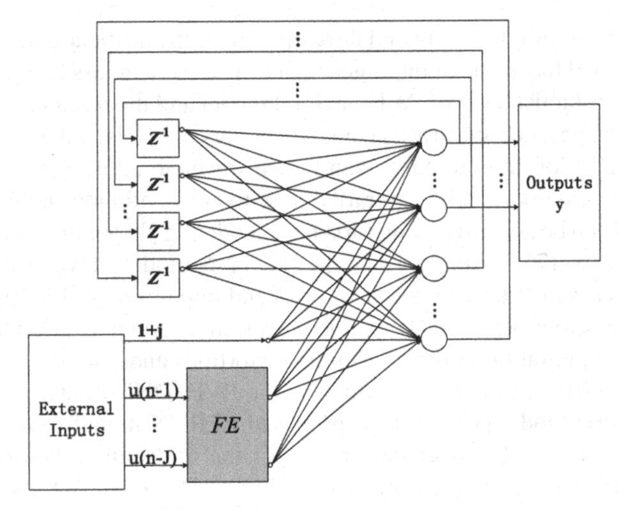

Fig. 1. FCRNN model sturcture

For the transmitter behavioral modeling, the I/Q components of the input signals and its nonlinear terms should be considered together [20]. Its corresponding input signal vector can be expressed as follows

$$\begin{aligned} U_{FE}(n) = [&1, u(n-1), u(n-2), \ldots, u(n-J), \\ &u(n-1)|u(n-2)|, \ldots, u(n-(J-1))|u(n-J)|, \\ &2u(n-1)|u(n-1)|-1, \ldots, 2u(n-J)|u(n-J)|-1, \\ &4u(n-1)|u^2(n-1)|-3u(n-1), \ldots, \\ &4u(n-J)|u^2(n-J)|-3u(n-J)]^T \end{aligned} \tag{3}$$

The entire network is constituted by a two-layer structure, where the external delay input layer and feedback output layer are the input for the model. In the proposed CPRNN model, the delayed input signals are extended by the "FE" nonlinear function, and the complex output of each neuron can be calcuted as $y_l(n)$. Then the entire input of the proposed network model can be expressed by the polynomial functional expansion of the input signals and feedback signals, which is given as follows

$$\begin{aligned} X(n) &= [S_{FE}(n), 1+j, y_1(n-1), y_2(n-1), \ldots, y_L(n-1)]^T \\ &= X_l^r(n) + jX_l^i(n), \quad l = 1, \ldots, p+L+1 \end{aligned} \tag{4}$$

Then, the *sth* neuron output in the CPRNN model can be defined as:

$$\begin{aligned} y_s(n) &= \varphi^r(u_s^r(n)) + j\varphi^i(u_s^i(n)) \\ &= y_s^r(n) + jy_s^i(n), s = 1, \ldots, L \end{aligned} \tag{5}$$

$$u_s(n) = \sum_{s=1}^{p+L-1} w_{t,s}(n) X_s(n) \tag{6}$$

Here, the complex-valued nonlinear activation function of the neuron is represented by φ, and the input signal of the activation function at time n can be represented by (6). Then the linear sum of all the output of the activation function after the weights are applied for the network output. The weight matrix of the CPRNN model is defined as

$$W = [\omega_1, \ldots, \omega_L] \tag{7}$$

where the weight vector in the network can be given as

$$\omega_l = [\omega_{l,1}, \ldots, \omega_{l,p+L+1}]^T \tag{8}$$

And the total length of the weight matrix is $(p + L + 1) * L$.

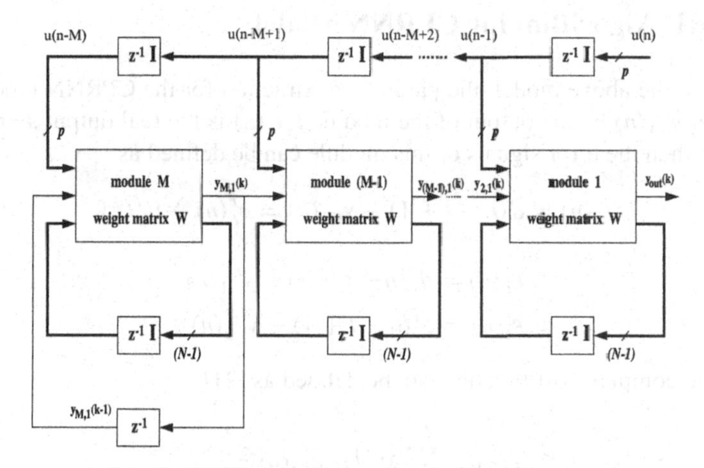

Fig. 2. CPRNN model structure for the transmitter

Furthermore, the complex-valued PRNN (CPRNN) can be designed using the proposed FCRNN structure, which is defined as an extension of real-valued PRNN and shown in Fig. 2. In the proposed CPRNN structure, the FCRNN with N neuron is the basic unit of each module. The $L - 1$ outputs of each module of the CPRNN are the feedback of the module input, the other outputs of each module are directly accessed to the next module. Then the complex-valued weight matrix of all modules in the CPRNN model can be given as

$$W(n) = [\omega_1(n), \ldots, \omega_l(n), \ldots, \omega_L(n)] \tag{9}$$

Accordingly, the complete expression of the CPRNN model is

$$\begin{aligned} y_{t,l}(n) &= \varphi^r(u_l^r(n)) + j\varphi^i(u_l^i(n)) \\ &= y_{t,l}^r(n) + jy_{t,l}^i(n), \quad t = 1, 2, \ldots, L \end{aligned} \tag{10}$$

here, $y_{t,l}(n)$ is the output of the lth neuron of the tth module at time n. For each module, the input vector can be defined as

$$X_t^T(n) = [U_{FE,t}(n), 1 + j, y_{t+1,1}(n-1), y_{t,2}(n-1), \ldots, y_{t,N}(n-1)] \tag{11}$$

$$X_M^T(n) = [U_{FE,M}(n),\ 1+j, y_{M,1}(n-1), y_{M,2}(n-1),\ \ldots, y_{M,N}(n-1)] \tag{12}$$

where $X_t^T(n)$ is the input signal vector for the tth module, t = 1… M–1. $X_M^T(n)$ is input signal vector for the *Mth* module. As can be seen in Fig. 2, the input of the $M-1$ modules consists of the the output $y_{t+1,l}(n-1)$ of the last module, and the input of the last module M only contains the it's own feedback delay. Accordingly, the output of the first PRNN module is the total output of the network, which can be defined as

$$y_{out}(n) = y_{1,1}(n) \tag{13}$$

3 CRTRL Algorithm for CPRNN Model

According to the above model, the parameter extraction for the CPRNN model can be derived. Let $y_{t,1}(n)$ be the output of the module t, $d(n)$ is the real output signals of the transmitter, then the error signals of this module can be defined as

$$\varepsilon_t(n) = d(n-t+1) - y_{t,1}(n) = \varepsilon_t^r(n) + j\varepsilon_t^i(n) \tag{14}$$

$$\begin{aligned} \varepsilon_t^r(n) &= d^r(n-t+1) - y_{t,1}^r(n) \\ \varepsilon_t^i(n) &= d^i(n-t+1) - y_{t,1}^i(n) \end{aligned} \tag{15}$$

Then the complex cost function can be defined as [21]

$$\begin{aligned} J(n) &= \sum_{t=1}^{M} \lambda^{t-1}(n)|\varepsilon_t(n)|^2 \\ &= \sum_{t=1}^{M} \lambda^{t-1}(n)[\varepsilon_t(n)\varepsilon_t^*(n)] \\ &= \sum_{t=1}^{M} \lambda^{t-1}(n)[(\varepsilon_t^r)^2 + (\varepsilon_t^i)^2] \end{aligned} \tag{16}$$

Where $\lambda(n)(0 < \lambda \leq 1)$ is the forgetting factor. The weight can be updated in the steepest descent direction

$$\Delta\omega_{l,s}(n) = -\eta \frac{\partial}{\partial\omega_{l,s}(n)} \left(\sum_{t=1}^{M} \lambda^{t-1}(n)|\varepsilon_t(n)|^2 \right) \tag{17}$$

Then the sensitive function for each module of the CPRNN model at the time n can be defined as [22]

$$\begin{bmatrix} \Lambda_{l,s,t}^{rr\,j}(n) & \Lambda_{l,s,t}^{ri\,j}(n) \\ \Lambda_{l,s,t}^{ir\,j}(n) & \Lambda_{l,s,t}^{ii\,j}(n) \end{bmatrix} = \begin{bmatrix} \dfrac{\partial y_{t,j}^r(n)}{\partial\omega_{l,s}^r(n)} & \dfrac{\partial y_{t,j}^r(n)}{\partial\omega_{l,s}^i(n)} \\ \dfrac{\partial y_{t,j}^i(n)}{\partial\omega_{l,s}^r(n)} & \dfrac{\partial y_{t,j}^i(n)}{\partial\omega_{l,s}^i(n)} \end{bmatrix} \tag{18}$$

According to the definition of the sensitive function matrix, the changing degree of the *lth* neuron output to the weight can be represented by the element. And the update equation for the sensitive functions can be given as

$$\begin{bmatrix} \Lambda_{l.s,t}^{rr}(n) & \Lambda_{l.s,t}^{ri}(n) \\ \Lambda_{l.s}^{ir}(n) & \Lambda_{l.s}^{ii}(n) \end{bmatrix} = \begin{bmatrix} \varphi\psi^{r}(n-1) & 0 \\ 0 & \varphi\psi^{i}(n-1) \end{bmatrix} \times \left\{ \sum_{\alpha=1}^{N} \left(\begin{bmatrix} \omega_{l,\alpha+p+1}^{r}(n-1) & -\omega_{l,\alpha+p+1}^{i}(n-1) \\ \omega_{l,\alpha+p+1}^{r}(n-1) & \omega_{l,\alpha+p+1}^{i}(n-1) \end{bmatrix} \times \begin{bmatrix} \Lambda_{l.s,t}^{rr,\alpha}(n-1) & \Lambda_{l.s,t}^{ri,\alpha}(n-1) \\ \Lambda_{l.s,t}^{ir,\alpha}(n-1) & \Lambda_{l.s,t}^{ii,\alpha}(n-1) \end{bmatrix} \right) + \begin{bmatrix} \delta_{\ln} X_{s}^{r}(n-1) & -\delta_{\ln} X_{s}^{i}(n-1) \\ \delta_{\ln} X_{s}^{i}(n-1) & \delta_{\ln} X_{s}^{r}(n-1) \end{bmatrix} \right\} \tag{19}$$

Further simplify:

$$(\Lambda_{l,n}^{t}(n))^{*} = \{\psi^{*}(n)\}' \times \left[\sum_{\alpha=1}^{N} \omega_{l,\alpha+p+1}^{*}(n) \left(\Lambda_{l,s}^{t,\alpha}(n-1) \right)^{*} + \delta_{\ln} X_{t,s}^{*}(n) \right] \tag{20}$$

Finally, the update equation for the weight of the CPRNN model can be obtained

$$\omega_{l,s}(n+1) = \omega_{l,s}(n) + \eta \left(\begin{array}{l} \sum_{t=1}^{M} \lambda^{t-1}(n) e_{t}(n) \{\varphi^{*}(u_{t,l}(n))\}' \\ \times \left[\sum_{\alpha=1}^{N} \omega_{1,\alpha+p+1}^{*}(n) \left(\Lambda_{l,s}^{t,\alpha}(n-1) \right)^{*} + \delta_{\ln} X_{t,s}^{*}(n) \right] \end{array} \right) \tag{21}$$

4 Simulation and Experimental Results

In order to verify the performance of the proposed CPRNN model, the behavioral model for the transmitter is carried out firstly. Here, the normalized mean square error (NMSE) is adopted to evaluate the model accuracy [20]. The RVFTDNN model [13], the parallel Hammerstein (PH) model [12], and the FCRNN model are selected for the transmitter model performance comparison. In this section, a wideband high-efficiency GaN Class-AB PA over 27–31 GHz is designed for the experimental verification. The Class-F PA worked at 29 GHz, which has the average output power of 36 dBm. The baseband input signals are the high-order spectrally-efficient 64 amplitude/phase-shift keying (64APSK) modulations, which are adopted widely in Satellite communication system [23]. The synthesized 64APSK signals have a signal bandwidth of 400 MHz and are sampled at 3.2 GHz. Considering the practical application, the I/Q imbalance, dc-offset and

PA nonlinear distortions of the transmitter are all considered together. The amplitude imbalance of the I/Q branch is set to 2 dB, and the phase imbalance of the I/Q branch is set to 3°. And the dc-offset values for the I and Q channel are set to 3% and 5%, respectively.

The structure of the FCRNN model, the CPRNN model and the RVFTDNN model can be detemined using the trial and error method. Finally, the number of input and output neurons of the FCRNN model is set to 4, the forgetting factor $\lambda = 0.5$, and the learning rate $\eta = 0.05$. The structure and parameter settings for each module in the CPRNN model are set to the same, which is consists of M FCRNN modules. Here the the value of M is set to 4 by using the trial and error method. The structure of the RVFTDNN model is a three-layer network, and the numbers of neurons in the hidden layers can be determined by the optimization process, which is 7 and 15, respectively, and output layer contains two linear neurons. Once the structure of these models is determined, the corresponding comparison results of these compensation models are obtained in Table 1 in detail. As can be seen in the table, the CPRNN model has more accurate modeling effect for the transmitter, which can give 4 dB improvement of NMSE value than the conventional PH model.

Table 1. Model performance comparison

Model	Neurons	NMSE(dB)
PH model	P = 9, M = 3	−34.87
RVFTDNN	7-15-2	−36.83
FCRNN	P = 4, N = 4	−36.55
CPRNN	P = 4, N = 4, M = 4	−38.76

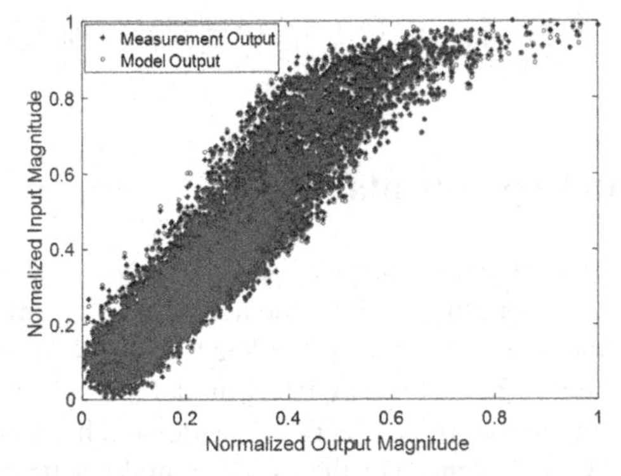

Fig. 3. The dynamic AM/AM characteristics comparison from the measurement output and the model predicted output

Considering the nonlinear memory effects of the transmitter, the amplitude and phase of the transmitter output signals will change nonlinearly with the amplitude of the input signal, and the I/Q imbalance and dc-offset will further exacerbate its distortion. To represent the nonlinear characteristics of the transmitter, the the dynamic AM/AM and AM/PM curves of the measured output and the modeled output are given in Fig. 3 and Fig. 4, respectively. As can be seen from the figures, the proposed CPRNN model can replicate the nonlinear curve well. It can be concluded that the CPRNN model can describes the nonlinear imfluence of the transmitter I/Q imbalance and dc offset on the gain and phase distortions.

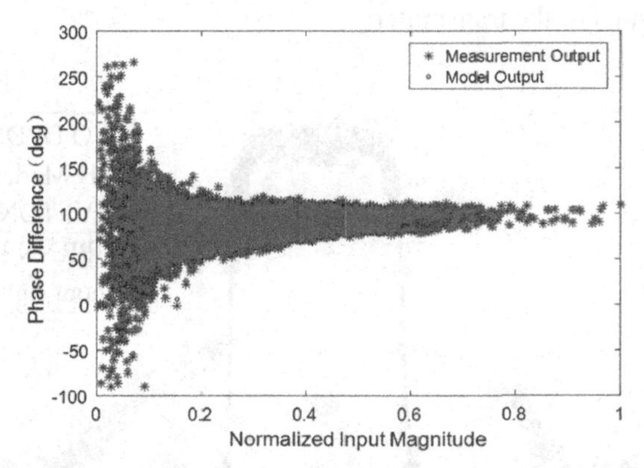

Fig. 4. The dynamic AM/PM characteristics comparison from the measurement output and the model predicted output

Furthermore, the power spectrum density (PSD) of the 64APSK signals can be plotted for the comparison of the model performance in the frequency domain. Figure 5 presents the PSD comparison of the model prediction outputs and the experimental outputs. The lower the frequency spectrum of the error signal, the better the prediction performance of the model.

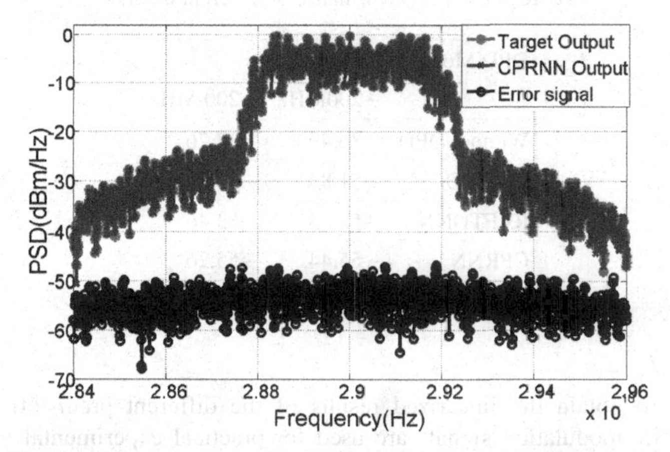

Fig. 5. Measured and modeled PSD comparison of 64APSK signals

The accurate model performance of the CPRNN model has been validated in the previous section. In theory, the more accurate the behavior model results, the better the linearization results. In order to verify the performance of the CPRNN model in the DPD system, the proposed model is applied to a complete transmitter system, where the PA nonlinearities, I/Q imbalance and dc-offset are considered together. According to the obtained input and output signals of the transmitter, the DPD inverse model can be obtained. Then the transmitter input signals can be processed through the inverse model to get the DPD signals. Then, the DPD output signals pass through the transmitter to get the linearizaed results of the transmitter.

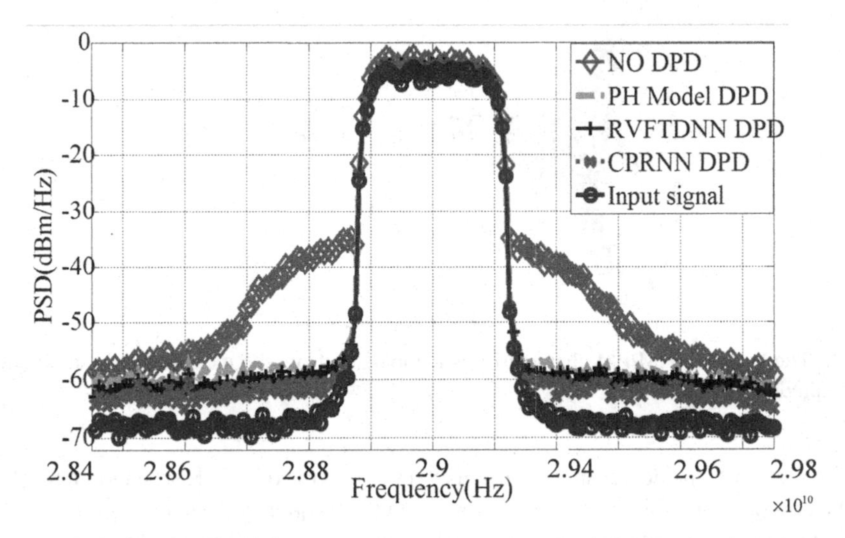

Fig. 6. DPD comparison of different models for 64APSK signal

Table 2. ACPR performance of different models.

DPD Models	ACPR(dB)	
	−200MHz	+200 MHz
Without DPD	−36.49	−37.76
PH DPD	−51.85	−52.02
RVFTDNN	−53.63	−53.46
CPRNN	−55.44	−55.26
Input Signals	−59.88	−59.89

In order to obtain the linearized results of the different predistorters the proposed 64APSK modulation signals are used for practical experimental validation in the transmitter system. The first is the comparison of the PSD after linearization, which is given in Fig. 6. It can be seen from the figure that the PSD of the transmitter distortion outputs can be compensated to different degrees by these DPD models. Here, the PH DPD models presents the worst compensation effect. The compensation results of the RVFTDNN and the FCRNN DPD model almost have the same linearization results, and the linearized results of the proposed CPRNN model presents the best ACPR results. The quantitative representation of the linearization results is given in Table 2. As can be seen from Table 2, only 15 dB ACPR improvement can be obtained by the PH DPD model. And the RVFTDNN and the FCRNN DPD model can give the ACPR improvement of about 17 dB. As a comparison, the proposed CPRNN DPD model can achieve 19 dB ACPR improvement. Both the measured and quantitative results prove that the proposed CPRNN DPD model can compensate jointly the nonlinear distortions and RF impairments of the transmitter very well.

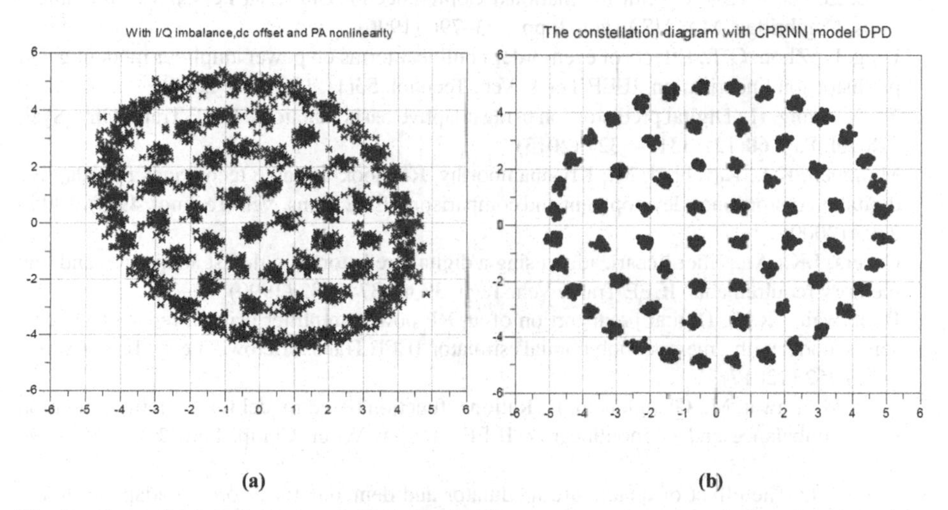

Fig. 7. Constellation diagrams of 64APSK signals. (a) shows the constellation diagram without DPD. (b) shows the constellation diagram with CPRNN model DPD.

The constellation diagrams of 64APSK modulation is given in Fig. 7, where Fig. 7(a) shows the constellation diagram without DPD and Fig. 7(b) shows the constellation diagram with CPRNN DPD model. As can be seen in Fig. 7, the distortions of the 64APSK constellation in Fig. 7(a) can be significantly compensated using the proposed CPRNN DPD model, and the compensated constellation diagrams in Fig. 7(b) can be used directly for digital demodulation.

5 Conclusion

In this paper, the CPRNN model consisted of the M-order FCRNN module is proposed for transmitter joint compensation. For the model parameter extraction, and the CRTRL learning algorithm is derived in detaill. The orthogonal polynomial structure is used in the PRNN structure for fitting the nonlinear characteristics of the transmitter. In practice, the optimal model order M and the appropriate complex activation function of the CPRNN model can be obtained through the iterative simulations. To verify the linearization ability of the proposed model, the GaN Class-AB PA driven by the 400MHz 64APSK signals including quadrature modulator I/Q imbalance and dc offset is used for the experimental measurements. Experimental results show that the proposed CPRNN DPD model can give better linearization results for the transmitter including I/Q imbalance and dc-offset compared with the other common compensation models when the complex-valued signals of the transmitter is processed simultaneously.

References

1. Harris, F.: Digital filter equalization of analog gain and phase mismatch in I-Q receivers. In: Proceedings of ICUPC - 5th International Conference on Universal Personal Communications, Cambridge, MA, USA, vol. 2, pp. 793–796 (1996)
2. Ding, L., Zhou, G.T.: Effects of even-order nonlinear terms on power amplifier modeling and predistortion linearization. IEEE Trans. Veh. Technol. **53**(1), 156–162 (2004)
3. Yu, X., Jiang, H.: Digital predistortion using adaptive basis functions. IEEE Trans. Circ. Syst. I Regul. Pap. **60**(12), 3317–3327 (2013)
4. Muhonen, K.J., Kavehrad, M., Krishnamoorthy, R.: Look-up table techniques for adaptive digital predistortion: a development and comparison. IEEE Trans. Veh. Technol. **49**(5), 1995–2002 (2000)
5. Cavers, J.K.: Amplifier linearization using a digital predistorter with fast adaptation and low memory requirements. IEEE Trans. Veh. Tech. **39**(4), 374–382 (1990)
6. Braithwaite, R.N.: Digital predistortion of an RF power amplifier using a reduced Volterra series model with a memory polynomial estimator. IEEE Trans. Microw. Theory Tech. **65**(10), 3613–3623 (2017)
7. Aziz, M., Rawat, M., Ghannouchi, F.: Rational function based model for the joint mitigation of I/Q imbalance and PA nonlinearity. IEEE Microw. Wirel. Comp. Lett. **23**(4), 196–198 (2013)
8. Cavers, J.: The effect of quadrature modulator and demodulator errors on adaptive digital predistorters for amplifier linearization. IEEE Trans. Veh. Technol. **46**(2), 456–466 (1997)
9. Kim, Y., Jeong, E., Lee, Y.: Adaptive compensation for power amplifier nonlinearity in the presence of quadrature modulation/demodulation errors. IEEE Trans. Sig. Process. **55**(9), 4717–4721 (2007)
10. Hilborn, D., Stapleton, S., Cavers, J.: An adaptive direct conversion transmitter. IEEE Trans. Veh. Technol. **43**(2), 223–233 (1994)
11. Cao, H., Tehrani, A., Fager, C., Ericsson, T., Zirath, H.: I/Q imbalance compensation using a nonlinear modeling approach. IEEE Trans. Microw. Theory Techn. **57**(3), 513–518 (2009)
12. Anttila, L., Handel, P., Valkama, M.: Joint Mitigation of power amplifier and I/Q modulator impairments in broadband direct-conversion transmitters. IEEE Trans. Microw. Theory Tech. **58**(4), 730–739 (2010)
13. Rawat, M., Rawat, K., Ghannouchi, F.M.: Adaptive digital predistortion of wireless power amplifiers/transmitters using dynamic real-valued focused time-delay line neural networks. IEEE Trans. Microw. Theory Tech. **58**(1), 95–104 (2010)
14. Liu, T., Boumaiza, S., Ghannouchi, F.M.: Dynamic behavioral modeling of 3G power amplifiers using real-valued time-delay neural networks. IEEE Trans. Microw. Theory Tech. **52**(3), 1025–1033 (2004)

15. Woo, Y.Y., et al.: Feedforward amplifier for WCDMA base stations with a new adaptive control method. In: IEEE MTT-S International Microwave Symposium Digest, vol. 2, pp. 769–772 (2002)
16. Isaksson, M., Wisell, D., Ronnow, D.: Wide-band dynamic modeling of power amplifiers using radial-basis function neural networks. IEEE Trans. Microw. Theory Tech. **53**(11), 3422–3428 (2005)
17. Wang, D., Aziz, M., Helaoui, M., Ghannouchi, F.M.: Augmented real-valued time-delay neural network for compensation of distortions and impairments in wireless transmitters. IEEE Trans. Neural Netw. Learn. Syst. **30**(1), 242–254 (2019)
18. Jaraut, P., Rawat, M., Ghannouchi, F.M.: Composite neural network digital predistortion model for joint mitigation of crosstalk, I/Q imbalance, nonlinearity in MIMO transmitters. IEEE Trans. Microw. Theory Tech. **66**(11), 5011–5020 (2018)
19. Lajnef, S., Boulejfen, N., Abdelhafiz, A., Ghannouchi, F.M.: Two-dimensional cartesian memory polynomial model for nonlinearity and I/Q imperfection compensation in concurrent dual-band transmitters. IEEE Trans. Circ. Syst. II Exp. Briefs **63**(1), 14–18 (2016)
20. Li, M., Liu, J., Jiang, Y., Feng, W.: Complex-Chebyshev functional link neural network behavioral model for broadband wireless power amplifiers. IEEE Trans. Microw. Theory Tech. **60**(6), 1979–1989 (2012)
21. Haykin, S., Li, L.: Nonlinear adaptive prediction of nonstationary signals. IEEE Trans. Sig. Process. **43**(2), 526–535 (1995)
22. Kechriotis, G., Manolakos, E.S.: Training fully recurrent neural networks with complex weights. IEEE Trans. Circ. Syst. II Analog Digit. Sig. Process. **41**(3), 235–238 (1994)
23. Morello, A., Mignone, V.: DVB-S2: the second generation standard for satellite broad-band services. Proc. IEEE **94**(1), 210–227 (2006)

An Off-Grid Sparse Representation Based Localization Method for Near-Field Sources

Li Yang(✉), Yi Jin, Changzhi Xu, Xiaoran Li, Jinzhong Zuo, and Dizhu Wang

China Academy of Space Technology of Xian, Xian 710100, China
87701726@qq.com, john.0216@163.com, sandy_xu@126.com, lixr_504@126.com, zuojinzhong111@163.com, dz82@163.com

Abstract. Near-field source localization is a potential research topic in next-generation wireless communications. Most existing methods focus on traditional subspace based methods or on-grid sparse methods. In this paper, we propose an off-grid sparse representation localization method. First, by obtaining a high order cumulant matrix we construct an angle based off-grid signal model and then employ the alternatively iterating optimization method to estimate the angles. For range estimation, a range based off-grid signal model is constructed by using the angle estimations and solved by alternatively iterating method. Simulation results reveal that, the proposed method not only enjoys high estimation accuracy, but also can realize auto-pairing of angles and ranges.

Keywords: Near-field localization · Sparse representation · Off-grid signal model · Alternative iteration

1 Introduction

In the traditional wireless communication, the distance between the user and the base station is generally much larger than the antenna size of the base station, so the traditional array receiving model is based on the far-field hypothesis, that is, the signal sent by the user incident to the base station antenna can be regarded as a plane wave. In this case, the channel information is determined by the channel attenuation coefficient and the arrival angle of the incident signal relative to the base station antenna (Direction-of-Arrival: DOA) In order to obtain DOA information, researchers proposed a number of estimation algorithms under the far-field hypothesis. The most famous algorithms are MUSIC (Multiple Signal Classification: MUSIC) [1–4], ESPRIT (Estimation of Parameters by Rotational Invariant Techniques) [2] and L1-SVD (L_1 reconstruction after Singular Value Decomposition) [3], where the subspace class methods represented by MUSIC and ESPRIT are known for their high resolution. In a good environment with known signal number and large snapshot, the method can realize superresolution estimation and has approximate optimal estimzation performance. However, the subspace class method relies on the orthogonality of Signal subspace and Noise subspace to achieve direction finding. In some harsh scenarios, such as multi-path, small snapshot and low

Q. Wu et al. (Eds.): WiSATS 2020, LNICST 358, pp. 462–470, 2021.
https://doi.org/10.1007/978-3-030-69072-4_37

(Signal-to-Noise Ratio: SNR) scenarios, the orthogonality between two subspaces will be destroyed, which will seriously affect its direction finding performance. The sparse direction-finding method that is based on the hypothesis of spatial angle sparsity represented by L1-SVD has high scene adaptability, able to fit the above harsh scenarios so as to achieve the correct positioning. However, this method is based on the spatial Angle division and assumes that the incident signal will fall on the divided grid without errors. When the number of grids is small, this method is difficult to achieve the required estimation accuracy, otherwise, when the number of grids is large, it will be restricted by RIP(Restricted Isometry Property). At the same time, a large number of grids will bring high computation, thus greatly reducing the computing efficiency. For this reason, the researcher proposed an off-grid class direction finding method [5, 6], which is independent of the above assumptions, thus greatly improving the application scope of the sparse representation direction-finding method. The signal is no longer assumed to fall on the prearranged grid, but can be distributed in the whole angle space in the off-grid method. The array guidance vector is approximated by the first-order Taylor expansion formula, so a signal model based on sparse signal and agger deviation as joint variables is established. Based on this model, the researchers put forward multi-factor to solve the sparse signal and the offset, and then get the signal direction. Zhu etc. studied the error of the reconstructed matrix in the compressed sensing algorithm and proposed a new method called Sparsity-cognizant total least-squares method [7]. Yang etc. proposed a Basis Pursuit Denoising (BPDN) model to jointly solve the signal and offset [8]. Based on Sparse Bayesian Learning theory, literature [6] proposed an efficient direction finding method. In literature [9], a direction finding method based on two-step iterative optimization is proposed, which is accomplished alternately optimizing sparse signals and offset.

In the next generation wireless communication system, it is an important research direction to enhance the spatial resolution of the base station and improve the spatial reuse capability. For this reason, researchers proposed the concept of Extremely Large Aperture Array (ELAA) [10]. The aperture size of ELAA ranges from several meters to tens of meters, and its near-field area can reach several kilometers. Therefore, the traditional signal model which relies on the far-field hypothesis cannot be applied to the ELAA scenario. So it is necessary to study the localization method based on the near-field signal model. When the user is located in the near-field area of the base station antenna array, the base station receives the signal in the form of spherical wave. The positioning information of the user is determined by the DOA and the distance between the user and the base station. Therefore, the two-dimensional parameters of the signal source, DOA and distance, need to be solved simultaneously for the near-field positioning. Because of the complexity of the guidance vector in the near-field signal model, the spherical wave signal model is generally simplified by using the second-order Taylor expansion. Based On this model, the researchers put forward a series of near field positioning methods, such as Oblique Projection MUSIC (Oblique the Projection MUSIC: OPMUSIC) method [11]. Two step MUSIC (Two - Stage MUSIC: TSMUSIC) method [12], and the Sparse (On - grid point Approach: OSA) [13], etc. Among them, OPMUSIC and TSMUSIC are traditional subspace class methods and can simultaneously realize the positioning of near and far field hybrid source. These two methods inherit the advantage of high precision of subspace class method, but lose the array aperture. OSA is a sparse representation class method, The DOA and distance parameters are obtained by dividing the grid in Angle space and distance space respectively and using the weighted norm minimization model. At the same time, OSA can realize the automatic matching of DOA and distance. However, this method is also restricted by meshing effect. That is, the mesh needs to be subdivided to improve the estimation accuracy, and is limited by the RIP criterion and high computational efficiency. Therefore, a positioning method with high estimation accuracy without increasing mesh density is urgently needed.

In this paper, we propose an off-grid sparse representation based localization method for near-field sources. First, This method establishes an off-grid signal model based on angle parameters by obtaining a high-order cumulant matrix and then realizes the estimation of Angle by means of alternating iterative optimization method. Then an off-grid signal model based on distance parameter is established according to the Angle estimation and solved by alternatively iterating method.

The symbols used in this paper are as follows: for A matrices, A^T and A^H represent the transpose matrix and conjugate transpose matrix of the matrix A respectively. $\|A\|_2$ and $\|A\|_F$ represent the two norm and Frobenius norm of the matrix A respectively. $\odot$ represents Hadamard product. diag means taking the diagonal elements of a matrix or converting a vector to a diagonal matrix. $\Re$ represents a real part operation.

2 Signal Model

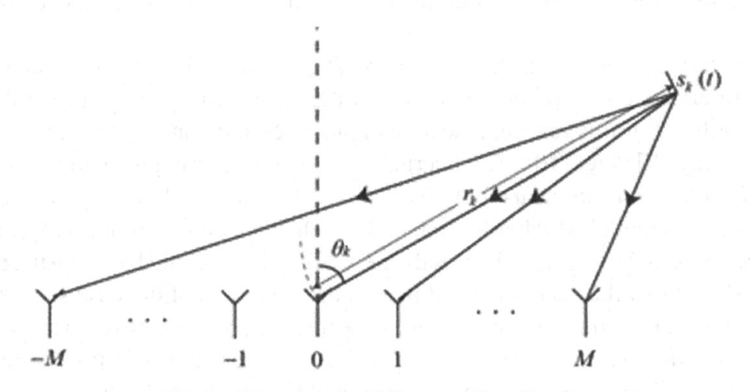

Fig. 1. Illustration of NF source localization

Suppose there are k narrow band near-field signals incident on a Uniform Linear Array (ULA) with N array elements. The index value of the array element is $\Omega = \{-M, \cdots, M\}$. As shown in Fig. 1, the incident Angle of the k-th incident signal relative to the array normal is θ_k. If the middle array element is taken as the reference array element, the distance between the k-th source and the reference array element is r_k. The output of the entire array is,

$$x(t) = As(t) + n(t) \tag{1}$$

Where, x(t) is the array output at time t, $A = [a(\theta_1, r_1), \cdots a(\theta_K, r_K)]$ is the array manifold matrix, $a(\theta_k, r_k) = \left[e^{j[-M\omega_k+(-M)^2\phi_k]}, \cdots, e^{j[M\omega_k+M^2\phi_k]}\right]^T$ is the guide vector of the k-th signal, s(t) is the incident signal at time t, n(t) is the zero mean additive gaussian white noise at time t, and

$$\omega_k = -2\pi\frac{d}{\lambda}\sin(\theta_k) \tag{2}$$

$$\phi_k = \pi\frac{d^2}{\lambda r_k}\cos^2(\theta_k) \tag{3}$$

Where, d represents the spacing between elements and λ represents the signal wavelength. Our purpose is to recover DOA parameters $\theta = \{\theta_1, \cdots, \theta_K\}$ and distance parameters $r = \{r_1, \cdots, r_K\}$ of k-th signals through the array reception model (1) and complete the pairing.

Before introducing the method proposed in this paper, we propose the following hypothesis:

(1) in order to avoid Angle ambiguity, the matrix interval d should satisfy: $d \le \lambda/4$;
(2) the incident signal is a narrow-band zero-mean stationary random process, and its fourth-order cumulant is not zero;
(3) array received noise is independent of the signal and is additive zero-mean gaussian white noise.

3 Methods Mentioned

The proposed method consists of two steps: first, the fourth-order cumulant matrix is obtained according to the array output information, and the angle-based off-lattice signal model is established to solve the Angle information. Secondly, the off-grid signal model based on distance parameter is established to realize the solution of distance parameter.

3.1 Solution of Angle Parameters

The fourth-order cumulant of array output is defined as:

$$\begin{aligned} c(m, n, p, q) &= \mathrm{cum}\left\{x_m(t),\ x_n^*(t),\ x_p(t),\ x_q^*(t)\right\} \\ &= \sum\nolimits_{k=1}^{K} c_{s_k} e^{j[(m-n)-(p-q)]\omega_k} e^{j[(m^2-n^2)-(p^2-q^2)]\phi_k} \end{aligned} \tag{4}$$

Where, c_{s_k} represents the fourth-order cumulant of the k-th signal. Let $\overline{m} = m + N + 1$, $\overline{n} = n + N + 1$, we get the following fourth-order cumulant matrix:

$$\begin{aligned} C(\overline{m}, \overline{n}) &= \mathrm{cum}\left\{x_m(t), x_{-n}^*(t), x_{-n}(t), x_n^*(t)\right\} \\ &= \sum\nolimits_{k=1}^{K} c_{s_k} e^{j2(m-n)\omega_k} \end{aligned} \tag{5}$$

The matrix can be further expressed as follows:

$$C = \sum_{k=1}^{K} c_{s_k} \bar{a}(\theta_k)\bar{a}^H(\theta_k) \\ = \overline{A}(\theta)C_s\overline{A}^H(\theta) \tag{6}$$

Where, $C_s = \text{diag}([c_{s_1}, \cdots, c_{s_K}])$, $\overline{A}(\theta) = [\bar{a}(\theta_1), \cdots, \bar{a}(\theta_K)]$, $[e^{j2(-N)\omega_k}, \cdots, 1, \cdots, e^{j2N\omega_k}]^T$. From formula (6), it can be seen that the matrix C is only related to the Angle parameter, but not to the distance parameter. Let $\overline{S} = C_s\overline{A}^H(\theta)$ it be the input signal of virtual array, then model (6) can be regarded as the output of virtual array in a far-field source scenario, that is,

$$C = \overline{A}(\theta)\overline{S} \tag{7}$$

The Angle space is divided into Q grids, and the grid set is $\vartheta = \{\vartheta_1, \cdots, \vartheta_Q\}$, $\vartheta_{q_k}(q_k \in \{1, \cdots, Q\})$ is defined as the nearest grid point from θ_k. As θ_k is evenly distributed throughout the Angle space, the error between θ_k and ϑ_{q_k} will always exist, and is defined as $\delta_{q_k} = \theta_k - \vartheta_{q_k}$. Then the guidance vector of the k-th incident signal $a(\theta_k)$ can be expressed by the first-order Taylor expansion as,

$$a(\theta_k) = a(\vartheta_{q_k}) + b(\vartheta_{q_k})\delta_{q_k} \tag{8}$$

Where, $b(\vartheta_{q_k})$ represents the derivative of $a(\vartheta_{q_k})$ at ϑ_{q_k}, Definition$B^{\circ} = [b(\vartheta_1), \cdots, b(\vartheta_Q)]$, $\Delta = \text{diag}(\delta)$, $\delta = [\delta_1, \cdots, \delta_Q]^T$ then model (7) can be extended to the following off-grid signal model,

$$C = \left(\overline{A}^{\circ} + B^{\circ}\Delta\right)\overline{S}^{\circ} \tag{9}$$

Where, $\overline{A}^{\circ} = [\bar{a}(\vartheta_1), \cdots, \bar{a}(\vartheta_Q)]$, $\overline{S}^{\circ}$ is the sparse signal after expansion, and its non-zero value position represents the size ϑ_{q_k}. According to the sparse representation theory, we propose the following model based on ℓ_1 norm minimization:

$$\min_{\overline{S}^{\circ},\delta} \beta\left\|\overline{S}^{\circ}\right\|_{2,1} + \frac{1}{2}\left\|C - \left(\overline{A}^{\circ} + B^{\circ}\Delta\right)\overline{S}^{\circ}\right\|_F^2 \tag{10}$$

Where, $\beta > 0$ is a user-defined parameter. It can be seen from model (10) that the model is a non-convex problem due to the existence of bilinear variables $\Delta\overline{S}^{\circ}$, so it is difficult to solve in polynomial time. In order to solve the problem effectively. We do this by iterating between variables $\overline{S}^{\circ}$ and Δ.

In the Q-th iteration, fix Δ first and update $\overline{S}^{\circ}$ by solving the following optimization problem,

$$\overline{S}^{\circ(q+1)} = \min_{\overline{S}^{\circ}} \beta\left\|\overline{S}^{\circ}\right\|_{2,1} + \frac{1}{2}\left\|C - \left(\overline{A}^{\circ} + B^{\circ}\Delta^{(q)}\right)\overline{S}^{\circ}\right\|_F^2 \tag{11}$$

Since model (11) is a convex optimization problem, it can be solved by CVX and other optimization toolkits. After the optimal solution $\overline{S}^{\circ(q+1)}$ is obtained, Δ is updated according to the following optimization problems

$$\delta^{(q+1)} = \min_{\delta} \beta \left\| \overline{S}^{\circ(q+1)} \right\|_{2,1} + \frac{1}{2} \left\| C - \left(\overline{A}^{\circ} + B^{\circ} \Delta \right) \overline{S}^{\circ(q+1)} \right\|_F^2 \tag{12}$$

It is noted that model (12) is essentially a weighted least squares estimation about δ, so its closed solution can be obtained through a series of derivations. According to literature [9], the solution of model (12) can be obtained as

$$\hat{\delta}^{(q+1)} = \Re\left\{ D^{-1} f \right\} \tag{13}$$

Among them,

$$D = \left(B^{\circ H} B^{\circ}\right) \odot \left(\overline{S}^{\circ(q+1)} \overline{S}^{\circ(q+1)H} \right) \tag{14}$$

$$f = \mathrm{diag}\left(\overline{S}^{\circ(q+1)} \left(C - \overline{A}^{\circ} \overline{S}^{\circ(q+1)} \right)^H B^{\circ} \right) \tag{15}$$

When the iteration ends, we can obtain the spatial power spectrum P^{final} and the new grid set in the case of off-grid,

$$\vartheta^{\circ} = \vartheta + \hat{\delta}^{final} \tag{16}$$

Where P^{final} is generated by the optimal solution of model (11) at the end of iteration, and $\hat{\delta}^{final}$ is the size at the end of iteration $\hat{\delta}^{(q+1)}$. Then the estimated value $\hat{\theta}$ of DOA can be obtained by searching for P^{final} the corresponding size of the first K peak index values in ϑ°.

3.2 Solve the Distance Parameter

By taking the angle estimated value $\hat{\theta}$ Angle into model (1),

$$x(t) = A\left(\hat{\theta}, r\right) s(t) + n(t) \tag{17}$$

Where $A\left(\hat{\theta}, r\right)$ is the array manifold matrix with respect to distance r. The distribution space of the source distance r is $\left[0.62\left(\frac{D^3}{\lambda}\right)^{\frac{1}{2}}, \frac{2D^2}{\lambda} \right]$, where D is the aperture size of the array. Referring to the DOA solving process, we grid the spatial range of r to obtain the grid point set $\overset{\circ}{r} = \{r_1, \cdots, r_V\}$, and then obtain the sparse expansion model in the off-grid scenario.

$$x(t) = [A^{\circ}\left(\hat{\theta}, r^{\circ}\right) + B^{\circ}\left(\hat{\theta}, r^{\circ}\right) \Delta_r] s^{\circ}(t) + n(t) \tag{18}$$

Where, $A^{\circ}\left(\hat{\theta}, r^{\circ}\right) = \left[A^{\circ}\left(\hat{\theta}_1, r^{\circ}\right), \cdots, A^{\circ}\left(\hat{\theta}_K, r^{\circ}\right)\right]$, $B^{\circ}\left(\hat{\theta}, r^{\circ}\right)$ represents the derivative of r with respect to $A^{\circ}\left(\hat{\theta}, r^{\circ}\right)$, $s^{\circ}(t)$ represents the extended equivalent sparse signal, and Δ_r is similarly defined as Δ. We establish the following sparse reconstruction model

$$\min_{s^{\circ}(t), \Delta_r} \eta \sum_t \left|s^{\circ}(t)\right| + \frac{1}{2} \sum_t \left\| x(t) - [A^{\circ}\left(\hat{\theta}, r^{\circ}\right) + B^{\circ}\left(\hat{\theta}, r^{\circ}\right)\Delta_r] s^{\circ}(t) \right\|_2^2 \quad (19)$$

Where $\eta > 0$ is a user-defined parameter. This model is also a non-convex problem, and the solution method is similar to formula (11)–(16). At the same time, the model (19) is used to solve the distance parameters, which can realize the automatic pairing of Angle and distance parameters.

4 Simulation Experiment

We will verify the effectiveness of the proposed algorithm through some simulation experiments. In the simulation experiment, we selected OPMUSIC [11], TSMUSIC [12] and OSA [13] which are representative in the field of near-field positioning. The array adopted is a 7-element uniform linear array with an interval of $d = \lambda/4$. The incident signal is $e^{j\psi}$, where the phase ψ is uniformly distributed in the interval of $[0, 2\pi]$.The index to measure the performance of the algorithm is the RMSE (Root Mean Square Error) of the estimated results, which is defined as,

$$RMSE = \sqrt{\frac{1}{MoK} \sum_{n=1}^{Mo} \left\| \theta_n^{Est} - \theta_n^{True} \right\|_2^2} \quad (20)$$

Where Mo represents the number of simulation, θ_n^{True} and θ_n^{Est} corresponds to the real value and estimated value of angle in the n-th simulation experiment respectively. Meanwhile, we used CRLB (Crammer-Rao Lower Bound) as a reference to measure the estimated performance.

4.1 Changes of RMSE with SNR

In the first simulation experiment, it is assumed that two narrowband near-field signals are incident on the array at the position of $\{0^{\circ}, 1.3\lambda\}$ and $\{20^{\circ}, 3\lambda\}$. The number of quick beats collected is 600. Let the SNR range from −15 dB to 25 dB. The variation of RMSE estimated by each method with SNR is shown in Fig. 2.

It can be seen from Fig. 2(a) that off-grid signal method proposed in this paper (MM) can approach CRLB at a fast speed and continue to decline with the improvement of SNR and always keep close to CRLB. In contrast, although OSA can approach CRLB first, but its RMSE cannot continue to decrease with the increase of SNR, which shows a performance "saturation" phenomenon. OPMUSIC has low performance due to the loss of array aperture caused by the introduction of smoothing method. TSMUSIC exhibits similar estimation performance. It can be seen from Fig. 2(b) that the method in this paper is always close to CRLB when the SNR is greater than −5 dB. OPMUSIC can only approach CRLB when the SNR is greater than 5 dB. OSA deviated from CRLB even when the SNR was relatively high. TSMUSIC, on the other hand, performed poorly.

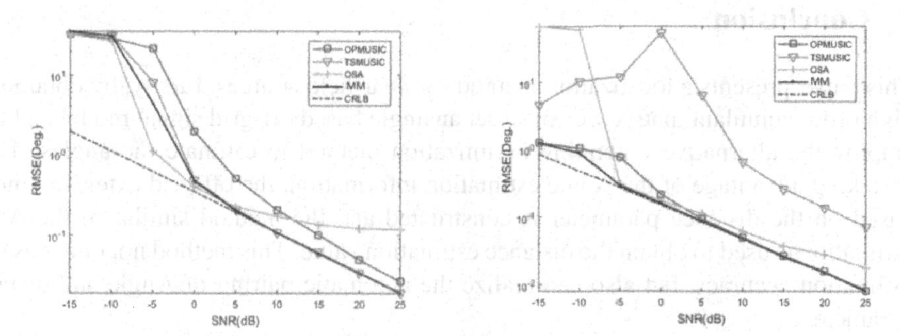

(a)comparison of angle estimation results (b)comparison of distance estimation results

Fig. 2. Performance analysis of RMSE with varying SNR.

4.2 RMSE Changes with the Number of Quick Beats

In the second simulation experiment, we compared RMSE of each method under different number of snapshots. The experimental parameters are basically the same as the first simulation experiment, except that the number of snapshots varies from 100 to 800 and the SNR is set to 10 dB. The experimental results are shown in Fig. 3.

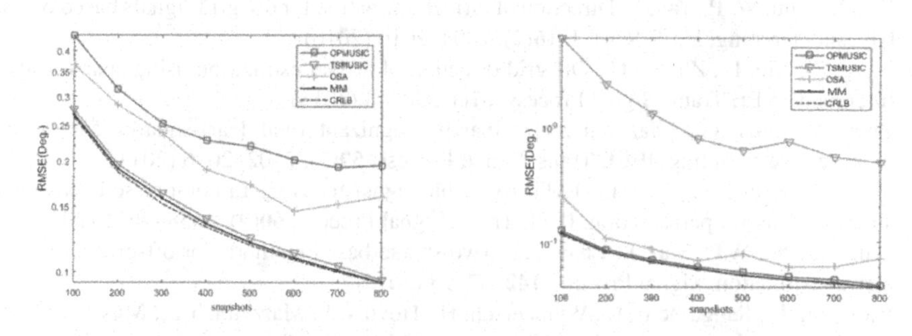

(a)comparison of angle estimation results (b)comparison of distance estimation results

Fig. 3. Performance analysis of RMSE with varying number of snapshots.

It can be seen from Fig. 3(a) that the method in this paper can approach CRLB well in the whole range of snapshots.TSMUSIC shows similar estimated performance to the method in this paper. OPMUSIC and OSA have underperformed. It can be seen from Fig. 3(b) that the method mentioned still provides excellent estimation capability in the aspect of distance estimation. OPMUSIC performs similarly, while the other two methods perform less well. It can be seen from the above two simulation experiments that the method presented in this paper has a stable and excellent near-field source location capability.

5 Conclusion

This paper presents a localization method for near-field sources. Firstly, by obtaining a high order cumulant matrix we construct an angle based off-grid signal model and then employ the alternatively iterating optimization method to estimate the angles. Then, by taking advantage of the Angle estimation information, the off-grid extension model based on the distance parameter is constructed and the method similar to the Angle estimation is used to obtain the distance estimation value. This method not only has high estimation accuracy, but also can realize the automatic pairing of Angle and distance parameters.

References

1. Schmidt, R.: Multiple emitter location and signal parameter estimation. IEEE Trans. Antennas Propag. **34**(3), 276–280 (1986)
2. Roy, R., Kailath, T.: Esprit-estimation of signal parameters via rotational invariance techniques. IEEE Trans. Acoust. Speech Signal Process. **37**(7), 984–995 (1989)
3. Malioutov, D., Çetin, M., Willsky, A.S.: A sparse signal reconstruction perspective for source localization with sensor arrays. IEEE Trans. Signal Process. **53**(8), 3010–3022 (2005)
4. Liu, Z.: Spatial sparsity-based theory and methods of array signal processing. National University of Defense Technology, Changsha Hunan (2012)
5. Wu, X., Zhu, W.-P., Yan, J.: Direction of arrival estimation for off-grid signals based on sparse bayesian learning. IEEE Sens. J. **16**(7), 2004–2016 (2016)
6. Yang, Z., Xie, L., Zhang, C.: Off-grid direction of arrival estimation using sparse Bayesian inference. IEEE Trans. Signal Process. **61**(1), 38–43 (2013)
7. Zhu, H., Leus, G., Giannakis, G.: Sparsity-cognizant total least-squares for perturbed compressive sampling. IEEE Trans. Signal Process. **59**(5), 2002–2016 (2011)
8. Yang, Z., Zhang, C., Xie, L.: Robustly stable signal recovery in compressed sensing with structured matrix perturbation. IEEE Trans. Signal Process. **60**(9), 4658–4671 (2012)
9. Wu, X., Zhu, W.P., Yan, J., Zhang, Z.: Two sparse-based methods for off-grid direction-of-arrival estimation. Signal Process. **142**, 87–95 (2018)
10. Bjornson, E., Sanguinetti, L., Wymeersch, H., Hoydis, J., Marzetta, T.L.: Massive MIMO is a reality-what is next? Five promising research directions for antenna arrays. Digit. Signal Process. **94**, 3–20 (2019)
11. He, J., Swamy, M., Ahmad, M.: Efficient application of MUSIC algorithm under the coexistence of far-field and near-field sources. IEEE Trans. Signal Process. **60**(4), 2066–2070 (2011)
12. Liang, J., Liu, D.: Passive localization of mixed near-field and far-field sources using two-stage MUSIC algorithm. IEEE Trans. Signal Process. **58**(1), 108–120 (2009)
13. Wang, B., Liu, J., Sun, X.: Mixed sources localization based on sparse signal reconstruction. IEEE Signal Process. Lett. **19**(8), 487–490 (2012)

Space-Borne Multifunctional Integrated Hardware Processing Platform Design

Yi-Fan Ping(✉), Su-jun Wang, Wei Wen, Chang-zhi Xu, and Ying-zhao Shao

China Academy of Space Technology, Xi'an 710100, China
pingyf1982@126.com, 1036727331@qq.com, wenwei8114@163.com, sandy_xu@126.com, daisyshao1983@126.com

Abstract. This paper presents a design scheme of space-borne multifunctional integrated hardware processing platform. This platform is characterized by low power consumption, small size and light weight. At the same time, the scheme has the feature of reconfiguration, which maximizes the function of software. Different software is loaded according to different application to build hardware platforms for satisfying requirements in different environments. It provides a new way to solve the problem of traditional hardware specialization, which is the trend of hardware platform in the future.

Keywords: Multifunctional · Universal · Configuration · Hardware platform

1 Introduction

With the rapid development of microelectronics, computers, signal processing and other technologies, as well as the wide application in the field of satellite communications, the requirements for multifunctional and universal hardware platform have increased significantly [1–3]. The traditional hardware processing platform generally has the characteristic of specificity. It develops specific hardware platform for specific application scenarios, and its functions have been solidified to meet specific requirements. At the same time, when the functional requirements of users in orbit change, the product will not be replaced, and these problems have seriously restricted the development and application of the product. In order to solve these problems of satellite traditional hardware platform, it is necessary to study a hardware architecture platform with versatility, flexibility and freedom to upgrade. Secondly, it is necessary to build a high-performance digital signal processing platform that is suitable for a variety of needs. Third, the development of low power consumption, miniaturization, lightweight characteristics of hardware architecture. These requirements greatly heighten the implementation difficulty of the hardware platform.

At present, the concept of new software radio technology partly solve the problem that the functions can't be changed or upgraded, and gets rid of the traditional design method [4–8]. It is based on general and re-configurable hardware platform through loading software. Thus various functions can be implemented on a single platform. Although

Q. Wu et al. (Eds.): WiSATS 2020, LNICST 358, pp. 471–479, 2021.
https://doi.org/10.1007/978-3-030-69072-4_38

the new software radio platform has many advantages, such as re-configurable, openness and extensible feature, there are also some problems. The integration degree of platform is relatively low, the power consumption is high, and the volume is big. So the platform can not adapt to the characteristics of miniaturization and lightweight. How to design a more compact signal processing architecture is a very important issue.

In order to solve the above problems, this paper proposes a design scheme of space-borne mufti-functional integrated hardware platform to realize the characteristics of lower power, miniaturization and light weight. This platform also has the characteristic of reconfiguration which can load different software programs according to different functions. This paper provides a new idea and method which is the trend of future hardware platform.

2 Overall Design of New Hardware Platform

Traditional hardware platform include ADC, DAC, FPGA, DSP, CPLD, peripheral storage and interface chips. The main problem is that area and power consumption will be increased sharply. The overall design of traditional hardware platform is as follows (Fig. 1).

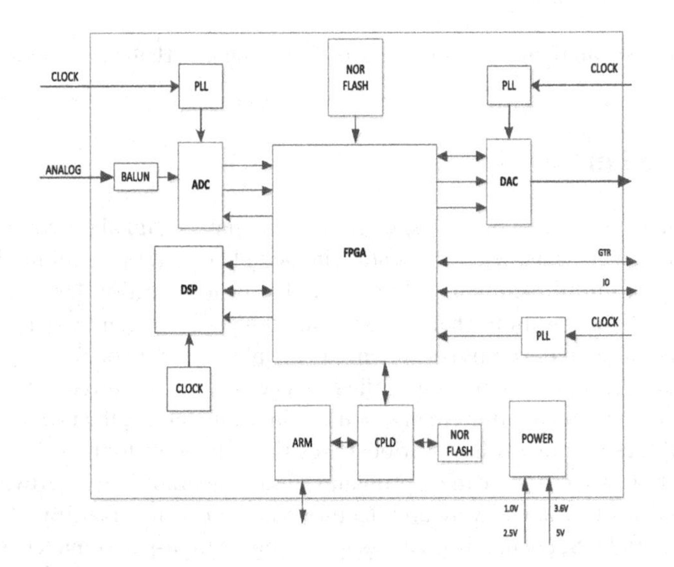

Fig. 1. Traditional hardware processing platform solution

This new space-borne mufti-functional integrated hardware platform is include RFSoc, DSP, DDR4, interface chips and so on. The overall design of new platform is as follows (Fig. 2).

The RFSoc chip selected for this hardware platform is equipped with dual-core ARM Cortex-A9 processor [9–12]. The processor has 6.25M logic units, more than 2000 DSP. In addition, four 16-bit DDR4 devices are integrated on the platform to provide high-bandwidth interfaces for ARM and FPGA logic resources in the RFSoc chip. And it can

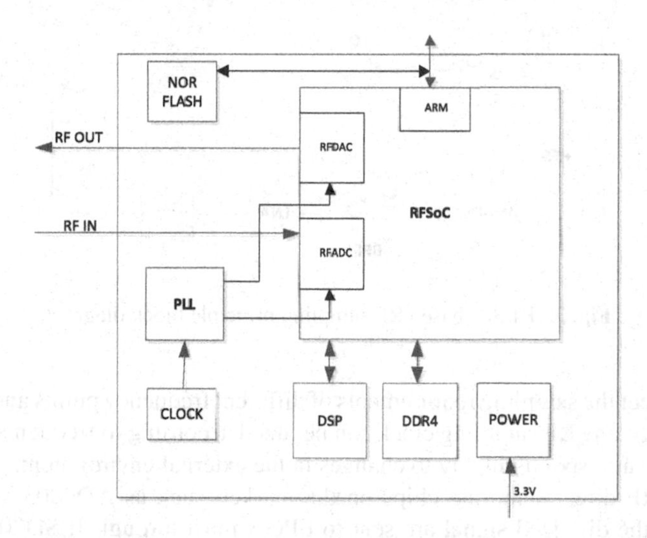

Fig. 2. Multifunctional integrated hardware processing platform

realize heterogeneous processing between ARM and FPGA. It is the most comprehensive and extensible hardware platform with the highest performance.

2.1 Direct RF Sampling Design of New Platform

The RF signal are converted to IF signal by one or two analog down-conversion which is traditional method. Then the IF signal is sampled by ADC. The traditional RF front requires a relatively complex design scheme with many discrete analog devices. And down-conversion circuits include mixers, oscillators, band-pass filters and so on, all of these requiring the specific design. Moreover, if the receiving frequency is variable and the bandwidth of filter can be set, the volume of the system will increase. This architecture can not satisfy the needs of miniature and lightweight.

In order to solve this problem, the new platform designed in this paper adopts the direct RF sampling technology. It moves the A/D and D/A as close to the antenna as possible. It has the advantages of less devices required, low cost, low power consumption and easy to obtain higher performances. It has great significance to the miniaturization, integration and low power consumption of equipment.

The selected RFSoc devices in the platform can directly sample the incoming and outcoming RF signals of frequency band below 6GHz. After the signal is digitized, digital signal processing technology is used to perform down-conversion and other signal processing in digital domain. Moreover, RF-ADC/RF-DAC integrated in RFSoc support a high sampling rate, which can better balance between dynamic range and SRN. The schematic diagram of integrated direct sampling subsystem in shown in Fig. 3. By eliminating the analog devices and adopting integrated method, the power consumption and packaging are reduced by nearly 50%–75%. At the same time, the development cycle of the whole system is greatly reduced.

Subsystem include mixer, CNC oscillator, extraction, interpolation, gain/phase compensation and other digital signal processing techniques for each channel. In addition,

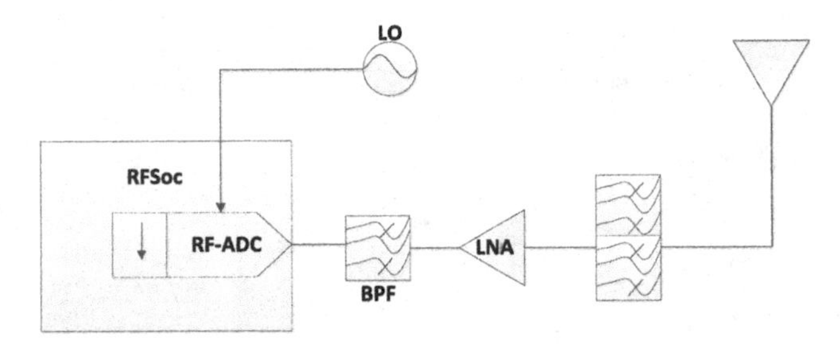

Fig. 3. RFSoc based RF sampling principle block diagram

RFSoc can meet the sampling requirements of different frequency points and bandwidth. In the RF range, the RF sampling clock can be tuned according to frequency. Therefore, the platform can respond quickly to changes in the external environment.

If other RF direct sampling chips on the market, such as AD9003 and AD9371, are adopted, the digitized signal are sent to FPGA must through JESD204B interface based on high-speed SERDES. This is because with the continuous improvement of the sampling rate of ADC/DAC, the data throughput is getting lager and lager. And the data throughput rate is often several Gbit/s. It is difficult to meet the design requirements with the traditional LVDS, so the manufacturers of high-speed ADC/DAC devices adopt JESD204B interface.

However, the IP core of JESD204B interface standard is not only expensive, but also has very high requirements for the design of high-speed data line of the circuit board. At the same time, it will increase the circuit delay and design complexity of up to 80 sampling cycles. Meanwhile, it is difficult to debug, and the power consumption is large up to 8 W. Therefore, in order to solve these problems, it is necessary to remove the JESD204B interface. The platform scheme proposed in this paper breaks through the bottleneck of JESD204B and solve these problems. Because RFSoc used in this scheme integrates high-performance ADC/DAC, it is unnecessary to use the IP core of JESD204B and it also reduces the complexity of wiring on the circuit board.

2.2 High Integration Design of the Platform

In this deign RFSoc has sixteen channel transceiver. It is obviously that the new platform does not need extra ADC/DAC, ARM controller and power conversion chips correspond to these devices. Therefore, it also reduces the difficult of distributing the printed board and difficulty of dividing the power plane layer.

RFSoc, the core chip of the whole processing platform, integrates processing system and programmable logic resources. The processing system includes application processing unit (APU), real-time processing unit (RTU), DDR controller, system controller, security module, platform management module and various common interface management. Programmable logic resources include RF signal chain, common I/O, storage module and DSP resources. The core idea of space-borne multifunctional integration platform is to integrate FPGA + ARM + RF sampling as much as possible.

2.3 Multi-core Processor Chip Selection

DSP processing chip uses TMS320C6678, including a total of eight DSP kernel. The chip uses the keystone structure which can carry out high-performance fixed-point operation and floating point operation. The kernel speed of TMS320C6678 can reach 1.25 GHz. Thus the whole chip can provide 10 GHz operating frequency.

TMS320C6678 not only provides powerful operation ability of up to 9600MIPS, but also integrates a variety of digital signal interface, including EMIF, GPIO and SRIO interface. SRIO can realize the high-speed data transmission between DSP and FPGA, which to some extent can meet the requirements of the high-speed real-time signal processing and transmission. TMS320C6678 is used to execute a one-million-point FFT under the operating frequency of 1 GHz. It takes only 6.4 ms for 8 cores to run simultaneously. Such high-speed DSP kernel can be fully used to perform high-speed real-time computation, such as radar and electronic warfare.

The development flow of platform based on TMS320C6678 in shown in Fig. 4 below. Specifically, the signal processing process is firstly built based on the signal processing requirements and set module parameters, connection parameters and hardware parameters. Then the signal processing module is mapped to the C6678 hardware platform to generate the C6678 code. After that, the project code is compiled, loaded and debugged. If it does not meet the requirements of the system design, the above steps are executed again.

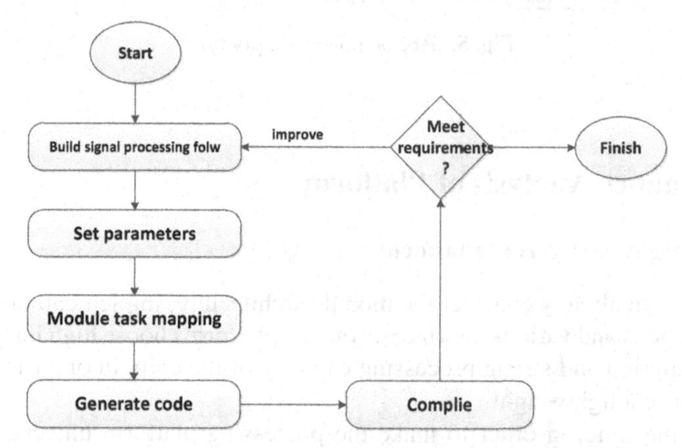

Fig. 4. TMS320C6678 based development process

2.4 Power Module Design of Platform

The power supply of RFSoc is the most complex part of the processing system. As shown in the Fig. 5 below, there are as many as fourteen power types. The selection and design of power module is an important factor that restricts the size and weight of the platform. For decrease the volume of platform, LINTER power modules are selected in this paper. LTM4650 has two power channels, each 25 A. And the two channels of LTM4650 can parallel to obtain 50 A ability. The size of it is only 16 mm × 16 mm. Another power module of LINTER is LTM4644, which has four power channels, each 6 A. LTM4644 is also used in this new platform and the four channels of LTM4644 can parallel to obtain 24 A ability. The size of it is only 9 mm × 15 mm. The new platform has two LTM4650s and four LTM4644. These power modules can provide the complete power scheme for RFSoc, DSP, DDR4 and other chips.

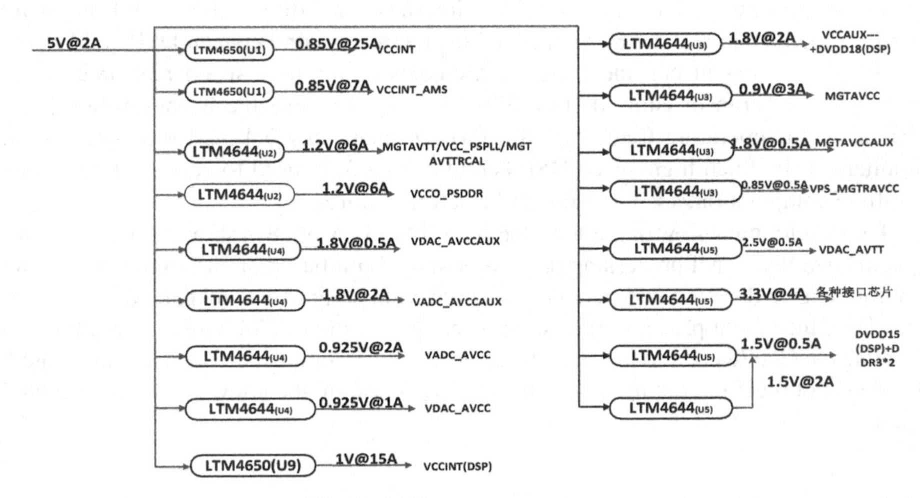

Fig. 5. RFSoc power supply type

3 Performance Analysis of Platform

3.1 Lightweight Analysis of Platform

The new platform already consider the module architecture, implementation of the different applications and various interfaces. And the platform choose high integration, low power consumption and strong processing capacity of the chip, in order to support the establishment of a lightweight.

At the same time, in order to make the processing platform universal, RFSoc is selected. RFSoc integrates RF-ADC, RF-DAC, ARM, FPGA and high-speed interfaces. So the hardware platform in nearly half the size. The input RF frequency of RFSoc can reach 6 GHz. If the input RF frequency is below 6 GHz, the mixer, oscillator, bandwidth is no needed. It greatly reduces the power consumption, size and development cycle of entire system.

3.2 Low Power Consumption of Platform

In the new platform, the power consumption of the DSP is estimated at about 10 W. And the core voltage of RFSoc is 0.85 V, the static current is less than 2.5 A, and the static power consumption is less than 2.1 W. When the program runs, the power consumption of RFSoc is less than 25 W. So the total power consumption of processing platform is less than 35 W. When the power conversion efficiency is 90%, the total power consumption is less than 40 W.

Using Xpower of Xilinx, the current of RFSoc voltages can be calculated. When using XCZU49DR, for example, working at 25 °C, we can set the utilization rate of LUT to 70%, BRAM to 50%, DSP to 50%, parallel processing rate to 250 MHz, DDR3 interface to 36 bit, operating clock rate to 1333 Mb/s. Under this condition, RFSoc static consumption current is nearly 2.0 A. Operating at 25 °C, the temperature of thermal resistance is 69.6 °C and the power consumption of 22 W. RFSoc power consumption varies with the junction temperature. When the junction temperature changes from 10 °C to 100 °C, the chip's power consumption changes from 20.97 W to 25.01 W.

When using the traditional hardware platform, the power consumption is much greater than 40 W if the processing capacity is to be achieved similar to that of the new platform proposed in this paper. The power consumption of 16-channel ADC alone has reach more than 30 W.

3.3 Reconfiguration of Platform

RFSoc and DSP are the main components of hardware platform, which can realize different functions by loading different programs. By storing different software packages and corresponding control instructions, users can switch processing tasks.

The re-configurable characteristics of the hardware platform are shown in the Fig. 6 below. The numerical control method can adjust the frequency band of filter, and the SPI control method can change the gain amplitude of the RF signal. Sampling clock and NCO clock are adjustable.

The programmable logic devices and DSP devices are controlled and configured by the control unit to realize the desired functions. Algorithmic programs with different processing flows can be configured according to applications.

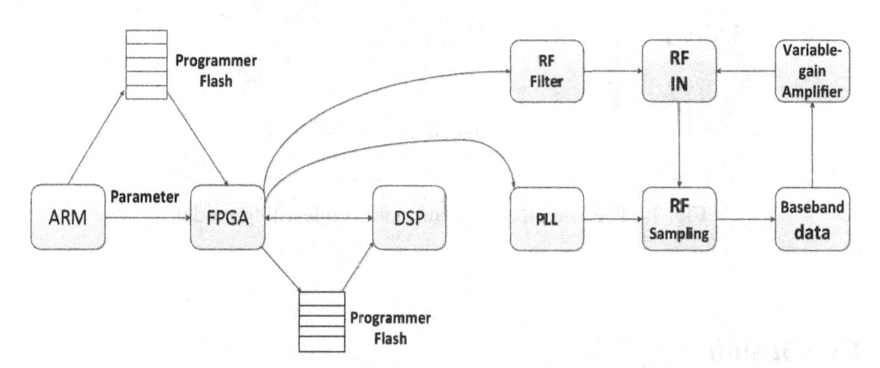

Fig. 6. Hardware processing platform re-configurable design

3.4 Deep Learning of Platform

In this design, the RFSoc is used to implement the deep learning algorithm. Firstly, the selected neural network structure type and deep learning framework are determined according to relevant tasks. Second, the network training is completed on the PC, so that the accuracy of the network meets the expected requirements. Third, the specific architecture of the deep learning model is determined and the neural network IP core is written by using high-level comprehensive tools. Fourth, a neural network computing engine matching the trained deep neural network is constructed on the RFSoc. Finally, the program running on the ARM within RFSoc is written to test the whole classifier.

According to the results analysis of hardware and software co-design during the implementation of deep learning algorithm model based on RFSoc, the acquisition of target data and weight data, the post-processing of the prediction results of deep neural network, the data scheduling and other control parts can be put into the processing unit (PS) part of the RFSoc hardware platform. The convolution of neural network, which contains a large number of multiplier and parallel computing, is implemented in the powerful programmable logic part (PL). The processing platform mainly includes external memory DDR4, processing unit (PS), on-chip cache, programmable logic (PL), and bus interconnection. Among them, the PS is responsible for data scheduling of the whole neural network and the PL is responsible for neural network acceleration. The overall architecture of deep learning model based on RFSoc is shown in Fig. 7.

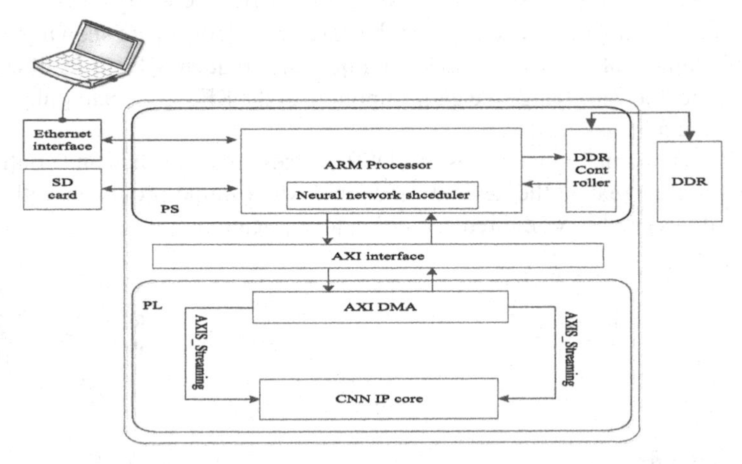

Fig. 7. The overall architecture of deep learning model

4 Conclusion

In this paper, a design scheme of space-borne multifunctional integration platform is presented. The platform has the ability of direct RF sampling and high-speed data processing. At the same time, the platform is characterized by low power consumption, small size, light weight and reconfiguration. It provides a new way to solve many problems of traditional hardware platform. Therefore the designed platform can be widely used in aerospace equipment, which can greatly reduce the hardware cost of the upgrade system and can improve the data processing capacity.

References

1. Wang, Y.: Design and implementation of hardware platform for high-speed data acquisition and playing system. Mod. Electron. Tech. **39**(17) (2016)
2. Shan, Y., Xie, L., Yang, Y., Wang, D.: Design of hardware platform for flight control system based on DSP and FPGA. Fire Control Command Control **42**(11) (2017)
3. Jia, C., Chen, S., Yang, X.: A design of multichannel universal baseband processing hardware platform. J. Telemetry Tracking Command **33**(4) (2012)
4. Cheng, Q., Liu, X., Liu, Z.: Design of reconfigurable mode for hardware platform based on software definition radio technology. Mod. Electron. Tech. **42**(11) (2017)
5. Xiao-niu, Y.: From software radio to cognitive radio: prospect of wireless communication development. Chin. Acad. Electron. Sci. J. **3**(1), 1–7 (2008)
6. Zhang, P., Zhang, C., Zhao, Y., Xu, X.: Design of software radio platform based on ZYNQ-7000 FPGA and AD9361. Exp. Technol. Manage. **36**(8) (2019)
7. Yang, Y., Yuan, Y., Tian, L.: Experimental teaching of communication based on software platform. Exp. Technol. Manage. **34**(4) (2015)
8. Zhu, J.: Software radio platform SoftBand Software Radio Summarize. Microprocessors **4** (2000)
9. Zynq UltraScale+ RFSoC Data Sheet: Overview
10. UltraScale Architecture and Product Data Sheet: Overview
11. Zeng, D., Ding, G.: Heterogeneous multicore architecture software and hardware platform for baseband processing. Microcontrollers Embed. Syst. (2017)
12. Crockett, L.H.: The Zynq book: embedded processing with the ARM Cortex-A9 on the Xilinx Zynq-7000 all programmable SoC. Strathclyde Academic Media (2014)
13. Liu, W., Tang, J., Xu, H., Zhang, N.: Design of software radar signal processing platform based on TMS320C6678. Sci. Technol. Eng. **16**(20) (2016)
14. Deng, B.: Boot loader configuration and implement based on multicore DSP TMS320C6678. Aeronaut. Comput. Tech. **47**(1) (2017)
15. Zhang-ru, Z., Hong-min, W., Dong, L., et al.: Design of radar signal processor based on TMS320C6678. Ind. Control Comput. **25**(11), 14–15 (2012)

Research on Total Probability Digital Channelization Technique Without Blind Zone

Ding-kun Ma(✉), Yu Du, Chang-Zhi Xu, Ying-zhao Shao, Su-jun Wang, and Yi-Fan Ping

China Academy of Space Technology (Xi'an), Xian 710100, China
madingkun@163.com, yangweichao2008@163.com, sandy_xu@126.com, daisyshao1983@126.com, 1036727331@qq.com, pingyf1982@126.comss

Abstract. Based on the problems of blind zone and overlap in the traditional digital channelization model, it is hard to meet the requirements of total probability detection in modern electronic reconnaissance receiver. The paper proposes a kind of overlapping digital channelization model, the processed signal is joint together seamlessly in frequency domain, making the detection of cross channelization signal possible. The proposed algorithm is simulated and tested by actual data sampled by AD, the results validate high efficiency of the proposed algorithm, and it can be applied in the situation of total probability detection for non-cooperation signal receiving.

Keyword: Broad-band signal receiver · Total probability detection · No-blind-zone · No-overlap · Channel division with overlap

1 Introduction

Electronics' probing receiver is an Indispensable part of electronic reconnaissance system, it can intercept, analyze and identify a target radiation, playing an important role in the battlefield district [1, 2]. Ideal electronics' probing receiver can detect and process various signals in all frequency band by 100% timely. The receiver based on digital channelization technique without blind zone provides a solution for this requirement [3].

Digital channelization technique that the paper studies, adopts the trick of parallel channel processing and efficient poly-phase filter, FFT transform simplifies the process of realization and raises the real-time process capability. The overlap channelization and frequency patching techniques that the algorithm adopted resolve the problem of blind zone among the channels, and avoid the filter boundary effect, so that the receiver can intercept signals in all cases. The techniques raise the performance of receiver and can be applied in various situations.

Q. Wu et al. (Eds.): WiSATS 2020, LNICST 358, pp. 480–486, 2021.
https://doi.org/10.1007/978-3-030-69072-4_39

2 Algorithm Principle

2.1 Channelization Division Without Blind Zone

The way to divide channel and choose stack are the key for digital channelization technique, it determines the complexity of following signal processing and receiver's performance [4]. In order to establish the model of digital channelization receiver [6, 7], the channel can be devised as follow:

$$w_k = \left[k - (2D-1)/4\right] \times 2\pi/D \tag{1}$$

$$k = 0, 1, 2, \Lambda, \quad D-1$$

w_k is the center frequency for k channel, $D(D = 8)$ is data extracting rate, in order to realize the signal intercept capability without blind zone. The most simple way is to make use of the signal's spectrum symmetry, the study divides the channel in odd number. Widening the filter's pass-band properly, enable that the channel pass-band overlaps and lowers the blind zone, special channel from symmetry spectrum can be chosen for signal detecting. According to sampling theory, lowing the sampling rate, then widening the filter pass-band, can avoid signal overlapping between the signals, the channel dividing without blind zone is shown as follow (Fig. 1):

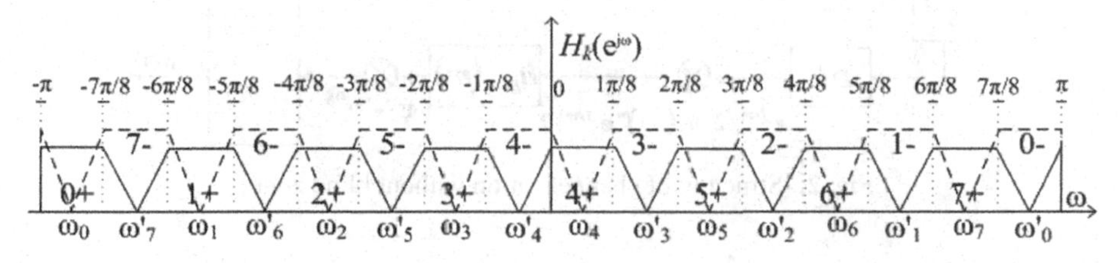

Fig. 1. Way to divide channle.

2.2 Principle of Digital Channelization Model Without Blind Zone

The principle of digital channelization model without blind zone is as follow:

$$\begin{aligned} y_k(m) &= \left\{\left[x(n)e^{jw_k n}\right] * h(n)\right\} n = mD \\ &= \left\{\sum_{i=-\infty}^{+\infty} \left[x(n-i)e^{jw_k(n-i)}\right] \cdot h(i)\right\} n = mD \\ &= \sum_{i=-\infty}^{+\infty} \left[x(mD-i)e^{jw_k(mD-i)}\right] \cdot h(i) = \sum_{p=0}^{D-1} \sum_{i=-\infty}^{+\infty} \left[x(mD-iD-p)e^{jw_k(mD-iD-p)}\right] \cdot h(iD+p) \end{aligned} \tag{2}$$

Assume that $x_p(m) = x(mD - p)$
$h_p(m) = h(mD + p)$
Replace Eqs. (2), it can be derived as follow

$$y_k(m) = \sum_{p=0}^{D-1} \sum_{i=-\infty}^{+\infty} x_p(m-i)e^{jw_k(m-i)D} \cdot h_p(i)e^{-jw_k p}$$

$$=\sum_{p=0}^{D-1}\left\{\left[x_p(m)e^{jw_kmD}\right]*h_p(m)\right\}\cdot e^{-jw_kp}$$
$$=\sum_{p=0}^{D-1}\left\{\left\{\left[x_p(m)e^{jw_kmD}\right]*h_p(m)\right\}\cdot e^{-j\frac{(2D-1)\pi}{2D}p}\right\}e^{-j\frac{2\pi}{D}kp}$$
$$=DFT\left\{\left\{\left[x_p(m)e^{jw_kmD}\right]*h_p(m)\right\}\cdot e^{-j\frac{(2D-1)\pi}{2D}p}\right\} \quad (3)$$

The structure of channelization without blind zone is shown as Fig. 2 . If number D is even, the first item should be $e^{j\pi m/2}$, otherwise, the first item should be $(-1)^m e^{j\pi m/2}$. Assume the pass sub-band requirement for receiver is B_w, the number of channel is $D = f_s/2B_w$, the frequency interval between channel is $2\pi/D$.

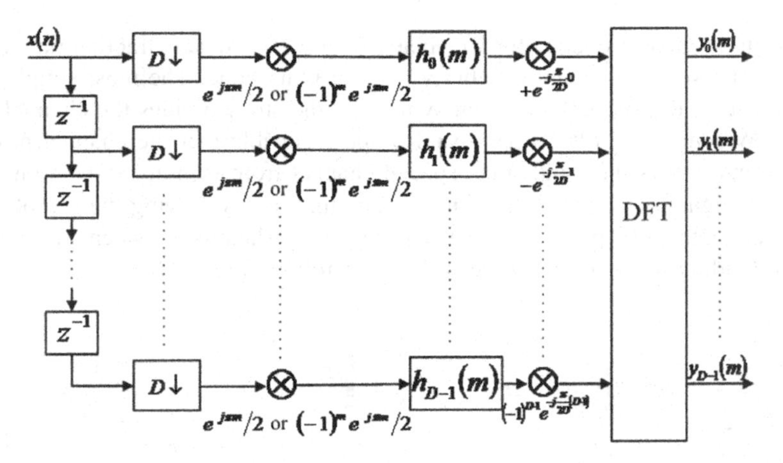

Fig. 2. Structure of channelization without blind zone

The interested signal must be pre-processed after channelization. First, the zone between channels does not mix in frequency domain, signal can be got by cutting blind zone. Second, the channel order should be adjusted to get non-distortion signal. It has two cases,

1) if the channel number D is even, sub-frequency band order "1,3,5,……,*D*-1" should be channel order "*D*/2, D/2 + 1,……,*D*-1", sub-frequency band order 2,4,6,……,*D*" should be channel order "*D* /2–1,*D* /2–2,……,0".
2) if the channel number D is odd, sub-frequency band order "1,3,5,……,*D*-1" should be channel order "(D-1)/2,(D-1)/2–1,……,0", sub-frequency band "2,4,6,……,*D*" should be channel "(*D* + 1)/2,(*D* + 1)/2 + 1,……,*D*-1".

In order to detect the interested signal that bestride two channels with total probability, signal distributing at full frequency band should be got, the channelization result should be joint such as in Fig. 3.

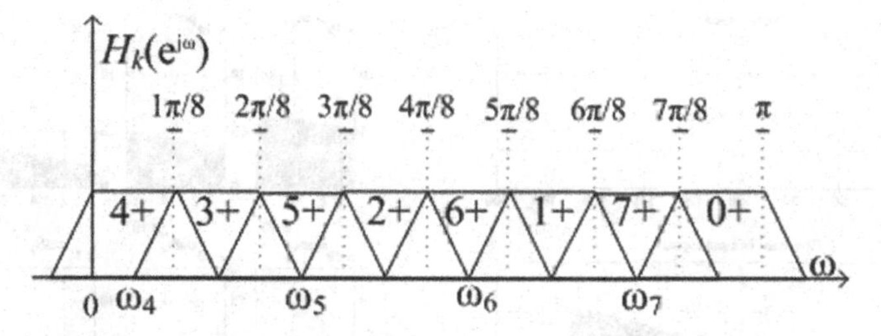

Fig. 3. Signal analysis mode in wide pass band

3 Experiment Validation

The line frequency modulation signal and sampling signal by AD are adopted to verify the algorithm proposed in this paper.

3.1 Line Frequency Modulation Signal

As process of float computing is very complicated in FPGA, and consume much more hardware resource. In order to make algorithm running more efficient, float number is adjust to integer number in the algorithm computing.

In order to verify the advantage of algorithm more efficient, line frequency modulation signal is designed, the frequency band is from 1 MHz to 256 MHz, step is 0.5 MHz, sampling rate is 512 MHz, the amplitude is positive to the value of instantaneous frequency. The order of poly-phase filter is 16×8, the channel band is 64 MHz, experiment results is as shown in Fig. 4.

It can be seen from the Fig. 4 that, the spectrum have been jointed reflects the basic current of signal, unitary err is less than 2.5%, there is not any signal loss in the joint spectrum, and the jointed spectrum result meet the requirement of total probability for signal detecting. At the same time, on the condition that processing capability of the same point of FFT, the spectrum of channelization without blind zone can raise the frequency resolution by 400% (D = 8). The method can be applied in situation for higher frequency resolution and lower FFT points, the method resolves problem of large number of FFT points with limited FFT points in hardware(FPGA).

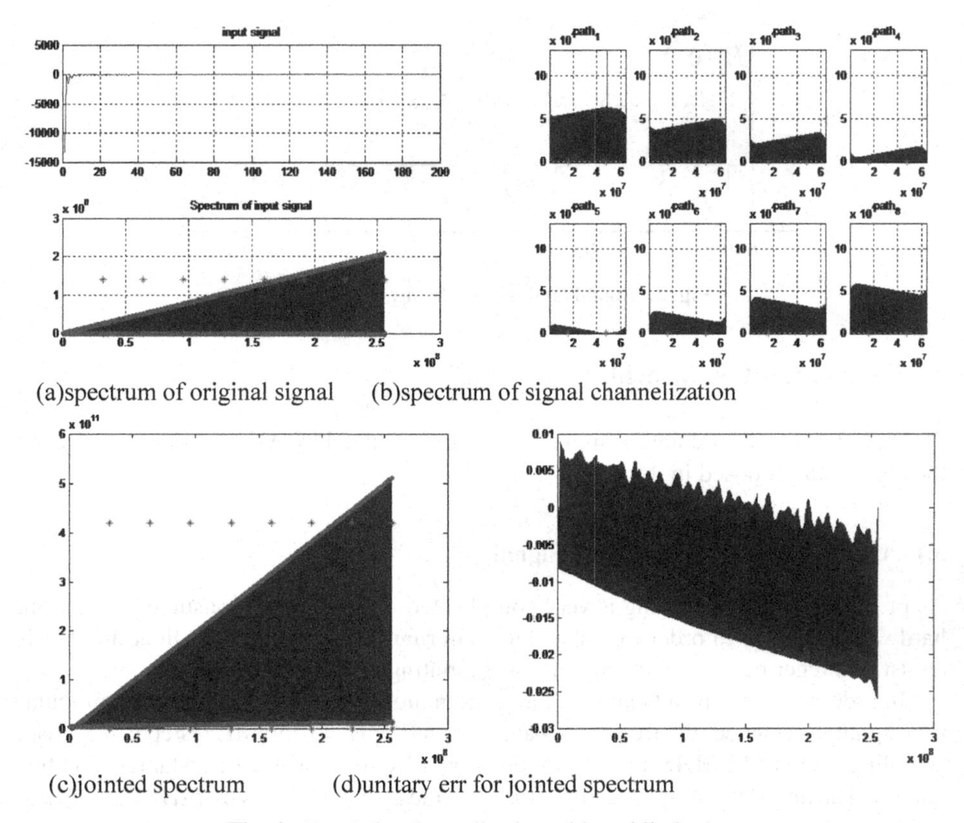

(a)spectrum of original signal (b)spectrum of signal channelization

(c)jointed spectrum (d)unitary err for jointed spectrum

Fig. 4. Result for channelization without blind zone.

3.2 Sampling Signal by AD

The composite communication signal in this section is generated by sampling actual signal with AD, it is consist of BPSK, AM, QPSK, 16QMAM, sampling rate is 70 MHz, order of poly-phase filter is 16×8, sub-band width is 4.375 MHz. The result is shown in Fig. 5.

It can be seen from the Fig. 5 that, the jointed spectrum can reflects the frequency character of composite communication signal, unitary err for jointed spectrum can be seen in Fig. 5(d). One thing need to explain is that, the power of composite communication signal in frequency domain distributes asymmetrically, unitary err is computed based on maxim of spectrum power, resulting that maxim appears in strongest part in spectrum.

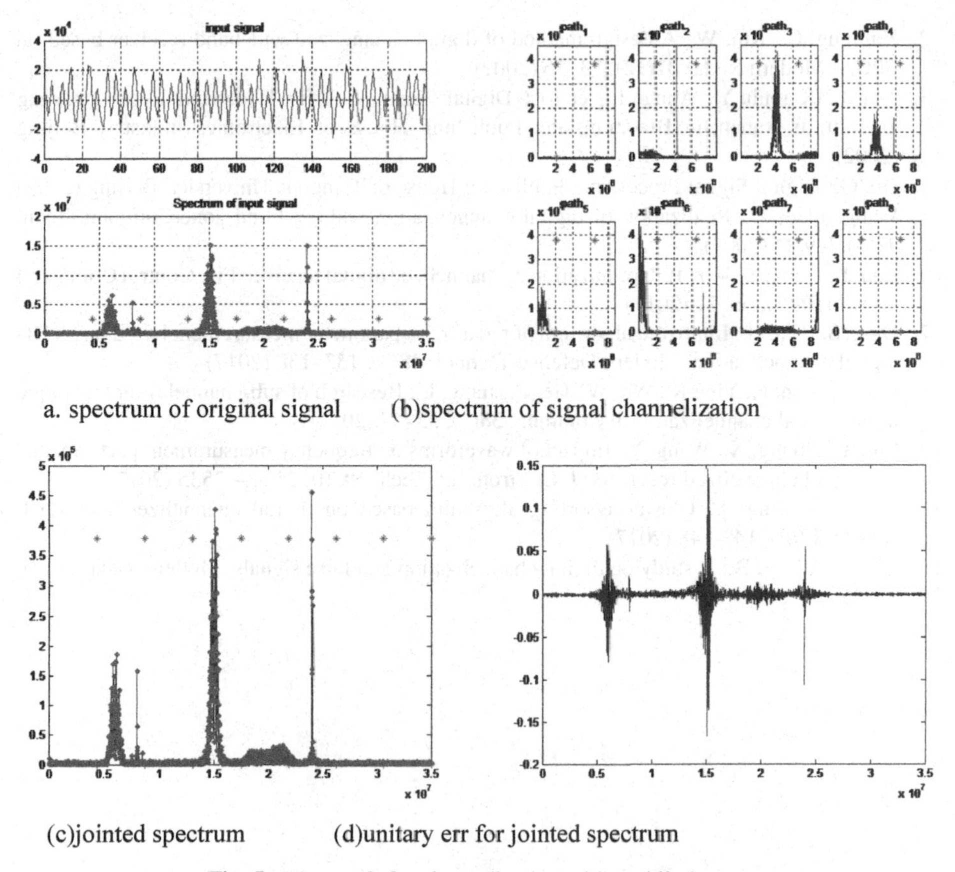

Fig. 5. The result for channelization without blind zone.

4 Conclusion

The paper proposes a method for digital channelization technique without blind zone, the channel is divided with overlapping by 50%, so that the signal can be detected with total probability in frequency domain. At the same time, the method adopts FFT structure, simplifying the complexity for designing, solving the problem that digital channelization technique can be realized more effectively. The method can sort the signal in frequency domain, lower the velocity of signal stream. Weakening the pressure for signal processing, so that the hardware can work in a lower clock. The method has been applied in a electronics' probing receiver successfully, it can meet the requirement for detecting non-cooperative signal continually in frequency domain.

References

1. Zhou, X., Wu, Y.: The research and improvement of a high efficient channelized algorithm based on polyphase filter . Signal Process. **24**(1), 45–48 (2008)

2. Haihong, C., Xin, W.: A design method of digital channelized wideband receiver based on FPGA. Modern Radar **31**(12), 73–76 (2009)
3. Tsui,J., Xiaoniu,Y., Annan,L., et a1.: Digital Techniques for Wideband Receivers.Yang xiaoniu,Lu Annan,Jin Biao,translate. Publishing House of Electronics Industry, Beijing (2002)
4. Hu, G.: Digital Signal Processing. Publishing House of Tsinghua University, Beijing (2003)
5. Wang, J,Ge, X.: Realization of digital channelization without blind zone.Commun. Tech. **42**(3):7–9,24 (2009).
6. Zou, J., Wang, Z., Yan, P.: Optimization of channelized digital receiver. Fire Control Command Control **36**(7), 68–71 (2011)
7. Ding, S., Xia, H.: Improved algorithm of radar pulse parameter measurement based on STFT-digital channelization. Modern Defence Technol. **48**(3), 133–138 (2017)
8. He, D., Wen, F., Ying R., Wu, W., He, C., Jiang, L.: Research of sub-channel filter technique in the digital channelization.J. Commun. **38**(1), 53–57 (2017)
9. Liu, Y., Huang, X., Wang, Y.: Impact of waveforms on frequency measurement performance for digital channelized receivers. J. Electron. Inf. Tech. **39**(10) 2531—2535 (2017)
10. Zhang, Y.,Tang, J.: Clusteringsorting algorithm based on digital channelized receiver.J. CAEIT **12**(2), 143-148 (2017)
11. Gui, Y., Wang, B.: A study on digital channelization and false signals. Modem Radar **38**(3), 23–27 (2016)

Multi-modem Implementation Method Based on Deep Autoencoder Network

Peng Wei[1], Ruimin Lu[1](✉), Shilian Wang[2], and Shijun Xie[1]

[1] 63rd Research Institute, National University of Defense Technology, NanJing 210007, China
weipengcss@163.com, Luruiminpaper@163.com, xsjxsj520@163.com
[2] College of Electronic Science, National University of Defense Technology, Changsha 410073, China
wangsl@nudt.edu.cn

Abstract. With the fierce competition for electromagnetic spectrum, the development of intelligent satellite communication systems with intelligent waveform generation and reconstruction capabilities is an effective means to adapt satellite communication system to the harsh electromagnetic environment. In this paper, a 10-layer deep autoencoder network (DAN) is designed, and 2-ary to 64-ary modem are implemented based on this 10-layer DAN. During this process, a unified loss function and a unified optimization algorithm are utilized to train and test the 10-layer DAN. Finally, the demodulation performance, that is close to, consistent with or better than that of traditional MPSK or QAM is obtained. The above-mentioned DAN and its training method provide a new way for waveform generation and reconstruction in intelligent communication satellites. In addition, the high-order modulation constellation generated by this 10-layer DAN is quite different from the traditional modulation method and very difficult to distinguish linearly, which is beneficial to improve the anti-intercept ability of the satellite communication waveform.

Keywords: Satellite communications · Deep learning · Deep autoencoder network · Modem · Anti-interception

1 Introduction

Satellite communication has been more and more widely used due to its advantages of wide coverage, long distance transmission, and freedom from terrain. However, there are many aspects that need to be resolved, such as single satellite function, difficulty in upgrading and maintaining, and weak ability to adapt to complex electromagnetic environments. On the other hand, the third wave of artificial intelligence represented by deep learning and reinforcement learning is infiltrating or even subverting the traditional industry at an unprecedented

Q. Wu et al. (Eds.): WiSATS 2020, LNICST 358, pp. 487–501, 2021.
https://doi.org/10.1007/978-3-030-69072-4_40

speed, depth and breadth. In strategic games, image detection classification, target recognition, voice processing, automatic translation, unmanned driving and other fields, it has shown "wisdom" beyond the human brain [1]. Therefore, combining artificial intelligence with satellite communications and using the most advanced artificial intelligence research results to improve or reshape traditional satellite communications can effectively improve the performance and security of satellite communication systems and increase their ability to adapt to complex electromagnetic environments. This is critical to winning the future intelligent warfare.

Adaptive code modulation (ACM) as a technology that can achieve a good compromise between signal capacity and reliability by adjusting the coding rate and modulation order under different channel conditions has been widely used in wireless communication systems [2]. However, this method usually needs to implement multiple coding and modulation with different orders and different rates separately, and then select a certain combination of coding and modulation to complete the communication according to the perception and decision of the channel environment. This way makes the design, implementation and hardware cost of the communication system multiply. To this end, a realization method of 2-ary to 64-ary modem based on the unified DAN [3], which is different from the traditional modem based on expert design, is proposed in this paper. In this new method, a 10-layer DAN is adopted, training set is generated using random number, and a unified optimization algorithm, a unified loss function, and some certain signal-to-noise ratio (SNR) are utilized to train the 10-layer DAN. Test results show that, the 10-layer DAN can convergence in a relatively short time for all of 2-ary to 64-ary modem, and the demodulation performance is close to, consistent with or batter than that of traditional modem. So it provides a new way of realizing the waveform generation and reconstruction or ACM for satellite communication intelligent.

The research related to this paper mainly includes the end-to-end communication system based on unsupervised learning proposed by T. J. O'Shea et al. [4–7]. Among them, unsupervised representation learning of radio communication signals was studied in raw sampled time series representation, and convolutional autoencoder was used to learn the modulation basis function and visually recognize their relationship to the analytic bases used in digital communications in [4]. By optimizing the reconstruction loss during channel autoencoder through a series of channel regularizes, new modulation schemes were learned in [5], which blurs the boundary between modulation and error correction decoding, and provides similar capacity and error performance with lower complexity and without expert design. By Combining with random delay, frequency difference, phase difference, delay extension and other channel impairments, the bit error performance under different loss functions, different network connection methods (DNN, CNN), and different activation functions was evaluated in [5]. Results showed that the bit error performance can exceed the traditional QPSK demodulation under certain conditions. Furthermore, in order to solve the performance degradation in the case of large delay expansion, an attention mechanism was introduced to expand the use of the model. In [7], the advantages of deep learning in the field of communication, such as complex channel learning, overall optimization, efficient approximation of arbitrary functions, distributed parallel architecture and dedicated high-efficiency processing chips were pointed out, end-to-end modeled with autoencoder network was setup, and performance close to that of traditional communication systems was achieved under some specific parameters. In [6], the design and training method of the wireless communication physical layer based on the deep generation adversarial network (GAN) were proposed, in which the deep GAN was used to learn wireless channel characteristics and establish a passed back from receiver to sender. Hao He et al. also completed a similar work in [8], and the performance similar to the traditional communication was acquired under additive Gaussian noise or Rayleigh fading channels. Using software radio and open source deep learning software library, S. Dorner et al. [9] built, trained and run a complete communication system based entirely on deep neural networks (DNN), extended block-based transmissions to continuous data transmission. An additional frame synchronization module based on deep network was introduced to solve the synchronization problem. Without a lot of overparameter tuning, the performance deteriorated within 1 dB compared with traditional software radio demodulation. Yang Yaodong et al. [10] applied the stack sparse autocoder (SSAE) network to the demodulation of multi-position phase shift keying (MPPSK), and obtained a demodulation performance of 1–2 orders of magnitude better than the traditional demodulation. Huang Yuanyuan et al. [11] applied the deep confidence network to the feature extraction and recognition of communication signals, and the simulation showed a 0.4 dB performance improvement over the traditional modem method for MPSK modem.

In the overview of applying deep learning to wireless communication, Q. Mao et al. [1] comprehensively introduced the advantages of deep learning and deep reinforcement learning applied to wireless networks. On this basis, they listed the application of deep reinforcement learning at all layers of the system and analyzed the future research trends and challenges. Zhang Jing et al. [12] summarized the development history of wireless communication. Based on the introduction of various deep learning network structures, they focused on summarizing the channel estimation of deep learning in large-scale MIMO scenarios, signal detection in OFDM systems, CSI feedback and reconstruction, channel decoding, and end-to-end wireless communication system applications. From the perspective of system design mode, adaptability to channel changes and the current powerful computing power based on parallel GPU, Guiguan et al. [13] pointed out the potential of deep learning in the field of communication, provided the application of deep learning network in modulation recognition and beam forming, and analyzed its structure and superior performance. Finally, they pointed out the lack of common data sets, the lack of common models suitable for communication scenarios, the excessive number of parameters in the application to small terminals, as well as the physical layer security problems, and gave a preliminary solution.

In above work, the most similar to the research in this paper is [5,6]. In these two references, modems of multiple (n, k) combinations, including (2, 2), (4, 4), (7, 4), (8, 8), were realized through autoencoder network. When a symbol $s \in M$ is sending, the width of the input layer is $M = 2^k$, the width of the output layer the sending end is n, and the receiving end performs M classification output to restore the sending symbol $\hat{s} \in M$. A total $(2M + 1)(M + N) + 2M$ of training parameters are required. The minimization cross-entropy loss function is used as the optimization goal, and the minimum gradient descent method (SGD) is used for training. Although the performance of this method consistent with or better than that of traditional code modulation method. But a different network structure was utilized for each (n, k), which is not conducive to the efficient implementation and reconstruction of multiple code modulations. In addition, only I and Q signals can be transmitted on the actual channel, while in [5,6], n-channels of data are transmitted directly, which brings about spatial diversity gain, thus obtains superior performance to the traditional encoding and modulation. Therefore, this comparison is little far from reasonable.

In view of the deficiencies of above work, we focus on the realization of multi-modem based on a unified DAN architecture, in the hope of providing a new implementation method for intelligent and efficient waveform generation and reconstruction for satellite communication systems, and improving the anti-intercept ability of the waveform. Practical work is as follows:

1) A 10-layer DAN is designed, and base on this 10-layer DAN, 2-ary to 64-ary modems are realized with a unified DL network architecture, a unified loss function and a unified optimization algorithm. The parameters of each layer and the optimization training method are given.
2) For each of 2-ary to 64-ary modem, the modulation constellation, symbol mapping relationship, network convergence speed and performance comparison with traditional demodulation methods are simulated. The results show that, under the white noise channel, the performance of 2-ary and 4-ary modem based on the 10-layer DAN is completely consistent with that of BPSK and QPSK respectively, the performance of 8-ary and 64-ary modem is better than that of 8QAM and 64QAM respectively, and the performance of 16-ary and 32-ary modem is close to that of 16QAM and 32QAM respectively.

The following chapters of this paper are arranged as follows: In Sect. 2, the 10-layer DAN architecture is designed, and the parameter configuration of each layer, loss function and optimization algorithm are tried and selected. The training results and demodulation performance of multi-modem based on the 10-layer DAN are presented in Sect. 3. In Sect. 4, a brief summary of the paper is given, and further research directions is proposed.

2 Multi-modem Model Based on DAN

After many trial and error, we find that the 10-layer DAN model shown in Fig. 1 can achieve the best performance for 2-ary to 64-ary modem with fewer parameters. The 10-layer DAN is mainly composed of a compression encoder for modulation at the sending end, a decompression decoder for demodulation at the receiving end, a optimization goals which minimize the loss function, and a optimization algorithm for updating all trainable parameter.

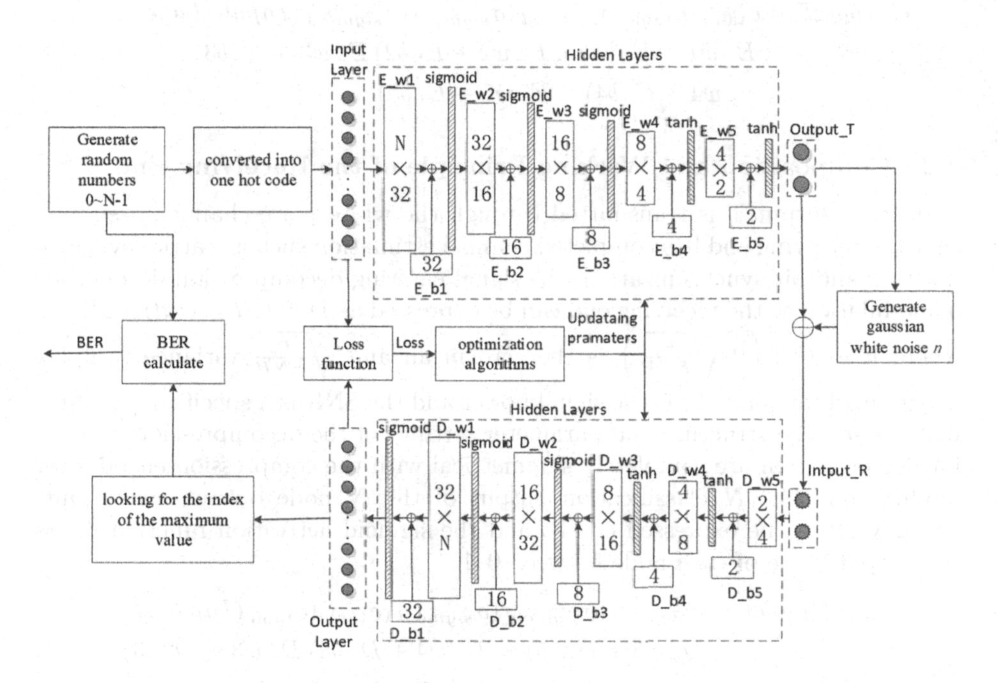

Fig. 1. Multi-modem model based on DAN.

2.1 Composition and Working Principle of the Sending End

At the sending end, random transmission symbols $s \in \{0, 1, 2, \cdots, N-1\}$ are generated according to N, which is the ary of the transmission symbol. Then, they are converted into a one hot code and input the compression encoder for modulation. The compression encoder consists of an N-node input layer (Input_Layer), 5 hidden layers (Hidden_Layers) and a 2-node output layer (Output_T). Among them, the five hidden layer weight parameters E_w1, E_w2, E_w3, E_w4 and E_w5 are $N \times 32$, 32×16, 16×8, 8×4 and 4×2 matrices respectively, and the offset parameters E_b1, E_b2, E_b3, E_b4 and E_b5 are 32, 16, 8, 4 and 2 column vectors respectively. The output of the Hidden_Layers 1, 2, and 3 uses the sigmoid activation function [14], as shown in (1), and the layers 4 and 5 use the tanh activation function [14], as shown in (2). After passing through Hidden_Layers, Output_T can be equivalent to the modulated I and Q signals of the sending end, as shown in (3), its value is limited to -1–1 by the tanh activation function.

$$\sigma_{sigmoid}(x) = \frac{x}{1+e^{-x}} \tag{1}$$

$$\sigma_{\tanh}(x) = \frac{e^{x}-e^{-x}}{e^{x}+e^{-x}} \tag{2}$$

$$\begin{aligned} Output\_T = {} & \sigma_{\tanh}(\sigma_{\tanh}(\sigma_{sigmoid}(\sigma_{sigmoid}(\sigma_{sigmoid}(Input\_Layer \\ & \times E\_w1 + E\_b1) \times E\_w2 + E\_b2)\, E\_w3 + E\_b3) \\ & \times E\_w4 + E\_b4) \times E\_w5 + E\_b5) \end{aligned} \tag{3}$$

2.2 Composition and Working Principle of the Receiving End

After the Output_T is transmitted through the white noise channel, assuming that the receiving end has completed channel estimation such as carrier synchronization and bit synchronization, the signal entering decompression decoder for demodulation at the receiving end can be expressed as $Input\_R = Output\_T + n$, where $n \sim CN\left(0, \sqrt{\frac{P_s}{SNR}}\right)$ is the zero mean and $\sqrt{\frac{P_s}{SNR}}$ variance complex gaussian white noise, P_s is the signal power and the SNR is a specified signal-to-noise ratio. The structure and parameter settings of the decompression decoder for demodulation are completely symmetrical with the compression encoder for modulation. The N classification output of the N node output layer (Output_Layer) can be expressed as (4), and the sigmoid activation function limits the output value of each node between 0–1.

$$\begin{aligned} Output\_Layer = {} & \sigma_{sigmoid}(\sigma_{sigmoid}(\sigma_{sigmoid}(\sigma_{\tanh}(\sigma_{\tanh}(Input\_R \\ & \times D\_w5 + D\_b5) \times D\_w4 + D\_b4)\, D\_w3 + D\_b3) \\ & \times D\_w2 + D\_b2) \times D\_w1 + D\_b1) \end{aligned} \tag{4}$$

The estimate of transmitted symbols $\hat{s}$ are obtained by looking for the index of the maximum value in the N nodes of $Output\_Layer$, and the bit error rate (BER) can be obtained by comparing $\hat{s}$ with transmit symbols s.

2.3 Optimization Objective and Optimization Algorithm

The optimization objective is to minimize the mean square error (MSE) loss function between the Input_Layer and the Output_Layer of the 10-layer DAN, as shown in (5). Where π is the parameter set that contains all the weight parameters and bias parameters to be optimized, and B is the number of symbols for each training in the mini-batch training process.

$$\min_{\pi}(loss) = \frac{1}{B}\min_{\pi}\left(\sum_{n=1}^{B}\sum_{i=1}^{N}(Output\_Layer[i] - Input\_Layer[i])^2\right) \tag{5}$$

AdaDelta algorithm [15] is chosen as the optimization algorithm, whose parameter update formula is shown in (6)

$$\pi_{t+1} = \pi_t - \frac{\eta}{\sqrt{E(g^2)_t + \varepsilon}} \times g_t \tag{6}$$

Where η is the initial learning rate and g_t represents the gradient at the t th iteration, ε is a minimum value added to prevent the denominator from being 0, $E(\cdot)$ represents expectation operation, and $E(g^2)_t = \rho E(g^2)_{t-1} - (1-\rho)\, g_t^2$ is the weighted average of the historical gradient squared and the current gradient squared, ρ represents the attenuation coefficient, and its value range is 0–1.

3 Training and Test Verification of the Multi-modem Based on DAN

3.1 Training of the Multi-modem Based on DAN

All parameters to be trained are initialized to small random numbers. The training set includes 4000 random integers ranging from 0 to N−1. After many experiments, it has been verified that 7 dB SNR and 10,000 rounds of training, 12 dB SNR and 20,000 rounds of training, and 13 dB SNR and 30,000 rounds of training are suitable for 16-ary and its below, 32-ary, and 64-ary modem respectively.

Using small batch training method [16], each batch is trained with 1000 symbols, and the white noise added into Output_T is regenerated during each batch training process. This method of generating white noise can be used as a Tikhonov regularization [17], which effectively prevents the 10-layer DAN from overfitting. The initial learning rate is set to $\eta = 0.2$, the attenuation coefficient is set to $\rho = 0.95$, and the minimum constant to prevent the denominator from being 0 when updating gradient is set to $\varepsilon = 1 \times 10^{-8}$. The test set contains regenerated 100,000-symbol random numbers. During the process of training, the MSE loss is outputted and the BER is calculated every each 200 rounds of training. simultaneously, the generalization ability of the 10-layer DAN is also detected.

The 10-layer DAN for Multi-modem uses TensorFlow [18] and single CPU for training. It takes about 5–8 totally for 200 rounds of training, a MSE loss calculating, a performance testing of 0–14 dB SNR, and an outputting of observed variables and graphics, which is increasing gradually from 2-ary to 128-ary. Therefore, the training for a certain modem can be completed within a few minutes.

Every set of parameters, which are trained and verified against one certain modem, can be stored, and then loaded according to the recognition and decision results of the channel environment in practice use. Transfer learning can be carried out against a specified layer or newly added layers, so that the trained Multi-modem based on DAN can quickly adapt to the new channel environment, and even be able to suppress malicious interference. These contents will be studied in depth in the follow-up works.

In addition, we also tried to use the minimized cross-entropy loss function as the optimization target to train the 10-layer DAN. When N is small, the 10-layer DAN can quickly converge, and the performance is consistent with that of the traditional modem, but when N is large, The 10-layer DAN cannot converge. For example, when $N = 16$, only 9 or 10 constellation points are formed with the cross-entropy loss function. When the Gradient Descent optimization algorithm is used, the loss value is often invalid, which result in the all parameters invalid after updating.

3.2 Training and Test Results of Multi-modem Model Based on DAN

The training and test results based on the above 10-layer DAN for 2-ary, 4-ary, 8-ary, 16-ary, 32-ary, 64-ary, and 128-ary are shown in Fig. 2, Fig. 3, Fig. 4, Fig. 5, Fig. 6, Fig. 7, and Fig. 8 respectively. Among each figure, a constellation diagram for the modulation under training SNR is shown in subfigure (a). Relationship between the MSE loss and the number of training rounds, which is output once every 200 training rounds, is shown in subfigure (b). Training symbol modulation coding constellation without noise is shown in subfigure (c). And the performance comparison between modem based the 10-layer DAN and traditional method is displayed in subfigure (d), where, "DL (N = X)" represents the performance of X-ary modem based on the 10-layer DAN under white noise channel, and "theory of XXXX" represents the theoretical performance of XXXX modem under white noise channel.

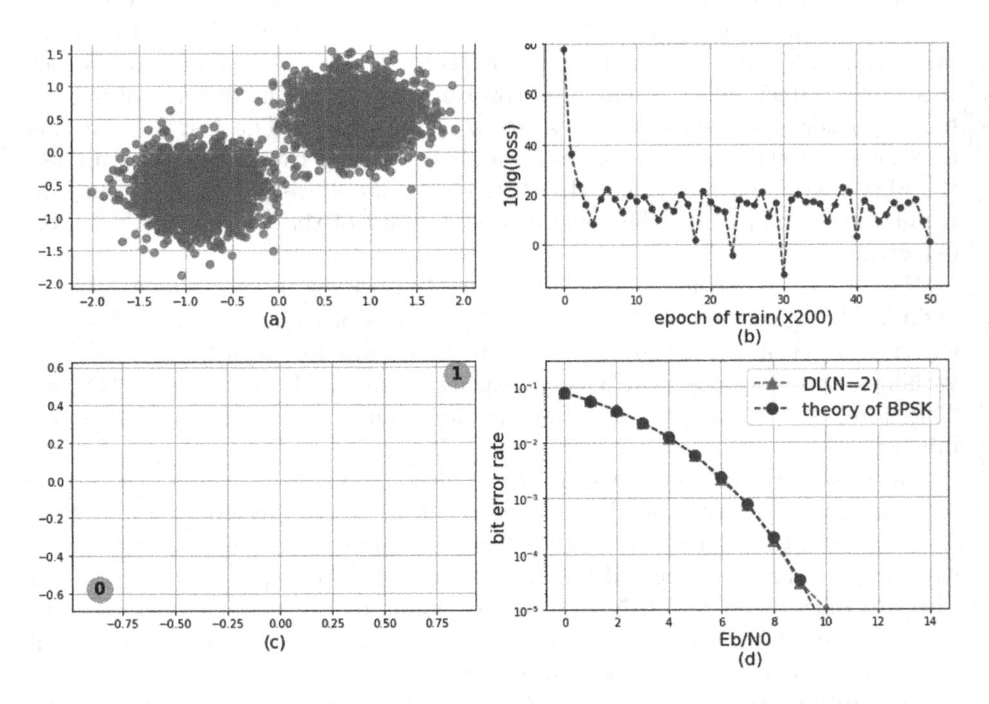

Fig. 2. 2-ary modem training results and performance comparison with BPSK.

Figure 2 and Figure 3 show that the constellation of 2-ary and 4-ary modulation based on the 10-layer DAN are consistent with traditional BPSK and QPSK

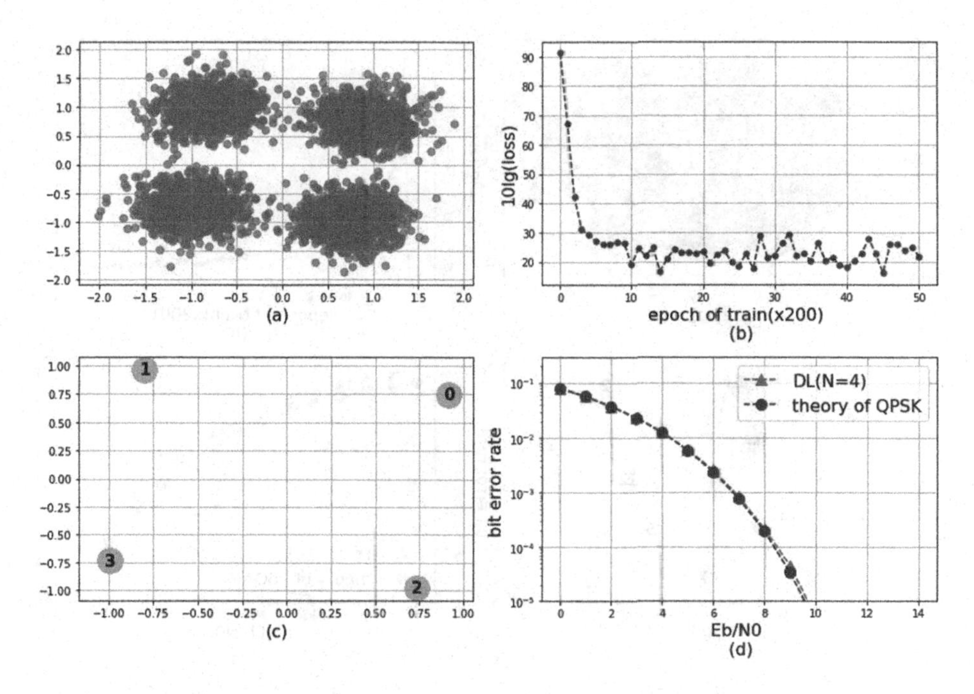

Fig. 3. 4-ary modem training results and performance comparison with QPSK.

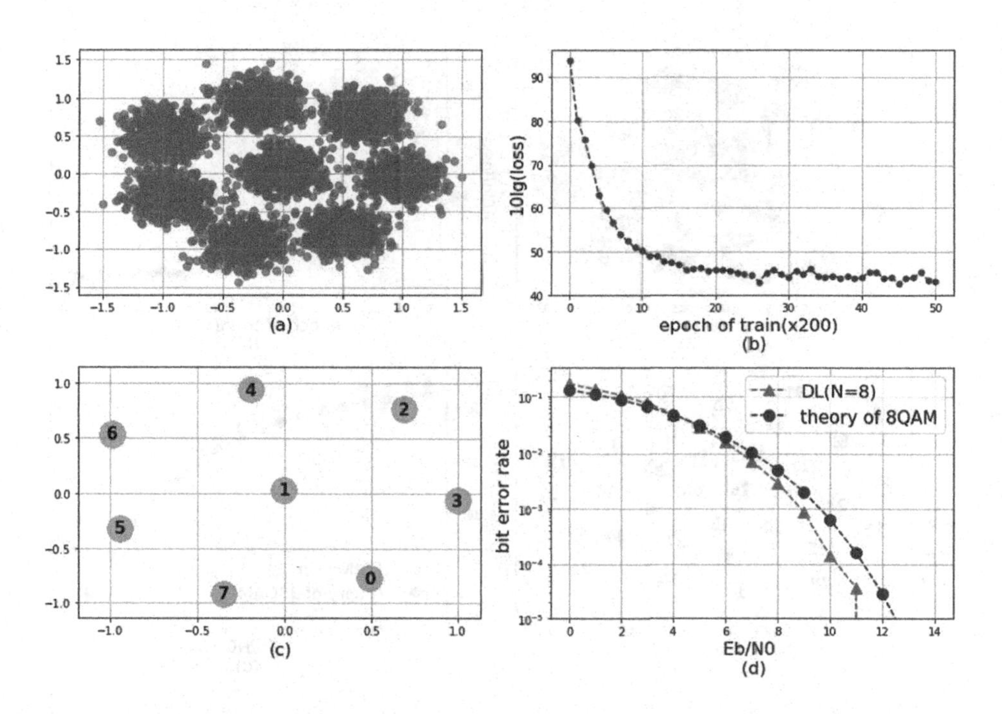

Fig. 4. 8-ary modem training results and performance comparison with 8QAM.

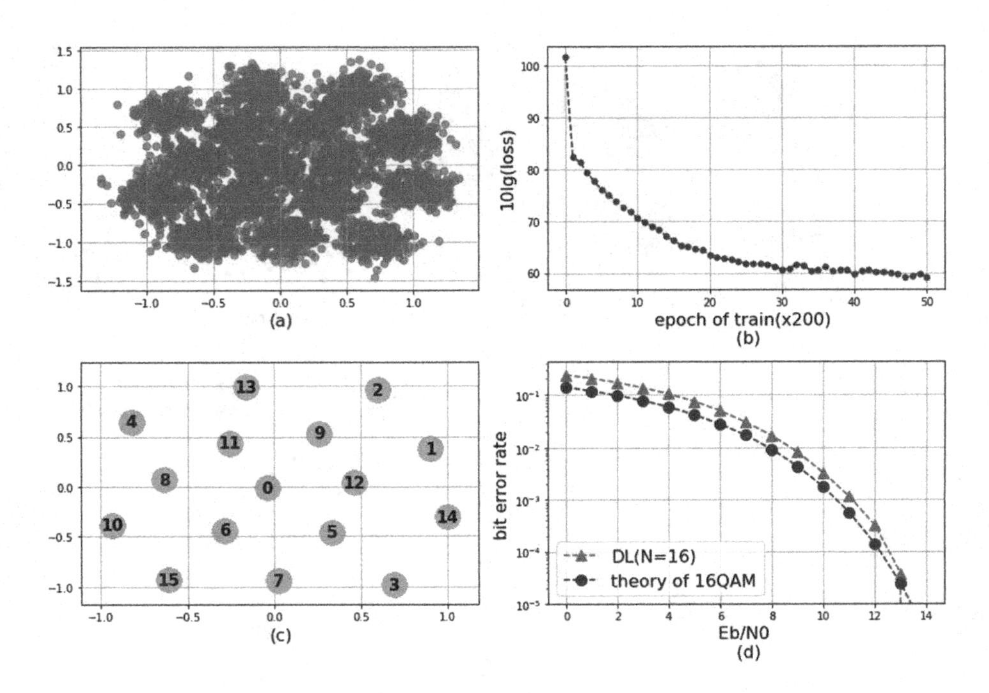

Fig. 5. 16-ary modem training results and performance comparison with 16QAM.

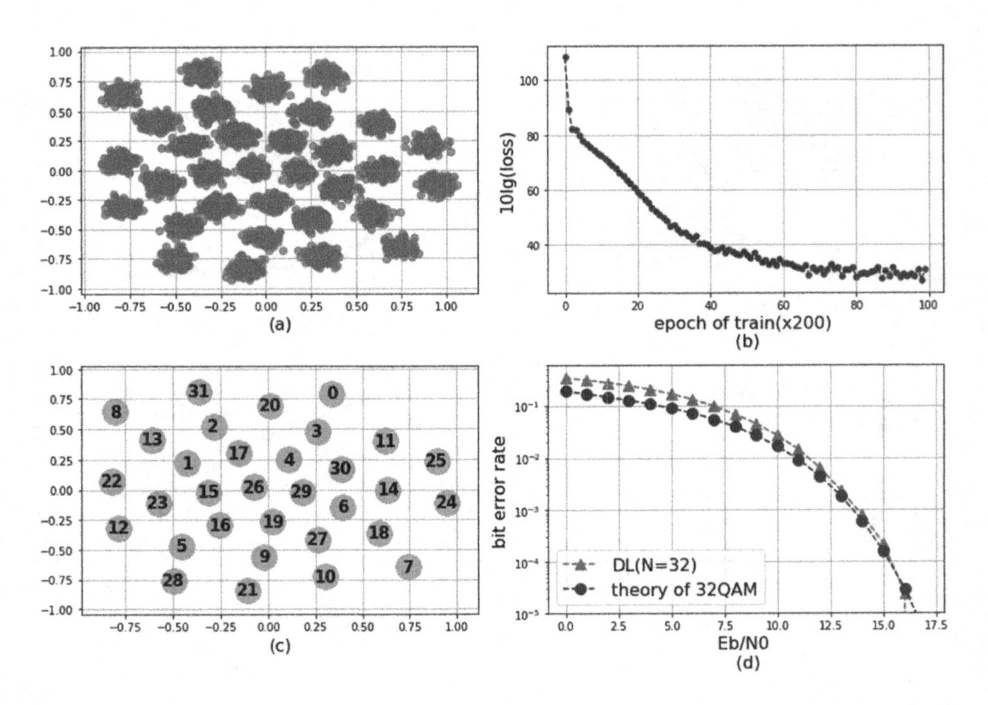

Fig. 6. 32-ary modem training results and performance comparison with 32QAM.

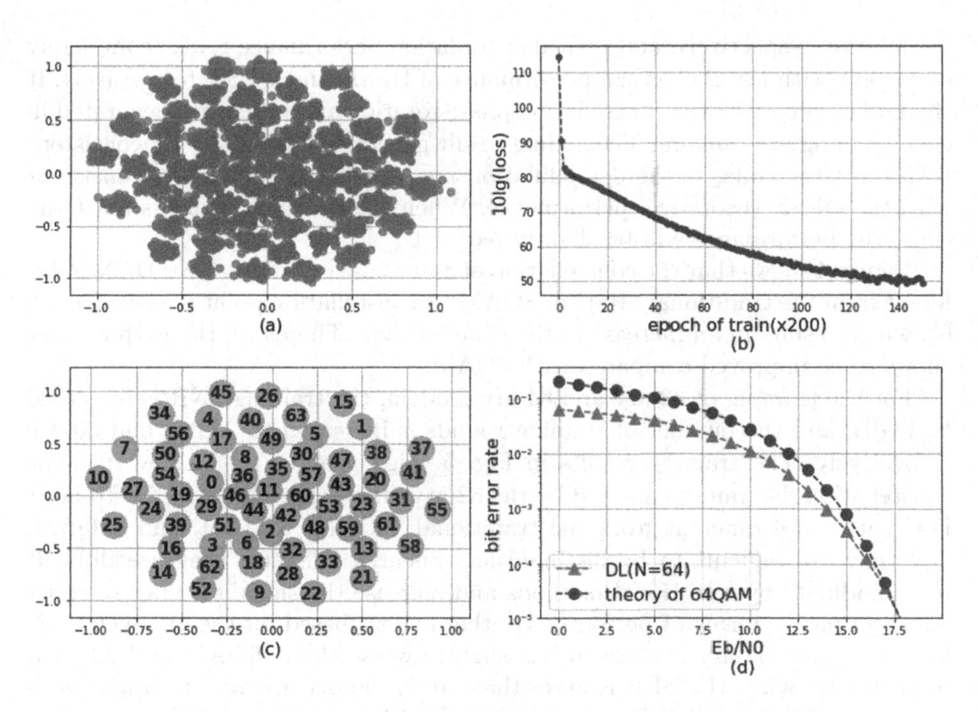

Fig. 7. 64-ary modem training results and performance comparison with 64QAM.

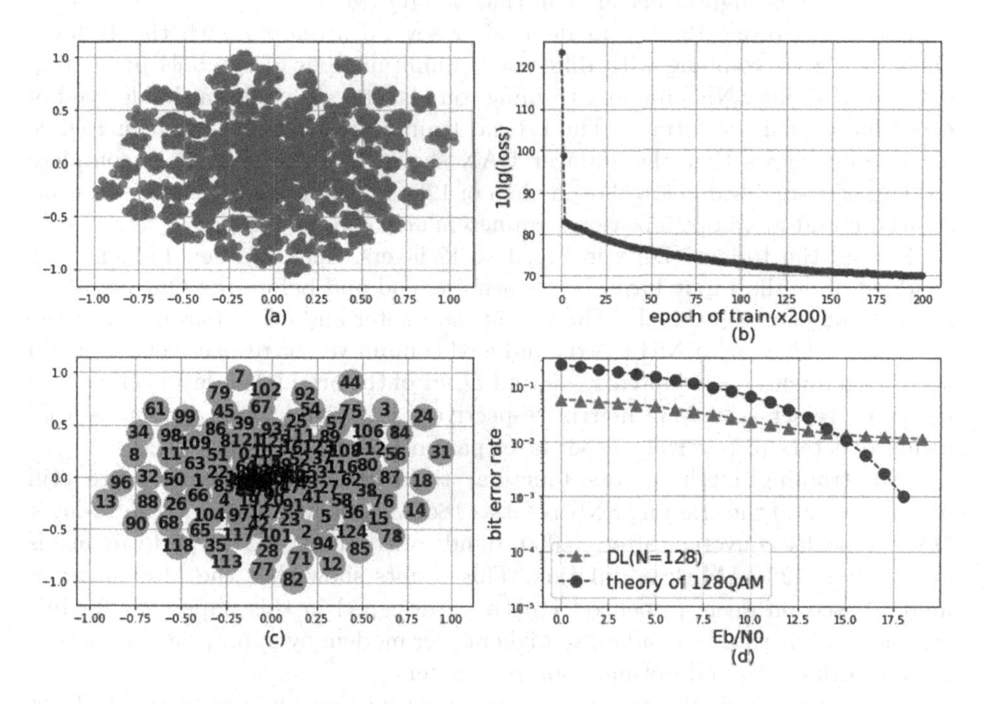

Fig. 8. 128-ary modem training results and performance comparison with 128QAM.

modulation respectively, and their demodulation performance is also completely consistent with the theoretical performance of BPSK and QPSK respectively. It should be noted that the constellation phase rotation and bit coding generated in each training are random. The coding result generated in Fig. 3(c) is consistent with the Gray code, so the demodulation performance is completely consistent with the QPSK theoretical performance. When the encoding result is not Gray code, the performance will be slightly reduced.

Figure 4 shows that the constellation of 8-ary base on the 10-layer DAN is different from the traditional 8PSK or 8QAM. A constellation point is placed at (0, 0), which results in an increase in the code interval. Therefore, the performance shows some improved compared with 8QAM.

For the training of 32-ary and 64-ary modem, the training SNR is increased to 13 dB, and the number of training rounds is increased to 20,000 and 30,000 respectively. The training results in Fig. 5, Fig. 6, and Fig. 7 show that the constellation diagrams generated by the 32-ary and 64-ary based on the 10-layer DAN are quite different from the traditional 16QAM, 32QAM, and 64QAM, and they are difficult to be distinguished linearly. Therefor they are difficult to demodulate by traditional methods and increase the signal's ability to resist interception. In terms of performance, the modem based on the 10-layer DAN for 16-ary and 32-ary is close to but slightly worse than 16QAM and 32QAM respectively (when the BER is lower than 10^{-3}, the performance degradation is less than 0.5 dB and 0.2 dB respectively). For 64-ary, the modem based on the 10-layer DAN is slightly better than that of 64QAM.

For higher-order 128-ary modem, after several attempts with the 10-layer DAN of Fig. 1, combing with different training number of symbols per batch, different training SNR, different training rounds, etc., no distinguishable symbol constellation can be formed. The typical training results are shown in Fig. 8. This result shows that the 10-layer DAN shown in Fig. 1 can only complete modem of 64-ary and below. For modem of 128-ary and above, a deeper network structure and more optimization parameters are required.

Extend the 10-layer DAN in Fig. 1 to 12 layers, that is, a new hidden layer is added after the Input_Layer of the sending end and before the Output_Layer of receiving end respectively. The weight parameter and offset parameter of the new hidden layer are a N64 matrix and a 64 column vector respectively. Sigmoid activation function is adopted.E_w1 and D_w1 of the original 10-layer self-coding network are set as a 6432 matrix respectively, E_b1 and D_b1 are set as a 64 column vectors respectively, other layer parameters remain unchanged.

The training method, loss function, training set and test set are still unchanged, and the training SNR is set as 18dB. As shown in Fig. 9, the 12-layer DAN basically converges after 40,000 rounds of training, and its performance is better than 128QAM demodulation. This results show that the Multi-modem model based on deep autoencoder network designed in this paper has flexible expansion ability and can adapt to higher order modem by appropriately increasing network depth and optimization parameters.

In order to show the training parameters and performance of the 10-layer DAN for Multi-Modem, a summary is presented in Table 1.

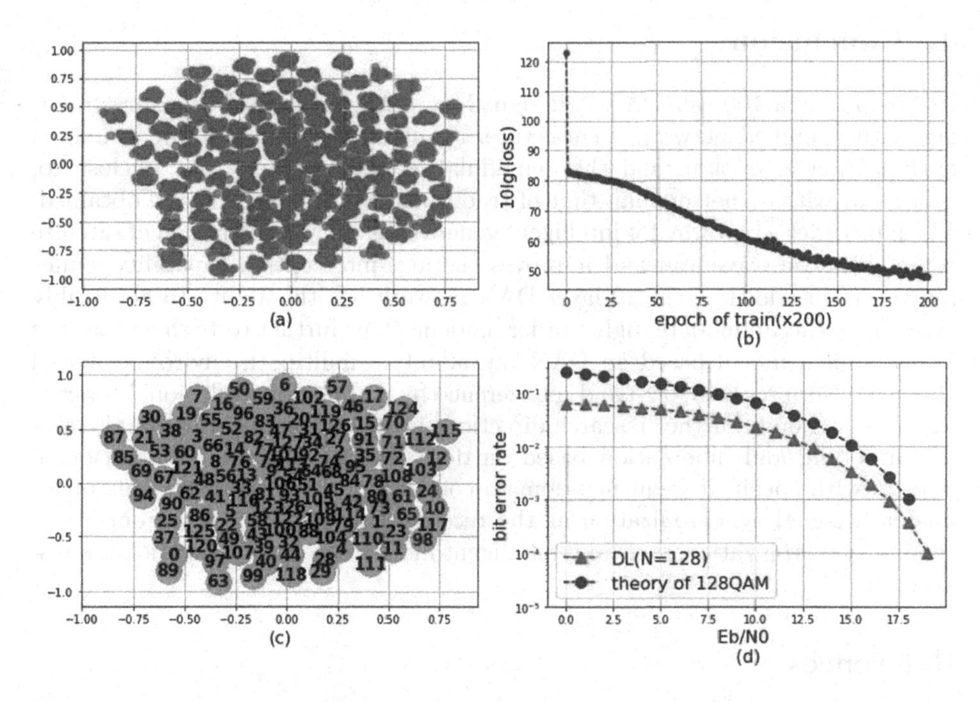

Fig. 9. 128-ary modem training results and performance comparison with 128QAM with 12-layer DAN.

Table 1. Training parameters and performance of the 10-layer DAN for Multi-modem.

10-layer DAN	Training SNR	Training epoch	Performance compared with traditional modulation	Constellation features
2-ary modem	7 dB	10,000	Consistent with BPSK	Consistent with BPSK
4-ary modem	7 dB	10,000	Consistent with QPSK	Consistent with QPSK
8-ary modem	7 dB	10,000	Better than 8QAM	Different from 8QAM, but easy to be differentiated linearly
16-ary modem	13 dB	10,000	Close to 16QAM	Different from 16QAM, and difficult to be differentiated linearly
32-ary modem	13 dB	20,000	Close to 32QAM	Different from 32QAM, and difficult to be differentiated linearly
64-ary modem	13 dB	30,000	Better than 64QAM	Different from 64QAM, and difficult to be differentiated linearly
128-ary modem	18 dB	40,000	Failure with 10-layer DAN, but better than 128QAM with 12-layer DAN	Different from 128QAM, and difficult to be differentiated linearly

4 Conclusion

In this paper, a 10-layer DAN is designed to realize modems from 2-ary to 64-ary with a unified network architecture, a unified loss function and a unified optimization algorithm, and the demodulation performance, that is close to, consistent with or better than that of traditional MPSK or QAM are obtained, which provides a new way for intelligent generation and reconstruction of satellite communication waveform and improves the anti-interception capability simultaneously. In addition, the 10-layer DAN network has the ability to be flexibly extended to accommodate higher order modems. Our further tests show that the Multi-modem model based on DAN can adapt to multipath environment and effectively suppress narrow-band interference by adding a convolutional layer at the receiving end. Further research directions include overall learning and training of coding and modulation based on deep learning network, generation of modem with specified frequency domain constraints (such as continuous phase modem), signal synchronization at the receiving end (carrier synchronization, symbol synchronization, etc.) and intelligent interference detection and suppression, etc.

References

1. Mao, Q., Fei, H., Hao, Q.: Deep learning for intelligent wireless networks: a comprehensive survey. IEEE Commun. Surv. Tutor. **20**(4), 2595–2621 (2018)
2. Zhang, J., Sheng, C., Maunder, R.G., Rong, Z., Hanzo, L.: Adaptive coding and modulation for large-scale antenna array-based aeronautical communications in the presence of co-channel interference. IEEE Trans. Wirel. Commun. **17**(2), 1343–1357 (2018)
3. Hinton, G.E., Salakhutdinov, R.R.: Reducing the dimensionality of data with neural networks. Science **313**(5786), 504–507 (2006)
4. O'Shea, T.J., Corgan, J., Clancy, T.C.: Unsupervised representation learning of structured radio communication signals. In: First International Workshop on Sensing (2016)
5. O'Shea, T.J., Karra, K., Charles Clancy, T.: Learning to communicate: channel auto-encoders, domain specific regularizers, and attention (2016)
6. O'Shea, T.J., Roy, T., West, N., Hilburn, B.C.: Physical layer communications system design over-the-air using adversarial networks (2018)
7. Oshea, T., Hoydis, J.: An introduction to deep learning for the physical layer. IEEE Trans. Cogn. Commun. Netw. **3**(4), 563–575 (2017)
8. Ye, H., Li, G.Y., Juang, B.-H.F., Sivanesan, K.: Channel agnostic end-to-end learning based communication systems with conditional GAN (2018)
9. Dorner, S., Cammerer, S., Hoydis, J., ten Brink, S.: Deep learning based communication over the air. IEEE J. Sel. Top. Sign. Process. **12**(1), 132–143 (2018)
10. Yaodong, Y., Le'nan, W.: Realization of SSAE demodulator of MPPSK communication system. J. Electro. Meas. Instrum. **32**(4), 144–150 (2018)
11. Huang, Y., Zhang, J., Zhou, X., Lu, J.: Demodulation with deep learning. Telecommun. Eng. **57**(7), 741–744 (2017)
12. Zhang, J., Jin, S., Wen, C., Gao, F., Jiang, T.: An overview of wireless transmission technology utilizing artificial intelligence. Telecommun. Sci. **34**(8), 46–55 (2018)

13. Gui, G., Wang, Y., Huang, H.: Deep learning based physical layer wireless communication techniques: opportunities and challenges. J. Commun. **4**(2), 19–23 (2019)
14. Gomar, S., Mirhassani, M., Ahmadi, M.: Precise digital implementations of hyperbolic tanh and sigmoid function. In: Asilomar Conference on Signals (2016)
15. Zeiler, M.D.: Adadelta: an adaptive learning rate method. Computer Science (2012)
16. Masters, D., Luschi, C.: Revisiting small batch training for deep neural networks (2018)
17. Bishop, C.: Training with noise is equivalent to Tikhonov regularization. Neural Comput. **7**(1), 108–116 (1995)
18. Haque, Z., Cheng, H.-T., Hong, L.: Tensorflow estimators. In: the 23rd ACM SIGKDD International Conference on Knowledge Discovery and Data Mining, pp. 1763–1771 (2017)

A Secure Storage and Transmission Method of Space Cloud Privacy Data

Yingzhao Shao(✉), Xiaobo Li, and Mingming Zhang

China Academy of Space Technology, Xi'an 710100, Shannxi, China
daisyshao1983@126.com

Abstract. With the rapid development of satellite Internet and space cloud, space cloud data security will become an important problem to be solved. In this paper, a method for secure storage and transmission of user privacy data in space cloud in the future is presented. By employing a large number of image data in the cloud, the Joint Photographic Experts Group (JPEG) image is decompressed into the quantized Discrete Cosine Transform (DCT) coefficients, and the mapping relationship between the DCT coefficients and the code stream is established. The maximum frequency of the non-zero coefficient is taken as the marked point, and the user privacy data is encrypted and embedded into each original code stream according to the Huffman code table. Finally, the final marked file with privacy data is obtained by merging the code streams of all code blocks. The marked file with embedded privacy data can be decompressed normally, and the decoded image can be displayed in a normal way. After the privacy data is extracted by legitimate users, the original carrier data can be recovered lossless. The experimental results show that this method ensures the secure storage and transmission of privacy data in the cloud without destroying the integrity and sharing of the original carrier data.

Keywords: Satellite internet · Cloud data security · User privacy data

1 Introduction

In recent years, innovative enterprises such as Space X and OneWeb in the United States have planned to build low-orbit satellite constellations, which has triggered an upsurge in the development of satellite Internet. Cloud computing is the third IT information revolution after the Internet. With the gradual construction of the satellite Internet system, space cloud will become an important space-based infrastructure. The United States has unveiled the "Space Belt" (SpaceBelt) Cloud Constellation program [2]. The space belt company plans to launch three geosynchronous orbit relay satellites and 10 data storage satellites at an altitude of 36,000 km from the earth. Among them, the data storage satellite will form a closed link (cloud constellation) in the low-Earth orbit, and communicate with each other and back up each other. A secure cloud server system with stable performance is installed on the data storage satellite, and through the communication between the

Q. Wu et al. (Eds.): WiSATS 2020, LNICST 358, pp. 502–513, 2021.
https://doi.org/10.1007/978-3-030-69072-4_41

synchronous orbit relay satellite and the special ground receiving station, the secure transmission of data in space and the secure storage of private data can be realized to meet the security requirements that can not be completely satisfied on the ground, such as preventing network attacks, data injection, data theft and so on. On March 22, 2019, Galactic Sky of the United States announced that its first software-defined satellite, GSky-1, has successfully completed the whole satellite integration in the Space Engineering Research Center (SERC) at the Information Sciences Institute (ISI) of the University of Southern California. The satellite uses Citrix virtualization technology, which will verify the functions of multi-customer satellite resource sharing, cloud node flexibility scalability, and cloud status monitoring and recovery in the cloud environment. On March 20, 2019, Lockheed Martin said it will test the space-based cloud computing infrastructure in the first star of the Pony Express project, which will eventually support the construction of a space cloud data center in the future. In addition, on November 20, 2018, Tianzhi-1, led by the Institute of Software of the Chinese Academy of Sciences, was launched from the Jiuquan Satellite launch Center and successfully entered the scheduled orbit of space. The satellite carries a "miniaturized cloud computing platform", which is mainly adopted to verify space-based cloud computing technology [3].

At present, almost all the data in cloud storage services are stored in clear text in the cloud, which is relatively simple to design, develop and deploy, and its users can easily share data. However, as this kind of cloud system can view all users' data directly, there is a great risk for the protection of users' private data. In order to protect the privacy and security of users' cloud data, it is a common method of encrypting the data and uploading it to the cloud server. However, this cloud data storage method poses a serious obstacle to data sharing, that is, the cloud server cannot directly send the ciphertext data of its owner to the sharer, because the sharer is incapable of decrypting the ciphertext that is not encrypted by his own key. In addition, due to the openness of space links, attackers are likely to steal or destroy cloud privacy or confidential data through illegal intrusion. How to strike a balance between the convenience of space cloud data sharing and private data security in the future is an urgent problem to be solved. Considering that a large number of cloud data are remote sensing image data, in order to solve the problem of secure storage and transmission of user privacy or confidential data, in this paper, a secure storage and transmission algorithm of privacy data for the cloud JPEG stream is proposed. Using this algorithm, the user privacy data is encrypted and hidden in the code stream corresponding to the highest frequency of non-zero coefficients for storage and transmission. For illegal users, even if the image data embedded with privacy data is obtained, it is difficult to find any anomalies; for shared users, the code stream embedded with privacy data can still be displayed with high quality after decompression, and does not affect the data sharing application; after the privacy data is extracted by legitimate users, the carrier image data can be restored in a lossless way for ensuring the integrity of the carrier data. With this method not only can the security of privacy data be ensured, but also the sharing of cloud space-based big data is satisfied. In this case, it has a broad application prospect in cloud private data storage and transmission.

2 Related Works

At present, there are four kinds of data embedding techniques based on JPEG format: re-quantizing DCT coefficients [4–6], modifying the quantization table [7, 8], modifying the Huffman coding table [9–12], and embedding data in encrypted JPEG code streams [13, 14]. These methods well adapt to the rules of JPEG coding and improve the application range of JPEG image data embedding, but most of the embedded images can not be shown normally, or the information of the carrier file is lost.

Wang et al. [7] first proposed the algorithm to achieve high-quality display and large embedding capacity, and the file expansion is also limited. He not only modified the quantized DCT coefficients, but also changed the quantization table. Although the expansion has been restrained, the expansion problem is still very serious, and it is not suitable for the case that QF is 100. Huang et al. [8] proposed a histogram shift algorithm for DCT coefficients of JPEG images. Coefficients with values of -1 and 1 in each DCT block are used to embed secret information, and a block selection strategy is added to further improve the capacity with the number of zeros in DCT blocks. However, there is a certain deviation between the theoretical value and the actual value of this method, and the expansion is also very obvious. Hou et al. [9] optimized Huang et al.'s [8] algorithm, that he selects K frequency points with the smallest deviation in the DCT block, and shifts the coefficients of the frequency points whose values are -1 and 1. In the same embedding capacity, it has better image quality and less expansion. Liu et al. [10] proposed a simple and efficient algorithm in which all non-zero coefficients in each DCT block are changed to embed data, such that capacity is greatly improved and the file expansion is relatively small. Zhang et al. [11] proposed an adaptive hiding algorithm for JPEG code stream, which truncates the code stream corresponding to high-frequency coefficients and hides information with spare space. The marked images can be displayed normally, but the original data is lost to some extent. Zhang et al. [12] proposed a lossless hiding algorithm for JPEG code stream, which recompresses the high-frequency coefficients to hide secret information. The algorithm can restore the image lossless, but the modified file can not be decompressed normally in the process of transmission.

3 The Proposed Method

In order to ensure the secure transmission of JPEG remote sensing images in space cloud, an information embedding algorithm is proposed in this paper. Secret information is preprocessed and put behind the code stream corresponding to the non-zero coefficients with the highest frequency, so that the marked images can be displayed with high quality. This method ensures both the security of secret information and the integrity of image data.

In the Huffman code table of JPEG, Run/Size is the joint coding of Alternating Current (AC) coefficients. For each non-zero coefficient, Run represents the number of coefficients before the non-zero coefficient is 0; Size indicates the binary coding length of the non-zero coefficient; Value refers to the value of the non-zero coefficient; code length is the length of Run/Size joint coding; Codes are the corresponding codeword, and the binary coding length of Variable Length (VL) is the sum of code length and VL. In other words, DCT coefficient coding is the joint coding concerning the number of non-zero coefficients and non-zero coefficients. For example, in the coefficients sequence {0,0,0,4}, Run is 3, Size is 3, the corresponding Run/Size code is "111111110101", added with the binary code "100" of 4, and the joint coding of the sequence {0,0,0,4} is "111111110101,100" (Table 1).

Table 1. Huffman coefficient encoding

Run/Size	Value	Code length	Codes	Sum length	VL
0/0(EOB)	0	4	1010	4	0
0/1	−1, 1	2	00	3	1
0/2	−3, −2, 2, 3	2	01	4	2
0/3	−7, −6, −5, −4, 4, 5, 6, 7	3	100	6	3
0/4	−15, −14,...,−8, 8,...,14, 15	4	1011	8	4
0/5	−31, −30,...,−16, 16,...,30, 31	5	11010	10	5
1/1	−1, 1	4	1100	5	1
1/2	−3, −2, 2, 3	5	11011	7	2
1/3	−7, −6, −5, −4, 4, 5, 6, 7	7	1111001	10	3
1/4	−15, −14,...,−8, 8,...,14, 15	9	111110110	13	4
2/1	−1, 1	5	11100	6	1
2/2	−3, −2, 2, 3	8	11111001	10	2
2/3	−7, −6, −5, −4, 4, 5, 6, 7	10	1111110111	13	3
3/1	−1, 1	6	111010	7	1
3/2	−3, −2, 2, 3	9	111110111	11	2
3/3	−7, −6, −5, −4, 4, 5, 6, 7	12	111111110101	15	3

In each DCT block, as the value of the high frequency coefficient is small and sparse, a small modification to the high frequency coefficient will not cause great attenuation of the image quality. In order to ensure the blind extraction of secret information at the receiver and the unchanging original coefficient, it is necessary to find a suitable high-frequency termination point T and embed secret data in the high-frequency termination point. When the value of the non-zero coefficient exists in $\{-3, 2, 2, 3\}$, the corresponding coding length is 2 bits, and its effect on image quality at high frequency is negligible. Corresponding to the selected termination point T, it should be ensured that there is no non-zero coefficient above it. Below this point, there are several zero coefficients, and the number of zero coefficients is M. In this paper, the 2-bit mapping for secret data can be established, as shown in Table 2. For example, when the secret data is "00", the non-zero value at point T is −3. Then, the final bit data is obtained according to Table 3. In this case, the Size is all 2, or the coding length of non-zero coefficients is 2 bits, and Run/Size can be regarded as Run/2. Table 3 shows a simplification of the Huffman code table, and its coding process is fully in line with the JPEG coding standard. When T is less than 64, all the high frequency coefficients above T are 0, and it is necessary to add "1010" for indicating the end of coding. For example, when T is 53, secret data is "01", and the number of zero coefficients Size below the high frequency point T is 3, then the non-zero value in the point T is changed from 0 to −2, and the joint coding is "111110111,01". With "1010" as the ending identifier End Of Bits (EOB), the changed code stream is "111110111,01,1010". The coefficients below T are not changed as well as the corresponding code stream, indicating that there is no harm to the original low-frequency coefficients, and the carrier data can be recovered lossless after the secret data at the receiver is extracted completely. The cost is a certain degree of file expansion, which is negligible compared with the protection of secret data.

Table 2. Relationship between secret data and value

Secret data	00	01	10	11
Value	−3	−2	2	3

Table 3. Joint coding table of secret data

Run	Value			
	−3	−2	2	3
0	01,00	01,01	01,10	01,11
1	11011,00	11011,01	11011,10	11011,11
2	11111001,00	11111001,01	11111001,10	11111001,11
3	111110111,00	111110111,01	111110111,10	111110111,11
4	1111111000,00	1111111000,01	1111111000,10	1111111000,11
5	11111110111,00	11111110111,01	11111110111,10	11111110111,11

In this way, the changed DCT coefficient at the highest frequency T point is limited to $\{-3, -2, 2, 3\}$, which not only guarantees a certain hiding capacity, but also maintains the high quality display of the marked image or the invisibility of secret data. The PSNR of the marked image is kept above 35 dB, and the distortion between the marked image and the original JPEG image is extremely small. Therefore, it is difficult for human eyes to distinguish. In each block, the high-frequency termination point T is adaptive, and its value is the corresponding highest frequency of the original non-zero coefficient added with 1. When the original non-zero highest point is 64, it means that there is no additional frequency for embedding secret data. In order to ensure the generalization ability of this algorithm, the maximum frequency corresponding to the original non-zero coefficient is 62. In this case, the high-frequency termination point T is 63. When there is a non-zero value at frequency 63 or 64 in the original DCT block, the code block cannot hide the data. In extreme cases, as shown in Table 4, even if there are non-zero values in the original frequencies 62 and 63, and the values are in {−3, −2, 2, 3}, a value of 7 can be selected as a marker on frequency 64. According to a large number of experimental statistics, in the highest frequency 64, only a few non-zero values are −2 or 2. When the highest frequency of the non-zero coefficient is 62, and its value is in {−3, −2, 2, 3}, and the value of the non-zero value of the secret data in frequency 63 is at {−3, −2, 2, 3}, the coefficient in the frequency 64 is set to zero, so that whether the code block is embedded in the secret message can be judged by the coefficient value of the highest frequency 64. In this way, it is possible to determine whether the code block is embedded in the secret data by the coefficient value of the highest frequency 64. When the coefficient in the 64 frequency point is zero, the secret data is embedded, while when its value is not zero, the secret data is not embedded.

Table 4. Extreme case handling table

Embedding situation	Frequency		
	62	63	64
Original coefficient	−3, −2, 2, 3	−3, −2, 2, 3	7
Embedding coefficient	−3, −2, 2, 3	−3, −2, 2, 3	0

The data embedding process of an 8 × 8 DCT block is shown in Fig. 1. The original DCT block is displayed in Fig. 1(a); the highest frequency corresponding to its non-zero value is 31, and the frequency diagram is shown in Fig. 1(b); 32 is taken as the high-frequency termination point T, and the data is embedded at this point, assuming that the secret data is "10", while the corresponding value is 2, and the marked DCT block is shown in Fig. 1(c). It can be seen that the information on the DCT block is changed only slightly, and the distortion of the image corresponding to the spatial domain is very small. In terms of the code stream, the code stream below frequency 31 has not changed. Above this point, the code stream changes from "1010" to "01101010", where "0110" is the encoding with a Value of 2, and "1010" indicates the end of the encoding.

At the sender in the cloud, the data embedding can be divided into four steps, as shown in Fig. 2.

1. Decompress the JPEG file to the DCT blocks, and establish the corresponding relationship between the DCT coefficients and the code stream.
2. Make statistics of each DCT block which can be embedded in data to get the final embedding capacity.

(a)

12	17	10	-5	0	-2	0	0
15	8	0	0	0	0	0	0
-9	0	0	0	0	-1	0	0
-3	4	0	0	0	0	0	0
0	0	0	0	0	0	0	0
1	0	0	0	0	0	0	0
0	0	0	0	0	0	0	0
0	0	0	0	0	0	0	0

(b)

1	2	6	7	15	16	28	29
3	5	8	14	17	27	30	43
4	9	13	18	26	31	42	44
10	12	19	25	32	41	45	54
11	20	24	33	40	46	53	55
21	23	34	39	47	52	56	61
22	35	38	48	51	57	60	62
36	37	49	50	58	59	63	64

(c)

12	17	10	-5	0	-2	0	0
15	8	0	0	0	0	0	0
-9	0	0	0	0	-1	0	0
-3	4	0	0	0	0	0	0
0	0	0	0	0	0	0	0
1	0	0	0	0	0	0	0
0	0	0	0	0	0	0	0
0	0	0	0	0	0	0	0

Fig. 1. An 8 × 8 DCT block data embedding schematic diagram

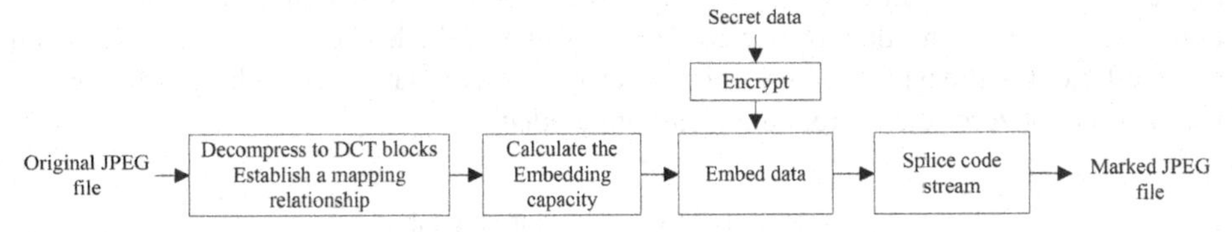

Fig. 2. Data embedding flowchart

3. The secret data is encrypted and embedded in the DCT blocks with a set of 2 bits according to the proposed coding algorithm.
4. All the changed code streams are spliced together to form a marked JPEG file.

At the receiver in the cloud, the data extraction and recovery can be divided into four steps, as shown in Fig. 3.

1. Decompress the JPEG file to the DCT blocks, and also establish the corresponding relationship between the coefficients and the code stream.
2. Judge the utilization of each block according to Table 4.
3. For the utilized code blocks, the coefficient corresponding to the highest frequency is decoded into a bit stream, and the coefficient is set to 0; for the unused code block, the original coefficient is repaired according to the coefficient at the 64 frequency point.

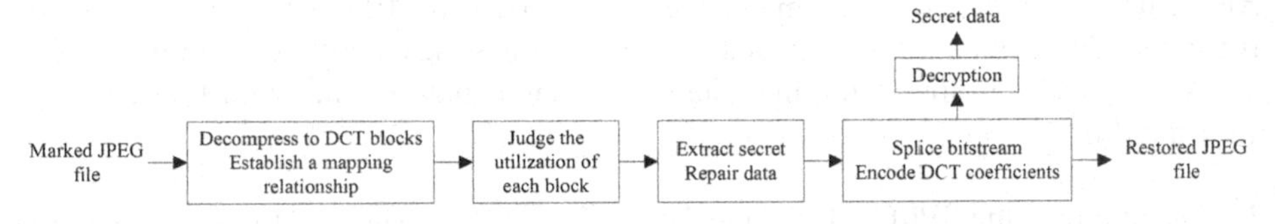

Fig. 3. Data extraction and recovery flowchart

4. Continue to encode the repaired coefficients to get the final recovered compressed file. The extracted bitstream is spliced and decrypted to get the final extracted data.

4 Experimental Results

In this paper, 38 images in the dataset of Southern University are adopted to verify the algorithm, and the test images are all lossless TIFF grayscale images with the 512×512 format. When the QF is greater than 20, the visual quality of the image is higher. Thus, the QF is set as 30, 50, 70 and 90 to compress the image. The secret data is a random binary bit stream. The key data is shared in the sender and the receiver, and the key data is a pseudo-random seed. In the sender, a pseudorandom 0,1 sequence is generated, and it is XOR with the original secret data. In addition to that, the encrypted secret data is obtained. In the receiver, the same sequence is XOR with the extracted secret data, and the final secret data is gained.

The experimental platform is MATLAB 2013a; the operating system is 64-bit windows 7; the CPU is i5-5200u; the main frequency is 2.2 GHz, and the memory is 8 GB. Peak signal-to-noise ratio (PSNR) and embedding capacity (EC) are employed to evaluate the performance. PSNR refers to the value of the marked JPEG image relative to the original JPEG image. It is worth noting that the higher the PSNR, the better the image quality and the invisibility of secret data, while the higher the EC, the stronger the ability of the image to carry information.

The EC and PSNR of the first 10 remote sensing images are shown respectively in Table 5 when the QF is 30, 50, 70 and 90. When the QF is small, the quantization step is large, and a large amount of data is removed, so that the coefficient on the high frequency is extremely small. For the 512×512 image, there are a total of 4096 blocks, each of which can be embedded with 2 bits. Hence, in theory, up to 8192 bits of information can be embedded. With the increase of the QF, the quantization step decreases and a large amount of data is retained. In this case, the coefficients in high frequencies become larger and denser, and some blocks that fail to meet the coding of this paper appear, but the number of these blocks is very small and can be ignored. When the QF is small, the retained coefficient is less. Although the change is the same, the proportion of the existing DCT coefficient is larger, and the PSNR value is lower. With the increase of the QF, more coefficients are kept, and these slight changes are smaller than the existing DCT coefficient, and the PSNR value is larger. However, on the whole, the PSNR values are all around 40 dB, and the human eyes are unable to distinguish the distortion.

When the QF is 30, 50, 50, 70 and 90, the comparison between the 2nd and 10th images is shown in Fig. 4 and Fig. 5. Figure (a) is the original JPEG image with QF 30; (b) shows the original JPEG image with QF 50; (c) displays the original JPEG image with QF 70; (d) is the original JPEG image with QF 90; (e) is the marked JPEG image with QF 30; (f) is the JPEG image with QF 50; (g) shows the JPEG image with QF 70, while (h) displays the JPEG image with QF 90. It can be seen in Table 6 that the texture of the second image is complex; the PSNR value of the same QF is lower; there are a large number of non-zero high-frequency coefficients; the texture of the 10th image is relatively simple; the PSNR value of the same QF is higher, and there are a small number of non-zero high-frequency coefficients. However, whether the simple image

Table 5. EC and PSNR of the first 10 remote sensing images

Number	QF							
	30		50		70		90	
	EC (:bits)	PSNR (:dB)	EC (:bits)	PSNR (:dB)	EC (:bits)	PSNR (:dB)	EC (:bits)	PSNR (:dB)
1	8192	37.02	8192	38.10	8192	38.12	8188	41.69
2	8192	34.72	8192	37.73	8190	36.93	8188	39.20
3	8192	41.08	8192	43.44	8192	44.35	8186	48.00
4	8192	37.14	8192	38.47	8192	38.83	8188	42.26
5	8192	38.32	8190	41.37	8190	41.74	8184	45.89
6	8192	37.42	8192	39.48	8192	40.11	8190	43.68
7	8192	39.56	8192	40.87	8192	41.57	8190	46.28
8	8192	40.44	8192	44.50	8190	46.03	8186	57.04
9	8192	41.59	8192	43.83	8192	46.08	8190	52.50
10	8192	38.91	8192	40.84	8192	41.90	8188	45.68

or the complex image, the distortion amplitude of the image is still within the range acceptable to the human eyes, or in other words, the human eyes fail to distinguish the distortion.

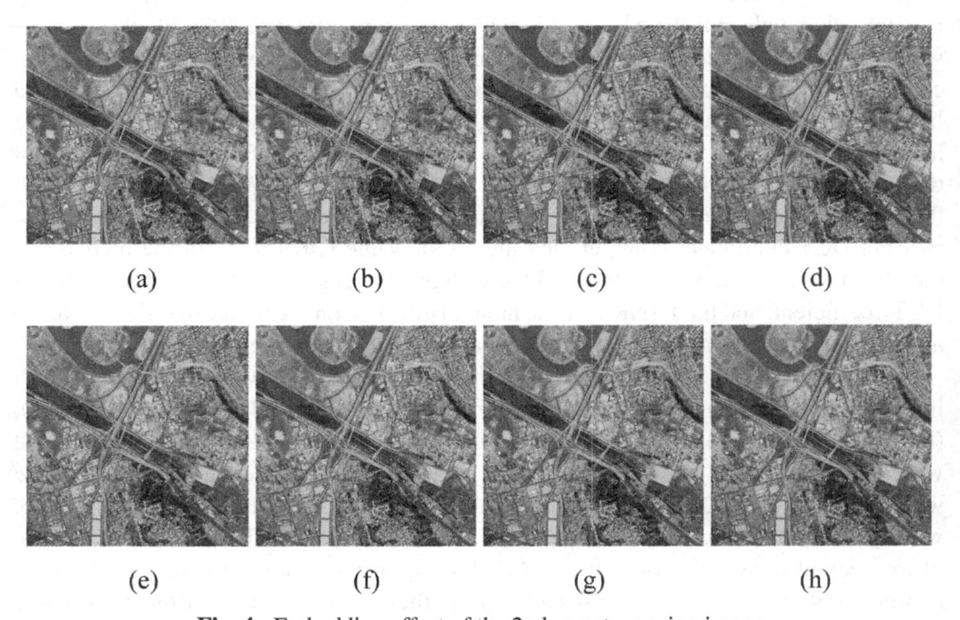

Fig. 4. Embedding effect of the 2nd remote sensing image

In order to further elaborate the effectiveness of this algorithm, in this paper, EC and PSNR are compared, with Wang et al.'s [7], Huang et al.'s [8], Hou et al.'s [9] and Liu et al.'s [10]. These algorithms can guarantee that the image can be restored lossless in the receiver, and the hidden marked image can be displayed normally, while the cost is more consistent, which will cause file expansion to a certain extent. The average EC comparison of 38 images under different QFs is shown in Fig. 6, and the average PSNR comparison is displayed in Fig. 7. It can be seen that the EC of this paper is relatively low, while the PSNR is relatively high, because the modified DCT coefficient of this algorithm only corresponds to a separate high frequency point, and the change appears in a small range. In algorithm [7], Wang et al. embed data by modifying quantization step size. In algorithm [8], Huang et al. embed data through DCT block histogram shift, while in algorithm [9], Hou et al. embed data by selecting frequency and blocks. The frequency point which is most suitable for hiding is selected to embed the data. In algorithm [10], Liu et al. multiply the whole coefficients to obtain redundant space to embed data. These algorithms modify the coefficients in a large range of DCT blocks, and the corresponding EC is also relatively large, but the image quality is not high. In this way, even though the marked image can be displayed, there will be modified traces, which can be easily found, and the security of the image can not be satisfied. In this paper, we make a compromise between EC and PSNR, lay emphasis on PSNR, make the secret data in the marked image with high invisibility, and carry a certain amount of secret data.

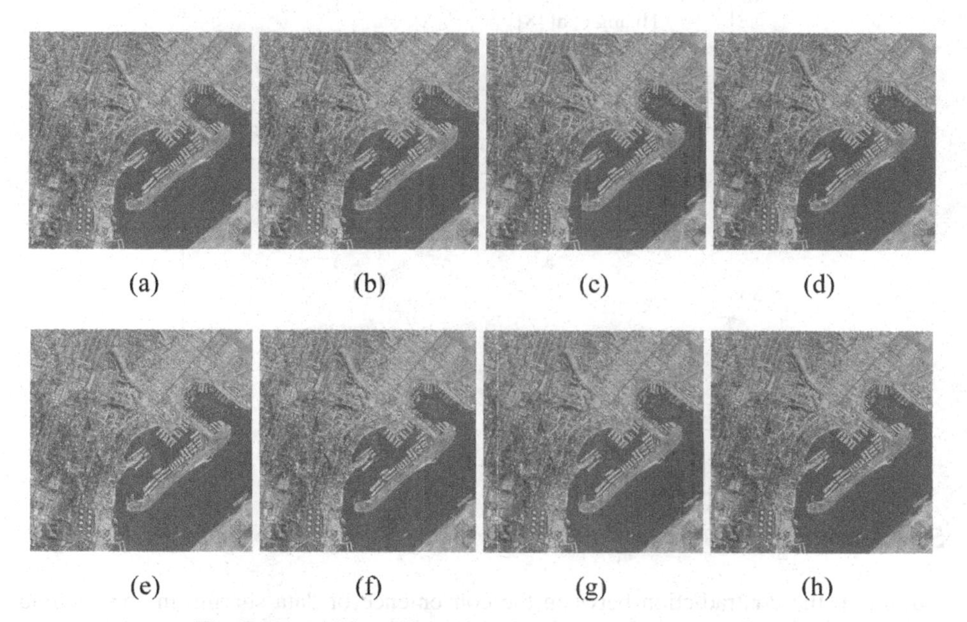

Fig. 5. Embedding effect of the 10th remote sensing image

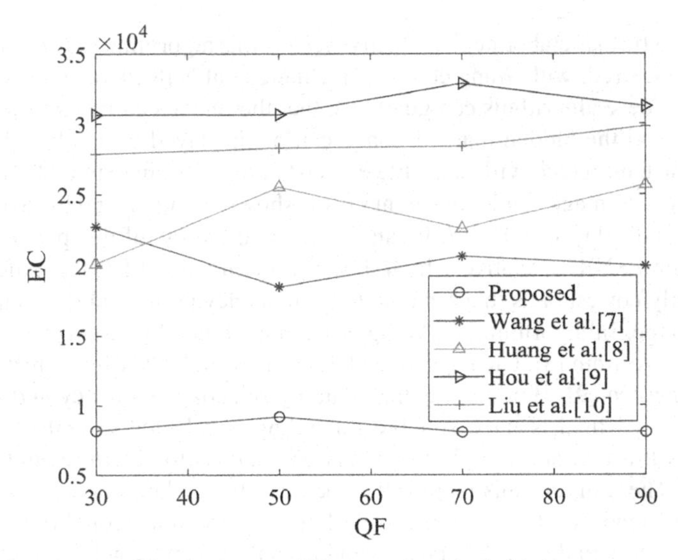

Fig. 6. Average EC comparison (unit: bits)

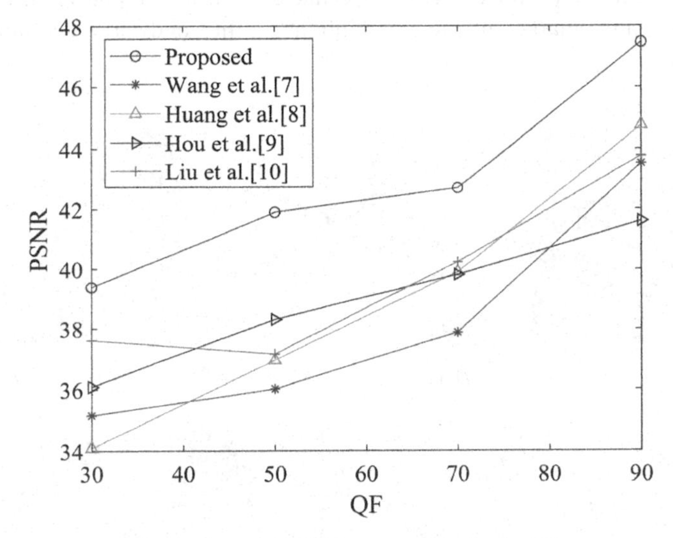

Fig. 7. Average PSNR comparison (unit: dB)

5 Conclusions

Aiming at the contradiction between the convenience of data sharing in space cloud and the security of privacy data in the future, this paper proposes a method based on the secure storage and transmission of privacy data belonging to space cloud users in the future. By using a large amount of image data in the cloud, the user privacy data is embedded in the image stream for secure storage and transmission. On the premise of ensuring the integrity and sharing of the original carrier data, it meets the requirements of the secure storage and transmission of private data in the cloud. Furthermore, it can be taken as a reference for solving data security problems in open and shared environments such as ground clouds and future space-based clouds.

References

1. Gao, Y.Y., Wang, N.W., Lu, Z.: The development research and construction suggestion of satellite internet constellations. J. China Acad. Electron. Inf. Technol. **14**(8), 875–881 (2019)
2. Cloud Constellation Corporation Selects LeoStella to Manufacture the SpaceBelt Constellation. https://www.parabolicarc.com/tag/spacebelt/. Accessed 12 Nov 2019.
3. China's first software-defined satellite, Tianzhi-1, was successfully launched. https://www.cas.cn/cm/201811/t20181121_4671546.shtml. Accessed 20 Nov 2018
4. Huang, F.J.: Reversible data hiding in JPEG images. IEEE Trans. Circuits Syst. Video Technol. **26**(9), 1610–1621 (2016)
5. Hou, D.D.: Reversible data hiding in JPEG image based on DCT frequency and block selection. Signal Process. **148**(10), 41–47 (2018)
6. Liu, Y.J., Chang, C.C.: Reversible data hiding for JPEG images employing all quantized non-zero AC coefficients. Displays **51**(2), 51–56 (2018)
7. Wang, K., Lu, Z.M., Hu, Y.J.: A high capacity lossless data hiding scheme for JPEG images. J. Syst. Softw. **86**(7), 1965–1975 (2013)
8. Di, F.Q.: Reversible data hiding in JPEG images based on zero coefficients and distortion cost function. Multimedia Tools Appl. **78**(24), 34541–34561 (2019)
9. Hu, Y.J., Wang, K., Lu, Z.M.: An improved VLC-based lossless data hiding scheme for JPEG images. J. Syst. Softw. **86**(8), 2166–2173 (2013)
10. Qiu, Y.Q.: Lossless data hiding in JPEG bitstream using alternative embedding. J. Vis. Commun. Image Represent. **52**(2), 86–91 (2018)
11. Qian, Z.X., Zhang, X.P., Wang, S.Z.: Reversible data hiding in encrypted JPEG bitstream. IEEE Trans. Multimedia **16**(5), 1486–1491 (2014)
12. Nasrullah, N.: Reversible data hiding in compressed and encrypted images by using Kd-tree. Multimedia Tools Appl. **78**(13), 17535–17554 (2019)
13. Zhang, M.M., Zhou, Q., Hu, Y.L.: A reversible data hiding scheme in JPEG bitstreams using DCT coefficients truncation. KSII Trans. Internet Inf. Syst. (TIIS) **14**(1), 404–421 (2020)
14. Zhang, M.M., Zhou, Q., Hu, Y.L.: Lossless data hiding in JPEG images with segment coding. Journal of Electronic Imaging (JEI) **28**(5), 053015(1–14) (2019).

International Workshop on Satellite Network Transmission and Security (SNTS)

Wavelet Threshold Denoising for High Speed Satellite Communication

Shulin Xiao[1,2], Lintao Han[1,2], Jiabian An[1,2], Luyao Gao[1,2], and Changhong Hu[1(✉)]

[1] Changchun Institute of Optics, Fine Mechanics and Physics, Chinese Academy of Sciences, Changchun 130033, China
13263073168@163.com, hlintao1997@gmail.com, 872731105@qq.com, 2657095331@qq.com, changhonghu@rocketmail.com

[2] University of Chinese Academy of Sciences, Beijing 100049, China

Abstract. The principle of wavelet threshold de-noising is described in detail. Daubechies wavelet function is selected to denoise the sinusoidal signal with noise. The relationship between the order of wavelet function, the number of decomposition layers, the number of signal samples and the signal-to-noise ratio of denoised signal is demonstrated. At the same time, the calculation methods of fixed threshold, unbiased risk estimation threshold, mixed threshold and mini threshold max threshold are summarized, and then the denoising effects of hard threshold, soft threshold and semi soft threshold functions are compared. By analyzing the distribution of wavelet decomposition coefficients and combining with the characteristics of other threshold functions, a new wavelet threshold function is designed and compared with other threshold functions.

Keywords: Wavelet threshold denoising · Threshold function

1 Introduction

Generally speaking, after the data acquisition system collects the data, we need to process the data. In the process of signal detection and transmission, we will inevitably suffer from noise interference, so the measurement accuracy and accuracy in complex environment become an important factor affecting its practical application, so it is necessary to filter the noise.

Traditional signal theory, mainly based on Fourier analysis theory, directly or indirectly transforms the signal from time domain to frequency domain for analysis and processing. Because the set of analysis functions selected by Fourier analysis is a sinusoidal function set in an infinite time domain, Fourier transform lacks the ability to distinguish signals in time domain, that is, to know the frequency or frequency distribution of signals at different times. In view of the shortcomings of Fourier transform, the short-time Fourier transform (STFT) has been developed, which solved the problem of the lack of time resolution of Fourier transform to a certain extent, but because the

Q. Wu et al. (Eds.): WiSATS 2020, LNICST 358, pp. 517–530, 2021.
https://doi.org/10.1007/978-3-030-69072-4_42

width of the sliding window function of STFT is fixed, the short-time Fourier Transform (STFT) has insufficient time domain resolution when the signal frequency changes rapidly and irregularly with time [1].

Wavelet transform is a new method of signal analysis. It decomposes the signal by using the wavelet function which decays rapidly in the whole-time domain, the average amplitude is 0, and the time-frequency window is variable, so as to realize the signal analysis in time domain and frequency domain. Wavelet transform can be divided into two categories: continuous wavelet transform (CWT) and discrete wavelet transform (DWT). In the field of digital signal processing, discrete wavelet transform (DWT) decomposes digital signal by discrete scale and discrete translation wavelet function. By processing the decomposed wavelet coefficients and reconstructing them, signal processing tasks such as signal compression and denoising can be completed. Among them, the wavelet threshold denoising algorithm is a filtering algorithm that thresholds the discrete wavelet transform coefficients of the digital signal, and then reconstructs the signal to achieve the denoising effect. Compared with other filtering methods, the wavelet threshold denoising algorithm has a better effect for the denoising problem of time-varying and non-stationary random signals such as sound [2]. Next, the process of wavelet threshold de-noising is described step by step, and some skills in the algorithm are demonstrated. Finally, a new threshold function and its denoising effect are shown.

2 Wavelet Threshold Denoising Process

Assume that the signal with Gaussian white noise is:

$$f(t) = s(t) + n(t) \tag{1}$$

Where $s(t)$ is the original signal without noise, $n(t)$ is the Gaussian white noise of variance σ^2, that is to say, it obeys $N\left(0, \sigma^2\right)$ distribution. The discrete-time signal $f[n] = f(nT_s)$ is obtained by Nyquist sampling with sampling interval $T_s \le \frac{2}{f_{max}} (f_{max}\ \textit{is the maximum frequency of}\ f)$.

Generally speaking, compared with noise, the energy of signal is larger and its distribution is more concentrated. Because wavelet transform has the characteristics of sparsity and decorrelation [3], most of the energy of the signal is concentrated in the wavelet approximation coefficients, while the wavelet detail coefficients are the coefficients after the decomposition of the signal high frequency part and high frequency noise, and the energy of signal wavelet transform is concentrated in the low frequency part. The wavelet transform of Gaussian noise is still Gaussian distribution, the energy of noise is more evenly distributed on all wavelet coefficients, and the corresponding wavelet coefficient amplitude is also small. Therefore, the appropriate threshold is selected in different wavelet transform scales, and the corresponding wavelet coefficients are processed by threshold quantization. Finally, the denoising signal is obtained by inverse wavelet transform, so that the noise can be effectively suppressed. On the other hand, compared with FIR filter or IIR filter, wavelet threshold de-noising can also preserve the peak and mutation of the signal. Wavelet threshold denoising process can be divided into the following three steps [4]:

1. Discrete wavelet transform for noisy signal $f[n]$. According to the characteristics of the signal, the appropriate wavelet function is selected, and the decomposition level $Ndec$ is determined, then the decomposition calculation is carried out to obtain a group of wavelet detail coefficients $cD_j(j = 1 \cdots Ndec)$ and wavelet approximation coefficients cA_{Ndec}.
2. The detail coefficients after wavelet decomposition are quantized by threshold. Selecting a suitable threshold value for the detail coefficients cD_j of each decomposition scale to quantize the threshold value and get the processed wavelet coefficients sD_j.
3. The signal is reconstructed by inverse wavelet transform to get the denoised signal. According to the approximation coefficient cA_{Ndec} of wavelet decomposition and the detail coefficient sD_j after threshold quantization of each layer, the estimated signal s is obtained, that is, the denoising signal.

The process of wavelet threshold denoising is shown in Fig. 1.

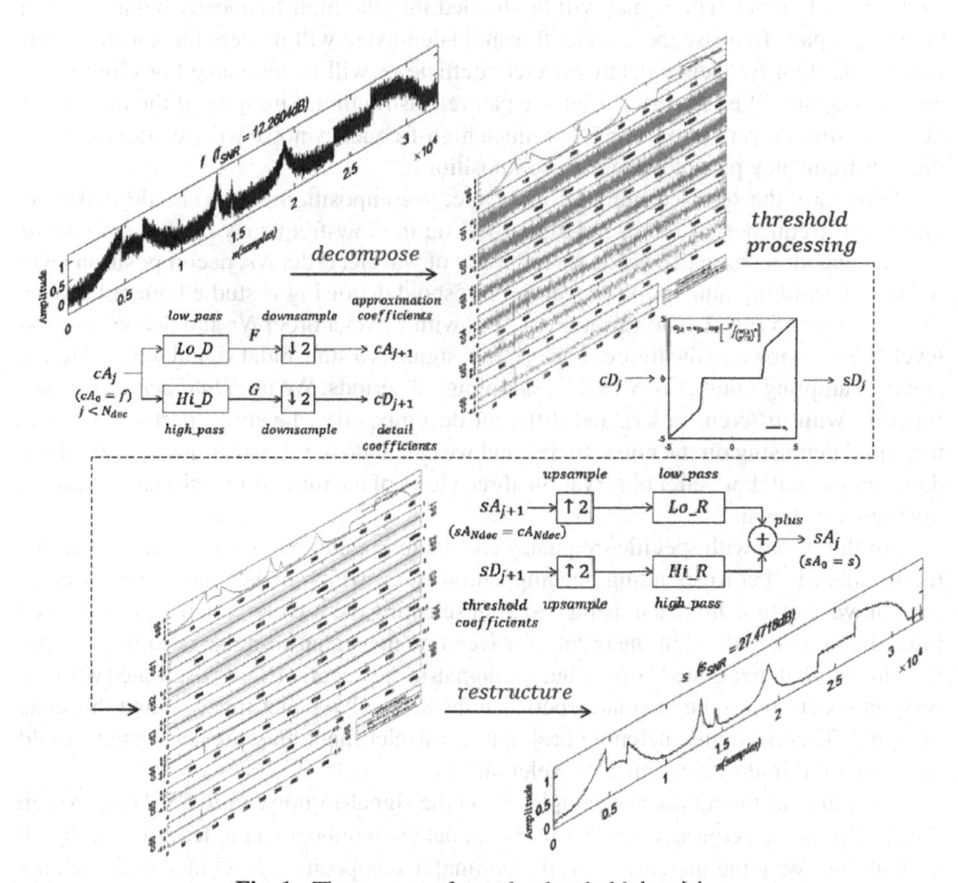

Fig. 1. The process of wavelet threshold denoising

Mallat algorithm is used for wavelet decomposition and reconstruction [5].

3 Selection of Wavelet and Determination of Decomposition Level

According to the properties of wavelet function, it can be seen that the vanishing moment reflects the smoothness of the wavelet function. The higher the vanishing moment, the smoother the wavelet, but it also means that the tightly supported interval is larger, which is not conducive to localized analysis [6]. For fast wavelet transform (FWT), the longer the filter length required, the greater the amount of calculation, and the denoising effect cannot be greatly improved. Therefore, for smoother signals, wavelet functions with higher vanishing moments should be selected appropriately. For example, for *Daubechies* wavelets, *Symlet* wavelets and *Coiflet* wavelets, wavelet functions with higher orders should be selected. On the contrary, for abrupt signal, the wavelet function with small vanishing moment and short support length should be selected.

The selection of decomposition layers is related to the maximum frequency and sampling frequency of the signal. There are too many decomposition layers. The cut-off frequency of the wavelet decomposition low-pass filter is less than the maximum frequency of signal. The signal will be divided into the high-frequency detail wavelet coefficient part. Because the wavelet threshold denoising will process the wavelet coefficient, the high frequency detail wavelet coefficients will be attenuated or eliminated, and the signal will be distorted after wavelet reconstruction. Similarly, if the number of decomposition layers is too small, too much high-frequency noise will be classified into the low-frequency part of wavelet decomposition.

Therefore, the selected number of wavelet decomposition layers should make the maximum frequency of the useful signal fall on the low-frequency coefficient part of wavelet decomposition [7]. Next, the influence of wavelet order *Nr*, decomposition level *Ndec* and sampling number N on wavelet threshold denoising is studied quantitatively.

As shown in Fig. 2. The variation of *SNR* with wavelet order *Nr* and decomposition level *Ndec* is shown in the figure. The original signal is a sinusoidal signal with period 1, and the sampling number is $N = 2^{15}$, sampling 10 periods. We use *Daubechies* wavelet function with different orders and different decomposition layers to perform wavelet threshold denoising on the noisy signal, and we calculate the signal-to-noise ratio of the denoising signal. For better observation, three views of the three-dimensional coordinate diagram are shown.

For the signal with specific frequency and sampling number, it can be seen from the figure, there is a corresponding decomposition level, which makes the signal-to-noise ratio of wavelet threshold denoising best after selecting the wavelet function. At the same time, the influence trend of the order of wavelet on the signal-to-noise ratio is generally the same as that mentioned before, but the signal-to-noise ratio (SNR) oscillates with the wavelet order due to the mismatch between the scale of wavelet function and the scale of signal. Therefore, the matching problem of wavelet function scale and signal should be considered in the selection of wavelet order.

The effect of the number of samples N on the signal-to-noise ratio *SNR* is shown in Fig. 3. The signal is the same as that in Fig. 2, but the number of samples N of the signal is changing. With the increase of N, the optimal decomposition level increases, and the corresponding signal-to-noise ratio also increases. In fact, for a discrete-time sinusoidal signal with a fixed number of periods, its frequency and sampling rate are equivalent, so the number of samples increases and the signal frequency decreases. From the previous

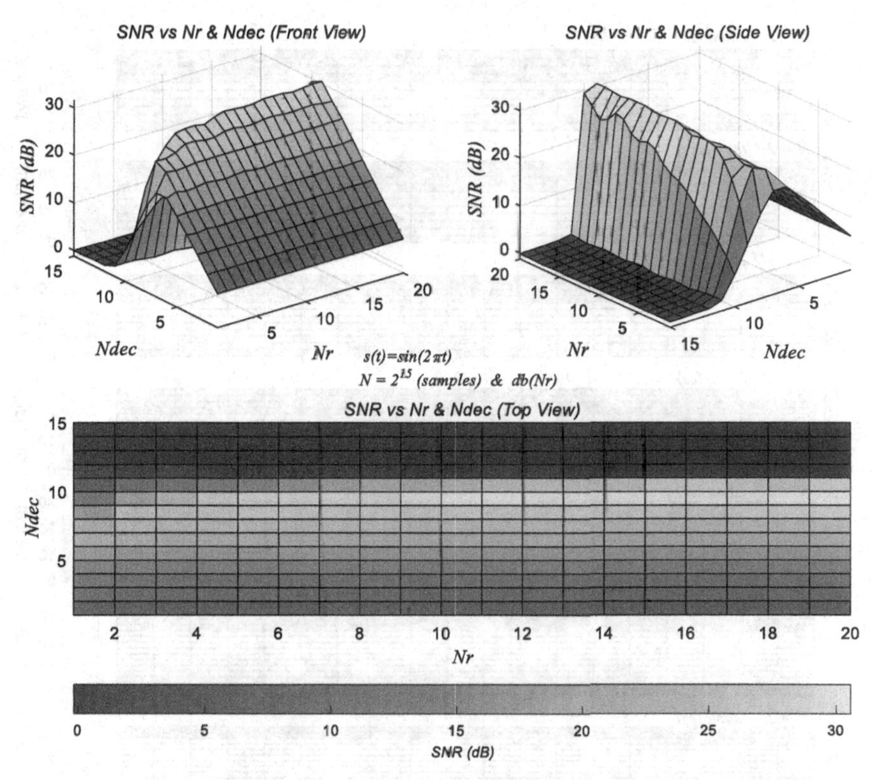

Fig. 2. The influence of *Ndec* and *Nr* on *SNR*

analysis, it can be seen that the number of decomposition levels should be increased. The increase of signal-to-noise ratio is due to the decrease of noise power spectral density with the increase of sampling rate while the signal power remains unchanged.

4 Threshold and Threshold Function

4.1 Threshold Calculation

Fixed Threshold Criterion (Sqtwolog)

$$Tr = \sigma\sqrt{2\log N} \tag{2}$$

N is the signal length and Tr is the global threshold. In soft thresholding, the fixed thresholding can get the visual direct denoising effect, so it is called VisuShrink [8].

Unbiased Risk Assessment Criteria (Rigrsure)
That is, an adaptive threshold selection method based on Stein's unbiased likelihood estimation principle. For each threshold value, the corresponding risk value is calculated. The one with the lowest risk is selected. The specific algorithm is as follows.

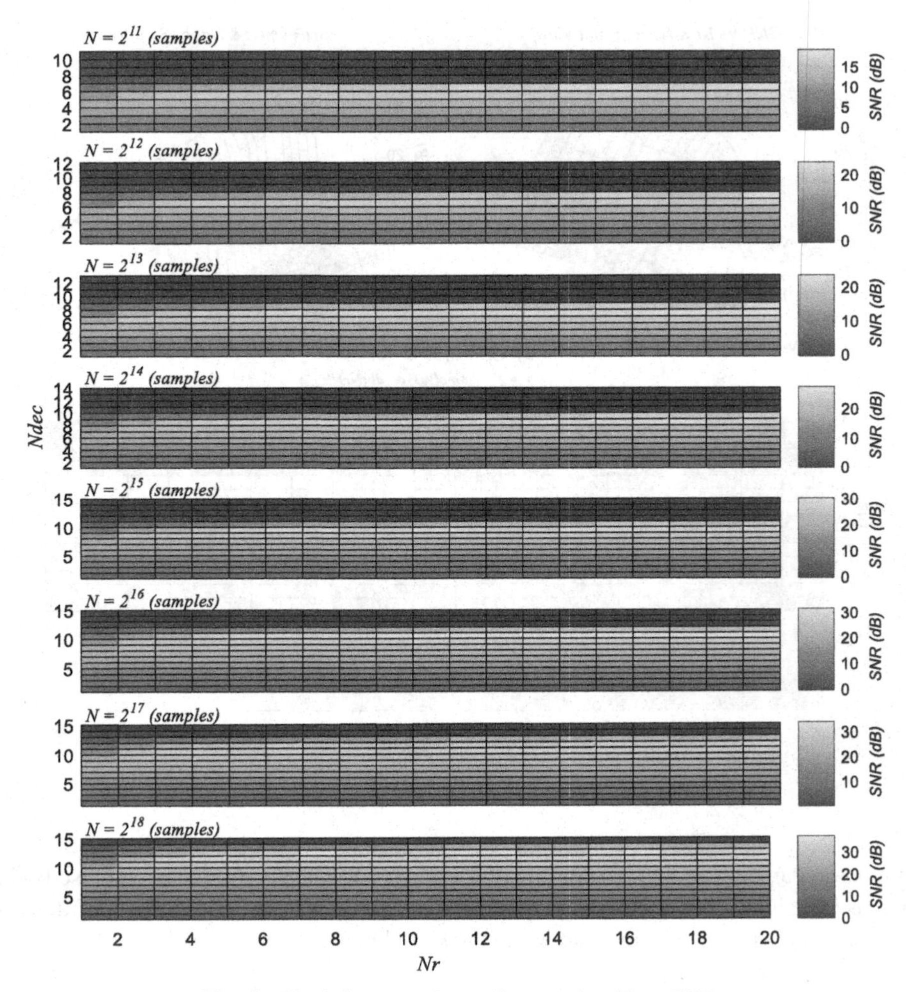

Fig. 3. The influence of sampling number N on SNR

- The wavelet coefficient vector (whose length is n) used to estimate the threshold value is squared, and then sorted from small to large to get a new vector NV to be estimated.
- For each element subscript k of NV, calculate the risk vector as follows:

$$Risk(k) = \frac{n - 2k + \sum_{i=1}^{k} NV(i) + (n - k) \cdot NV(k)}{n} \tag{3}$$

- The value of subscript k corresponding to the minimum point of risk vector *Risk* is obtained, and the threshold *Tr* is obtained as follows:

$$Tr = \sqrt{NV(k)} \tag{4}$$

Mixed Criterion (Heursure)
It is a mixture of fixed threshold criteria and unbiased risk estimation criteria. When the signal-to-noise ratio is very low, unbiased risk estimation criteria has a lot of noise, so fixed threshold is used. The calculation method of the threshold value is: first, judge the size of two variables *Eta* and *Crit*, their expressions are respectively.

$$\begin{cases} Eta = \frac{\sum_{j=1}^{n} |w_{j,k}|^2 - n}{n} \\ Crit = \sqrt{\frac{1}{n}(log_2 n)^3} \end{cases} \tag{5}$$

Where n is the length of the wavelet coefficient vector to be estimated, if $Eta < Crit$, the fixed threshold is selected, otherwise, the smaller of unbiased risk estimation criterion and fixed threshold criterion is selected as the threshold of this criterion.

Minimax Criterion (Minimaxi)
Minimax criterion is also a fixed form of threshold selection, which is used in statistics for the design of estimators. Since the denoising signal can be assumed to be the estimator of unknown regression function, the minimax estimator is the one to achieve the minimum mean square error under the worst condition [9]. The calculation formula of the threshold value is [9]:

$$Tr = \begin{cases} 0, \ N \leq 32 \\ 0.3936 + 0.1829 \cdot log_2 N, \ N > 32 \end{cases} \tag{6}$$

The above threshold is for Gaussian white noise with standard deviation (wavelet domain) of 1, so the actual threshold should be $Tr{\cdot}\sigma$, where σ is the standard deviation of noise. Generally speaking, the wavelet coefficients on the minimum scale are mostly caused by noise, so the estimated value is used. The estimation method is as follows: if M_x is the median of absolute value vector of wavelet coefficient on the minimum scale of noisy signal, then:

$$\sigma = \frac{M_x}{0.6745} \tag{7}$$

The mixed criterion and minimax criterion in the above criteria are relatively conservative (only part of the coefficients are set to zero), so these two thresholds are more suitable when a small part of the high-frequency information of the signal is in the noise range. The other two threshold selection rules, especially the fixed threshold method, can eliminate more noise, but may also remove the high-frequency part of the useful signal [10].

4.2 Selection of Threshold Function

Hard-threshold function:

$$\hat{w}_{j,k} = \begin{cases} w_{j,k}, \left|w_{j,k}\right| \geq \lambda \\ 0, \left|w_{j,k}\right| < \lambda \end{cases} \tag{8}$$

Soft threshold function:

$$\hat{w}_{j,k} = \begin{cases} sign\left(\left|w_{j,k}\right|\right)\left(\left|w_{j,k}\right| - \lambda\right), \left|w_{j,k}\right| \geq \lambda \\ 0, \left|w_{j,k}\right| < \lambda \end{cases} \tag{9}$$

Semi-soft threshold function:

$$\hat{w}_{j,k} = \begin{cases} 0, \left|w_{j,k}\right| \leq \lambda_1 \\ sign\left(\left|w_{j,k}\right|\right)\frac{\lambda_2\left(\left|w_{j,k}\right| - \lambda_1\right)}{\lambda_2 - \lambda_1}, \lambda_1 < \left|w_{j,k}\right| \leq \lambda_2 \\ w_{j,k}, \left|w_{j,k}\right| > \lambda_2 \end{cases} \tag{10}$$

And λ_2 is the upper threshold and λ_1 is the lower threshold [11].

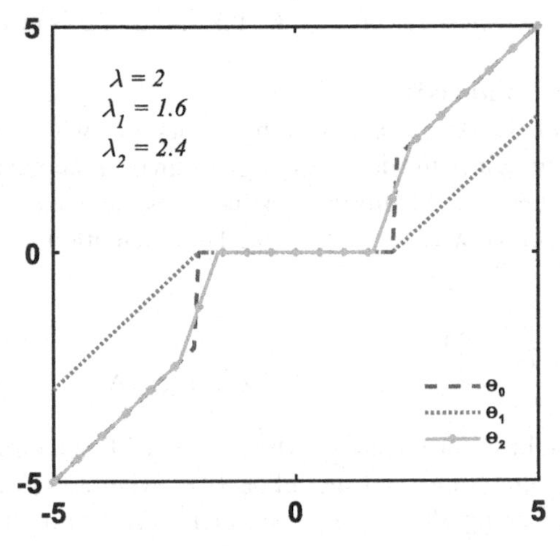

Fig. 4. Threshold function

In Fig. 4, Θ_0, Θ_1, Θ_2 are hard threshold function, soft threshold function and semi-soft threshold function curves respectively.

The following figure shows the processing effect of each threshold function under the fixed threshold value.

In Fig. 5, s_0 is the original signal, f is the noisy signal, $SNR = 12.2049$ dB, $s_{\theta 0}$ is the reconstructed signal processed by hard threshold function, and the *SNR* is 24.4302 dB. $s_{\theta 1}$ is the reconstructed signal processed by the soft threshold function with an *SNR* of 25.3501 dB. $s_{\theta 2}$ is the reconstructed signal processed by the semi-soft threshold function, and the *SNR* is 24.4488 dB. From the aspect of *SNR*, the processing effect of soft threshold and semi-soft threshold function is better than that of hard threshold function.

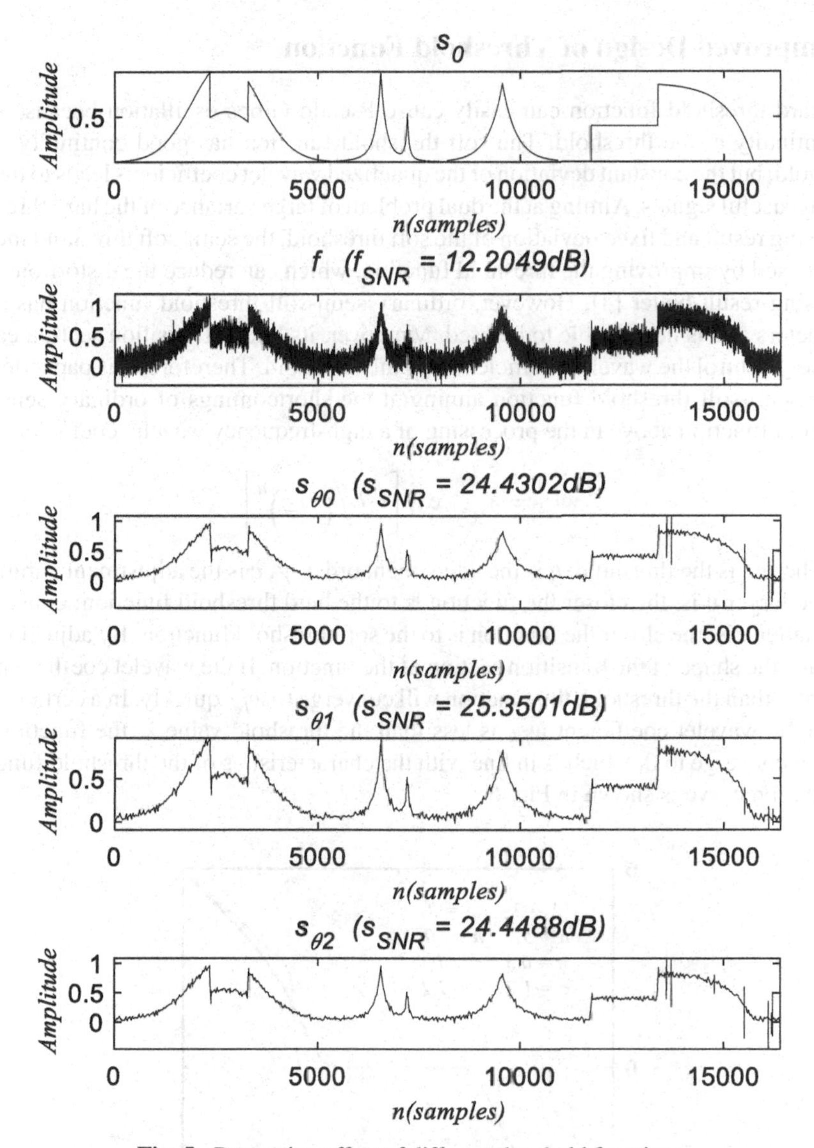

Fig. 5. Processing effect of different threshold functions

5 Improved Design of Threshold Function

The hard threshold function can easily cause Pseudo-Gibbs oscillation because of its discontinuity at the threshold. The soft threshold function has good continuity at the threshold, but the constant deviation of the quantized wavelet coefficients leads to the loss of some useful signals. Aiming at the dual problem of large variance of the hard threshold denoising result and fixed deviation of the soft threshold, the semi-soft threshold method is proposed by improving the threshold function, which can reduce the distortion of the denoising result better [4]. However, ordinary semi-soft threshold function has a few parameters and is not flexible to be used. Moreover, its linear Transition section cannot precisely control the wavelet coefficient near the threshold. Therefore, this paper designs a new semi-soft threshold function aiming at the shortcomings of ordinary semi-soft threshold function above in the processing of a high-frequency wavelet coefficient [12].

$$\hat{w}_{j,k} = w_{j,k} \cdot \exp\left[-\gamma \Big/ \left(\frac{w_{j,k}}{c \cdot \lambda}\right)^n\right] \tag{11}$$

Where λ is the threshold, n is the adjustment order, γ, c is the adjustment parameter, and the larger n is, the closer the function is to the hard threshold function; conversely, the smaller n is, the closer the function is to the soft threshold function. By adjusting γ, c to adjust the shape of the transition section of the function. If the wavelet coefficient $w_{j,k}$ is greater than the threshold, the function will converge to $w_{j,k}$ quickly. In a certain range where the wavelet coefficient $w_{j,k}$ is less than the threshold value λ, the function will quickly converge to 0, which is in line with the characteristics of the threshold function. Its function curve is shown in Fig. 6.

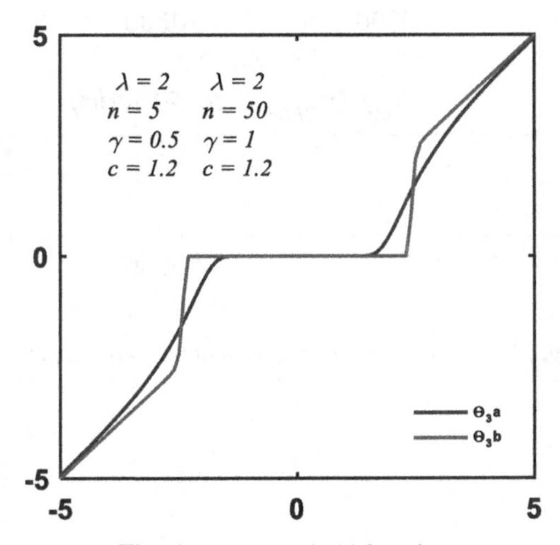

Fig. 6. New threshold function

The main advantage of this threshold function is that the function can be adjusted flexibly, which fully combines the advantages of soft and hard thresholds, and the function quickly converges to zero in the range of $[-\lambda, \lambda]$, and the cut-off effect is obvious.

Of course, the disadvantage is that in theory, using this threshold function for threshold processing cannot completely filter out high-frequency noise, because the function is only zero at the zero points, but because the value within the threshold range is very small (10^{-9}), so In practical applications, in addition to the accuracy of the algorithm or the accuracy of the machine, it can be set to zero, to achieve the purpose of making the high-frequency noise completely zero.

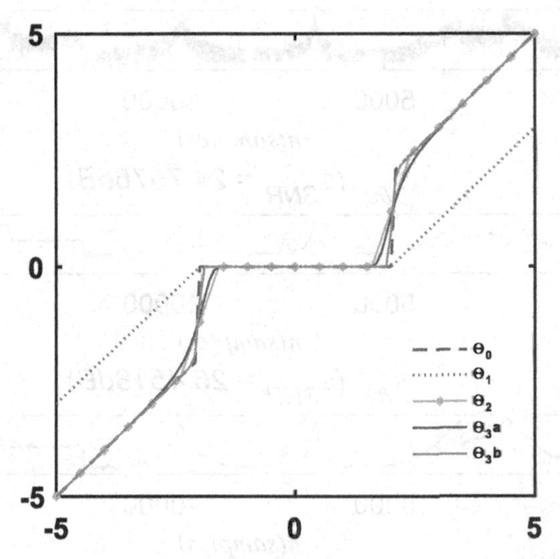

Fig. 7. Comparison of the new threshold function with the general threshold function

As shown Fig. 7, Θ_0, Θ_1, Θ_2 respectively hard threshold function, soft thresholding function, and semi-soft threshold function curve, $\Theta_3 a$, $\Theta_3 b$ is the new threshold function curve under different order numbers, you can see, choose different parameters, a new threshold function is a good way to approach the hard threshold function, and semi-soft threshold function, according to the different parameters, can approximate the optimal threshold function.

The specific denoising effect is shown in Fig. 8.

Compared with the hard threshold functions, the newly designed threshold function has a better processing effect, and it is equivalent to that of the soft threshold function.

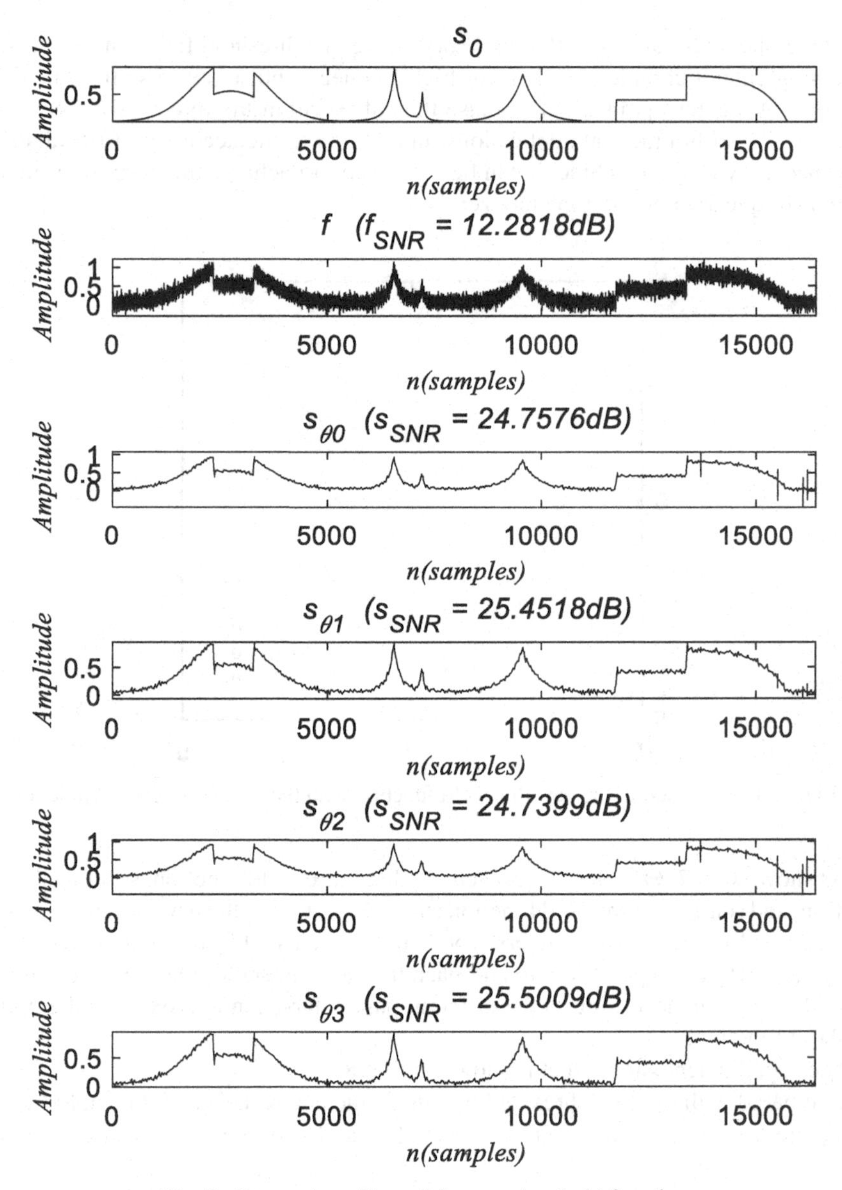

Fig. 8. Processing effect of the new threshold function

6 Conclusion

This paper mainly discusses the basic principle of wavelet threshold denoising, and analyzes the choice of wavelet function: that is, for the signal with higher smoothness, the wavelet function with higher disappearance moment should be selected, and for the sudden signal, the choice of small disappearance moment and Support a short wavelet function. Discuss the choice of decomposition layers: The choice of decomposition layers is related to the frequency of the signal and the sampling frequency. Too many decomposition layers. The cutoff frequency of the wavelet decomposition low-pass filter is greater than the signal frequency. The signal will be divided into high-frequency wavelet coefficients. Because wavelet threshold denoising will process wavelet coefficients and high-frequency wavelet coefficients will be eliminated, the signal will be eliminated, and the signal will not be restored during wavelet reconstruction; too few decomposition layers will cause excessive high-frequency noise Into the low-frequency part of the wavelet decomposition so that the reconstructed signal will contain these noises. Therefore, the number of wavelet decomposition layers should be selected so that the coefficient of the maximum frequency component of the useful signal falls exactly on the low-frequency coefficient part of the wavelet decomposition.

Then the characteristics of the threshold function are studied, and a new type of threshold function is designed. The function is flexible and convenient and can approximate other ordinary threshold functions. That is, by changing the parameters, the new threshold function has the characteristics of its ordinary threshold function. Experiments show that the new threshold function has a better denoising effect than other ordinary threshold functions.

Wavelet threshold denoising is a flexible and effective denoising method. Threshold calculation is the key problem of wavelet threshold denoising. If the threshold calculation is too large, the high-frequency details of the signal will be lost. If the threshold calculation is too small, there will be too many high-Frequency noises is reconstructed into the signal. At present, wavelet thresholds have fixed thresholds, unbiased risk estimation thresholds, heuristic thresholds, and maximum and minimum thresholds. Different threshold calculation methods should be selected for different types of noise and noise levels. Threshold function is a major focus of wavelet threshold denoising, and its function curve around the threshold determines the difference between this threshold function and other threshold functions. From my point of view, the key to improving the effect of wavelet threshold denoising is the threshold function. On the other hand, for the fine selection of wavelet coefficients, can we use neural networks instead of wavelet threshold functions to obtain the optimal threshold function for signals? This is a question to be demonstrated.

Acknowledgement. Aided by Scientific and Technological Developing Scheme of Ji Lin Province No. 20190302082GX and CHINESE NATIONAL PROJECT No. JZX2G201911TJ006601.

References

1. Hu, G., et al.: Modern Signal Processing Course. Tsinghua University Press, Beijing (2004)
2. Zhaowen, R., et al.: Research on speech enhancement method based on acoustic model and wavelet transform. University of science and technology of China, Anhui (2009)
3. Mallat, S., Zhong, S.: Characterization of signal from multiscale edges. IEEE Trans. Pattern Anal. Mach. Intell. **14**, 710–732 (1992)
4. Ye, Z., Huang, Y.: New improvement of wavelet threshold denoising algorithm. Comput. Eng. Appl. **47**(12), 141–145 (2011)

5. Mallat, S.: A theory for multiresolution signal decomposition: the wavelet representation. IEEE Pattern Anal. and Machine Intell **11**(7), 674–693 (1989)
6. Yongmin, Z.: Study on speech denoising method based on wiener - wavelet threshold. Guangdong: Guangdong University of Technology (2018)
7. Srivastava, M., Anderson, C.L., Freed, J.H.: A new wavelet denoising method for selecting decomposition levels and noise thresholds. IEEE Access. **4**, 3862–3877 (2016)
8. Donoho, D.L., Johnstone, I.M.: Ideal spatial adaptation by wavelet shrinkage. Biometrika **81**, 425–455 (1994)
9. Sardy, S.: Minimax threshold for denoising complex signals with waveshrink. IEEE Trans. Signal Process. **48**, 1023–1028 (2000)
10. Zhu, D.D., Wang, H.F.: The application of wavelet denoise in sampled grating comb filter. Advanced materials research, vol. 1042, pp. 135–138, October 2014, Trans Tech Publications, Ltd.
11. Hao, W., Tingquan, C., Xianghong, H., et al.: Improved Semi-soft threshold algorithm for Random walk Denoising in GNSS time series and its evaluation . J. Survey. Mapp. **45**(S2), 22–30 (2016)
12. He, l., et al.: Study on linear fiber Sagnac interferometer acoustic sensor and its denoising method. Acta instrumentation **40**(9), 71-77 (2019)

International Workshop on Satellite Internet of Things, Trusted Data sharing, Secure Communication

Research on Network Fault Detection and Diagnosis Based on Deep Q Learning

Peipei Zhang(✉), Mingxiao Wu, and Xiaorong Zhu

Nanjing University of Posts and Telecommunications, Nanjing, China
1342113203@qq.com

Abstract. In order to improve the efficiency and quality of service of the network, network convergence and the development of heterogeneous network have became inevitable. It is a challenge to detect and diagnose the various network faults efficiently in the complex network environment. To solve this problem, a network fault detection and diagnosis algorithm based on deep Q-learning is proposed. Combining deep learning and reinforcement learning model to classify network faults, we can classify some obvious network states via using less features, and filter irrelevant or redundant features at the same time. Results show that the algorithm can use less features to achieve higher classification accuracy, and the accuracy can reach 96.7%.

Keywords: Heterogeneous wireless networks · Deep Q learning · Fault diagnosis · Fault prediction

1 Introduction

With the development of 5G and 6G, we can forecast that in order to meet the needs of users, the network environment will be complex in the future. Under the trend that network develops more and more heterogeneous and intensive, how to diagnose and predict network faults effectively has become a huge challenge, which has been studied by many experts. Szilagyi [1] proposed a complete fault diagnosis framework. The fault detection process mainly monitors the radio measurement data and compares it with the normal behavior captured by the profile, and the diagnosis of the root cause depends on the historical fault cases, and we should figure out these cases' impact on the performance indicators. Three key performance indicators (KPI) are considered in the research process in that literature, namely, channel quality, call drop and early handover time. Khanafer [2] used the simulation data and the actual data to verify, but the identification of the faulty cells only depends on one KPI, that is, the call drop rate. Khatib [3] proposed a diagnosis method based on supervised genetic fuzzy algorithm. Using genetic algorithm to learn fuzzy rule base depends on labeled training set. The experiment is based on a simulation data set and a real data set with 72 records, four kinds of KPIs and four fault causes are considered in the process of fault diagnosis. From the experts' studies on network fault diagnosis, the traditional network fault diagnosis algorithms are based on supervised

Q. Wu et al. (Eds.): WiSATS 2020, LNICST 358, pp. 533–545, 2021.
https://doi.org/10.1007/978-3-030-69072-4_43

learning and rely on a huge number of data sets. What's more, these algorithms only consider a few kinds of faults and the process of fault identification only relies on a small number of KPIs. However, in the complex heterogeneous wireless network environment, network faults will become more diversified, and the identification of network faults will also rely on more KPIs. Therefore, we propose a network fault detection and diagnosis algorithm based on deep reinforcement learning, which is used to solve the situation that the network state is diverse.

Reinforcement learning (RL) [4] is an important branch of machine learning. The essence of reinforcement learning is to describe and solve the problem that the agent learns strategies to maximize rewards or achieve specific goals in the process of interaction with the environment. Unlike supervised learning, reinforcement learning does not tell the agent how to take correct actions. It only evaluates the actions and corrects the action selection and strategy according to the feedback signals. Therefore, the return function of reinforcement learning needs less information and is easier to design, which is suitable for solving more complex decision problems. Recently, with the rise of deep learning (DL) [5] technology and its brilliant achievements in many fields, deep reinforcement learning (DRL) [6], which integrates deep neural network and RL, has become a research hot spot of all parties, and has made great breakthroughs in computer vision, robot control, large real-time strategic games and other fields.

The main contribution of this paper is combining deep learning and reinforcement learning model to classify network faults, specifically, classifying some obvious network states via using less features, and filtering irrelevant or redundant features. Simulation results show that the proposed algorithm can achieve accurate network fault diagnosis and prediction.

2 System Model

2.1 Network Scenario

Figure 1 shows a heterogeneous wireless network scenario in which macrocell, microcell and femtocell overlap each other. In this scenario, due to the diversity of the network, the system becomes more complex and the network management becomes more difficult. We take the network fault diagnosis and prediction in this scenario as an example to verify the value of the network fault detection and diagnosis method based on deep reinforcement learning.

2.2 Network Fault Data Set

The network fault data set comes from the simulation environment set up, which is generated by OPNET 18.6. In this simulation environment, the building of cellular network and the setting of base station parameters are shown in Table 1.

In the simulation, 11 kinds of network status categories are mainly set, which can be divided into five categories: normal, interference, coverage, hardware and transmission. Among them, normal is $\{FC_1\}$, interference is divided into two types: uplink and downlink interference $\{FC_2, FC_3\}$, coverage fault $\{FC_4\}$, hardware is divided into four

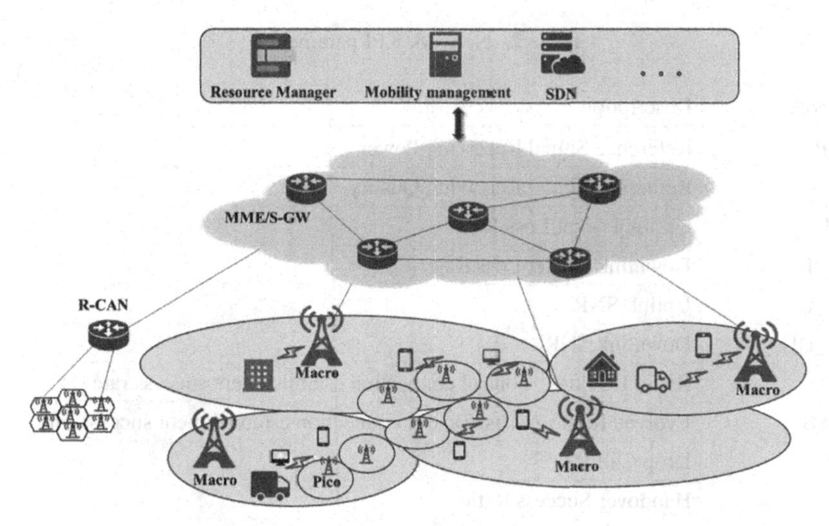

Fig. 1. Heterogeneous wireless network scenario

Table 1. Network simulation parameters

Simulation parameters	Marcocell	Mircocell
Number of base stations	3	8
Number of users/base station	30	10
Transmission power/dBm	46	30
Standard deviation of shadow fading/db	8	10
Propagation loss model	Free Space	Indoor office environment
Antenna gain/dBi	15	8
Operation mode	LTE,5 MHz,FDD	LTE 10 MHz FDD
Receiving sensitivity/dBm	−110	−107
Base station selection strategy	Best suitable eNodeB	Best suitable eNodeB
User distribution	Random distribution	Random distribution

different base station faults $\{FC_5, FC_6, FC_7, FC_8\}$, and transmission is divided into three different link failures $\{FC_9, FC_{10}, FC_{11}\}$. That is, $C = \{FC_1, FC_2, FC_3,\ldots, FC_{11}\}$.

For each network state, 16 kinds of key performance indicators are used to measure in the simulation, and the specific indicators are shown in Table 2. Then, the occurrence time of these network states is set in advance in order to generate data labels manually. Each simulation time is set to 2 h, and the occurrence time of each network state is 20 min. In the end, about 10000 pieces of data were obtained.

Table 2. Network KPI parameters

Symbols	Description
RSRP	Reference Signal Receiving Power
RSRQ	Reference Signal Receiving Quality
PD_UL	Uplink Packet Loss Rate
PD_DL	Downlink Packet Loss Rate
SNR_UL	Uplink SNR
SNR_DL	Downlink SNR
RRC	Radio Resource Control connection establishment success rate
E-RAB	Evolved Radio Access Bearer connection establishment success rate
DCR	Drop Call Rate
HO	Handover Success Ratio
CUAT	Cell Uplink Average Throughput
CDAT	Cell Downlink Average Throughput
LT (→)	Average Link Throughput (→)
LT (←)	Average Link Throughput (←)
HO_d	Handover Delay
LER	Link Error Rate

3 Markov Decision Process of Network Fault Identification

In order to use reinforcement learning algorithm to solve the problem of network fault identification, it is necessary to model the problem of network fault identification as Markov decision process. As shown in Fig. 2, when an agent is carrying out a task, it first interacts with the environment to generate a new state, and the environment returns a reward. As the cycle goes on, the agent and environment constantly interact to generate more new data. Reinforcement learning algorithm [4] is to generate new data through a series of action strategies and environment interaction, and then use the new data to modify their own action strategies. After several iterations, the agent will learn the action strategies needed to complete the correct fault diagnosis.

We define (x, y) as a sample in data set, vector x as the value of feature set $k \in K = \{k_1, k_2 \ldots k_n\}$ composed of key performance indicators, and $y \in Y$ as the target label. c is defined as the cost function. When a new feature k_i is adopted, the cost is $c(k_i)$. This paper defines environment state space S, observation state o, action space A, reward function $r(s, a)$, environment transformation function $t(s, a)$ as follows:

$s = \left(x, y, \tilde{K}\right) \in S$ consists of a set of samples (x, y) and the currently selected feature set $\tilde{K}$. The observation state $o = \{x_i, k_i\}$ is the state accepted by the agent, and it has no target label. Action is $A = \{A_C, A_K\}$, where A_K represents selecting a new feature that has not been selected before, and A_C means to use a classification action to predict

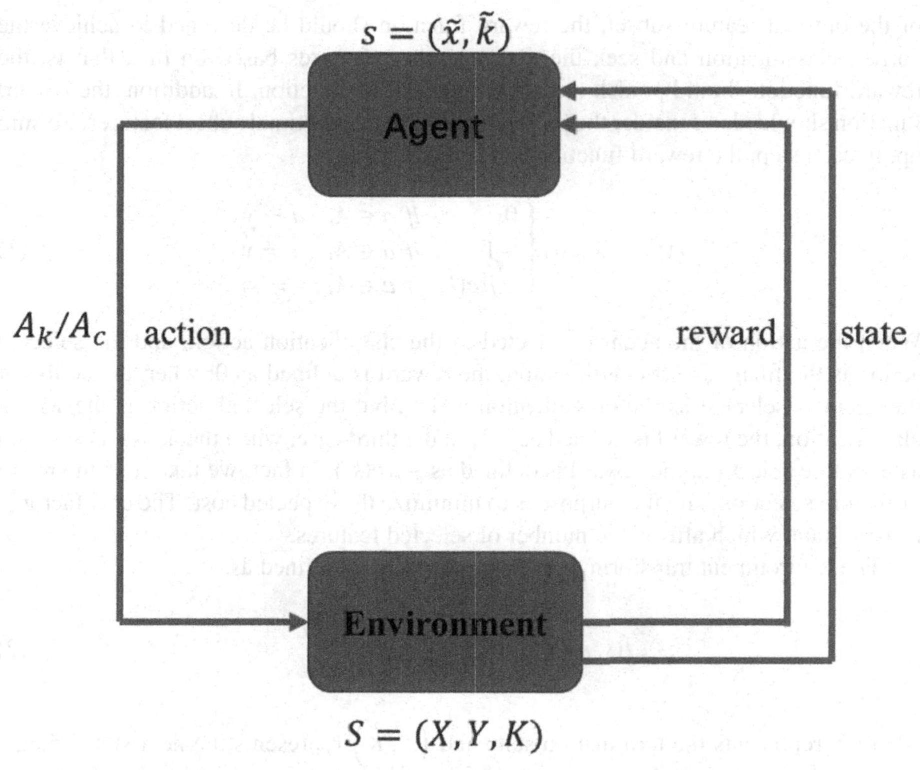

Fig. 2. Markov decision process for network fault identification

which category the sample belongs to. We provide that if $A = A_C$, the event will end (see Fig. 3).

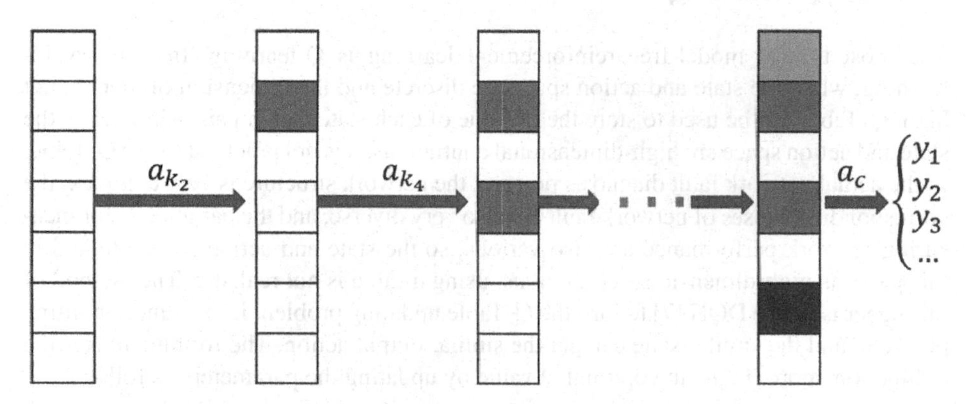

Fig. 3. Classification process

The reward function $r(s, a)$ is a quantitative evaluation performed for each state. Since the purpose of the algorithm is to achieve the correct classification and the selection of the optimal feature subset, the reward function should be designed to achieve the correct classification and seek the optimal subset features based on this, that is, the reward function should punish the wrong classification action. In addition, the reward function should also consider the problem of finding the optimal subset features. To sum up, in each step, the reward function can be defined as:

$$r((\tilde{x}, y, k), a)\begin{cases} 0 & \text{if } a \in A_C, a = y \\ -1 & \text{if } a \in A_C, a \neq y \\ -\mu c(k_i) & \text{if } a \in A_k, a = k_i \end{cases} \tag{1}$$

When the action of the agent is selected as the classification action, and the selected action is the final correct classification, the reward is defined as 0; when the action of the agent is selected as the classification action, but the selected action is the wrong classification, the reward is defined as -1; in the third case, when the action is selected as a feature selection, the reward is defined as $-\mu c(k_i)$, in fact, we take it as the result of feature selection, and the purpose is to minimize the expected cost. The cost factor μ is a constant, which affects the number of selected features.

The environment transformation function $t(s, a)$ is defined as:

$$t(s, a) = \begin{cases} T & \text{if } a \in A_C \\ \left(x', y, \tilde{K}\right) & \text{if } a \in A_k \end{cases} \tag{2}$$

where T represents the termination state and $\left(x', \tilde{K}\right)$ represents the next state when a new feature is selected. In one cycle, the most states are converted to $|K| + 1$. When $a \in A_C$, the environment changes to the termination state. When $a \in A_k$, it enters the next state of selecting new features.

4 Deep Q Learning

The most typical model-free reinforcement learning is Q-learning. In ordinary Q-learning, when the state and action space are discrete and the dimension of them is not high, Q-Table can be used to store the Q value of each state action pair, while when the state and action space are high-dimensional continuous, it is not practical to use Q-Table. In the actual network fault diagnosis process, the network structure is very complex, the corresponding causes of network fault are also very diverse, and the parameters for measuring network performance are also various, so the state and action space studied in this paper is high-dimensional continuous, using q-table is not realistic. The method of this paper is to use DQN [7] to turn the Q-Table updating problem into a function fitting problem, and the similar state can get the similar output action. The formula makes the Q function approximate the optimal Q value by updating the parameters as follows:

$$Q(s, a; \theta) \approx Q^*(s, a) \tag{3}$$

We define the state-action value $Q(s, a)$, which represents the state-action value function that takes action a while following the strategy π when the agent is in the state s.

Strategy π refers to the probability distribution of actions under a given state, defines the behavior of the agent in a specific environment at a specific time, and can be regarded as a mapping from environmental state to actions. Here, the strategy determines how the fault recognition task should identify the fault category correctly or select the appropriate feature subset in the current state. $Q^*(s, a)$ represents the optimal state-action value function, it subjects to the Bellman equation [4]. If the optimal value of s' at the next time step is known to all actions a', then the optimal strategy is to choose action a' to maximize expected value:

$$Q^*(s, a) = E_{s' \sim t(s,a)}\left[r + \gamma \max_{a'} Q^*\left(s', a'\right)|s, a\right] \quad (4)$$

γ is the discount factor, and r represents the reward value of the current state taking action.

DQN uses a neural network function with weight θ as an approximator, called a Q network. One Q network can be iteratively trained by minimizing the loss function of the decision sequence:

$$Loss(\theta) = E\left[\left(Q_{target} - Q(s, a; \theta)\right)^2\right] \quad (5)$$

where $Q_{target} = r + \gamma \max_{a'} Q^*\left(s', a'; \theta'\right)$, and θ' is the parameter of the fixed target network.

The DQN training process is shown in Fig. 4. It uses two key technologies. One is the experience reply. The function of the experience reply is mainly to solve the problems of correlation and non-static distribution. The specific method is to store the transfer samples $\left(s, a, r, s'\right)$ obtained from the interaction between the agent and the environment at each time step in the playback memory unit, and randomly take out a minibatch of them to train when training is needed. This treatment breaks the correlation between samples and makes samples independent of each other. The other one is a fixed target value network (Fixed Q-target): calculating the network target value requires the use of the existing Q value, now a network with slower updating rate is used to provide this Q value. This improves the stability and convergence of training. To make the algorithm performance more stable, establish two neural networks with the same structure: one network that has been always updating neural network parameters (MainNet) and another one network for updating Q values (TargetNet).

Initially, assign MainNet's parameters to TargetNet, then MainNet continues to update the neural network parameters, while the TargetNet parameters are fixed. After a while, the MainNet's parameters are assigned to TargetNet, and so on.

In this way, the target Q value is stable for a period of time, which makes the algorithm update more stable.

5 Algorithm

To facilitate the simulation, we map the observation state o to $(\overline{x}, \text{m})$, the vector $\overline{x}$ is a masked vector of the feature set x composed of key performance indicators, it contains

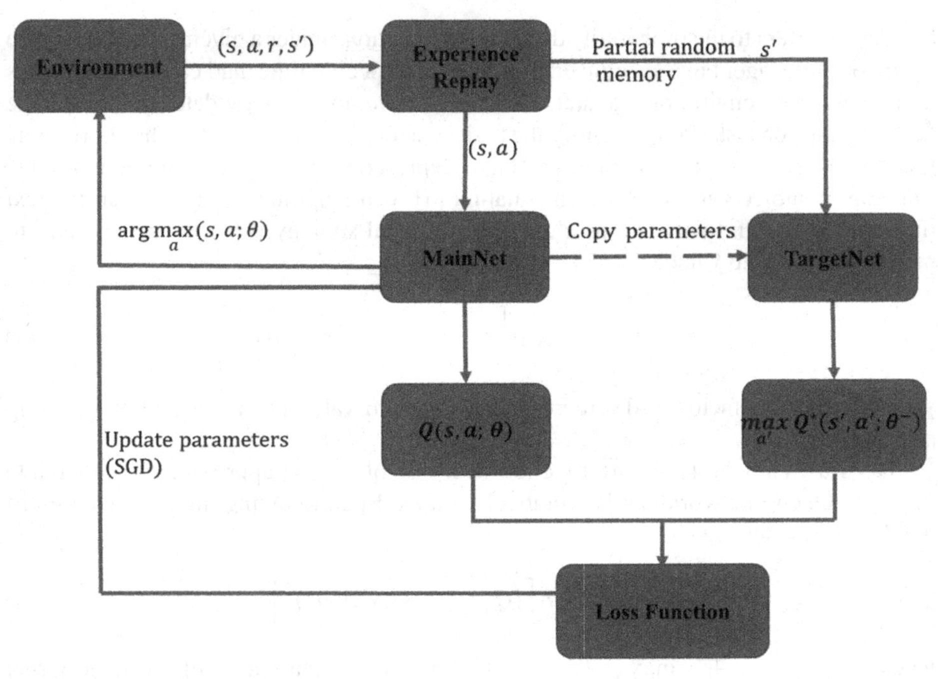

Fig. 4. DQN training process

two parts, one is a optional feature value, another one is 0, indicating that an unknown value is selected.

$$x_i = \begin{cases} x_i \; if \; k_i \in K \\ 0 \; otherwise \end{cases} \tag{6}$$

Mask m $\in (0, 1)^n$ is a vector, and different values indicate obtaining different types of features. If the obtained feature value $k_i \in K$, value is 1, otherwise it is 0.

$$m_i = \begin{cases} 1 \; if \; k_i \in K \\ 0 \; otherwise \end{cases} \tag{7}$$

The architecture of the model is shown in Fig. 5. The input layer consists of feature vector $\overline{x}$ and binary mask m, then a neural network, and the final fully connected layer outputs the q value of classification and feature selection actions. Algorithm 1 and Algorithm 2 describe the algorithm and environment simulation.

Fig. 5. DQN model framework

Algorithm 1 Environment simulation

---

function STEP(s, a)

if $a \in A_k$ **then**

Select a corresponding position feature:k= $k + k_a$

Create the mask $m^{(i)} = 1$ if $k_i \in K$, *otherwise* zeros

Return (k, m), $-\mu c(k_i)$

else if $a \in A_c$ **then**

$$r = \begin{cases} 0 & if\ a = y \\ -1 & if\ a \neq y \end{cases}$$

Draw a new sample from the data-set reset the environment

Return $(done, r)$

end if

end function

Algorithm 2 DQN Training

Randomly initialize networks parameters θ and θ'

Initial the environment E with $s_0 \in (x, y, \varnothing)$

Initial the experience pool P with size N

For episode =1, EPOCHS **do**

for $e \in E$ **do**

repeat

Simulate one step with ε -greedy police π

$a = \pi(s),\ (s', r) = STEP(s, a)$

Store the transition (s, a, r, s') into pool P

until $|P| > N$

Start to train the net and update P circularly, choose a mini batch of experience from P, Set:

$$y^{DQN} = \begin{cases} r \\ r + \gamma \max_{a'} Q(s', a'; \theta') \end{cases}$$

Perform a gradient descent step on:

$$loss(\theta) = (y^{DQN} - Q(s, a; \theta))^2$$

end for

end for

6 Experimental Results

The data obtained by setting the simulation environment is input into the DQN model as input parameters, and the reward is obtained through continuous iteration. The accuracy of network fault classification is shown in Fig. 6 and Fig. 7. As can be seen from Fig. 6, in the initial stage of training, the average reward convergence rate is very fast, and then tends to be stable. Since we narrowed its range to [−1,0], this effectively overcomes the numerical explosion. It can be seen from Fig. 7 that the optimal classification accuracy rate is 96.7%. During the initial training, the DQN algorithm selects almost all features to make classification decisions, which makes the accuracy rate increase rapidly. As the number of iterations increases, the number of selected features will gradually decrease. After a period of exploration, the agent will find the smallest subset composed of important features, and as the number of iterations increases later, the total number of choices changes slowly and tends to be stable. In this process, the agent will continue to change the best subset of feature combinations to improve accuracy, but it has not improved a lot. Therefore, the classification accuracy rate increases rapidly at the beginning, and gradually converges to a stable value after reaching higher accuracy.

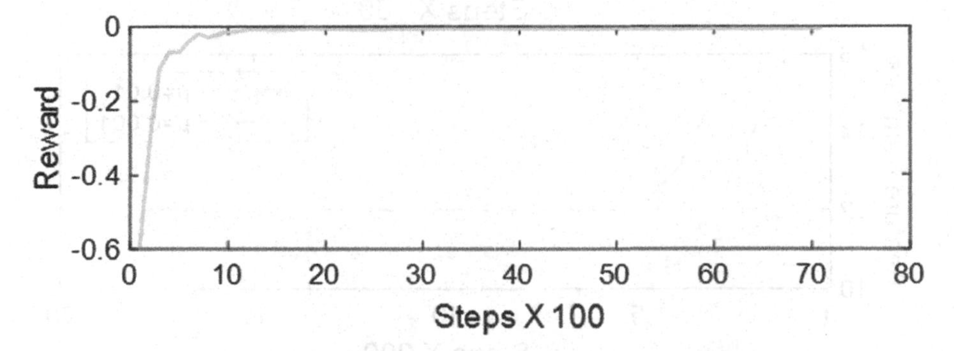

Fig. 6. Changes of reward value under different iterations

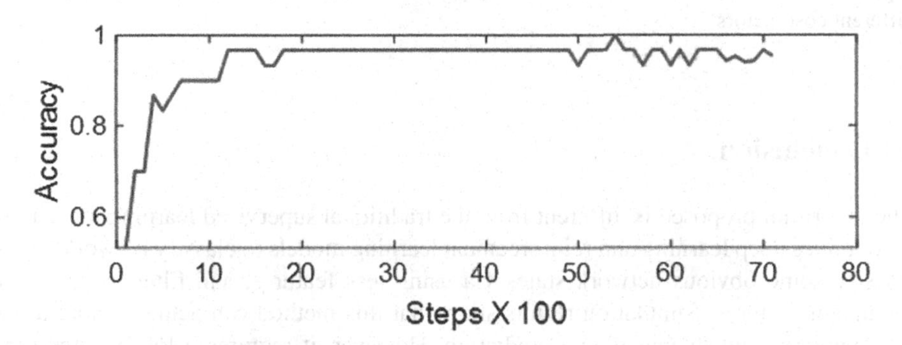

Fig. 7. Changes of fault classification accuracy under different iterations

Figure 8 is a simulation result for selecting different cost factors μ. From the picture, we can see that the smaller μ is, the smaller the absolute value of the cost generated by feature selection, then the agent will iterate more times to search for the optimal feature subset. At first, the algorithm selects almost all features, then as the number of iterations increases, then it starts filtering redundant features. The speed of filtering redundant features at $\mu = 0.001$ is significantly lower than the rate at $\mu = 0.01$. As the curve stabilizes, the difference in classification accuracy between the two is very small. So we can choose to control the best choice and convergence speed by adjusting to cost factor μ.

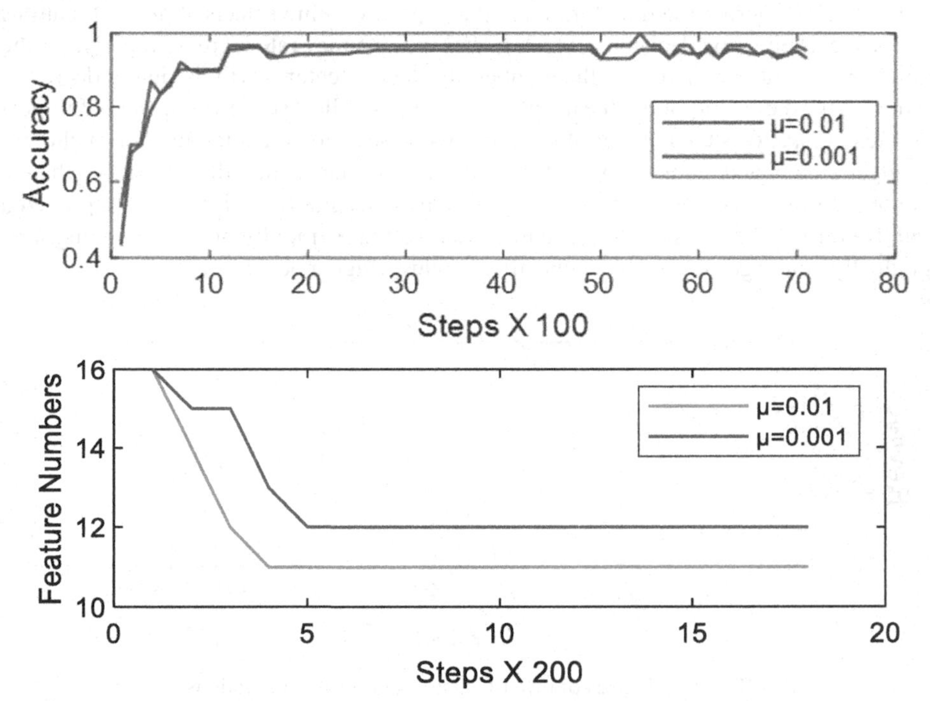

Fig. 8. Changes of fault classification accuracy and number of feature combinations under different cost factors

7 Conclusion

The algorithm proposed is different from the traditional supervised learning algorithm. It combines deep learning and reinforcement learning models to classify network faults, classify some obvious network states via using less features, and filter irrelevant or redundant features. Simulation results show that this method can achieve more accurate network fault diagnosis and prediction. However, it requires a lot of computing resources during the training process, and the training time is slow, so other enhancement technologies can be selected in the future to improve performance.

References

1. Szilagyi, P., Novaczki, S.: An automatic detection and diagnosis framework for mobile communication systems. IEEE Trans. Netw. Serv. Manage. **9**(2), 184–197 (2012)
2. Khanafer, R.M., Solana, B., Triola, J., et al.: Automated diagnosis for UMTS networks using bayesian network approach. IEEE Trans. Veh. Technol. **57**(4), 2451–2461 (2008)
3. Khatib, E.J., Barco, R., Andrades, A.G., et al.: Diagnosis based on genetic fuzzy algorithms for LTE self- healing. IEEE Trans. Veh. Technol. **65**(3), 1 (2015)
4. Sutton, R.S., Barto, A.G.: Introduction to Reinforcement Learning. MIT Press, Cambridge (1998)
5. LeCun, Y., Bengio, Y., Hinton, G.: Deep learning. Nature **521**(7553), 436–444 (2015)
6. Henderson P, Islam R, Bachman P, et al.: Deep reinforcement learning that matters. In: Thirty-Second AAAI Conference on Artificial Intelligence (2018)
7. Janisch, J., Pevn, T., Lis, V.: Classification with Costly Features using Deep Reinforcement Learning (2017)

attr2vec: Learning Node Representations from Attributes of Nodes

Pengkun Zheng[1], Yan Wen[1](✉), Ming Chen[2], and Geng Chen[3]

[1] College of Computer Science and Engineering, Shandong University of Science and Technology, Qingdao, China
wenyan84@hotmail.com

[2] State Grid Shandong Electric Power Company, Qingdao Power Supply Company, Qingdao, China

[3] College of Electronic and Information Engineering, Shandong University of Science and Technology, Qingdao, China

Abstract. In recent years, the research in the multiple fields of representation learning has led to the emergence of many excellent Network Embedding algorithms. Here we propose *attr2vec*, a completely unsupervised algorithmic framework for learning the latent representations for nodes. In *attr2vec*, we have adopted an attribute processing method similar to GCN, that is, taking the average of the attribute of the node's neighbors as the attribute for the node. We also consider first-order neighbors and second-order neighbors separately to achieve an effect similar to multiple convolutional layers in GCN. In summary, our algorithm utilizes similar attribute processing idea of GCN, which can learn the graph topology and node attribute to generate latent representations for nodes, but implemented it with a completely unsupervised way. In some experiments on citation networks we demonstrate that our algorithm outperforms related unsupervised techniques by a significant margin.

Keywords: Network embedding · Unsupervised · Feature learning

1 Introduction

In many real-world problems, information is often organized as networks. Nodes in the network represent entities, and edges represent relationships between entities. We need to perform various prediction tasks on the network, such as visualization [1], node classification [2], and link prediction [3]. Therefore, it is necessary to accurately learn useful knowledge from the networks. Learning the network representations of network is a useful strategy: represent each node of the network with a low-dimensional vector which captures meaningful relational, structural and semantic information conveyed by the network.

Almost all recent efforts in network embedding are based on these intuitions: 1) Nodes should have similar latent representations with its neighbors. 2) Nodes that have neighbors with similar sets of nodes should have similar latent representations. Specifically, these efforts define a general concept of node's neighborhood, which is a random walk of nodes. Then transforms a network into a sample collection of linear

Q. Wu et al. (Eds.): WiSATS 2020, LNICST 358, pp. 546–555, 2021.
https://doi.org/10.1007/978-3-030-69072-4_44

sequences consisting of nodes using uniform sampling. The skip-gram model [4], a technique originally designed for learning latent representations of words in linear sequences, can also use these linear sequences of nodes as input to generate latent representations of the nodes.

These techniques for learning the representations of nodes in networks have been achieved great success in performing visualization, classification and prediction tasks. But neighborhood is a local concept usually composed of nodes that are close to each other in the network. A fundamental limitation is that network environmental similar nodes will never share the same context if their distance (hop count) in original network is larger than the skip-gram window. Thus, a pair of nodes in a network that are environmentally similar but that are far apart in distance will not have similar representations because they will not appear frequently in the same skip-gram input sequence. This is also the reason for representations such as DeepWalk [5] and node2vec [6] fail in classification tasks that depend more on structural identity.

struc2vec [7] provide an alternative methodology, one based on unsupervised learning of representations for the structural identity of nodes. It builds a multi-layer graph, making the similarity of nodes independent of their network position and labels. While struc2vec performs well in some completely structure-based classification tasks, it completely discards the neighbor similarity which contains important network topology information in real world network. Therefore, struc2vec does not perform well in general networks. However, struc2vec gives us an important revelation that we can build a new graph for random walk in order to find similar nodes that are far away from the original graph.

In short, these Network Embedding technologies generally samples the nodes in the network through specific strategies to learn the similarity of the nodes in the network, which can be regarded as a method of learning latent representation of the topology of the network. However, in the real world, the nodes in network also contain several attributes information, such as user portrait information in social networks, text information in citation networks, etc. For such information, the method based on Network Embedding usually splices the attributes to the nodes for downstream tasks.

In this paper, we propose *attr2vec*, which is a network embedding algorithm inspired by GCN [8]. GCN can directly generate node representations by learning the network topology and nodes attribute information, but it is a semi-supervised algorithm and requires a certain number of labeled nodes. Our main contribution is a completely unsupervised framework for generating latent representation for nodes by directly learning network topology and node attributes, called *attr2vec*. The key ideas of *attr2vec* are:

- Assess attributes similarity between nodes independently of their position in the network. If two nodes have similar attributes and their neighbors have similar attributes, they will have a high degree of similarity, regardless of their position in the network and the labels of their neighbors. For example, in the citation network, nodes represent articles, and the attribute of node are the known information of article, such as key words that appeared in the article. If two articles have similar attributes (such as key words), and the neighbor articles in citation network are also similar to each other, they will be similar in our access.

- Establish a multi-layer hierarchy to find nodes with similar attribute, allowing more stringent notion of similarity at higher layer. In particular, at the first level of the hierarchy, similarity between nodes depend only on their node attribute, while the similarity at the second level depends not only on their own attributes, but also on the attributes of their neighbors. This hierarchy can continue to expand until that at the top of the hierarchy the similarity between nodes depends on the entire network. As more and more layers of the hierarchy, the information obtained is getting richer, but the interference information has also increased.
- Generate random contexts for nodes by weighted random sample in the K-layer hierarchy, the random contexts for nodes are sequences of nodes that have similar attributes. Thus, nodes that frequently appear in similar contexts are more likely to have similar attributes. These contexts can be used as input to language models to learn the latent representation for nodes.

We implemented an example of *attr2vec* and confirmed its effect on several real networks through numerical experiments. We compared its performance with DeepWalk and node2vec, which are two latest learning techniques for latent representation for nodes. Our results show that *attr2vec* can make better use of the attribute information of the nodes and have better performance in classification task.

The rest of this paper is organized as follows. In Sect. 2, we briefly summarize the recent related work on learning latent representations for nodes. We present the technical details of *attr2vec* in Sect. 3. Section 4 shows experimental evaluation and comparison with other methods on classification tasks. Finally, we conclude in Sect. 5.

2 Related Work

Recent advancements in natural language processing have provided new method for learning latent representations for nodes in network. Specially, the skip-gram model is invented as a tool for learning representations for text data. It is based on the idea that words that frequently appear in similar contexts should be similar. Thus, skip-gram formulate a neighborhood preserving likelihood objective and optimize it using SGD [9] with negative sampling [10].

Inspired by the skip-gram model, recent research treats the network as sequences of nodes, the specific method is to randomly walk in the original network according to some rules to generate sequences of nodes. However, there are many feasible random walk strategies, which will result in different node sequences and different representations of nodes.

DeepWalk is the first algorithm to learn node representations using a language model. It obtains sequences of nodes by performing random walks in the original network, and then uses these sequences as input to the skip-gram model. This idea has been extended in node2vec, which propose a biased second order random walk strategy that increases flexibility when generating sequences of nodes. But one limitation is that if the distance between two nodes exceeds the window size in the skip-gram model, they will not have closely representation even if they are similar.

In order to make similar pairs of nodes that are far away in the original network appear in the same node sampling sequence, struc2vec construct a fully connected weighted hierarchical network and performs node sampling on this network (not the original network). Although struc2vec has succeeded in structure-based prediction tasks, it is not suitable for general real-world networks.

The concept of graph neural network (GNN) [11] improves the existing neural network so that it can process data represented by the network. The important difference between GNN and the previous technology is that it is semi-supervised and it can not only learn the topology of node but also the attributes of node. Experiment results show that GCN is a powerful model for data in network domain.

3 attr2vec

For the problem of learning the representation of nodes in a network, almost all recent efforts in network embedding are based on this intuition: nodes should have similar latent representations with its neighbors. However, the reason why a node exhibits property similar to its neighbors is because they are in a similar network environment, not whether they are close in distance. Moreover, in many real-world networks nodes and their neighbors do not show similarities, because sometimes they are not similar in degree although they are close in distance, or their neighbors are completely different sets of nodes. In summary, we believe that the attributes of node are the key to determining the role of node. So, we think a successful method should have these two properties:

- The similarity of the representations for nodes should depend on the similarity of the attributes of nodes. Therefore, nodes with identical attribute should have the same representations, while two nodes that have different attribute should be far apart.
- The representation of nodes should be independent of their position in the network. Thus, two nodes that have similar attribute but are far away in the network should also have similar representations.

Based on the above ideas we propose *attr2vec*, in the following part we make a detailed explanation of *attr2vec* at each step.

3.1 Generating Represent of Attributes

The first step of *attr2vec* is to generate K attribute vectors for each node. First of all, we assume that each node in the network has its own attribute. For example, in a citation network, the nodes are different articles, the edges are the citation relations between the articles. The attribute of the node are the key words in articles. It can be extracted in a unified way and represented by a series of numbers of equal length. We assume that the attribute of nodes is already in our train data. Now what we have to do is to generate K attribute vectors for each node. In particular, the k-th attribute vector of u is generated by averaging attributes of nodes that at distance exactly k from u in original network (u in a node in network).

Let $G = (V, E)$ denote the undirected, unweighted network under consideration with vertex set V and edge set E, where $n = |V|$ denotes the number of nodes in G, K is a hyper parameter and let $R_k(u)$ denote the set of nodes at distance (hop count) exactly $0 \leq k < K$ from u in G. Let *attribute(s)* denote attribute of s (s may be a node or a collection of nodes) and $attr\_vec_k(u)$ denote the k-th attribute vector of u. In particular, we define:

$$attr\_vec_k(u) = mean(attribute(R_k(u))) \tag{1}$$

where *mean(set)* means to average the target *set*. The above-described process of generating $attr\_vec_k(u)$ is shown in Fig. 1 (See Fig. 1).

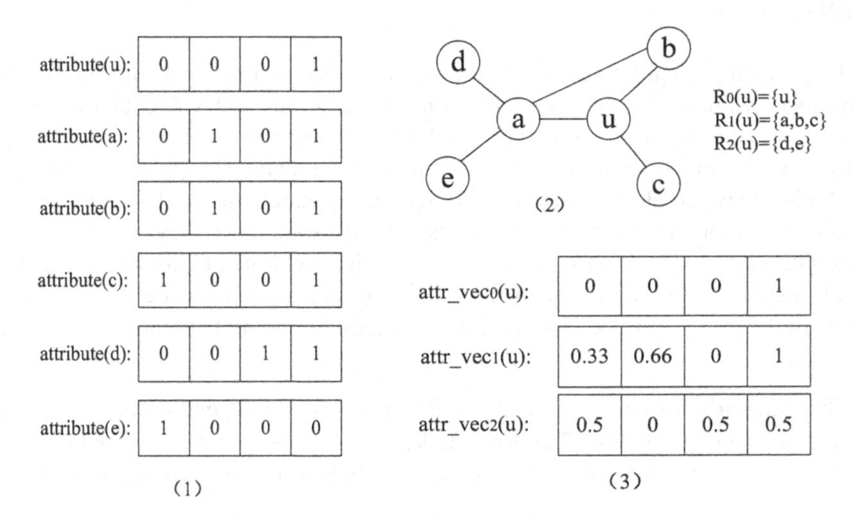

Fig. 1. Illustration of $attr\_vec_k(u)$ generation in *attr2vec*. The original attributes of nodes in network is shown in (1), and (2) is the structure of original network. Thus, we get $attr\_vec_0(u)$, $attr\_vec_1(u)$ and $attr\_vec_2(u)$ in (3).

3.2 Measuring Attribute Similarity

By comparing the $attr\_vec_k(u)$ and $attr\_vec_k(v)$ we can impose a hierarchy to measure similarity. In particular, we define:

$$D_k(u,v) = D_{k-1}(u,v) + \frac{g(attr\_vec_k(u), attr\_vec_k(v))}{\alpha_k}, k \geq 0 \tag{2}$$

where $g(attr\_vec_1, attr\_vec_2) \geq 0$ measures the distance between $attr\_vec_1$ and $attr\_vec_2$, α_k are hyper parameter for value scale adjustment to and $attr\_vec_{-1} = 0$. Note that by definition $D_k(u,v)$ is increasing and is defined only when at least one of u and v have nodes at distance k (If only u has nodes at distance k, then every element of $attr\_vec_k(v)$ is 0).

We also need to define a function g that calculates the distance between $attr\_vec_k(u)$ and $attr\_vec_k(v)$. Note that $attr\_vec_k(u)$ and $attr\_vec_k(v)$ are the same size and its elements are arbitrary decimals. We adopt Euclidean Distance to measure the distance between them, which a technique that can cope better with sequences of same sizes. We adopt the following distance function:

$$g(x,y) := \sqrt{(x_1 - y_1)^2 + (x_2 - y_2)^2 + \cdots + (x_n - y_n)^2} = \sqrt{\sum_{i=1}^{n} (x_i - y_i)^2} \quad (3)$$

Note that when $x = y$ then $g(x, y) = 0$. Thus, the distance between two identical attribute vectors is 0.

3.3 Constructing the Context Graph

We construct a weighted multi-layer graph to save the similarity between attributes of the nodes. Each layer $k = 0, 1, \ldots, K - 1$ of this weighted multi-layer graph is composed of all nodes in the network and the weighted edges between nodes. Thus, every layer is formed by a weighted undirected complete graph with node set V, and $n(n - 1)$ edges. The edge weight between two nodes in a layer is given by:

$$W_k(u, v) = e^{-D_k(u,v)}, k = 0, \ldots, K - 1 \quad (4)$$

Note that weights are inversely proportional to attribute distance, and assume values of $W_k(u, v)$ smaller than or equal to 1, it being equal to 1 only if $D_k(u, v) = 0$.

We connect the layers using directed edges as follows. Each vertex is connected to its corresponding vertex in the layer above and below. The edge weight between layers are as follows:

$$\begin{aligned} W(u_k, u_{k+1}) &= \log(\Gamma_k(u) + e), k = 0, \ldots, K - 1 \\ W(u_k, u_{k-1}) &= 1, k = 1, \ldots, K \end{aligned} \quad (5)$$

Where $\Gamma_k(u)$ is number of edges incident to u that have weight larger than the average edge weight of the complete graph in layer k. In particular:

$$\Gamma_k(u) = \sum_{v \in V} \left(W_k(u, v) > \overline{W_k} \right)$$

$$\overline{W_k} = \sum_{(u,v) \in \binom{V}{2}} \frac{W_k(u, v)}{\binom{n}{2}} \quad (6)$$

$\Gamma_k(u)$ represents the number of edges connected to u with a weight greater than the average weight of layer k. Note that the attribute information of farther neighbors is captured in the higher layer, so if there are many nodes similar to u in this layer, then you should go to the higher layer to find more refined similar nodes. And when going to the upper layer, there will be fewer similar nodes because there are more neighbors participating in the calculation. Imagine that two nodes that are similar at the first layer become dissimilar after considering further neighbors, and two nodes that are not similar at the first layer are unlikely to be similar at the upper layer.

3.4 Generating Context for Nodes

In the previous work we constructed a multi-layer graph M and calculated the weights of it, M can be used to generate context for each node in the network. *Attr2vec* uses random sampling to generate context of each node, which is the sequence of nodes. In particular, we randomly sample L times on M according to the weight of the edge connected to u to generate a context of length L for u. Before each step, random sampling first determines whether need to change the layer or sample at current layer (with probability $q > 0$ the random sampling stays in the current layer, q is a hyperparameter).

Given that it will stay in the current layer, the probability of stepping from node u to node v in layer k is given by:

$$p_k(u, v) = \frac{e^{-F_k(u,v)}}{Z_k(u)} \tag{7}$$

where $Z_k(u)$ is the normalization factor for vertex u in layer k, simply given by:

$$Z_k(u) = \sum_{\substack{v \in V \\ v \neq u}} e^{-F_k(u,v)} \tag{8}$$

Note that random sampling tends to sample nodes that have similar attributes to the current node. If the attribute of two nodes are similar and the attributes of their neighbors are similar too, then they are likely to appear in the context of each other. Thus, a node is more likely to have nodes similar to it in its context, regardless of the position of the node in the original network.

3.5 Embedding with Skip-Gram

Skip-gram models have been widely used to learn word embedding and only require a collection of sentences to generate meaningful representations. Now we just need to input these sequences of node that we generated in previous section into skip-gram and the output are embeddings of nodes.

4 Experimental Evaluation

We tested our model in the following experiment, we used *attr2vec* to learn the latent representations for the nodes in the reference network, and then used these node representations for visualization and classification tasks. We also compared with the state-of-the-art techniques that learning potential representations for nodes.

4.1 Datasets

Cora: Data collected from the Collective classification in network data [12]. The dataset is a citation network dataset, it contains sparse bag-of-words keywords vectors for each document and a list of citation links between documents. The network has 2708 nodes, 5429 edges, and 7 different labels.

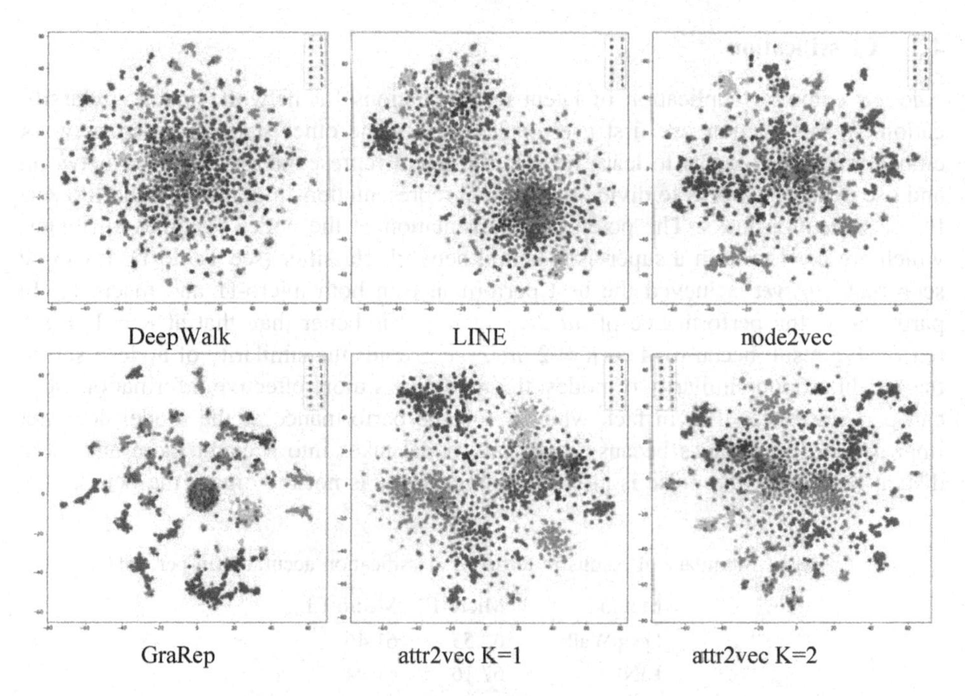

Fig. 2. Visualization of Cora network. Each point indicates one node. Color of a point indicates the label of node.

4.2 Visualization

An important application for network embedding is to visualize a network in a two-dimensional space. In this paper we visualized the representations learned from Cora network through different models. t-SNE [13] is currently the most popular method for dimension reduction and visualization of data. Therefore, we use the latent representations learned by different graph embedding models as the input to t-SNE. As a result, each node in Cora network is mapped as a two-dimensional vector. Then we can visualize each vector as a point on a two-dimensional space. For nodes labeled with different labels, we use different colors for corresponding points. Therefore, a good visualization result should be that the points with different color are separated by boundaries and the points with same color are clustered together. The visualization figure is shown in Fig. 2.

From Fig. 2, we can see that the visualization of DeepWalk and LINE [14] are not acceptable because the points with different labels are mixed with each other. For node2vec and GraRep, the clusters of points with same labels are formed. However, in the center part are still the points with different colors mixed together. Obviously, the visualization of *attr2vec* performs best in both the aspects of clustering same nodes and separate different nodes.

4.3 Classification

Another common application of latent representations for network nodes is classification. In this section, we first use *attr2vec* and some other state-of-the-art network embedding technologies to learn meaningful latent representations for Cora network, and use neural networks to divide these latent representations into training and test sets for classification tasks. The potential representation of the nodes becomes attributes, which are used to train a supervised neural network classifier (see Table 1). It can be seen that *attr2vec* achieved the best performance in both micro-f1 and macro-f1. In particularly, the performance of *attr2vec* at $K = 2$ is better than that at $K = 1$. It's a reasonable result because when $K = 2$ *attr2vec* extends the similarity of nodes itself to the neighborhood similarity of nodes, the model gets more effective information, so it can perform better. But in fact, when $K = 3$ the performance of the model does not improve, we think that's because when the model takes into account more and more distant neighbors, the noise is also increasing. So, K is not the bigger the better.

Table 1. Summary of results in terms of classification accuracy (in percent).

Method	Micro-F1	Macro-F1
DeepWalk	62.55	61.46
LINE	67.16	67.04
node2vec	73.25	72.78
GraRep	78.60	77.73
attr2vec $K = 1$	80.55	79.31
attr2vec $K = 2$	**82.94**	**81.91**

5 Conclusion

In this paper we propose *attr2vec*, a novel unsupervised network embedding algorithm that can capture network topology and node attributes. We show that attr2vec is powerful in finding similar nodes and learning the latent representation of node. Compared with the traditional DeepWalk and node2vec, it removes the limitation that it can only randomly walk on the original network and it can find similar nodes at long distances. At the same time, it expands the similarity of nodes itself to the similarity of the neighborhood, which can mine more potentially effective information. It can also learn the attribute information of nodes, instead of just learning the structure of the network, so that the nodes get a more meaningful representation.

Acknowledgments. This work was supported by the Qingdao Philosophy and Social Sciences Planning Project (QDSKL1801131), the 2018 Postgraduate Tutors'Guidance Ability Improvement Project of Shandong Province (84), the National Natural Science Foundation of China under Grant No.61701284, the Innovative Research Foundation of Qingdao under Grant No. 19–6-2–1-cg.

References

1. Van der Maaten, L., Hinton, G.: Visualizing data using t-sne. J. Mach. Learn. Res. **9**(2579–2605), 85 (2008)
2. Bhagat, S., Cormode, G., Muthukrishnan, S.: Node classification in social networks. In: Social Network Data Analytics, pp. 115–148. Springer, Heidelberg (2011)
3. Liben-Nowell, D., Kleinberg, J.: The link-prediction problem for social networks. J. Am. Soc. Inf. Sci. Technol. **58**(7), 1019–1031 (2007)
4. Mahoney, M.: Large text compression benchmark (2011).www.mattmahoney.net/dc/textdata
5. Perozzi, B., Al-Rfou, R., Skiena, S.: DeepWalk: online learning of social representations. In KDD (2014)
6. Grover, A., Leskovec, J.: node2vec: Scalable Feature Learning for Networks. In: ACM SIGKDD (2016)
7. Ribeiro, L.F.R., Saverese, P.H.P., Figueiredo, D.R.: struc2vec: learning node representations from structural identity. In: KDD (2017)
8. Kipf, T.N., Welling, M.: Semi-supervised classification with graph convolutional networks. In: ICLR (2016)
9. Bottou, L.: Stochastic gradient learning in neural networks. In: Proceedings of Neuro-Nimes 91, Nimes, France (1991)
10. Mikolov, T., Sutskever, I., Chen, K., Corrado, G.S., Dean, J.: Distributed representations of words and phrases and their compositionality. In: NIPS (2013)
11. Scarselli, F., Gori, M., Tsoi, A.C., Hagenbuchner, M., Monfardini, G.: The graph neural network model. IEEE TNN **20**(1), 61–80 (2009)
12. Sen, P., Namata, G., Bilgic, M., Getoor, L., Galligher, B., Eliassi-Rad, T.: Collective classification in network data. AI Mag. **29**(3), 93 (2008)
13. Van der Maaten, L., Hinton, G.: Visualizing data using t-sne. JMLR **9**(2579–2605), 85 (2008)
14. Tang, J., Qu, M., Wang, M., Zhang, M., Yan, J., Mei, Q.: LINE: large-scale information network embedding. In: WWW (2015)

Hashgraph Based Federated Learning for Secure Data Sharing

Xiuxian Zhang[1,2], Lingyu Zhao[1], Jinfeng Li[1], and Xiaorong Zhu[1(✉)]

[1] Nanjing University of Posts and Telecommunications, Nanjing 210003, China
xrzhu@njupt.edu.cn
[2] Nanjing Xiaozhuang University, Nanjing 211171, China

Abstract. As the key technology of connected intelligence, the importance of artificial intelligence has increased rapidly. It is worth to note that the most critical challenge is the secure data sharing which is stored in different area and belonged to different organization. With this in mind, a hashgraph based federated learning for secure data sharing model is proposed to protect user privacy and detect the dishonest model provider. In terms of technologies, detection of the local model is added to the hashgraph consensus processing, and only if the supermajority (more than 2/3) of the participants agree, the local model could be adopted. Therefore, the accuracy and convergence rate of the federated learning both increased largely. On the other hand, the asynchronous working mode of hashgraph can greatly reduce network overload. Simulation results show that the hashgraph based federated learning enables the data sharing more secure and reliable.

Keywords: Hashgraph · Federated learning · Blockchain · Gossip · Virtual voting

1 Introduction

With the advent of the 6G, connected things have gradually transformed into connected intelligence. Artificial intelligence, as the key technology of connected intelligence, has attracted more and more attention of the researchers. However, up to now, there are two big challenges of artificial intelligence. The first one is data sharing, which is stored in different areas and belonged to different organizations. The second one is to guarantee the privacy and security of the shared data during model training. The federated learning (FL), which obtains a central model on the server by aggregating models trained locally on clients [1], can solve the problems.

In FL, the distributed local devices compute their local model based on local data samples and send them to a central server. The central server trains a shared model by aggregating the local models received from different devices [2]. Therefore, the raw data stays in the local devices all the time during the training. Notably, not only data shared but also privacy protection both realized in FL. Nonetheless, there are several limitations in FL. For the first, the reliable privacy of the learning model from each device cannot be

Q. Wu et al. (Eds.): WiSATS 2020, LNICST 358, pp. 556–565, 2021.
https://doi.org/10.1007/978-3-030-69072-4_45

guaranteed. Secondly, dishonest users can have an adverse impact on the global model by offering the low-grade local model. Besides, users also lack the motivation to participate in the FL using their own computing resources and data. The last one is the problem of network overload. Massive amounts of models are transmitted at the same time during FL, which will cause network overload under the constraint of bandwidth.

In recent years, lots of researchers have been engaged in the research of FL combined with blockchain to solve the above problems. The blockchain was used to store the retrieval data and access rights in paper [3], which could prevent malicious users to temper the models. And, the differential private algorithm was used to protect personal privacy data. However, the use of differential private algorithm leads to a sharp decline of the data availability due to the random noise interference. FL was investigated based on the fabric channel in paper [4]. The decentralized FL request was proposed in one channel with the same type of user data to guarantee the personal privacy of users in different channels, but it does not involve the personal privacy protection among users in the same channel. The blockchain and FL are coupled to ensure the privacy of the user data. The trained learning model parameters can be stored on the blockchain securely in an immutable manner against unauthorized access and malicious actions [5]. Y. J. Kim et al. [4] proposed a blockchain-based FL to provide an incentive mechanism and prevent malicious users from changing the models according to the natural trading attributes and immutable ledger of blockchain. Besides, a fast and stable target accuracy convergence joint learning model was proposed to reduce the network overload.

To summarize, although there exist a number of studies on blockchain based on FL, the results in those studies fail to consider the dishonest model provider. To fill this gap, a hashgraph based FL is proposed to detect dishonest model provider. The main contributions of this paper are mainly given as following:

- In order to detect the dishonest model provider, detection of the local model is added to the hashgraph consensus processing. Theoretically, the local model will be adopted only if the supermajority (more than 2/3) of the participants agree.
- The hashgraph with shorter consensus time is adopted to reduce the training time. Typically, the asynchronous working mode of hashgraph can greatly reduce network overload.

The remainder of this paper is organized as following. In Sect. 2, the system model is established. And, the hashgraph for data sharing is proposed in Sect. 3. Then, FL is described in detail in Sect. 4, Numerical results are presented in Sect. 5, followed by a conclusion in Sect. 6.

2 System Model

In this paper, a common distributed data sharing scenario with multiple parties is considered. The system can be divided into two parts shown as Fig. 1: the blockchain platform and communication network. The blockchain platform adopts hashgraph consensus to reduce the consensus time and network overload. Specifically, the blockchain platform is used to record the local model retrieval (the raw model parameters are stored in local devices), the availability of local models, and all the sharing data events which can trace the use of data for further audit. The communication network takes charge of data communication.

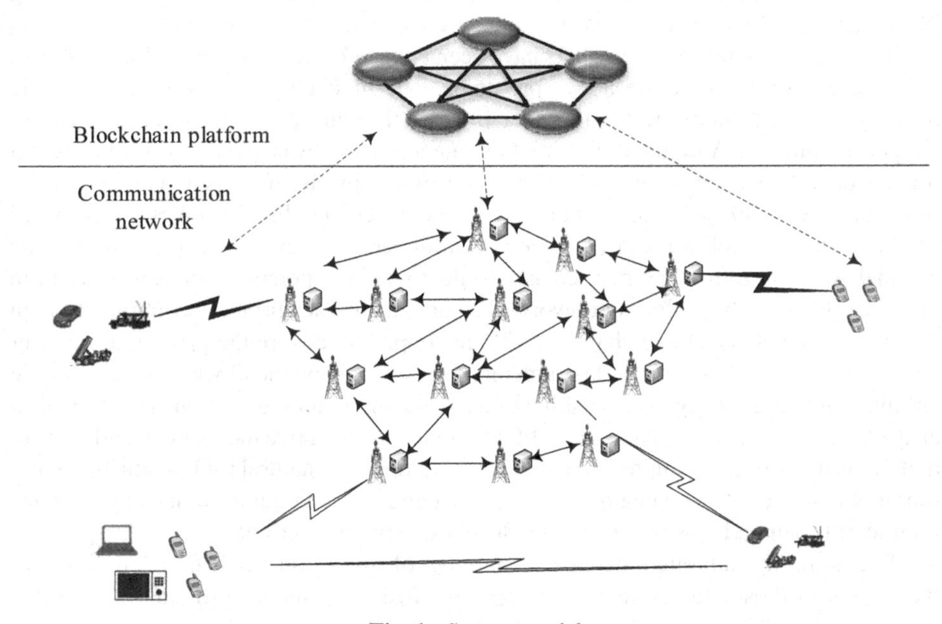

Fig. 1. System model

All users who want to provide data sharing service can apply to join the blockchain platform. A data sharing requester lunches a request to the blockchain platform, the blockchain will check whether the request has been processed before. If there is a hit, the request will be forwarded to the node that has cached the results and the cached results are then sent to the requester as a reply. In contrast, a new FL request with data categories and incentive mechanism will be published in the platform, then, the data provider participated in the blockchain will choice whether join the FL or not according to the matched-degree of the data they have with the data requested and incentive mechanism. All nodes participated in the FL are regarded as committee nodes which are responsible for driving the consensus in the blockchain.

3 The Hashgraph for Secure Data Sharing

In this paper, we consider the problem of privacy-preserving and dishonest model provider checking in the data sharing process with decentralized multiple parties. In order to protect the privacy of local models, homomorphic encryption is used to encrypt the local models and then transmit the encrypted models to the next node. The local models are transmitted among the committee nodes. All the committee nodes check the availability of the local models and vote on them. Only more than 2/3 of the committee nodes agree. The local models are legitimate.

Hashgraph [6] is a relatively novel DAG (Directed Acyclic Graph) technology, which is a consensus of blockchain 3.0. Theoretically, the hashgraph is an aBFT (Asynchronous Byzantine Fault Tolerance) system, with no node that can prevent the network from reaching consensus or modify data after consensus has been reached, and it can achieve bank-level security. Lots of problems of the traditional blockchain can be solved in hashgraph, such as long consensus time, the lack of concurrent processing mechanism to meet the large scale application scenario, and too high transaction costs in small transactions. To this end, the hashgraph is adopted in this paper. In terms of technologies, the hashgraph is different from the previous blockchain, the nodes of the hashgraph package the transactions into events, which are the smallest data units, communicate with other nodes through gossip protocol, and reach the consensus relying on the virtual voting protocol.

3.1 Event Structure

Events as the smallest unit of the hashgraph mainly include a timestamp, transaction information, self-parent hash, other-parent hash, and a digital signature, as shown in Fig. 2. Where the self-parent hash is the hash of the last event on this node and other-parent hash is the hash of the last event on the other nodes. Transaction information is the main content of the event mainly includes local model retrieval, sharing data information, the support number of the local model. In more detail, the local model retrieval is to record the retrieval information of the local model, the sharing data information contains data categories and data quantity. The support number of the local model is the number of the node who vote “yes” to the local model.

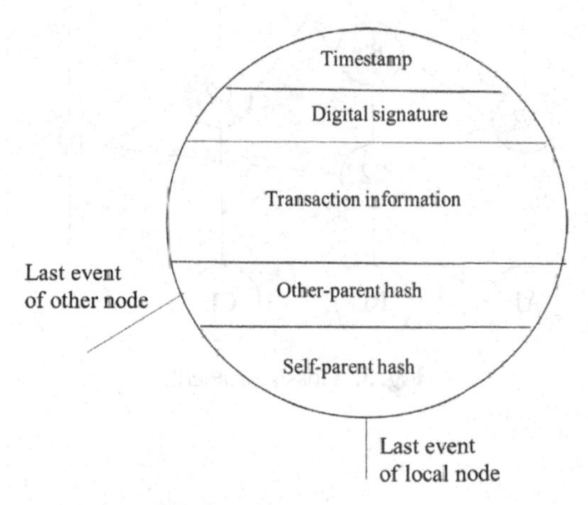

Fig. 2. The event structure

3.2 Gossip Protocol

The communication mechanism uses gossip protocol. In the gossip protocol, the node randomly selects another node and sends data known in this node but not known in the selected node to the selected node. When the node receives the data containing new transactions, it first executes all the new transactions and checks the availability of the local model, and then repeats the same process by selecting another random node. Therefore, the protocol of gossip spreads exponentially until all the nodes receive the event.

For the sake of simplicity, assume that there are four nodes A, B, C, D in hashgraph, as depicted in Fig. 3. And, define the event generated by the node A as A1, A2, A3…in order, define the node B, C, D in the same way. At the beginning of the gossip protocol, node A randomly selects a node from B, C, D, here select B for example, to send transactions that are known in A but not known in B and package the transactions into events A1. After node B receiving event A1, it will deal with the new transactions, which is local model checking in this paper, contained in event A1. Additionally, Node B repeats the same process of node A that select node D to transmit event B2 which includes the information of event A1 if node D hasn't received the transactions before. It is obvious to note that, the transactions of event A1 will be known by all nodes A, B, C, D ultimately.

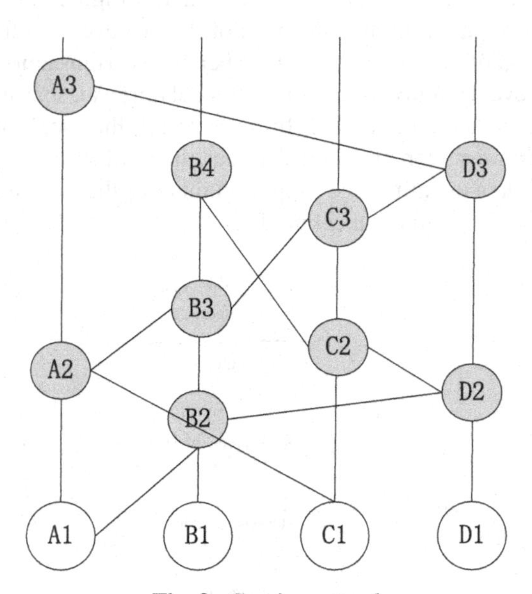

Fig. 3. Gossip protocol

3.3 Virtual Voting Protocol

As evident from above, the communication of each node has been completed. Ultimately, all nodes participated in the FL have stored the complete history of the transaction. But, this is just a communication step, and a virtual voting protocol is needed to reach a consensus among the nodes. When a consensus is proposed, there is no need for large-scale message communication due to the gossip protocol, each node performs the voting algorithm independently, and all nodes will reach the same consensus result [7]. Therefore, zero bandwidth is used, beyond simply gossiping in the hashgraph. Therefore, it can sharply reduce the network overload. Virtual voting processing is divided into 3 steps: divide rounds, decide famous witnesses, determine round received and consensus time.

To understand the process of virtual voting, it's worth describing some terminology about hashgraph, such as witnesses, round, seeing, strongly seeing, and famous witness, before discussing the specific voting steps. Conventionally, the first event created by the node is called witness and the witness is the beginning of the round (r) for the node. As such, an event Y could see event X only if event Y can find X by the pointer of hash. Typically, when all paths of event Y could find Event X go through supermajority (more than 2/3) of nodes called Y strongly sees X. Correspondingly, if a witness of round r can be seen by supermajority of witnesses of round $r+1$, then the witness of round r is a famous witness.

Divide Rounds: A witness event is the beginning of a round (r) known from the definition of round. Assume that node B receives the event X send by node A and node B will create event Y to send to node C. Before creating event Y, node B should check whether need to start a new round, if event X can see supermajority of witnesses of r round, the event Y is the beginning of $r+1$ round. Meanwhile, Y is the witness of $r+1$ round. Otherwise, event Y is still in r round.

Decide Famous Witness: A witness in round r is called famous if and only if it can be seen by supermajority witnesses in round $r+1$. If witness Y of node B in round $r+1$ could see witness X of node A in round r, then witness Y will vote yes to witness X. Witness Z in round $r+2$ will collect the votes about the event X from the witnesses that are seen strongly by Z in round $r+1$. If the amount of votes is not less than the number of the supermajority nodes, then the event X is a famous witness. Hashgraph has proved mathematically that if any of the witnesses in $r+2$ round make a decision on the result of the vote, the result will be the conclusion of the network, and if the witnesses in $r+2$ round can not make a decision, the next round of witnesses will collect the votes until a firm conclusion is reached [7].

Determine Round Received and Consensus Time: Assuming that all witnesses in round r have been determined whether they are famous witnesses or not, the receiving round of event X is r when all known witnesses of round r can see the event. Find all first events $Y = \{Y_1, Y_2, Y_3, \ldots\ldots Y_m\}$ that can see X on the paths from X to all famous witnesses in round r. Then, the median of the timestamp of event $Y_i i = [\frac{1+m}{2}]$ is the consensus time.

4 The FL for Data Sharing

In this section, the FL model based on hashgraph is described in detail showed in Fig. 4. The process of the FL can be divided into two parts: the global model and the local model. At global iteration t, the local model $w_i(t)$ is trained based on its own data set D_i

on each device. Then, the encrypted model parameter $w_i^{'}(t)$ is transmitted to the other participants of the blockchain platform to check the availability of the local model. When the consensus of the event include the local model is complete, the global model will be concluded based on the local model and the vote result of the committee nodes.

Local Model: In this paper, the local machine learning adopts linear regression. As known to all, the learning objective of node i is to minimize the loss function $l(w_i)$ over all the data samples $D_i = \{x_{ij}, y_{ij}\}$ where $x_{ij} \in \Re^d$, $y_{ij} \in \Re$. Then, the local model$w_i(t)$, local loss function (w_i), and global loss function $L(w)$ is described as:

$$l(w_i(t)) \triangleq l\left(w_i(t), x_{ij}, y_{ij}\right) = \frac{1}{2} \parallel y_{ij} - w_i^T(t)x_{ij} \parallel^2 \tag{1}$$

$$w_i(t) = \underset{w_i(t)\epsilon\Re^d}{arg\ min}\ l(w_i(t)) \tag{2}$$

$$L(w(t)) = \frac{1}{N_i}\sum_{i=1}^{i=I} m_i * l(w_i(\mathrm{t})) \tag{3}$$

Where N_i is the number of the committee nodes who support $w_t^{'}(t)$ and $m_i = 0$, if the node i is a dishonest model provider, otherwise, $m_i = 1$.

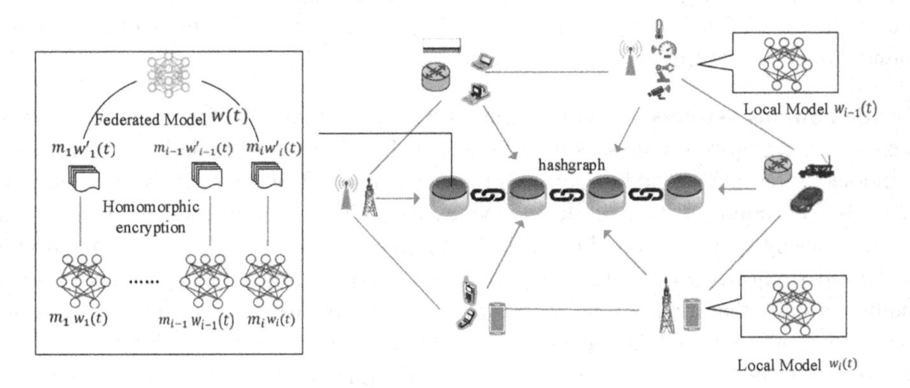

Fig. 4. FL model

For each global model iteration t, assume that the local model of the device i is updated for R epochs. At epoch r, the local model for device i is updated by stochastic variance reduced gradient (SVRG) as [8]:

$$w_i^r(t) = w_i^{r-1}(t) - \lambda\nabla\varphi \tag{4}$$

$$\nabla\varphi = \left[\nabla l\left(w_i^{r-1}(t)\right) - \nabla l(w_i(t)) + \nabla L(w(t))\right] \tag{5}$$

Where $\lambda > 0$ is step-size and after R local epochs $w_i(t) = w_i^R(t)$. $\nabla L(w) = \frac{1}{N_i}\sum_{i=1}^{i=I} m_i{*}\nabla l(w_i)$. Furthermore, after the local model $w_i(t)$ is trained, $w_i(t)$ and local loss function $\nabla l(w_i(t))$ are encrypted to $w_i^{'}(t)$and$\nabla l^{'}(w_i(t))$. Correspondingly, they are transmitted to the other participants of the blockchain platform to check the availability of the local model.

Global Model: The preliminary weight parameters at global iteration $t = 0$ are randomly chosen from pre-selected range $w_i(0), w(0) \in [0, w_{max}]$, $\nabla l(w(0)) = (0, 1]$. When the consensus of the event including the local model $w_i^{'}(t)$and$\nabla l^{'}(w_i(t))$ is complete, read the number of the committee nodes N_i who support $w_i^{'}(t)$ from blockchain. And, if it is less than 2/3 amount of committee nodes, the node i is a dishonest model provider and $m_i = 0$, otherwise, $m_i = 1$. When all local models of the committee nodes are confirmed, the global model can be concluded as:

$$w(t) = \sum_{i=1}^{i=I} m_i * \mu_i * w_i^{\prime}(t) \tag{6}$$

Where $0 \leq \mu_i \leq 1$, $\mu_i = \frac{|D_i|}{|D|} * \frac{N_i}{I}$ is the weight coefficient of $w'_i(t)$ with $D = \sum_{i=1}^{i=I} D_i$ is the data set of all devices. Then all the nodes update $w(t)$ from blockchain and start a new round of local and global training.

5 Performance Evaluation and Analysis

For the sake of presentation, the performance of the proposed method with the detection of dishonest providers is compared with the conventional FL. Where the total number of the local model provider I is 10, and assume that there is one dishonest provider. Then, divide the dataset into 9 fragments. Simultaneously, randomly generate a dataset as the dishonest provider's dataset and assume that the proportion of the data provided by the dishonest provider is 0.2. It is worth to notice from Fig. 5 that the performance of the FL based on hashgraph is better than the conventional FL in the aspects of precision, recall, f-measure and accuracy. As shown in Fig. 6, it is obvious that the more proportion of the data provided by the dishonest provider, the lower accuracy of the FL model will be in the conventional FL. But, it makes no difference in the proposed FL.

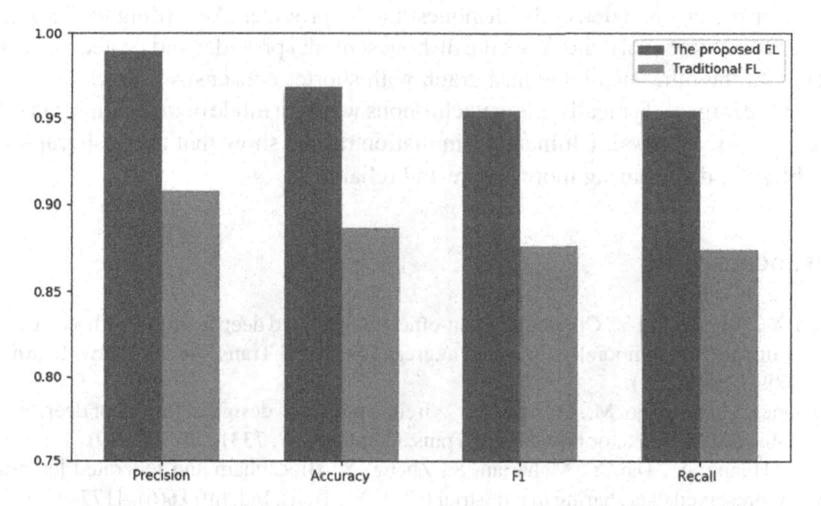

Fig. 5. Performance of the FL proposed comparing with the conventional

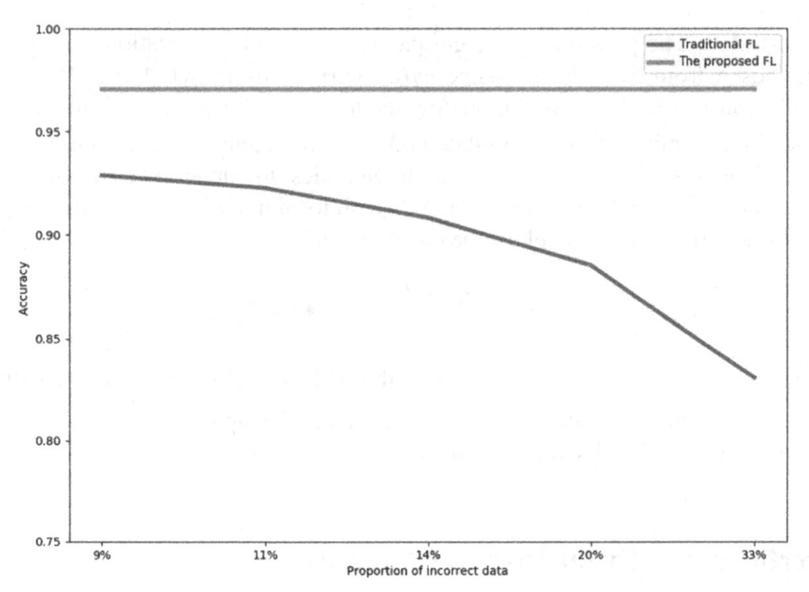

Fig. 6. The accuracy with different proportion of incorrect data provided by dishonest providers

Through the above evaluation, it is important to note that the performance of the hashgraph based FL is better than the conventional FL due to the detection of the dishonest provider. As pointed by the previous work, the hashgraph based FL enables the data sharing more secure and reliable.

6 Conclusion

To summarize, a hashgraph based FL for secure data sharing model is proposed to protect user privacy and detect the dishonest model provider. According to the analysis, the system can effectively check out the dishonest model provider and protect the privacy of users. On the other hand, the hashgraph with shorter consensus time can reduce the training time largely. Typically, the asynchronous working mode of hashgraph can greatly reduce network overload. Ultimately, simulation results show that the hashgraph based FL enables the data sharing more secure and reliable.

References

1. Chen, Y., Sun, X., Jin, Y.: Communication-efficient federated deep learning with asynchronous model update and temporally weighted aggregation. IEEE Trans. Neural Netw. Learn. Syst. **31**, 4229–4238 (2019)
2. Zappone, A., Di Renzo, M., Debbah, M.: Wireless networks design in the era of deep learning: model-based, AI-based, or both? IEEE Trans. Commun. **67**, 7331–7336 (2019)
3. Lu, Y., Huang, X., Dai, Y., Maharjan, S., Zhang, Y.: Blockchain and federated learning for privacy-preserved data sharing in industrial IoT. IEEE Trans. Ind. Inf. **16**(6), 4177–4186 (2020)

4. Majeed, U., Hong, C.S.: FLchain: federated learning via MEC-enabled blockchain network. In: 20th Asia-Pacific Network Operations and Management Symposium (APNOMS), Matsue, Japan, pp. 1–4 (2019)
5. Salah, K., Rehman, M.H.U., Nizamuddin, N., Al-Fuqaha, A.: Blockchain for AI: review and open research challenges. IEEE Access **7**, 10127–10149 (2019)
6. Baird, L., Harmon, M., Madsen, P.: Hedera: A Public Hashgraph Network & Governing Council. Hedera Hashgraph, LLC., Whitepaper V.2.0, August 2019. https://www.hedera.com/hh-whitepaper-v2.0-17Sep19.pdf.
7. Baird, L.: The swirlds hashgraph consensus algorithm: fair, fast, byzantine fault tolerance, May 2016. https://www.swirlds.com/downloads/SWIRLDS-TR-2016-01.pdf
8. Konen, J., Mcmahan, H.B., Ramage, D., et al.: Federated optimization: distributed machine learning for on-device intelligence. Edinburgh Research Explorer - University of Edinburgh (2016)

Design of Fast-SSC Decoder for STT-MRAM Channel

Jianming Cui[1], Zengxiang Bao[1](✉), Xiaojun Zhang[1,2], Hua Guo[1], and Geng Chen[1]

[1] Shandong University of Science and Technology, Qingdao 266590, China
bzx5699@163.com

[2] State Key Laboratory of High-End Server and Storage Technology, Jinan, China

Abstract. In order to achieve fast decoding and improve the throughput, this paper uses the polar code to encode the spin transfer torque MARAM (STT-MRAM) channel. Based on the Fast-SSC algorithm, a (256, 220) hardware architecture is designed, including the controller, processing element, Kronecker product and memory module. This paper reduces the complexity of data process by splitting the data of nodes, and reduces the memory bandwidth by increasing the reusability of data. The decoder is synthesized on Stratix V 5SGXEA7N2F45C2, the decoding latency is 0.68us, and it can achieve 375 Mbps at 167 MHz.

Keywords: STT-MRAM channel · Polar code · Fast-SSC decoder

1 Introduction

With the development of the memory fields, STT-MRAM is regarded as the most promising replacement for dynamic random access memory (DRAM) in the future due to nanosecond high-speed read and write. In this paper, the spin transfer torque MRAM (STT-MRAM) [1, 2] channel is studied, combined with its reliability, which is susceptible to process changes and thermal fluctuations leading to writing errors, read interference and read decision errors [3, 4]. Researches have shown that for a (1024, 512) polar code under an additive white Gaussian noise (AWGN) and binary phase-shift keying (BPSK) modulation, it has a performance gain of 0.3–0.7 dB than low-density parity-check (LDPC). Polar code with excellent error correction performance is selected for channel coding.

The decoding latency of polar codes increases significantly with the increase of code word length [5], which increased hardware consumption. The successive-cancellation SC [6, 7] decoder hardware architecture, however, due to the serial nature, the hardware resource utilization rate is low and suffers from the high decoding latency. Successive-Cancellation list (SCL) [8] will greatly improve the decoding performance, but the decoding complexity also increases. W. J. Gross et al. proposed the Fast-SSC algorithm [9–11], and they proposed the hardware architecture with the dedicated instruction set. In this paper, polar codes is adopted as coding scheme with Fast-SSC algorithm. The decoder is constructed with (256, 220) polar codes and 32 processing elements (PEs) are used in this paper, which not only achieves better parallelism and high throughput, but also greatly reduces hardware resource consumption.

Q. Wu et al. (Eds.): WiSATS 2020, LNICST 358, pp. 566–575, 2021.
https://doi.org/10.1007/978-3-030-69072-4_46

2 Preliminary

2.1 STT-MRAM Channel

The basic storage unit of STT-MRAM is Magnetic Tunnel Junction (MTJ), control and access to MTJ through N-MOS transistors. In this paper, the Binary Asymmetric Channel - Gaussian Mixture Channel (BAC-GMC) series channel model is used to simulate the STT-MRAM magnetic channel (see Fig. 1), and the writing error P_0, P_1 and read interference error P_r of the STT-MRAM channel are simulated by combining the transition probabilities of the BAC channel.

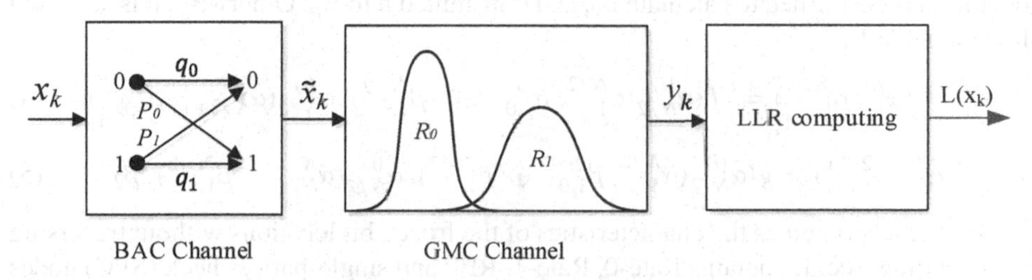

Fig. 1. BAC-GMC channel model

In the GMC channel, R_0 and R_1 present the low-resistance state and the high-resistance state of the MTJ unit respectively, so that R_0 and R_1 follow the Gaussian distribution of mean value μ_0, μ_1 and variance σ_0^2, σ_1^2 respectively.

$$y_k = \begin{cases} R_0 \; if\,(\tilde{x}_k = 0) \\ R_1 \; f\,(\tilde{x}_k = 1) \end{cases} \tag{1}$$

Considering channel symmetry, this paper defines $\alpha(x_k)$ as the LLR of the data bit x_k in the k-th memory cell:

$$\alpha(\tilde{x}_k) = ln(\sigma_0/\sigma_1) + ln((p_0 + q_1)/(q_0 + p_1)) - (y_k - \mu_1)^2/(2\sigma_1^2) + (y_k - \mu_0)^2/(2\sigma_0^2) \tag{2}$$

$$\alpha(x_k) = ln((p_0/(p_0 + q_1))e^{L(\tilde{x}_k)} + (q_0/(q_0 + p_1))) - ln((q_1/(p_0 + q_1))e^{L(\tilde{x}_k)} + (p_1/(q_0 + p_1))) \tag{3}$$

3 Decoding Algorithm

As shown in Fig. 2, V_p represents the parent node of V, V_l and V_r represent the left and right child nodes of V respectively. When the node V is activated, it calculates α_v through (6), and transmits the result α_{vl} to V_l. If V_l is not leaf node, V_l is activated and the f operation is repeated until the left child is leaf node. If V_l is leaf node, β_{vl} is obtained by performing hard decision on α_{vl}. Then transmits it to its parent node V, calculate α_{vr} by (5), and transmits α_{vr} to V_r. If V_r is leaf node, perform hard decision on α_{vr}, calculate bit estimates β_{vr}, and transmits it to V. Further, according to (7), the c

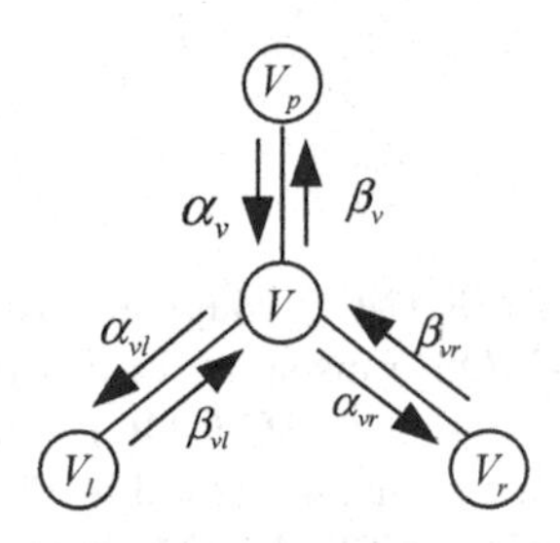

Fig. 2. Fast-SSC algorithm decoding rules

operation is performed to calculate β_v, and transmitted it to V_p. Otherwise, it is activated like the node V.

$$\alpha_{vl}^{(2i-1)}(\alpha_1^N, \beta_1^{2i-2}) = f(\alpha_{N/2}^{(i)}(\alpha_1^{N/2}, \beta_{1,0}^{2i-2} \oplus \beta_{1,\ell}^{2i-2}), \alpha_{N/2}^{(i)}(\alpha_{N/2+1}^N, \beta_{1,\ell}^{2i-2})) \quad (4)$$

$$\alpha_{vr}^{(2i)}(\alpha_1^N, \beta_1^{2i-1}) = g(\alpha_{N/2}^{(i)}(\alpha_1^{N/2}, \beta_{1,0}^{2i-2} \oplus \beta_{1,\ell}^{2i-2}), \alpha_{N/2}^{(i)}(\alpha_{N/2+1}^N, \beta_{1,\ell}^{2i-2}), \beta_{2i-1}) \quad (5)$$

Fast-SSC combines the characteristics of the frozen bit locations without traversing the decoding tree. It contains Rate-0, Rate-1, REP and single-parity check (SPC) nodes [12].

3.1 Rate-0, Rate-1 Nodes

The leaves of the Rate-0 node are all frozen bits, which means the bit estimate of the Rate-0 node is an all-zero vector.

The leaves of the Rate-1 node are all information bits, its estimate can be obtained by hard decision as

$$\beta_v[i] = \begin{cases} 0, \text{ when } \alpha_v[i] \geq 0; \\ 1, \text{ otherwise.} \end{cases} \quad (6)$$

3.2 REP Node

The last leaf of the REP node is an information bit, and the others nodes are frozen bits. It has only two decoding results, all-zero and all-one sequence. Its estimate can be calculated by

$$\beta_v = \begin{cases} 0, \text{ when } (\sum_{i=0}^{N_v-1} \alpha_v[i]) \geq 0; \\ 1, \text{ otherwise.} \end{cases} \quad (7)$$

3.3 SPC Node

The first leaf of the SPC node is a frozen bit, and the others are information bits, it is necessary to perform threshold detection and get the parity check by

$$parity = \bigoplus_{i=0}^{N_v-1} \beta_v[i] \quad (8)$$

Then, if the parity constraint is satisfied, the estimated bit vector is generated by reusing the β_v calculated above. Otherwise, the least reliable bit is founded and flipped if the parity constraint is not satisfied by (9)(10).

$$i = \arg \quad \min(|\alpha_v[i]|) \tag{9}$$

$$\beta_v[i] = \begin{cases} \beta_v[i] \oplus parity, & \text{when } i = j \\ \beta_v[i], & \text{otherwise.} \end{cases} \tag{10}$$

Unlike traditional SC decoding, at the end of Fast-SSC decoding, the result of bit estimation needs to be multiplied by the corresponding size of the generator matrix G_{Nv}, and the final bit estimation u_1^{Nv} according to

$$u_1^{N_v} = \beta_1^{N_v} \mathrm{G}_{\mathrm{N}_v} \tag{11}$$

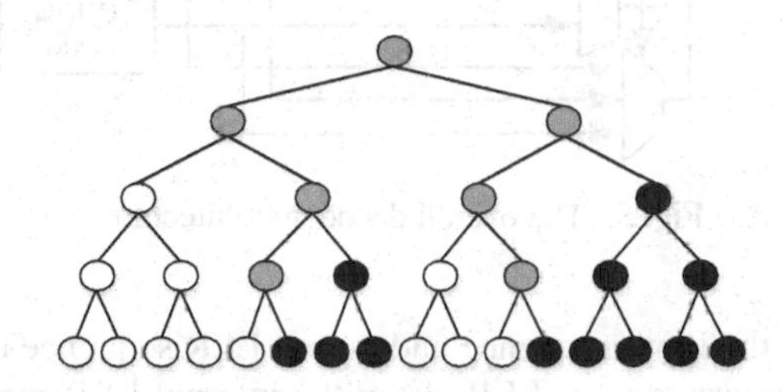

Fig. 3. SC algorithm decoding tree ($N = 16$, $R = 1/2$)

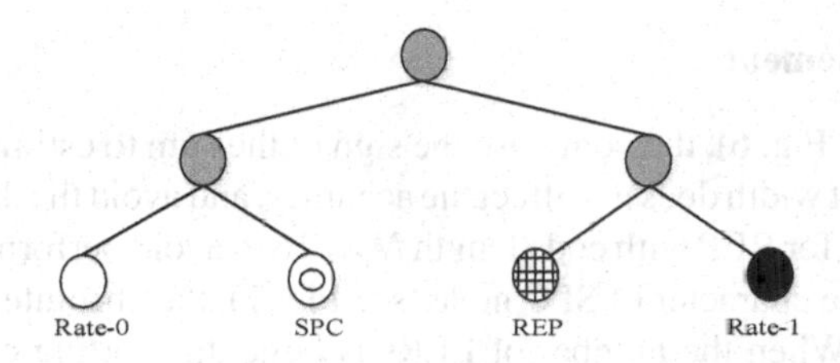

Fig. 4. Fast-SSC algorithm decoding tree ($N = 16$, $R = 1/2$)

Compared with the SC algorithm, the number of nodes in the Fast-SSC decoding tree is significantly reduced (see Fig. 4), which improves decoding the parallelism (Fig. 3).

4 Decoder Architecture

This paper designs a decoder based on the Fast-SSC algorithm (see Fig. 5), which is mainly composed of processing element (PE), controller, Kronecker product and memory module.

We transmit the channel-LLR to the PE, which is used to perform decoding of *f*, *g*, *c* and special nodes. The entire decoding process is manipulated by the controller, which decides whether the data transmitted to the PE is read from the register or the memory. If the results of current stage are not used immediately by the next stage, it will be stored into internal-LLR memory or internal-β memory. Due to the decoding result of every constituent node needs to multiply G_{Nv}, we use Kronecker product to implement it, where $Nv = 2, 4, 8, 16, 32$.

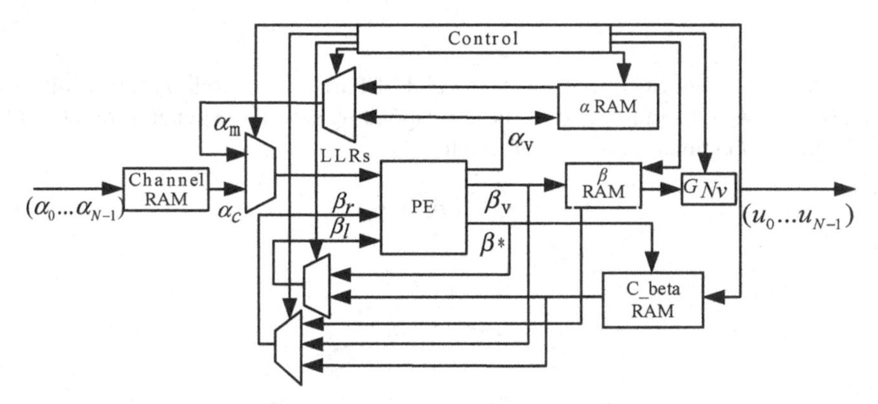

Fig. 5. The overall decoder architecture

LLRs and α_v are the input sequence and output LLR sequence of PE, α_c are LLRs from the channel memory, α_m are LLRs from the internal-LLR memory, respectively, β_v are bit estimations, β^* are the result of *c* operation, β_l and β_r represent bit estimates of the left and right children, respectively.

4.1 Processing Element

For REP nodes (see Fig. 6), they only use the sign of the sum to estimate the codewords. To ensure that the bit width does not affect the accuracy, and avoid the data saturation, they use zero fill method for REP with code length $N_v < 16$ to avoid performance degradation.

According to the character of SPC node (see Fig. 7), the absolute value of the LLRs need to be sorted. When the number of LLRs is large, the sorting complexity is high, which limits the operating frequency of this module, we constrain the length of the SPC to four. The 4MIN1 module selects the smallest LLRs by comparison operation, D0 ~ D3 are calculated to determine which bit to be flipped together with parity. For instance, when D0 = 1, it denotes that the estimate of bit 0 in SPC node is need to flipped.

The *g* operation has two inputs, α and β (see Fig. 8). When β is zero, $\alpha[2i]$ adds $\alpha[2i + 1]$, when β is one, $\alpha[2i + 1]$ subtracts $\alpha[2i]$, and we use two-sign complement operation to avoid overflow during addition.

We use one comparator, one XOR gate and a combination logic to implement *f* operation (see Fig. 9). Where the comparator is used to select the data with the smaller absolute value, and then combine with the sign bit to get the result.

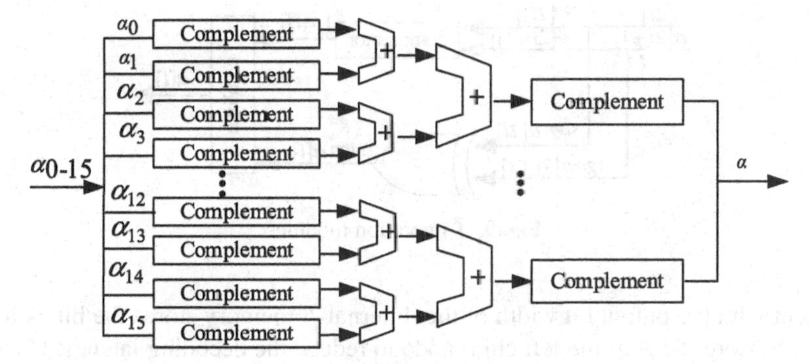

Fig. 6. REP module

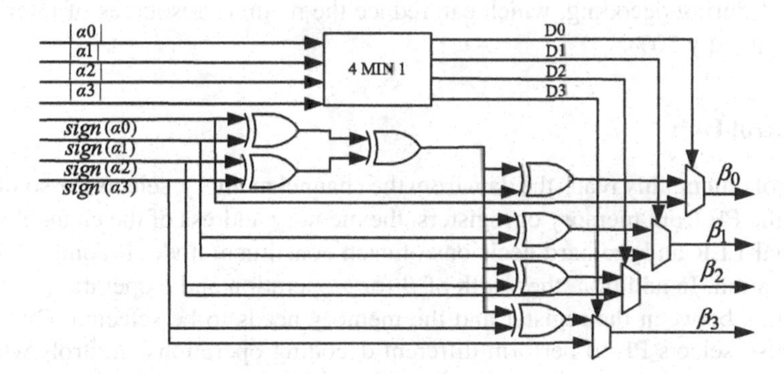

Fig. 7. SPC-4 decoding module

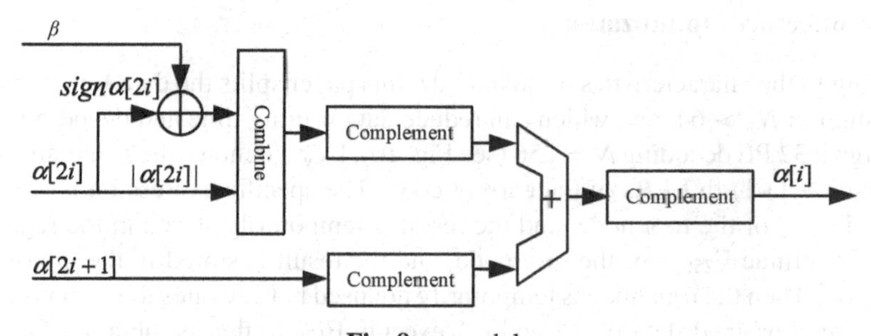

Fig. 8. *g* module

4.2 Memory

The memory mainly includes channel memory, internal-LLR memory, internal-β memory, codeword memory and register. Among them, channel memory stores the channel-LLRs. To reduce the resources of the decoder, the width of this memory is consistent with the data processed by the PE to minimize the memory read and write time. Internal-LLR memory stores the α generated by the *f* and *g* operations, therefore this memory is also the most frequent memory for data access, the width of the memory is 192 bits, which is

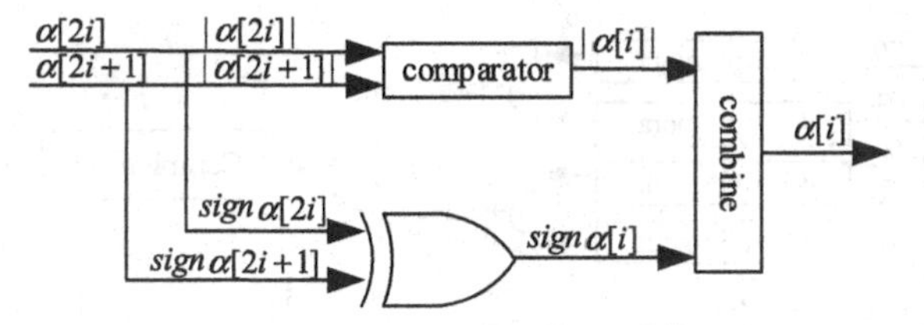

Fig. 9. f operation module

consistent with the output bit width of the. Internal-β memory stores the bit estimation β, we only store the β of the left child node to reduce the decoding latency. Codeword memory stores the bit estimates related to the operation of c, and its bit width is 64. In order to balance the hardware consumption, the right edge Rate-1 node is divided into two Rate-1 during decoding, which can reduce the memory resources of internal-LLR and internal-β by 50%.

4.3 Control Unit

The control unit mainly reads the data from the channel memory, selects the source of the LLRs of the PE from memory or registers, the memory address of the channel memory, the internal-LLR and the hard decisions of each constituent node. It controls the β for the g operation. In addition, the width of β for g operation and c operation is different, and the data between the register and the memory needs to be selected. On the other hand, it also selects PE to perform different decoding operations, controls whether to perform f, g, c operations and outputs the codeword estimates.

4.4 Architecture Optimization

According to the characteristics of polar code, this paper splits the data for nodes with a code length of $N_v > 64$, and which can reduce data waiting time and decoding latency. We design a 32 PE decoding $N = 256$ (see Fig. 10), F_{Nv_i} denotes the f operation on the ($64i$ ~ $64(i + 1)$-1)-th LLRs of the current code. The specific expression is as follows: perform F_{256_0} of the root node, and the result is temporarily stored in the register $\alpha*$, and then continue F_{256_1} of the root node, and the result is stored in the internal-LLR memory $\alpha\hat{}$. Then the root node is temporarily not used but activates the next node. After reading the combined data of $\alpha*$ and $\alpha\hat{}$, execute F_{128_0}, that is, obtain α_v of its left child node by the f operation, and store it in $\alpha\hat{}$. Return to the root node, execute F_{256_2} and F_{256_3} respectively, and store the result in $\alpha\hat{}$. Then execute F_{128_1} using the LLR of the left child V of the root node, the resulting LLR is combined with the F_{128_0}, and finally execute F_{64} to obtain α_{vl} with $N_v = 32$ node, and the subsequent lower layers still follow the Fast-SSC for sequential decoding.

In the case of the same hardware consumption, the decoder can reduce the entire decoding process by 10 clocks by splitting the node data. For nodes with $N_v > 64$, the c and g operations use the same rule to split the LLR sequence, and combine the registers to update the data in time to ensure the accuracy of the controller data selection.

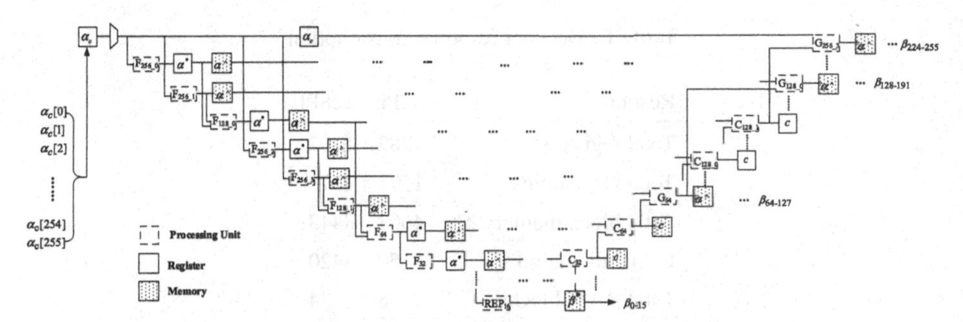

Fig. 10. Decoding flow

In order to read data quickly, it is convenient for the register and the memory to transmit data alternately, and reduce the memory bandwidth. We use three multiplexers to select the data required by each node (see Fig. 11), split the register data to have more flexible selects for the data required by the PE, effectively avoiding memory read-write conflicts, while reducing the number of accesses to the memory. Under the same circumstances, this method does not require additional registers with a bit width of 192.

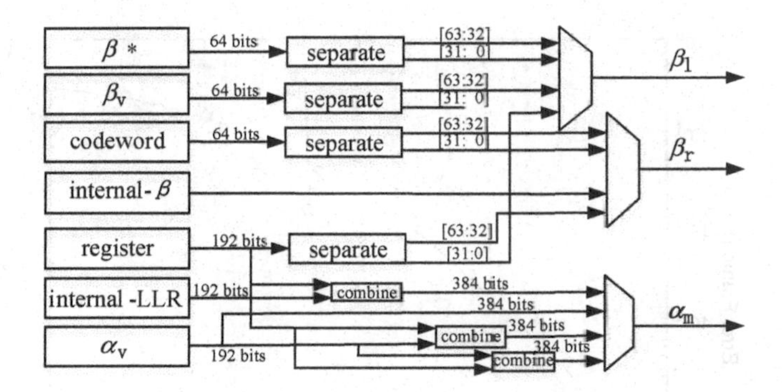

Fig. 11. Data access control

5 Performance Analysis

This paper synthesizes the Fast-SSC decoder on the Stratix V 5SGXEA7N2F45C2, and performs performance comparison between the two decoders. The resource consumption and decoding performance are shown in Table 1 and Table 2.

By comparison, it is found that the operating frequencies of the two decoders have reached 167 M, and the decoding latency of the 32-PE decoder is 0.68 μs, which is 16.18% more than the 128-PE decoder. But the hardware resource consumption is greatly reduced, among them, consumption of total register 782, total block storage bit 4608, logic utilization rate 3150 and total ram blocks 8, resource consumption was reduced by 34.94%, 45.45%, 28.73% and 66.67%, respectively (Fig. 12).

Table 1. Decoder resource consumption

Resources	32PE	128PE
Total registers	782	1202
Total virtual pins	1571	1571
Total block memory bits	4608	8448
Logic utilization	3150	4420
Total RAM blocks	8	24

Table 2. Comparison of decoding latency

	32PE	128PE
Frequency (MHz)	167	166.75
Decoding latency (μs)	0.68	0.57
Throughput (Mbps)	375	449

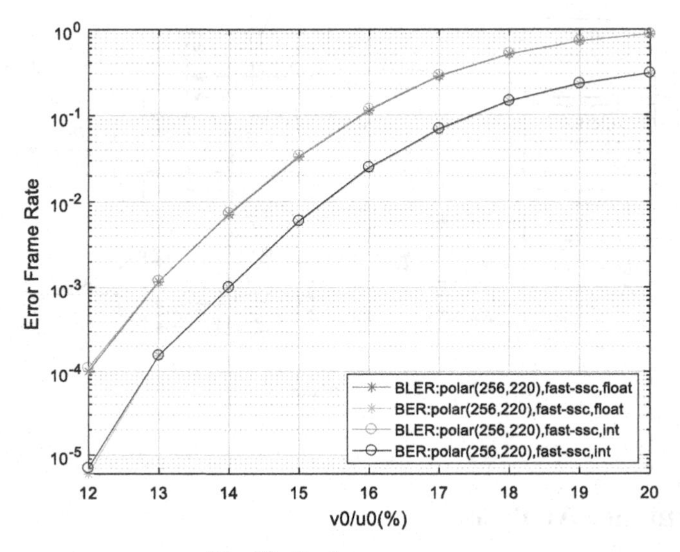

Fig. 12. Performance curve

In this paper, the channel-LLR is quantified with six bits including one fractional bit. When $v0/u0 = v1/u1$, $q0 = 0.999999$, $q1 = 0.999898$, $u0 = 1000$ and $u1 = 2000$, simulations result show that decoding performance with the quantified data is very close to that of the floating-point performance in term of BER and BLER.

6 Conclusion

This paper designs a high-throughput Fast-SSC decoder for STT-MRAM channel, synthesizes it on the FPGA. Simulation results show that the fixed-point decoding performance is very close to that of the floating point algorithm. By splitting the node data, adjusting the data processing order to optimize the architecture, the proposed decoder reduces the complexity of data selection and the decoding latency.

Acknowledgements. This work was supported in part by Joint Fund for Smart Computing of Natural Science Foundation of Shandong Province (ZR2019LZH001), Shandong University Youth Innovation Supporting Program (2019KJN020, 2019KJN024), Shandong Key Research and Development Project (2019GGX101066), the Natural Science Foundation of China (61701284), the Innovative Research Foundation of Qingdao (19-6-2-1-cg).

References

1. Van Beek, S., et al.: Impact of self-heating on reliability predictions in STT-MRAM. In: IEEE International Electron Devices Meeting (IEDM), San Francisco, CA, pp. 25.2.1–25.2.4 (2018)
2. Song, Y.J., et al.: Demonstration of highly manufacturable STT-MRAM embedded in 28 nm logic. In: IEEE International Electron Devices Meeting (IEDM), San Francisco, CA, pp. 18.2.1–18.2.4 (2018)
3. Zhang, M., Wu, F., Huang, H., Xia, Q., Zhou, J., Xie, C.: FPGA-based failure mode testing and analysis for MLC NAND flash memory. In: Design, Automation & Test in Europe Conference & Exhibition (DATE), Lausanne, pp. 434–439 (2017)
4. Yang, K., Zhao, Y., Yang, J., Xue, X., Lin, Y., Bae, J.: Impacts of external magnetic field and high temperature disturbance on MRAM reliability based on FPGA test platform. In: 2015 IEEE 11th International Conference on ASIC (ASICON), Chengdu, pp. 1–4 (2015)
5. Tal, I., Vardy, A.: List decoding of polar codes. IEEE Trans. Inf. Theory **61**(5), 2213–2226 (2015)
6. Arikan, E.: Channel polarization: a method for constructing capacity-achieving codes for symmetric binary- input memoryless channels. IEEE Trans. Inf. Theory **55**(7), 3051–3073 (2009)
7. Hassan, H.G.H., Hussien, A.M.A., Fahmy, H.A.H.: A simplified radix-4 successive cancellation decoder with partial sum lookahead. AEUE – Int. J. Electron. Commun. **96**, 267–272 (2018)
8. Xu, Q., Pan, Z., Liu, N., You, X.: A low-latency list decoder for polar codes. Sci. China Inf. Sci. **61**(10), 1–10 (2018). https://doi.org/10.1007/s11432-017-9312-9
9. Wang, W., Li, L., Niu, K.: An efficient construction of polar codes based on the general partial order. EURASIP J. Wireless Commun. Netw. **2019**(1), 1–12 (2019). https://doi.org/10.1186/s13638-018-1327-7
10. Hashemi, S.A., Condo, C., Gross, W.J.: Fast simplified successive-cancellation list decoding of polar codes. In: 2017 IEEE Wireless Communications and Net-working Conference Workshops, pp. 1–6 (2017)
11. Sarkis, G., Giard, P., Vardy, A., et al.: Fast list decoders for polar codes. IEEE J. Sel. Areas Commun. **34**(2), 318–328 (2016)
12. Zhang, X., et al.: High-throughput fast-SSC polar decoder for wireless communications. Wireless Commun. Mob. Comput. **2018**, 1–10 (2019)

Pipelined BP Polar Decoder with a Novel Updated Scheme

Xiaojun Zhang[1,2](✉), Na Li[1], Jun Li[1], Chengguan Chen[1], Hengzhong Li[1], and Geng Chen[1]

[1] Shandong University of Science and Technology, Qingdao, China
zhangxiaojun@sdust.edu.cn
[2] State Key Laboratory of High-End Server and Storage Technology, Jinan, China

Abstract. Compared with the SC decoder, BP decoder provides a higher throughput and lower decoding latency for its inherent parallel nature. However, the functional units of existing BP decoders are not fully utilized. In this paper, we propose a new update scheduling scheme and hardware optimization design to improve the hardware efficiency of BP decoder. First, a pipelined decoder architecture is proposed to reduce the consumption of functional units. Then, a new update scheduling scheme is proposed, when updating the messages, both new-value and old-value approaches are used to improve the utilization of functional units and reduce the decoding latency. The analysis and synthesis results have shown that, compared with the existing methods, the proposed decoder suffers from a slight the decoding performance degradation, but the utilization rate of basic computational blocks (BCB) can be increased to 50.58%. The storage resource dissipation can be reduced by 20.1%–34.09% .

Keywords: Polar code · Belief propagation (BP) · VLSI · Pipelined architecture · Hardware efficiency

1 Introduction

Polar code has been proved theoretically to be able to achieve the Shannon capacity over binary-input discrete memoryless channels (B-DMCs), and the codec has a lower algorithm complexity [1]. It is a major breakthrough in the history of channel coding and a research hotspot in the field of coding. There exist mainly two decoding algorithms: successive cancellation (SC) decoding [1] and belief propagation (BP) decoding algorithms [2]. The SC algorithm has low decoding complexity and excellent error-correction performance, but the decoding latency is very high, which limits the system throughput and hinders the wide applications of polar codes, especially for high-speed applications.

Unlike SC decoding algorithm, BP decoding is an iterative algorithm that is highly parallel, which provides high throughput and low decoding latency [3, 4]. In 2013, B. Yuan and K. K. Parhi proposed an improved architecture of polar BP decoder in order to improve throughput and efficiency [5]. The following year, they also utilized early

Q. Wu et al. (Eds.): WiSATS 2020, LNICST 358, pp. 576–587, 2021.
https://doi.org/10.1007/978-3-030-69072-4_47

stopping techniques to reduce energy consumption and decoding latency [6]. Subsequently, several architecture transformation techniques are given to further improve the hardware performance [7]. Jin Sha et al. exploited a stage-combined decoding scheme to advance the memory efficiency of BP decoder [8]. S. Sun and Z. Zhang [9] proposed an architecture and optimization of BP decoder that eliminates data dependencies by using forward flood scheduling to improve the error correction performance, throughput and reduce the decoding delay. Junmei Yang et al. [10] presented both feed-forward (FFD) and feed-back (FBK) pipelined architecture for BP decoder to achieve a balance between performance, throughput, latency, area, and utilization. However, owing to the underutilization of the functional units, the hardware performance of the decoder is still not competitive.

Assume that the message that has been updated in current iteration is referred to new value (NV). Otherwise, if the message that has been not updated in current iteration, namely, it is still the value in last iteration, which is defined as old value (OV). In conventional BP decoding, the decoder needs to wait when the new value is not valid, which brings in large decoding latency and costs more memories to store internal messages. To improve hardware efficiency, this paper presents an update scheduling scheme. During the iterations. it updates and calculates the messages with old values directly does without waiting old value. Based on it, a pipelined architecture with new and old value (NOV) based on folding technology is presented. The utilization rate of BCB (basic computational block) can be improved to 100%. Simulations show that the proposed scheme can obtain similar decoding performance as other schemes. Meanwhile, it consumes less hardware resources.

The remainder of this paper is organized as follows. Section 2 briefly reviews polar codes and BP decoding algorithm. In Sect. 3, we present a novel update scheduling scheme and hardware architecture of BP decoder. Section 4 compares the performance among different decoders. Conclusions are drawn in Sect. 5.

2 Conventional BP Decoding of Polar Code

2.1 Polar Codes

Polar codes can be defined by a parameter vector (N, K, A, u_{A^c}), where $N = 2^n$ denotes the codeword length, K denotes the number of information bits, A and A^C represents the set of information bits' indices and its complement, u_{A^c} represents frozen bits. The source vector $u_1^N = (u_1, u_2, \cdots, u_n)$ can be obtained by mixing K information bits and $N - K$ frozen bits. The codeword vector $x_1^N = (x_1, x_2, \cdots, x_n)$ is generated as follows. Subsequent paragraphs, however, are indented.

$$x_1^N = u_1^N G_N = u_1^N B_N F^{\otimes n} \tag{1}$$

Where G_N is a generator matrix, $F^{\otimes n}$ is the n-th Kronecker power of $F = \begin{bmatrix} 10 \\ 11 \end{bmatrix}$, and B_N is a bit-reversal permutation matrix.

2.2 Polar BP Decoding Algorithm

The BP algorithm can be illustrated through factor graph. Figure 1 depicts the factor graph of an (8, 4) polar code, which consists of $n = \log_2 N$ stages and $N(n + 1)$ nodes. Each stage contains $N/2$ 2×2 BCBs [8], which has two inputs and two outputs as shown in Fig. 2.

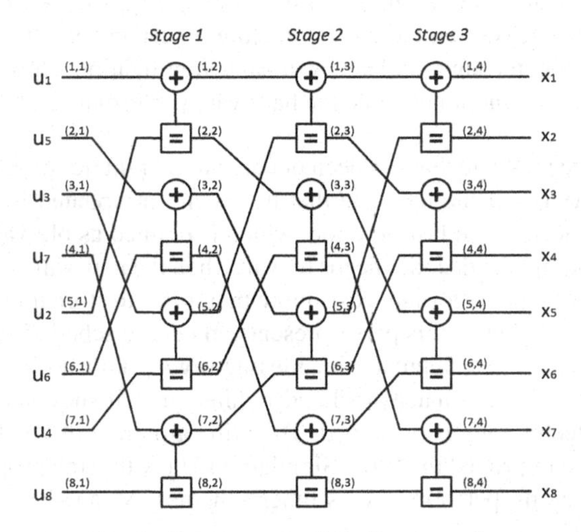

Fig. 1. Factor graph of (8, 4) polar code.

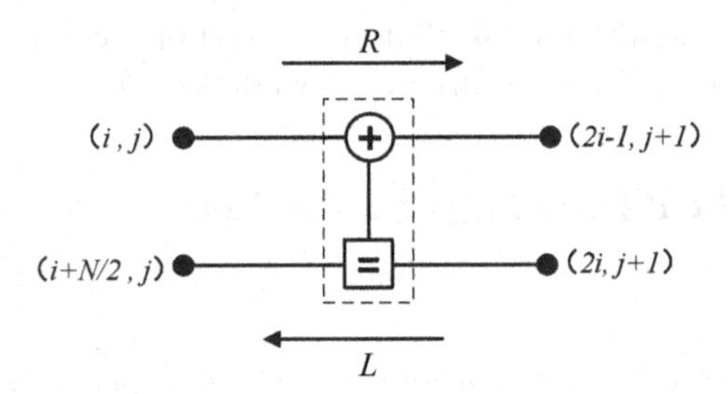

Fig. 2. Factor graph of 2×2 BCB.

The node (i, j) represents the i-th input bit of the j-th column, which is associated with two types of messages: left-to-right messages $R_{i,j}$ and right-to-left messages $L_{i,j}$. During the decoding iterations, these soft messages are updated and propagated among adjacent nodes. The decoder can be initialized as follows.

$$L_{i,n+1} = \ln\left(\frac{p(y_i|x_i = 0)}{p(y_i|x_i = 1)}\right) \tag{2}$$

$$R_{i,1} = \begin{cases} 0, & if\ i \in A \\ \infty, & if\ i \in A^c \end{cases} \tag{3}$$

In BP decoding, messages are passed iteratively from left to right and then from right to left through the factor graph. In each iteration, the BCB calculates $R_{i,j}$ and $L_{i,j}$ messages according to (4).

$$\begin{aligned} L_{i,j} &= f\left(L_{2i-1,j+1}, L_{2i,j+1} + R_{i+N/2,j}\right) \\ L_{i+N/2,j} &= f\left(L_{2i-1,j+1}, R_{i,j}\right) + L_{2i,j+1} \\ R_{2i-1,j+1} &= f\left(R_{i,j}, R_{i+N/2,j} + L_{2i,j+1}\right) \\ R_{2i,j+1} &= f\left(R_{i,j}, L_{2i-1,j+1}\right) + R_{i+N/2,j} \end{aligned} \tag{4}$$

Where $f(x, y)$ can be further simplified to (5) by using the min-sum approximation [11], and the scaling factor is set to 0.9375.

$$f(x, y) \approx 0.9375 \cdot sign(x)sign(y)\min(|x|, |y|) \tag{5}$$

After the BP decoder reaches the preset maximum number of iterations $I_{\max}$, $\hat{u}_1^N$ can be determined by calculating the LLR values of the leftmost node according to (6).

$$\hat{u}_i = \begin{cases} 0, & if\ L_{i,1} \geq 0 \\ 1, & else \end{cases} \tag{6}$$

3 Proposed Nov Update Scheme and Hardware Architecture

3.1 Existing Pipelined BP Decoder

When designing the hardware architecture of the decoder, each stage needs $N/2$ BCBs for an N-bit fully parallel BP polar decoder. The direction of messages update iteratively is from 1-th stage (RS_1) right to (n-1)-th stage (RS_{n-1}), and then from n-th stage (LS_n) left to the 2-th stage (LS_2). After updating messages ($R_{i,j}$) messages or $L_{i,j}$ messages) of each stage takes only one clock cycle, and each iteration takes a total of $2(n-1)$ clock cycles.

Different from the design of the fully parallel BP polar decoder, the whole decoder needs $2(n-1)$ BCBs when using a BCB at each stage [10]. Based on (4) and the FFD pipelined architecture, each BCB updates one pair of messages (or $L_{i,j}$ messages) every clock cycle. When the messages generated by each $R_{i,j}$ BCB update can not consumed immediately in the next cycle, the generated messages should be delayed. For each BCB, if the required input messages is not generated in time during this cycle, it needs to wait for those messages to arrive before it is activated. FFD architecture uses one BCB at each stage, for the N-bit BP polar decoder, the total number of BCBs is

$$Q_{BCB} = 2(\log_2 N - 1) \tag{7}$$

The decoding latency can be evaluated by

$$D_{\text{latency}} = \left(\sum_{i=1}^{\log_2 N-1} 2^i + 2(\log_2 N - 1)\right)I + N/2 \tag{8}$$

The BCB utilization is given by

$$U_{BCB} = \frac{N/2}{\sum_{i=1}^{\log_2 N-1} 2^i + 2(\log_2 N - 1)} \tag{9}$$

3.2 Proposed NOV Updating Scheme

In the FFD pipelined architecture, since the ability of one BCB to update messages is insufficient at each stage, the generated messages need to be delayed if it cannot be immediately consumed. Accordingly, the corresponding register resource will be increased. When BCB updates the messages, it will wait until the required messages is arrived. Subsequently, the overall decoding delay will be increased and the utilization of BCB will also be declined.

For the aforementioned analysis, a novel update scheduling scheme is proposed to overcome those flaws based on the overlapped scheduling method used in the iteration level and codeword level [6]. During the current iteration, the updated messages are called NVs, and the messages that are not updated are called OVs. The OV is essentially the result of last iteration. Similarly, only one pair of $L_{i,j}$ messages (or $R_{i,j}$ messages) can be updated for each BCB in one clock cycle. If the NV that is generated cannot be immediately consumed in the next cycle, it needs to be delayed. However, when the BCB of each stage is updated, if the required messages do not arrive yet, it does not have to wait until those messages are the NV, instead of dealing with the corresponding OV. The BCB of each stage is activated by rotation in the above manner until the preset $I_{\max}$ is reached. In the above decoding process, since two kinds of messages, NV and OV, are always involved, this method is called NOV update scheduling scheme. By adopting this scheme, without considering whether all messages is updated or not. Thus the idle cycle of BCB can be greatly reduced, and the cycles of one iteration will be significantly reduced. On the other hand, the messages that needs to be delayed will be avoided, which can reduce the memories. Similarly, this scheme can also be adopted in the multi-level pipeline architecture.

To further illustrate the NOV scheduling process, an 8-bit polar decoder is shown in Fig. 3. The red dotted line represents the boundary of adjacent iterations, with the first iteration on the left and the second iteration on the right. For RS_1 stage, BCB will be activated in the first cycle to produce right messages: $R_{1,2}$ and $R_{5,2}$, that is NV. Then, $R_{1,2}$ will be consumed by BCB of RS_2 stage in the second cycle, while $R_{5,2}$ is not the right messages required by RS_2 stage in this cycle, so it needs to be delayed. For RS_2 stage, BCB will be activated in the second cycle, and right messages it needs is $R_{1,2}$ and $R_{3,2}$, while $R_{3,2}$ is updated in the third cycle of the first iteration. At this point, instead of waiting for $R_{3,2}$ to be NV, BCB is activated by replacing $R_{3,2}$ with corresponding OV. Each BCB is activated as described above until $I_{\max}$ is reached and decoding is terminated.

3.3 Hardware Architecture

According to (4), assume that the 4-input ports and the 2-output ports of BCB are *a*, *b*, *c*, *d*, and *out1*, *out2*, respectively. Then (4) can be further simplified to (10). The logical

Clock Cycle	1	2	3	4	5	6	7	8	9	...
RS1	$R_{1,2}$ $R_{5,2}$	$R_{2,2}$ $R_{6,2}$	$R_{3,2}$ $R_{7,2}$	$R_{4,2}$ $R_{8,2}$	$R_{1,2}$ $R_{5,2}$	$R_{2,2}$ $R_{6,2}$	...			
RS2		$R_{1,3}$ $R_{3,3}$	$R_{2,3}$ $R_{4,3}$	$R_{5,3}$ $R_{7,3}$	$R_{6,3}$ $R_{8,3}$	$R_{1,3}$ $R_{3,3}$	$R_{2,3}$ $R_{4,3}$	...		
LS3			$L_{1,3}$ $L_{2,3}$	$L_{3,3}$ $L_{4,3}$	$L_{5,3}$ $L_{6,3}$	$L_{7,3}$ $L_{8,3}$	$L_{1,3}$ $L_{2,3}$	$L_{3,3}$ $L_{4,3}$	...	
LS2				$L_{1,2}$ $L_{3,2}$	$L_{2,2}$ $L_{4,2}$	$L_{5,2}$ $L_{7,2}$	$L_{6,2}$ $L_{8,2}$	$L_{1,2}$ $L_{3,2}$	$L_{2,2}$ $L_{4,2}$	...

Fig. 3. NOV updating schedule of 8-bit polar code. (Color figure online)

architecture of BCB is illustrated in Fig. 4, and its hardware architecture is shown in Fig. 5. Here T2C module converses sign-magnitude (SM) to 2's complement, and C2T is inversely converted. Moreover, SU module performs the scaling function, MIN module can get the minimum value. The BCB updates the $R_{i,j}$ (or $L_{i,j}$) messages from left to right (or right to left) as shown in Fig. 6. Obviously, the BCB is a bidirectional update function.

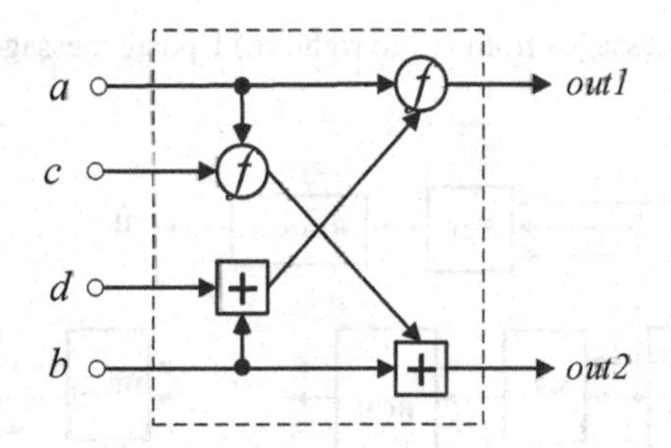

Fig. 4. Architecture of BCB.

$$out1 = f(a, b + d), out2 = f(a, c) + b \tag{10}$$

An N-bit pipelined BP decoder architecture with the NOV update scheme is shown in Fig. 6. The switch module has 4-input ports and 4-output ports, which updates $L_{i,j}$ messages of the LS_1 from right to left for the last iteration and is controlled by the signal I, when $I = I_{\max}$, the switch module is activated. The same BCB can be used with the assistance of the switch module because of RS_1 and LS_1 just update the messages in different directions. The hard decision module is composed of the sign module and the reorder module, which determines the codeword estimation value $\hat{u}$, and is also activated when $I = I_{\max}$. The sign module is used to gain the sign bit of the LLR. The reorder module is employed to perform bit reversal operation. The MR_n and ML_n modules are utilized to deposit $R_{i,j}$ and $L_{i,j}$ messages of the n-th stage generated by the BCB respectively, but they are not pure memories, as shown in Fig. 8. Here switch acts

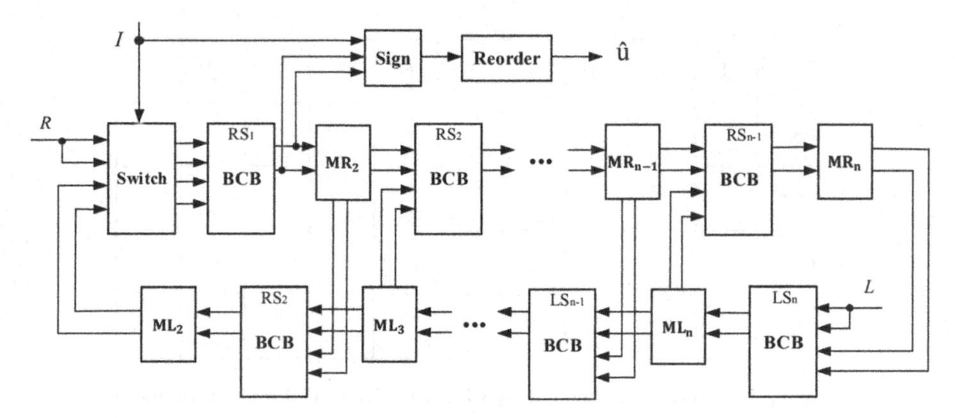

Fig. 5. Hardware architecture of BCB.

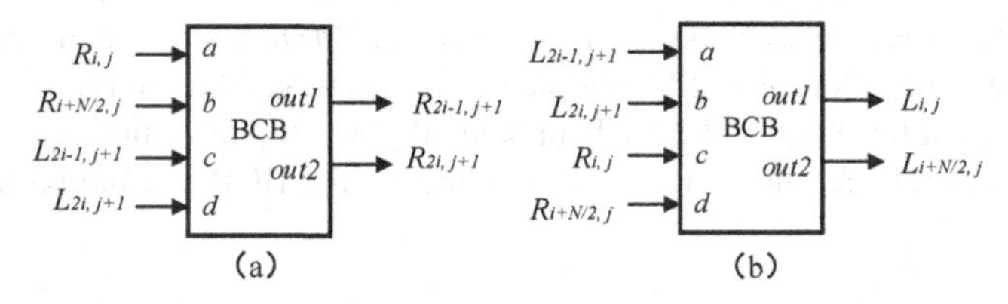

Fig. 6. (a) Update messages from left to right. (b) Update messages from right to left.

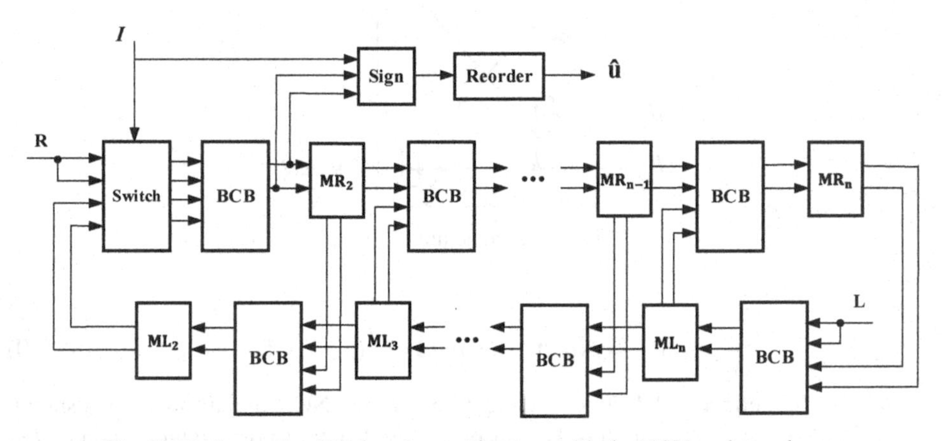

Fig. 7. N-bit pipeline BP decoder architecture with the NOV update scheme.

as a commutator, FIFO is used to store NVs that needs to be delayed, RAM is used to store part of OVs, where the corresponding OVs will be overwritten by the result of the next iteration.

For an 8-bit pipelined BP decoder architecture with the NOV update scheme, one BCB is adopted for each stage, and a total of 4 BCBs is required. Each iteration takes 4 clock cycles. Moreover, BCB takes 4 clock cycles just to update the messages of this

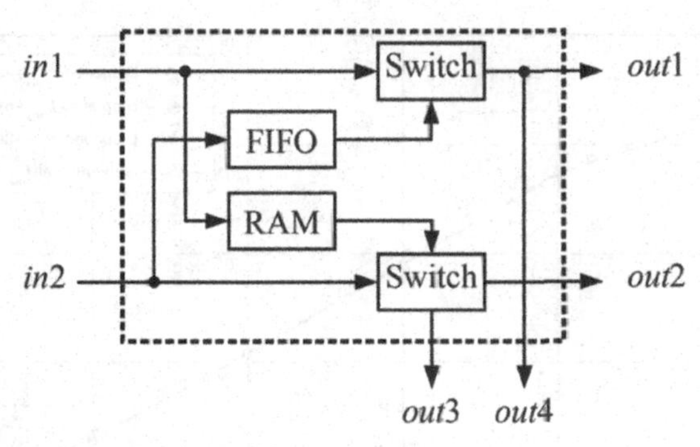

Fig. 8. Memory module.

stage during that time, thus the utilization rate of BCB is 100%. If the decoding result is outputted, it also takes 4 clock cycles, and the decoding latency is $4I + 4$ clock cycles.

In Fig. 7, the total number of BCBs is

$$Q_{BCB} = 2(\log_2 N - 1) \tag{11}$$

The decoding latency is calculated by

$$D_{latency} = \frac{N}{2} I + N/2 \tag{12}$$

The BCB utilization is

$$U_{BCB} = \frac{N/2}{N/2} \tag{13}$$

4 Implementation and Comparison

In this section, we analyze and compare the decoding performance and hardware performance under different polar BP decoder architectures, in order to illustrate the advantages of the proposed architecture with the NOV scheduling scheme.

To evaluate the decoding performance of the proposed scheme, A (1024, 512) polar code is simulated under AWGN (Additive White Gaussian Noise) channel with BPSK(Binary Phase Shift Keying) modulation. Simulation results are depicted in Figs. 9 and 10. Compared with the conventional BP decoding, the proposed has a slight decoding performance degradation in the low SNR regions. This is mainly because we used some old values during iterative process, which lowers the convergence rate of decoding. But it is very close to the performance of the conventional BP decoding in high SNR regions. When $I_{max} = 80$, the proposed scheme is very close to the conventional one.

Table 1 lists the comparison of BCB number, BCB utilization and decoding latency of FFD and the proposed NOV at different code lengths. From the table, it can be shown that the number of BCB required that of the proposed in this paper is the same as the FFD. Under different code lengths, the BCB is always in active state for the duration of

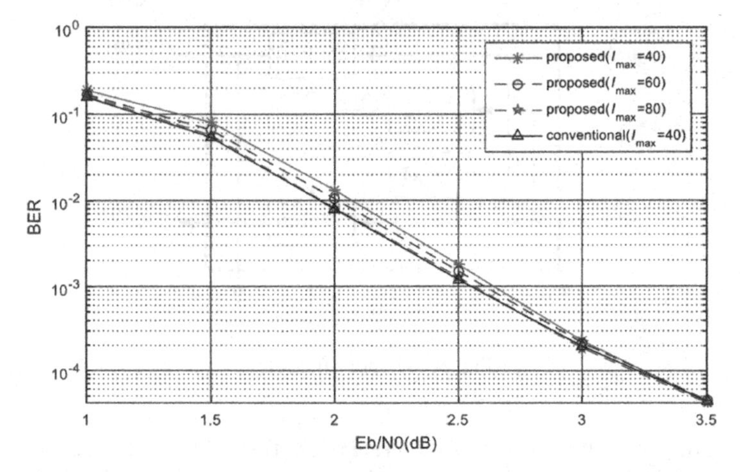

Fig. 9. BER performance for (1024, 512) polar codes with different $I_{\max}$.

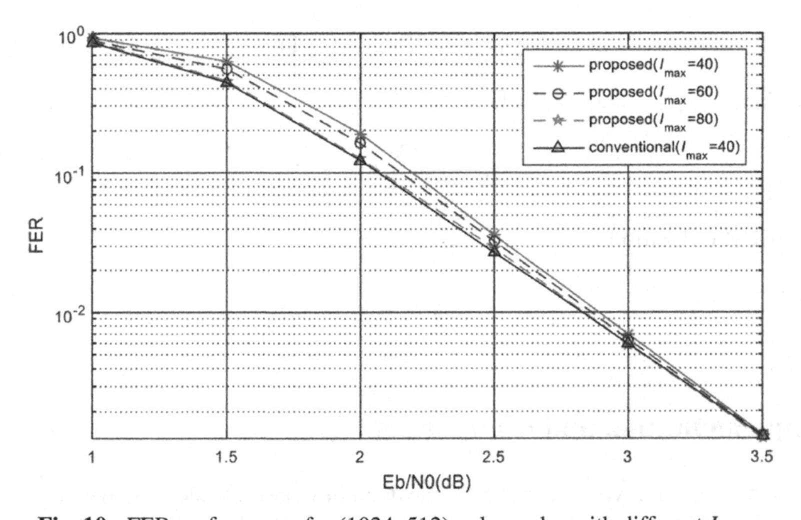

Fig. 10. FER performance for (1024, 512) polar codes with different $I_{\max}$.

iteration with the NOV scheduling strategy. Accordingly, under different code lengths, one iteration and without decoding results, the decoding latency can be reduced by 50.7%, and the utilization ratio of BCB can be increased to 50.6%.

Table 2 shows the comparison of the decoding latency between the proposed NOV and FFD with the average number of iterations with two early stopping schemes (minLLR and G-matrix [8]), when $I_{\max} = 40$ at SNR = 3.5 dB. According to Table 2, compared with FFD, the average number of iterations of NOV increases about three times with two early stopping schemes, this is also caused by using some old values. Furthermore, the decoding latency is increased by 40.7% with the average number of iterations, but the decoding latency can be reduced by 50.2% with the same iteration number.

Table 1. Comparison of decoding latency, BCB number, and BCB utilization for different code lengths

Code length (bit)	Decoding latency		Number of BCB		BCB utilization	
	FFD [10]	NOV	FFD [10]	NOV	FFD [10]	NOV
512	782	512	16	16	48.67%	100%
1024	1552	1024	18	18	49.23%	100%
2048	3090	2048	20	20	49.56%	100%
4096	6164	4096	22	22	49.76%	100%
8192	12310	8192	24	24	49.87%	100%

Table 2. Comparison of the decoding delay under the average number of iterations

Design	SNR (dB)	Average number of iterations		Decoding latency	
		FFD [10]	NOV	FFD [10]	NOV
Proposed without stopping criteria	3	40	40	42112	20992
	3.5	40	40	42112	20992
Proposed with minLLR	3	6.70	19.53	7480	10511.3
	3.5	5.53	16.45	6263.2	8934.4
Proposed with G-matrix	3	6.20	17.85	6960	9651.2
	3.5	5.12	15.04	5836.8	8212.4

The synthesis results of BP polar decoder with different decoding schemes are shown in Table 3. Let (Q_s, Q_i, Q_f) denote the quantization scheme, where Q_s presents the quantization bits of sign bit, Q_i and Q_f denotes the integer bits and fractional bits respectively. The quantization scheme (1, 8, 3) is adopted to quantize the LLRs of BP decoders. From Table 3, it can be seen that compared with FFD and FBK architectures under the 12-bit quantization scheme, NOV architecture can reduce the consumption of register and block memory by 25.8% to 38.9%, respectively, and the frequency can be increased by 1.9 to 2.1 times.

Table 3. Synthesis and simulation results under different methods

Hardware overheads	Existing methods		NOV
	FFD [10]	FBK [10]	
Logic unit	2,738	2,942	212,408
Storage resource	225,099	185,674	148,364
Throughput (Mbps)	17.28	10.82	10.74
Frequency (MHz)	105.69	96.02	93.75

5 Conclusion

In this paper, we propose a new update scheduling scheme and an optimized hardware architecture to improve the hardware efficiency of polar BP decoder. This research have been implemented and verified at FPGA platform. Synthesis results show that the proposed architecture can significantly improve the hardware utilization, and lower memory consumption compared with the existing methods.

Acknowledgements. This work was supported in part by Joint Fund for Smart Computing of Natural Science Foundation of Shandong Province (ZR2019LZH001), Shandong University Youth Innovation Supporting Program (2019KJN020, 2019KJN024), Shandong Key Research and Development Project (2019GGX101066), the Natural Science Foundation of China (61701284), the Innovative Research Foundation of Qingdao (19-6-2-1-cg).

References

1. Arıkan, E.: Channel polarization: a method for constructing capacity-achieving codes for symmetric binary-input memoryless channels. IEEE Trans. Inf. Theory **55**(7), 3051–3073 (2009)
2. Pamuk, A.: An FPGA implementation architecture for decoding of polar codes. In: International Symposium on Wireless Communication Systems, pp. 437–441 (2011)
3. Yu, Y., Pan, Z., Liu, N., You, X.: Belief propagation bit-flip decoder for polar codes. IEEE Access **7**, 10937–10946 (2019)
4. Wang, X., Zheng, Z., Li, J., Shan, L., Li, Z.: Belief propagation bit-strengthening decoder for polar codes. IEEE Commun. Lett. **23**(11), 1958–1961 (2019)
5. Yuan, B., Parhi, K.K.: Architecture optimizations for BP polar decoders. In: IEEE International Conference on Acoustics, Speech and Signal Processing (ICASSP), pp. 2654–2658 (2013)
6. Yuan, B., Parhi, K.K.: Early stopping criteria for energy-efficient low-latency belief-propagation polar code decoders. IEEE Trans. Signal Process. **62**(24), 6496–6506 (2014)
7. Yuan, B., Parhi, K.K.: Architectures for polar BP decoders using folding. In: Proceedings of the International Symposium on Circuits and Systems (ISCAS), Melbourne, Australia, pp. 205–208 (2014)
8. Sha, J., Xing, L., Wang, Z., Zeng, X.: A memory efficient belief propagation decoder for polar codes. China Commun. **12**(5), 34–41 (2015)

9. Sun, S., Zhang, Z.: Architecture and optimization of high-throughput belief propagation decoding of polar codes. In: 2016 IEEE International Symposium on Circuits and Systems (ISCAS), pp. 165–168 (2016)
10. Yang, J., Zhang, C., Zhou, H., You, X.: Pipelined belief propagation polar decoders. In: IEEE International Symposium on Circuits and Systems (ISCAS) (2016)
11. Kschischang, F.R., Frey, B.J., Loeliger, H.A.: Factor graphs and the sum-product algorithm. IEEE Trans. Inf. Theory **47**(2), 498–519 (2001)

Recommendation Based Heterogeneous Information Network and Neural Network Model

Cong Zhao[1], Yan Wen[1](✉), Ming Chen[2], and Geng Chen[3]

[1] College of Computer Science and Engineering, Shandong University of Science and Technology, Qingdao 266590, China
wenyan84@hotmail.com
[2] State Grid Shandong Electric Power Company, Qingdao Power Supply Company, Qingdao 266500, China
[3] College of Electronic and Information Engineering, Shandong University of Science and Technology, Qingdao 266590, China

Abstract. With the advent of the Internet era, the recommendation system has developed rapidly. Heterogeneous information networks representation learning is widely used in recommendation systems due to its advantages in complex information modeling. Although the performance of the recommendation system has been improved, there are still two shortcomings: 1. There is a lot of noise data in the instances of the meta-path generated by random walks of meta-paths, which will reduce the performance of the recommendation system. 2. Traditional recommendation algorithms fail to make full use of the relevant meta-path information in heterogeneous information networks, which makes the recommendation results lack of interpretability. To solve these problems, we propose a recommendation system based on heterogeneous network representation learning and neural network model. Firstly, use the matrix factorization and the similarity calculation to select the meta-path instances with good quality as the pre-training vectors of the recommendation system. Then, we combine LSTM with Attention mechanism to learn the user, item and meta-path embeddings, and use MLP to make prediction after fusion to jointly improve the recommendation effect. We conducted experiments on Movielens datasets to evaluate the performance of our proposed recommendation.

Keywords: Heterogeneous information network representation learning · Neural network · Recommendation system

1 Introduction

The rapid development of the Internet era has brought the huge amount of information resources, which makes users can't accurately obtain the information they need. Therefore, as a kind of information retrieval tool in the Internet era, the recommendation system has developed rapidly.

Q. Wu et al. (Eds.): WiSATS 2020, LNICST 358, pp. 588–598, 2021.
https://doi.org/10.1007/978-3-030-69072-4_48

Currently, heterogeneous information networks (HIN) [1] are widely used in recommendation systems due to their advantages in complex information modeling. In Fig. 1, we can see that the HIN contains multiple types of entities connected by different types of relations. Meanwhile, network representation learning [2], which aim at learning the low-dimensional representation vectors of each node has shown certain potential in structural feature extraction. Heterogeneous information network representation learning is an extension of the homogeneous network representation learning, which emphasizes both on the complex structure and rich semantics, and has shown effectiveness in many recommendation tasks.

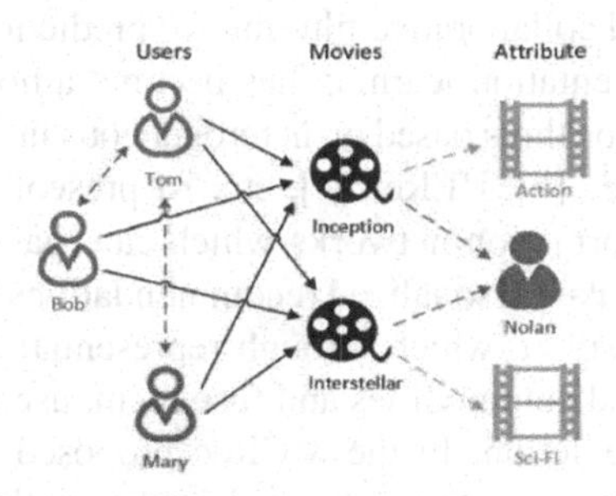

Fig. 1. Movie heterogeneous information network sample diagram

Although existing recommendation methods based on heterogeneous network representation learning have achieved performance improvement to some extent, they still face some challenges: (1) In most existing HIN representation learning works, there is a lot of noise data in the instances of the meta-path generated by random walks of meta-paths, which will reduce the performance of the recommendation system. (2) Most existing the recommendation algorithms only model the interaction between users and items, and fails to make full use of the meta-paths in HIN with abundant auxiliary information, which makes the recommendation results lack of interpretability.

In order to solve the above problems, we propose a recommendation system based on heterogeneous network representation learning and neural network model. The main contributions of this paper are as follows: (1) In order to filter out noisy meta-path instances, the matrix factorization algorithm is used to generate the latent factors for users and items, which are future used to calculate the similarity between nodes guide the meta-path based random walk, calculate the cosine similarity between nodes, and Top-k meta-path instances with high score are selected. (2) We propose a neural network recommendation framework that combines LSTM with Attention mechanism. This framework can learn the three feature representations of user, item and meta-path information, and make predictions after the integration of the three to improve the recommendation effect. (3) We conducted experiments on Movielens dataset to evaluate the performance of our methods. The results show that we prove the good performance of the proposed model in the recommended task.

2 Related Work

In the early work on recommendation system, the classical recommendation algorithm matrix factorization, is to model users' and items' preferences by learning two latent semantic matrices which are used as a prediction function for the recommended items. However, the matrix factorization algorithm will generate cold start problem, we try to improve the effect of recommendation by adding auxiliary information. For example, Ma et al. [1] proposed adding auxiliary data such as social relations to matrix decomposition to recommend users. The model proposed by Ling et al. [4] not only considers scoring information, but also adds comment information to it, realizing the combination of content-based filtering and collaborative filtering for prediction.

In recent years, representation learning has become a hot research. Among them, representative learning algorithms based on heterogeneous information network include metapath2vec [5], HIN2vec [6], HERec [7], etc. At present, most online services are typical heterogeneous information networks which can make full use of various rich semantic information to make personalized recommendations for users. Chuan Shi et al. [7] proposed HERec algorithm, which through representation learning, obtain vector representations of users and commodities and fuse them, use matrix factorization algorithm to complete the prediction. In the MCRec proposed by Binbin Hu et al. [8], Using PCRW sampling sequence, the embedded representation of different meta-paths is obtained through the convolutional neural network, using attention mechanisms to fuse embedded representations, then, a layer of fully connected neural network is used to predict the user's rating of the item.

3 Preliminary

Definition 1. Heterogeneous information network [1]. A HIN is denoted as G = (V, E), node set V and edge set E. It is also associated with an object type mapping function $\varphi: V \rightarrow A$ and a link type mapping function $\delta: E \rightarrow R$. A and R denote the sets of predefined object and link types, where $|A| + |R| > 2$.

Definition 2. The network schema is denoted as S = (A; R). It is a meta template for an information network G = (V, E) with the object type mapping $\varphi: V \rightarrow A$ and the link type mapping $\delta: E \rightarrow R$, which is a directed graph defined over object types A, with edges as relations from R.

Definition 3. Meta-path [9]. The meta-path ρ defined as $A_1 \xrightarrow{R_1} A_2 \xrightarrow{R_2} \cdots \xrightarrow{R_t} A_{t+1}$ (abbreviated as $A_1 A_2 \cdots A_{t+1}$) on the network schema S = (A, R), represents a compound relationship between node type A_1 and A_{t+1} through node type sequence $A_1, A_2, \ldots A_t$, and $R = R_1 \circ R_2 \circ \cdots \circ R_t$ represents the compound operator on the relationship. Some meta-paths with difference semantics are defined as in Table 1.

4 The Proposed Model

4.1 Model Overview

The main framework of this paper is the combination of heterogeneous information network representation learning and neural network. First, matrix factorization algorithm

Table 1. Examples of meta-path

Meta-path	Meaning	Examples
U-U (User-User)	Friend	Tom-Mary, Tom-Bob
U-M-U (User-Movie-User)	Users who watch the same movie	Tom-Avater-Bob
U-M-D-M-U (User-Movie-Director-Movie-User)	Users who watch movies made by the same director	Tom-Avatar-Cameron-The Titanic-Bob

is used to evaluate the meta-path instances generated by meta-path-based random walks. For each meta-path, the instances are assessed by average similarity between adjacent nodes along the instance path, and TOP-K instances are selected as pre-training vectors for the recommendation system. Then a neural network recommendation framework combining LSTM and Attention mechanism (in Fig. 2) is proposed. This framework can learn the feature representations of user, item and meta-paths, and make prediction by using MLP, so as to jointly improve the recommending performance.

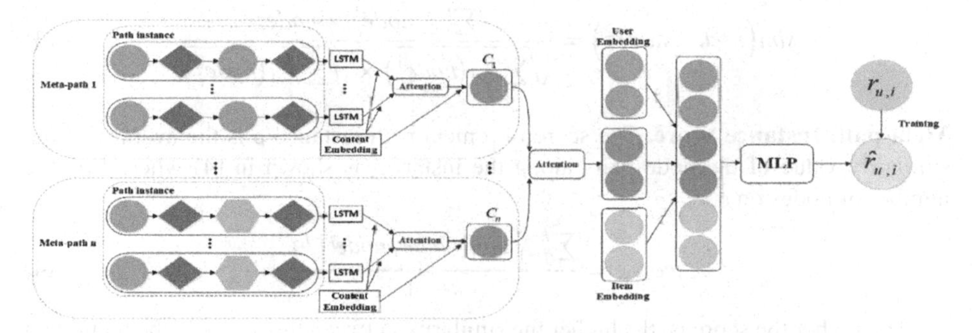

Fig. 2. Overall framework

4.2 Selection of Meta-path Instances

A meta-path instance is a sequence of nodes generated by random walks a meta-path. The average similarity of the edges in the meta-path instance can be taken as its score, then the Top-k instances are selected as the input data.

Matrix Factorization on Edge Type. For a give edge type R = <A1, A2 >, all the edges with the type R is, the corresponding matrix is defined as M, the element $r_{u,i}$ means the value of uth row and i^{th} column in M, and is set to 1 when there is an edge between u and i, and 0 otherwise. The matrix M can be factorized into two latent matrix X and Y as $M \approx X^T \cdot Y$, where X = [x1,x2,...,xn] and Y = [y1, y2,...,ym] represent latent matrices for node type A1 and A2 under edge type R respectively, and xi and yj represent the latent vectors. The latent vector for each node can be obtained by optimizing formula (1).

$$\min_{U,L} \frac{1}{2} \sum_{i=1}^{M} \sum_{j=1}^{N} \|W_{i,j} - U_{i.}^{T} L_{.j}\|_F^2 + \frac{\lambda}{2}\left(\|U\|_F^2 + \|L\|_F^2\right) \tag{1}$$

Meta-path-based random walks on heterogeneous networks is based on following transition probability:

$$P(n_{t+1} = x | n_t = v, \rho) = \begin{cases} \frac{1}{\left|N^{A_{t+1}}(v)\right|}, (v, x) \in \varepsilon \ and \ \emptyset(x) = A_{t+1}; \\ 0, otherwise, \end{cases} \tag{2}$$

Where n_{t+1} is the next node, n_t is the current node, v is the node type, ρ is the meta-path, and the denominator $\left|N^{A_{t+1}}(v)\right|$ represents the number of candidate nodes according to the meta-path.

Similarity Measure for Node Pairs on a Mate Path Instance. Suppose the meta-path ρ is *umum*, and one of its instances is $node^1, node^2, node^3 \ldots\ldots, node^k$, and each node can be represented by an n-dimensional vector. The similarity between adjacent nodes in the meta-path instance is based on the cosine similarity measure shown in Eq. (3).

$$sim\left(node^1, node^2\right) = \frac{\sum_{i=1}^{n} node_i^1 \times node_i^2}{\sqrt{\sum_{i=1}^{n}\left(node_i^1\right)} \times \sqrt{\sum_{i=1}^{n}\left(node_i^2\right)}} \tag{3}$$

Meta-path Instance Score. The score of a meta-path instance ρ is the average of the similarity value of the node pairs along the instance as shown in (4) where k is the number of nodes on σ.

$$score_\sigma = \frac{\sum_{j=1}^{k-1} sim\left(node^j, node^{j+1}\right)}{k-1} \tag{4}$$

The higher the score is, the higher the similarity between the nodes in the meta-path instance is, which makes the semantics of the meta-path instance more explicit.

4.3 User and Item Embedding

As look up can simplify the operation and low time complexity, we use look up to produce the user embedding and item embedding. Formally, given a user-item pair < user, item> , let a_u and b_i denote their one-hot representations.

The lookup layers correspond to two parameter matrices A and B, which store the latent factors for users and items respectively. And d is the dimension size of user and item embeddings, and U and I are the total number of users and items respectively. The lookup operation is implemented as follows:

$$x_u = A^T \cdot a_u \tag{5}$$

$$y_i = B^T \cdot b_i \tag{6}$$

4.4 Meta-path Embedding

In order to capture particular semantics for different meta-paths, each meta-path is processed separately. As LSTM is good at sequence modeling and the Attention mechanism can obtain the importance of each meta-path instance. We combine the LSTM and the Attention mechanism to produce the meta-path instances embedding, content embedding and path instances' weight distribution, then, concatenate path instance embedding obtained by the Attention mechanism and content embedding to obtain a single meta-path embedding (in Fig. 3(a)). Similarly, different meta-paths play different roles for determining the nodes relevance, so we introduce the Attention mechanism to put different weight on each meta-path embedding. Each individual meta-path embedding is fused into one final meta-path representation (in Fig. 3(b)).

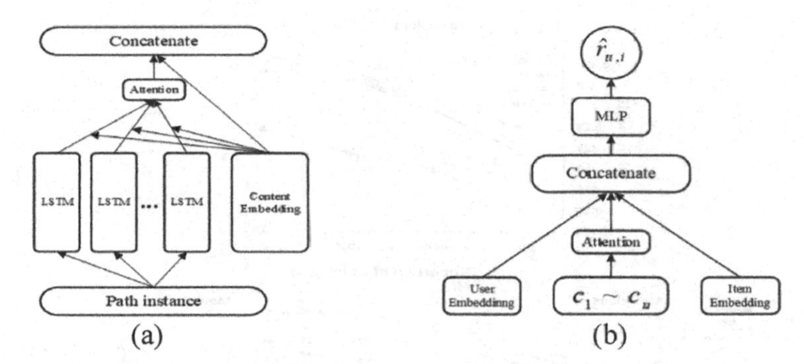

Fig. 3. Model processing

Use the Combination of LSTM and Attention Mechanism to Obtain the Embedding of a Single Meta-path. While extracting each meta-path instance embedding, we also trained content embedding. When all path instances under this meta-path are trained, content embedding includes the representation of the content of this meta-path.

We use LSTM to learn the sequence embedding of path instance i, where X^i is the node embedding matrix, and θ represents all relevant parameters in LSTM, as follows:

$$h_i = LSTM\left(X^i; \theta\right) \tag{7}$$

Then, through the Attention mechanism to put different weight on each meta-path instance embedding. Where, h_i is the sequence embedding of the meta-path instance obtained by LSTM, u_i is the feature matrix after nonlinear transformation, u_p represents the content embedding, it is continuously updated as the model training, α_i represents the Attention mechanism distribution coefficient of different meta-path instances, o is the output result of Attention mechanism,

$$u_i = tanh(W_s h_i + b_s) \tag{8}$$

$$\alpha_i = \frac{\exp\left(u_i^T u_p\right)}{\sum_i \exp\left(u_i^T u_p\right)} \tag{9}$$

$$o = \sum_i \alpha_i h_i \tag{10}$$

We concatenate the Attention mechanisms' result o and the content embedding u_p together to form a single meta-path embedding p_j, as follows:

$$p_j = concatenate(o, u_p) \tag{11}$$

Obtained Different Weight of Different Meta-paths Embedding. Different metapaths play different roles for determining the nodes relevance. In Fig. 4, we use the Attention mechanism to obtain the weight of different meta-paths ($C_1 \sim C_n$).

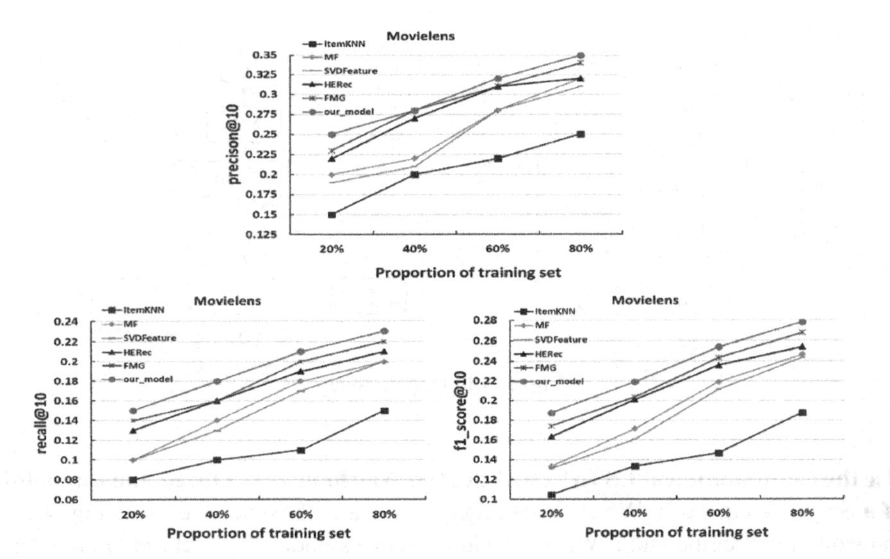

Fig. 4. The precision and recall on the Movielens dataset

$$v_j = tanh(W_k p_j + b_k) \tag{12}$$

$$\beta_j = \frac{\exp\left(v_j^T u_m\right)}{\sum_j \exp\left(v_j^T u_m\right)} \tag{13}$$

$$v = \sum\nolimits_j \alpha_j p_j \tag{14}$$

Where, p_j represents the embedding of each meta-path, and β_j represents the Attention mechanism distribution coefficient of different meta-path. v is the result of weight of different meta-paths embedding.

4.5 Interaction of User, Item and Meta-path Embedding

In Fig. 4, we concatenate the meta-path embeddings with user embedding and item embedding, as follows:

$$out = concatenate(x_u, v, x_i) \tag{15}$$

4.6 Model Prediction

In Fig. 4, we feed the *out* to the MLP component, in order to model the complex non-linear interaction among the three embeddings.

$$\hat{y}_{\mathrm{u,i}} = MLP(\mathrm{out}) \tag{16}$$

Defining objective functions for model optimization is the key to learning a good recommendation model. In our task, the objective for an interaction <u, i> can be formulated as follows:

$$l_{u,i} = -log\,\hat{y}_{u,i} - E_{j \sim P_{neg}}\left[\log\left(1 - \hat{y}_{u,j}\right)\right] \tag{17}$$

Where the first term models the observed interactions and the second term models the negative feedback from the noise distribution P_{neg}.

5 Experiment

We conducted experiments on Movielens datasets and proved the effectiveness of our proposed method by comparing it with other methods.

5.1 Dataset

We use Movielens datasets, which contains data for users and their ratings on movies, including 943 users and 1,682 movies.

The meta-paths used are shown in Table 2. The user and item have an embedded dimension of 128, a random walk path length of 10, and a window size of 3. The learning rate is set to 0.001, the Gaussian distribution is used to randomly initialize the model parameters, the batch size is 128, the optimizer uses Adaptive Moment Estimation (Adam), and the number of iterations is set to 100. When the loss has not dropped for 20 consecutive rounds, stop training.

Table 2. Meta-paths selected for each dataset

Dataset	Meta-paths
Movielens	UMU, UMDMU, UMAMU, UMTMU, UUM

We consider comparing with the following methods:

- ItemKNN [10]: A classic collaborative filtering method that recommends similar items based on previous items.
- MF [11]: Standard matrix factorization method, which uses the cross-entropy loss function to modify its optimization loss.
- SVD Feature$_{mp}$: A variant of SVDFeature [12], which uses the HIN embedding method meta-path2vec ++ to extract user and project embedding.
- FMGrank: Based on FMG [13], the optimization objective was modified to the paired ranking loss in BPR for scoring prediction.
- HERec [7]: A recommendation method based on heterogeneous networks embeddings, which is fused with matrix methods for recommendation.

5.2 Overall Performance

We divide the entire dataset into a training set and a test set. We use different proportions of data (20%, 40%, 60%, 80%) as the training set. We use ranking-based accuracy (Prec @ K), recall (Recall @ K) and f1 value (F1-score @ K) as to the metrics to evaluate the recommended performance of our model. In Fig. 4, The result shows that: (1) Our proposed method is always superior to all comparison models. Compared with other HIN-based methods, our model uses a method based on heterogeneous network representation learning combined with LSTM and Attention mechanism to fuse the three aspects of user, item and meta-path information for recommendation tasks, making recommendation result more accurate. (2) The model's performance improves as the training data increases.

5.3 Meta-path Instances Selection

In order to verify the effectiveness of the meta-path instance selection method, we compare the performance (F1-score) between model with filtered and unfiltered meta-path instances as data input, as shown in Fig. 5. The results show that by filtering out the noisy instances, the recommendation performance can be effectively improved. the recommended model.

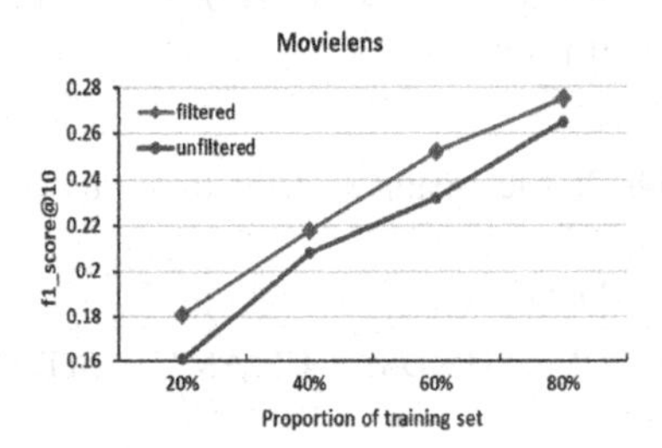

Fig. 5. Meta-path instance selection

5.4 Meta-path Attention Weight Visualization

The attention weights for different meta-paths is visualized in Fig. 6, which shows the impact of different meta-paths on recommendation performance. We can find that for the Movielens dataset, the "UMDMU" meta-path takes more weight than other meta-paths. Therefore, we believe that some meta-paths can improve the performance of the model more than others.

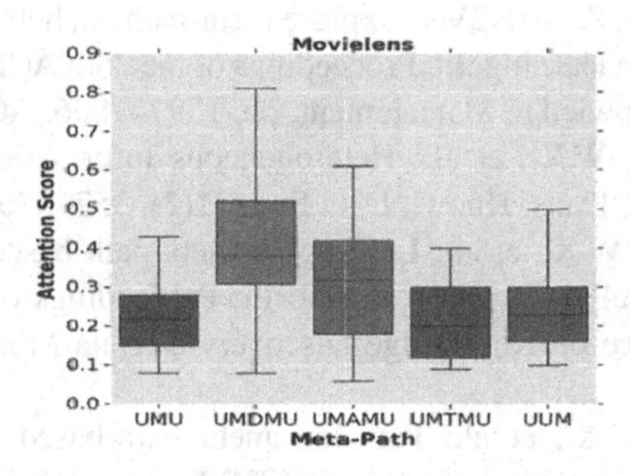

Fig. 6. Meta-path attention weight visualization

6 Summary

In this paper, we propose a recommendation system based on heterogeneous network representation learning and neural network model. We selected meta-path instances with better quality as the pre-training vectors of the recommendation system. We combine the LSTM and Attention mechanism to learn the three aspects of user, item, meta-path information, use the MLP to predict, so as to improve the recommendation effect. In the experiment, we prove that our model improves the performance of the recommendation system. By concatenate with users, items and meta-path embedding, the embedded vector information is enriched, which not only improves the recommendation effect, but also makes full use of the meta-path information to enhance the interpretability of the recommendation results.

Acknowledgements. This work was supported by the Qingdao Philosophy and Social Sciences Planning Project (QDSKL1801131), the 2018 Postgraduate Tutors' Guidance Ability Improvement Project of Shandong Province (84), the National Natural Science Foundation of China under Grant No. 61701284, the Innovative Research Foundation of Qingdao under Grant No. 19-6-2-1-cg.

References

1. Sun, Y., Han, J.: Mining heterogeneous information networks: principles and methodologies. Synth. Lect. Data Min. Knowl. Discov. **3**, 1–159 (2012)
2. Chen, H., Perozzi, B., Al-Rfou, R., et al.: A Tutorial on Network Embeddings (2018)

3. Ma, H., Zhou, D., Liu, C., et al.: Recommender systems with social regularization. In: Proceedings of the Forth International Conference on Web Search and Web Data Mining, WSDM 2011, Hong Kong, China, 9–12 Feb 2011. DBLP (2011)
4. Ling, G., Lyu, M.R., King, I.: Ratings meet reviews, a combined approach to recommend. In: Proceedings of the 8th ACM Conference on Recommender Systems, pp. 105–112 (2014)
5. Dong, Y., Chawla, N.V., Swami, A.: metapath2vec: scalable representation learning for heterogeneous networks. In: ACM SIGKDD International Conference on Knowledge Discovery & Data Mining. ACM (2017)
6. Fu, T.Y., Lee, W.C., Lei, Z.: HIN2Vec: explore meta-paths in heterogeneous information networks for representation learning. In: Proceedings of the 26th ACM International Conference on Information and Knowledge Management, pp. 1797–1806. ACM Press (2017)
7. Shi, C., Hu, B., Zhao, W.X., et al.: Heterogeneous information network embedding for recommendation. IEEE Trans. Knowl. Data Eng. **31**(2), 357–370 (2019)
8. Hu, B., Shi, C., Zhao, W.X., et al.: Leveraging meta-path based context for top-n recommendation with a neural co-attention model. In: Proceedings of the 24th ACM SIGKDD International Conference on Knowledge Discovery & Data Mining, pp. 1531–1540. ACM (2018)
9. Sun, Y., Han, J., Yan, X., et al.: Pathsim: meta path-based top-k similarity search in heterogeneous information networks. Proc. VLDB Endow. **4**(11), 992–1003 (2011)
10. Sarwar, B., Karypis, G., Konstan, J., Riedl, J.: Item-based collaborative filtering recommendation algorithms. In: Proceedings of the 10th international conference on World Wide Web, pp. 285–295 (2001)
11. Koren, Y., Bell, R., Volinsky, C.: Matrix factorization techniques for recommender systems. Computer **42**, 30–37 (2009)
12. Chen, Tianqi., Zhang, Weinan., Qiuxia, Lu., Chen, Kailong., Zheng, Zhao, Yong, Yu.: SVDFeature: a toolkit for feature-based collaborative filtering. J. Mach. Learn. Res. **13**(2012), 3619–3622 (2012)
13. Zhao, H., Yao, Q., Li, J., Song, Y., Lee, D.L.: Metagraph based recommendation fusion over heterogeneous information networks. In: Proceedings of the 23rd ACM SIGKDD International Conference on Knowledge Discovery and Data Mining, pp. 635–644 (2017)

Performance Analysis of Video-Flow in Mobile Edge Computing Networks Based on Stochastic Network Calculus

Jindou Shi(✉) and Xiaorong Zhu

College of Telecommunications and Information Engineering, Nanjing University of Posts and Telecommunications, Jiangsu, China
1018010222@njupt.edu.cn

Abstract. Mobile edge computing (MEC) networks can provide a variety of services for different applications. End-to-end performance analysis of these services serves as a benchmark for the efficient planning of network resource allocation and routing strategies. In this paper, we propose a performance analysis framework for the end-to-end data-flow in MEC networks based on stochastic network calculus (SNC). Due to the random nature of routing in the MEC networks, we introduce a probability parameter set in our proposed analysis model to characterize this randomness into our derived expressions. Taking actual communication scenarios into consideration, we analyze the end-to-end performance of video with the interference with voice over internet protocol (VoIP) and file transfer protocol (FTP). For scheduling of these network data-flows, we consider the preemptive priority scheduling scheme. Based on the arrival processes of the video-flow, the effect of interference on its performances and the service capacity of each node in the MEC network, we derive closed-form expression for showing the relationship between delay upper bound and violation probability of the video-flow. Simulation and analytical results show that delay performances of the video-flow is influenced by the number of hops in the network and the random probability parameters of interference-flow.

Keywords: Delay · Mobile edge computing · Random routing · Stochastic network calculus

1 Introduction

With the increasing popularity of mobile terminal devices, data-flows related to the different business applications are also on a constant rise. The delay due to the increasing number of users in the network poses a great challenge in its capacity to handle high throughput. Mobile edge computing (MEC) networks provide the end-users with closer computing service, which reduces the end-to-end delay and energy consumption. This means that the storage and computing resources in the edge nodes are deployed closer to the user terminal. MEC networks can carry the data of a variety of applications.

Q. Wu et al. (Eds.): WiSATS 2020, LNICST 358, pp. 599–610, 2021.
https://doi.org/10.1007/978-3-030-69072-4_49

Software-defined network (SDN) technology is introduced into MEC to flexibly control the forwarding of the network traffic, leading to the random routing of data-flows. To obtain a proper analytical model for different applications in MEC networks, it is important to characterize and incorporate the random routing nature of the network into the analytical model.

In [1–3], end-to-end performance analysis of different applications in various network scenarios has been studied. However, most of them adopted the queuing theory in their analysis. The results obtained by the queuing theory are the average analysis results in steady states. Moreover, the queuing theory has a specific requirement of restricted distribution of the arrival process of data-flows and service processes at the servers. On the other hand, stochastic network calculus (SNC) is a suitable option to overcome these shortcomings. As a tool for network performance analysis, SNC can transform complex nonlinear problems into easily solvable linear problems by using the min-plus algebra and max-plus algebra. Moreover, it has the characteristic of being relatively simple and flexible for the analysis of different network scenarios. Therefore, in this paper, we adopt SNC to analyze the end-to-end performance of different applications in MEC networks with random routing.

End-to-end delay of the through-flow was analyzed by using the SNC in [4–6], in case of interference-flow in wireless sensor networks. The performance of the system with multi-servers was analyzed in [7]. Based on SNC, authors in [8] showed the influence of the signaling and data channel capacity allocation on packet delay in the wireless multi-channel scenario. In [9], SNC was used to analyze the access delay in the narrow-band internet of things (NB-IoT) and two effective optimization schemes are also proposed to improve network performance. System performance based on SNC under the priority scheduling scenario was analyzed in [10]. In [11], SNC was used to compare the delay upper bounds of data-flows in the multi-server scenario under first-in-first-out (FIFO) scheduling, static priority (SP) scheduling, and the combination of both scheduling schemes.

Some other researches adopted the moment generating function (MGF), a kind of method in SNC, to analyze the performance of the networks [12–14]. Other than the system delay analysis using SNC, the throughput analysis of the networks was extensively studied in some literature [15, 16]. Lyapunov's inequality was used in [17] to improve the output bound calculation. SNC was also used to analyze the performance of heterogeneous networks. A recursive formula was proposed in [18] to analyze the end-to-end performance of heterogeneous networks where the service process of each node is assumed to be different.

To the best of our knowledge, the performance analysis and modeling of a framework for different applications in MEC networks with random routing using SNC have not been reported in any existing literature. The major innovations and contributions of this paper are as follows:

- A multi-hop system model of the MEC network with random routing is proposed. A mathematical model of this system is presented and extensively analyzed.
- The end-to-end performance of the video-flow in MEC networks is analyzed using SNC based on the MGF. In our derived expression, the random routing is represented by the probability parameter set. We also derived closed-form expression that show

the relationship between delay upper bound and violation probability of video-flow. Simulation and numerical results show the impact of the number of hops and the probability parameter set of interference-flows on the end-to-end performance of video-flow.

Notations: Throughout this paper, we use the notations of the interference-flows described in Table 1. Expectation and probability are represented by E{·} and P{·}, respectively.

Table 1. Summary of notations.

Notations	Definition
$\mathfrak{R}$	The type of the data flow
$\tilde{A}^{j}_{\mathfrak{R}}(s,t)$	The cumulative data which has a probability to arrive at node *j* of $\mathfrak{R}$ flow during the time interval (s, t).
$\tilde{A}^{j,j+1}_{\mathfrak{R}}(t)$	The cumulative data of $\mathfrak{R}$ flow from node *j* to node *j* + *1* during the time interval $[0, t)$
$I^{j}_{\mathfrak{R}}(s,t)$	The cumulative data of $\mathfrak{R}$ flow during the time interval (s, t) need to be processed on node *j*.
$\tilde{\lambda}^{j}_{\mathfrak{R}}$	The average arrival rate of $\mathfrak{R}$ flow which has a probability to arrive at node *j*
$P^{j}_{\mathfrak{R}(a)}$	The probability of $\mathfrak{R}$ flow from other service chains arrives at node *j*
$P^{j}_{\mathfrak{R}(b)}$	The probability of $\mathfrak{R}$ flow transmits from node *j* to node *j* + *1*
$P^{j}_{\mathfrak{R}(c)}$	The probability of $\mathfrak{R}$ flow needs to be processed by node *j*
θ	Free parameter

2 System Model

In this section, we propose a multi-hop model in the MEC network with random routing. The network topology of this model is shown in Fig. 1. Various data-flows will access edge clouds through nearby base stations or access points. There are interconnections between different edge clouds through agents. Although, the edge clouds also share interconnections with the core cloud.

The data of different applications are transmitted through multiple network elements. A network element can be a terminal, a router, an access device, etc. Each network element corresponds to a node. The communication link between anytwo nodes can be a single-hop or multi-hop. A node can have multiple neighboring nodes. As long as these neighboring nodes are within the transmission range, they can be chosen to create a communication path. In this paper, we denote the through-flow and interference-flow of data as TF and IF, respectively. Through-flow is defined as the intended data transmitted

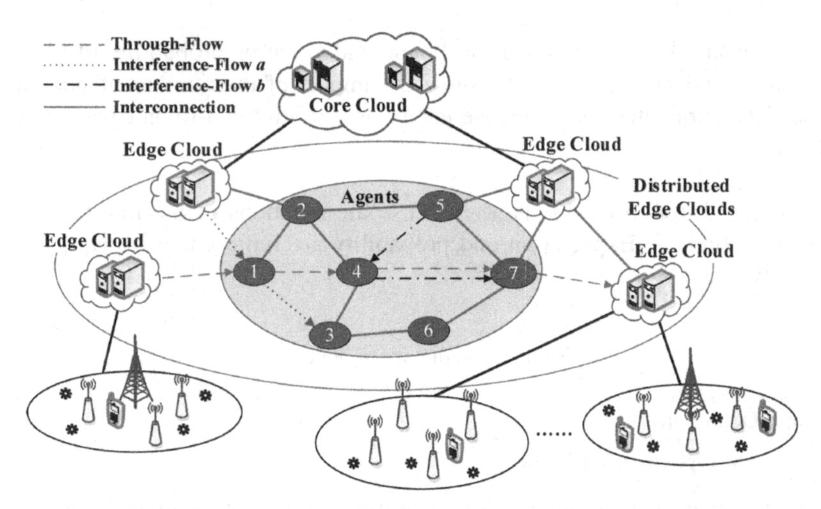

Fig. 1. Network topology of the multi-hop model in the mobile edge computing network.

through an established path. Whereas, Interference-flow is the data that share the nodes on the same path used by the TF. Moreover, the services provided by the nodes in that path are also shared. IF may affect the performance of the TF. Since SDN is introduced into the MEC network, multiple routes are used by the same pair of the source and destination node. Each TF selects its path randomly to reach its destination node and complete its task. This means that the selection of each hop is random.

In real networks, there are multiple numbers of source and destination node pairs. Since all the node pairs have multiple paths to communicate, data-flows randomly choose their paths. For a single agent, the quantity of data needed for different services is also random. The impact of IF on the performance of the TF is also not fixed. There are two interference scenarios adopted in this paper, which are elaborated as follows:

- Data-flows that are from different service chains, which reach the agent on the path of TF and need to share data processing at the agent.
- Data-flows on the current agent have the same next hop choice as the through flow and need to share data processing on the next agent.

The agents, which connect an edge cloud with others as shown in Fig. 1, consist of intelligent components such as routers and edge computing servers. Some agents on the path may be shared by multiple data-flows. For example, agent 1 in Fig. 1 may need to share service to TF and Interference-Flow a (IF_a). Whereas, agent 4 and agent 7 may need to share the data processing service to TF and Interference-Flow a (IF_b).

This paper assumes three types of data-flow in the system: VoIP, video, and FTP flow with decreasing priority, respectively. Preemptive priority scheduling is adopted for efficient scheduling of these different data-flows. If a data-flow with higher priority request service when a lower priority data-flow is being served, the agent will immediately stop the current service process and provide service to the highest priority data-flow. Data-flows with the same priority are scheduled according to the FIFO.

3 Mathematical Model of Arrival and Service Processes of Video-Flow

In this section, SNC is explored to set up a mathematical model for the analysis of arrival and service processes of data-flows in the MEC network. We configure the agent nodes and the path selected by the TF in the system model as service nodes and the service chain in the mathematical model, respectively. In our analysis, we assume to fix video-flow as the TF, whereas, VoIP-flow and FTP-flow are IFs. The performance of the video-flow will be analyzed in this paper. The flow of data and interference in the network is shown in Fig. 2.

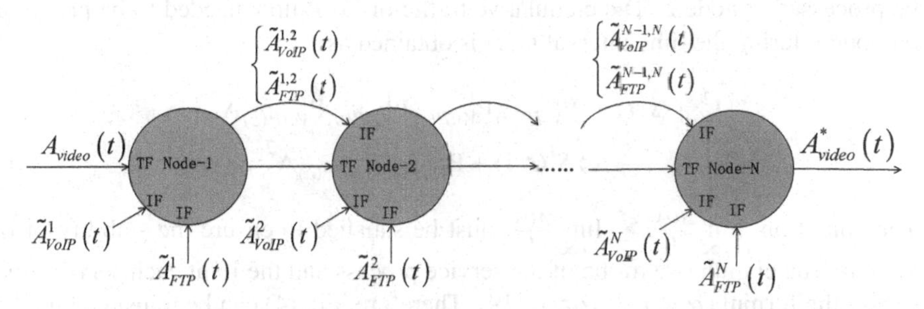

Fig. 2. Illustration of the data-flows when video-flow is assumed to be the TF.

3.1 Arrival Process

We denote the cumulative arrival traffic during the time interval (s, t) as $\mathrm{A}_{video}(s, t)$. Moreover, the arrival rate is constant and we represent this constant by r. According to [19], the MGF of $\mathrm{A}_{video}(s, t)$ is derived as follows:

$$M_{A_{video}}(\theta, s, t) = E\left(e^{\theta A_{video}(s,t)}\right) = e^{r\theta(t-s)} = \pi_{video}^{t-s}(\theta) \tag{1}$$

3.2 Interference Analysis

For interference analysis of data-flows, we denote the probability parameter set of $\mathfrak{R}$-flow on node j as $(\mathrm{P}^j_{\mathfrak{R}(a)}, \mathrm{P}^j_{\mathfrak{R}(b)}, \mathrm{P}^j_{\mathfrak{R}(c)})$, where $\mathfrak{R}$-flow is IF. Therefore, when VoIP, video, and FTP-flow are IF, we denote their probability parameter sets as $(\mathrm{P}^j_{VoIP(a)}, \mathrm{P}^j_{VoIP(b)}, \mathrm{P}^j_{VoIP(c)})$ and $(\mathrm{P}^j_{FTP(a)}, \mathrm{P}^j_{FTP(b)}, \mathrm{P}^j_{FTP(c)})$, respectively.

Theorem. 1. When the video-flow is TF, the cumulative traffic which will interfere with the QoS of the video-flow on node j, is given by

$$\mathrm{O}^j_{video}(s, t) = \sum_{m=1}^{j} \mathrm{P}^m_{VoIP(a)}\mathrm{P}^j_{VoIP(c)}\tilde{\mathrm{A}}^m_{VoIP}(s, t)\prod_{n=m}^{j-1} \mathrm{P}^n_{VoIP(b)}\mathrm{P}^n_{VoIP(c)} \tag{2}$$

Proof. The priority of the video-flow is higher than the FTP-flow and lower than the VoIP-flow, therefore, its performance is only affected by the VoIP-flow. We will use mathematical induction to derive the expression for the cumulative traffic of VoIP-flow needed to be processed on node j during the time interval (s, t).

- Case 1: For node 1, we have

$$\mathrm{I}_{VoIP}^{1}(s,t) = \mathrm{P}_{VoIP(a)}^{1}\mathrm{P}_{VoIP(c)}^{1}\tilde{\mathrm{A}}_{VoIP}^{1}(s,t) \tag{3}$$

- Case 2: Now, we analyze the cumulative traffic of the VoIP-flow on node 2. Except for the data traffic from other service chains, the traffic from node 1 needs to be processed at node 2. The cumulative traffic of VoIP-flow needed to be processed on node j during the time interval (s, t) is obtained as:

$$\begin{aligned}\mathrm{I}_{VoIP}^{2}(s,t) = {} & \mathrm{P}_{VoIP(a)}^{1}\mathrm{P}_{VoIP(c)}^{1}\mathrm{P}_{VoIP(b)}^{1}\mathrm{P}_{VoIP(c)}^{2}\tilde{\mathrm{A}}_{VoIP}^{1} \\ & \otimes S^{j}(s,t) + \mathrm{P}_{VoIP(a)}^{2}\mathrm{P}_{VoIP(c)}^{2}\tilde{\mathrm{A}}_{VoIP}^{2}(s,t)\end{aligned} \tag{4}$$

The condition $\lim_{t\to\infty}\frac{S(t)}{t} \geq \lim_{t\to\infty}\frac{A(t)}{t}$ must be satisfied to ensure the stability of the system. The cumulative traffic of the service process and the IF at each service node satisfy the formula $\alpha \otimes \beta \leq \alpha \wedge \beta$ [19]. Therefore, Eq. (4) can be translated into:

$$\mathrm{I}_{VoIP}^{2}(s,t) = \mathrm{P}_{VoIP(c)}^{2}\left(\mathrm{P}_{VoIP(a)}^{1}\mathrm{P}_{VoIP(b)}^{1}\mathrm{P}_{VoIP(c)}^{1}\ \tilde{\mathrm{A}}_{VoIP}^{1}(s,t) + \mathrm{P}_{VoIP(a)}^{2}\tilde{\mathrm{A}}_{VoIP}^{2}(s,t)\right) \tag{5}$$

- Case 3: On node 3, the cumulative traffic of VoIP-flow is:

$$\begin{aligned}\mathrm{I}_{VoIP}^{3}(s,t) = {} & \mathrm{P}_{VoIP(b)}^{2}\mathrm{P}_{VoIP(c)}^{2}\mathrm{P}_{VoIP(c)}^{3}\left(\mathrm{P}_{VoIP(a)}^{1}\mathrm{P}_{VoIP(b)}^{1}\ \mathrm{P}_{VoIP(c)}^{1}\tilde{\mathrm{A}}_{VoIP}^{1}(s,t)\right. \\ & \left. + \ \mathrm{P}_{VoIP(a)}^{2}\tilde{\mathrm{A}}_{VoIP}^{2}(s,t)\right)\mathrm{P}_{VoIP(a)}^{3}\mathrm{P}_{VoIP(c)}^{3}\tilde{\mathrm{A}}_{VoIP}^{3}(s,t)\end{aligned} \tag{6}$$

- Case j: From the above analysis and by mathematical induction, we can obtain the cumulative traffic of VoIP-flow needed to be processed on node j as

$$\mathrm{I}_{VoIP}^{j}(s,t) = \sum_{m=1}^{j}\mathrm{P}_{VoIP(a)}^{m}\mathrm{P}_{VoIP(c)}^{j}\tilde{\mathrm{A}}_{VoIP}^{m}(s,t)\prod_{n=m}^{j-1}\mathrm{P}_{VoIP(b)}^{n}\mathrm{P}_{VoIP(c)}^{n} \tag{7}$$

Then, according to the superposition property, we can obtain the expression for the cumulative traffic that affects the performance of video-flow.

$$\mathrm{O}_{video}^{j}(s,t) = \sum_{m=1}^{j}\mathrm{P}_{VoIP(a)}^{m}\mathrm{P}_{VoIP(c)}^{j}\tilde{\mathrm{A}}_{VoIP}^{m}(s,t)\prod_{n=m}^{j-1}\mathrm{P}_{VoIP(b)}^{n}\mathrm{P}_{VoIP(c)}^{n} \tag{8}$$

3.3 Service Process

The cumulative service provided by node j during the time interval (s, t) is denoted by $S^{j}(s, t)$. In this paper, the service rate of all agents is assumed to be the same, denoted by a constant C. According to [19], we can write the expression for the service process of node j as:

$$S^j(s,t) = C(t-s) \tag{9}$$

Hence, the MGF of the service process is obtained as:

$$\bar{M}_{S^j}(\theta,s,t) = E\left(e^{-\theta S^j(s,t)}\right) = e^{-\theta(C(t-s))} = \varphi^{t-s}(\theta) \tag{10}$$

Now, when the video-flow is the TF, the service it receives will only be affected by the VoIP-flow. According to leftover service [19], the service process of the video-flow on node j is derived as follows:

$$S^j_{video}(s,t) \geq S^j(s,t) - O^j_{video}(s,t) \tag{11}$$

When VoIP-flow is an IF, we denote the average arrival rate of VoIP-flow at node j as $\tilde{\lambda}^j_{VoIP}$. According to [19], we can derive the MGF of $\tilde{A}^j_{VoIP}(s,t)$ as follows:

$$M_{\tilde{A}_{VoIP}}(\theta,s,t) = e^{\tilde{\lambda}^j_{VoIP}(t-s)(e^{\theta}-1)} = \tilde{\pi}^{t-s}_{VoIP(j)}(\theta) \tag{12}$$

According to Eq. (8) and Eq. (12), we can derive the MGF of $O^j_{video}(s,t)$ as follows:

$$\begin{aligned}
M_{O^j_{video}}(\theta,s,t) &= \prod_{m=1}^{j} e^{\tilde{\lambda}^j_{VoIP}(t-s)\left(e^{P^m_{VoIP(a)} P^j_{VoIP(c)} \prod_{n=m}^{j-1} \theta P^n_{VoIP(b)} P^n_{VoIP(c)}}-1\right)} \\
&= \left(\prod_{m=1}^{j} e^{\tilde{\lambda}^j_{VoIP}\left(e^{P^m_{VoIP(a)} P^j_{VoIP(c)} \prod_{n=m}^{j-1} \theta P^n_{VoIP(b)} P^n_{VoIP(c)}}-1\right)}\right)^{(t-s)} \\
&= \rho_j^{t-s}(\theta)
\end{aligned} \tag{13}$$

Therefore, the MGF of Eq. (11) can be transformed into the following formula:

$$\begin{aligned}
\bar{M}_{S^j_{video}}(\theta,s,t) &\leq \bar{M}_{S^j - O^j_{video}}(\theta,s,t) \\
&= \bar{M}_{S^j}(\theta,s,t) \cdot \bar{M}_{O^j_{video}}(\theta,s,t) \\
&= \varphi^{t-s}(\theta)\rho_j^{t-s}(\theta)
\end{aligned} \tag{14}$$

4 Derivation of Delay Upper Bound of Video-Flow

In this section, we derive the delay upper bound of the video-flow used in the system model. The closed-form expression are derived for showing the relationship between its delay bound and the violation probability, which are derived according to its arrival and service processes.

Theorem. 2. The cumulative traffic of the video-flow during the time interval $(0, t)$ is $A_{video}(t)$, and the cumulative service provided to the video-flow by the whole system is $S_{video}^{net}(t)$. Moreover, the cumulative traffic of the video-flow departing from the system during the time interval $(0, t)$ is $A_{video}^{*}(t)$. The relationship between the delay upper bound and the violation probability satisfies

$$P\{D_{video}(t) > x\} \leq M_{A_{video} \emptyset S_{video}^{net}}(\theta, t + x, t) \tag{15}$$

Proof.

$$\begin{aligned} P\{D_{video}(t) > x\} &= P\left\{A_{video}(t) > A_{video}^{*}(t + x)\right\} \\ &\leq P\left\{A_{video}(t) - A_{video} \otimes S_{video}^{net}(t + x) > 0\right\} \\ &= P\left\{A_{video}(t) - \inf_{0 \leq s \leq (t+x)} \left\{A_{video}(s) + S_{video}^{net}(s, t + x)\right\} > 0\right\} \\ &= P\left\{\sup_{0 \leq s \leq t+x} \left\{A_{video}(t) - A_{video}(s) - S_{video}^{net}(s, t + x)\right\} > 0\right\} \\ &= P\left\{A_{video} \emptyset S_{video}^{net}(t + x, t) > 0\right\} \leq M_{A_{video} \emptyset S_{video}^{net}}(\theta, t + x, t) \end{aligned}$$

According to [12], it can be known that the MGF of the form of deconvolution in this paper can be written as follows:

$$M_{A_{video} \emptyset S_{video}^{net}}(\theta, t + x, t) \leq \frac{(\pi_{video}(\theta))^{-x}}{(1 - \phi_{video}(\theta)\pi_{video}(\theta))^{N}} \tag{16}$$

Where $\phi_{video}(\theta) = \max_{1 \leq j \leq N} \left\{\left(\bar{M}_{S_{video}^{j}}(\theta, s, t)\right)^{\frac{1}{t-s}}\right\}$.

Therefore, the relationship between the delay upper bound and the violation probability of video-flow

$$P\{D_{video}(t) > x\} \leq \frac{e^{\theta(-rx)}}{\left(1 - \phi_{video}(\theta)e^{\theta r}\right)^{N}} \tag{17}$$

where $\phi_{video}(\theta) = \max_{1 \leq j \leq N} \left\{\varphi(\theta)\rho_{j}(\theta)\right\}$.

5 Numerical Results

To demonstrate the accuracy of our derived expressions, we compare the results from analytical equations and simulations based on queuing theory. In this section, we also study the impact on the end-to-end performance of the TF by the number of hops and the probability parameter set of IFs.

We assume that when a data-flow is IF, the average arrival rate and parameter set of each service node are the same, i.e. we use $\tilde{\lambda}_{VoIP}$ and $\tilde{\lambda}_{FTP}$ to uniformly represent $\tilde{\lambda}_{VoIP}^{j}$ and $\tilde{\lambda}_{FTP}^{j}$. And for the simplicity of our analysis, the probability parameter sets of all nodes are uniformly defined in a single set, i.e. ($P_{Vo(a)}$, $P_{Vo.(b)}$, $P_{Vo(c)}$) and ($P_{F(a)}$, $P_{F(b)}$, $P_{F(c)}$).

The default value of system configuration used in simulation and numerical analysis are set as follows: service rate is set to be 350 packets/s; average arrival rate of the video-flow is set to be 284 packets/s; the average arrival rate of VoIP and FTP-flow are set to be 202.5 packets/s and 119.2 packets/s; free parameter θ is set to be 1.

5.1 Performance Evaluation

We use MATLAB to evaluate the simulation and analytical results. We compare the delay upper bound predicted by the mathematical expression derived in this paper with that generated by the simulation experiment as shown in Fig. 3. The number of nodes is set to be 1. The probability parameter sets of IFs of each data-flow is uniformly set to be (0.5, 0.2, 0.5).we can observe that the result from the proposed mathematical expression of the delay upper bound match well with that of the simulation.

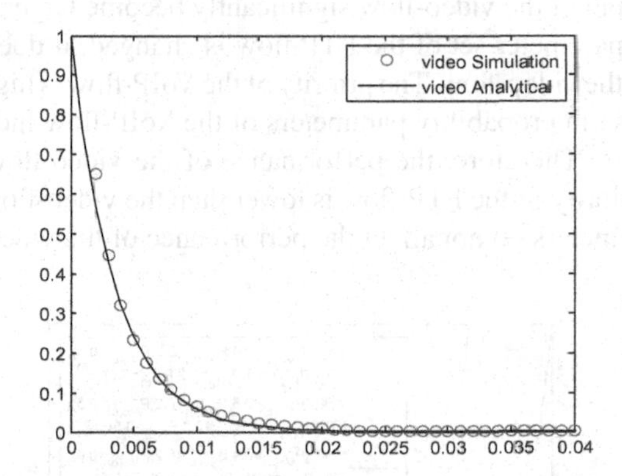

Fig. 3. Comparison of the simulation and analytical results of the delay upper bounds

5.2 Performance Analysis

In this subsection, we analyze the performance of video-flow in different system configurations by changing the number of hops and the parameter sets of IFs.

1) *Impacts of the number of hops on end to end performance of the video-flow*: the probability parameter sets of IFs are uniformly set to be (0.5, 0.2, 0.5). In Fig. 4, the numerical results of the delay upper bounds and violation probability of each data-flow are shown when the number of nodes '*N*' is 5, 9 and 15. In Fig. 4, we note that by increasing the number of hops, the end-to-end delay upper bound increases.
2) *Impacts of probability parameters of VoIP flow and FTP flow on the end-to-end performance of the video flow:* we fix the number of nodes used in the system configuration as 5. In Fig. 5, we evaluate the performance of the video-flow by changing the probability parameter set of IFs (i.e. VoIP-flow and FTP-flow). We

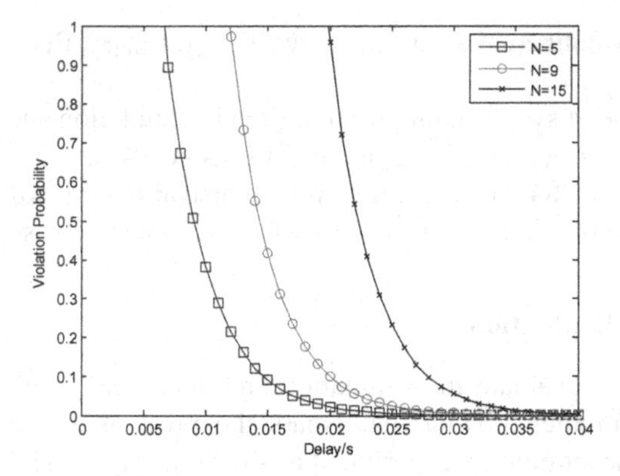

Fig. 4. Comparison of the delay upper bounds of video-flow under different number of nodes

can observe that when the probability parameter set of the VoIP-flow increases, the delay upper bound of the video-flow significantly become larger. Meanwhile, when the probability parameter set of the FTP-flow is changed, it does not influence the performance of the video-flow. The priority of the VoIP-flow is higher than the video-flow, the increase in probability parameters of the VoIP-flow indirectly grabs more service resources. Therefore, the performance of the video-flow becomes poorer. However, the priority of the FTP-flow is lower than the video-flow, the change in its probability parameters do not affect the performance of the video-flow.

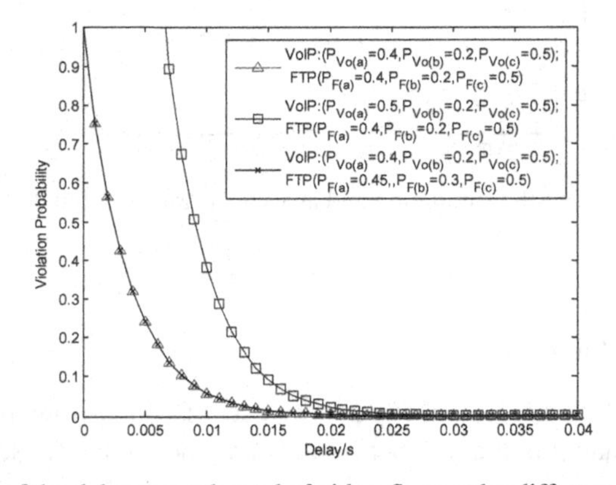

Fig. 5. Comparison of the delay upper bound of video-flow under different probability parameter sets of interference flows

6 Conclusion

We proposed an analysis model for the end-to-end performance of video-flow in MEC networks with random routing. The delay and bound of video-flow is studied and the closed-form expression for the relationship between delay upper bound and violation probability was derived using SNC. The impact of the number of hops and the probability parameter set of IFs on the end-to-end performance of the video-flow is explored in this paper. Through the results obtained from our analysis, we observe that the delay upper bound of the video-flow will increase with the increase in the number of hops. We also note that by changing the probability parameter set of the IF whose priority is higher than that of the TF, will impact the end-to-end performance of the TF.

References

1. Alaslani, M., Nawab, F., Shihada, B.: Blockchain in IoT systems: end-to-end delay evaluation. IEEE Internet Things J. **6**(5), 8332–8344 (2019)
2. Liu, J., Sheng, M., Xu, Y., Li, J., Jiang, X.: End-to-end delay modeling in buffer-limited MANETs: a general theoretical framework. IEEE Trans. Wireless Commun. **15**(1), 498–511 (2016)
3. Aloqlah, M.: End-to-end performance analysis of dual-hop relaying systems over extended generalized K-fading channels. In: ICT 2013, Casablanca, pp. 1–4 (2013)
4. Deng, Y., Ren, F., Lin, C.: An end-to-end stochastic delay bound analysis in sensor networks. In: 2010 3rd International Conference on Advanced Computer Theory and Engineering (ICACTE), Chengdu, pp. V3-370–V3-374 (2010)
5. Li, C., Yu, L.: End-to-end delay bound analysis in multimedia sensor network using stochastic network calculus. In: 2012 1st IEEE International Conference on Communications in China (ICCC), Beijing, pp. 126–131 (2012)
6. Azuaje, O., Aguiar, A.: End-to-end delay analysis of a wireless sensor network using stochastic network calculus. In: 2019 Wireless Days (WD), Manchester, UK, pp. 1–8 (2019)
7. Li, Z., Gao, Y., Salihu, B.A., Li, P., Sang, L., Yang, D.: Network calculus delay bounds in multi-server queueing networks with stochastic arrivals and stochastic services. In: 2015 IEEE Global Communications Conference (GLOBECOM), San Diego, CA, pp. 1–7 (2015)
8. Li, Z., Gao, Y., Li, P., Sang, L., Yang, D.: Packet delay analysis in wireless multi-channel networks: a network calculus perspective. In: 2015 International Conference on Wireless Communications & Signal Processing (WCSP), Nanjing, pp. 1–5 (2015)
9. Wang, X., Chen, X., Li, Z., Chen, Y.: Access delay analysis and optimization of NB-IoT based on stochastic network calculus. In: 2018 IEEE International Conference on Smart Internet of Things (SmartIoT), Xi'an, pp. 23–28 (2018)
10. Liu, Y., Lang, L.: Modeling and performance analysis of scheduling system for cloud service based on stochastic network calculus. In: 2014 IEEE 7th Joint International Information Technology and Artificial Intelligence Conference, Chongqing, pp. 473–477 (2014)
11. Luo, C., Zheng, J., Yu, L.: Performance analysis of stochastic multi-server systems. In: 2015 10th International Conference on Communications and Networking in China (ChinaCom), Shanghai, pp. 562–566 (2015)
12. Miao, W., et al.: Stochastic performance analysis of network function virtualization in future internet. IEEE J. Sel. Areas Commun. **37**(3), 613–626 (2019)
13. Yang, G., Xiao, M., Poor, H.V.: Low-latency millimeter-wave communications: task dispersion or network densification? IEEE Trans. Commun. **66**(8), 3526–3539 (2018)
14. Al-Zubaidy, H., Fodor, V., Dán, G., Flierl, M.: Reliable video streaming with strict playout deadline in multihop wireless networks. IEEE Trans. Multimedia **19**(10), 2238–2251 (2017)
15. Zheng, J., Yu, L., Yang, P.: Throughput analysis of cognitive radio networks via stochastic network calculus. In: 2014 Sixth International Conference on Wireless Communications and Signal Processing (WCSP), Hefei, pp. 1–6 (2014)

16. Li, Z., Gao, Y., Li, P., Sang, L., Yang, D.: A network calculus approach to throughput analysis of stochastic multi-channel networks. In: 2015 IEEE/CIC International Conference on Communications in China (ICCC), Shenzhen, pp. 1–5 (2015)
17. Nikolaus, P., Schmitt, J.: Improving output bounds in the stochastic network calculus using Lyapunov's inequality. In: 2018 IFIP Networking Conference (IFIP Networking) and Workshops, Zurich, Switzerland, pp. 1–9 (2018)
18. Petreska, N., Al-Zubaidy, H., Knorr, R., Gross, J.: On the recursive nature of end-to-end delay bound for heterogeneous wireless networks. In: 2015 IEEE International Conference on Communications (ICC), London, pp. 5998–6004 (2015)
19. Liu, Y., Jiang, Y.: Stochastic Network Calculus. Springer, London (2008). https://doi.org/10.1007/978-1-84800-127-5

A Bio-inspired Smart Access Algorithm for Large Scale Self-organizing Wireless Networks

Enfu Jia(✉), Jiaming Cao, Xiaorong Zhu, and Jinfeng Li

Nanjing University of Posts and Telecommunications, Nanjing 210003, China
1018010223@njupt.edu.cn

Abstract. Efficient wireless access of a large number of nodes is one important issue for large scale self-organizing wireless networks. In order to achieve this goal, collision problem between nodes must be resolved. Bio-inspired algorithms provide some significant characteristics such as stability, adaptability, and scalability, and hence many researchers have attempted to apply bio-inspired algorithms to solve some problems in networks. In this paper, we propose a smart access algorithm for large scale self-organizing wireless networks, which is inspired by Stigmergy, which is able to make group members implement information interaction symmetry in some ways, and members are able to influence and interact with each other to avoid collision. Then we build an analysis model based on Markov chain for the proposed algorithm. Simulation results show that the proposed algorithm can maintain a low collision probability with the increasing number of competing nodes even in a dynamically changing network topology. In addition, the results show that compared with traditional algorithms, the proposed algorithm has better performances on channel throughput and access delay.

Keywords: Bio-inspired · Stigmergy · Self-organizing · Large scale wireless networks

1 Introduction

With the rapid development of the Internet of Things, it brings unprecedented opportunities and challenges. For example, with the explosive growth of the number of nodes, in order to implement efficient access without or with little collision between nodes, the nodes need to have a high degree of self-organization in the current network. As is known that self-organizing phenomenon is a very common phenomenon in nature. It is caused by the cooperative interaction between individual organisms. The full openness of self-organizing phenomena, autonomous interaction, decentralized control, complexity, and emergence have promoted the development of various disciplines. For example, Grasse studied nesting and foraging behavior of ant colonies in 1959 [1, 2]. He called this phenomenon "Stigmergy", which has been widely studied in aspect of social insects [3] and applied in different scenes [4–6].

Q. Wu et al. (Eds.): WiSATS 2020, LNICST 358, pp. 611–623, 2021.
https://doi.org/10.1007/978-3-030-69072-4_50

Stigmergy is an information coordination mechanism for biological individual autonomy. It is an indirect coordination mechanism between agents or individual behaviors [7]. In the absence of central control and direct contact with communication, the group implements information interaction symmetry through some methods, such as co-oscillation. Individuals act independently and influence and interact with each other on the basis of perceiving changes in the external environment, which can generate more complex and highly intelligent group structures through the adjustment and modification of members within the group. Therefore, it can be considered to resolve the collision problem that is easy to happen among the distributed multi nodes competing to access the same channel in the future complex and changing network environment. To the best of our knowledge, using Stigmergy for collision in wireless network has not been considered. The contributions of this work are as follows:

- We propose a smart access algorithm for large scale self-organizing wireless networks, which is inspired by Stigmergy, which is able to make group members implement information interaction symmetry in some ways, and members are able to influence and interact with each other to avoid collision.
- We build an analysis model based on Markov chain for the proposed algorithm, which mainly analyzes collision probability, channel throughput and access delay.
- Simulations results including collision probability, channel throughput and access delay are compared with the CSMA/CA mechanisms.

The rest of this article is organized as follows. In Sect. 2, a suitable system model is built by analyzing the current network topology. Moreover, we propose a new access algorithm. In Sect. 3, the proposed algorithm is divided into three phases, and each phase is analyzed and described in detail. In Sect. 4, according to the proposed algorithm, the system performance is analyzed. In Sect. 5, the proposed algorithm is compared with the CSMA/CA mechanisms. In the simulations results, the efficiency and advantages of the algorithm are verified. Finally, we summarize and prospect this paper.

2 System Model

As shown in Fig. 1, it is a self-organizing wireless network composed of multiple distributed nodes. Learning from the Stigmergy mechanism, a coordination mechanism between a large-scale number of nodes in the wireless network is implemented, which is based on the pheromone communication interaction. It provides an effective solution to reduce collision that is prone to occur in the network.

In this paper, a similar cooperation mechanism model is established between nodes in a wireless network through the Stigmergy cooperation mechanism model, as shown in Fig. 2. Each node is regarded as a different agent. As the agent's behavior state changes and if the state reaches a certain condition, it will send broadcast information in the network. This process is regarded as the agent leaving pheromone in the environment. The other agents adjust their current behavior state through receiving the information.

According to the established cooperative mechanism model, we propose a bio-inspired smart access algorithm (BSAA). This algorithm is a kind of de-synchronization

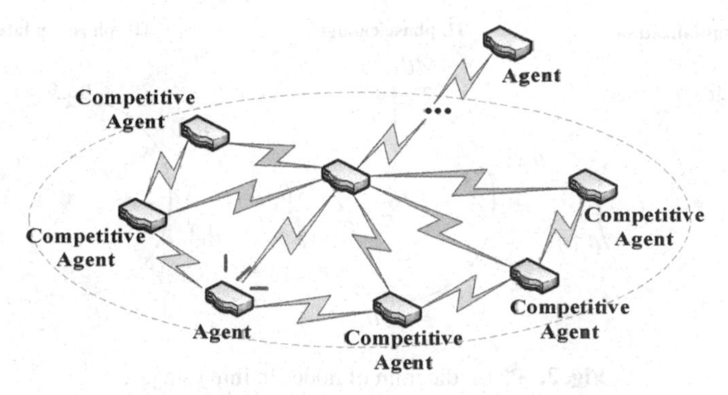

Fig. 1. A self-organizing wireless network composed of multiple distributed nodes.

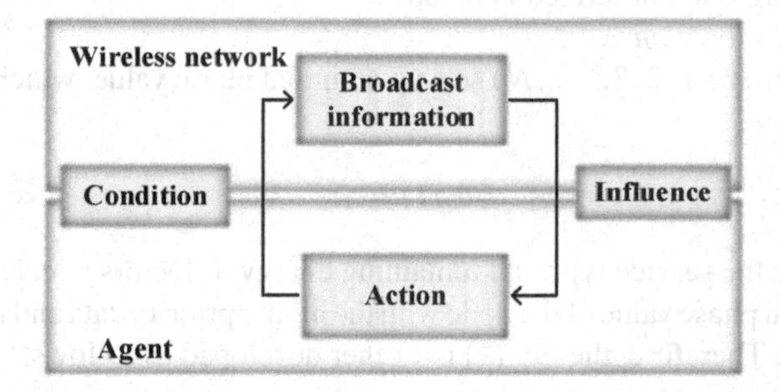

Fig. 2. Cooperative mechanism model between nodes in wireless network.

[8, 9] that is implemented in the paper by means of combining the cooperative mechanism model and the phase oscillation model in synchronization theory. We make the phase represent the state of node. Then node modifies its own behavior to achieve desynchronization by means of interacting with other nodes.

3 Algorithm Introduction

The state of each node at time t is regarded as a phase value $\theta(t)$. The behavior of the node includes phase change and phase update. Each node has an initial phase value, which is determined by the service type of the data and the remaining energy of the current node. The phase change of a node is similar to the oscillation of a phase oscillator. When the phase value of the node reaches 2π, the node can access the channel to transmit data packets and inform the adjacent nodes of the current status by the way of sending broadcast information. If a node receives the broadcast information from adjacent node during the phase change, it will extract the information and immediately send broadcast information to the adjacent node as well. At the same time, the node updates the phase to avoid collision with the node that is transmitting data. According to the process, this paper divides the algorithm into three stages, as shown in Fig. 3.

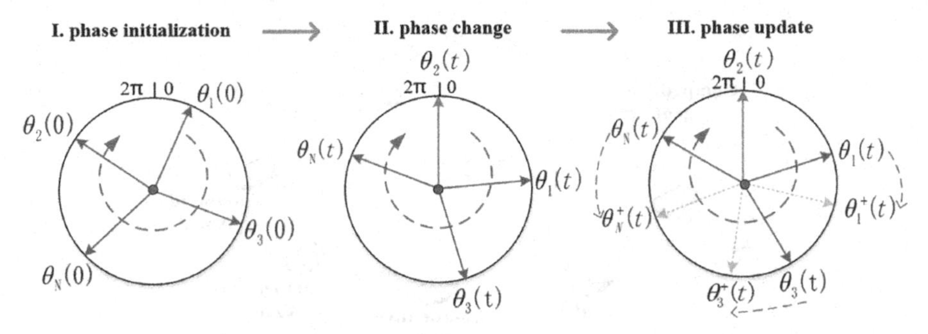

Fig. 3. Phase diagram of nodes in three stages.

The three stages are described in detail.

1) Phase Initialization

Each node $n(n = 1, 2, 3, \ldots, N)$ sets up an initial phase value, which is represented as follows:

$$\theta_n(1) = w_n \tag{1}$$

We consider the service type and remaining energy as factors to calculate the initial phase. The initial phase value of the node with the higher priority data and large remaining energy is larger. Therefore, the Eq. (1) is further developed as follows:

$$w_n = \begin{cases} \left(\alpha \frac{[T]}{k_1+[T]} + (1-\alpha)\frac{E_{rest}/E_{max}}{k_2+E_{rest}/E_{max}}\right) * \frac{2\pi}{N}, N > 1 \\ 2\pi \qquad\qquad\qquad\qquad\qquad\qquad , N = 1 \end{cases} \tag{2}$$

where, $[T]$ represents the proportion of the current data type of the node to all data types, which satisfies $0 < [T] \leq 1$. k_1 and k_2 are constants. E_{rest} represents the remaining energy of the node. E_{max} represents the total energy of the node. E_{rest}/E_{max} represents the remaining energy rate of the node, which satisfies $0 < E_{rest}/E_{max} \leq 1$. N represents the number of nodes in the range of the node n. This formula indicates that when there is only one node competing for the channel, the data is sent directly and when there is more than one node, different initial phases values must be calculated.

2) Phase Change

The phase value of node n is a discrete and time-varying function, then the phase change should satisfy as follows:

$$\theta_n(t) = w_n t \tag{3}$$

When $\theta_n(t)$ reaches 2π at time t, the node n will send adjacent nodes broadcast information including the phase value of the current node and the estimated time of the occupied channel. Then it starts transmitting data packets, and resets its phase value to 0. If the node n receives broadcast information from an adjacent node during the phase change, it will immediately carry out the phase update and send a broadcast information including the phase value of the current node.

In order to improve system performance, the phase value of a node is updated up to x times after reaching 2π. If the number of updates exceeds x, the node no longer carries out the phase updates, and if a collision occurs, the data packet is discarded.

3). Phase Update

After receiving the broadcast information from adjacent node m, the node n extracts the information to carry out the phase update. The phase of the updated node is expressed as follows:

$$\theta_n(t^+) = \theta_n(t) + F_n(t) = w_n t + F_n(t) \tag{4}$$

where, $\theta_n(t^+)$ represents the phase value for the node n after updating and the t^+ satisfies $\lim\limits_{t}(t^+ - t) = 0$. $F_n(t)$ represents the value of phase update.

The node n makes different update rules based on the broadcast information of different adjacent nodes. We divide them into two cases.

- When $\theta_n(t) \geq \theta_m(t)$, it indicates that when the phase value of node n is larger than the phase values of other nodes except the node that is transmitting the data packet. Due to the phase update is only related to the node that is transmitting the data packet, the updated phase value of node n is calculated based on the estimated time T_m(the channel occupied by the broadcast information sent by the node m). Hence, the value of phase update satisfies as follows:

$$\theta_m(t) - \theta_n(t^+) = \frac{d\theta_n(t)}{dt} * T_m \tag{5}$$

- When $\theta_n(t) < \theta_m(t)$, it indicates that there are $M\,(M = 1, 2, 3, ..., N - 1)$ nodes whose phase value is larger than node n. In this paper, we only consider the influence of two nodes with the smallest phase difference from node n. Therefore, the value of phase update function is expressed as follows:

$$F_n(t) = K \sum_{m=1}^{2} G_{mn}(t) \sin(\theta_m(t) - \theta_n(t) - \theta_\alpha) \tag{6}$$

where, K is a coupling coefficient. In order to make the value of the phase difference between the two nodes in $[0, 2\pi)$, the Mod function is applied to the phase difference of the nodes, that is,

$$\varnothing_{m,n}(t) = mod(\theta_m(t) - \theta_n(t), 2\pi) \tag{7}$$

When the node's phase difference $\varnothing_{m,n}(t) = 0$, in order to avoid the value of the phase update function being 0, a phase delay θ_α is introduced into the phase difference function, which is used to solve the problem between adjacent nodes.

$G_{mn}(t)$ represents the weight function of the phase difference, which is defined as follows:

$$G_{mn}(t) = \begin{cases} e^{-\varnothing_{m,n}(t)}, 0 \leq \varnothing_{m,n}(t) < \pi \\ e^{-2\pi + \varnothing_{m,n}(t)}, \pi \leq \varnothing_{m,n}(t) < 2\pi \end{cases} \tag{8}$$

4 System Performance Analysis

4.1 Research Model

This paper analyzes packet transmission probability, channel throughput and access delay. Assuming that there are a fixed number of nodes and an ideal single channel. According to the BSAA, the scenario where multiple nodes access the same channel is modeled as a two-dimensional Markov model with the number of updates and time slice as state variables, as shown in Fig. 4. Let $s(t)$ represent the number of node updates at time t, which satisfies $s(t) \in [0, m]$. m is the maximum number of updates. Let $b(t)$ represent process of reducing the node's time slice (TS). The TS is a value of size L. t and $t + 1$ represent the starting time of two adjacent slot time. And at the beginning of each slot time, L is reduced by one unit of time. Therefore, $\{s(t), b(t)\}$ can be regarded as a two-dimensional Markov model in discrete time. Let p represent the probability of the channel busy, and $(1 - p)$ be the probability that a node can transmit a data packet. Moreover, each node corresponds to an L value on each update, that is, $L_i = \frac{\emptyset_{m,n}(t) - F_n(t)}{W_n}$, $i \in (0, N - 1]$, and the value of L_i will change accordingly after each update.

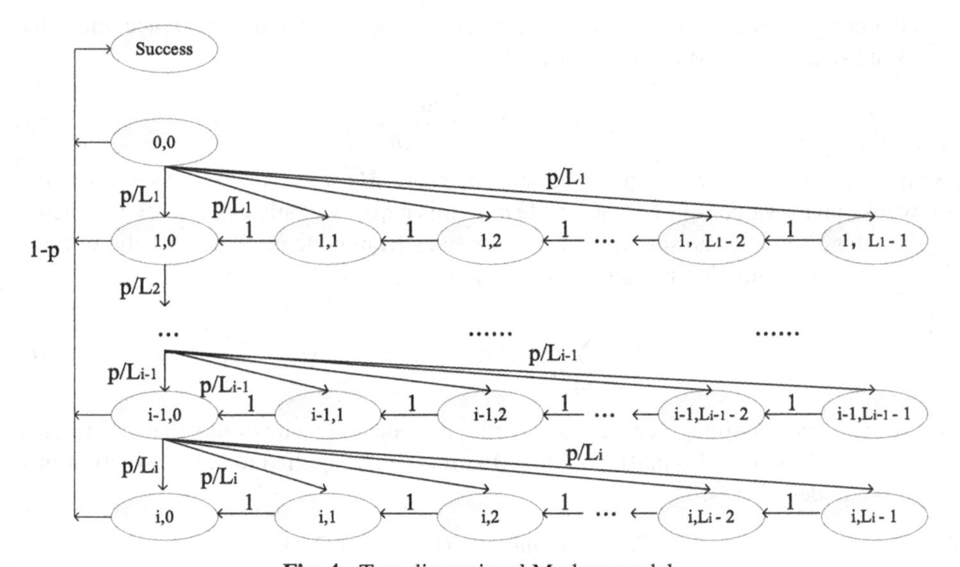

Fig. 4. Two-dimensional Markov model.

From the Markov model shown in Fig. 4, one step state transition probability can be obtained as follows:

$$\begin{cases} P\{i, k|i, k+1\} = 1, i \in (0, N-1+x), k \in [0, L_i - 2] \\ P\{i, k|i-1, 0\} = \frac{p}{L_i}, i \in (0, N-1+x), k \in [0, L_i - 1] \end{cases} \tag{9}$$

where, the first formula indicates that at the beginning of each slot time, the value of L_i will decrease by one unit, and it is inevitable that $k+1$ will become k. The second formula indicates that after the $i-1$th update, if a node receives broadcast information from an adjacent node at a certain time k, it will update its own phase again and recalculate the phase value.

4.2 Packet Transmission Probability

In order to calculate the channel throughput, it is necessary to obtain the packet transmission probability. Let τ represent the probability that the phase value of the node reaches 2π in a slot time. According to the BSAA, the node is able to transmit data packets only when the phase value reaches 2π, and there should be only one node in the channel for data packet transmission. Let $b_{i,k} = \lim_{t\to\infty} P\{s(t) = i, b(t) = k\}, i \in [0, N-1+x], k \in [0, L_i - 1]$ represent the steady-state distribution of the two-dimensional Markov model. From Eq. (9), the steady state distribution for any state is obtained as follows:

$$b_{i,k} = \frac{L_i - k}{L_i} b_{i,0} = \frac{L_i - k}{L_i} p^i b_{0,0}, \quad i \in [0, N-1+x] k \in [0, L_i - 1] \tag{10}$$

From the nature of the Markov model, the probability sum of the states is 1, that is,

$$1 = \sum_{i=0}^{N-1+x} \sum_{k=0}^{L_i - 1} b_{i,k} \tag{11}$$

According to the definition of τ, the phase value of the node reaches 2π when L_i decreases to 0, and its probability is calculated as follows:

$$\tau = \sum_{i=0}^{N-1+x} b_{i,0} \tag{12}$$

The probability that a node transmits a packet but the channel is busy is equivalent to the probability that at least one node has a phase value of 2π in the same slot time. Therefore, p can be expressed as follows:

$$p = 1 - (1-\tau)^{N-1} \tag{13}$$

4.3 Channel Throughput

According to the definition of throughput, the channel throughput is expressed as the ratio of the payload to the time of successful transmission in the channel. Let P_u represent the probability that the phase value of at least one node reaches 2π, which is equivalent to the probability of a node carrying out the phase update. P_u can be expressed as follows:

$$P_u = 1 - (1-\tau)^N \tag{14}$$

Let P_s represent the probability of successfully transmitting a data packet when the phase value of a node reaches 2π, which can be expressed as follows:

$$P_s = \frac{N\tau(1-\tau)^{N-1}}{P_u} = \frac{N\tau(1-\tau)^{N-1}}{1-(1-\tau)^N} \tag{15}$$

Let S represent the channel throughput, which can be expressed as follows:

$$S = \frac{E[P_s]}{E[t_s]} \tag{16}$$

where, $E[P_s]$ represents the expectation of the size of a successfully transmitted data packet in a slot time, and $E[t_s]$ represents the expectation of the length of a slot time.

Assuming that the expectation of a data packet size is $E[P]$, the amount of data successfully transmitted in a slot time is $P_u P_s E[P]$. A slot time consists of a slot time with no nodes with a phase value of 2π, a slot time with no phase update when the phase value of a node reaches 2π, and a slot time with the phase update when the phase value of a node reaches 2π. Therefore, the throughput S can be further expressed as follows:

$$S = \frac{P_u P_s E[P]}{(1 - P_u)\sigma + P_u P_s T_s + P_u(1 - P_s)T_u} \tag{17}$$

where, σ represents a complete length of slot time. T_s represents the time required for a node to transmit a data packet without the phase update. T_u represents the time required for a node to carry out the phase update. The expressions for T_s and T_u are as follows:

$$\begin{cases} T_s = H + E[P] + T_{bro} \\ T_u = H + E\left[P^*\right] + \delta + T_{bro} \end{cases} \tag{18}$$

where, $H = PHY_{hdr} + MAC_{hdr}$ represents the sum of the physical layer header length and the MAC layer header length. δ represents the propagation delay. T_{bro} represents the time required to send broadcast information. $E\left[P^*\right]$ represents the expectation of the data packet size of the node that finally sends data packet in the channel when the phase update occurs. In order to facilitate calculation, the length of all transmitted packets is the same.

4.4 Access Delay

In the BSAA, the access delay mainly includes the phase change delay and the phase update delay of the node. It can be known that the phase update delay exists with a certain probability. Therefore, the access delay is analyzed based on whether there is the phase update during the phase change.

Assuming that T_s^* represents the delay of successfully transmitting a data packet when there is no phase update during the phase change. Then,

$$T_s^* = (1 - P_u)\left(\frac{\theta_n}{w_n} + T_s\right) \tag{19}$$

Assuming that T_u^* represents the delay of successfully transmitting a data packet when there is the phase update during the phase change. Then,

$$T_u^* = P_u\left(\sum_{i=1}^{N-1+x}\left(\frac{\theta_{n,i} - \theta_{n,i-1}}{w_n} + L_i\right) + T_u\right) \tag{20}$$

where, $\frac{\theta_{n,i}-\theta_{n,i-1}}{w_n}$ represents the time that it takes for a node to change the phase value before the next phase update, and $\theta_{n,0} = 0$. i represents the update times.

In summary, the access delay T can be expressed as follows:

$$T = T_s^* + T_u^* = (1 - P_u)\left(\frac{\theta_n}{w_n} + T_s\right) + P_u\left(\sum_{i=1}^{N-1+x}\left(\frac{\theta_{n,i} - \theta_{n,i-1}}{w_n} + L_i\right) + T_u\right) \tag{21}$$

5 Experimental Simulation

According to the analysis in the previous section, this paper uses MATLAB to verify them and compare with the CSMA/CA mechanisms meanwhile. The number of nodes in the simulation experiment starts from 5. There are at most 50 competing nodes at the same time, and each time it increases by 5 nodes. The service types of data are divided into three categories: emergency services, streaming media services, and ordinary data services. Nodes are randomly selected among the three service types. Other simulation parameters are shown in Table 1.

Table 1. Simulation parameters.

Parameter name	Parameter value
Packet payload	3808 bits
MAC header	240 bits
PHY header	192 bits
ACK	112 bits + PHY header
RTS	160 bits + PHY header
CTS	112 bits + PHY header
Propagation delay	1 μs
Slot time (σ)	20 μs
SIFS	10 μs
DIFS	50 μs
Channel bit rate	2 Mbit/s
E_{max}	50000 J
x	6

In the experiment, we determine whether a collision has occurred by calculating the phase difference between each node and the remaining nodes. As shown in Fig. 5 and Fig. 6, they show the time series data of the phase difference between this node and the other nodes when the number of competing nodes is $N = 20$ and $N = 40$. It can be seen from Fig. 5 that the phase difference is 0 at about $t = 650$, but at this time the number of updates x is 1. Therefore, no collision will occur, and the node will continue to carry out the phase update. While in Fig. 6, there are two moments that the phase difference is 0, where the number of node updates x is 3 when $t = 750$, and x is 5 when $t = 1350$. Compared to Fig. 5, the number of node updates x is bigger. The reason is the number of competing nodes increases, which causes the probability that the phase value of the node reaches 2π at the same time to increase. However, the phase difference between the two nodes is randomly distributed between $(0, 2\pi)$ at most of time, which indicates that the probability of packet collision between nodes is very small.

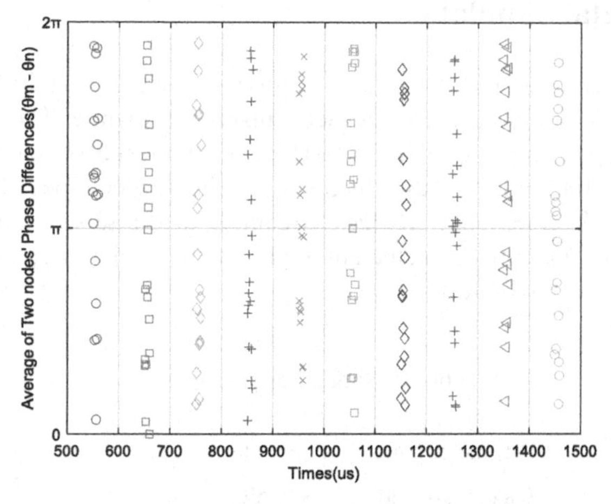

Fig. 5. Time series data of phase difference with adjacent nodes when $N = 20$.

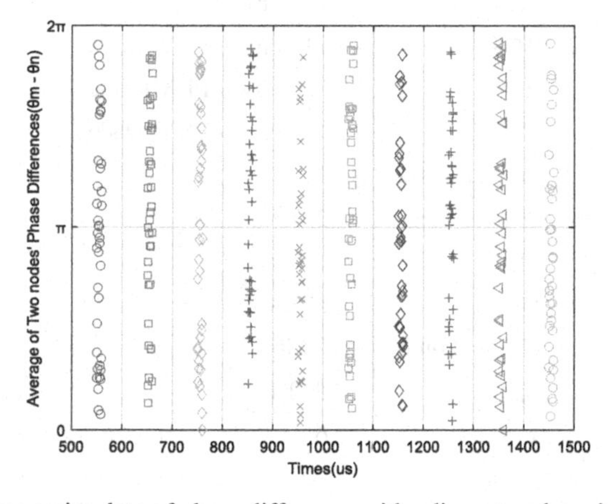

Fig. 6. Time series data of phase difference with adjacent nodes when $N = 40$.

Figure 7 shows the comparison graph of the collision probability between the BSAA and the CSMA/CA mechanisms. It can be seen from the Fig. 7 that as the number of competing nodes increases, the curves of the collision probability of all three show an upward trend.

In the BSAA, nodes are able to adjust their behaviors to avoid sending data packets at the same time, therefore, the probability of collision is relatively smaller than the CSMA/CA mechanism. In addition, the larger the number of competing nodes, the greater the gap between the two, which indicates that our proposed algorithm is able to avoid collisions better in the case of a large number of nodes.

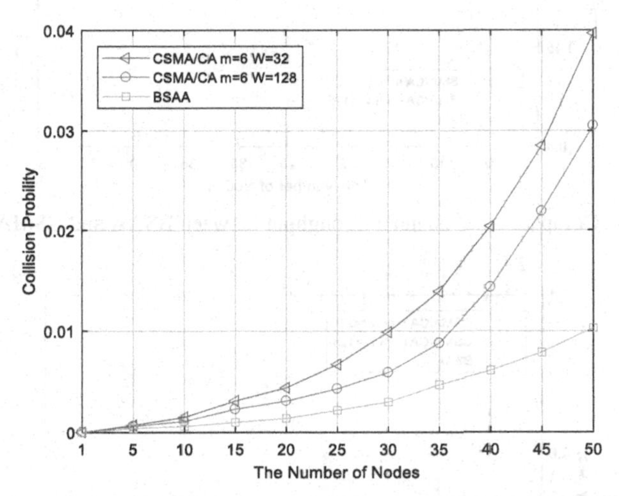

Fig. 7. Comparison of the collision probability between BSAA and CSMA/CA.

Figure 8 is a comparison graph of the channel throughput performance. It can be seen from the Fig. 8 that the channel throughput performance of the BSAA is overall improved by about 12%–15% compared to the CSMA/CA mechanisms. The throughput here refers to the average time of the payload successfully transmitted in a time slot to the length of the entire time slot. For the BSAA, the node is more likely to get access to the channel, and the length of the entire time slot is smaller than the CSMA/CA mechanisms, therefore, the BSAA is able to get better performance.

Figure 9 is a comparison graph of the access delay performance. It can be seen from the Fig. 9 that when the number of competing nodes is small, the access delay of the BSAA is slightly longer than the CSMA/CA ($m = 6$, $W = 32$) mechanisms. This is because when there are fewer nodes, the backoff waiting time of the nodes will not be long in the CSMA/CA mechanisms. While each node needs to go through the phase change and the phase update in the BSAA, and its time may be slightly longer than the backoff waiting time. Therefore, when the number of nodes is small, the delay performance of the BSAA is not as good as the CSMA/CA mechanisms. However, with the increase in the number of competing nodes, the time for backoff retransmission and backoff waiting is increasing, and the delay is also increasing in the CSMA/CA mechanisms. While in the BSAA, the increase in the time spent by the nodes on the phase change and the phase update is not very large. Therefore, in the case of a large number of competing nodes, the delay performance of the BSAA is better than the CSMA/CA mechanisms.

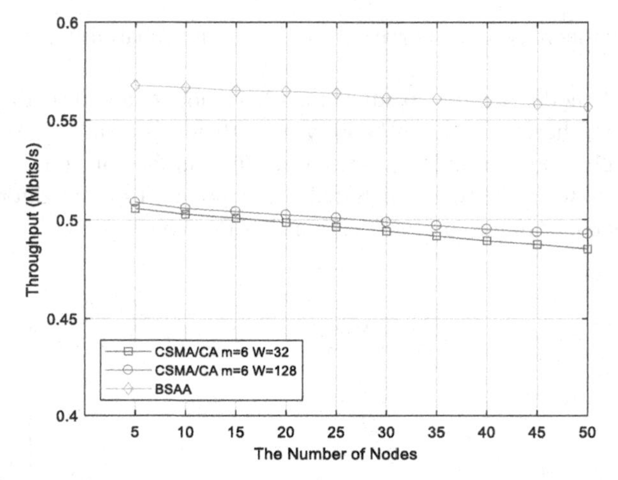

Fig. 8. Comparison of channel throughput between BSAA and CSMA/CA.

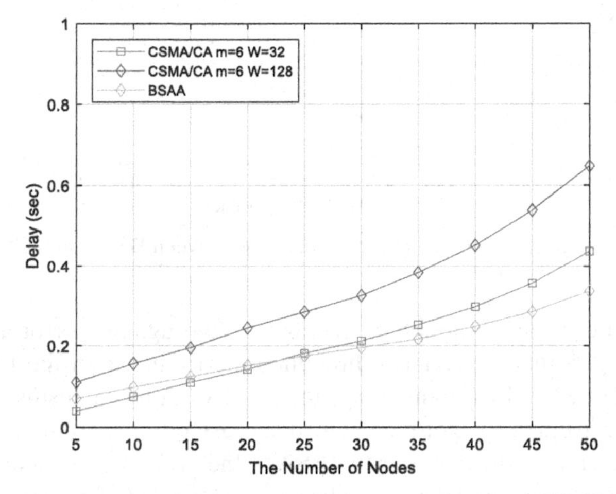

Fig. 9. Comparison of access delay between BSAA and CSMA/CA.

6 Conclusion

Inspired by Stigmergy, this paper proposes an algorithm to resolve access collisions between massive nodes in wireless networks. The algorithm makes each node completely self-organize. In addition, by means of analyzing the initialization status and update status of the nodes in different situations, adjacent nodes are able to self-adjust the current behavior to avoid collisions when one node is transmitting data packets. Simulation results show that the proposed algorithm is able to maintain a low collision probability with the increasing number of competing nodes even in a dynamically changing network topology. Moreover, comparing the proposed algorithm with CSMA/CA mechanisms in terms of collision probability, channel throughput and access delay. The results show that the collision probability and access delay of our proposed algorithm performs better in the case of the large number of competing nodes, and the performance of channel throughput is overall improved by about 12%–15%.

References

1. Grassé, P.P.: La reconstruction du nid et les coordinations inter—Individuelles chez Bellicositer- mes natalis et Cubitermes sp. La théorie dela stigmergie. Insectes Sociaux **6**(1), 41–80 (1959)
2. Göllner, U.: Grassé, Pierre-P.: Fondation des société—Construction. termitologia. 2. 624 S., 452 Figure., 28 Tab., Masson, Paris, New York, Barcelona, Milan, Mexico, Sao Paulo. Deutsche Entomologische Zeitschrift **32**(4–5), 379–379 (1984)
3. Dorigo, M., Bonabeau, E., Theraulaz, G.: Ant algorithms and stigmergy. Future Gener. Comput. Syst. FGCS **16**(8), 851–871 (2000)
4. Kassabalidis, I., El-Sharkawi, M.A., Marks, R.J., et al.: Swarm intelligence for routing in communication networks. In: Proceedings of the IEEE Global Telecommunications Conference on, San Antonio, TX, USA, 25–29 November 2001, pp. 3613–3617 (2001)
5. Werfel, J., Nagpal, R.: Extended stigmergy in collective construction. IEEE Intell. Syst. **21**(2), 20–28 (2006)
6. Alfeo, A.L., Cimino, M.G.C.A., Egidi, S., et al.: A stigmergy-based analysis of city hotspots to discover trends and anomalies in urban transportation usage. IEEE Trans. Intell. Transp. Syst. **19**(7), 2258–2267 (2018)
7. Tummolini, L., Castelfranchi, C.: Trace signals: the meanings of stigmergy. In: Weyns, Danny, Parunak, H Van Dyke., Michel, Fabien (eds.) E4MAS 2006. LNCS (LNAI), vol. 4389, pp. 141–156. Springer, Heidelberg (2007). https://doi.org/10.1007/978-3-540-71103-2_8
8. Degesys, J., Rose, I., Patel, A., et al.: DESYNC: self-organizing desynchronization and TDMA on wireless sensor networks. In: 6th International Symposium on Information Processing in Sensor Networks 2007, Cambridge, MA, USA, 25–27 April 2007, pp. 11–20 (2007)
9. Degesys, J., Nagpal, R.: Towards desynchronization of multi-hop topologies. In: 2008 Second IEEE International Conference on Self-adaptive and Self-organizing Systems, Venezia, Italy, 20–24 October 2008, pp. 129–138 (2008)

Single-Satellite Interference Source Locating Based on Four Co-efficiency Beam

Laiding Zhao[1,2], Li Zhiwei[3], Cen Ruan[1,2](✉), and Yue Zheng[2]

[1] Key Laboratory of Broadband Wireless Communication and Sensor Network Technology, Nanjing University of Posts and Telecommunications, Nanjing 210003, China
1018010327@njupt.edu.cn

[2] College of Communication Engineer, Nanjing University of Posts and Telecommunications, Nanjing 210003, China

[3] College of Information Science and Electronic Engineering, ZheJiang University, ZheJiang 310058, China

Abstract. With the previous method based on the signal strength of the three-beam interference source [1], after studying and deriving the antenna gain pointing model, this paper proposes a single-star interference source localization method based on the signal strength of the four-beam interference source. As for solving the nonlinear directional equations, this paper proposes an improved particle swarm optimization algorithm to obtain its numerical solution, which is compared with the previous ordinary particle swarm optimization algorithm [2]. Then, using the least square method, the multi-group data is used to determine the interference source with the smallest error. First orientation and then positioning. After the simulation test of the proposed positioning method, the feasibility of the algorithm for positioning is proved. The method proposed in this paper is compared with the previous positioning method to prove the robustness of the algorithm.

Keywords: Satellite communication · Interference source locating · Swarm optimization algorithm · Antenna gain pointing model

1 Introduction

Whether in daily life or in special activities such as wild patrols, military operations, earthquake relief, and other special activities, mobile communication systems are essential for communication. The satellite mobile communication system has the characteristics of wide coverage, good reliability and no geographical limitation, which makes up for the shortcomings of the ground mobile communication system and improves the robustness and reliability of the communication system [3]. Internationally, the development of satellite mobile communication systems is very rapid, a number of global or regional mobile communication systems including Iridium, Eurostar and international mobile communication satellite systems have been established. In personal communications, maritime transportation, satellite mobile communication systems are widely used

Q. Wu et al. (Eds.): WiSATS 2020, LNICST 358, pp. 624–635, 2021.
https://doi.org/10.1007/978-3-030-69072-4_51

and providing an effective means of communicating in all terrain conditions. With the continuous development of satellite communication technology, more and more spectrum resources are used, and the interference received by satellites is increasing [4]. In the military and civilian fields, the positioning of satellite interference sources has always been a hot issue. The single-satellite interference source of the geosynchronous orbit multi-beam satellite has a small Doppler shift due to its operation in the geosynchronous orbit, and can only be positioned by a single star, and the commonly used satellite positioning method cannot be used. The interference source localization method based on the signal strength of the interference source and the interference source localization method based on the movable spot beam obtain the incident direction of the interference source by establishing the relationship between the antenna gain and the interference source pointing direction. For the existing single-star interference source localization algorithm, the antenna pointing angle, satellite orbit height, signal source power and other data measured by the tracking telemetry system have different degrees of deviation [5], which influence the result of the pointing direction of interference source. At the same time, the particle swarm algorithm used in the positioning algorithm proposed by the predecessors tends to be unable to converge due to the random generation of the population position. The correct result cannot be obtained when calculating the incident direction of the interference source. This algorithm is designed for the geosynchronous orbit satellite mobile communication system. According to the limitations of the existing single-star interference source localization algorithm, a new interference source localization method is designed (Fig. 1).

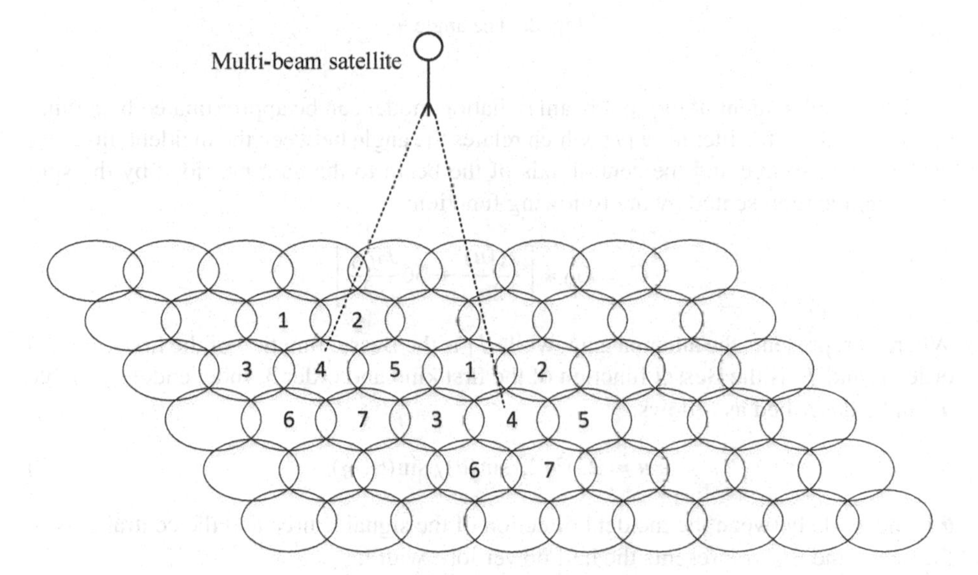

Fig. 1. Beam multiplexing schematic diagram

2 Previous Method

2.1 Antenna Gain Pointing Model

The antenna gain is the ratio of the power density of the signal generated by the actual antenna to the ideal radiating element at the same point in space under the condition of equal input power [6]. That is, it describes the ability of antenna radiating the input power directionally. Antenna gain is related to the angle $\boldsymbol{\theta}$ between the central axis of the antenna and the incident direction of the signal source (Fig. 2).

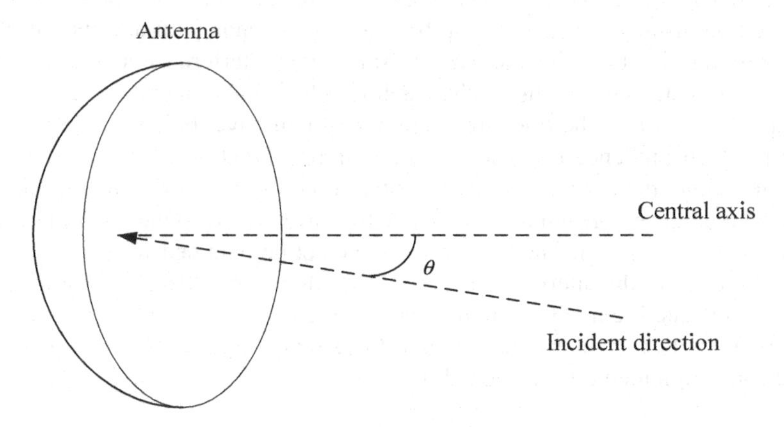

Fig. 2. The angle θ

The establishment of the spot beam radiation model can be approximated by a function provided by the literature [7], which relates the angle between the incident direction of the signal source and the central axis of the beam to the gain provided by the spot beam, and is represented by the following function:

$$G = G_0 * \left[\frac{J_1(u)}{2u} + 36\frac{J_{3(u)}}{u^3} \right] \tag{1}$$

Where $\boldsymbol{G}$ represents the antenna gain, while $\boldsymbol{J}_1$ is the Bessel function of the first kind and order 1, and $\boldsymbol{J}_3$ is the Bessel function of the first kind and order 3. Independent variable $\boldsymbol{u}$ can be described as follows:

$$u = 2.07123 \sin(\theta)/\sin(\theta_{3dB}) \tag{2}$$

$\boldsymbol{\theta}$ is the angle between the incident direction of the signal source and the central axis of the beam and θ_{3dB} represents the half power lobe width:

$$\theta_{3dB} = 70 \cdot \frac{\lambda}{D} \tag{3}$$

$\boldsymbol{\lambda}$ is the wavelength of the Radiation signal, $\boldsymbol{D}$ represents the Antenna paraboloid diameter.

G_0 can be obtained as follows:

$$G_0 = \frac{\pi^2 D\eta^2}{\lambda^2} \tag{4}$$

Where η is the antenna efficiency.

The incident direction of the interference source signal is represented by two angles. In order to derive the antenna gain pointing model, the angle between the incident direction and the center axis of the spot beam needs to be related to the incident direction of the signal source.

Through simple geometric derivation, following formula can be obtained:

$$\cos\theta = \frac{1}{2}\cos\varphi_0 \cdot \cos\varphi\left[\frac{1}{cos^2\varphi_0} + \frac{1}{cos^2\varphi} - (\tan\alpha_0 - \tan\alpha)^2 - (\tan\beta_0 - \tan\beta)^2\right] \tag{5}$$

$$\varphi_0 = arctan\sqrt{tan^2\alpha_0 + tan^2\beta_0} \tag{6}$$

$$\varphi = arctan\sqrt{tan^2\alpha + tan^2\beta} \tag{7}$$

Where the angle α is the angle between the incident direction of the interference source signal in the direction parallel to the satellite's movement and the point right under the satellite. The angle β is the angle between the direction of the interference source signal in the direction perpendicular to the satellite's movement and the point right under the satellite. Also, α_0 and β_0 are the angles of the central pointing direction of the beam. Using the above formula, the antenna gain pointing model can be obtained (Fig. 3).

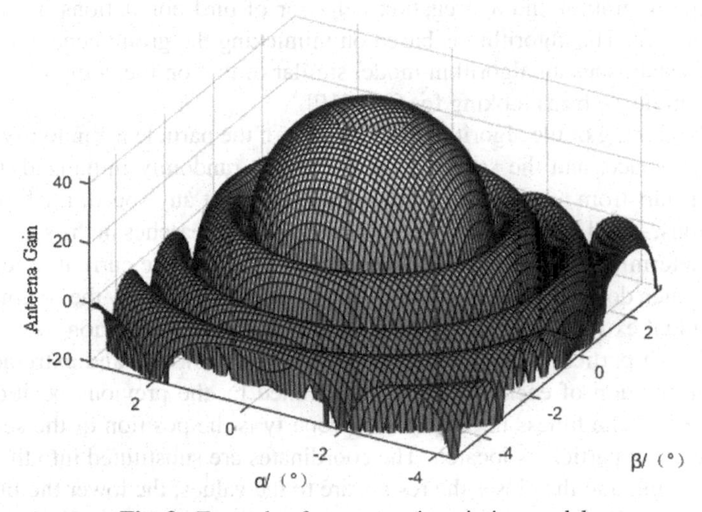

Fig. 3. Example of antenna gain pointing model

2.2 Orientation Equations

Assume that the closest three spot beams around the interference source: beam 1, beam 2 and beam 3 have received the interference source signal. When the interference source signal passes through the uplink, there will be free space transmission loss, atmospheric attenuation [8], multipath effect [9] and other losses. Set all losses on the uplink to $\boldsymbol{L}$, the signal transmission power of the interference source is set to $\boldsymbol{P_t}$, The antenna gain obtained by the interference source is set to $\boldsymbol{G_t}$, After the signal passes the uplink, the signal power received by the satellite is set to $\boldsymbol{P_{R1}}$, the pointing direction of beam 1 can be described as $(\boldsymbol{\alpha}_1, \boldsymbol{\beta}_1)$, while the incident direction of interference source is $(\boldsymbol{\alpha}, \boldsymbol{\beta})$.With the antenna gain pointing model, It can be obtained that the antenna gain obtained by the interference source in beam 1 is $\boldsymbol{G}_1(\boldsymbol{\alpha}, \boldsymbol{\beta})$, then we can get the following equation:

$$[P_{R1}] = [P_T] + [G_T] + [G_1(\alpha, \beta)] - [L] \tag{8}$$

For spot beam 2 and spot beam 3, we can also get the following equations:

$$\begin{cases} [P_{R2}] - [P_{R1}] = [G_2(\alpha, \beta)] - [G_1(\alpha, \beta)] \\ [P_{R3}] - [P_{R2}] = [G_3(\alpha, \beta)] - [G_2(\alpha, \beta)] \end{cases} \tag{9}$$

Using the particle swarm algorithm, we can solve equations and get $(\boldsymbol{\alpha}, \boldsymbol{\beta})$. When we have the incident direction, we can easily calculate the interference coordinate with the satellite ephemeris.

3 Ordinary Particle Swarm Optimization

The particle swarm optimization (PSO) algorithm is a global search algorithm that simulates the migration and aggregation behavior of bird populations in the foraging process in nature. The algorithm is based on mimicking the group behavior of birds in nature, and establishes an algorithm model similar to that on the computer, that is, the behavior of multiple birds looking for food [10].

At the beginning of the algorithm, the position of the particle is randomly initialized in the search space, and the speed of the particle is randomly initialized, that is, the particle can start from any position in the search space at any speed. Each particle has three positions, speed and fitness. Attribute, each particle searches in the search space by itself, and determines the location of an extremum based on the current fitness value of the particle, then determines the extremum position of the group by the optimal solution in all individual extremums, and in order to make the search direction Sex, the current velocity of each particle is determined by the previous velocity and extreme position. The current position of each particle is determined by the previous position and the current velocity. The fitness in the particle property is the position of the search space where the current particle is located. The coordinates are substituted into the nonlinear equations sought, and the closer the results are to the values, the lower the fitness [11].

Assume in a D dimension search, there are n particles $\boldsymbol{X} = (\boldsymbol{X}_1, \boldsymbol{X}_2, \cdots, \boldsymbol{X}_n)$, and initialization location of each particle is $\boldsymbol{X}_i = (\boldsymbol{X}_{i1}, \boldsymbol{X}_{i2}, \cdots, \boldsymbol{X}_{iD})^T$, while the initialization speed is $\boldsymbol{V}_i = (\boldsymbol{V}_{i1}, \boldsymbol{V}_{i2}, \cdots, \boldsymbol{V}_{iD})^T$. Initial individual extremum as $\boldsymbol{P}_i =$

$(P_{i1}, P_{i2}, \cdots, P_{iD})^T$, and population extremum as $P_g = (P_{g1}, P_{g2}, \cdots, P_{gD})^T$, we can use the following formula to update the speed and position of each particle.:

$$V_{id}^{k+1} = \omega \cdot V_{id}^{k} + c_1 \cdot r_1 \cdot \left(P_{id}^{k} - X_{id}^{k}\right) + c_2 \cdot r_2 \cdot \left(P_{gd}^{k} - X_{id}^{k}\right) \tag{10}$$

$$X_{id}^{k+1} = X_{id}^{k} + V_{id}^{k+1} \tag{11}$$

Where d represents the serial number of the coordinate dimension, i represents the serial number of particles, k means the number of iterations. $\mathbf{c}_1$ and $\mathbf{c}_2$ are Acceleration factors, r_1 and r_2 are two random numbers within [0, 1]. These four coefficients are used to limit and control the position and velocity of the particles, preventing them from blindly searching. And ω represents the linear decreasing inertia weight [12] (Fig. 4).

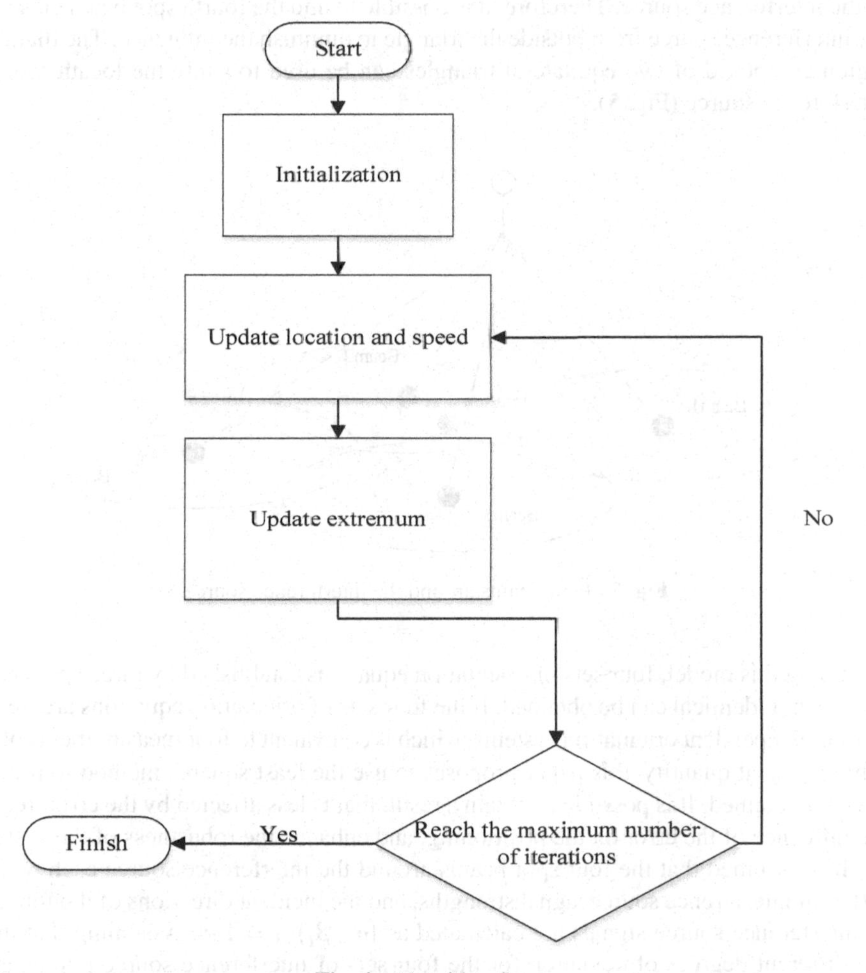

Fig. 4. Algorithm flow

4 New Method

4.1 Improvements to Orientation Methods

The method proposed by the predecessor to use the interference source signal strength received by the three spot beams interfered by the interference source and the antenna gain pointing model to establish the directional equations has good accuracy. However in the actual measurement process, because of the spot beam center pointing measured by the tracking telemetry earth station subsystem in the satellite communication system and the data of the interference source signal strength measured by the satellite side is deviated from the true value, at the time the satellite operates at a synchronization of about 35786 km from the ground, systematic error is inevitable, and the combination of measurement error and systematic error has a great influence on the accurate direction of the interference source. Therefore, it is possible to find the fourth spot beam closest to the interference source from outside the triangle to diminish the influence. The diamond region composed of two equilateral triangles can be used to study the location of the interference source (Fig. 5).

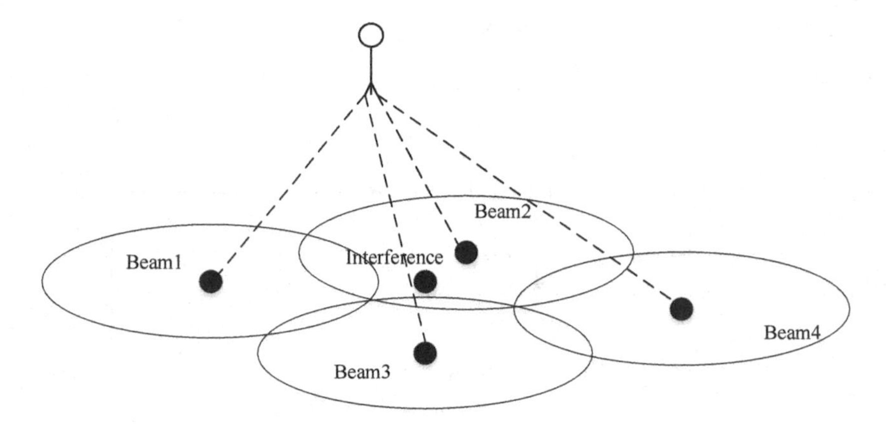

Fig. 5. Four beams around the interference source

Using this model, four sets of orientation equations established by three spot beams that are not identical can be obtained. If the four sets of orientation equations are treated as four independent orientation systems, which is equivalent to four measurements of the same physical quantity, this paper proposes to use the least squares method to process the data obtained. It is possible to obtain a result that is less affected by the error, reduce the influence of the error on the positioning, and enhance the robustness of the system.

It is assumed that the four spot beams around the interference source each receive different interference source signal strengths, and the incident directions of the four sets of interference source signals are calculated as (α_i, β_i), i = 1~4, Assuming that there are different degrees of deviation for the four sets of interference source points, after processing the four sets of data using the least squares method, the interference source direction with the degree of deviation between the minimum and the maximum can be obtained. Find a point that satisfies the following formula $(\boldsymbol{\alpha}, \boldsymbol{\beta})$:

$$\gamma_{min} = \sum_{i=1}^{4} \left[(\alpha_i - \alpha)^2 + (\beta_i - \beta)^2 \right] \tag{12}$$

This pointing direction is the most reliable value sought.

4.2 Improvements to the PSO Algorithm

As an advanced intelligent algorithm, the PSO algorithm has the characteristics of fast search speed and high efficiency, and the PSO algorithm is simple, which is very suitable for dealing with real value problems. However, the problem of the PSO algorithm is also very obvious. As shown in Fig. 6, the PSO search algorithm is performed 100 times, and there is a case where it does not converge and falls into local optimum.

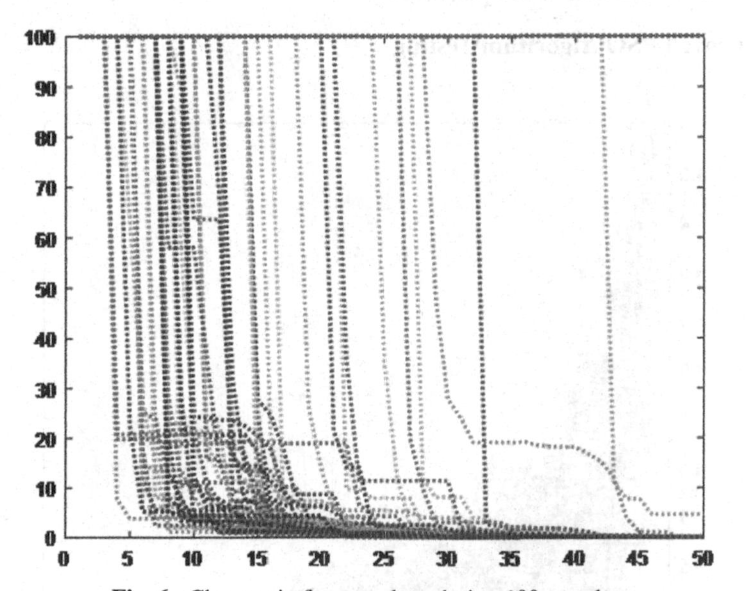

Fig. 6. Changes in fitness values during 100 searches

When the external fitness of the search space is set to a fixed value of 100, the algorithm cannot converge because the particle does not fall into the search space when the position is initialized. As the number of iterations increases, the fitness value does not change. In the figure, the value is 100. Straight line. In some cases, when the algorithm terminates, the particle still does not find the optimal solution, but falls into the local optimum. In most cases, the particle finds the optimal solution when the number of iterations is 45. In order to speed up the convergence, in order to speed up the convergence, the fitness function outside the search space is always taken to a larger value. When most of the particles are initialized outside the search space, it is easy to cause the generated particles to be global. The optimal solution is far away. In a limited number of iterations, it is easy to cause the convergence speed to be slow, or to fall into local optimum, or even to converge. That is to say, when the PSO algorithm cannot reach the vicinity of the optimal solution at the beginning of the iteration, we may not get the right answer.

Therefore, this paper proposes an improvement to the original PSO algorithm, changing the random initialization of the position of the particles to grid initialization, listing the center of the four spot beams on the ground, and meshing them to make the initial position of the particles. It is distributed in the search space, which can increase the probability that the particle will reach the optimal solution in the initial iteration, which is close to 100%, which improves the speed and reliability of the algorithm convergence.

The algorithm proposes to divide multiple grids in the diamond-shaped area, select multiple points in each grid randomly, and find the optimal solution grid by analyzing the fitness value of each point. Then the particle swarm algorithm is executed in the optimal solution grid.

5 Test Results and Comparison

5.1 Improved PSO Algorithm Testing

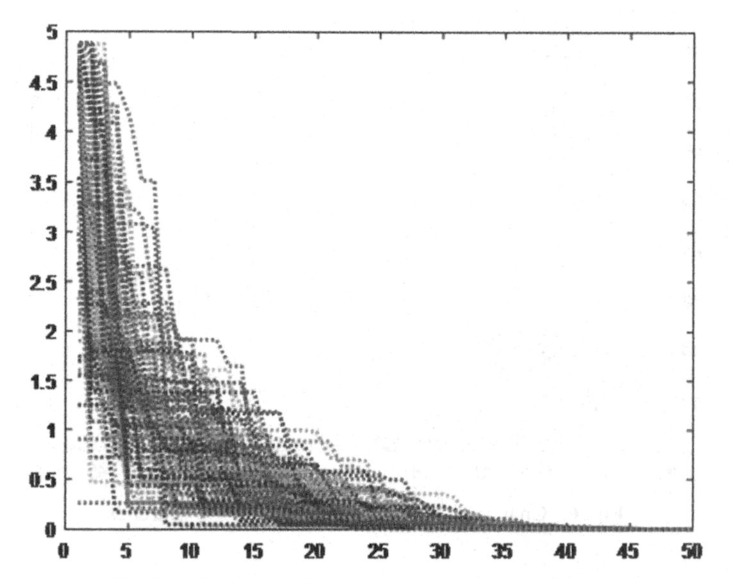

Fig. 7. Changes in fitness values during 100 searches

As shown in Fig. 6, in the search process of the original PSO algorithm, there is a non-convergence condition in which the fitness is always fixed, and there is also a case where the local optimal cannot reach the optimal solution. Although most of the search process converges, it has a large impact on the results when averaging.

In Fig. 7, the non-convergence disappears, and each search converges after 45 iterations, and the convergence speed is faster, improving the reliability of the previous algorithm.

It can be seen from the 100 average results in Table 1, the original algorithm is less reliable, and its correct orientation is (6°, 0.25°).

Table 1. Algorithm solution result.

Group	Solution result (average)
Improved algorithm	(6.000000624044548, 0.250000841961512)
Original algorithm (all)	(3.208875514278203, 0.142658280846434)
Original data (valid)	(6.000160308574986, 0.250032228895439)

5.2 Directional System Test

In this experiment, the results of the change when the center of the spot beam 1 is changed from 4° to 6° are simulated, and the changes obtained by the original method and the proposed method are compared (Figs. 8 and 9).

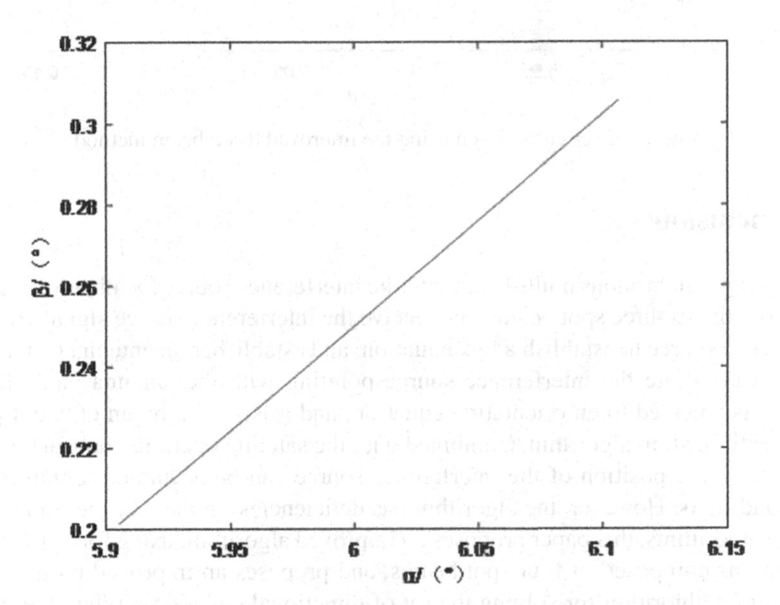

Fig. 8. Error curve when using the original three-beam method

As shown in the figure, the maximum error of the angle α is about 0.1° and the maximum angle error of β is about 0.003°, which is much better than the original method. And when the error is larger, since the satellite is in the GEO orbit, the 0.2° orientation error will produce an error of about one hundred kilometers. The curves in the previous two graphs are linked by 20 experimental results.

According to the experimental results, it is proved that the proposed method has better robustness and reliability than the original method in the presence of measurement deviation.

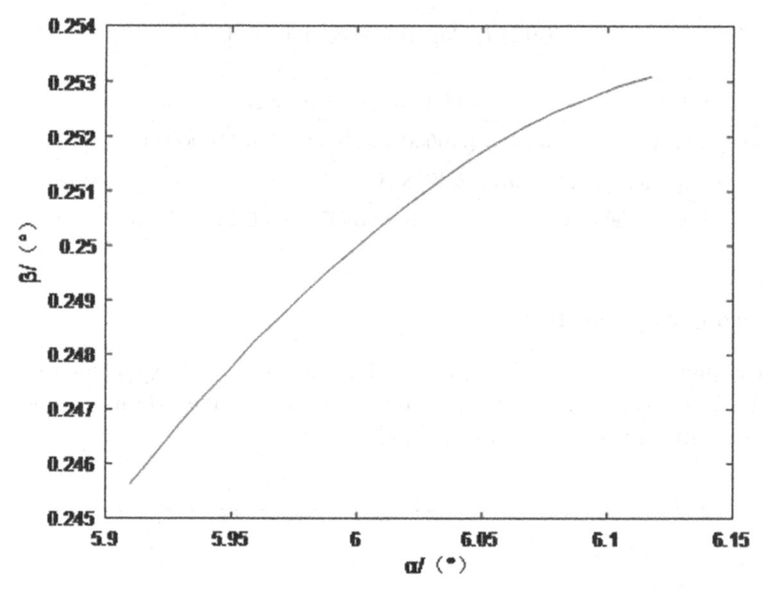

Fig. 9. Error curve when using the improved three-beam method

6 Conclusion

The existing synchronous multi-beam satellite interference source localization algorithm skillfully utilizes three spot beams that receive the interference source signal around the interference source to establish a link equation, and establishes an antenna gain pointing model to associate the interference source pointing with the antenna gain. The link equation is changed to an orientation equation, and it is solved by an efficient particle swarm optimization algorithm. Combined with the satellite operation data and the earth information, the position of the interference source can be accurately obtained under ideal conditions. However, the algorithm has deficiencies. In view of the limitations of existing algorithms, this paper proposes an improved algorithm, using four different sets of equations composed of four spot beams, and proposes an improved particle swarm optimization algorithm for solving the set of directional equations. When the particles are meshed and initialized, the reliability and convergence speed of the particles are improved. In the treatment of the four sets of interference source pointing data, this paper uses the least squares method to diminish the error influence.

References

1. Zhong, X., Yao, K., Xie, Z., et al.: The method of interference source locating based on multi-beam antenna and analysis of locating accuracy. In: International Conference on Electronics Information & Emergency Communication. IEEE (2016)
2. Eberhart, Shi, Y.: Particle swarm optimization: developments, applications and resources. In: Proceedings of the 2001 Congress on Evolutionary Computation (IEEE Cat. No.01TH8546). IEEE (2002)

3. Neely, M.J., Modiano, E., Rohrs, C.E.: Power and server allocation in a multi-beam satellite with time varying channels. In: Joint Conference of the IEEE Computer & Communications Societies IEEE. IEEE (2002)
4. Rhee, I.-K., Kim, S.-A., Jung, K., Serpedin, E., Park, J.-M., Lee, Y.-H.: Uplink interference adjustment for mobile satellite service in multi-beam environments. In: Kim, T.-H., Adeli, H., Robles, R.J., Balitanas, M. (eds.) UCMA 2011. CCIS, vol. 151, pp. 371–380. Springer, Heidelberg (2011). https://doi.org/10.1007/978-3-642-20998-7_46
5. Xue-Yuan, L., You, H.E.: Location method and error analysis for three-star time-difference system using digital map. J. Univ. Electron. Sci. Technol. China **36**(4), 688–691 (2007)
6. Klein, B.: Optical antenna gain. Appl. Opt. **13**, 2134–2141 (1974)
7. Caini, C., Corazza, G.E., Falciasecca, G., et al.: A spectrum- and power-efficient EHF mobile satellite system to be integrated with terrestrial cellular systems. IEEE J. Sel. Areas Commun. **10**(8), 1315–1325 (1992)
8. Lawrence, B.D., Simmons, J.A.: Measurements of atmospheric attenuation at ultrasonic frequencies and the significance for echolocation by bats. J. Acoust. Soc. Am. **71**(3), 585–590 (1982)
9. Encheng, W., Zhuopeng, W., Zhang, C.: A wideband antenna for global navigation satellite system with reduced multipath effect. IEEE Antennas Wirel. Propag. Lett. **12**, 124–127 (2013)
10. Yu, J., Piao, Z., Sun, R., et al.: Application of GIS and particle swarm optimization in rural substation locating. Nongye Gongcheng Xuebao/Trans. Chin. Soc. Agric. Eng. **25**(5), 146–149 (2009)
11. Kennedy, J.: Particle swarm optimization. In: Proceedings of 1995 IEEE International Conference on Neural Networks, Perth, Australia, 27 November–December (1995)
12. Huang, C., Zhang, Y., Jiang, D., et al.: On some non-linear decreasing inertia weight strategies in particle swarm optimization. In: Chinese Control Conference (2007)

Spectrum Data Reconstruction via Deep Convolutional Neural Network

Xiaojin Ding(✉) and Lijie Feng

Telecommunication and Network" National Engineering Research Center, Nanjing University of Posts and Communications, Nanjing 210003, China
dxj@njupt.edu.cn

Abstract. In the paper, we explore the spectrum-data reconstruction of a spectrum-sensing system. In order to decease the demand on the sensed spectrum data, we proposed a deep convolutional neural network (DCNN) based spectrum data reconstruction scheme relying on three stages, thus the satellites are allowed to perform spectrum sensing with the aid of down-sampling, and transmit the low-resolution (LR) and small amount of high-resolution (HR) spectrum data to earth stations. Specifically, in the first stage, the received LR and HR spectrum data will be first preprocessed. Then, the preprocessed HR spectrum data will be sent into the DCNN model for training purposes in the second stage. In the third stage, the preprocessed LR spectrum data will be fed into the trained model with the aid of the optimized hyperparameters, and the trained DCNN can generate the HR spectrum data. Additionally, performance results show that the proposed reconstruction scheme can obtain the reconstructed HR spectrum data in terms of the low mean absolute error.

Keywords: Spectrum data reconstruction · Down-sampling · Deep convolutional neural network

1 Introduction

Satellite spectrum sensing has the advantages of wide sensing range, efficient spectrum utilization and low energy consumption, which has received increasing research attention as a benefit of its ability of seamless coverage [1, 2]. With the increasing number of sensing tasks, the amount of data transmitted by the satellite spectrum sensing system become enormous. However, these huge amount of data may not be transmitted, due to the limited transmission capability of wireless links spanning from satellites to earth stations [3].

At present, there are two kind ways to solve the problem of limited data transmission, which are data compression and down-sampling. To be specific, data compression [4] relies on high timely processing ability on-satellite. In contrast, down-sampling is more easier to implement on-satellite, and the unsampled data can be reconstructed at the Earth station. The data reconstruct methods are mainly concentrated in the field of image processing, such as super-resolution (SR) [5], and image interpolation [6], etc.

Q. Wu et al. (Eds.): WiSATS 2020, LNICST 358, pp. 636–644, 2021.
https://doi.org/10.1007/978-3-030-69072-4_52

Image Super-resolution can reconstruct low-resolution (LR) images as high-resolution (HR) images [7, 8]. Especially, with the continuous development of deep learning [9], the super-resolution Convolutional Neural Network (SRCNN) was designed to recover LR images [10]. To be specific, Bicubic interpolation method [11] was used to preprocess the image, and then sent the preprocessed data into the network to learn the end-to-end features between LR images and HR images, which achieved a better recovery performance compared with the traditional image recovery technology. Due to the adaptability and robustness, in [12], deep convolutional network was utilized to reconstruct LR images.

Inspired by this, the spectrum data with time-frequency domain can also be regarded as an image. Through our investigation and research, there is no deep learning-based method introduced into the spectrum reconstruction. In this paper, we propose a super-resolution reconstruction method for LR spectrum relying on DCNN. Moreover, the Adam optimization [13] is adopted, and the zero interpolation method [14] is also used to improve the efficient of data preprocessing. The main contributions of this paper are as follows: we propose a spectrum-data super-resolution reconstruction with the aid of deep convolutional neural network, thus, the spectrum sensing satellites can perform spectrum sensing relying on down-sampling, and the proposed reconstruction method can generate HR spectrum data. Furthermore, performance evaluations show that the proposed spectrum-data reconstruction scheme has a good reconstruction quality.

2 Data Preprocessing

Similar to image recovery, the LR spectrum data can also be reconstructed based on Convolutional Neural Networks. In the image recovery, the Bicubic interpolation method is an effective way that usually used for preprocessing to obtain the LR samples [11]. In contrast, the spectrum data has two-dimensional nature and correlation in time and space, where time-domain and frequency-domain are equivalent to the height and width of the grayscale image, respectively, and the power spectral density (PSD) value is equivalent to the pixel value. Thus, the spectrum data of the time-frequency domain can be considered as the grayscale image for processing. However, differing form the image, the time-frequency domain interval of spectrum data is inconsistent, and the LR spectrum data should also exist in the HR case. Then, the zero interpolation method is adopted for spectrum data construction, without using Bicubic method.

Real-world spectrum data are collected and stored as PSD value. To reduce the impact of random noise and avoid direct reconstruction of the PSD value, the sensed data should be preprocessed, including normalization and zero interpolation. Then, the normalized HR spectrum data is considered as a HR spectrum image, which can be used as the training label. Moreover, for training purposes, the HR spectrum image can be converted into LR spectrum image via down-sampling. Moreover, the LR spectrum image will be inserted with zero by the factor of d in both time domain and frequency domain. Taking the factor $d = 2$ as an example, the specific zero interpolation can be shown in Fig. 1.

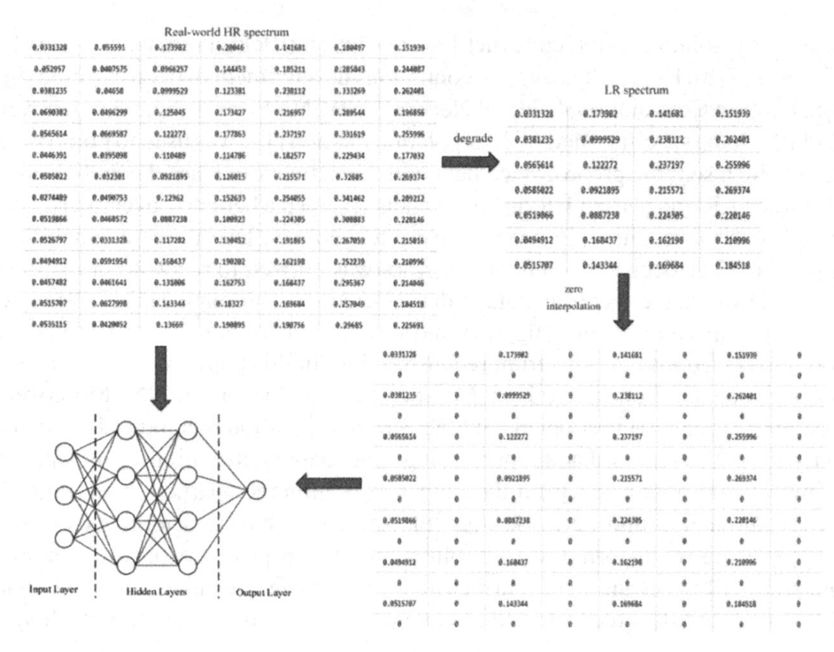

Fig. 1. Data preprocessing in training phase

The data preprocessing in the reconstruction phase only relies on normalizing the acquired LR spectrum data, and carries out zero interpolation operation. Then, the pre-processed can fed into the model to achieve recovery and reconstruction, as shown in Fig. 2.

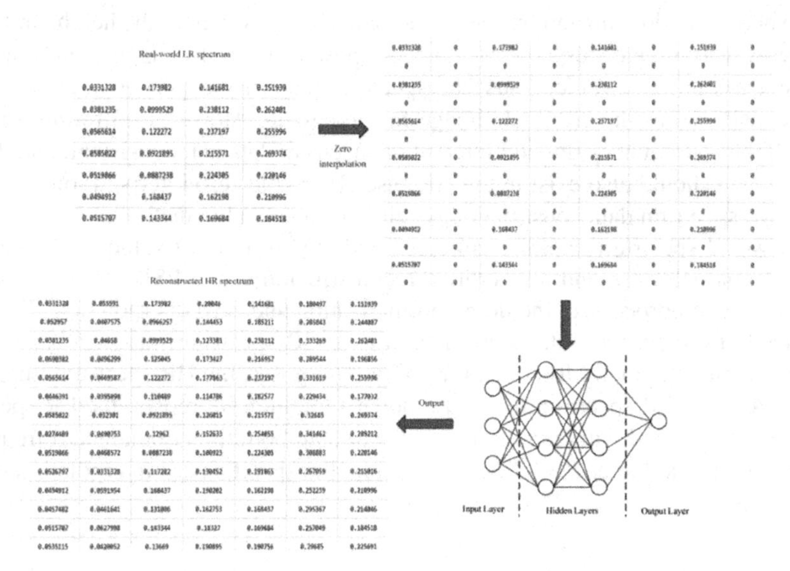

Fig. 2. Data preprocessing in the testing phase

3 Deep Convolutional Neural Networks for Spectrum Data Reconstruction

3.1 Deep Convolutional Neural Networks

Compared with other neural networks, DCNN has the advantages of sparseness, parameter sharing, non-linearity, translation invariance, etc. Moreover, it has advantage of learning the correlation in space [15]. Therefore, it can achieve excellent performance in image processing and classification, leading to extensive research [9]. In order to perform super-resolution reconstruction of the spectrum based on DCNN network, a three-layer neural network is constructed, which can process a large amount of data, and learn an end-to-end feature mapping between LR spectrum and HR spectrum. Moreover, it also can estimate missing HR information in the LR spectrum in order to complete reconstruction of spectrum data, relying on spectrum data preprocessing, spectrum feature extraction, non-linear mapping and final reconstruction. The specific model is shown in Fig. 3:

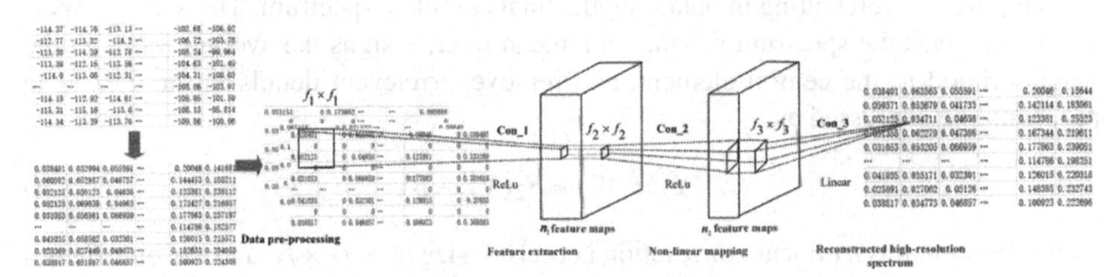

Fig. 3. DCNN-based spectrum super-resolution reconstruction

As shown in Fig. 3, no pooling layer is used to prevent the loss of information. The rectified linear unit (ReLU) has been proven to keep the gradient from decaying and effectively overcome the problem of gradient disappearance and gradient explosion, which is prone to occur during the reverse transfer of the parameters of the model. Moreover, it can also accelerate the model's convergence rate and improve the performance of the convolutional network [16]. Hence, ReLu is used as the activation function of the convolution layer for the hidden layer neuron output, which can be shown as:

$$y = \max(0, x) \tag{1}$$

The preprocessed LR spectrum date, denoted by $\boldsymbol{X}$, will be sent into the constructed DCNN. Each neuron in the first layer consists of both learnable weights and biases, and the features of LR spectrum are extracted and expressed. In particular, the input spectrum $\boldsymbol{X}$ is weighted and summed, and it will be passed to an activation function and be converted into high-dimensional vector. Finally, all these vectors are spatially recombined to output a feature map. Upon denoting this operation as F_1, which can be expressed as:

$$F_1(\boldsymbol{X}) = \max(0, \boldsymbol{W}_1 * \boldsymbol{X} + \boldsymbol{B}_1) \tag{2}$$

where $\boldsymbol{W_1}$ is the set of n_1 convolution kernels, and the size of each convolution kernel in the set is $c \times f_1 \times f_1$. Moreover, $\boldsymbol{B}_1$ represents the bias, and its each element corresponds to a convolution kernel.

The first layer uses n_1 convolution kernels for convolution operations (*), and every convolution kernel outputs a feature map to form a n_1-dimensional feature map. In contrast, the second layer is a non-linear mapping. A convolution kernel of 1×1 size is used. This is due to that it can reduce the number of parameters by cutting back the number of input channels. Moreover, this layer output n_2-dimensional feature map, and the operation process be expressed as:

$$F_2(\boldsymbol{X}) = \max(0, \boldsymbol{W_2} * F_1(\boldsymbol{X}) + \boldsymbol{B_2}) \tag{3}$$

where the weight $\boldsymbol{W_2}$ has n_2 convolution kernels of size $n_1 \times f_2 \times f_2$, and the bias $\boldsymbol{B}_2$ is a n_2-dimensional vector. This convolution layer can be used to perform non-linear mapping, and to obtain the characteristic information of the reconstructed HR spectrum.

The third layer of the convolutional network can be used to reconstruct the high-resolution spectrum, and to perform the average operation to process the data with overlapping areas, resulting in obtaining the final complete spectrum. The average operation convolves the spectrum relying on a mean filter, assigns the average value in the neighborhood to the central element, and removes irrelevant details in the data. The procedure be expressed as:

$$F(\boldsymbol{X}) = \boldsymbol{W}_3 * F_2(\boldsymbol{X}) + \boldsymbol{B_3} \tag{4}$$

where W_3 contains n_3 linear convolution kernels of size $n_2 \times f_3 \times f_3$, and the bias $\boldsymbol{B_3}$ is a n_3-dimensional vector. Finally, a complete reconstructed HR spectrum is obtained. The optimization of related hyper-parameters will be detailed later.

3.2 Loss Function, Optimizer and Evaluation Metric

In order to evaluate the reconstruction performance, the mean-square error (MSE) is used as the loss function of DCNN, which can indicate the distance between the reconstructions and the targets by loss scores, and can be formulated as:

$$L(\theta) = \frac{1}{K} \sum_{k=1}^{K} \|F(X_k; \theta) - Y_k\|^2 \tag{5}$$

where K denotes the total number of spectrum training samples, k is the sample number, $\{\boldsymbol{Y}_k\}$ is a set of real-world HR spectrum, and $\{\boldsymbol{X}_k\}$ is the corresponding set of LR spectrum. The purpose of network training is to update parameters $\boldsymbol{\theta} = \{\boldsymbol{W_1}, \boldsymbol{W_2}, \boldsymbol{W_3}, \boldsymbol{B_1}, \boldsymbol{B_2}, \boldsymbol{B_3}\}$ with input data iteratively, and establish end-to-end feature mapping F between LR spectrum and HR spectrum.

In the SRCNN model [10], a stochastic gradient descent (SGD) optimizer is used to update the network parameters and to minimize the loss function [17]. The SGD algorithm updates the weights with the aid of using the same fixed learning rate set in advance for all parameters. A large number of parameters are often involved in the model, and the updating frequencies of different parameters are often different. If the learning rate is set too large or too small, it will increase the number of iterations, and slow down the convergence rate. Considering these problems, the Adagrad algorithm determines the updating amplitude by calculating the sum of the squares of all gradients [18], which gradually reduces the learning rate of each parameter. Differing from Adagrad, based on [19], RMSProp algorithm gradually discards past gradients and adds the rest in an exponential moving average manner to achieve a customized learning rate for each parameter. From [13], the adaptive moment estimation (Adam) algorithm uses gradient first moment estimation and second raw moment estimation to dynamically design different adaptive learning rates for each parameter. Thus, Adam algorithm is utilized, which is more suitable for processing spectrum data. Specific experimental results will be evaluated later.

The model reconstruction performance is evaluated with the aid of the mean absolute error (MAE) value [20], which is used to evaluate the normalized PSD error between the real-world HR spectrum and the reconstructed, and can be given by:

$$\mathrm{MAE} = \frac{1}{M \times N} \sum_{i=1}^{M} \sum_{j=1}^{N} \left| y(i,j) - \hat{y}(i,j) \right| \tag{6}$$

where M is the total number of frequency points, and N is the total time slots. $y(i,j)$ is the normalized PSD that i-th frequency point at the j moment in the real-world HR spectrum, $\hat{y}(i,j)$ is the normalized PSD of the reconstructed spectrum correspondingly. i and j are the frequency point and time slot, respectively.

4 Experiments and Evaluations

4.1 Experimental Precondition

The experiment platform is Inter(R) Core(TM) i7-9700K CPU @ 3.60 GHz, GPU is NVIDIA RTX2080ti, memory is 64.00 GB, and convolutional neural network is built on the Tensorflow framework. The dataset used in the experiment is the spectrum data of the GSM1800 downlink, ranging from 1820 to 1875 MHz, and the time span is two weeks. The minimum sampling interval in the frequency domain of the dataset is 200 kHz, and the minimum interval in the time domain is 1.8 s. To save computing resources and reduce data redundancy, we resample the original dataset at 18 s interval.

4.2 Selection of Network Hyper-Parameters

Hyper-parameters (network depth, convolution kernel size and the number, etc.) are important factors, which can affect the performance of model. The specific selection process can be shown as follows. First, the width of the network is changed by the number of convolution kernels, which means that the width of the network refers to the number of convolution kernels per layer. In order to output the complete reconstructed spectrum, the number of convolution kernel in the last layer is fixed to 1. Four groups of different convolution kernel number combinations are selected. From Table 1, it is clear that the performance of the network improves as the network width increases. But considering the time overhead, the wider the network width costs more time. Hence, we have $n_1 = 128, n_2 = 64, n_3 = 1$.

Table 1. Evaluation of different convolution kernel combinations

n_1	n_2	Total params	Time ($\mu s/step$)	Test MAE
256	128	57089	93	0.0258
128	**64**	**20353**	**55**	**0.0261**
64	32	8129	38	0.0266
32	16	3353	29	0.0271

Second, different convolution kernel sizes are also evaluated. The convolution kernel size of the second layer is set to 1×1, which adds non-linear features without loss of resolution, improves the network expression ability and reduces the computational complexity [21]. From Table 2, we have $f_1 = 9, f_2 = 1, f_3 = 5$.

Table 2. Evaluation of different convolution kernel sizes

f_1	f_2	f_3	Total params	Time ($\mu s/step$)	Test MAE
11	1	9	29057	80	0.0260
9	**1**	**5**	**20353**	**55**	**0.0261**
7	1	3	15233	52	0.0267

Finally, the effect of the model depth is analyzed. The model parameters are shown in Table 3. The comparison results of the reconstruction performance of the model are shown in Fig. 4. It can be seen that the convergence speed of the three-layers network is slightly faster than that of the four-layers network, and the three-layers network has a better performance than that of the four-layer network. Therefore, the selection of model depth is 9-1-5.

Table 3. Model parameter settings

Network depth	Network composition	Hyper-parameter combination
3	**9-1-5**	$\boldsymbol{n_1 = 128, n_2 = 64, n_3 = 1}$
4	9-1-1-5	$n_1 = 128, n_2 = 64, n_3 = 32, n_4 = 1$
4	9-1-1-5	$n_1 = 128, n_2 = 64, n_3 = 16, n_4 = 1$
4	9-7-1-5	$n_1 = 128, n_2 = 64, n_3 = 32, n_4 = 1$

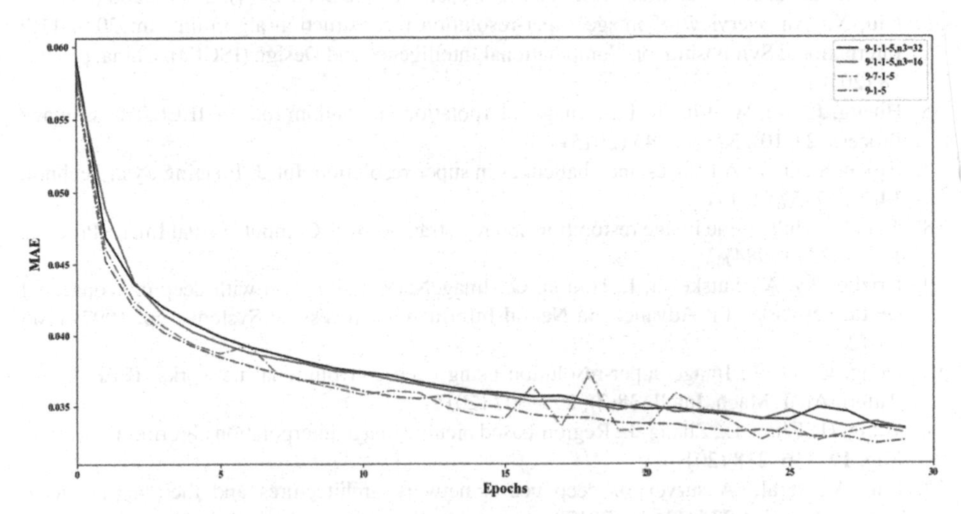

Fig. 4. MAE values for Layer 3 and Layer 4 networks

5 Conclusion

In this paper, we investigated the reconstruction of LR spectrum data. In order to reconstruct LR data, a DCNN-based spectrum super-resolution scheme was designed. Specifically, in the training phase, a small amount of HR spectrum data may be preprocessed, and the preprocessed data will be fed into the designed DCNN model. Then, the model can mine correlation between the LR spectrum and the HR spectrum in both time domain and frequency domain. Moreover, in the testing phase, the received LR data is normalized, and sent into the model, then the model can output the generated HR spectrum data. Experimental results have demonstrated that the proposed reconstruction scheme can achieve good reconstruction performance.

Acknowledgement. This work presented was partially supported by the National Science Foundation of China (No. 91738201), the China Postdoctoral Science Foundation (No. 2018M632347), and the Natural Science Foundation for Jiangsu Higher Education Institutions (No. 18KJB510030).

References

1. Abdelmohsen, A., Hamouda, W.: Advances on spectrum sensing for cognitive radio networks: theory and applications. IEEE Commun. Surv. Tutor. **19**(2), 1277–1304 (2016)
2. Zhang, L., et al.: A survey of advanced techniques for spectrum sharing in 5G networks. IEEE Wirel. Commun. **24**(5), 44–51 (2017)
3. Jia, M., et al.: Broadband hybrid satellite-terrestrial communication systems based on cognitive radio toward 5G. IEEE Wirel. Commun. **23**(6), 96–106 (2016)
4. Ghahremani, M., Ghassemian, H.: A compressed-sensing-based pan-sharpening method for spectral distortion reduction. IEEE Trans. Geosci. Remote Sens. **54**(4), 2194–2206 (2015)
5. Niu, X.: An overview of image super-resolution reconstruction algorithm. In: 2018 11th International Symposium on Computational Intelligence and Design (ISCID), China, pp. 16–18 (2018)
6. Huang, J., Siu, W., Liu, T.: Fast image interpolation via random forests. IEEE Trans. Image Process. **24**(10), 3232–3245 (2015)
7. Farsiu, S., et al.: Advances and challenges in super-resolution. Int. J. Imaging Syst. Technol. **14**(2), 47–57 (2014)
8. Tsai, R.: Multiframe image restoration and registration. Adv. Comput. Visual Image Process. **1**, 317–339 (1984)
9. Krizhevsky, A., Sutskever, I., Hinton, G.: ImageNet classification with deep convolutional neural networks. In: Advances in Neural Information Processing Systems, pp. 1097–1105 (2012)
10. Dong, C., et al.: Image super-resolution using deep convolutional networks. IEEE Trans. Pattern Anal. Mach. Intell. **38**(2), 295–307 (2015)
11. Wang, H., Zhou, L., Zhang, J.: Region-based bicubic image interpolation algorithm. Comput. Eng. **19**, 216–218 (2010)
12. Liu, W., et al.: A survey of deep neural network architectures and their applications. Neurocomputing **234**, 11–26 (2017)
13. Mehta, S., Paunwala, C., Vaidya, B.: CNN based traffic sign classification using Adam optimizer. In: 2019 International Conference on Intelligent Computing and Control Systems (ICCS), India, pp. 1293–1298 (2019)
14. Ionutiu, R., Rommes, J., Antoulas, A.: Passivity-preserving model reduction using dominant spectral-zero interpolation. IEEE Trans. Comput. Aided Des. Integr. Circuits Syst. **27**(12), 2250–2263 (2008)
15. Hu, W., et al.: Deep convolutional neural networks for hyperspectral image classification. J. Sens. **2015**(258619), 1–12 (2015)
16. Nair, V., Hinton, G.: Rectified linear units improve restricted Boltzmann machines. In: Proceedings of the 27th International Conference on Machine Learning (ICML-10), Israel, pp. 807–814 (2010)
17. Bottou, L.: Large-scale machine learning with stochastic gradient descent. In: Proceedings of COMPSTAT 2010 Physica-Verlag HD, Paris, pp. 177–186 (2010)
18. Duchi, J., Hazan, E., Singer, Y.: Adaptive subgradient methods for online learning and stochastic optimization. J. Mach. Learn. Res. **12**, 2121–2159 (2011)
19. Tieleman, T., Hinton, G.: Lecture 6.5-rmsprop: divide the gradient by a running average of its recent magnitude. COURSERA: Neural Netw. Mach. Learn. **4**(2), 26–31 (2012)
20. Willmott, C., Matsuura, K.: Advantages of the mean absolute error (MAE) over the root mean square error (RMSE) in assessing average model performance. Climate Res. **30**(1), 79–82 (2005)
21. Pang, Y., et al.: Convolution in convolution for network in network. IEEE Trans. Neural Netw. Learn. Syst. **29**(5), 1587–1597 (2018)

Author Index

Printed in the United States
By Bookmasters